7/03/2013

Ethnic Groups of the Americas

Recent Titles in
Ethnic Groups of the World

Ethnic Groups of Africa and the Middle East: An Encyclopedia
John A. Shoup

Ethnic Groups of Europe: An Encyclopedia
Jeffrey E. Cole, Editor

Ethnic Groups of South Asia and the Pacific: An Encyclopedia
James B. Minahan

Ethnic Groups of the Americas

AN ENCYCLOPEDIA

James B. Minahan

Ethnic Groups of the World

ABC-CLIO

Santa Barbara, California • Denver, Colorado • Oxford, England

Library of Congress Cataloging-in-Publication Data

Minahan, James.
  Ethnic groups of the Americas : an encyclopedia / James B. Minahan.
    pages cm. — (Ethnic groups of the world)
  Includes bibliographical references and indexes.
    ISBN 978-1-61069-163-5 (hardcopy : acid-free paper) — ISBN 978-1-61069-164-2 (ebook) 1. Ethnology—North America — Encyclopedias.   2. Ethnology—Latin America—Encyclopedias.   3. North America—Ethnic relations—Encyclopedias.
4. Latin America—Ethnic relations—Encyclopedias.   I. Title.
  E49.M56   2013
  305.80097—dc23   2012041224

ISBN: 978-1-61069-163-5
EISBN: 978-1-61069-164-2

17   16   15   14   13   1   2   3   4   5

This book is also available on the World Wide Web as an eBook.
Visit www.abc-clio.com for details.

ABC-CLIO, LLC
130 Cremona Drive, P.O. Box 1911
Santa Barbara, California 93116-1911

This book is printed on acid-free paper ∞

Manufactured in the United States of America

Contents

Preface

A greater understanding of ethnicity and ethnic groups is crucial to the tolerance and acceptance that is needed by our increasingly multiethnic world. Misunderstandings and intolerance of other cultures have contributed to the violence and wars that continue to make headlines around the world. The purpose of this guide to the peoples and ethnic groups of the Americas is to provide readers with an up-to-date, accurate, and easy-to-understand guide to the many ethnic groups inhabiting the Western Hemisphere. This series of books on the peoples and ethnic groups around the world is an essential guide to the world at a time when ethnic groups, ethnic relations, immigration, and regional conflicts are important factors in the modern world. The diversity of the world's many peoples and ethnic groups is the one most important element of modern world culture and an understanding of different cultures is an essential part of understanding the world around us.

This volume on the peoples and ethnic groups of the Americas forms part of a multivolume work that includes short chapters on each of the major groups inhabiting the enormous geographical region stretching from the Arctic Circle to the southern tip of South America. The individual surveys are devoted to the peoples of each country and the many ethnic groups that make up each country's population. The short entries highlight the social, political, cultural, and historical development of the major ethnic groups of the Americas. The value of this multivolume work is evident in its up-to-date information and the historical evolution of the New World's many and varied peoples and ethnic groups.

Many reference books published in the last decade about the ethnic groups of the Americas often address only the subject of the nations and their core populations, relegating the numerous nonstate peoples to brief paragraphs or footnotes. However, the selection process of which groups to include in this book presented numerous obstacles, not the least of which was the application of uniform criteria to the region's many distinct peoples. The peoples and ethnic groups presented in this volume range from the core populations of each of the Americas' nation-states to the many small, virtually unknown ethnic groups that are usually ignored in regional reference books. The peoples and ethnic groups introduced in this book include those groups that developed from ancient ethnicities, isolated societies, and the modern peoples that encompass the hemisphere's multiethnic cultures. Some of the groups developed relatively recently as distinct cultures arising from adherence to distinct religious or cultural traditions. The selection of the peoples to be included in this book required criteria based on language, common history, religion, geographic location, shared culture, self-identification, or identification by others. In general, strict adherence to information published by the region's nation governments has been avoided as these publications are often driven by local political considerations and the distinct government policies that govern ethnic policies in each country. The many groups selected for inclusion represent the core peoples of each of the American nations along with the most populous of the ethnic groups living in each country that have maintained their distinct cultures. The difficulties of researching the ethnic diversity of the Americas was complicated by a general lack of consensus on what attributes a group must display to be considered a distinct people or ethnic group. Part of the criteria applied to the selection process was the acceptance of groups that are not usually accepted as distinct peoples but who self-identify or view themselves as separate either culturally, historically, or religiously.

The book covers the evolution of the peoples of the Americas from the earliest periods of their known histories to the present day. Each survey includes information on the culture, language or languages, and the geographic distribution of each group. This collection of surveys of the region's peoples and ethnic groups is an indispensable guide to the many peoples that inhabit the vast region known as the Americas. These peoples, often misunderstood, ignored, or virtually unknown outside their homelands, represent a captivating kaleidoscope of the human geography of the New World. The surveys here highlight the historical, cultural, political, and religious development of each group and its relations with neighboring groups and with the country's national government.

Many of the peoples and ethnic groups presented in this book will be familiar as the core ethnic group or nationality of the nation-states of the Americas, but most of the surveys present groups that are less familiar, though their distinct histories, cultures, languages, and religions form important elements in each country's national society. Since many of the names of the groups will not be familiar to most readers, the group's preferred name and the alternative names are listed. The more familiar names for many of the region's surviving ethnic groups is often a colonial or imposed name that is now considered derogatory or represents a long history of abuse and cultural suppression.

Each individual survey is divided into several parts: the name and alternative names of the group; the major population concentrations and other areas with large representative communities; the estimated group population; a brief outline of the group's linguistic and religious affiliations; and the history of the group before the 19th century, the group's cultural traits, and its history from the 19th century to the present. Each group survey is accompanied by a suggested reading list. The group population figures are the author's estimates for 2012 based on a large number of sources, both official and unofficial. The population figures are gleaned from the latest census figures, where available, official and unofficial estimates, and figures published by the groups themselves. A number of regional governments do not enumerate the ethnic groups within their national borders, which makes reliance on other, perhaps less reliable, population estimates a necessity. As each of the groups included in the book has its own history of events, conflicts, and development, the largest part of each survey is devoted to the historical development of the group with a historical survey that encompasses the consolidation, evolution, and territorial dispersion of each group from its earliest known history to the present day.

This book presents both the historic ethnic and national groups associated with each of the American nation-states and the many ethnic groups that make up the remainder of each national population. The many ethnic groups that survived the colonization by Europeans of their historic homelands are increasingly demanding recognition of their distinct identities as part of the integrated modern world. The volume is presented as a unique reference source for the ethnic renaissance that is spearheading one of the most powerful and widespread political movements of the 21st century—the reemergence of regional and ethnic cultures as the basis of identity.

Introduction: Ethnicity in the Americas

The vast territory known as the Americas stretches from the Arctic Circle in the northern reaches of North America to Tierra del Fuego, the most southerly inhabited region of South America. The territory included in the Americas is home to a confusing variety of peoples and ethnic groups; these include the descendants of the original settlers who crossed the ancient land bridge from northern Asia to gradually populate the continents of the Americas; they also include the populations made up of immigrants from other continents, the so-called settler societies that now dominate most of the region. The cultural diversity is one of the strengths of the countries in the region but ethnicity, language, culture, and religion can also be a source of conflict and oppression. The modern political trend of many of the regional ethnic, religious, and linguistic groups demanding equality and recognition of their distinct cultures makes the issue of ethnicity of paramount importance. The ever-increasing number of peoples and ethnic groups asserting their right to equality within the national cultures must necessarily be an impediment to development unless the region's ethnic diversity is embraced, acknowledged, studied, and accepted.

The history of the Americas was drastically changed with the discovery of the New World by the Europeans in the late 15th century. Since that time vast movements of peoples from Europe, Africa, and Asia overwhelmed the original inhabitants as new cultures formed from a fusion of traditions brought to the Americas from distant homelands. The expansion of European empires brought disease, death, slavery, and ill-treatment to many of the indigenous peoples. Ethnic diversity was mostly ignored as European culture and traditions were transplanted to the region. The revolutionary spirit that swept most of the former European colonies to independence in the late 18th and early 19th centuries allowed the descendants of the Europeans to dominate the newly independent countries so that the oppression and abuse suffered by the indigenous peoples under colonial rule continued well into the 20th century and in some areas, continues to the present. The decolonization process that began in the 1950s dismantled the remains of the European empires and resulted in the independence of most of the remaining colonies in the Americas. But for the indigenous ethnic groups little has changed since the colonial period as they suffer poverty, marginalization, and discrimination.

Though most of the indigenous peoples of the Americas were and are tribal peoples with cultures adapted to their homelands, the Americas were also home to a number of advanced civilizations famous for their contributions to astronomy, mathematics, art, philosophy, and religious thought. All of the indigenous American cultures, of whatever level of sophistication, were overwhelmed by the superior weaponry of the European invaders. During the colonization of the Americas the indigenous peoples were pushed aside, their lands stolen, and their cultures denigrated. The descendants of the European colonizers, or their mixed race offspring, now make up the majority of the populations in most countries with a small number, particularly in the Caribbean area, now with majority populations descended from the African slaves imported by the Europeans. The ethnic diversity of the Americas is overly generalized as English-speaking North America and mostly Spanish- and Portuguese-speaking Latin America, but the reality is a mosaic of peoples and cultures that are asserting their right to be recognized as a distinct people within the multiethnic societies of the region.

The democratic political system, often accepted as the only system able to provide the basis of humane political and economic security, can also be a subversive political force. Multiparty democracy, promoted throughout the Americas with varied results, often generates instability and chaos as various ethnic groups within a country become rivals for advancement or political power. The volatility that is an inherent part of a free political system also allows long-suppressed ethnic groups to develop and thrive. The ethnic geography of the Americas, long suppressed in the name of stability, economic advantage, or colonial discrimination, in the 21st century has reaffirmed its existence as part of the territory of most of the region's nation-states. History, particularly the history written by the dominant groups, has a tendency to simplify ethnic realities and to identify ethnicity and culture with the state structures, but the stubborn refusal of ethnic groups to disappear into the wider cultures makes the understanding of ethnicity one of the most important undertakings that face modern American societies today.

The traditional emphasis on the rights of the region's nation-states, rather than on the rights of the ethnic groups and the individuals who make up their populations, has for long dictated the world's attitudes to ethnicity. Bolstered by historic discrimination, ignorance, and a failure to understand the diversity and dynamics of ethnicity, the continuing prominence of nationality or citizenship rather than ethnic identity continues to undermine development in much of the region. This book is dedicated to the hope that the world's politics and attitudes will someday accommodate the most basic of all cultural institutions: the ethnic group.

A

Acadians

The Acadians are a North American ethnic group of mostly French descent. The Acadian region of North America lies in the eastern Canadian provinces and the northeastern U.S. state of Maine. The estimated 500,000 Acadians are usually bilingual, speaking both their own French dialect known as Français Acadien and English. Many Acadians also speak standard French, the language used in the bilingual education institutions in the region. The Acadians are devoutly Roman Catholic, with small minorities of Protestants and other religions. Outside the region there are Acadian communities in Ontario, in other parts of the United States, and in France.

The region of Acadia, called Acadie in the French language, was colonized by French settlers beginning in 1604. Forming part of the French colony of New France, Acadia was mostly settled by the poor of France's large cities and by colonists from the poorer western provinces of Brittany and Normandy. Acadia was administered as a separate region of New France and was not part of the French colony of Canada, modern Quebec. The colonists mostly settled on individual farms and the region prospered. Colonists continued to arrive from France despite periodic incursions by adventurers or militias from the English colonies to the south. In

the 18th century, the region was caught up in the long war between France and England for supremacy in North America. In 1710, the Acadian capital at Port Royal in modern Nova Scotia was captured by the English. By the terms of the Treaty of Utrecht, Nova Scotia was ceded to England, leaving the other parts of Acadia under French rule. The British authorities ordered the Acadians in the newly ceded territory to swear allegiance to the English crown or to withdraw to the neighboring French territories. The Acadians did neither, although some took the oath in 1730. In spite of the ongoing war, the period from 1713 to 1748 is considered the golden age of Acadian culture. Between 1755 and 1763, some 11,500 Acadians—about three-quarters of the Acadian population in Nova Scotia—were forced out of their prosperous farms and towns at bayonet point. Later other Acadians were also deported, bringing the total to 18,000 uprooted, often separated from family members, and brutally expelled from their homeland. Herded onto overcrowded ships, many were deported to other parts of North America, other English colonies, or were forcibly returned to France. Approximately one-third of the Acadian deportees perished from diseases or drowning during the expulsion, known to Acadians as *Le Grand Dérangement*. Others fled south to the Madawaska River Valley in present-day northern Maine and eastern

New Brunswick. Some of the deportees were later allowed to return to the region but not to their former homes or towns, which had been taken by English settlers.

Acadian culture remains vibrant and is a unifying symbol for all Acadians. The culture survived the abandonment by the mother country, the horrors of the deportations, and the return of many Acadians from exile. The Acadian dialect is quite different from that spoken in neighboring Quebec and shows borrowings from both English and the local Algonquian languages. In 1968, the Acadians were finally allowed secondary education in French, but the Canadian language laws of 1969 and 1981 weakened the language in favor of the standard French, which is one of Canada's two national languages. The Roman Catholic faith that played such a large part in the formation of their culture remains an important Acadian institution. In rural areas Acadian cultural life continued to revolve around the local church, which is both the spiritual and secular center of village life. The church continues as a major force in the preservation of the unique Acadian culture, often providing French language education when local governments are unable or unwilling to provide it. The Acadians' national holiday falls on the feast of the Assumption, August 15 each year, and is celebrated as a form of carnival in the blue, white, red, and gold colors of the Acadian flag. A more subdued annual event is Acadian Remembrance Day, December 13, which commemorates the large number of Acadians who perished in the North Atlantic from hunger, diseases, and drowning during the years of the Acadian expulsions.

The mostly rural and Roman Catholic Acadians remained apart from the English-speaking population of the region but also refused to assimilate into the larger Québécois culture to the west. Language and education became rallying points for Acadian society. In 1864, the Canadian government introduced an English language curriculum that taught the glories of the British Empire but ignored the history and culture of Acadia. Activists seeking to safeguard their threatened culture began to mobilize. In 1884 the Acadians held their first national convention. Cultural symbols, including the distinctive Acadian flag and a national anthem, were adopted by representatives of Acadian communities in eastern Canada and the United States. The first institute of higher learning in the French language was opened in Nova Scotia but an infamous law known as Rule XVII, passed in 1912, abolished French as a medium of instruction and communication in regions outside the province of Quebec. The rule was not abolished until 1968. In 1969 the Official Languages Act made English and French equal throughout Canada. Language and religion remain the cornerstones of Acadian culture to the present. In 1990, the Canadian Supreme Court ruled that Francophone minorities should have some control over their children's education. In 1992 the first Francophone school and community center in Nova Scotia was opened. The deportation of their ancestors remains a central part of their culture and heritage. In 2003, at the request of Acadian representatives, the United Kingdom's Queen Elizabeth II issued a royal proclamation acknowledging the deportation and established a day of commemoration—July 28 of each year. The day is now marked on some official calendars as the "Great Upheaval."

Further Reading

Clark, Bill. *Acadia: The Story behind the Scenery.* Wickenburg, AZ: KC Publications, 2003.

Faragher, John Mack. *A Great and Noble Scheme: The Tragic Story of the Expulsion of the French Acadians from their American Homeland.* New York: W. W. Norton, 2006.

Hodson, Christopher. *The Acadian Diaspora: An Eighteenth-Century History.* New York: Oxford University Press, 2012.

African Americans

African Americans, sometimes referred to as Black Americans or Afro-Americans or in Canada as Black Canadians, are North Americans who have at least partial ancestry from sub-Saharan Africa. Others, immigrants from Africa, the Caribbean, other parts of the Americas, or their descendants, may also be identified or self-identify themselves as African Americans. The estimated 43 million African Americans make up the largest racial minority in the United States. In Canada, the estimated 800,000 African Americans are known as Black Canadians and are mostly of Caribbean origin. African Americans live throughout the United States, with larger populations in the Southern states and in large urban areas in other parts of the country. Black Canadians are mostly concentrated in the eastern provinces of Ontario and Quebec. African Americans are mostly Christian with Protestant sects, particularly the historically African American churches, predominating. Smaller numbers belong to various Muslim groups that emerged in the 20th century as part of the African American nationalist movement, belong to Jewish congregations, or practice other religions. An estimated 13 percent claim to follow no organized religion, a percentage that mirrors that of the total American public.

The first Africans arrived in North America as part of the San Miguel de Guadeloupe colony founded by Spanish explorer Lucas Vásquez de Ayllón in present-day South Carolina in 1528. The colony failed almost immediately due to a fight over leadership during which most of the African slaves fled the colony to seek refuge among local Native Americans. An epidemic further decimated the colony, which was abandoned, leaving the escaped slaves behind on North American soil. The Spanish colony of Saint Augustine, founded in present-day Florida in 1565, became the first permanent European settlement in North America. The colonists included an unknown number of free and slave Africans, who formed the first African American community on the continent. The first Africans in British North America were recorded in Jamestown, Virginia, in 1619. The Dutch imported the first Africans to New Amsterdam (New York) in 1625. Early settlements treated the Africans as indentured servants who traded several years of labor for their eventual freedom. Massachusetts was the first British colony to legally recognize slavery in 1641. Virginia was the first colony to rule that the children of a slave mother would remain slaves. The concept of a race-based system of slavery did not fully develop until the 18th century. By the time of the American Revolution in 1776, Africans, both slave and free, made up 20 percent of the population of the British American colonies, making them the second largest ethnic group after the British. Many African Americans joined the rebel forces and helped secure American independence. The first African American congregations and churches were established before 1800 and religion remains an important part of African American society.

African American culture is a subculture of American culture, sharing most cultural attributes with the other sectors of the American public. From the earliest African presence in North America, African Americans have contributed art, literature, agricultural skills, clothing styles, music, language, technological innovation, and new foods to the general American culture. The cultivation and use of many agricultural products such as peanuts, yams, rice, okra, sorghum, watermelon, grits, indigo dyes, and cotton can be traced to African and African American influences. Notable examples include George Crum, who invented the potato chip in 1853, and George Washington Carver, who created numerous products using peanuts, sweet potatoes, and pecans. African American music is one of the most pervasive cultural influences in the United States. African Americans dominate many forms of contemporary American music. Other musical forms originated in African American communities, including blues, ragtime, bluegrass, jazz, gospel, and hip-hop. African Americans have also greatly influenced American dance styles, clothing, and literature. African American literature

is a major genre of American literature. African American inventors, from the time of slavery to the present, have created many widely used devices and innovations. The first machine to mass produce shoes, the automatic lubrication devices for steam engines, the first system to allow moving trains to communicate, the first automatic traffic signal, and the gas mask are only a few of the inventions contributed to American culture by African Americans. More modern contributions include techniques of open heart surgery, participation in the development of nuclear reactors, and air conditioners. Three of the original nine patents for PC-based computers are held by African American Dr. Daniel Hale Williams. African American culture continues to flourish and as part of the overall American culture it remains an important component, influencing not just the culture of North America but cultures far beyond.

African slavery grew rapidly particularly in the labor-intensive plantations of the Southern states. The Atlantic slave trade brought tens of thousands of captured Africans to North America. The vast majority of the captives were Africans from the central and western parts of the African continent, usually sold by Africans to European slave traders who transported shiploads of captives to be sold in the slave markets of North America. The purchased slaves were forced to labor on agricultural plantations, work in mines, rice fields or the timber industry, or work as house servants. Some African American scholars label the slave trade the "African Holocaust" or the "Holocaust of Enslavement." The concept of slavery began to embitter relations between different parts of North America early in the 19th century. By 1860, there were an estimated 3.9 million enslaved African Americans in the United States and another half million lived free across the country and in Canada. During the American Civil War, President Abraham Lincoln signed the Emancipation Proclamation, declaring that all African American slaves held in states that had seceded from the Union were free. Many free and freed African Americans joined the Union forces to fight for the end of slavery. Advancing Union troops enforced the proclamation, with the state of Texas being the last to be emancipated in 1865. African Americans quickly set up their own churches, community and civic associations, and other institutions. The post-Civil War reconstruction era was initially a time of progress for African Americans; in the late 1890s, Southern states enacted the so-called Jim Crow laws that disenfranchised the African Americans and enforced racial segregation. Racial segregation was legally mandated in the South but also appeared at the local level of government in many areas of the country. The desperate situation of African Americans in the South sparked the Great Migration of the early 20th century with a mass movement of African Americans from the South to cities in the North. The migrants from the South moved north seeking better work and living opportunities, and to escape the pervasive Jim Crow laws and racial violence of the South. The Great Migration involved an estimated 6 million African Americans between 1916 and 1960. Local movements to fight racial violence and discrimination gradually evolved into the Civil Rights Movement from 1954 to 1968. The movement was aimed at abolishing racial discrimination against African Americans, particularly in the South. New laws were passed that banned discrimination and extended federal authority over the states to ensure African American participation in voter registration and elections. The Black Power movement, which lasted from 1966 to 1975, expanded on demands to include economic and political self-sufficiency and freedom. Economically and politically, African Americans have made substantial gains since the civil rights movements of the 1960s and 1970s. Many African Americans became prominent in business and entertainment, and successfully entered politics. In 2008, African American senator Barack Obama became the first African American to be elected president of the United States with the support of both African Americans and voters from across the spectrum of American ethnic groups.

Further Reading

Mintz, Sidney Wilfred. *The Birth of African-American Culture: An Anthropological Perspective.* Boston: Beacon Press, 1992.

Smallwood, Stephanie E. *Saltwater Slavery: A Middle Passage from Africa to American Diaspora.* Cambridge, MA: Harvard University Press, 2008.

Gates, Henry Louis Jr. *Life upon These Shores: Looking at African-American History, 1513–2008.* New York: Knopf, 2011.

Afro-Brazilians

Afro-Brazilians, known as Pretos or blacks in Brazil, form one of the five official categories of ethnicities recognized by the Brazilian government, along with Branco (white), Pardo (brown or multiracial),

Amarelo (yellow, East Asian), and Indigena (Amerindian). The estimated 13.5 million Afro-Brazilians make up about seven percent of Brazil's total population. Afro-Brazilians rarely refer to themselves as Afro-Brazilian or African Brazilian, and most do not identify their origin as African but see themselves as being of Brazilian origin. In recent years the term "afrodescendente" has been brought into use, but mostly in official or academic circles. Like the majority of the Brazilian population, Afro-Brazilians speak Portuguese, the official language of Brazil. The majority of Afro-Brazilians are Roman Catholic with a large and growing Protestant minority.

Most Afro-Brazilians are descendants of Africans who were taken captive and sold to Portuguese and Spanish slave traders. The Portuguese colonizers of Brazil realized early that without the mineral riches of other colonies, they would need to exploit the region agriculturally. The population of Portugal was insufficient to produce enough colonists, and the native peoples were deemed unsuited or were exterminated by war and disease; so the Portuguese began to resort to the importation of African slaves by 1550. The fact that Portugal already had colonies in present-day Angola and Mozambique facilitated the Atlantic slave trade. Between the 16th and 19th centuries, millions of African slaves were captured, shipped to Brazil in crowded slave ships, and sold in the slave markets of the South American colonies. The slave trade became an enormous economic undertaking that involved hundreds of ships and thousands of people in the Portuguese territories in Africa and Brazil. The huge profits from the trade made many slave traders, both among the tribes that dealt in slaves in Africa and among the colonists in the New World, extremely wealthy and powerful. Taxes paid on the sale of slaves became one of the most important sources of funds for local governments. In Africa an estimated 40 percent of captives died before reaching the slave ports on the coast. Another 15 percent died in the crowded and unsanitary slave ships crossing the Atlantic, a voyage that could take from 33 to 45 days. Ships sailing from Mozambique often took as much as 76 days for the Atlantic crossing. Once in Brazil, the slaves were sold and another 10–12 percent died wherever they were taken by their new owners. The consequences of the brutal capture and transport of slaves allowed only about 45 percent of all Africans captured in Africa to survive long enough to become slaves in Brazil. The Portuguese colonists of Brazil were mostly men, with very few women coming to the region from Europe. It became common practice for slave owners to choose the most beautiful ones from among the women slaves, leading to a large mulatto population of mixed heritage while the African population grew mostly by the importation of new slaves. Life expectancy for the slaves sold in Brazil in the late 18th century was a mere seven years.

The culture of the Afro-Brazilians varies from region to region due to the origins of the population. Captives from West Africa formed the largest group in Bahia and other regions of the north while Bantu peoples from Angola, Congo, and Mozambique were usually shipped to Rio de Janeiro, the interior region of Minas

Gerais, and the northeastern provinces of Brazil. Because the captives brought their indigenous cultures to the New World, the culture of the Afro-Brazilians is a combination of African traditions and traits and Portuguese culture. Most Afro-Brazilians are Christian, mostly Roman Catholic, al-though Afro-Brazilian religions such as Candomblé and Umbanda have many followers. The Afro-Brazilian religions are open to all Brazilians so over time they have ceased to be exclusively Afro-Brazilian. Evangelical Protestant groups have gained many followers since the late 20th century. The influence of the Afro-Brazilians is expressed in many facets of Brazilian culture, particularly in Brazil's regional cuisines, music, dance, and art. Feijoada, Brazil's national dish, started as a Portuguese stew that the Afro-Brazilians built upon. It is now available in all parts of Brazil and there are hundreds of ways to prepare it. Capoeira is a form of martial art initially developed by slaves from Angola or Mozambique. Beginning in the colonial period, Capoeira began as a form of combat involving a strong acrobatic component in some versions. It is always played to music, with Capoeira music now accepted as a distinct musical form. Most Brazilian music is a mixture of Portuguese, Amerindian, and African influences. The drums that enliven Brazilian music are a heritage of slave owners allowing their slaves to continue the African tradition of playing drums. In the United States slaves were forbidden by owners to have drums, as it was feared that they could be used for communications. Despite continuing prejudice against blacks in Brazil, many Afro-Brazilians have become prominent members of Brazilian society. Writers, sportsmen, musicians, singers, and other Afro-Brazilians have gained fame on a global scale.

In the first decades of the 19th century, the large number of slaves and growing discontent led to several serious uprisings—particularly serious in the southern Brazilian states. Tens of thousands of Afro-Brazilian slaves left their *fazendas* to support calls for the abolition of slavery. By 1887 the ongoing uprisings and the growing number of runaways seemed to indicate the real possibility of a widespread insurrection. Groups of slaves confronted police in many of the larger cities, chanting "long live freedom" and "death to the slave owners." Realizing that the slave labor system had almost completely collapsed, the Brazilian government officially abolished slavery on May 13, 1888. Many of the freed slaves migrated to the large towns, particularly in the coastal areas where they had worked on large cane plantations. The end of slavery was accompanied by the ruin of many wealthy planters and the abandonment of much fertile land. Many of the former slaves settled as subsistence farmers raising just enough to feed their families. The end of slavery allowed the Afro-Brazilian population to quickly grow. Discrimination and a complicated scale of racial classifications running from white to black prevented many Afro-Brazilians from achieving the prosperity of those Brazilians at the lighter end of the scale. In the late 19th and 20th centuries, Brazilian society promoted racial integration and mixing. However, most former slaves were not able to find employment for wages as ideas of the superiority of the "white race" persisted. Instead of offering employment to millions of former slaves, the government promoted immigration from Europe and elsewhere to fill the job market. Although rejected by the Brazilian Congress, laws attempting to restrict immigration by nonwhites were proposed as late as the 1920s. In 1945, the Brazilian government adopted a decree favoring the entrance of European immigrants into the country. The racial mixing that accompanied the colonization of the Brazilian territories resulted in a very racially mixed population. Unlike the United States, where race is usually based on parentage or ancestry, race in Brazil is based on a person's appearance. Within the same family siblings may be classified as belonging to different races. A common saying in Brazil—"money whitens"—is an example of the upwardly mobile Afro-Brazilian movement in the 1950s and 1960s. Opportunities based on criteria other than race also impacted the Afro-Brazilians, whose educational level was lower than that of other groups. Modernization and industrialization gradually allowed more Afro-Brazilians to leave behind the traditional poverty of their parents, but racial barriers remained. In 2010, a survey of the wealthiest Brazilians showed that only 12 percent were Afro-Brazilians or Pardos, while whites accounted for over 85 percent of the group. Among the poorest in Brazil, nearly 75 percent are Afro-Brazilian or Pardo against 25 percent of whites.

Further Reading

Klein, Herbert S. *Slavery in Brazil.* Cambridge: Cambridge University Press, 2009.

Reichmann, Rebecca. *Race in Contemporary Brazil: From Indifference to Inequality.* University Park, PA: Pennsylvania State University Press, 1999.

Twine, Francine Winddance. *Racism in a Racial Democracy: The Maintenance of White Supremacy in Brazil.* Piscataway, NJ: Rutgers University Press, 1997.

Afro-Cubans

Afro-Cubans are a Cuban ethnic group with roots in sub-Saharan Africa. The estimated 1.4 million Afro-Cubans speak the Cuban dialect of Spanish, often mixed with words or phrases originally brought from Africa. Although Afro-Cubans are found throughout the island, eastern Cuba, particularly Havana, has the higher concentrations of Afro-Cuban populations. The Afro-Cubans are traditionally Roman Catholic, but decades of official atheism and the popularity of specific Afro-Cuban religions have reduced the Catholic population.

Slavery in Cuba began with the Spanish conquerors enslaving the local indigenous peoples. The colonists used the *encomienda* system, slavery, and production quotas to force the slave laborers to ensure a return on the costs of the expedition and the colonization investments. After decades of pressure, primarily from priests who argued that enslaving the indigenous peoples was incompatible with Christianity, the Council of the Indies—the Spanish governing body officially mandated to protect the indigenous groups under the Laws of the Indies—stopped the *encomienda* system. However, the intervention of the Council came too late for the indigenous peoples, who had mostly disappeared due to the widespread and abusive forced labor. The colonists needed a new source of labor and began to import African slaves in 1502. The Spanish contracted with British slavers in 1713 to supply the island with needed laborers. The number of slaves in Cuba remained low until the 1760s, when the British took control of Havana. In 1762, the British began the import of a total of 10,000 slaves into Cuba, using the island to send slaves to other British islands in the Caribbean and to the 13 British colonies in the North American mainland. After the Spanish returned to Cuba, the British continued, along with the Portuguese, to bring African slaves to the island while the Spanish outlawed their own slave trade of the Africans. The island's slaves were generally divided into two groups. One group was urban and directed by the needs of the Spanish colonial government and the elite populations of Havana and other cities; the other group was rural and was used for the production of agricultural products, particularly sugar. Until the last decades of the 18th century, Cuba was a relatively underdeveloped colony with an economy based on tobacco farms and cattle. The Spanish authorities were faced with several large-scale slave revolts in the 18th century, which were brutally crushed with leaders and free Afro-Cubans helping the insurrection summarily executed.

Afro-Cuban culture is an important part of the overall Cuban culture. The importance of African influences on the island's cuisine, music, art, literature, and dance cannot be understated. The blending of Hispanic culture with the imported African influences began in the 16th century, but most of today's Afro-Cuban culture is a product of the 19th century when Cuba's culture began to develop independently of that of the Spanish motherland. The most visible of the cultural assets of the Afro-Cubans is the island's music and dance. The combination of African drums and Spanish guitars was the first tentative blending that resulted in the specifically Afro-Cuban music, sometimes known as the Afro-Cuban beat. In the 20th century this style of music, mixing the African percussion and European melody, gained fame throughout the world. Like the music, Afro-Cuban dance has also gained international fame.

The intensive cultivation of sugarcane began at the turn of the 19th century with a corresponding need for slave labor. The influence of the French and American revolutions was important in the Spanish-American wars of independence in the early 19th century. The wars emancipated most of Spain's colonies in the Americas and brought to an end the near-feudal existence of most inhabitants of the colonies. The islands of Cuba and Puerto Rico remained part of the Spanish Empire after the loss of most of Spain's American territories. In 1820, the Spanish government officially outlawed slavery in its territories except for the Caribbean islands. The important sugar industry in the islands needed slave labor, so slavery remained legal in Cuba until 1866. A widespread rebellion against Spanish rule swept the island in 1868. Many Afro-Cuban slaves were granted freedom to fight with the rebel forces. The rebellion resulted in the Ten Years' War, which ended with the Spanish government promising greater autonomy for the island. In the 1880s the abolition of slavery on the

Afro-Cuban group Ban Rra Rra at the San Francisco Cuban Festival in 1999 on their first tour of the United States. (AP Photo/Susan Ragan)

island was completed. Freed slaves often found work on the remaining sugar plantations as wage laborers. Another rebellion against the Spanish began in 1895, bringing much death and misery to the island, and particularly to the poorest part of the population—the Afro-Cubans. The rebellion was caught up in the Spanish-American War in 1898. Defeated Spain ceded its remaining few colonies and relinquished all claim to Cuba. Under American rule after the war, Cuba gained full independence in 1902. Under a series of weak or dictatorial governments, the Afro-Cuban population of the island made little economic progress, although during the years following World War II their music, dance, and cuisine formed part of the burgeoning Cuban culture. By 1958, Cuba was a relatively advanced country—by Latin American

standards—but modernity was mostly for the country's European-descended elite and foreigners. Economic disparities and poverty among the disadvantaged portions of the population resulted in widespread support for the revolution led by Fidel Castro in 1959. Castro's successful revolt ended the long line of weak and authoritarian governments with promises of racial and economic equality. Cuba's one-party communist government has ruled the country since the early 1960s and instituted programs that led to advances in medicine, education, and literacy, particularly among Afro-Cubans. The path to equality for Afro-Cubans is often stymied by successive economic crises, patronage politics, and profound racial tensions. Afro-Cuban social clubs and organizations continue to seek respectability and socioeconomic equality without running afoul of the Cuban authorities. Many Afro-Cuban activists are among the most well known of the political dissidents seeking greater freedom for all the people of Cuba.

Further Reading

Daniel, Yvonne. *Rumba: Dance and Social Change in Contemporary Cuba (Blacks in the Diaspora).* Bloomington, IN: Indiana University Press, 1995.

Pappademos, Melina. *Black Political Activism and the Cuban Republic (Envisioning Cuba).* Chapel Hill, NC: University of North Carolina Press, 2011.

Afro–South Americans

South Americans of African ancestry are called Afro–South Americans, and sometimes referred to as Afro–Latin Americans. There are an estimated 19 million Afro–South Americans in the countries of South America other than Brazil. Because of a widespread lack of consensus regarding who is Afro–South American and confusion in enumeration, there are no reliable population figures for most South American countries. The largest percentages of Afro–South Americans are in Colombia, French Guiana, Guyana, Peru, and Venezuela with smaller populations in Argentina, Bolivia, Chile, Paraguay, Suriname, and Uruguay. The major language of the Afro–South Americans is Spanish, with English, French, and Dutch spoken in Guyana, French Guiana, and Suriname. Many Afro–South Americans also speak Creole languages, which are usually a mixture of African languages, Spanish, and other influences. Most Afro–South Americans are Roman Catholic, with smaller numbers of Protestants and other religious sects.

The first Afro–South Americans arrived in the Americas with the early Spanish colonists in the 16th century. Although many were brought to the region as slaves, others came as free men. The Atlantic slave trade grew rapidly as colonization spread across the continent. The indigenous peoples were quickly decimated through abuse, slavery, and imported European diseases. By the 1520s, African slaves were being imported into the colonies steadily to replace the rapidly declining indigenous population. As labor demands grew, more and more Africans were imported to work as agricultural hands, menials, domestic servants, or miners. Most of the slave ships arrived in South America from ports in West Africa and Central Africa. By the early 18th century there were sizable populations of African descent in most of the coastal regions, particularly those in the northern part of the continent where plantation agriculture and mining required larger numbers of laborers. African workers pioneered the extraction of alluvial gold deposits and the cultivation of sugarcane. Over time the Afro–South Americans born in the colonies began to be referred to as *ladinos*, slaves born into the Hispanic culture as opposed to *bozales*, slaves brought directly from Africa. Resistance to slavery was widespread and many Afro–South American slaves fought for their freedom as soon as they arrived. Numerous escaped slaves formed communities in the less accessible regions where sizable Afro–South American populations remain today. The escaped slaves, known as *cimarrones* in most of the colonies and as *maroons* in the Guiana colonies, often mixed with indigenous peoples and adopted a tribal formation. In other areas of northern South America the imported Africans also mixed with the indigenous peoples to produce a large mixed population known as Zambos. As few European women accompanied the Spanish colonists, they often took African or mixed-race women to produce a large and growing mulatto population. As the mixed population grew, a hierarchy based on pigmentation became increasingly important to protect the privileges of the Spanish masters and their Spanish and mestizo children. With the spread of this system the Spaniards formed the top of the hierarchy, the mestizos or mixed bloods were in the middle, and the Africans and indigenous peoples were at the bottom.

The culture of the Afro–South Americans varies from country to country, with local populations reflecting the regional cultures of each South American nation. The traditions brought to the New World by the early African slaves survive in many areas and influence the local culture beyond the Afro–South American communities. Religious traditions were also fused with Roman Catholicism, creating a creolized religion. The many saints correspond to African deities. Afro–South American priests were often known as "healers" as in Africa. The Catholic mass is typically held to the accompaniment of drumbeats. The important Roman Catholic celebration of Corpus Christi is celebrated with dancing, drums, and masks, traditions that can be traced to the Congo region of Africa. The mixture of African drums and Spanish melodies produced a number of regional music styles that form an important part of Afro–South American culture. Little

known outside their home countries until the 1950s and 1960s, many of these musical traditions now have international followings. The mix of the various African cultures with the Spanish, French, Dutch, and English colonial cultures and the indigenous cultures of the region has produced many unique forms of language, religion, music, and dance. Many of these Afro–South American cultural traits have become pervasive in South America.

Afro–South Americans played a significant role in the independence struggle that led to the liberation of Spanish South America in the early 19th century. The leaders of the independence movements initially refused to accept Afro–South Americans in their armies but soon realized they would never be victorious against the Spanish without the support of the blacks, Zambos, or mulattos. The slave trade continued to deliver slaves directly from Africa until the 1840s when buying African slaves became more expensive than purchasing slaves born locally. Some countries, such as Venezuela, banned slavery in 1845, mostly out of fear of a widespread slave revolt. The last slave imports from Africa arrived in South America in 1850. Most of the former Spanish colonies ended slavery in the 1850s, although discriminatory laws and denial of access to education kept most Afro–South Americans in rural areas as agricultural workers. Several countries promoted the ideology of *mestizaje* or miscegenation, the whitening of their national populations. In the early 20th century, laws were passed to prohibit dark-skinned immigrants from settling in the various countries. Some Afro–South Americans began to urbanize in the 1930s while others preferred to remain in isolated communities where they could practice their culture without interference. After World War II, some attempts to address disparities were made by providing education, health care, land reform, and trade union formations, but the problems of the Afro–South Americans were mostly ignored until the 1960s. The so-called Latin Africans led a black-power movement based on events in the United States. The movement quickly spread to communities throughout the region. Bans on black immigration were mostly removed and universities began to study Afro–South American history, art, music, and dance, but even with these reforms the Afro–South Americans remain at the bottom of the economic ladder in the 21st century.

Further Reading

Andrews, George Reid. *Afro-Latin America, 1800–2000.* New York: Oxford University Press, 2004.

Gates, Henry Louis Jr. *Black in Latin America.* New York: New York University Press, 2011.

Minority Rights Group, ed. *No Longer Invisible: Afro-Latin Americans Today.* London: Minority Rights Group, 1995.

Aguarunas

The Aguarunas, sometimes known as Awajún, their name for themselves, are an indigenous South American ethnic group living in the eastern Amazonia region of Peru. The estimated 45,000 Aguarunas speak a language belonging to the Jivaroan language family, a group of closely related dialects spoken in the Amazonian region. Nearly all Aguarunas are bilingual, also speaking Spanish, the language of education and administration. Most of the Aguarunas adhere to their traditional belief system that includes the veneration of many spirits and mythological figures. A growing minority have adopted Christianity, mostly belonging to several evangelical Protestant sects.

The Aguarunas are known to be fierce warriors, and for many centuries they have defended their homeland in the basins of the Marañón and Alto Mayo rivers. Legends and early accounts tell of attempts by the Incas Huayna Capac and Tupac Inca Yupanqui to unsuccessfully extend their empires into the homelands of the Aguarunas. The Spanish conquistadors first encountered Aguaruna groups in 1549. Two Spanish settlements, Jaén de Bracamoros and Santa Maria de Nieva, were founded in lands traditionally known as Aguaruna territory. A half century of worsening relations between the Spanish and the Aguarunas resulted in a widespread rebellion of the indigenous peoples. The Spanish were forced to abandon their settlements and farms and flee the region. Later Spanish attempts to colonize the territory in the 17th and 18th centuries failed due to armed Aguaruna resistance. The rough terrain of their homeland made incursions by enemies very difficult, with the invaders always at risk of attack in the lowland jungles. The Aguarunas continued to live a traditional lifestyle of hunting, fishing, and subsistence agriculture.

Because of their relative isolation, the Aguarunas' culture has survived nearly intact. Traditionally the Aguarunas relocated on a regular basis as soil fertility and wild game populations declined in the immediate vicinity of their villages. Most Aguarunas now live in permanent villages as relocations are difficult beyond their range-titled community lands. Some of their villages are now surrounded by the farms and villages of the growing nonindigenous populations. These populations have also greatly influenced the Aguaruna culture as new ideas and innovations replace traditions and historic ways. The Aguarunas have retained a strong traditional institution of mutual aid, known in their language as *ipáamamu*, with community groups constructing housing for young couples, clearing new fields, and aiding in the planting or harvesting of communal lands.

The Spanish authorities mostly ignored the region up to the wars of independence that ended with Peru becoming effectively independent in 1821. Tentative contacts by Peruvian authorities were rejected as were the earlier Spanish overtures. Attempts by Dominican and Jesuit missionaries to convert the Aguarunas were also largely unsuccessful. The Peruvian government finally established an agricultural colony at Borja in Aguaruna territory in 1865, but other colonies failed due to Aguaruna resistance. The Peruvian government, due to the distance and difficulties of supply, mostly left the Aguarunas to their traditional seminomadic life until the 1950s. The arrival of Christian missionaries, the building of roads, and the construction of an oil pipeline created tensions between the Aguarunas and the poor agricultural colonies, government agencies, and large profit-seeking corporations. In response to the threats to their traditional way of life

the Aguarunas began to organize to defend themselves based on the rights of indigenous peoples. Since the 1970s the leaders of the Aguarunas have increasingly become engaged in various economic activities. Most of the Aguarunas have given up their seasonal migrations to settle in small villages. Some communities have taken up the cultivation of rice, coffee, cocoa, and bananas for sale in local village markets or for transport to the cities of the coastal plain far to the west. Many Aguarunas have also become involved in the maintenance of the Transandean Oil Pipeline that traverses part of their traditional territory. The medicinal plant industry is playing an increasingly important role in their local economy. In the mid-1990s, the Aguarunas began to negotiate a unique bioprospecting agreement with a large American pharmaceutical company and a group of ethnobotanists from Washington University in Saint Louis. After several incidents and a long process of talks, the Aguarunas are still awaiting results. In the meantime they have developed an increasing range of plants and other goods from their jungles that have become a profitable way for them to manage their territory without the disruptions of big business or mining companies.

Further Reading

Berlin, Brent and Elois Ann Berlin. *Ethnobiology, Subsistence, and Nutrition in a Tropical Forest Society: The Aguaruna Jivaro.* Berkeley: University of California, 1977.

Brown, Michael F. *Tsewa's Gift: Magic and Meaning in an Amazonian Society.* Washington, D.C.: Smithsonian Institution Press, 1986.

Robinson, Lila. *Eight Years in the Amazon Headwaters: My Life in Three Peruvian Tribes.* Bloomington, IN: AuthorHouse, 2005.

Aleuts

The Aleuts, sometimes known as Unangan or Unanga, meaning original people, are an indigenous ethnic group inhabiting the Aleutian Islands of the American state of Alaska. The Aleut language is an Eskimo-Aleut language still spoken by just a few hundred people. The Aleuts usually use English, which is now the dominant language in the region. Most of the Aleuts are Christians, many belonging to the Russian Orthodox Church. The traditional beliefs are still practiced and are often part of Christian religious services.

The population of the Aleutian Islands has never been very large due to a lack of territory and resources. Because of the location of the islands, an archipelago of more than 300 small volcanic islands stretching like a broken bridge from Alaska to Asia, many anthropologists believe the islands were a route used by the first humans to cross from Asia to the Americas. The islands were settled by migrants from Asia approximately 7,000 years ago. The settled groups in the islands developed advanced skills in hunting, fishing, and basket weaving. Aleut hunters and warriors were skilled at making their own weapons and canoes. The Aleut population in the early 18th century was estimated at 25,000, spread through the archipelago in numerous small fishing villages. In 1741 the Russian government dispatched explorers Vitas Bering and Aleksei Chirikov in two ships to explore the northern Pacific region. Shipwreck and other disasters plagued the expedition, including Bering's death in the Aleutian Islands, but survivors reaching Russia's Kamchatka Peninsula reported the islands were rich in fur-bearing animals. Furs were in great demand so Siberian fur hunters flocked to the region, gradually moving eastward across the archipelago to the Alaskan mainland. The islands came under the authority of the Russian-American Company, leading to sporadic conflict between the colonizers and the Aleuts. The colonies established in the islands became more stable when the Russians instituted policies that allowed greater social status, education, and professional training to children of Aleut-Russian marriages. Within a generation or two the administration of the islands was largely in the hands of native-born Aleut speakers. In 1760, Russian citizenship was extended to the Aleut people and a detailed census of the islands was undertaken. A party of Russian Orthodox priests and monks arrived in the islands in 1793. Conversion to Russian Orthodoxy slowly spread among the population, even though within two years only one of the Russian priests remained alive. He settled on Spruce Island and often defended the Aleuts against the Russian trading companies. He is known to Russian Orthodox believers as Saint Herman of Alaska. The Russian hunters and traders took so many fur-bearing animals that the important otter population was decreasing year by year. In 1784, hundreds of Aleuts marched to the Russian compound but the Russians opened fire. The Aleuts again attempted to march but the Russians took around 40 Aleut women and children

Party of Aleuts and Chief (George C. Martin), near Katmai, Alaska, 1904. (USGS)

hostage. The Aleuts quickly surrendered. Four Aleut leaders were executed and many of the Aleuts left the islands with Russian compounds or trading posts. Warfare, hunger, and European diseases decimated the population, which dropped to just a few thousand by the end of the 18th century.

Aleut culture is a modern Alaskan culture that retains much of the traditions of the earlier culture. Some Aleuts continue to construct traditional houses known as *barabara*, which are built around a large pit. The *barabara* kept the occupants warm at all times, resisted the frequent rains, and sheltered the families from the high winds common to the islands. Fishing, hunting, and gathering are traditional pursuits with many Aleuts still working as fishermen. Traditional art forms are also maintained, particularly the prized Aleut carvings. The carvings are distinct in each part of the islands and have attracted buyers for centuries. Aleut basket weaving is considered

one of the finest in the world. The tradition began in prehistoric times and modern weavers continue to produce woven mats of a remarkable texture and works of art with roots in the traditional basket craft. Historically the Aleuts used piercings and tattoos to display their accomplishments and their religious views. Body art was believed to please the spirits of the animals they fished and hunted and to ward off any evil. While English is now the dominant language, there is a movement to revive the Aleut language, which is now spoken by several hundred people. The language was originally spoken in three dialects, one of which is now extinct. Russian Orthodoxy is the major Christian religion, although evangelical Protestant sects have won some followers in recent years.

As the fur-bearing animals were overhunted, many of the Russians left the region, leaving the Aleuts to return to their traditional pursuits. The population slowly

The Aleuts Own Saint Peter

An Aleut boy called Cungagnaq, born sometime before 1800 on the island of Kodiak, is now known as Saint Peter the Aleut by the Eastern Orthodox Church in the Aleutian Islands. He received the name Peter when he was baptized into the faith. According to Aleut tradition Peter and other Aleuts accompanied a Russian hunting expedition south to the California coast. Captured by the Spanish near San Pedro (now Pacifica), the Russians and the Aleuts were taken to Mission Delores in San Francisco for interrogation. Threatening torture, the Spanish Catholic priests attempted to force the Aleuts to convert to Roman Catholicism. When the Aleuts refused, the priests ordered that a toe be severed from each of Peter's feet. When he still refused, they slowly cut off his fingers and hands and eventually disemboweled him, making him a martyr to the Eastern Orthodox faith. Peter was canonized in 1980 and his martyrdom is commemorated on September 24.

began to recover but would never reach the precolonial population. As Russia lost interest in Alaska, the United States began negotiations to buy the region. After the American purchase of Russian Alaska in 1867, development in the islands accelerated. New building projects included a Methodist mission and orphanage, and the headquarters and docking facilities for a considerable fleet of revenue cutters that patrolled the hunting grounds close to the Pribilof Islands. The first public school was opened in the Aleut capital of Unalaska in 1883. American citizenship was extended to all indigenous peoples in 1924, giving the Aleuts greater access to local government and services. The first hospital was built at Unalaska in 1933. During World War II some of the outer islands were occupied by Japanese forces, but they were later driven out by American and Canadian troops. The islands were used as a refueling point for aircraft sent from California to Russia as part of the war effort. The United States government, over Aleut protests, conducted underground nuclear tests on Amchitka Island from 1965 to 1971. The events of World War II have been commemorated since 2002 in the islands as Dutch Harbor Remembrance Day.

Further Reading

Langdon, Steve. *The Native People of Alaska.* Anchorage, AK: Greatland Graphics, 2002.

Reedy-Maschner, Katherine L. *Aleut Identities: Tradition and Modernity in an Indigenous Fishery.* Montreal, Quebec: McGill-Queen's University Press, 2010.

Turner, Lucien and Raymond L. Hudson. *An Aleutian Ethnology.* Fairbanks, AK: University of Alaska Press, 2010.

Americans of European Descent

Americans of European descent, sometimes known as European Americans, are descendants of immigrants from Europe or from European populations in other parts of the world. Part of the extensive European diaspora, the estimated 224 million Americans of European descent mostly speak English, with a minority speaking other European languages. The majority of Americans of European descent are Christians, comprising both Roman Catholics and Protestants, with smaller numbers of Jews, Muslims, Buddhists, and people of other religions.

The continent of North America was mostly unknown when Christopher Columbus, sailing under the Spanish flag, encountered the continent in 1492. The Spanish settlers were the first Europeans to establish a continuous presence in the present United States.

The Treaty of Tordesillas, ratified by the Pope in 1494, divided the entire non-European world between Spain and Portugal. Other nations soon disputed the terms of the treaty and attempted to plant colonies in the New World. John Cabot, sailing for the Kingdom of England, landed on the North American coast in 1497. The first attempts were unsuccessful, but in the 16th and 17th centuries permanent colonies were founded by Spain, England, France, and the Netherlands. The majority of the colonies were in eastern North America north of the Spanish colonies in Florida. Martin de Argüelles, born at Saint Augustine, Florida in 1566, was the first person of European descent to be born in North America. Virginia Dare, born in 1587 on Roanoke Island, North Carolina, was the first child born to English parents. Eventually the entire continent came under the control of European governments, leading to profound changes in the population, landscape, and plants and animals. The largest European settlements were made by the English on the east coast of the continent starting in 1607. Early European territories in North America included the Spanish colonies of Florida and New Mexico, the English colonies of Virginia and New England, the Swedish colony of New Sweden, and the Dutch colony of the New Netherlands. In the 18th century, the Russians gained a foothold on the continent in Alaska. The European territorial claims took no note of the rights of the indigenous peoples, who often were enslaved and abused, or perished from the introduction of European diseases. The early colonies soon attracted immigrants from many parts of Europe drawn to the idea of unlimited space, vast natural resources, and freedom of worship. From the beginning of the English colonies the main source of labor and a large portion of the immigrants were indentured servants willing to trade years of their labor for transportation to the New World. Other immigrants, such as criminals, prisoners of war, and debtors, often became unwilling immigrants. Roman Catholics were the first large religious group to immigrate to the New World, as settlers in the Spanish colonies were required to belong to the Roman Catholic Church. The other European colonies tended to be more religiously diverse. Many groups of immigrants sailed to North America searching for the right to worship without persecution. The attractions of free or inexpensive farm land, religious freedom, and the right to improve themselves by their own hand were very attractive to those Europeans who wished to escape from persecution or poverty. The unintended introduction of European diseases resulted in large-scale epidemics that swept ahead of European contact. Between 1518 and 1618, an estimated half of the indigenous population perished. The accompanying political and cultural instability substantially aided the various colonies in seizing the great wealth in land and resources that had been used by indigenous societies. Gradually the English and French gained vast territories, which acerbated rivalries in Europe and led to skirmishes, attacks, and finally war for supremacy in the New World. The war fought between Great Britain and France in North America from 1754 to 1763 is known to Americans as the French and Indian War. The outcome of the war was one of the most significant developments in a long century of Anglo-French conflict. Defeated France ceded its colonies in Canada and Acadia to the British, who were then able to extend their territorial claims westward from the eastern coast to the Mississippi River. By the 1770s, the 13 British colonies had an estimated population of 2.5 million people. The colonies were prosperous and had developed their own legal and political systems. The British government's threat to American rights and self-government led to war in 1775 and the Declaration of Independence in 1776. In 1789, the Constitution of the United States became the basis of the federal government. By the turn of the 19th century the population of the United States was made up of citizens and immigrants from most European countries along with others not considered as citizens, such as indigenous peoples and slaves.

The culture of the Americans of European descent is the culture of the United States. As the largest component of the American population, the overall American culture reflects the European-influenced culture. The culture has been developing since long before the United States formed a separate country. The colonial heritage means that the major early cultural influences came from English, Irish, and Scottish settlers. Colonial ties to Great Britain spread the English language, legal system, and other cultural attributes. The ties of culture and language had a formative influence. Other important influences came from other parts of Europe and later from countries around the world. American culture includes many elements, including conservative and liberal influences, military and scientific competitiveness, risk taking, free expression, unique political structures, and material and moral elements. American culture, because of its geographic scale and demographic diversity, has a wide variety of expressions that vary greatly from region to region. There are many integrated but unique social and regional subcultures within the United States. The social affinities of Americans of European descent commonly depend on social class, political orientation, and a multitude of other considerations such as religious background, occupation, ethnic group membership, and regional elements. Although the United States has no official language at the federal level, over 30 states have passed legislation making English the official language and it is considered the de facto national language of the country. An estimated 97 percent of Americans speak and write English well, and for over 80 percent of American households it is the language spoken at home. The national dialect is widely known as American English, which is further divided into four major regional dialects and numerous subdialects. Besides English, there are numerous other European languages spoken in the country. Spanish is widely spoken and has official status in Puerto Rico and New Mexico. The United States is one of the most religious of the developed cultures. Nine of the original 13 colonies had official religions, but by the end of the Philadelphia Convention in 1787, the United States became one of the first countries in the world to codify religious freedom into law. Today an estimated 80 percent of Americans of European descent are nominally Christians, with smaller Jewish, Buddhist, Muslim, and other religious minorities.

The Americans fought a second war of independence in 1812 when the British attempted to reclaim their lost colonies. The territory of the United States expanded westward through conquest or purchase despite resistance from indigenous peoples and territorial claims by Mexico. African slavery was abolished in the North, but world demand for cotton allowed slavery to flourish in the South. Immigration from Europe went mostly to the North and its burgeoning industries. The secession of the slave states in 1861 began a bloody civil war that ended four years later in Southern defeat. In the years after the civil war, millions of European immigrants came to the United States. The growth in the number of immigrants from Europe continued unabated until it was stopped by World War I. In the 1920s, immigration was again a major factor in the rapid growth of the American population. Many of the immigrants believed they would someday return to their homelands, but having settled in, very few returned to the turbulence and uncertainties of Europe. The immigrants clustered in the large cities, often in separate neighborhoods that reflected the cultures of the home countries. Culinary traditions brought by the immigrants gradually evolved with increased access to meat and fresh vegetables. Despite the self-segregation into ethnic neighborhoods, mixed marriages increased and cultural borrowings broke down ethnic boundaries. As the immigrants prospered they came into contact with other European ethnic groups. During the 1930s the immigrant tide was diminished by totalitarian restrictions, but many frantic refugees continued to seek safety in the United States. World War II again stopped the flow of immigrants, but in the wake of the devastating war, many Europeans again decided to seek a better life in America. The Cold War mostly cut off immigration routes from eastern Europe, but a steady flow of refugees continued to arrive on America's shores from western and southern Europe. The children of the original immigrants grew up speaking English and became part of American culture, often retaining the traditions, cuisines, holidays, and nostalgia for the home country they inherited from their parents. The American culture became an overarching society that accepted and adapted the many cultures brought to its shores, but without losing the original elements that the early British, Irish, and Scots brought with them or the later additions from Germany, Italy, Spain, the Netherlands, and every other country in Europe. The integration of so many cultural traits from Europe, Asia, Latin America, and other parts of the world has given the American culture a resiliency and adaptability that is nearly unique in the modern world.

Further Reading

Jacobson, Matthew Frye. *Whiteness of a Different Color: European Immigrants and the Alchemy of Race.* Cambridge, MA: Harvard University Press, 1999.

Melzer, Milton. *Bound for America: The Story of the European Immigrants.* New York: Benchmark Books, 2001.

Walch, Timothy. *Immigrant America: European Ethnicity in the United States.* London: Routledge, 1994.

Amish

The Amish, sometimes known as Amish Mennonites, Plain People, Anabaptists, or Old Order Amish, are a North American ethnic group living mostly in the American states of Pennsylvania, Ohio, and Indiana and the Canadian province of Ontario. Outside these traditional Amish areas there are small communities found in 27 other states. The estimated 250,000 Amish speak Standard English with outsiders, but speak a German dialect known as Pennsylvania Dutch or Pennsylvania German among themselves. The Amish are members of a Protestant religious sect that can be traced back to the Anabaptist movement in 16th-century central Europe.

The Anabaptists began as a reform movement that spread through 16th-century Germany, the Netherlands, and Switzerland. The name Anabaptist means "rebaptizer," referring to the Anabaptist belief in adult baptism instead of the prevailing practice of infant baptism. The Anabaptists also promoted a strict literal interpretation of the teachings of Jesus. In seeking to pattern their lives around the teachings of the scriptures, they promoted a complete separation of the church from the government, which led to persecution and many deaths among the Anabaptists. In 1536, Menno Simons, a Roman Catholic priest in the Netherlands, became the leader of a small group of Anabaptists who became known as Mennonites. In 1693 the followers of a Swiss Anabaptist leader, Jacob Ammann, broke away from the movement to form their own church, whose members came to be called the Amish. Amman added ceremonial foot-washing, the strict shunning of excommunicated members, and the practice of dressing in plain garments to the basic Anabaptist doctrines of adult baptism and nonviolence. Government persecution and economic hardship pushed many of the Amish to begin immigrating to other parts of the world, particularly to North America. The first group settled Pennsylvania between 1727 and 1790. Under British rule, they migrated to the rich farmlands of central Pennsylvania where they formed self-sufficient communities that shunned the modern artifacts for a simple life based on their Anabaptist traditions. In the New World, the Amish settlers faced many hardships, including pressure to fight for the rebels during the American Revolution, but they found in their new communities the religious freedom they had long sought.

Amish culture reflects the culture prevalent during the immigration and settlement of the Amish communities in North America. Those communities that continue to practice strict adherence to Amish customs and precepts are known as Old Order Amish. They are easily recognizable to outsiders by their conservative, even somber clothing reminiscent of the 19th century, and by their continued use of horse-drawn buggies instead of automobiles. In their belief that the simplicity of the lives of their ancestors is a model for modern life, the Amish farm without tractors and live without telephones, electricity, central heating, or other modern conveniences. Living in traditional close-knit communities, they continue to rely on their neighbors and their devotion to their religious teachings to meet their needs and to ensure the continuation of their unique way of life. The Amish language is a combination of the original German and the English that the early Amish settlers learned in their new homeland. Called Pennsylvania Dutch, the language is a German dialect and the "Dutch" refers to the German word *Deutsch*, which means "German." The Amish are Christians, members of a sect that believes in the direct influence of the Holy Spirit on the heart of true believers. The Bible, specifically Luther's German Bible, is their primary source and the Amish consider its text to be the direct word of God. The Ordnung, meaning "order," is the collection of scripturally based principles and practices on which the Amish pattern their daily lives. The Ordnung is primarily a collection of traditional oral beliefs passed down from generation to generation. The Ordnung usually differs somewhat from one community to the next due to the existence of many local customs and interpretations of the scripture. There are four primary groups within the Amish community. The Old Order Amish are the most conservative with strict adherence to the traditional practices of plain dress, rural life and occupation, and separation from worldly customs. The Amish Mennonites and the Beachy Amish have split from the Old Order Amish and have fewer restrictions; for instance, the use of electricity and automobiles is allowed among them. The New Order Amish separated from the Old Order Amish, and while they continue to use horse and buggy for transportation, they allow the use of electricity and telephones in the home as well as tractors for farming. Having children, raising them, and frequently socializing with neighbors, relatives, and friends are the greatest functions of the Amish family. All Amish communities believe that large families are a blessing from God. Most Amish do not educate their children beyond the eighth grade, believing that basic knowledge is enough to prepare the students for the Amish way of life.

Between 1815 and 1865, a second wave of Amish immigrants left Europe to settle in Ohio, New York, Indiana, and Illinois. The Amish who remained in Europe eventually merged into the Mennonite movement or mainstream Protestant congregations. The Amish communities continued to practice their religion, were successful at farming, and the founding of new communities in other parts of the United States. Most of the Amish communities that were

Amish farm, Belmont Road, Paradise, Pennsylvania. (Corel)

established in North America did not retain their Amish identity. The major split that resulted in the loss of identity occurred in the 1860s. During the 1860s, *Dienerversammlunger* or ministerial conferences were held in Ohio concerning how the Amish communities should deal with the pressures of modern society. Because the meetings were a progressive idea, the more traditional leaders agreed to boycott the conferences. The more progressive groups, representing around two-third of the total Amish population, retained the name Amish Mennonite. Many of these progressive communities eventually merged with the Mennonite Church and other Mennonite denominations, especially in the early years of the 20th century. The more traditional communities became known as the Old Order Amish. By 1920 the Amish population was estimated at 5,000 people.

In the 1960s, another group split from the Old Order Amish to form separate communities of New Order Amish that allow some modern conveniences, although they retain the horse and buggy for transportation. The population grew rapidly due to large families, resulting in the founding of new communities in other parts of North America. By 1992, the population burgeoned to 125,000 and in just the last three decades, the Amish population has doubled to around 250,000. Since most of the Amish descend from about 200 18th-century founders, genetic disorders caused by inbreeding exist in many communities. Some of the disorders are quite rare and are often serious enough to increase the mortality rate among Amish children. The majority of the Amish accept these as "Gottes Wille" and reject the use of preventive genetic tests. Modern

Amish life often feels pressure from the outside world with issues such as taxation, education, law and law enforcement, and occasional cases of discrimination and hostility. The Amish way of life increasingly diverges from that of modern society. Like other citizens, the Amish pay sales and property taxes; however, Amish buggies, bicycles, and pedestrians use public roads and highways but pay no motor vehicle tax or motor fuel tax. The Amish have a religious objection to insurance and subscribe to Church Aid, which helps community members in need. The primary problem for many Amish communities is the struggle to main their traditional way of life away from the temptations of the modern world that surrounds them. The strict adherence to their traditional way of life means that problems such as alcoholism, drug addiction, homelessness, or domestic violence are very rare.

Further Reading

Clark, Mindy Starns. *A Pocket Guide to Amish Life.* Eugene, OR: Harvest House, 2010.

Kraybill, Donald B. *The Riddle of Amish Culture.* Baltimore: The John Hopkins University Press, 2001.

Nolt, Steven M. and Thomas J. Meyers. *Plain Diversity: Amish Cultures and Identities.* Baltimore: The John Hopkins University Press, 2007.

Anguillans

The Anguillans are a Caribbean ethnic group, the people of the island of the British Overseas Territory of Anguilla. The island is the most northerly of the Leeward Islands in the Lesser Antilles. The estimated 15,000 Anguillans are mostly blacks or mulattos, the descendants of African slaves. Outside their island there are Anguillan communities on other Caribbean islands, and in the United Kingdom and the United States. The Anguillans speak English, the official language of the territory, but the language of daily life is a Caribbean patois that developed from archaic English and the various African languages brought to the island by slaves from West Africa. The majority of the Anguillans belong to Protestant sects with small Roman Catholic and other religious minorities.

The island was uninhabited when the first European explorers visited the region. The French named the long and narrow island *anguille*, or eel. The island was first colonized between 1632 and 1650 by English settlers from Saint Kitts, who brought with them the first of the island's African slaves. The small population mostly engaged in fishing or salt gathering. The island changed hands several times before it was acknowledged as permanently British by the terms of the Treaty of Utrecht in 1713. With little economic importance the island remained sparsely populated. The English population grew very slowly but the number of African slaves and their descendants soon outnumbered the Europeans. The majority of the slaves, most purchased from neighboring islands, worked on the plantations owned by the small number of European residents.

Anguilla's cultural history began with the Taino Indians who left artifacts but had disappeared before the 17th century. The abolition of slavery in the British Empire ended the plantation agriculture of the island and most of the white population left Anguilla, leaving behind their former slaves as subsistence farmers and fishermen. The culture of the islanders evolved as a mixture of native Caribbean, African, Spanish, French, and English influences. The music, dance, art, and cuisine of Anguilla reflect the varied elements of the early cultural influences. Most Anguillans speak British-influenced Standard English; however, the most common language spoken, other than Standard English, is the island's own patois known as dialect or simply Anguillan. The dialect has its roots in English and in the languages brought from West Africa, and is similar to the dialects spoken in the other English-speaking Caribbean islands. Christianity is an important part of Anguillan culture. The majority of the islanders belong to the Protestant churches, particularly the Anglicans and the Methodists, with smaller numbers of other Protestant sects, Roman Catholics, and Jehovah's Witnesses. Some Anguillans are followers of the Rastafarian religion.

During the colonial period, Anguilla was administered by the British Authorities of Antigua, but in 1824 it was placed under the administrative control of nearby Saint Kitts. The abolition of slavery in the British Empire in 1833 ended the plantation economy. In 1875, the Anguillans petitioned the British government for separate status, but were turned down because of the island's small population and limited economic activity. Despite Anguillan resentment of rule from Saint Kitts, Anguilla was joined to Saint Kitts and Nevis to form a single British colony in 1882. The island remained a very minor part of the British Empire well into the

20th century, neither politically nor economically important. Anguilla became part of the Leeward Islands colony in 1956, and in 1958 the island, along with Saint Kitts and Nevis, became part of the British-sponsored Federation of the West Indies. In the 1950s some Anguillans, seeking better economic conditions or educational opportunities, began to leave the island for the larger English-speaking Caribbean islands, the United Kingdom, or the United States. The Anguillans continued to chafe under rule from Saint Kitts with minor tensions often bringing on a crisis in the relationship of the three islands. In 1962, as the larger member states opted for separate independence, the Federation of the West Indies was dissolved. In 1967 the Associated State of Saint Kitts, Nevis, and Anguilla was organized, independent except for defense, foreign affairs, communications, and currency. The Anguillans soon rejected their ties to the other two islands and demanded a separate self-governing state. Negotiations with the Saint Kitts and British governments failed to find an acceptable compromise. On February 10, 1969, the Anguillans announced the severance of all ties to the United Kingdom and declared their small island a free and independent republic. The dispatch of troops and London "bobbies" ended the secession, but the island was granted the status of a separate self-governing territory although it technically remained part of Saint Kitts-Nevis-Anguilla. In 1980 the island was officially separated, and Saint Kitts-Nevis achieved separate independence in 1983. In 1989 the Anguillans voted to retain their ties to the United Kingdom, which provides the population with economic aid and stability. Tourism is now an important industry and many Anguillans are employed at the new hotels and tourist facilities.

Further Reading

Dyde, Brian. *Out of Crowded Vagueness: A History of the Islands of St. Kitts, Nevis and Anguilla.* Northampton, MA: Interlink Publishing Group, 2006.

Icon Group International. *Anguilla: Webster's Timeline History, 1572–2007.* San Diego: Icon Group International, 2009.

Webster, Ronald. *Scrap Book of Anguilla's Revolution.* Anguilla, Seabreakers, 1973.

Antiguans and Barbudans

The Antiguans and Barbudans are a Caribbean ethnic group, the inhabitants of the island nation of Antigua and Barbuda. The two islands, separated by only a few nautical miles, are the only inhabited islands of the island groups, which also include a number of small, uninhabited islands. The estimated 85,000 Antiguans and Barbudans are mostly of Afro-Caribbean ancestry with a small mixed population and people of European and Asian ancestry. Outside Antigua and Barbuda there are communities of Antiguans and Barbudans in the United Kingdom, the United States, and Canada. English is the official language and is understood throughout the islands, but many of the local people speak a Creole language known as Antiguan Creole. The accent of the Barbudans is slightly different from that of the Antiguans. About three quarters of the population comprises Christians, the largest denominations being Anglican, Baptist, Presbyterian, and Roman Catholic.

Indigenous peoples inhabited the islands when Europeans first encountered the archipelago. Christopher Columbus visited the islands in 1493, naming the largest of the group Santa Maria de la Antigua. European diseases, malnutrition, and slavery decimated the indigenous population even before the first English settlement was established in 1632. Barbuda was settled in 1684. African slaves were imported to work in English sugar plantations from the late 17th century. Most of the slaves were imported from Africa's west coast. The Africans brought their languages, cultures, and religions to the islands. Despite the brutal working conditions, the African population of the islands grew rapidly as the sugar industry expanded. Profits from sugar made the European minority very prosperous, but the growing slave population lived in terrible conditions. By the middle of the 18th century, the islands were dotted with cane-processing windmills, each the most visible landmark of the many sizable plantations. By the end of the 18th century, Antigua became an important military port as well as a valued commercial colony.

The culture of the Antiguans and Barbudans fuses British and African traditions. Many of the cultural traditions are British, including the national sport of cricket. American popular culture also influences the region's fashion and media. Family and religion are important elements of everyday life in Antigua and Barbuda. Religious observances are important cultural events, including Antigua's famous national carnival held each August. African traditions are particularly evident in music and dance. Calypso and soca music are considered as island music, and dances originally brought from Africa have been modified to fit the island culture. The oldest form of music in the islands is calypso, which was begun by slaves forbidden to speak in the fields who used song to communicate. British and African traditions also combine in the Antiguan and Barbudan cuisine, which depends on fresh seafood and vegetables such as sweet potatoes, corn, and various greens. The official language of the country is English, which is understood by all Antiguans, but in daily life they use Antiguan and Barbudan Creole, a dialect heavily influenced by African structures. The Creole language uses many words of West African origin. These words are based on the dialects of the different tribes represented among the early slave population. Many of the proverbs that abound in the island Creole are derivatives of African sayings. Most Antiguans and Barbudans are Christians, about 75 percent of the total, with the Anglicans being the largest of several Christian demoninations that are active in the islands. Besides the Christian sects, there are communities of Muslims, Baha'is, and Rastafarians, with Rastafarianism being a particularly Caribbean belief system.

The political and social structure of the colony maintained the British at the top, controlling the local government and most of the island commerce. The plantation agriculture that sustained the colony required large numbers of slaves, brought from other islands or directly from slave ships sailing from West Africa. Although the slave population was the largest component of the population, the British retained tight control. Slavery in the British Empire was officially abolished in 1834, but most former slaves remained tied to the plantations because of a lack of available farming land, no access to credit, and a lack of experience. Between 1847 and 1852, some 2,500 Madeirans from the Portuguese archipelago in the Atlantic migrated to the islands, often establishing small businesses and joining the ranks of the mulatto and mixed race people. Many Antiguans and Barbudans are of partial Madeiran ancestry. The poor labor conditions persisted in the islands until 1939, when a member of a royal commission suggested the formation of a trade union movement. The Antigua Trades and Labour Union became the political vehicle for descendants of the former slaves. The Antigua Labour Party, formed by union leaders in 1946, became the majority political party by 1951. The racial structure of the society gradually gave way to a more egalitarian culture. In the 20th century, the former colonial social structure was phased out with the introduction of universal education and better economic opportunities. In the 1950s, Antiguans and Barbudans of African ancestry moved into the higher echelons of island society and government. Economically unstable since the end of the sugar era, tourism brought much-needed income and provided jobs for the growing population. Granted self-government by the British government, Antigua and Barbuda gained full independence in 1981. The Antiguans and Barbudans voted to remain part of the British Commonwealth and to retain ties to the British monarch as official head of the new nation. The descendants of African slaves now form the ruling elite of the islands and living standards have risen along with political power and education. The majority of the population is now involved in the lucrative tourist industry that provides jobs and foreign currency to sustain the Antiguans and Barbudans in the 21st century.

Further Reading

Clancy, Tomas. *Countries of the World: Antigua and Barbuda.* Seattle: CreateSpace, 2012.

Icon Group International. *Antigua and Barbuda: Webster's Timeline History, 1493–2007.* San Diego: Icon Group International, 2009.

Mottley, Marcus M., Ph.D. *An Anthology of Radical Thoughts and Empowering Perspectives.* Seattle: CreateSpace, 2010.

Apaches

Apache is a collective term for several historically and culturally related groups of Native Americans living in the southwestern states of Arizona and New Mexico. There are smaller numbers of Apaches in Oklahoma, Colorado, Texas, California, and other parts of the United States, particularly the large metropolitan areas in the west and southwest. The estimated 75,000 Apaches speak modern English and their own language, a Southern Athabaskan (Apachean) language, which is spoken in several distinct dialects. Most Apaches are nominally Christian, with the largest number belonging to the Native American Church. Minorities adhere to other Christian sects or to the traditional shamanistic tribal religion.

Historians and anthropologists believe that the Apaches are related to the Athabaskan-speaking peoples of Alaska and western Canada. Linguistic similarities indicate that the Apaches and Navajos were once a single ethnic group and that they probably migrated into the American Southwest after 1000 CE, possibly as late as the 14th or 15th centuries. In their new homeland the migrants scattered across a large territory extending into modern Mexico. Lacking any centralized tribal organization, the Apaches were divided into bands that were in turn divided into smaller local bands. The nomadic bands were small enough for every individual member to be aware of kinship ties to all other members. The early bands lived in tents, hunted bison and other game, and used large dogs to pull travois loaded with food and personal possessions. The early Spanish explorers of the region recorded encounters with several of the bands. Trade between the settled Pueblo peoples and the nomadic Apache bands was well established. The imposition of Spanish authority in the region disrupted that traditional trade. The Apache groups quickly acquired horses, introduced by the Spanish, which improved their mobility and their ability for quick raids on settlements. When the vast territory of New Mexico became a Spanish colony in 1598, hostilities between the Apache bands and the Spanish increased rapidly. Pressed by other tribes now mounted on horses, the Apaches had mostly abandoned the plains and the majority was concentrated in the dry, mountainous southwest by the middle of the 18th century. The Apaches attempted to retain friendly relations with the Spanish but when provoked, they proved to be difficult for the Spanish troops to subdue.

Culturally the Apaches are divided into two groups, an eastern group and a western group, both of which have adopted cultural traits from neighboring peoples. The name Apache is thought to come from a Yuma word meaning "fighting men," or from a Zuni word meaning "enemy." The name they use for themselves, Inde or Tinde, simply means "the people." The Apache ethnic group is divided into six regional groups—Kiowa Apache or Gataka, Lipan, Jicarilla, Mescalero, Chiracahua, and Western Apache. There are 13 different Apache bands in the United States, 5 in Arizona, 5 in New Mexico, and 3 in Oklahoma. The once nomadic people now occupy permanent homes, often outside reservation boundaries, and raise livestock, farm or work in tourism or in various tribal enterprises for their livelihood. The estimated 12,000 who live on the reservation lands are considered to be the heart of tribal life, keeping the traditional social and ritual activities alive for the entire Apache people. Traditionally the Apache bands were based on kinship through the lineage of women. The extended family of each band would usually consist of a primary couple, their unmarried children, their married daughters, the married daughters' husbands, and their married daughters' children. When a daughter married, a new dwelling was built near the family home for her husband and her. Several extended families worked together as a band for economic and military activities. The idea of "tribe" is still very weakly developed among the Apache peoples, with each cultural group remaining separate. The Apache language is divided into the seven traditional dialects that have similar grammatical structures and sound systems. The modern dialects are endangered as the use of English among the young is widespread. The Lipan dialect is already reported to be extinct. The traditional Apache religion is still practiced. It is centered on sacred geographical monuments and traditional rituals. The traditions retain their appeal and are often combined with the rituals of Christian sects, primarily Protestant rituals or the traditions of the Native American Church. Those individuals that retain and practice the traditional handicrafts and arts, such as basket weaving, ceramics, and painting, are now considered tribal treasures.

Periodic conflicts between the Apaches and the Spanish disrupted the lives of the various bands well into the 19th century. In 1821, their mountainous homeland was claimed by the new Mexican government, as the successor to the earlier Spanish claims to the region. The Apaches gained their greatest fame as warriors and guerilla fighters, defending their mountain strongholds against Mexican attempts to impose outside rule. The territory of the Apaches was acquired, without their consent, by the United States through agreements with the Mexican government between 1848 and 1853. The Apaches, as they did with the Spanish and the Mexicans, attempted to remain friendly with the new American presence in their homeland. The discovery of gold in California, in 1848, threatened the Apache with incursions of fortune hunters plundering their lands. Relations deteriorated rapidly leading to a series of wars between the Apaches and the military forces of the United States. Under a string of famous leaders, the Apaches resisted American expansion. The wars were among the fiercest fought on the frontier. The Apache wars lasted nearly a quarter of a century. Despite their adept use of swift horses and their superior knowledge of the terrain, most of the Apaches had been forced to surrender by 1873. Most agreed to settle on reserved lands known as reservations, but a large number of Apache warriors refused to give up their nomadic way of life or to meekly accept what they saw as permanent confinement. Skirmishes and raids continued, provoking renewed military campaigns against the Apache bands. The last Apache war ended in 1886 with the surrender of Geronimo and his few remaining fighters. The majority of the Apaches were settled on the reservations set aside by the American authorities but the Chiricahua, including Geronimo, were forced out of the Southwest and were held as prisoners of war for a total of 27 years. Geronimo died in 1909, and in 1913, the remaining prisoners were allowed to settle on tribal reservations in Oklahoma or New Mexico. The reservation Apaches mostly lived in poverty on the infertile reservation lands, dependent on government aid to survive. Since World War II, new government attitudes have allowed the Apaches to revive their traditional culture and to move into the mainstream of American life. Many problems continue in the lives of the Apaches, including high crime rates, alcoholism, and a larger than average population in jail, on parole, or on probation. Young members of the tribes, less amenable to past injustices, formed

Geronimo's camp before surrendering to General Crook, March 27, 1886. Geronimo's group included 18 men, women, and children. (Library of Congress)

the first activist organization, the Apache Survival Coalition (ASC) in 1989. The ASC has addressed such issues as a plan to transfer nuclear waste to storage on the Mescalero Reservation or the plan to construct an astronomical telescope on Mount Graham, one of the sacred monuments of the Apache tradition.

Further Reading

Haley, James L. *Apaches: A History and Culture Portrait.* Norman, OK: University of Oklahoma Press, 1997.

Verlade Tiller, Veronica E. *Culture and Customs of the Apache Indians.* Westport, CT: Greenwood, 2010.

Worcester, Donald E. *The Apaches: Eagles of the Southwest.* Norman, OK: University of Oklahoma Press, 1992.

Arab Americans

Arab Americans are citizens or residents of the United States who are of Arab descent. They are those Americans of Arab ethnic, linguistic, or cultural heritage who identify themselves as Arab. The estimated 3.5 million Arab Americans speak American English, often also speaking Arabic or other languages used in their homelands, such as Kurdish or French. The Arab American population is widely dispersed with populations in all 50 states. The majority lives in large metropolitan areas such as Detroit, New York, Los Angeles, Chicago, and Washington, D.C. In contrast to the majority of the population of the Arab countries which is composed of people of Muslim faith, the largest number of Arab Americans are Christians. According to estimates, some 63 percent are Catholic (including Roman Rite,

Eastern Rite, Maronites, and Melkites), some 18 percent are Orthodox (both Eastern Orthodox and Oriental Orthodox), 10 percent belong to various Protestant sects, and 25 percent are Muslims. The percentage of Muslims in the Arab American population has increased rapidly because new Arab migrants are mostly Muslim.

The history of Arab Americans in North America is long and very diverse. The first Arabs, probably slaves, are believed to have accompanied Spanish explorers in the 15th century. The European colonization of the Middle East and North Africa led to a stream of immigrants, first to the countries of Europe, then to the Americas. Relations between the new United States and the Barbary States of North Africa worsened as pirates from ports in the region attacked American shipping in the Mediterranean in the late 18th century. Despite skirmishes and ill feeling, small communities of Arabs were founded in a number of states along the eastern seaboard. The immigrants, mostly from North Africa and the Levant, were mostly Arab Christians seeking a new life free of persecution and uncertainty. In the late 18th century, the South Carolina House of Representatives ruled that the Moroccan Arabs living in the state would be treated according to the laws for whites, not the laws for people of African descent. The number of people of Arab descent remained small and mostly unnoticed well into the 19th century.

Arab American culture reflects the diversity of the Arab populations that settled in North America. Acculturation of the earlier Christian Arab populations was easier as the Christian religion provided a starting point into American culture. The Christian Arabs retained their distinctive cultural traits while embracing American culture. Arab Americans quickly adapted to the new culture, learning the language, and prospering. Like the other American ethnic groups they gradually moved to the suburbs, leaving the inner cities for the newer immigrant groups. Assimilation allowed many Arab Americans to triumph in business, sports, politics, and entertainment. Later immigrants, mostly Muslim, tended to live in Arab neighborhoods in the large cities where they could retain the language, traditions, cuisine, and religious observances of their home countries in the Middle East and North Africa. The diversity of the Arab American population in terms of culture, religion, and geographic background has prevented the blending of the various cultures into an Arab American culture. Each of the various Arab American groups retains its own cultural traditions. Attempts to bridge the gap between the many groups of Arab descent include the Arab American National Museum in Dearborn, Michigan. It features exhibits of the Arab civilization and its contributions to science, medicine, astronomy, and mathematics.

Arab migration to the United States was slow and mostly prohibited by quotas and prejudice. The first large number of Arab immigrants entered the United States during the era known as the Great Migration, between 1880 and 1924. Although most of the immigrants were from Europe, they also included more than 95,000 Arabs, mostly from the region known as Greater Syria, which is now Lebanon, Israel, and Syria. By 1924, there were some 200,000 Arab Americans living in the United States. As the number of Arab immigrants grew, resistance to Arab immigration also grew among Americans of European descent. Groups working to end immigration claimed that the Arab migrants were un-American, came from cultures that didn't fit with American culture, were more likely than European immigrants to be criminal and poor, and did not understand the American political system. These anti-immigrant movements gained strength, and a series of laws passed by the U.S. Congress in 1917, 1921, and 1924 restricted Arab immigration to a trickle. There were notable differences among the immigrants who came during the Great Migration. Some groups started family migrations and planned to remain in the United States. Others were mostly young men seeking work, who planned to return to their home countries after making enough to live well. Some groups clustered in certain large cities, while others moved to anywhere in the country where they found opportunities for work and prosperity. Arab immigration slowed greatly due to the Great Depression and the restrictive quota system. The next important group of immigrants began to arrive in 1948. The end of the quota system and the Arab-Israeli War sent a new wave of immigrants to the United States. From 1948 until 1966, some 80,000 Arabs arrived in the country as immigrants. The majority were ethnic Palestinians, with the second largest group arriving from Egypt. Many of the immigrants were Muslims and were better educated, often fleeing changes of governments due to popular revolutions or other upheavals. This trend continues to the present. The new immigration laws passed in 1965 began a third wave of Arab immigration. Between 1967 and 2003 over

750,000 Arabs immigrated to the United States. The large number of immigrants reflects the ongoing conflicts in their homelands, including intra-Arab warfare, and a marked increase in religious, ethnic, and sectarian tensions in the region. The rise of fundamentalist Islam added to the large numbers of Arab Christians seeking a new life away from the tensions and restrictions of the Middle East. The aftermath of the terrorist attacks in New York and Washington in 2001 led to some discrimination and incidents, particularly against some of the Arab American groups. In the years since the attacks, Arab Americans have made a great effort to eliminate radical elements in their own communities that could bring the whole group into conflict with the rest of the American public.

Further Reading

Ameri, Anan and Holly Arida, eds. *Daily Life of Arab Americans in the 21st Century.* Westport, CT: Greenwood, 2012.

Haddad, Yvonne Yazbeck. *Becoming American? The Forging of Arab and Muslim Identity in Pluralist America.* Waco, TX: Baylor University Press, 2011.

Kayyali, Randa A. *The Arab Americans.* Westport, CT: Greenwood, 2005.

Argentines

Argentines, sometimes known as Argentinians, Argentineans, or Argentinos in Spanish, are the people of the South American country of Argentina. Argentina is a multiethnic society that is home to people of many different ethnic backgrounds. Aside from the small indigenous population, nearly all Argentines or their ancestors immigrated to the region within the last five centuries. The estimated 42 million Argentines speak Spanish with a notable Italian lilt and often speak other European (particularly Italian), indigenous, or Middle Eastern languages. Outside Argentina there are sizable communities in Spain, the United States, Paraguay, Chile, Israel, Bolivia, Brazil, Uruguay, and Canada. The majority of the Argentines are nominally Roman Catholic with Protestant, Jewish, Muslim, and other religious minorities.

The earliest inhabitants were indigenous peoples who lived as early as 11000 BCE. The Inca Empire invaded and incorporated the present northwestern Argentina in 1480. Other tribes resisted the Inca incursions and remained independent. In the north, the Guarani developed an agricultural culture based on yucca, sweet potatoes, and yerba maté. In the south, the Pampas and Patagonia, nomadic tribes dominated the region. The first European expedition arrived at the mouth of the Rio de la Plata in 1516. The first Spanish settlement in modern Argentina was the fort of Sancti Spiritu, founded in 1527 on the Paraná River. Buenos Aires was established as a permanent colony in 1536, but was later destroyed by native peoples. The colony was established again in 1580 and became the center for the colonization of the vast region. The Spanish established a Viceroyalty of Peru in 1542, incorporating all Spanish settlements in South America. The Governorate of the Rio de la Plata was created in 1549 as the Spanish government of the region around the river. Colonial Spanish society in Argentina was organized in a system of *castas*. The Spanish born in Europe, the *peninsulars*, were at the top of the social hierarchy, as were people from other European countries. The Spanish born in the Americas, the *criollos*, formed the middle of the society, and the indigenous peoples and the African slaves imported by the Spanish formed the bottom. Relationships between Spanish males and native females resulted in a large mestizo population, mostly living in the countryside where they evolved into Argentine gauchos. Buenos Aires became the capital of the Viceroyalty of the Rio de la Plata in 1776, taking over the administration of the southern territories under Spanish rule.

Argentine culture is characterized by a significant European influence. The population is mostly of European descent with a conscious imitation of European styles in architecture, food, clothing, and entertainment. The other big influence on Argentine culture is that of the gauchos with their traditional rural lifestyle of self-reliance and independence. Indigenous Amerindian traditions such as yerba maté, now a popular caffeinated drink made from the leaves of the maté tree, have also been absorbed into the Argentine culture. Argentines are generally well-educated and literate, giving the culture a rich literary history and one of South America's most active publishing industries. The visual arts, such as architecture, painting, and sculpture are highly prized and have achieved renown throughout the world. The Argentine television and film industry is one of the largest in South America, creating around 80 full-length motion pictures each year. The television industry is large and diverse. Widely viewed in Latin America, its productions are now seen around the world. Argentines enjoy a high availability of cable and satellite television, similar to percentages in North America. Buenos Aires is one of the world's great capitals of theatre. The Teatro Colón is one of the city's national landmarks for opera and classical performances; in terms of its acoustics, it is considered to be the best among the opera houses in the world. Music is another important element of the Argentine culture. Tango is considered as Argentina's national musical symbol. The golden age of tango, from the 1930s to the mid-1950s, mirrored that of swing and jazz in the United States. Other musical forms such as Argentine rock have also developed distinct musical styles. The Argentine national sport is *pato*, played with a six-handle ball on horseback, but the most popular sports are association football and basketball. Argentine cuisine is an integral part of the culture; it not only features many of the pasta, sausage, and dessert dishes brought from continental Europe, but also a wide variety of indigenous and Creole dishes. The most famous Argentine culinary tradition is Argentine barbecue, which includes various types of meat, particularly steaks from cattle raised on the pampas. The highest consumption of red meat in the world is found among Argentines. The Argentine wine industry, one of the largest outside Europe, has grown rapidly in recent years with much foreign investment.

During the Napoleonic Wars in Europe, two ill-fated British invasions were launched against Buenos Aires. The local resistance was led by the Frenchman Santiago de Linieres, who later became viceroy through popular acclaim. The ideas of the French and American revolutions generated growing criticism of Spain's absolute monarchy and its overbearing rule of the American colonies. The overthrow of the Spanish king Ferdinand VII during the Peninsular War created opportunities for the opponents of continued Spanish rule. The Rio de la Plata colony deposed the authorities appointed by the monarch and appointed new officials who embraced the new political ideas. This began the Spanish-American wars of independence across the continent. The revolution in Buenos Aires began with the May Revolution in 1810, leading to the Argentine War of Independence fought between Argentine patriots and Spanish royalists. Argentina was declared independent in 1816, but further conflict quickly erupted between the Centralists and the Federalists. The Centralists favored a strong central government at Buenos Aires and wanted to encourage immigration from Europe while the Federalists wanted a loose federation of provinces. The ideas of the Centralists ultimately prevailed, but conflicts between adherents of federalism continued into the 1840s, a situation complicated by a French blockade from 1838 to 1840, and an Anglo-French blockade from 1845 to 1850. A new constitution was adopted in 1853, but the province of Buenos Aires rejected it and declared itself the State of Buenos Aires. The war between Buenos Aires and the other provinces lasted nearly a decade, ending with the victory of Buenos Aires. Buenos Aires rejoined the Confederation of Argentina under a unified government in 1862. During the political conflicts the population continued to grow rapidly and to move into the huge territories of the indigenous peoples. Most successive

Argentine governments attempted to kill the indigenous peoples, to push them into the far corners of the country, or to forcibly assimilate them into Argentina's European culture. Argentina has always attracted large numbers of European immigrants. During the 19th century, waves of Europeans—many Italians, but also Basques and Galicians from Spain and France, Welsh, English, Irish, French, Scandinavians, Germans, Slavs from Eastern Europe, and immigrants from other parts of Europe—poured into Buenos Aires. During the late 1800s, Argentina exported meat and grain to Europe. By the first decade of the 20th century, Argentina had become one of the world's wealthiest nations. Mass politics erupted into Argentine political life in the first half of the 1900s due to the rapid expansion of the working class. Many socialist and democratic experiments were tried, but the 1929 world economic crisis brought an end to experimentation. After a period of rule by an oligarchy of prominent Buenos Aires families, Colonel Juan Domingo Perón won the 1946 presidential elections with the support of the strong labor unions. With his charismatic wife, Eva Duarte de Perón, he created a regime based on import substitutions and the massive empowerment of the working class. The power of the traditional ruling oligarchy was broken, but under his rule the formerly wealthy country quickly declined. Between the mid-1950s and the 1970s military or weak civilian governments held power but escalating political violence, often supported by the labor unions, ended with a takeover by the military from 1976 to 1983. The military government launched the so-called Dirty War against "subversives," which saw the death of tens of thousands of innocent victims. Paramilitary death squads, operating with the approval of the government, were responsible for widespread torture and the "disappearing" of victims. A rapidly declining economy and growing public outrage brought huge demonstrations to the streets of Buenos Aires and other large cities. In an effort to channel Argentine resentment the military rulers launched an abortive invasion of the Falkland Islands, setting off with the United Kingdom. The Argentine defeat brought an end to the military government and a return to elected civilian governments. Attempts by successive governments to stabilize the economy mostly failed. The 1998 world financial crisis culminated in the Argentine economic crisis of 2001. The government froze bank accounts and devalued the currency bringing massive demonstrations to the streets. The tradition of populist government continues up to the present with the old Peronist traditions still evident in the Argentine government. Since 2001, an estimated half a million Argentines have abandoned the country to seek work and stability in the countries of Europe, North America, and Oceania. The European economic crisis of 2011–2012 forced many to return to Argentina putting a strain on the already unstable society.

Further Reading

Nouzielles, Gabriela and Graciela Montaldo, eds. *The Argentine Reader: History, Culture, Politics.* Durham, NC: Duke University Press, 2002.

Shumway, Nicholas. *The Invention of Argentina.* Berkeley, CA: University of California Press, 1993.

Tanzi, Vito. *Argentina: An Economic Chronicle. How one of the Richest Countries in the World Lost its Wealth.* New York: Jorge Pinto Books, 2007.

Arhuacos

The Arhuacos, sometimes known as Arucos, Bintuks, Bintukuas, Icas, Ikas, or Ijcas, are a Native American ethnic group inhabiting a highland region in the Sierra Nevada de Santa Marta in northern Colombia. The estimated 30,000 Arhuacos speak the Arhuaco language, also known as Ika, a language of the Chibchan language family spoken in northern South America. The majority of the Arhuacos follow their own traditional belief system with a small Roman Catholic minority.

The Arhuacos formed one of the groups of chiefdoms that go back to the first century CE. Known as the Taironas, the group formed one of the two principal groups of Chibcha speakers. Archaeological evidence shows a relatively dense population of the region by at least 200 BCE. Settled agriculture—mostly the cultivation of maize and yucca—allowed for population growth and the rapid deforestation of the chiefdom's territory. The Tairona civilization was known for advanced ceramics, artifacts made of gold, and an advanced society. Historically the Arhuacos lived closer to the Caribbean coast where cultivation of the plains was the mainstay of their society. In the 16th century, Spanish explorers visited the Arhuaco region. Contact with the Europeans was tolerated by the Tairona peoples, but by 1600 skirmishes and confrontations led to violence. Tairona resistance to Spanish attempts to take women and children as slaves led to widespread conflict. A part of the Tairona population migrated south to the higher elevations of the Sierra Madre de Santa Marta. The Arhuacos are only one of several indigenous groups in the highlands descended from the early-17th-century Tairona migrants. The relative inaccessibility of their new homeland allowed the Arhuacos to escape the worst of the Spanish colonial system imposed on Colombia in the 17th and 18th centuries. The Spanish continued to use the name Tairona for all the chiefdoms in northern Colombia. The individual tribes were indistinguishable to the Spanish and that tradition was carried on by modern archaeologists and anthropologists.

Arhuaco culture shows many of the traditions of the ancient Tairona culture often overlaid with later Spanish traditions and borrowings from neighboring cultures. The main economic activity of the Arhuacos is subsistence agriculture, traditionally with each family in the community farming its own plot of land. Each Arhuaco usually has two houses, one in the highlands where the weather is cooler during the hot season, and another in the warmer lowland mountain valleys although the disruption of Spanish colonial rule and confiscation of traditional lands ended this practice for many Arhuacos. Each of the areas of their homeland, the highlands, the midlands, and the lowlands are cultivated with different crops, now mostly for commercial purposes. Traditional handicrafts, such as handmade bags and woven fabrics, are also produced for sale in major Colombian cities. The Arhuaco language is a Chibchan language still spoken by the highland

Arhuacos. About 90 percent of the Arhuacos are monolingual, speaking only their own language, with a minority that is bilingual in Arhuaco and Spanish. The Arhuacos are a profoundly spiritual people who have retained their unique philosophy that globalizes their surroundings. They believe in a "father" or "creator" named Kakü Serankua, who is believed to have created the first gods and all living things. Other "fathers" and "mothers" are also venerated, such as the sun, the snowy peaks, and the moon. They consider the Sierra Nevada de Santa Marta to be the center or the heart of the world, and firmly believe that the well-being of the rest of the world depends on the well-being of their homeland.

In their mountainous region the Arhuacos remained isolated and mostly ignored once the most fertile of their lowlands had been taken leaving them the less accessible highlands. Some contacts with Colombian authorities took place in the mid-19th century, but their contacts with the outside world were mainly with intermediaries who bought their agricultural and handicraft products for sale in Colombia's market towns and cities. In 1916, the Arhuaco leaders asked the Colombian government for teachers so they could learn to read and write and study mathematics. Instead of the teachers, the government sent Capuchin friars. The friars soon prohibited the Arhuaco children from learning about their own culture and established a "regime of terror" by taking many Arhuaco children and placing them in a Capuchin orphanage. The friars also established a system of forced labor with government approval. The government finally withdrew the Capuchins but the experience continues to color Arhuaco relations with the government authorities. In 1943, provincial politicians, allied with Roman Catholic missionaries, and officials of the Ministry of Agriculture, expropriated some of the best lands in the region without compensation. The lands were used to build a state-owned commercial agricultural farm. The intrusion began a series of conflicts and incidents that drove the Arhuacos to create a self-defense organization, the Liga de Indios de la Sierra Nevada (Sierra Nevada Amerindian League) in 1944. The league, which allowed the Arhuacos to vocalize their complaints and became a center of Arhuaco life, was outlawed by the military government of Colombia in 1956. In 1962, the government appropriated land on Mount Alguacil, considered a sacred peak by the Arhuacos. A communications tower for television was built on the sacred mountain. When the Arhuacos protested, the government established a military post in their midst to maintain order and intimidate Arhuaco leaders. Ignoring the repeated threats, the Arhuacos reestablished their league. In 1972, the league was converted into the Cabildo Gobernador, a more widely accepted organization to defend their traditional values and land. After four decades of abuse, the Arhuacos rebelled against the Capuchin friars. Rebels took over the mission buildings and pleaded with the government to intervene. The Capuchins were finally removed from Arhuaco lands in 1983. In the early 21st century, the cultivation of marijuana by non-Arhuacos in the region has caused many problems with the Colombian military and the paramilitary groups of the drug trafficker clans.

Government attempts to construct hydroelectric dams and ecotourism routes in their territory have been actively opposed by the Arhuacos.

Further Reading

Bengt, Arne. *Arhuaco: Sierra Nevada.* Managua: Ministry of Culture of Nicaragua, 1986.

Elsass, Peter. *Strategies for Survival: The Psychology of Cultural Resilience in Ethnic Minorities.* New York: New York University Press, 1992.

Lizarralde, Roberto. *Indigenous Survival among the Bari and Arhuaco: Strategies and Perspectives.* Copenhagen: International Work Group for Indigenous Affairs, 1987.

Arubans

The Arubans, sometimes known as Orubans, are a Caribbean ethnic group, the inhabitants of the island of Aruba in the southern Caribbean Sea just north of the Venezuelan coast of South America. The estimated 106,000 Arubans are usually bilingual, speaking both of the island's official languages, Dutch and Papiamento. Many Arubans also speak Spanish or English. There are Aruban communities in the Netherlands, the United States, and on other Caribbean islands. The majority of the Arubans are Roman Catholics, with minorities of Protestants and other religions.

The island was home to the Arawak people when the first European explorer, Alonso de Ojeda, visited the region in 1499. The island soon became a center of smuggling and piracy, but the indigenous Arawaks were not exterminated as happened on the other Caribbean islands. In the early 16th century, the Spanish established a base on the island but territorial claims by other European colonial powers made Aruba a center of contention. The Dutch conquered the island in 1634, with Dutch authority confirmed by the other European powers in compensation for the Dutch cession of New Amsterdam to the English. Aruba and five other Caribbean islands were united as the Dutch colony of Curaçao. Initially the administration of Aruba was under Peter Stuyvesant, who left New Amsterdam (New York) for the Dutch Caribbean islands. The Dutch maintained the earlier Spanish use of the island, a huge cattle ranch staffed by the indigenous Arawaks. As the island was unfit for plantation agriculture only a few African slaves were imported. The population grew slowly during the 18th century, with a few Dutch landowners and administrators dominating the Arawak majority and the small African population.

The culture of the Arubans has evolved through the influences of the various peoples who have settled on the island. In 2005, there were 92 different nationalities living on the island. Dutch influences can be seen in the traditional architecture, the national holidays, and the traditional foods of the island. The original mixture that produced the Arubans included Spanish, Dutch, and Arawak traditions and customs that have become part of the modern Aruban culture. Physically the Arubans are mostly a mixture of the many groups that have settled on the island, although the physical appearance of the Arawak Indians continues to predominate. The Arubans speak standard Dutch and also Papiamento, a patois based on a Spanish creole language that now combines elements of Arawak, Spanish, Portuguese, and Dutch. An estimated 25 percent of the Papiamento vocabulary is of Dutch origin. Dutch is the language of administration and education and Papiamento is the language of daily life. The Papiamento language is also spoken on the other Dutch islands of Curaçao and Bonaire. The language now has official status, since 2003, and is recognized as a separate language while historically it was dismissed as a pidgin Spanish. The grammar and syntax have been changed and simplified, and this modified Papiamento is not intelligible to Spanish speakers. The major religion on the island is Roman Catholicism, with a number of Protestant sects also represented. The Catholic Church historically had great influence on the Arubans' daily lives, but the advent of tourism and the secularization of Dutch society in general decreased Catholic influence in the latter half of the 20th century.

The mixed population of the island intermarried freely, and by the early 1800s a distinct Aruban nationality with its own culture and language was evident. The first government statement written in Papiamento dates back to 1803. During the Napoleonic Wars the island was first occupied by French troops, and then by the British in 1805–1806. Following the final defeat of Napoleon Bonaparte and the liberation of the Netherlands, the island was returned to Dutch rule in 1816. Gold was discovered on the island in 1824, drawing in fortune seekers from many parts of the world. Gold remained the mainstay of the island economy until after the turn of the 20th century. Slavery was abolished in the Dutch possessions in 1863 and the island's economy quickly declined. Gold production ceased in 1913, deepening the economic depression in Aruba. Much of the island's European population returned to Europe, leaving behind the Aruban population of mixed European, Arawak, and African descent. The advent of petroleum production in nearby Venezuela quickly brought new prosperity for the Arubans. In 1924, the Lagos Oil and Transport Company established its first oil refinery in Aruba. Standard Oil constructed a second refinery in 1929, and in 1930, Lagos became part of the American oil company Exxon. The huge oil refineries revived the Aruban economy and brought an influx of oil workers to settle on the island. National sentiment grew as the Aruban culture evolved. In 1933, the Arubans sent the first petition to the Netherlands government for separate status and autonomy for the island. In World War II, the island was part of the self-governing Netherlands Antilles during the German occupation of the Netherlands. The war also brought great prosperity as the energy needs of the Allies meant more work and money for the Arubans. In 1951 Aruba and the other Dutch islands in the Caribbean gained greater autonomy as part of the Netherlands Antilles, which formed a federation under loose Dutch authority. From the beginning of the federation, the Arubans resented rule from the rival island of Curaçao. Tourism, beginning in the 1960s, brought a new source of income and greater prosperity. The Arubans, seeing themselves as a distinct ethnic group, demanded greater autonomy. Tourism replaced the refineries as the most important economic resource around 1985. Politically the Arubans supported several pro-independence and pro-autonomy organizations. In a referendum held in 1977 a majority voted for immediate independence, but the Aruban government was replaced as a consequence. The Arubans took on the trappings of independence while maintaining their ties to the Netherlands. In 1986, Aruba separated from the Netherlands Antilles to form a separate country as part of the Dutch nation. Support for full independence has since waned as prosperous, stable Aruba and its people are self-governing but enjoy the protection of Dutch nationality and the benefits of continued ties to the European Union.

Further Reading

Icon Group International. *Aruba: Webster's Timeline History, 1499–2007.* San Diego: Icon Group International, 2009.

Jeffrey, S. B. *A Brief History of the People and Culture of Aruba.* San Diego: Webster's Digital Services, 2011.

Saunders, Nicholas J. *The Peoples of the Caribbean: An Encyclopedia of Archaeology and Traditional Culture.* Santa Barbara, CA: ABC-CLIO, 2005.

Asháninkas

The Asháninkas, sometimes known as Asháninkas or Antis, are an Amazonian ethnic group living in the rain forests of eastern Peru with a small number across the border in the Brazilian state of Acre. The Asháninkas are sometimes referred to as Campa or Kampa, which they consider to be derogatory. The estimated 40,000 Asháninkas speak their own language, an Arawakan language, along with Spanish and some Portuguese. Most of the Asháninkas adhere to their traditional religious beliefs with a growing number embracing Christianity, both Roman Catholicism and the evangelical sects introduced by American and European missionaries.

The Asháninkas lived in isolation in the rain forests of the upper Amazonian region in prehistoric times. Known to the Incas, who called them the Anti or Thampa people, they gave their name to the Inca province of Antisuyu, but were notorious for their fierce independence and their warriors' skill in protecting their land and culture from intruders. Historically the Asháninkas lived in scattered bands in the forests of Junín, Pasco, Huánuco, and part of Ucayali. Traditional slash-and-burn cultivation of crops sustained the bands. The staple foods were yucca root and sweet potatoes. Hunting and fishing were important occupations, carried out using bows and spears. Women traditionally collected wild fruits and vegetables in the rain forest. Early Spanish explorers, in the 16th century, also noted the Asháninkas for their bravery and independence. The Spanish adopted the Inca name for the Asháninkas, Campa or Kampa, which means disheveled or ragged and dirty in the Quechua language, a name the Asháninkas found offensive. The Spanish first attempted to take control of the river valleys in 1595, creating several small forts garrisoned by Spanish or indigenous troops. The European incursion made little difference to the daily lives of the Asháninkas, but as time went on conflicts and skirmishes increased. In 1742 the colonizers were driven from the area by a general uprising of the tribes of the region led by the legendary Juan Santos Atahualpa. The uprising continued until 1752 by which time all missionaries and colonists had fled the region. The Asháninkas and the neighboring tribes had control over their ancestral lands for the next century.

Asháninka culture retains much of its traditions and customs due to the relative isolation of the Asháninka homeland. The difficult access to the region allowed the tribal groups to remain isolated from outside influences until relatively recently. Asháninka culture explains history and nature through its ancient myths and heroes. According to legend the dangerous insects of the region, such as red ants or wasps, are the transformations of evil men. The Asháninka religious beliefs also form part of the ancient myths. Instead of a creator they revere a hero, Avireri, who is believed to have transformed humans into animals, plants, rivers, and mountains. Their beliefs are based on the living forms that can be seen, and also a host of invisible beings or spirits. Among the good spirits are the sun and the moon. Shamans known as *sheripiári* are the intermediaries between the people and the supernatural beings. Central to their beliefs is an apocalyptic vision of the world. They believe that this world is so plagued by evil forces that it will someday be destroyed. After the destruction, there will be a new world free of violence, sickness, and death. Village life is communal with many economic activities, such as hunting and fishing, done collectively. Trade with other indigenous peoples of the region has greatly enriched the culture.

The Asháninkas remained isolated and secure until the beginning of the rubber boom in the Amazon Basin in 1839. The

Asháninka Indian, Moises Pianco, smokes a pipe during the 20th Moitara, in the headquarters of the National Foundation of Indians in Brasilia, Brazil, April 19, 2000. Moitara is an exhibition of indigenous crafts in commemoration of the Indian's Day. Ceremonies will mark the anniversary of the Portuguese arrival in Brazil in 1500. (AP Photo/Beto Barata)

rubber boom resulted in the invasion of their lands by various groups of rubber trappers. Many Asháninkas were taken by the rubber trappers as slaves to do the hard work of finding and trapping the rubber. Rubber trappers took women from the villages and often destroyed homesteads or villages after they were finished with trapping a district. An estimated 80 percent of the Asháninka population was killed between the 1840s and the end of the rubber boom in 1913. Loggers then moved into the region for the hardwood trees of the rain forest. Their treatment of the indigenous peoples was nearly as ruthless as that of the rubber trappers before them. Since the 1950s, Asháninka lands have been reduced

and their villages systematically destroyed, forcing many of the survivors to retreat into the jungle. Some fled across the border into Brazil, where a small community still exists. The near civil war in Peru in the 1980s and 1990s between the Shining Path rebels and the Peruvian military caused massive disappearances, displacement, and death among the Asháninka communities. Traditional occupations such as hunting and fishing were disrupted, an estimated 10,000 were displaced, some 6,000 died in the attacks and violence, and 5,000 were forced to join the Shining Path during this time. Between 30 and 40 small Asháninka communities completely disappeared. Malaria and other diseases brought to the region by loggers and colonists are a continuing threat to the ethnic group. In the mid-2000s the Asháninkas gained legal title to a portion of their lands, which became part of a newly created national park and reserved zone. Most of the refugees have returned to their ancestral lands, and many are now involved in projects to protect and strengthen their ancient culture. The Asháninkas continue to be threatened by oil companies, drug traffickers, colonists seeking farm land, illegal loggers and roads, well-meaning but inept conservation and missionary groups, and diseases, alcoholism, and disruption brought to the region by outsiders.

Further Reading

King, David C. *Peru: Lost Cities, Found Hope.* New York: Benchmark, 1998.

Lewington, Anna. *Rainforest Amerindians.* Austin, TX: Raintree Steck-Vaughan Publishers, 1993.

Varese, Stefano. *Salt of the Mountain: Campa Ashaninka History and Resistance in the Peruvian Jungle.* Norman, OK: University of Oklahoma Press, 2004.

Asian Americans

Asian Americans are Americans of Asian origin. This refers to persons having origins in any of the regions of the Far East, Southeast Asia, or the Indian subcontinent. The estimated 14.7 million Asian Americans, up to 17.4 million counting people with mixed Asian and other heritage, speak standard American English and often speak the languages they or their forefathers spoke in their original homelands in Asia. Asian Americans live in all parts of North America but are concentrated in Hawaii, the states of the West Coast, western Canada, and large metropolitan areas across the continent. Asian Americans come from varied backgrounds, and this variety is visible in the large number of religions practiced among them, from agnosticism and atheism to Buddhism, Christianity, Hinduism, Islam, and other religions brought from their original homelands.

The first Asian communities in North America were founded in the late 18th century. In 1763, a group of Filipino men established a small settlement at Saint Malo, Louisiana. The men fled mistreatment aboard Spanish ships as Spain controlled the region at that time. As they were seamen with no Filipino women with them, the Manilamen, as they came to be known, married local women, mostly Cajuns or Native Americans. Chinese sailors first arrived in Hawaii in 1778, the same year that Captain James Cook encountered the Hawaiian Islands. Many of the Chinese sailors settled in the islands and married Hawaiian women. Some of the descendants of these Chinese sailors can claim to be seventh generation islanders.

The cultures of the many groups that form part of the Asian American population are as varied as the groups themselves. Each group retains much of its traditional culture and increasingly adopts American culture. The first generation of immigrants normally held to their culture for protection, often settling in areas, towns, or cities with others from their home regions in Asia. Gradually, as they prospered and acculturated, they began to leave the ethnic ghettos to follow the overall American pattern of moving into better neighborhoods, often in the fast-spreading suburbs. Despite distrust and difficulties placed in their path by mainstream American society, the Asian Americans have prospered and flourished with high rates of educational achievement and a visible presence in many of the arts and professions. Among America's major ethnic and racial categories, Asian Americans have the highest educational qualifications, although this varies for each individual ethnic group. Asian influences on North American culture have added many Asian words to the English language, particularly the names of foods, food types, and religious terminology. Asian Americans are sometimes referred to as a model minority due to the cultural emphasis on a strong work ethic, a respect for elders, professional and academic success, and a high value on family, education, and religion. Statistics such as high personal income rates and low levels of incarceration plus higher-than-average life expectancy and low rates of many diseases adds to the positive image of Asian Americans.

The Chinese immigrants were the first to arrive in North America in large numbers, mostly on the West Coast in the 1850s and 1860s to work in mines or on the rapidly extending railroads. The immigrants often encountered very strong opposition, such as the violent rioting and physical attacks that forced them out of the gold mines of California. In 1854 the California Supreme Court ruled that the testimony of a Chinese man who was a witness to a murder committed by a white man was inadmissible. The Central Pacific railroad hired thousands to help build the rail lines through the rugged mountains of the West, but after the line was finished in 1869, the Chinese workers were mostly hounded out of many railroad towns in Wyoming, Nevada, and other areas. Many fled to the burgeoning Chinatowns, areas of large cities usually ignored by the local police. They were often attacked as undesirable strangers who brought with them disease, prostitution, and opium, along with economic

Murder Solidifies the Asian American Movement

Vincent Jen Chin, a Chinese American, was beaten to death in June 1982 in the Detroit suburb of Highland Park. His attackers, former Chrysler plant supervisor Ronald Ebens and his stepson Michael Nitz, confessed to outrage at the increasing market share of Japanese carmakers, which they blamed on all Asians. They initially received lenient sentencing in a plea bargain, which outraged the Asian communities across the country. The case became a rallying point for Asian Americans, and Ebens and Nitz were put on trial in federal court for violating Chin's civil rights as a result of the public pressure from a coalition of many Asian ethnic organizations. The murder of Vincent Chin is now considered the beginning of a nationwide pan-ethnic Asian American movement.

competition with other immigrant groups. Japanese immigrants arrived in large numbers between 1890 and 1907, many settling in Hawaii and others continuing on to the West Coast. In Hawaii the Japanese formed the largest component of the multiethnic population of the territory by 1910. In other areas they often faced discrimination and hostility, but these protests were mostly nonviolent. In 1869, the Fourteenth Amendment gave full citizenship to every baby born in the United States, allowing a number of Asians to become citizens rather than remain strangers and immigrants. However, in 1878, Chinese migrants were ruled ineligible for naturalized citizenship. The Chinese Exclusion Act was passed in 1882, banning further immigration of Chinese laborers, although students and businessmen were allowed to enter the United States. Hawaii joined the United States in 1898 and all its citizens, including the Asian majority of Japanese, Chinese, and Filipino ethnicity, were granted immediate citizenship. Immigration from other Asian countries and territories brought new ethnic groups to the country. The commonwealth status given to the Philippines in 1935 allowed for open immigration and thousands of Filipinos left their islands to settle in North America. When the United States ended World War II in 1941, many Japanese leaders in Hawaii and the mainland were arrested for being pro-Japanese. The government of the United States, along with Canada, Mexico, and other American nations, forced people of Japanese birth or descent into internment camps. The 100,000 people interred in the West Coast states mostly lost their businesses, homes, and other properties even as soldiers of

Japanese descent in the military services were winning fame as brave and loyal warriors. In 1946, naturalization opportunities were extended to Filipino Americans and Indian Americans, which included people from present-day Pakistan and Bangladesh. Activism grew from the 1960s to the 1980s as the term Asian American was adopted and Asian American rights were defended. Asian Americans were already moving into mainstream American culture, holding high political positions and producing noted teachers, entertainers, sports figures, politicians, and professionals of every occupation. By the 1990s Asian Americans were integrated into American culture and became visibly active in all parts of the country and in all walks of life. Asian Americans have only recently emerged as a cohesive, self-identified group among the American people.

Further Reading

Han, Arar and John Hsu, eds. *Asian American X: An Intersection of Twenty-First Century Asian American Voices.* Ann Arbor, MI: University of Michigan Press, 2004.

Lee, Jennifer and Min Zhou. *Asian American Youth: Culture, Identity and Ethnicity.* London: Routledge, 2004.

Zia, Helen. *Asian American Dreams: The Emergence of an American People.* New York: Farrar, Straus and Giroux, 2001.

Aymaras

The Aymaras are a South American ethnic group inhabiting the high Altiplano, a vast and windy plateau in the central Andes in Bolivia and Peru, with smaller numbers in northern Chile and Argentina.

The estimated 2.6 million Aymaras speak the Aymara language, which remains the dominant language of the region. Many Aymaras also speak Andean Spanish. The majority of the Aymaras are nominally Roman Catholic, with many continuing to practice their traditional Andean religion or a mixture of both.

The Aymaras first appeared in the altiplano region after the decline of the Tiahuanaco civilization in the 12th century CE. The early Aymaras probably migrated north from the southern part of the continent. Some historians and anthropologists believe that the Aymaras have inhabited parts of the altiplano for over 2,000 years and that they developed the little-known Tiahuanaco culture in the basin of Lake Titicaca. After resisting for over a century, the Aymaras finally succumbed to the invading Incas under Huayna Capac, who ruled the Inca Empire from 1483 to 1523, although the exact date of the Inca conquest of the Aymara homeland is unknown. Under Inca rule, the Aymaras retained some autonomy within the empire. The various ethnically and linguistically related groups were considered as separate ethnic groups. Groups such as the Lupaca, Pacaje, Uru, and Canchi did not see themselves as part of a larger Aymara ethnicity. The Aymaras adopted many Inca cultural traits and religious customs, but retained their separate languages and traditions. The Aymaras later joined the Incas to fight and subdue other indigenous cultures. The invaders from Europe, known as the Spanish conquistadores, conquered the Inca Empire between 1524 and 1533. The Spanish government was based in Lima in Peru, while the Aymara homeland came to be known as Upper Peru. The Spanish adopted the practice of calling all related cultural groups by the name Aymara. In 1570, the Spanish viceroy in Lima decreed the use of forced labor in the rich silver mines of the altiplano. The mine at Potosi was the richest silver mine in the world. Millions of Aymaras perished in the wretched conditions of the Spanish mines. The spread of European diseases further decimated the Aymara population. Colonial abuses and exploitation accelerated the rapid decline of the Aymara population in the region. A young leader of the Aymaras, calling himself Túpac Katari, led a widespread rebellion against Spanish rule in the 1780s. He raised an army of over 40,000 and surrounded and laid siege to the city of La Paz in 1781. After 184 days and 20,000 deaths, the siege was finally broken when colonial troops arrived from Lima and Buenos Aires. Katari besieged La Paz later the same year but the city was again saved by the arrival of Spanish troops. Túpac Katari was betrayed by his people and arrested by the Spanish after a feast. After undergoing torture he was executed by being torn into four pieces while still alive. Túpac Katari became a folk hero and later a national hero of the Aymaras.

Aymara culture combines the ancient traditions and customs of the preconquest cultures of the region with later borrowings from the imposed Spanish culture. Much of contemporary Aymara urban culture developed in the working-class Aymara neighborhoods of La Paz, the Bolivian capital. The distinctive bowler hats have been worn since the 1920s when the first shipment of bowlers was sent from Europe for use by Europeans working on the construction of railroads in the region. The hats were found to be too small to be used by the Europeans, so they were distributed among the local Aymaras. Apart from the bowler hats, Aymara women are known for the Chola dress of heavy skirts that also evolved in the urban areas. The distinctive Aymara costume became an ethnic symbol, even though it is an urban tradition and not a rural one. The Aymara language, originally known as *jaqi aru* or "the language of the people," is still the dominant language in the Bolivian altiplano and in southeastern Peru. In the urban areas most Aymaras are bilingual, speaking both Aymara and Spanish, with some also speaking a third language, Quechua, the language of the Incas. The religious practices of the Aymaras are a unique fusion of their traditional belief system and the religion imposed on them by the colonial Spanish. Many Aymaras have Christian first names but preserve their traditional family names in the Aymara form. The Aymara culture shows the cultural and religious traditions of both the Incas, the first to conquer the Aymaras, and the later Spanish colonizers. The Spanish suppressed the native Andean religions but the Aymara conversion to Roman Catholicism was only superficial. Modern Aymara society lives in a multispirit world. Many categories of magicians, medicine men, diviners, and witches maintain the traditional Aymara beliefs while belief in the afterlife, a Christian tradition, has become part of the modern belief system.

The Aymaras attend mass and celebrate baptisms in the Catholic tradition, but the religious festivals, based on the feast days of Spanish saints, show the importance of their traditional beliefs and customs, such as the regular offerings to Mother Earth, and the belief in the spirits that reside in the sky, the mountains, or natural forces such as lightning. The basic unit of Aymara culture is the extended family, which has been negatively affected by the expansion of cities and the Aymara migration to urban areas.

Unrest in the Spanish colonies grew into the wars of independence in the early 19th century. The wars raged over the region for many years with both factions, the patriots and the royalists, often forcibly enlisting Aymaras or taking food and other goods from the Aymara communities. After 16 years of war and violence, Bolivia was finally proclaimed an independent state in 1825. Wars between the newly independent South American nations resulted in more years of violence and devastation for the Aymara people. A period of political and economic instability in the mid-19th century meant continued hardship for the Aymaras. War between Bolivia and Chile in 1879–1983 ended with a small portion of the Aymara territory being transferred to Chilean authority. In the late 19th century, the price of precious metals increased bringing a modest prosperity and new jobs to the Aymaras, but the living conditions of the communities remained deplorable. Work opportunities were limited to the dangerous and primitive conditions in the mines, or to being serfs on the large estates that

Bolivian Aymaras offer ashes of coca, llama, salt, and sugar to the Mother Earth while receiving first rays of sunlight to celebrate Aymara New Year in the highest mountain near the village of Curahuara de Carangas, Bolivia, June 21, 2006. Aymaras, the country's most politically influential ethnic group, celebrate year 5514 on a calendar based mainly on the agricultural cycle, paying tribute to Mother Earth. (AP Photo/Dado Galdieri)

were held in near-feudal conditions by a small European elite. The majority of the Aymaras lived on subsistence farming or began to migrate to the cities in search of a better life. The Aymaras had no access to education, political participation, or economic opportunities. In the mid-1950s the idea of universal suffrage was finally introduced, allowing the Aymara to vote in some elections. Sweeping land reforms and the promotion of rural education was followed by the nationalization of most of the area's mines. Many Aymaras left the traditional communities to move to La Paz, Cuzco, and other cities of the Andean highlands. Large Aymara neighborhoods appeared in the large cities. A distinct Aymara urban culture evolved from the fusion of the rural traditions and the modern urban customs. Desperation and the influence of radical movements in other South American countries resulted in the organization of a number of Aymara groups demanding greater political power and more control over their lives and a say in the decisions that affect the Aymara people. Government attempts to suppress the cultivation of coca, which can be processed into cocaine, brought renewed violence and hardship in the 1970s and 1980s. The coca leaf has a long history and has been part of Aymara culture.

Aymara workers traditionally chewed the leaf for its properties as a mild stimulant and appetite suppressant. In the 1990s governments in the region began to campaign for greater indigenous rights and to promote programs to benefit the indigenous peoples of the region. Bilingual education, greater access to health care, work training programs, and rural development brought new vigor to the Aymara communities both in the countryside and in the cities. In 2005 an Aymara coca farmer, Juan Evo Morales, was elected president of Bolivia. A new constitution was adopted that gave more power to the Aymaras and the other indigenous peoples that formed the majority of the Bolivian population. Morales—who was reelected in 2009—remains the champion of indigenous rights in South America with widespread Aymara support.

Further Reading

Egan, James. *The Aymara of South America.* Minneapolis: Lerner Publishing Group, 2002.

Icon Group International. *Aymara: Webster's Timeline History, 1582–2007.* San Diego: Icon Group International, 2010.

Kolata, Alan L. *Valley of the Spirits: A Journey into the Realm of the Aymara.* Hoboken, NJ: Wiley, 1996.

B

Bahamians

The Bahamians are a North American ethnic group, the inhabitants of the Commonwealth of the Bahamas, a nation of more than 3,000 islands, cays, and islets located in the Atlantic Ocean just southeast of the Florida Peninsula. The estimated 350,000 Bahamians are mostly of African descent with smaller minorities of European descent, Asians, and Hispanics. Sizable Bahamian populations live in the United Kingdom and the United States. The official language of the Bahamas is English, but a regional patois known as Bahamian or Bahamian English is the language of daily life. The Bahamians are mostly Protestant with Roman Catholic and other religious minorities, such as Jews, Muslims, Baha'is, Hindus, followers of Obeah, and Rastafarians.

The Lucayan people settled in the southern islands of the group from Hispaniola and Cuba around the 11th century CE. At the time of Christopher Columbus's first landfall in the Americas, probably on the Bahamian island of San Salvador, there were an estimated 30,000 Lucayans living in the islands. Smallpox, brought to the islands by Columbus's expedition, wiped out half of the Lucayan population. The remainder were rounded up and shipped to Hispaniola as slaves. A group of English Puritan settlers established the first English settlement in the uninhabited islands on the island they named Eleuthera in 1649, a name derived from the Greek word for freedom. Puritan settlers later established a settlement known as New Providence. To survive, the early settlers depended on salvaged goods from the many wrecks in the treacherous waters around the islands and cays of the group. The islands were granted by King Charles II to the Lord Proprietors of the Carolinas. The king rented the islands with the rights to trade, taxes, appointing governors, and general administration. Under their rule the islands were mostly abandoned and became a haven for pirates, including the notorious Blackbeard. To restore orderly administration, the Bahamas were made a British crown colony in 1718. The new governor suppressed piracy and a local militia was formed to protect the islands. At the end of the American Revolution some 7,300 American Loyalists and their slaves migrated to the islands, mostly from Florida, Georgia, and the Carolinas. These Loyalists established plantations and became a political force in the islands. The small population of the islands was made up of a European-descended elite and a majority of African-descended slaves.

Bahamian culture is an island culture of African, British, and American influences. In the outer islands the traditional handicrafts, such as basketry and dolls made from palm fronds, are popular tourist items. The Bahamian culture has a rich mixture of myths and legends, especially those related to specific islands. The islands' history as a base for pirates in the 17th and 18th centuries has spawned many traditional tales of buried treasure and sunken pirate ships. Modern Bahamian culture is largely urban and the traditional roles have diminished with the incorporation of women into the work force, politics, and other aspects of the modern Bahamian society. The culture includes the urban centers of Nassau and Freeport, with a majority of the population, and the rural traditions of the Family Islands, sometimes known as the Out Islands, where a simpler, more traditional way of life continues. The impact of tourism has greatly influenced the culture with modernizing influences from North America and Europe. Standard or British English is the official language of the islands, but most of the population speaks an English-based Creole language called Bahamian English or the Bahamian dialect. This dialect has absorbed vocabulary and usages from the influx of Haitian migrants since the mid-20th century. Most of the Bahamian population is Christian, with the Baptists alone making up about 35 percent. Anglicans, Roman Catholics, and other Protestant sects are also important. Gospel music, part of many Christian services, is an important element of the Bahamian culture. Other forms of island music, such as the indigenous Bahamian *goombay* or goat-skin drum music, soca, calypso, and reggae, are also popular. The African-based Junkanoo, a mixture of music, dancing, and art, is a popular expression of Bahamian culture. Junkanoo festivals are held throughout the year.

When the British government abolished the slave trade in 1807, thousands of Africans liberated from slave ships by the Royal Navy landed on the islands. Slavery itself was abolished in 1834 with many of the plantation owners leaving the islands. Most of the former slaves turned to subsistence farming to survive. The islands remained a poor territory of the British Empire, mostly neglected and ignored. Major development began soon after the end of World War II. Tourism and offshore banking became the twin pillars of the Bahamian economy. New hotels and tourist attractions brought work and modest prosperity. The Bahamians began to demand a greater say in the administration of their islands. The first political parties were formed in the 1950s, and the Bahamas was granted internal self-government in 1964. The first premier of African descent took office in 1967 resulting in majority rule and new opportunities for the black majority in the islands. In 1973, the Bahamas became an independent country within the British Commonwealth. The prosperity of the tourism and banking industries raised living standards for the entire population. The portion of the population descended from early Puritan and Loyalist settlers remained in the islands, giving the Bahamas a mixed population that has remained stable into the 21st century. The Bahamians have continued to prosper and their country is now one of the wealthiest in the Americas. However, there remain significant problems in fields such as education, housing, health care, and the increasing threat from drug traffickers and illegal immigration from Haiti. Constitutional guarantees include freedom of speech, press, worship, association, and movement, giving the islands a stable administration that has benefited the population as a whole.

Further Reading

Bethel, Clement E. *Junkanoo: Festival of the Bahamas.* London: Macmillan, 1992.

Craton, Michael and Gail Saunders. *Islands in the Stream: A History of the Bahamian People.* Athens: University of Georgia Press, 2000.

Saunders-Smith, Gail. *The Bahamas: A Family of Islands.* London: Macmillan, 2002.

Barbadians

The Barbadians, sometimes known as Bajans, are a Caribbean ethnic group, the inhabitants of the island nation of Barbados. The estimated 285,000 Barbadians speak Standard English, the language of education and administration, and also speak an English-based patois called Bajan, the language of daily life. The majority of Barbadians are Christian, and the Anglican Church has the largest membership followed by Seventh-Day Adventists, Roman Catholics, Pentecostals, Methodists, Jehovah's Witnesses, and small numbers of Baptists, Moravians, and Mormons. Other religions are also represented, including Jews, Muslims, Baha'is, and Rastafarians.

Although previously inhabited by Arawak and Carib peoples, the island was uninhabited when the first English expedition landed in 1625. The Spanish and the Portuguese both claimed the island from the late 16th century to the 17th century but never colonized, although the Spanish may have taken the indigenous population as slaves. The English established a settlement in 1627–1628 and Barbados remained under uninterrupted rule from London until independence in 1968, becoming the only Caribbean island not to change hands during the turbulent colonial times. The early population of the island was mostly made up of English farmers who cultivated tobacco, cotton, ginger, and indigo. Labor was provided by European indentured labor or Irish prisoners until the start of the sugar industry in the 1640s. The cultivation of sugar was introduced by Dutch colonists from the Dutch Brazilian territories. Plantation agriculture needed larger numbers of laborers than was available from Europe, so African slaves were imported. Soon the Africans formed the largest portion of the island population. The English Civil War resulted in large numbers of both Parliamentarians and Royalists coming to the island. The growing number of slaves and the deplorable condition of their lives resulted in the first slave uprising in 1675. Slavery forced many of the former European workers to leave, mostly to the Carolinas and Jamaica. The island prospered with the English elite gaining power in Parliament in London. During the 18th century, the sugar industry remained the most important activity and the British government established a permanent land force to protect the island and to guard against slave unrest in 1795.

Barbadian culture is known as the Caribbean culture to retain more British influence in the region. The island's national sport, cricket, reflects that influence. Although officially known as Barbadians, most locals call themselves Bajans, an abbreviation of the British pronunciation of

Barbadian that sounds like "Barbajians." Around 90 percent of the Barbadian population is of African or mixed-African descent, known as Afro-Bajans, about 4 percent is of European descent, the Anglo-Bajans or Euro-Bajans, with some Irish and Scottish Bajans. Others include a small Chinese-Bajan community, Muslim-Bajans, and people from the other Caribbean islands, Europe, the United States, and Canada. The Indo-Guyanese community, immigrants from Guyana, introduced roti and other popular Indian dishes to the Barbadian cuisine. Standard British English is the language of education, administration, and public services while the local dialect, known as Bajan, is the language of daily life, especially in informal settings. Bajan is somewhat different from the other Caribbean English dialects. Spanish is increasingly spoken as the number of Hispanic immigrants is growing. An estimated 95 percent of the population is nominally Christian, with the Anglican faith having the largest number of followers. Other significant groups are the Roman Catholics, Pentecostals (Evangelicals), Jehovah's Witnesses, Seventh-Day Adventists (Mormons), and Spiritual Baptists, a local denomination. Religious minorities include Hindus, Muslims, Jews, Baha'is, and a small group of Wiccans. Music, dance, and art are important cultural elements and are showcased in frequent festivals and shows. The annual carnival-like celebration known as Crop Over draws locals and thousands of tourists every year and is a showcase of Barbadian culture with music competitions and other traditional activities. The literacy rate of the island is ranked close to 100 per-

cent, placing the Barbadians alongside the industrialized countries of the world.

The British outlawed the slave trade in 1807, although slaves were illegally landed on the island as the demand for slave laborers continued to grow. In 1816, an African-born slave known as Bussa led a slave rebellion in Barbados. He eventually had some 400 fighters and many followers but was defeated by British firepower. The scale of the uprising frightened many plantation owners and support for the end of slavery grew. Slavery in the British Empire was finally banned completely in 1834. Many of the plantation owners, economically ruined, left the island for the Southern states of the United States. The former slaves mostly settled on small plots as subsistence farmers. The descendants of the African slaves formed the largest segment of the island population and in the early 19th century, began making inroads into the government and administration of the island. British efforts to add Barbados to a crown colony consisting of the British Windward Islands led to widespread rioting in 1875. Efforts to form a confederation of British islands in the Caribbean were finally abandoned due to Barbadian opposition in 1885. In the 1930s, the first black Barbadians were elected to the local House of Assembly. Rioting broke out in 1937 with demands for greater rights. The first black political party, the Barbados Progressive League, was founded to promote social, economic, and political reform. The right to vote was extended to women in 1944. After World War II, provisions were made for an excellent system of universal health care that greatly reduced the incidence of infectious diseases and other ailments common to the Caribbean islands. A stable government, including representatives of the majority population, gave Barbados a prosperous economy and added to the island's allure as a tourist destination in the 1950s and 1960s. The British government granted the island full self-government in 1961. Full independence was achieved in 1966, with Barbados, sometimes known as Little England, voting to remain within the British Commonwealth of Nations. In 1989 the island marked the 350th anniversary of the opening of the local Barbadian parliament. By the 1990s, Barbados had achieved one of the highest standards of living in the Caribbean and was among the 51 wealthiest countries in the world. Most Barbadians belong to the island's large middle class that includes both skilled blue-collar workers and white-collar professionals and management personnel. The labor force is made up of equal numbers of men and women.

Further Reading

Beckles, Hilary. *Natural Rebels: A Social History of Enslaved Women in Barbados.* Piscataway, NJ: Rutgers University Press, 1989.

Elias, Marie Louise. *Barbados.* New York: Benchmark Books, 2010.

Toy, Mike. *Barbados: An Island Portrait.* London: Macmillan, 2005.

Belizeans

The Belizeans are a Central American ethnic group, the inhabitants of Central America's only country with a British heritage. The estimated 350,000 Belizeans are a people of many different backgrounds who share the country's unique culture. Outside Belize there are sizable communities in the United States and the United Kingdom. The official language of Belize is Standard English with Kriol, Spanish, Maya, Garifuna, and Plautdietsch recognized as regional languages. An estimated 80 percent of the Belizeans are Christian, about 50 percent are Roman Catholic, and 30 percent are Protestant. Other Christian denominations (including Pentecostals, Mennonites, Mormons, and Jehovah's Witnesses), Baha'is, Hindus, and other religions are also present.

The Mayas, the indigenous peoples of the region, constructed several major cities and ceremonial centers in the territory now forming part of Belize. The brilliant Maya civilization had collapsed by the 16th century, when Spanish expeditions reached the coast. Diseases such as smallpox and yellow fever decimated the remaining Mayan population. The Spanish colonizers controlled the western part of present-day Belize, but the coastal regions came under the control of English pirates as a base for their raids on Caribbean shipping. English loggers followed to exploit the region's forests. British settlers established a colony in 1638 and began to import African slaves to work the plantations and the logging crews. The extraction of logwood, which yielded a fixing agent for clothing that was vital to the European woolen industry, became the primary economic resource in the 18th century. The Spanish, who continued to claim the entire region, granted the British settlers the right to live in the coastal regions and to cut logwood in exchange for an end to raids on Spanish shipping. The British finally recognized the unplanned colony and appointed a superintendent in the region called British Honduras in 1786. The Spanish repeatedly attempted to gain control of the region by force but were unsuccessful. In a last try at winning control of the region, a Spanish fleet sailed into coastal waters in 1798, but was defeated by a small force of British loggers known as the Baymen. The conflict, without casualties on either side, is known as the Battle of St. George's Caye, and the date, September 10, 1798, is now celebrated as a national holiday in Belize.

Belizean culture is made up of a mixture of distinct influences from the Kriols (of mixed European and African descent), the Maya, the Garifuna, the Mestizo (of mixed Spanish and Native American descent), and the Mennonites of German descent, with additions from other cultures such as the Chinese and the Lebanese. The culture is a unique blend that has evolved through the country's long and occasionally violent history. A culture with so many different influences remains a vital and evolving entity. Belizean folklore is a unique combination of European, African, and Mayan beliefs. Many supernatural beings are part of the local folklore and many Kriols and Garifuna believe in *obeah*, or witchcraft. For many people in Belize, particularly among the poor and rural residents, a formal marriage is not necessary. However, family ties to an extended family are strong. Many poor households are headed by a single parent, usually women. Marriage and relationships between the different groups in the country are very common, which has resulted in the mixing of traditions that has evolved into the Belizean culture. The Belizean cuisine is also a mixture of many different traditions, including distinct dishes brought to the region by its many settlers. Belizean music and dance also show the many influences, such as the marimba music of the Mestizos, and *brukdown*, a type of Kriol music played on the guitar, banjo, accordion, and steel drums; calypso and reggae are also popular. Garifuna musicians, since the 1980s, made their *punta* rock the most popular style of music in the country. Belize has one of the highest standards of living in Central America, along with high educational standards and health care. The country has a high birthrate but suffers from a serious shortage of workers. The migration of Spanish-speaking illegal immigrants from other Central American countries has become a major problem, along with rising crime in the cities and the growth of youth gangs.

The settlements along the coast continued to receive migrants in the early 1800s. In 1836, following the independence of most of Central America from Spanish rule, the British government claimed the right to administer the region known as British Honduras. In the early 19th century, the British authorities in the Caribbean sought greater control over the coastal settlements, particularly over the question of slavery. The British threatened to suspend the informal local legislature, the Public Meeting, unless the settlers accepted government instructions to eliminate slavery. Slavery was officially abolished in the British Empire in 1834, but in Belize the slaves were valued for their superior abilities in the work of mahogany logging. The

British government finally paid the slave owners in compensation for freeing their slaves. Because a small English-speaking elite controlled the settlement's commerce and most of the land, the former slaves had little choice but to continue in the timber industry. The British government formally declared British Honduras a crown colony, subject to the colonial administration of Jamaica, in 1862. Although the original Maya population was wiped out by disease and conflicts with the European settlers, three Mayan groups settled in the region. These included the Yucatec Maya, fleeing war in the Yucatan Peninsula in the 1840s, the Mopan, who moved into the region to escape slavery in Guatemala, and the Kekchi, also fleeing slavery in the Spanish-speaking territories. The Kriols evolved as the largest ethnic group in the colony as a result of the mixing of Europeans and African slaves with later arrivals from Jamaica. The Garinagu or Garifuna were a mixture of African, Arawak, and Carib descent. Originally from the Caribbean island of Saint Vincent, the Garifunas entered the region through Spanish Honduras to settle in coastal communities. The officially recognized "Garifuna Settlement Day" is based on the settlement of Dandriga, their largest town, in 1832. In the 1840s, Mestizos, mostly a mixture of Maya and Spanish, began to settle in the region along with some Spanish-speakers of European descent. They now form Belize's largest group. Smaller groups include the German-speaking Mennonites who came to the region seeking religious freedom, and migrants from India who began to settle in the region in the 1860s. Since the 1980s many Mestizo refugees

from conflicts in El Salvador, Guatemala, and Honduras have come to Belize in significant numbers. The worldwide depression of the 1930s caused a near-collapse of the colonial economy as British demand for timber products plummeted. A severe hurricane in 1931 brought further misery, and inadequate British relief efforts marked the beginning of demands for self-government. Demonstrations and riots erupted in 1934, which are considered the beginnings of the independence movement. Economic conditions improved during World War II with greater support for full independence in the years following the war. Territorial claims by Guatemala, based on early Spanish claims to the region, delayed independence until 1981. Guatemala has refused to recognize Belizean independence and continues to claim the territory. A British garrison has remained in Belize as a guarantee of Belizean independence.

Further Reading
Grant, C.H. *The Making of Modern Belize: Politics, Society and British Colonialism in Central America.* Cambridge: Cambridge University Press, 2008.

Thomson, Peter. *Belize: A Concise History.* London: Macmillan, 2005.

Twigg, Alan. *Understanding Belize: A Historical Guide.* Pender Harbor, British Columbia: Harbour Publishing, 2006.

Bermudians

The Bermudians, sometimes known as Bermudans or Bermuda Islanders, are a North American ethnic group, the inhabitants of the North Atlantic territory of Bermuda, situated 570 miles (917 kilometers) southeast of Cape Hatteras, North Carolina. The estimated 70,000 Bermudians speak Standard English, the language of education and administration. Outside Bermuda there are Bermudian communities in the United Kingdom and the United States. The majority of the Bermudians belong to Protestant churches, the largest being the Anglican congregation, with sizable Methodist and Seventh-Day Adventist groups, and a Roman Catholic minority.

The group of small islands was named after the Spanish explorer Juan Bermudez, who sighted it in 1503 or 1505. Although claimed by Spain, the islands remained uninhabited until an English expedition bound for Virginia under Sir George Somers on the ship *Sea Venture* landed on them after being shipwrecked in 1609. The passengers and crew of the *Sea Venture* lived on birds and fish for a year while they built another ship, but when it sailed the majority decided to stay on in the pleasant islands. An English company was organized for the Plantations of the Somers Islands, as the archipelago was first called. The early colonists created the House of Assembly, the first parliamentary body to be formed in the English colonial possessions in 1620. In 1684, the English crown revoked the island charter and took direct control of the colony, making Bermuda the first crown colony. English planters in the islands needed imported labor, so African slaves were brought to work and agriculture flourished in Bermuda's mild climate. The African slaves and their descendants eventually formed the largest segment of the island population. The two groups, the English colonists and the African slaves,

remained officially separate but over time a large number of mixed-race people were found to be living in the islands. Bermuda became the base of the Royal Navy's important Atlantic Fleet in 1767 and the islands became an important stop on the trans-Atlantic trade routes. The prosperous colony, known for its equitable climate, attracted many settlers from the British Isles and smaller numbers from the Portuguese Azores. Unlike most British Caribbean colonies, Bermuda developed a sizable population of European descent. During the Revolutionary War on the American mainland, Bermuda became a refuge for United Empire Loyalists fleeing the new United States between 1776 and 1781.

The Bermudian culture is a mixture of British and Afro-Caribbean influences with many borrowings from American culture. About 55 percent of Bermuda's population consists of people of Afro-Caribbean descent; 34 percent consists of people of European descent; 6.5 percent consists of people of mixed background; and the rest consists of people representing different nationalities and groups. Each of the population groups has maintained many early cultural traits and customs that are not part of the overall island culture. The culture shows strong British influences in education, language, administration, and entertainment, with many Afro-Caribbean traditions being reinforced by a continuing migration from the West Indies. The infusion of Caribbean traditions has diversified the culture with music such as Jamaican reggae and calypso becoming popular. Bermuda's proximity to the United States allows significant aspects of American culture to be adopted by the islanders. The English spoken in Bermuda is a blend of British, North American, and West Indian English. The religious observances in Bermuda are based on British traditions, particularly among the Anglicans, the largest denomination. Other Protestant and Roman Catholic groups often reflect Bermuda's ties to the United States and Canada. Evangelical sects have gained converts in Bermuda since the first churches were created in the 1970s. Until the late 20th century, the population of the island was identified as being mostly of Afro-Caribbean descent or as British subjects. Since the late 1970s, a sense of Bermudian nationality has evolved embracing all the people living in the islands.

Bermuda formed a prosperous colony at the turn of the 19th century. Ship building, whaling, and trade provided for the population while plantation agriculture produced a surplus for trade with the American mainland and other British colonies. The increasingly busy port town of Hamilton became the capital of the colony in 1815. The abolition of slavery in the British Empire in 1834 temporarily crippled the island culture. Laborers were imported from the Azores and Madeira, with many staying on to form an important population group in the islands. Much of Bermuda's trade was with the American states known as "the South." While the islands remained carefully neutral during the American Civil War, many Bermudians sympathized with the Confederate cause. Trade boomed during the conflict with the South paying premium prices for weapons that came through Bermuda from the United Kingdom. During the later decades of the 19th century, the export of

vegetables, particularly the onions known as Bermuda Onions, provided the island population with a steady income. When the agricultural market fell, a new industry—tourism—brought income and development in the form of new hotels and other tourist amenities staffed by Bermudians. Tourism waned after World War I, but the Furness Steamship Company in England picked Bermuda as the new destination for its vacation cruise ships when the situation seemed most critical. In the 1920s, the era of Prohibition on the American mainland, Bermuda became a popular escape where wealthy tourists could drink on cruise ships and in the island hotels. Tourism carried the Bermudians through the Great Depression without great hardship. The island served as a center of Allied operations during World War II. After the war, racial tensions grew, as the Bermudian blacks, influenced by events on the mainland, began to protest against unfair treatment. Riots erupted in 1968, and in 1973, Bermuda's British governor and one of his aides were assassinated by activists. Bermuda became self-governing in 1968, but the white minority continued to dominate politics and the economy. A royal commission recommended full independence for Bermuda in 1978. Many blacks supported independence but the white population opposed it as premature. In the 1980s, the islands became a major offshore banking center bringing greater prosperity. In 1995, the Bermudians were asked to vote on the question of independence. The vote showed that 74 percent were against immediate independence. The question of independence continues to be debated, but the prosperous Bermudians of all population groups are wary of any changes that could harm the lucrative tourist and financial industries.

Further Reading

Jarvis, Michael J. *In the Eye of All Trade: Bermuda, Bermudians, and the Maritime Atlantic World, 1680–1783.* Chapel Hill, NC: University of North Carolina Press, 2010.

Nausbaum, Donald. *Bermuda.* London: Macmillan, 2008.

Orr, Tamra B. *Bermuda.* New York: Marshall Cavendish, 2009.

Blackfoot

The Blackfoot, also known as Niitsítapi (Original People), Nizitapi (Real People), or Blackfeet, are a North American ethnic group made up of four closely related bands speaking the Blackfoot language, an Algonquian language, as well as sharing a common culture. The estimated 32,000 Blackfoot people mostly live in Alberta in western Canada, and across the border in the American state of Montana. The majority of the Blackfoot are Christians, often blending their Christian beliefs with their earlier traditions and customs.

Language and cultural affinities, according to anthropologists, originally coalesced as a group in the forest zone of eastern North America, in the region now forming the border between Canada and the state of Maine. By 1200, the Niitsítapi moved west and settled in the region just north of the Great Lakes. Competition with other tribes pushed them farther west. The early Blackfoot were successful warriors and controlled a territory that stretched from present-day Edmonton, Alberta, to the Yellowstone River in Montana. Their territory, known as Nitawahsin-nanni, meaning "Our Land," was expanded following the adoption of the horse, probably around 1730. Until that time the Blackfoot traveled on foot and used dogs to carry and pull some of their goods on travois. The horse gave them greater mobility and expanded range as well as advantages in hunting. The basic social unit above the family level was the band, usually made up of between 10 and 30 lodges housing between 80 and 250 people. Early European explorers mistakenly referred to all the related Niitsítapi peoples as Blackfoot, although only one was called Siksika or Blackfoot. The name is reportedly derived from the black-dyed moccasins worn by some tribal members. The bands remained small for flexibility but were large enough to defend against attackers or for the communal hunts. The bands were constantly forming and reforming, often across the lines that separated the various related peoples. During the summers, the various groups sometimes assembled for a gathering of the nation. Buffalo hunting played an important part in the communities, providing meat, leather, bone implements, and other necessities. In midsummer, the four peoples would gather for their major ceremony, the *Okan* or Sun Dance ceremony. The gathering reinforced the bonds between the various groups and allowed young people to marry across group lines. After the *Okan* the groups again separated to follow the buffalo. The members of the confederation included the South Piegan or Pikuni, the Blood or Kainai, the North Piegan, and the Siksika or North Blackfoot.

The groups freely intermarried, spoke a common language, shared a common culture, and fought the same enemies. In the mid-18th century, fur trappers exploring the western territories were the first non-indigenous people to visit the vast region controlled by the Blackfoot peoples. The first extensive written record of the Blackfoot way was by David Thompson, an agent of Hudson's Bay Company, who visited the region in 1787.

The Blackfoot culture, the common culture of the Niitsítapi peoples, is based on the early plains culture of their ancestors. Traditionally the culture relied on the buffalo for clothing, food, shelter, and much of its military and domestic equipment. After the disappearance of the buffalo herds, log cabins replaced the traditional tipi, and became a symbol of the sedentary Blackfoot lifestyle. Ranching and farming became the primary occupations and remain so to the present. Many of the ancient traditions remain, such as the avoidance of eating fish or using canoes. Their ancestors believed that lakes and rivers held special powers through the habitation of spirits or underwater beings known as *Suyitapis*. These beings were believed to be the power source for medicine bundles, painted tipi covers, and other items sacred to the traditional belief system. The disdain for fishing has continued to the present, with many refusing to eat fish despite the rich fisheries on the Blackfoot lands. Historically, the Blackfoot bands had numerous dance societies, each with a social and religious function. Dances, usually performed at summer gatherings, reflected the culture's emphasis on hunting and war.

Blackfoot man and woman wearing striped trade blankets with a horse and travois. (Library of Congress)

Blackfoot Activist Sues the United States

Elouise Pepion Cobell, also known as Yellow Bird Woman, while she was the Treasurer of the Blackfeet Tribe in the 1980s, found many irregularities in the management of funds held in trust by the United States for the tribe and for individual tribal members. These were funds derived from fees collected by the government for lumber, oil production, gas and mineral rights, and grazing on tribal lands, and the government was supposed to use them to pay royalties to the tribal owners. Cobell sought unsuccessfully to reform the royalty process. She then joined other tribal leaders and lawyers in bringing a class action suit that forced an accounting of the trust funds. Filed in June 1996, the case known as *Cobell v. Salazar* brought a negotiated settlement of $3.4 billion to be distributed to thousands of individuals affected by the trust fund irregularities in 2009. After receiving numerous awards between 1997 and 2011, Elouise Cobell died in Montana on October 16, 2011, after a brief battle with cancer. As the heroine of the Blackfoot people, her funeral also honored her position as the former president of Montana's Elvis Presley fan club, whose activities Cobell had to relinquish in order to focus on her landmark lawsuit.

The tradition continues as the Blackfoot host the North American Indian Days Celebration at Browning, Montana, every July. The great powwow draws tribal groups from across the West for singing, dancing, and socializing. Currently, the language most often used is English, although the Blackfoot language is being taught in primary grades. The Blackfoot language is related to several regional languages of the plains, the woodlands, and the Great Lakes. As the Blackfoot groups moved west they incorporated borrowings from other tribes, which makes their Algonquian language very distinct. In an effort to ensure the survival of their language, young Blackfoot scholars led an initiative to bring about a resurgence of the language, beginning at the end of the 20th century. The majority of Blackfoot peoples are now Christian, mostly Roman Catholic, while a minority have retained their ancient spiritual beliefs. Catholic rituals are often blended with the older religious customs and traditions in a unique religious experience.

The Niitsítapi, having driven the hostile Shoshone and Arapaho from the northwestern plains, began in 1800 a phase of sharp competition for the fur trade with their former allies, the Crees. The Niitsítapi domination of the plains gave them tremendous advantages in hunting and in war. The competition with the Crees often escalated into violence. Both groups required an adequate supply of horses, which had become a question of survival. Horse theft became proof of courage for young warriors, but often it was also a desperate contribution to the survival of the tribe as many distinct ethnic groups competed for hunting in the grasslands of the plains.

Blackfoot war parties sometimes rode for hundreds of miles on raids. During a long conflict between the Blackfoot confederation and that of the Crees, the so-called Buffalo Wars, from 1850 to 1870, the Crees penetrated further and further into Blackfoot territory, forcing the Blackfoot to withdraw to safer hunting grounds. The first Americans, of the Lewis and Clark expedition, encountered the Blackfoot groups in 1806. By the 1820s, some Blackfoot groups temporarily put aside cultural prohibitions having to do with water to trap enormous numbers of beaver, whose fur they could trade for manufactured goods, particularly guns. In Canada, the Hudson's Bay Company established a number of trading posts in the Niisítapi region, including some of the most profitable ones on the western frontier. To the south, the American Fur Company entered Blackfoot territory in 1822, with peaceful trading relations finally established in 1830. The first American trading post was established in 1831, with Fort MacKenzie being built in 1833. The Americans offered better trading terms and were more interested in buffalo skins than were the Canadians. Contact with the Canadians and Americans caused a rapid spread of infectious diseases. Smallpox and cholera decimated the Blackfoot peoples. The death of some 6,000 during a smallpox epidemic in 1837 marked the end of their dominance among the plains tribes. By the mid-1800s, the Blackfoot hunters faced a dwindling food supply, as American and European hunters were taking too many of the native bison. Settlers were also encroaching on their traditional territory. Without the buffalo herds, the Niitsítapi were forced to depend on government agencies for their food and supplies. In 1855, the Niitsítapi chief Lame Bull signed a peace treaty with the United States, which promised $20,000 annually in food and goods in exchange for their moving to a reservation. By 1860, very few buffalo were left, making the Blackfoot completely dependent on government supplies. Often cheated or given spoiled food, Blackfoot warriors raided settler colonies for food and supplies, bringing conflict with the United States and Canadian military. A war with the Crees in 1870 ended with a decisive Blackfoot victory near Lethbridge, Alberta. The next winter, hunger compelled the Crees and the Blackfoot to make a final and lasting peace. The American authorities, without consulting the Blackfoot leaders, passed laws greatly reducing their reservation lands. In response, the Kainai, Piegan, and Siksika groups moved across the border to join their people in Canada, leaving only the Pikuni in Montana. The winter of 1883–1884 became known as "starvation winter" as no government supplies arrived, leaving hundreds to perish from hunger. Government policies aimed at the assimilation of the native peoples brought much suffering in the early 20th century. In 1934 the Indian Reorganization Act ended many of the cruel practices and allowed the tribes to choose their own governments. They were again free to practice their cultures and their ancient religions. The Blackfoot wrote and passed their own constitution, giving them an elected representative government. The four nations of the Blackfoot Confederacy continue to have their own governments under a head chief, but regularly come together for social and religious celebrations. Many Blackfoot now live on reservations in Canada and one reservation in Montana. To find work, younger Niitsítapi often leave the reservations to live in towns and cities.

Further Reading

Dwyer, Helen and Mary Stout. *Blackfoot History and Culture*. Milwaukee, WI: Gareth Stevens, 2011.

Ewers, John C. *The Blackfeet: Raiders of the Northwestern Plains*. Norman, OK: University of Oklahoma Press, 1983.

Kehoe, Alice Beck and Darrell Kipp. *Mythology of the Blackfoot Indians*. Lincoln, NE: University of Nebraska Press (Bison Books), 2008.

Bolivians

The Bolivians are a South American people made up of a majority belonging to 36 indigenous ethnic groups, mestizos of mixed European and indigenous background, people of European descent, and smaller groups descended from African slaves. The estimated 11 million Bolivians speak the local Spanish dialect with many also speaking Quechua, Aymara, or other indigenous languages. Outside Bolivia there are sizable Bolivian communities in Chile and Argentina in South America, and in Spain and the United States. The majority of the Bolivians are nominally Roman Catholic, although Protestant denominations and the resurgent traditional ethnic Inca religious practices are expanding rapidly. Smaller groups include the Baha'is, the Muslims, the Jews, and the Mennonites.

The region that now forms the Bolivian state has been inhabited for over 2,000 years. The earliest settlers, the Aymara, are associated with the advanced civilization that arose around Lake Titicaca and formed an important regional power in the southern Andes between 600 CE and 800 CE. The civilization of Tiwanaku (Tiahuanaco) declined around 1000 CE due to a significant drop in rainfall and hence, in food production. Between 1438 and 1527, the Inca Empire of present Peru, in its last great expansion, incorporated much of what is now western Bolivia. The Spanish conquest of the internally weak Inca Empire began in 1524. By 1533, most of the former Inca territories were under Spanish control. The highland territory now called Bolivia was called Upper Peru and was under the authority of the Spanish viceroy at Lima. Spanish explorers found the massive mountain of silver at Potosî, which was founded in 1545, and using the local Aymaras and other indigenous peoples as slaves, soon produced fabulous wealth. Potosí became the largest city in the New World with a population exceeding 150,000 by 1600. By the late 16th century, Bolivian silver was an important revenue source for the Spanish Empire. Disease, abuses, and the deplorable conditions of the mines decimated the indigenous population. Unrest finally erupted in a widespread indigenous uprising led by Túpac Katari. The rebels besieged the city of La Paz in 1781, with 20,000 people dying of hunger and disease during the siege. The rebels were defeated by Spanish troops sent from Lima and Buenos Aires, and the Latin American pattern of rule by a small European-descended oligarchy over a large population of indigenous and mestizo people became firmly entrenched.

Bolivian culture is a mixture of influences from the large indigenous populations, the Quechua and the Aymara, as well as the popular culture of Latin America. The arts, music, dance, and cuisine of Bolivia are a blend that reflects the largest groups making up the population. The largest portion of the population, about 55 percent, is made up of the Quechuas and the Aymaras and 34 smaller indigenous peoples, and they continue to maintain their own individual cultures while participating in the overall Bolivian culture. Many of the traditions and customs of the indigenous peoples have been adopted by all Bolivians. The second largest group comprises of the Mestizos, who make up about 30 percent of the total population; they are mostly of mixed Spanish and indigenous background and combine the influences that dominate the Bolivian culture. The descendants of Spanish and other European settlers make up about 15 percent of the population. Smaller numbers of other groups, including the descendants of African slaves, make up the rest of the population. The major language is Spanish, with Quechua and Aymara also being widely spoken, and all three—along with 34 other indigenous languages—are now official languages in Bolivia. The large number of different cultural traditions within Bolivia has contributed greatly to an impressive diversity in fields such as cuisine, art, literature, and music. Spanish cultural traditions, including the celebrations of saints' days, mark the annual round of national celebrations in Bolivia. Although the majority of the Bolivians are nominally Roman Catholic, pre-Columbian traditions are often blended into religious services to produce a unique belief system that bridges both cultures. Bolivia was declared free of illiteracy in 2008 by UNESCO, but a lack of education, continued discrimination, and high unemployment continues to affect the large indigenous and Mestizo populations. In the 1990s, the Bolivian government introduced the *Plan de Todos*, which led to the decentralization of government and the introduction of bilingual education. Under the government of Evo Morales the indigenous peoples of Bolivia have been given greater opportunities and the centuries of rule by the descendants of the Spanish conquistadores has officially ended.

As the Spanish royal administration weakened with soldiers withdrawn for service in Europe's Napoleonic wars, sentiment among the local population against continued colonial rule quickly grew. The ideals of the French and American revolutions galvanized the small educated classes. The Chuquisaca Revolution began in 1809 with another revolution in La Paz, but the revolutionaries were defeated by Spanish troops and royalist local militias. The following year the South American wars of independence erupted across the continent. Royalists and patriots fought, captured, and recaptured the towns and cities of Bolivia. After 16 years of war Bolivia was proclaimed a republic in 1825, and named in honor of freedom fighter Simón Bolivar. Bolivia and Peru formed a confederation, but war with Chile and tensions between the two halves of the union ended the alliance and Bolivia was recognized as a separate republic in 1847. Political and economic instability weakened the state in the mid-19th century. The War of the Pacific, between 1879 and 1883, brought the loss of Bolivia's access to the Pacific Ocean and the adjoining territories conquered by the Chileans. Those that suffered the most from the wars and instability were the majority indigenous peoples, who faced prejudices and abuses at the hands of the ruling European-descended elite.

The living conditions of the indigenous majority and many of the mestizos remained deplorable. With work limited to the mines and large estates, they had no access to economic opportunities, education, or political participation. Bolivia's defeat by Paraguayan forces in the Chaco War in the early 1930s, with Bolivia having to cede a great part of the Gran Chaco region to Paraguay, marked a turning point in Bolivian history. Revolutionary movements, often with large indigenous memberships, became active and by the late 1940s, had formed into political parties. Land reform, universal suffrage, and the promotion of rural education were introduced in the 1950s. The 1960s and 1970s were decades of unrest and political and economic upheavals. Governments dominated by the descendants of the European colonists dominated the country until the election of an Aymara coca grower, Evo Morales, in 2005. The introduction of many leftist ideas failed to stabilize the economy, but the indigenous majority in the country was recognized and granted greater rights. A new constitution gave even greater power to the indigenous majority. After the new constitution was adopted the historic Republic of Bolivia ceased to exist. A new socialist state known as the Plurinational State of Bolivia was created to acknowledge the multicultural population of the country. Although Evo Morales and his government have adopted many controversial laws that have alienated many of the Mestizo people and people of European descent, he was reelected in 2009 with nearly 65 percent of the vote.

Further Reading

Galvan, Javier A. *Culture and Customs of Bolivia.* Westport, CT: Greenwood, 2011.

Lagos, Maria L. *Autonomy and Power: The Dynamics of Class and Culture in Rural Bolivia.* Philadelphia: University of Pennsylvania Press, 1994.

Werner, Robert J. *Bolivia in Focus: A Guide to the People, Politics, and Culture.* Northampton, MA: Interlink Publishing, 2009.

Bonaireans

The Bonaireans are a Caribbean ethnic group inhabiting the Dutch island of Bonaire in the southern Caribbean just north of Venezuela on the South American mainland. The estimated 22,000 Bonaireans speak Dutch, the language of education and administration, along with Papiamentu, a creole language also spoken in Curaçao and Aruba. Outside Bonaire there is a sizable Bonairean community in the Netherlands. The majority of the Bonaireans are Protestant, with smaller Roman Catholic and other religious minorities.

The earliest inhabitants of Bonaire were the Caquetio people, a branch of the Arawaks who came by canoe to the island from the South American mainland around 1000 CE. The archaeological remains are few, but rock paintings and petroglyphs have been preserved in several caves on the island. The Caquetios were apparently a very tall people as the early Spanish explorers in the Caribbean called the ABC Islands (Aruba, Bonaire, and Curaçao) Las Islas de Los Gigantes, the Islands of the Giants. In 1499, a Spanish expedition led by Alonso de Ojeda is believed to have visited the island. The Spanish claimed the islands in the region but without the attraction of precious metals or other resources they were considered useless. In 1515, the indigenous peoples were rounded up and deported to work in the copper mines of Hispaniola. In 1526, Juan de Ampies was appointed the Spanish commander of the three ABC Islands. He returned some of the surviving Caquetios to Bonaire. He also imported animals from Spain, including cows, goats, donkeys, horses, pigs, and sheep. The island was turned into a large cattle ranch worked by the surviving Caquetios. The hides were a valuable commodity. Beginning in 1623, Dutch ships stopped at Bonaire to obtain meat, water, and wood. The Eighty Years' War between the Dutch and the Spanish, fought between 1568 and 1648, brought conflict to the Caribbean. Bonaire was conquered by a Dutch expedition in 1636. While nearby Curaçao became a center of the slave trade, Bonaire was set up as a plantation by the Dutch West India Company. A small number of slaves imported from Africa were set to work in the fields and saltpans alongside the Caquetios and a number of convicts.

The Bonairean culture is a blend of the cultures brought to the island by settlers from many areas. The major influences are the Afro-Caribbean culture of the largest portion of the population, the Dutch culture brought to the island during the colonial period, remnants of the Caquetio culture, and other influences such as popular American culture and the Latin American culture of nearby Venezuela. The culture is based on traditions that go back many generations and are remembered in the songs and dances that are traditionally performed during festivals and ceremonies. The culture is based on strong family ties and a respect for nature and the environment. The islanders all speak Dutch, as their island forms a part of the Dutch state, but the language of daily life is Papiamentu, a creole language derived from Spanish, Portuguese, African languages, and some influences from Arawak, English, and especially Dutch. The language is spoken in two major dialects, Papiamento, spoken primarily in Aruba, and Papiamentu, the language of Bonaire and Curaçao. The name Bonaire is thought to have come from the Caquetio word *bonay*, meaning low country. The early Spanish and Dutch modified its spelling to Bojnaj, or Bonaire. Religion is an integral part of Bonairean culture and there are a number of churches represented on the island. The majority of people are Protestants but the island also has Roman Catholics and others, including a growing Muslim population.

During the Napoleonic Wars in the early 19th century, the ownership of Bonaire and its uninhabited sister island, Klein Bonaire, changed hands a number of times. The island was finally returned to Dutch rule in 1814. Bonaire remained a government plantation from 1816 to 1868. The population consisted of some Dutch administrators and a few others plus several hundred slaves. By the late 1830s, Bonaire was a thriving center of salt production.

Gradually many of the slaves were freed and became freemen with an obligation to render some service to the government. The remaining slaves were officially freed when the Dutch finally outlawed slavery in 1862. Some of the plantation or public lands on the island were sold by the Dutch government, and in 1870 they sold the salt-pans. The entire population of Bonaire became dependent on two large landlords, which caused hardship and suffering. Many Bonaireans left the island to move to Aruba, Curaçao, or Venezuela. During the first decades of the 20th century, the governor constructed the first ship's pier in the harbor, allowing passenger boats and later cruise ships to visit. Tourism quickly became an important part of the local economy. During World War II, Bonaire was held as a self-governing protectorate under American and British auspices. In 1943, the Allies constructed a modern airport that made communications with the outside world even easier. The experience of self-government remains to the present. After the end of the war hotels began to be built and tourists from Europe, South America, North America, and other areas began to visit the island. Tourism brought prosperity to the growing population. Salt production resumed in 1966 and an oil transshipment terminal was constructed in 1975. Tensions within the Dutch islands belonging to the Netherlands Antilles federation led to the end of the federation in 2010. Bonaireans voted in December 2010 to become a direct part of the Netherlands as a special municipality. Many Bonaireans already live in the Netherlands giving the islanders economic, political, and family ties to the Dutch kingdom.

Further Reading

Greey, Madeleine. *Aruba, Bonaire and Curaçao.* London: Macmillan, 2006.

Warner-Lewis, Maureen. *Central Africa in the Caribbean: Transcending Space, Transforming Cultures.* Mona, Jamaica: University of the West Indies Press, 2002.

West-Duran, Alan. *African Caribbeans: A Reference Guide.* Westport, CT: Greenwood, 2003.

Brazilians

The Brazilians, called Brazileiros in Portuguese, are the inhabitants of the South American country of Brazil, the continent's largest and most populous nation. The estimated 193 million Brazilians speak the Brazilian dialect of Portuguese along with a number of indigenous, group, and regional languages. Outside Brazil there are sizable Brazilian communities in neighboring Paraguay, the United States, Japan, Portugal, Switzerland, Spain, Italy, Argentina, Chile, Germany, the United Kingdom, and Canada. Around 68 percent of the Brazilian population is nominally Roman Catholic; about 20 percent belongs to various Protestant churches, with smaller groups adhering to spiritism or Afro-Brazilian religions.

The indigenous peoples of western South America were mostly Stone Age societies speaking the languages of the Tupi-Guarani family. The tribes often fought amongst themselves for hunting and fishing rights, women, or trophies. The Treaty of Tordesillas, signed by Spain and Portugal and endorsed by the Pope, arbitrarily divided the New World between the two countries. A Portuguese expedition commanded by Pedro Álvares Cabral visited the coast in 1500. The first Portuguese settlement was founded in 1532, although colonists only began to arrive in 1534. The Portuguese king, Dom João III, divided the huge territory claimed by Portugal into 12 hereditary captaincies. When this arrangement proved problematic the king appointed a governor-general to administer all the Portuguese colonies together. The early Portuguese colonists, mostly young men but including a few women and children, often took women from the tribal peoples. Other tribes were taken as slaves or exterminated by abuses and violence. European diseases, to which the local population had no immunity, further decimated the indigenous peoples. By the mid-16th century, sugar production had become the most important activity in the territory. Sugar plantations required large numbers of laborers but the indigenous peoples had mostly disappeared or been killed, so the Portuguese began to import African slaves, primarily from the Portuguese colonies in Angola and Mozambique. Other European nations also founded settlements along the coasts. The French, the English, and the Dutch established several colonies that occupied important natural harbors or had other advantages. By means of wars against the other Europeans, the Portuguese slowly expanded their territory. They took Rio de Janeiro from the French in 1567, and expanded by taking the French settlements in the northwest in 1615. The Portuguese sent military expeditions inland to explore the Amazon rainforests and to expel the Dutch and the English from several settlements beginning in 1669. By 1680 the Portuguese

had extended their control of the coastal region in the south to the north bank of the Rio de la Plata. The decline of the sugar trade in the late 17th century was offset by the discovery of gold in the interior region later called Minas Gerais or General Mines. Gold seekers came from all over the Portuguese colonies in Brazil and thousands more arrived from Portugal. Competition with the Spanish colonies, which were also expanding into the interior of the continent, led to many skirmishes and wars. In 1777, a Spanish expedition succeeded in conquering the so-called Eastern Strip, the present-day country of Uruguay.

The Brazilian culture is traditionally derived from the culture of Portugal, the mother country. Because of the strong colonial ties to Portugal, the Portuguese language, Roman Catholicism, cuisine, and architecture remain heavily influenced by Portuguese traditions. Other influences have also had a large impact on the culture, particularly the traditions and customs brought to the region by the millions of Africans, and the traits adopted from the indigenous peoples. Regional cultures have developed with more African influence in the north and northeast, and a more European culture in the south and southeast which received large numbers of Italian, German, Slavic, Spanish, and other European groups in the 19th and early 20th centuries. The indigenous peoples' most notable influences are on the language and cuisine. The Africans added their words to the language, and greatly influenced the regional cuisines, as well as the music, dance, and religious practices of the country. The Europeans, first the Portuguese, then other European immigrants, maintained the core culture of the Portuguese language, the European cuisines, arts, architecture, and ties to many parts of Europe. Famous elements of the culture, such as Brazilian music, encompass various regional styles influenced by indigenous, African, and European forms. Distinctive musical styles such as the samba, the choro, the brega, the frevo, and the bossa nova are known far beyond Brazil's borders. The Brazilian cuisine varies greatly from region to region, reflecting each region's distinctive mix of indigenous and immigrant populations. These regional cuisines add to the national cuisine while maintaining the regional differences. Dishes such as Feijoada, considered the national dish, are prepared throughout the country, often with regional ingredients and variations. Along with art, music, and dance, sport is another important element of the culture, particularly association football. The vast country and population share the Portuguese language, the official language of Brazil and virtually the only language used in radio, television, and newspapers, as well as for administration. Brazil is the only Portuguese-speaking nation in South America, making the language an important part of Brazilian national culture and making Brazilian culture distinct from its Spanish-speaking neighbors. Religion plays an important part in the culture. The blending of Roman Catholic traditions with belief systems brought from Africa or borrowed from the indigenous peoples gives Brazilian culture a spiritual context that is unique to the continent. In recent years Protestants, particularly Pentecostal groups, have won many followers even as the proportion of Roman Catholics continues to drop.

War in Europe resulted in the flight of the Portuguese royal family and a majority of the Portuguese nobility in 1808. The invasion of Portugal by the troops of the French emperor Napoleon I greatly changed the status of the Brazilian territories. The king and the court were established in Rio de Janeiro, which became the center of the entire Portuguese Empire. In 1815, Brazil was elevated from the status of a colony to that of a sovereign kingdom united with Portugal. After Napoleon's defeat, the Portuguese king João Vi returned to Europe in 1821. He left his eldest son, Prince Pedro de Alcântara as regent to rule the Brazilian territories. The Portuguese government attempted to return Brazil to its former colonial status but the Brazilians refused to give up their achievements and Prince Pedro joined them, declaring Brazil independent of Portugal in 1822. Prince Pedro was declared the emperor of Brazil—Dom Pedro I. The majority of the Europeans and those of European descent in Brazil supported the monarchy. The subsequent Brazilian War of Independence pitted the colonial population against the remaining Portuguese garrisons in various parts of the vast territory. In 1825 Portugal recognized the independence of Brazil. The extension of plantation agriculture required the continued importation of African slaves, who were often purchased in the Caribbean or from local slave breeders as slaves were increasingly difficult to obtain directly from Africa. Wars with neighboring countries consolidated the country's borders. The end of the international slave trade in 1850 made the acquisition of new slaves very difficult and began the slow but steady decline of slavery in Brazil. Slavery was finally outlawed completely in 1888. Millions of emancipated slaves continued to work on the plantations or settled as subsistence farmers on marginal lands. The end of slavery ruined many of the plantation families and spread discontent that resulted in the overthrow of the monarchy in 1889. The new republican constitution restricted political rights to the portion of the population of European descent. Voting rights and other basic rights were denied to the large numbers of people of African, mixed, and indigenous origin. The country entered a long cycle of political, economic, and social instability. Civilian and military rebellions were countered by military rule and a restriction on the rights of the entire population. In the 1930s, communist and fascist attempts to take over the government prolonged military rule. Democracy was reinstated at the end of World War II in 1946. Economic expansion in the 1950s created a rapidly growing middle class, including some people of mixed race. Military regimes and instability again unsettled the country in the 1960s and 1970s. Only in the 1990s did the economy begin to expand allowing millions of Brazilians to rise out of poverty, including members of formerly neglected groups such as the Afro-Brazilians and the poorest groups in the northeast. Economic and political stability continued into the 21st century with Brazil finally beginning to grow into the long-held belief that the country could be among the most advanced and prosperous in the world.

Further Reading

Hawthorne, Walter. *From Africa to Brazil: Culture, Identity, and an Atlantic Slave Trade, 1600–1830*. Cambridge: Cambridge University Press, 2010.

Hollander, Malika. *Brazil: The Land*. New York: Crabtree, 2003.

Levine, Robert M. and John Crocitti, eds. *The Brazil Reader: History, Culture, Politics*. Durham, NC: Duke University Press, 1999.

Bribris

The Bribris are a Central American ethnic group, the indigenous people of the Talamanca region of Costa Rica and adjacent regions of Panama. The estimated 35,000 Bribris speak their own language (of the Chibchan language family) and some of them are bilingual, also speaking Spanish. Most of the Bribri continue to adhere to their traditional belief system; a minority has adopted Christianity, primarily Roman Catholicism, with smaller numbers of Protestants.

The Bribris have lived for thousands of years in the isolated Talamanca highlands. Originally they inhabited a larger territory but attacks by hostile tribes and pressure on resources drove them into the less accessible highlands hundreds of years ago. In the early 16th century, Spanish explorers began to move inland from Central America's East Coast searching for gold, silver, and other riches. European diseases reached the Bribris before the Europeans, devastating the population. Colonial abuses further reduced the Bribri population. Some were captured and taken as slaves; others were exterminated or dispersed from their home territories. The survivors moved further into the region known as the Cordillera de Talamanca where they continued to live as their ancestors had always done. The lack of gold and silver meant that the region of Costa Rica was mostly ignored. The region was described as "the poorest and most miserable Spanish colony in all America" by a Spanish governor in 1719. The lack of a large indigenous population was significant historically for Costa Rica, as without a population of slaves the establishment of large haciendas was not possible. The settlers in the region worked their own land and settled the region in the European manner. The Bribris and other small ethnic groups in the highlands were ignored following the devastation of the first decades of colonization. The Bribris survived as hunters, fishermen, and farmers. They maintained their traditional culture and their language while other indigenous groups in Central America were absorbed into the colonial system and mostly disappeared as distinctive ethnic groups.

Modern Bribri culture maintains the traditional culture developed over centuries of living in isolation in the highlands of Central America. The social system is based on clans, with inheritance through the maternal line. Women have high status as they are the only ones who can inherit land or prepare the sacred cacao drink that is essential for ceremonies and rituals and also used for medicinal purposes. Cacao has a special significance in Bribri culture. Cacao branches are never utilized as firewood and only Bribri women are allowed to prepare and serve the sacred drink. There are now several Bribri women's associations that produce organic, handmade cacao products to sell to the lowland populations. The shaman or medicine man, known as the *awa*, has a very important role in Bribri culture. Only members of certain clans are allowed to become shamans. As clan relationships are based on the mother's line, an *awa* cannot teach his own sons, but must pass on his knowledge to the sons of his female relatives. Bribri spiritual belief centers on the

Matilda Fernandez, president of the group of Bribri women, piles up some of the crops that they grow on the Bribri indigenous reservation in the Talamanca mountains, Costa Rica, August 30, 2003. The Fabio Baudrit Experimental Biological Station of the University of Costa Rica was helping the Bribri Indians to improve their quality of life by teaching them new agricultural methods and providing them with disease-resistant varieties of chickens and crops. (AP Photo/Kent Gilbert)

conical house. Conical houses are found in many related Chibchan cultures; they are considered as the symbolic representation of the universe. The roof is supported by eight pillars representing the animals that helped Sibu, the supreme being, construct the universe. Conical houses have four levels, symbolizing the four levels of the world, with the ground level representing our world. The next two levels are believed to be inhabited by the spirits of plants and animals, and the spirits of diseases and calamities. The top level is reserved for Sibu and his helpers. The culture is based on the main activities, including agriculture. The Bribri language belongs to the Talamanca branch of the Chibchan languages that are spoken in Central America and South America. The language remains the first language of the Bribris, with some speaking Spanish or understand at least enough Spanish to understand outsiders. Bribri is spoken in three major dialects corresponding to the three major population centers, Coroma, Amubre, and Salitre.

The circumstances of the colonial settlement of Costa Rica resulted in a "rural democracy" in the region with no oppressed mestizo or indigenous class. In the early 19th century the lowland settlers turned to the hills, where they found rich volcanic soils and a milder climate than in the tropical lowlands. Much of the Bribri lands were taken for cultivation but the culture of the Bribri highlands was not uprooted. After the final Spanish defeat in Mexico's War of Independence in 1821, the authorities in Guatemala declared the independence of Central America. Costa Rica became a province of the new Federal Republic of Central America, which exercised only loose authority over the various provinces. In 1838 Costa Rica formally withdrew from the federation and proclaimed

El Indio

Benjamin Mayorga Mora, also known as El Indio (The Indian) or by his nickname of Mincho, is the most famous representative of the Bribri people of Central America. Born in 1966, Mincho was educated in the lowlands and began playing football while still in primary school. When he was 16 he began playing semi-professional football for Municipal Turrialba. A year later he joined the Asociación Deportiva Belén, known as the "equipo con estrella" or the "team of stars." When Mincho was just 17, he was contracted by A. D. Belén, then in the premier league of Costa Rica. He later moved to Deportivo Saprissa in San José where he helped the club to win four national championships and two Central American Champions cups. He played on the Costa Rican national team during the late 1980s and the 1990s, becoming the only pure-blooded indigenous player in the world during that time. Since his retirement in 1998, he has pursued a coaching career. He continues to represent the Bribri nation with pride and has become a national hero of the Bribri people.

itself a sovereign republic. Coffee became Costa Rica's most important export with new lands in the highlands taken for coffee production. Some Bribris found work on the coffee farms, often making their first acquaintance with the non-Bribri populations. An American named William Gabb visited the Bribri people in the early 1870s and in 1875, published an article titled "On the Indian Tribes and Languages of Costa Rica." Other American and European anthropologists and linguists visited the region in the next decades along with Christian missionaries. The missions brought modern medicine and education to some of the Bribris but the majority continued to live as their ancestors had for hundreds of years. The Bribris near the mission stations sometimes adopted the Protestant religion of the missionaries. Since the 1970s health clinics have been constructed in the region, apart from schools that now teach in Bribri and Spanish. The modern Bribris are renowned for living in remarkable synchronization with their highland rainforest world. Some live on small reservations but the majority live outside the reserves. They are dependent on hunting, fishing, and farming for survival but also gather forest medicines and prepare building materials for sale. Most Bribris continue to barter for their needs as money economy is still considered a lowland cultural trait.

Further Reading

Clancy, Tomas. *Countries of the World: Republic of Costa Rica.* Seattle: CreateSpace, 2012.

Franke, Joseph. *Costa Rica's National Parks and Preserves.* Seattle: Mountaineers Books, 2009.

Moody, Roger, ed. *Indigenous Voice: Visions and Realities.* New York: International Books, 1993.

C

Cajuns

The Cajuns are a North American ethnic group living mostly in the southern parishes of the state of Louisiana. There is a sizable Cajun population in the neighboring parts of Texas with smaller groups. The estimated 2 million Cajuns speak English along with their own Cajun French (Français Acadien), a creole version of French, and a French-influenced dialect of English known as Cajun English. The Cajuns are predominately Roman Catholic with small minorities of Protestant and Evangelical Christian denominations.

The region around the delta of the Mississippi River was explored by French expeditions in the 17th century. In 1731, the region, called Louisiana, became a French crown colony. The population mostly consisted of a French planter elite and many African slaves. Far to the north, in present-day Nova Scotia and New Brunswick, another French colony known as Acadia was created. The frequent colonial wars between the French and the English resulted in a part of Acadia coming under British rule in 1713. British rule was later extended to all of Acadia and in 1755, for obscure reasons, the British forced thousands of Acadians to leave their farms and villages at bayonet point. Pushed onto any ship sailing from the region, the dispersal of the Acadians became known as *Le Grande Dérangement*. Scattered by sea to many parts of the British Empire, they faced discrimination as enemies and Catholics. Most British colonies prohibited Catholics from settling within their borders. Between 1756 and 1788, thousands of displaced Acadians made their way to French Louisiana. The exiles established new communities but did not mix with the resident French population. The Acadian language and culture gradually changed to fit their new circumstances. Their name for themselves changed from "Acadian" to "Cajun" as they spread across southern Louisiana. Their French language absorbed many indigenous, African, and English words and forms to become a distinct dialect. France ceded Louisiana to Spain in 1764, but the Cajuns living in the swampy delta region were mostly ignored. The Spanish retroceded Louisiana to French control in 1800.

The Cajun culture has a strong correlation with the geography of southern Louisiana. The 22 southern parishes of Louisiana are officially designated as Acadiana. Descendants of 18th-century exiles from Canada, the Cajuns remain clannish and suspicious of outsiders, known to them as Teixannes (which stems from the discovery of gas and oil in the region and the influx of small-time Texas oil men). The traditional hostility to outsiders from beyond their bayous was not overcome until the building of roads across the region in the 1930s. The relative isolation of the Cajuns until the mid-20th century helped to preserve the Cajun culture with its distinctive music, dance, and cuisine. Cajun music evolved from its roots as the folk music of the French-speaking population of Acadia in present eastern Canada. The music gained national attention in 2007, when a new category called "Best Zydeco or Cajun Music Album" was created as part of the Grammy Awards. Cajun cuisine developed as a rural method of cooking that utilized wild game, pork products, local vegetables, and grains such as rice. Cajun cuisine is now an integral part of the various cuisines available throughout Louisiana and in many American cities across the country. The Cajun French language is a creole language with extensive borrowings from other European, indigenous, and African languages. Many older Cajuns have little knowledge of English, but younger Cajuns normally speak Standard English and a mixed dialect known as Cajun English. Three dialects of Cajun French are still distinguishable. In the 19th century there were as many as seven distinct dialects spread across Cajun Acadiana. Roman Catholicism remains an integral part of the culture with village and town churches remaining the cultural and social center of Cajun life. Some Cajuns have converted to Protestantism, particularly evangelical sects, but many Cajuns shun family members if they convert to Protestantism because of the extreme persecution and hardships the Cajuns suffered at the hands of the Protestant British during the Great Expulsion of 1755.

The French and Spanish plantation owners built great fortunes on the river trade based on slave labor. From the beginning of their settlement in Louisiana, the Cajuns refused to engage in slave-supported agriculture but worked their small farms themselves. Fears that Napoleon would close the Mississippi River to American commerce prompted President Thomas Jefferson to offer to buy the Ile Orleans region at the mouth of the river. To the surprise of the American government, the French offered to sell all of the huge Louisiana territory from the Mississippi Delta north to the Canadian border. In 1803 the Louisiana Purchase was official and American authorities took control of the region, including the bayous inhabited by the Cajuns. The Cajuns remained clannish and mostly rejected contact with outsiders. Between 1815 and 1880, the traditionally large families resulted in the growth of the Cajun population from just 35,000 to over 270,000. The Cajuns remained small landowners, very religious, self-sufficient, and isolated from the society around them. In their rural parishes the Cajuns developed a strong culture and dialect, quite unlike the French culture of cosmopolitan New Orleans. In 1847, the poem "Evangeline," a commemoration of the hardships of the Acadian diaspora, was published. In the first half of the 19th century, Louisiana experienced a great economic boom generated by the flourishing plantation economy built on slave labor. Politics in the region created divisions between the French and English speakers, between the plantation aristocracy and the Cajun farmers, and between the slaveholders and the antislavery sector. A large portion of the Cajun population opposed Louisiana's secession from the United States in 1861, although many Cajuns fought for the Confederacy. The disrupted plantation system was replaced by share-cropping and subsistence farms while the Cajuns remained on their bayou farms shunning contact with the outside world. In the 20th century teaching and speaking Cajun French was outlawed in Louisiana schools. Oil and gas, discovered in the delta region, brought new prosperity to the Cajun population. By the 1950s and 1960s, work in the oil fields became a staple of the Cajun economy. A cultural revival, beginning in the 1970s, accelerated over the next decades with new interest in the Cajun traditions and dialect. Cajun studies were begun in area schools and universities. Renewed contact between the Cajuns and the Acadians of Canada helped to revive forgotten music and dance forms and cultural interchanges revitalized the culture.

Further Reading

Bernard, Shane K. *The Cajuns: Americanization of a People.* Jackson, MS: University Press of Mississippi, 2003.

Brasseaux, Carl A. *Acadiana: Louisiana's Historic Cajun Country.* Baton Rouge, LA: Louisiana State University Press, 2011.

Jobb, Dean W. *The Cajuns: A People's Story of Exile and Triumph.* Hoboken, NJ: Wiley, 2005.

Cambas

The Cambas, sometimes known as Cruceños, are a South American group living in the lowland provinces of eastern Bolivia known as El Oriente or Santa Cruz. The majority of the Cambas are of mixed European and Native American descent; Cambas of European descent, Native American descent, and those from other parts of South America also exist in smaller numbers. The estimated 2.6 million Cambas speak a dialect of Latin American Spanish known as Camba or Kamba. Most Cambas are members of the Roman Catholic Church, around 90 percent of the total according to recent studies. Protestant sects, particularly evangelical groups, have been gaining followers among the Cambas since the 1960s.

The region—which includes the llanos or plains, the rain forests, and the river lowlands that occupy the region east of the high Andes Mountains in western Bolivia—was sparsely populated by indigenous tribes when it came under the influence of the highly advanced civilizations of the Andean highlands. Spanish explorers entered the region in the early 16th century searching for riches. Finding little gold or other treasure, the Spanish mostly ignored the fertile llanos for several decades. Spanish settlers moving north from Paraguay settled the plains in the mid-16th century, founding their first settlement in 1561. The settlement was repeatedly attacked by local tribes until it was moved to a new location on the Piray River and renamed Santa Cruz de la Sierra. Physically isolated, the inhabitants of the region known as El Oriente, or "the East," developed their own cultural traditions and a regional character quite distinct from the centers of Spanish power in the Andean highlands. Dominated by European settlers and locally born people of European or mixed race, the region's trade and cultural links were with the Rio Plate region to the south. In 1776 the Spanish authorities separated the El Oriente region from the Andean provinces and added it to the Viceroyalty of La Plata in Buenos

Aires. The region, known as Santa Cruz after its capital city, was organized as a separate province in 1782.

The Cambas are a lowland, tropical people also known as Cruceños after their largest city, Santa Cruz de la Sierra. Most Cambas are of mixed European and indigenous background, with a substantial unmixed population of European descent that comprises a Guarani minority in the southeast and a small Mennonite community. Physically, culturally, and historically separate from the culture of highland Bolivia centered in the Andes Mountains, the Cambas have traditionally been farmers on the fertile llanos or plains although in recent decades work in the natural gas fields has became part of Camba culture. The Camba dialect of Spanish combines influences from Guarani and Portuguese and is less influenced than the Bolivian Spanish by the widely spoken indigenous languages of the altiplano region in the Andes. Modern Cambas now normally speak Standard Spanish, but amongst themselves they continue to use the antiquated dialect that has been spoken in their region for more than two centuries. About 90 percent of the Cambas are nominally Roman Catholic, with church holidays, saints days, and feast days marking the annual cultural year. Traditional adherence to religious practices is declining but many of the religious traditions have become part of the Camba culture. Protestant sects, particularly evangelicals, have gained members from among the Cambas since the 1960s. A small Mennonite group has lived in the region since the 19th century.

The Cambas rebelled against Spanish colonial rule in 1809, one of the earliest colonial rebellions in South America. Two years later, in 1811, the rebels drove out the last of the Spanish troops from the region and declared the independence of the Republic of Santa Cruz. Spanish reinforcements from Buenos Aires ended the republican uprising, but rebellions quickly spread through the Spanish Empire. The Cambas joined the Kollas, the highlanders of the Altiplano, to form a combined force to fight the Spanish military units. In 1825 the rebels finally triumphed and a republic called Bolivia was proclaimed with its capital in the Andean highlands. The large province of Santa Cruz became a province of Bolivia in 1832. In 1842, to limit the size and power of the province, the region of El Beni was separated as a separate province. Isolated and often restive under the authority of the highland Kollas, the region remained the domain of the Camba culture with its European and mixed descent population distinct from the large indigenous population of the Andean highlands. The cultural and economic differences created tensions that erupted in rebellions in the Camba territories in 1892 and 1904. Each Camba uprising was ended by government troops dispatched from the highlands. Disputes between Bolivia and Paraguay over the Gran Chaco, a potentially rich region just south of El Oriente, increased in the early 20th century. Fearing Paraguayan influence in the lowlands, large garrisons were established, islands of culturally and physically distinct Kolla troops. Rebellion again erupted in 1920, and in 1921 the Cambas again declared their homeland a separate republic, but Kolla troops defeated the rebels. The uprising was renewed in 1924, becoming part of the growing conflict between Bolivia and Paraguay over the Gran Chaco. Fighting broke out between the two countries in 1932, with the Paraguayans announcing their support for an independent Camba republic in Santa Cruz. The end of the Chaco War and the negotiated partition of the territory allowed the government to once again put down the Camba uprising. The Cambas remained isolated until the 1950s and the construction of a railroad linking El Oriente to the coastal ports of Brazil. Economic and political ties to Brazil are often considered more important than ties to Andean Bolivia, which is seen by the Cambas as a distinct culture often oppressing their own. Unrest in recent decades revived support for an autonomous region of the Camba provinces. The government in La Paz, dominated by the descendants of the highland tribes, has given the indigenous peoples of Bolivia greater power, often seen by the Cambas as a new form of colonialism. The government's greater control of the region's huge natural gas deposits has become yet another reason for distrust between the two distinct regions of Bolivia.

Further Reading

Icon Group International. *The 2011 Economic and Product Market Databook for Santa Cruz, Bolivia.* San Diego: Icon Group International, 2011.

Lewis, Norman. *Eastern Bolivia: The White Promised Land.* Copenhagen: IWGIA, 1978.

Stearman, Allyn Maclean. *Camba and Kolla: Migration and Development in Santa Cruz, Bolivia.* Gainesville: University Press of Florida, 1985.

Canadians

The Canadians, sometimes known as Canucks, are a North American people, the inhabitants of the northern part of North America included in the country of Canada. Outside Canada there are large Canadian communities in the United States, Hong Kong, the United Kingdom, Taiwan, Lebanon, China, Australia, Italy, and France. The estimated 35 million Canadians speak a version of Standard English known as Canadian English. French is spoken in Quebec, in the Maritime Provinces, and by smaller communities throughout Canada. Other languages include indigenous languages and a number of European languages spoken by immigrant groups.

Numerous indigenous peoples inhabited the land prior to the coming of the Europeans in the early 17th century. French settlers colonized New France in present-day Quebec in the early 1600s. French colonists also settled the Acadian territories in present-day New Brunswick, Nova Scotia, and Prince Edward Island. The English first settled in Newfoundland before moving on to found colonies on the Canadian mainland. European diseases devastated the indigenous peoples, often sweeping away whole populations long before the Europeans reached the region. A series of four French and Indian Wars, wars between the two colonial powers, were fought in Europe and North America between 1689 and

1763. Most of Nova Scotia came under British rule in 1713, with the rest of French Canada being ceded to the British by a defeated France in 1763. The British authorities made provision for large numbers of French-speaking residents in the Canadian territories. At the end of the American Revolution, the Treaty of Paris ceded British territories south of the Great Lakes to the United States. Many in the American colonies remained loyal to the British. Known as United Empire Loyalists, some 60,000 left the new United States to settle in other British territories, particularly in Canada where they formed a sizable portion of the population in many areas. To accommodate the English-speaking Loyalists, the Constitutional Act of 1791 divided Canada into French-speaking Lower Canada and English-speaking Upper Canada, which later became the provinces of Quebec and Ontario. Each of the new provinces was granted its own elected legislature. Few immigrants from Europe settled in Canada in the late 18th century, but the population grew rapidly due to large families in the Roman Catholic regions and continuing settlement of Loyalists from the new United States to the south.

The Canadian culture is a dynamic North American culture drawing influences from a broad range of Canadian nationalities. Policies that promote multiculturalism are protected by the Canadian constitution. Canadian culture comprises a number of regional, indigenous, and ethnic subcultures, each of which has absorbed traditions and traits from other Canadian subcultures. The proximity in geography, language, history, and lifestyles with the neighboring United States results in a strong American influence on Canadian culture. Historically the culture has been a blend of British, French, and indigenous influences, but large numbers of immigrants, especially from Europe but in recent decades from the Caribbean, Asia, and Latin America, have greatly changed the core culture. Canada is now a mosaic of many distinct cultural groups united by the overarching Canadian culture that draws from all the subcultures. Many cultural traits and cultural products are shared with the United States with films, television, and entertainers from both countries known and appreciated on both sides of the border. Canadian art is an important cultural element and from its beginnings to the 1930s it was mostly devoted to Canadian themes. Modern Canadian art is one of the major art centers of the world. Music and dance have also produced internationally known composers, musicians, dance ensembles, orchestras, and distinct forms of music. Sports are an important part of the culture with the national sports, ice hockey and lacrosse, played throughout the country and in international meets. Other sports are also very popular, including sports played as part of North American sports associations. Canadian culture is often depicted as progressive, diverse, and multicultural with strong social indicators that often show greater tolerance and a distinct evolution compared to the dominant culture of the neighboring United States.

Large scale immigration from England, Scotland, and Wales, began in 1815. Between that year and 1850 over 800,000 immigrants arrived in the colonies of British North America. The Irish Potato Famine in the 1840s sent tens of thousands of Irish to the New World, many to settle in the coastal towns and cities of eastern Canada. Westward migration of people followed the North American patterns with farmers opening new lands for crops, and as populations grew towns and cities appeared across the continent up to Canada's west coast. Beginning in the 1850s, Chinese immigrants began to arrive in sizable numbers to the colonies of Vancouver Island and British Columbia. The completion of the Canadian Pacific Railway linked the British colonies from the older east coast settlements to the rapidly expanding colonies in the west. The population of Canada grew rapidly as immigration accelerated, bringing new settlers from Europe, the Indian subcontinent, China, Japan, the Pacific, the Caribbean, and every other part of the world. The establishment of the Canadian Confederation in 1867 tied the former British colonies together as a nation. From mid- to late-19th century, the Canadian government maintained a policy of assisting immigrants from Europe, including an estimated 100,000 unwanted orphans from the United Kingdom. Legal restrictions on immigration that favored immigrants from Europe were amended in the 1960s allowing greater immigration from all parts of the world. In the 1950s and 1960s most immigrants were from Europe, but by the 1970s increasing numbers of Chinese, Indian, Vietnamese, and Caribbean peoples were settling in Canada. In the 1980s and 1990s Canada's growing trade with the countries of the Pacific brought renewed immigration from South Asia, mostly to settle in the western provinces, particularly British Columbia. Canada's cultural and historic ties to the United Kingdom

and Ireland remain strong even though the Canada Act of 1982 finally severed the last legal ties of dependence on the British Parliament. Modern Canada is one of the world's most developed countries with one of the highest standards of living and per capita incomes among world nations.

Further Reading

Bothwell, Robert. *The Penguin History of Canada.* London: Penguin Global, 2008.

Morton, Desmond. *A Short History of Canada.* Toronto: McClelland & Stewart, 2006.

Olson, Kay Mechisedech. *Canada.* Mankato, MN: Blue Earth Books, 2003.

Caymanians

The Caymanians, sometimes known as Cayman Islanders, are a Caribbean people, the inhabitants of the Cayman Islands. The estimated 55,000 Caymanians speak Standard English, with many of the Caymanians of African or mixed descent also speaking a creole dialect based on English mixed with African languages and Spanish. The majority of the Caymanians are Christians, the largest denomination being the United Church (Presbyterian and Congregational), with smaller groups of Anglicans, Baptists, Roman Catholics, and other Protestant groups, particularly the evangelical sects.

The small island group was reportedly sighted by Christopher Columbus during his fourth and final voyage to the New World in 1503. Because of the large number of sea turtles the Spanish called the islands "Las Tortugas." Although claimed by Spain, the islands were not colonized partly due to a lack of water. The first recorded English expedition, led by Sir Francis Drake, visited the island in 1586. He called the islands "Cayman" after the indigenous word for alligator, "caiman." For over 150 years the islands were visited by loggers, turtlers, and buccaneers of many nations. A variety of settlers came to the islands—pirates, refugees from the Spanish Inquisition on the nearby Spanish islands, shipwrecked sailors, and English army deserters from Jamaica. The English took control of the islands, along with Jamaica, under the terms of the Treaty of Madrid in 1670. Following several unsuccessful attempts at settlement, complicated by the numerous colonial wars of the late 17th century, the islands were finally colonized in 1734. English planters began to import slaves from Africa to work the plantations. Beyond the white sand beaches, much of the island land was either dense bush or limestone plains, so jagged and shot through with holes that many planters abandoned the new colony and returned to Jamaica. The Cayman Islands have always been a tax-exempt territory. On February 8, 1794, the Caymanians rescued the crews and passengers of a group of 10 merchant ships that floundered on the reefs, an incident that became known as the Wreck of the Ten Sail. According to Caymanian tradition, one of the passengers was William, Prince of Wales; so his father, King George III, rewarded the islanders' generosity with a promise never to introduce taxes. The story has been refuted by most historians but it remains a popular legend in the islands.

The Caymanians are a Caribbean people of mixed ancestry with a large portion of the population being of European descent, which is uncommon in the Caribbean. About 40 percent of the current population is of mixed background, mostly descended from early African slaves and European owners; 20 percent comprises people of European descent, and another 20 percent is made up of people of African descent; and the rest are of various backgrounds, representing more than 100 distinct nationalities. The remoteness of the islands and the integration that resulted following the emancipation of the slaves in 1834 have led to the evolution of a socially homogeneous society proud of its unique island culture. The Caymanians have the highest standard of living in the Caribbean and the 14th highest in the world. The islands are a major international financial center, which along with tourism, supports the Caymanian prosperity. Music and dance, incorporating both international forms and local traditions, are an important part of the culture. Cayman folk music is promoted through a number of yearly festivals, and the Pirate's Week Festival celebrates Caymanian culture and its past as a pirate lair. Sports are also very popular, including association football and cricket, with teams competing in many sports at an international level. The prosperity of the islands allows them to forego all development aid from the British government, which retains responsibility for defense and foreign relations. In recent years, illegal immigration has been a major problem, particularly of Cubans seeking to reach the United States or Europe, and other Caribbean islanders drawn to the Caymanians' prosperous economy. The Caymanians pay virtually no taxes, but they do pay import duties on goods, which makes the cost of living very high.

The first census taken in the islands in 1802 showed a population of 933 on the largest of the three islands, Grand Cayman, of which 545 were listed as slaves. Along with the other territories of the British Empire, slavery officially ended in 1834, when 116 Caymanian families emancipated some 950 slaves. The Cayman Islands was unusual as many of the white planters and their families remained in the islands following the emancipation. The ethnic mixture that resulted from their long shared history forms the basis of the majority of the Caymanian population. By the end of the 19th century, uncontrolled turtling had eliminated the native turtle population, usually the only resource available for poor Caymanians. The islands were governed as a dependency of the colony of Jamaica, with local authority on the three islands resting with the justices of the peace. The three small islands remained a backwater of the British Empire until after World War II, when air travel made the islands more accessible. Economic development began with the arrival of the first tourists in the early 1950s. The Cayman Islands joined the new British Federation of the West Indies as a unitary state in 1959. When the larger British Caribbean islands opted for separate independence the federation was dissolved in 1962. The Caymanians rejected forming part of newly independent Jamaica and voted to remain under British authority; they were granted a separate government as a British dependency. By the mid-1960s the long isolation of the Caymanian culture ended as tourism became a major part of the economy.

Tourism began with a few small hotels, but the increasing numbers of visitors resulted in a building boom for hotels, vacation homes, and condominiums. During the 1970s as a result of their tax-free economy, the islands became one of the major financial centers of the world. Full employment in the tourist and financial industries raised the Caymanian standard of living to being one among the highest in the world. Drug trafficking and money laundering quickly followed the financial boom, but new laws and greater cooperation with international policing agencies insured the Caymanian reputation as a reliable and stable haven. In the 21st century, the Caymanians pay virtually no taxes, but high import duties raise the cost of living. Despite the high costs the Caymanians are generally content with their present situation and control all aspects of their lives except for military and foreign affairs, the responsibility of the United Kingdom. The islanders, in recent opinion polls, display no great hurry to achieve full independence.

Further Reading

Craton, Michael. *Founded Upon the Seas: A History of the Cayman Islands and Their People.* Kingston, Jamaica: Ian Randle Publishing, 2003.

Jackson, Will. *Up from the Deep: The Beginnings of the Cayman Islands.* London: Lithofilms-Central Printers, 1996.

Smith, Roger C. *The Maritime Heritage of the Cayman Islands.* Gainesville: University Press of Florida, 2001.

Chatinos

The Chatinos, sometimes known as Kitse Cha'tño, are a Mexican ethnic group living mostly in the southeastern Mexican state of Oaxaca. The estimated 40,000 Chatinos speak their own language, known as Chatino or Cha'tña, along with Spanish, the language of education and administration. The Chatinos are predominately Roman Catholic, often blending Catholic rituals with their pre-Christian traditions and customs.

The early history of the Chatinos is mostly an oral history passed down from one generation to the next. The first Chatinos are believed to have been nomadic peoples who finally settled in the sedentary villages in the fertile valleys. The Chatinos were absorbed into the advanced civilizations that developed in Oaxaca's Central Valleys region. The powerful Zapotec and Mixtec peoples mostly left the Chatinos to their traditional way of life while taking a portion of the agricultural output as taxes. Domestication of maize is thought to have begun in the region. The growth of agriculture allowed the Chatinos to have a varied diet, which included corn, beans, tomatoes, chocolate, chili peppers, squash, and gourds. Not many animals were kept, but hunters provided wild turkey, deer, peccary, iguana, armadillo, and tepescuintle. Distinctive pottery and other handicrafts were produced for sale in the village markets. The Zapotecs gained dominance over the Central Valleys region around 500 BCE and extended their rule to the rolling hills and coastal plains inhabited by the Chatinos in the Juquila region. The Chatinos remained under loose Zapotec authority until the rise of the Mixtecs around 1325 CE. Like the Zapotecs, the Mixtecs took agricultural products as tribute, but mostly left the Chatinos to live as they always had.

The arrival of the Aztecs around 1457 began a new period for the Chatinos, who were forced to pay tribute, often in the form of humans for sacrifice, and to maintain Aztec military outposts in the region. Very soon after the fall of the Aztec Empire to the invading Spanish and their allies, a Spanish expedition arrived in the Central Valleys of Oaxaca. The Spanish, seeking gold or other treasure, mostly ignored the peaceful Chatinos. The indigenous peoples of the region, for the most part, chose not to fight the newcomers; instead, they negotiated to keep most of their old hierarchy under ultimate Spanish authority. Roman Catholic missions were established in the Central Valleys, from which they spread to eventually reach the Chatino region in the south. The Spanish conquest of Oaxaca had a devastating effect on the Chatinos. Thousands died of European diseases and forced labor. Some regions of the Chatino homeland were nearly depopulated.

Chatino culture remains a traditional indigenous culture even with the later influences of Spanish traditions and Catholicism. Traditional music and dance remain strongly tied to the precolonial traditions that celebrated the planting, harvest, and other events of the year. Some elements of Spanish culture and the Roman Catholic religion have become integral parts of modern Chatino culture. Celebrations of Catholic saints' days, Easter, Christmas, and other Catholic festivals and ceremonies are important events in the Chatino calendar. The Chatino cuisine remains one of Oaxaca's many regional cuisines with corn as the staple food, and corn tortillas called *blandas* accompanying most meals. Black beans are also very important to the Chatino diet. Dishes flavored with a variety of chili peppers are considered typical Chatino foods. Chocolate, grown by the Chatinos, plays an important part in the making of sauces but is best known as a typical beverage. Mezcal, produced from the maguey plant, is consumed both in alcoholic and nonalcoholic forms. In many parts of the Chatino homeland it is possible to buy mezcal from stores selling local products. Tourism, drawn to the region's sandy beaches and abundant wildlife, has greatly changed many Chatino communities. New hotels and tourist centers have brought work to the local population, whereas earlier many Chatinos were forced to leave their homes to work on the large coffee plantations. Most Chatino communities now have public services such as bilingual schools and high schools, and *telesecundarias*, which are educational programs for secondary and high school level for home learning. The traditional authorities are still organized on a system based on civil and religious duties, in which the advice of an elder is treated as the ultimate authority. The Chatinos, although they profess Roman Catholicism, believe in the Holy Grandmother, the Holy Father Sun, the Holy Mother Earth, and the Holy Mother Moon. They also revere the spirits of the wind, water, rain, mountains, and especially fire.

The poor treatment and abuses of the indigenous population by the Spanish authorities continued through the colonial period. The surviving Chatinos often moved higher into the mountains to escape the excesses of the lowlands. For most of the colonial period their region had few roads or other forms of communication. Most social issues were strictly local affairs. The Chatinos maintained their traditional culture and identity due to the geography of the land, which made the isolation of their communities a fact that persisted well into the 20th century. The Mexican War of Independence brought much misery as patriots and royalists fought for control of Oaxaca. The war ended in 1821 and Oaxaca became a state of the new federal republic in 1824. The Chatinos remained isolated until the late 19th century when the government introduced new agricultural techniques and revitalized the commercial networks linking the rural indigenous communities to the markets in the larger towns and cities. Severe earthquakes in 1928 and 1931 brought much destruction to the Chatino towns and villages. The Great Depression also forced many Chatinos to leave commercial farming and return to the subsistence farming of their ancestors. New dams and roads brought modernization in the 1950s and 1960s, including education in the Spanish language. Since the 1980s there has been much development of tourist facilities, particularly along the coast. Chatinos have found work in the industry, which has brought modernization through contacts with tourists from many parts of the world. Demands for education in their own language finally led to the introduction of bilingual education in the 1990s. Unrest in the Chatino areas in 2005–2006 focused on the marginalization of the rural communities and the poor.

Further Reading

Caplan, Karen. *Indigenous Citizens: Local Liberalism in Early National Oaxaca and*

Yucatan. Palo Alto, CA: Stanford University Press, 2009.

Eisenstadt, Todd A. *Politics, Identity, and Mexico's Indigenous Rights Movements.* Cambridge: Cambridge University Press, 2011.

Kuper, Peter. *Diario de Oaxaca: A Sketchbook Journal of Two Years in Mexico.* Oakland, CA: PM Press, 2009.

Cherokees

The Cherokees, sometimes known as Tsalagi, Tsaragi, Tslagi, Keetoowah, or Entarironnen, are a North American ethnic group. The estimated 540,000 Cherokees, including part-Cherokees, are the largest of the federally recognized Native American tribes in the United States. The Cherokees speak Standard English, with a small minority that has maintained the ancestral languages, the only language of the Southern Iroquoian languages that is still spoken. The majority of the Cherokees are Christians, with Methodist and Baptist denominations being the most numerous. Many also blend their Christianity with the teachings of the Four Mothers Society or are members of the Native American Church.

The early inhabitants of southeastern North America, known to scholars as the Mississippian Culture, developed a centralized and sophisticated society ruled by an established elite of chiefs and priests. The tribal groups, living in fortified towns built around large temple mounds, gradually spread across a vast area east of the Mississippi River. According to Cherokee historians, their ancient ancestors moved south following defeat by the Iroquois and Delaware tribes in the region of the Great Lakes. The Mississippian peoples, including the Cherokees, dominated a large territory that included present-day North and South Carolina, Tennessee, and Georgia, and parts of Alabama, Virginia, and Kentucky. The first recorded European contact with the Mississippian tribes was a Spanish expedition led by Hernan De Soto. Armed with guns, the Spanish looted sacred temples and kidnapped women in the territories of the related Choctaw and Chickasaw nations before moving into the territory of the Creek Confederacy. The more warlike Creeks fought the Spanish and forced them to fight their way through to Cherokee territory. The powerful Cherokees also resisted the Spanish, who fled west, but Hernan De Soto died before reaching the Mississippi River. The Cherokee remained a powerful nation until the settlement of Virginia by the English in 1609. European diseases decimated the tribe with an estimated 75 percent of the Cherokee population dying from the epidemics that swept their homeland between 1650 and 1755. The Cherokee, under pressure from settlers moving inland from the coastal colonies, established ties to the two colonial powers, the British and the French. In 1684 the Cherokee chiefs made their first treaty with the English of Carolina and eventually maintained an ambassador at the Court of St. James in London. Although broken treaties, diseases, and war took a toll on the tribe, the Cherokees increasingly adopted the lifestyle of the Europeans and attempted to maintain friendly relations. Tensions with the neighboring Creeks resulted in hostility and sporadic raids during the late 17th and 18th centuries. The Cherokees lived as well as, and often much better than, the European frontiersmen and settlers. The first Christian missionary, a Frenchman, established himself among the Cherokee leadership in 1736. He learned the Cherokee language and organized the first tribal government beyond the village or town level, and taught the principles of Christianity. Due to the ongoing rivalry between the British and the French in the region, he was eventually arrested and died in a British prison. The Cherokee allied with the British during the French and British wars in North America but the continuing encroachments on Cherokee lands finally brought on the Cherokee War of 1760–1762. Atrocities on both sides spread until the British troops destroyed the food supplies needed by the Cherokees for the approaching winter of 1761, forcing the chiefs to sue for peace. The defeated Cherokees were forced to cede most of their eastern territories in the Carolinas. Settlers from the coastal strip poured across the mountains once again encroaching on traditional Cherokee territory despite a British promise forbidding settlements west of the ridges of the Appalachia Mountains. New treaties during 1780–1785 confirmed previous land cessions, and additional Cherokee territory in Alabama, Kentucky, and Tennessee were taken.

Traditionally Cherokee culture was matrilineal, with inheritance through the

Sequoyah to His People

A Cherokee silversmith, called George Gist or George Guess in English but known as Sequoyah or Se-quo-ya to his people, studied the writing of the Americans in English and set out to apply a similar system to his native Cherokee language. In 1821 he completed his creation of a Cherokee syllabary, a phonetic table of 86 characters—the only such invention by a single man in history. His invention made reading and writing in the Cherokee language possible. After seeing its value the Cherokee National rapidly began to use his invention, and officially adopted the syllabary in 1825. Sequoyah's invention was soon used in publishing, education, and the republican constitution adopted by the Cherokee Nation in 1827. The Cherokee Phoenix, the first newspaper published in the United States by an indigenous people, began publishing using his syllabary in 1828. The Cherokee literacy rate quickly surpassed that of the surrounding European and American settlers. Sequoyah died while on a mission to extend the syllabary to the other Native American peoples sometime between 1843 and 1845. His home, Sequoyah's Cabin, where he lived from 1829 to 1843–1844, was designated a National Historical Landmark in 1965. Sequoyah has also been honored with a bronze figure in the Library of Congress, the Sequoyah Birthplace Museum in eastern Tennessee, and a stamp issued by the United States Postal Service as part of the Great Americans series.

female line. Women controlled property and their children were considered part of the mother's clan. Modern Cherokee culture is a blend of traditional customs and American cultural traits. The Cherokees are the largest of the Five Civilized Tribes, which also includes the Choctaws, Chickasaws, Seminoles, and Creeks. The Cherokee Nation, known as Tsalagihi Ayili in the Cherokee language, generally includes all people with at least a quarter or more of Cherokee blood, but membership is also open to anyone with Cherokee heritage. The most assimilated of the indigenous peoples of North America, an estimated 45 percent of all Cherokees are not registered as tribal members. Traditionally the Cherokees are divided into seven clans, some of which cross tribal lines among the related tribes of Oklahoma. Unlike the other Native American nations of the United States, the Cherokees and other peoples of the Five Civilized Tribes have no reserved tribal lands. The levels of education and living standards are among the highest of the indigenous Americans. A minority of the Cherokees are Black Americans, the descendants of black slaves who accompanied the Cherokees into exile in Oklahoma or later refugees who were fleeing from prejudice and abuses in other parts of the country. The Cherokee language belongs to the Southern Iroquoian language group spoken by a minority of the Cherokees. In recent decades there has been a concerted movement to ensure the survival and use of the language. The language is often used in Cherokee homes and in church services. English is the language of education and administration but private schools often teach the language.

The language is spoken in four major dialects that reflect the regional distribution of the Cherokee people. Most Cherokees are Protestants, with the Methodists and Baptists being the most popular, but their ancient belief system is also revered. Traditionally they followed a pantheist religion, holding in special reverence fire, water, and the sun. The great yearly ceremony, which is still celebrated annually, is the Green Corn Festival, a thanksgiving for the year's new crops. Since the early 1970s, many younger Cherokees have taken a new interest in their traditional belief system as part of the overall Cherokee cultural revival.

In the early years of the 19th century the Cherokees had assimilated American culture to a remarkable degree. An elected tribal government replaced the traditional clan system and a new Cherokee capital was constructed at New Echota. Educational institutions were widespread and a majority of the Cherokees lived much as their American neighbors did. The former ruling classes of chiefs and priests established themselves as an aristocratic class, often owning black slaves and employing white tutors for their children. Many Cherokees were much more prosperous and "civilized" than their increasingly envious white neighbors. The Rapid acquisition of American culture did not protect the Cherokees against the insatiable land hunger of the white settlers. Gold was discovered on Cherokee land in Georgia, bringing agitation seeking the removal of the entire Cherokee population from the state. President Andrew Jackson adopted a new policy in 1830 that provided for the forcible removal of North American peoples seen as an obstruction to American expansion into the West. On dubious legal grounds a few Cherokee chiefs were forced to sign the Treaty of New Echota, which bound all Cherokees to leave their homeland, for a payment of 5 million dollars and 70 million acres in Indian Territory far to the west. Most of the Cherokees repudiated the treaty and took their case to the U.S. Supreme Court. President Andrew Jackson refused to enforce the Supreme Court's ruling and preparations were made for the eviction of the Cherokees from their ancestral territory. Particularly in Georgia, armed militias rode through the Cherokee lands looting and burning. Many chose the mansions, plantations, and other Cherokee properties they would confiscate as soon as the removal of the Cherokees was completed. Driven from their homes at bayonet point, the Cherokees were herded into squalid camps, where starvation, filth, and disease decimated the youngest and oldest of the internees. In 1838 the Cherokees were taken from the camps and were forced westward accompanied by armed soldiers. Some Christian missionaries accompanied the deportees, and a sizable number of black slaves stayed with the former plantation owners. Thousands of Cherokees died in the concentration camps and during the forced migration to Indian Territory. Those who survived the ordeal suffered torments and humiliations unequaled in modern history until the atrocities of the 20th century. The various groups of deportees finally united as the Cherokee Nation, which was recognized as a sovereign nation by the U.S. government in 1846. During the American Civil War, the embittered Cherokees generally allied with the Confederacy against the hated American government. In 1865, having lost a quarter of the surviving tribal members during the Civil War, the Cherokees shared the South's defeat. All treaties were annulled and the Cherokees were restricted to the eastern districts of the Indian Territory. The western districts were taken for the settlement of other dispossessed tribes. In 1887 the U.S. authorities forced the Cherokees to abandon their communal lands and settle on individual plots. This produced a large quantity of surplus land, which was summarily confiscated for distribution to the growing number of American settlers moving into Indian Territory. In 1906 all tribal autonomy was ended and the Cherokees were given American citizenship. The Indian Territory became part of the new state of Oklahoma, which was admitted to the Union in 1907. Since the early 20th century, the Cherokees, mostly ignored or neglected by the state and federal governments, have organized to maintain their culture with an emphasis on education and self-help. Young activists have led a cultural resurgence in recent years, often demanding that the United States' government honor the treaties that recognized the Cherokees as a sovereign people. In 2010, the U.S. government issued an official apology for the long-running persecution of the indigenous Americans. The apology did not cover the Trail of Tears specifically; it does not restore stolen lands or lives, nor does it relieve the nightmare that visited upon the Cherokees of Georgia and the other states, but it finally addresses the country's sorry record of bigoted, ill-conceived, and often sadistic treatment of all the Native American peoples.

Further Reading

Conley, Robert J. *The Cherokee Nation: A History.* Albuquerque: University of New Mexico Press, 2008.

Ehie, John. *Trail of Tears: The Rise and Fall of the Cherokee Nation.* New York: Anchor Books Doubleday, 1997.

Perdue, Theda and Michael D. Green. *The Cherokee Nation and the Trail of Tears.* New York: Penguin, 2008.

Cheyennes

The Cheyennes are a North American ethnic group, a people of the Great Plains of the central part of the continent. The estimated 22,000 Cheyennes speak Standard English and a minority are able to speak the traditional Cheyenne language, which belongs to the Algonquian language family. Most Cheyennes are Christians, usually belonging to Protestant churches, with their belief system often blending traditional rites such as the Sun Dance with Christian rituals. A minority adheres to the Native American Church.

The Cheyennes are believed to have originated in the area of the Great Lakes. They may have branched off from the other Algonquian peoples as early as 1500 CE in present-day Minnesota. The earliest known historical account of the Cheyennes comes from the mid-17th-century visit to the French Fort Crevecoeur, near present-day Chicago. According to tribal tradition, the Cheyennes were driven from the Great Lakes region by the Assiniboine. They moved west, crossed the Mississippi River, and established new settlements in present-day Minnesota and North Dakota. The Cheyennes quickly adopted the horses brought to the New World by European explorers. Around 1730 the Cheyennes introduced their powerful neighbors, the Lakotas, to the horse culture that allowed greater range of territory, better hunting, and more tribal mobility. The Cheyennes were unusual as they formed a unified tribe in the early 19th century, with a more centralized authority and tribal structure than other peoples of the Great Plains. Through ritual ceremonies such as the Sun Dance and great tribal gatherings they maintained the unity of many seminomadic bands. Allied to the Arapaho tribe, they drove the competing Kiowas to the south, but in turn were pushed west by the more powerful and numerous Lakotas. The Cheyennes occupied the Black Hills and the Powder River region but bands of Lakotas followed them west and soon disputed Cheyenne control of the region. By 1776 the Lakotas had driven most Cheyennes farther west and had taken over much of their territory near the Black Hills. The Cheyenne Nation was made up of 10 bands that spread across the Great Plains from present-day southern Colorado north to the Black Hills of South Dakota. A unique feature of Cheyenne culture was the gathering to wage war at the tribal level, mostly against their traditional enemies, the Crows.

The Cheyenne culture evolved through several stages according to the geographic position of the group. They began their history in the eastern woodlands around the Great Lakes as a sedentary agricultural people raising corn, beans, and squash, and harvesting wild rice. Moving west they settled in present-day Minnesota and later on in South Dakota, where they established new farming communities. As they moved

Cheyenne camp near Arapaho, Oklahoma, in 1910. (USGS)

west they encountered the enormous herds of buffalo, which became the object of their hunters. The introduction of the horse by European explorers to the south made buffalo hunting more accessible. They gradually abandoned their farms near the Missouri River and acquired horses, the Cheyennes adopted the horse culture of the tribes of the Great Plains. Buffalo provided food, clothing, shelter, and other useful implements. Modern Cheyenne culture adapted to yet another geographic change when they were restricted to reservations in the late 19th century. The blend of traditional Cheyenne culture and the influences of American culture produced a mixed culture that embraced American modernity but continued to respect and adhere to many traditional values. Cheyenne women are not equal in the culture, but a Cheyenne woman has higher status if she is part of an extended family, is descended from distinguished ancestors, and gets on well with her female relatives. Younger Cheyennes are respected as hard working, modest, and skilled in traditional crafts; they are knowledgeable about Cheyenne history and culture and continue to speak the Cheyenne language. As in American culture in general, these attributes are ideals often lacking in the younger generation. The Cheyenne people are traditionally divided into two subtribes, the Só'taeo'o or Sutaio and the Tsétsêhéstâhese or Tsitsistas. The Cheyennes are now divided between the Northern Cheyennes who live in southeastern Montana and the Southern Cheyennes living in western Oklahoma. The Cheyenne language is still spoken by a minority with only a handful of vocabulary differences between the two groups. English is the mother language of the majority of the Cheyennes both in Montana and in Oklahoma. The majority of the Cheyennes are Christians, mostly Protestants, with minorities continuing to adhere to their ancient religious beliefs or belonging to the Native American Church.

The Lewis and Clark expedition passed through the Cheyenne territory in 1804. The surviving Cheyenne villages were mostly in present-day North Dakota and Montana as the more powerful Lakotas continued to expand their territory to the south. By the mid-19th century the Cheyennes had mostly abandoned their earlier agricultural traditions and moved west into the Great Plains. They quickly became a horse culture, adopting the classic nomadic plains lifestyle. They replaced their traditional earth lodges for portable tipis and changed their dietary habits from fish and agricultural products to the plains diet of mainly bison with wild vegetables and fruits. The horse allowed them to extend their range from the upper Missouri River into present-day Wyoming, Montana, Colorado, and South Dakota. Around 1820, explorers and traders reported contacts with the Cheyenne bands near the site of modern Denver and along the Arkansas River. Endemic warfare with other tribes, particularly the Crows, Utes, and Pawnees, were a regular feature of Cheyenne life into the 1860s. An American military expedition signed the first treaty with the Cheyennes of the upper Missouri River region in 1825. Increasing numbers of settlers moving west along the emigrant routes to the West in the 1840s often depleted resources or water and game. The Cheyennes gradually divided into the Northern Cheyennes and the Southern Cheyennes as they moved further north and south in search of adequate territory for sustenance. During the California Gold Rush, in the late 1840s, emigrants spread cholera through the gold camps and rivers due to poor sanitation.

Sun Dance

The Sun Dance or Sundance is a religious ceremony practiced by a number of indigenous peoples of the Great Plains. Each tribe has its own distinct practices and ceremonies. Many of the ceremonial protocols have features in common, such as songs and dances passed down from generation to generation. Many of the tribes use traditional drums, tobacco offerings, praying, fasting, and the sacred pipe in their ceremonies. Some also have a tradition of piercing the skin on the chests or backs of men and the arms of women. In March 2003 some bundle keepers and spiritual leaders of the Cheyennes issued a declaration that non-Native Americans would be banned from sacred altars and other ceremonies, especially the Sun Dance, because of increased desecration of the ceremony.

The cholera epidemic reached the Great Plains in 1849, decimating the Cheyennes with about a half to two-thirds of their population lost to the disease. The Cheyennes signed the Fort Laramie Treaty of 1851, which compensated the tribe for allowing emigrants and traders to travel through their territory with a string of forts to guard them. In 1856, the wounding of a Cheyenne warrior led to attacks on emigrant trains and reprisals by the U.S. Cavalry that continued into 1857. A new treaty, signed by some Cheyennes, created a small reservation but the majority refused to leave their home territories. In 1864, the governor of Colorado Territory, leading a citizen's militia, began a series of attacks on Cheyenne camps and hunting parties on the plains. They killed any Native American in sight, even women and children. A widespread war broke out with Cheyenne raids on the wagon trains. On November 29, 1864, the Colorado Militia mounted a surprise attack on a Cheyenne and Arapaho village even though the flag of truce indicating its allegiance to the United States flew above the tipis. The Sand Creek massacre resulted in the deaths of up to 200 Cheyennes, mostly unarmed women and children. Four years later, George Armstrong Custer and his troops attacked a Cheyenne band within the reservation leaving more than a hundred dead, again mostly women and children. The Northern Cheyennes joined other plains tribes at the Battle of the Little Bighorn on June 25, 1876. Custer and most of his Seventh Cavalry contingent were killed in one of the largest battles of the so-called Indian Wars. The U.S. Army increased its attempts to capture the hostile Cheyennes. Forced by hunger and unrelenting pursuit to finally surrender, the various bands were sent south to Indian Territory where conditions were harsh, rations were inadequate, and no buffalo survived. Eventually the Northern Cheyennes were given a reservation closer to their former homeland, in southern Montana. The Southern Cheyennes remained in Indian Territory, which in 1907 joined the Union as the state of Oklahoma. During the 20th century, the Cheyennes gradually assimilated American culture while retaining their own culture and traditions. The English language, the language of administration and education, replaced Cheyenne as the first language, but in recent decades the language has been revived as part of a cultural resurgence. A renewed pride in their past and a respect for their historic customs and traditions is an important part of the Cheyenne revival since the 1980s.

Further Reading

Grinnell, George Bird. *The Cheyenne Indians: Their History and Lifeways.* Bloomington, IN: World Wisdom, 2008.

Hoebel, E. Adamson. *The Cheyennes: Indians of the Great Plains.* Stamford, CT: Wadsworth, 1978.

Stands in Timber, John and Margot Liberty. *Cheyenne Memories.* New Haven, CT: Yale University Press, 1998.

Chickasaws

The Chickasaws, sometimes known as Chickashas, are a North American ethnic group, one of the Five Civilized Tribes of eastern Oklahoma. The estimated 55,000 Chickasaws speak Standard English with many also speaking the Chickasaw language, a member of the Muskogean language family. The majority of the Chickasaws are Christian, mostly Protestant, although the traditional religion is also respected and the old customs and traditions are often blended with Christian rituals.

The origin of the Chickasaws is uncertain. Many scholars and anthropologists believe that the Chickasaws and the related Choctaws coalesced as separate peoples in the 17th century from the remains of the Plaquemine culture that flourished in present-day Louisiana and Mississippi possibly as early as the 13th century CE. Others support the theory that they descend from the advanced Mississippian culture west of the Mississippi River in present-day Louisiana and Arkansas. Monumental mounds, built to elevate temples and other ceremonial structures, were constructed in northern Louisiana as early as 3500 BCE. Another theory speaks of their descent from the Nanih Waiya culture that left a great mound in Mississippi, a mound that is still considered sacred by the Chickasaws and Choctaws. The first Europeans to encounter the Chickasaws were the Spanish under Hernan De Soto in 1540. After a peaceful beginning, Spanish looting of temples and kidnapping of Chickasaw women led to a Chickasaw attack on the expedition, which fled from the Chickasaw territory. A few Europeans explored the region but the Chickasaws began to trade with the British following the settlement of Carolina in 1670. Supplied with guns, the Chickasaws raided the neighboring Choctaws, with the captives sold to the British as slaves. When the Choctaws acquired guns from the French, the slave raids were stopped. Allied to the British, the Chickasaws were often at war with the French and the Choctaws in the 18th century. A myriad of European diseases decimated the population as epidemics weakened the tribe. Skirmishes and raids continued until the French ceded all territory east of the Mississippi River following the French and Indian War in 1763. The Chickasaws remained British allies until the creation of the new United States. Peace between the new United States and the Chickasaws was signed in 1786. In 1793–1794, Chickasaws allied to the Americans fought against the indigenous peoples to the west. The first president of the United States, George Washington, formulated a plan for the assimilation of the indigenous peoples believing that once they settled on plots of land, built homes and farms, and embraced Christianity they would be accepted by the American people as equals. The Chickasaws signed the Treaty of Hopewell in 1796. A Scots trader, James Logan Colbert, settled in Chickasaw territory and lived there for over 40 years. He married several high-ranking Chickasaw women in succession as marriages to Americans and Europeans were viewed as advantageous to the tribe. Colbert fathered many children, including seven sons. The Colberts, through their mothers' inheritance, became the bilingual chiefs of the Chickasaws during the critical period beginning in the late 1700s.

The Chickasaw culture was a traditionally matrilineal system, with inheritance of property and titles through the female line. Modern Chickasaw culture has changed to the American tradition of male domination, but Chickasaw women retain high status and respect. The Chickasaw culture has always had its roots in the elements and nature, and a reverence for nature remains an important cultural element. The concepts and ideas that blend in modern Chickasaw culture came about through a long evolution that often pitted the full-blooded Chickasaws against those of mixed background. While many full-bloods wished to totally separate their people from the American culture, the mixed-bloods saw the benefits of modern trade goods, medicines, and improved implements and tools. The Chickasaws have their own government, laws, police, and services, but they are also American citizens. The governor and council members, a form of government based on the traditional council of hereditary clan chiefs, are now popularly elected. The English language is the language of the Chickasaws although the Chickasaw language is still spoken, especially by the elders of the tribe. The language is a Western Muskogean language closely related to the language of the Choctaws. In recent years there has been a concerted effort to extend the use of the language. The majority of the Chickasaws are Christians, mostly Protestants, with many people mixing earlier pre-Christian traditions with modern Christian rituals. Some of the Chickasaws are members of the Native American Church, the largest Native American church in the United States.

Several treaties were signed with the Americans ceding land as settlers moved west into the traditional Chickasaw territories. The Chickasaws joined Andrew Jackson in the Creek War, which brought them honor as invincible allies and brave warriors. The Chickasaws remained farmers and hunters, living in permanent towns and often adopting elements of American-European culture. But the continued encroachments of land-hungry emigrants from the American coastal regions brought conflict and finally expulsion. Unlike other tribes they agreed to cede territory, not in exchange for other land farther west but for a payment of 3 million dollars. With that money they negotiated the purchase of a part of the territory occupied by the related Choctaws in Indian Territory. But the U.S. government delayed the payment for over 30 years. Some of the former ruling class of chiefs and priests had adopted the local plantation agriculture and owned slaves. The Chickasaws were finally forced to leave their homes in 1837, often accompanied by black slaves. During the long journey to Indian Territory on the Trail of Tears, an estimated one in every six Chickasaws died of dysentery, smallpox, or exposure. In Indian Territory the Chickasaws were merged with the Choctaws for administrative reasons. In the 1850s, the Chickasaws wrote their own constitution. Distrust of the American government and sympathy for the South brought a Chickasaw alliance with the Confederacy during the American Civil War. Many young Chickasaws perished in the fighting which ended in 1865, many fighting for the Union as they opposed slavery and the mostly mixed blood slave owners. Because of their alliance with the Confederacy they signed a new peace treaty with the U.S. government in 1866. Because the freed slaves were not allowed full tribal membership as stipulated by the government, the Chickasaws were penalized by the confiscation of over half their lands with no compensation. After several decades of distrust between the Chickasaws and the Choctaws, the two peoples established separate governments.

Remnants of the Chickasaws in South Carolina, having escaped the deportation by hiding or passing as white, began to reorganize the remnants into a distinct tribe in the late 19th century. The U.S. Congress passed the Dawes Act, which mandated the breakup of Native American communal lands into individual allotments with the excess lands to be sold to American settlers. At first the Chickasaws were protected by their treaties, but the Curtis Act of 1895 dissolved the Chickasaw tribal government and the surplus lands were lost to the growing American population in their territory, keeping only a small portion as allotments. In 1888 Texas cattlemen moved some 150,000 cattle into the Chickasaw lands and refused to pay rent or grazing fees. The U.S. government intervened but was successful in removing only a part of the vast herd. Indian Territory, renamed Oklahoma, joined the Union as a separate state in 1907. For many years there were no formal Chickasaw tribes, until they finally reorganized and created a new tribal government in 1963. The Chickasaws were not allowed to elect their own leaders until 1970. A new constitution was adopted in 1983, which was recognized by the federal government. The Chickasaws remain a vital part of the population of Oklahoma, often attaining high office and succeeding in sports, entertainment, and other arenas. One among them is John Herrington, the first Native American astronaut.

Further Reading

Gibson, Arrell M. *The Chickasaws*. Norman, OK: University of Oklahoma Press, 1972.

Gray-Kanatiiosh, Barbara A. *Chickasaw*. New York: Abdo Publishing, 2007.

St. Jean, Dr. Wendy. *Remaining Chickasaw in Indian Territory 1930s–1907*. Tuscaloosa, AL: University of Alabama Press, 2011.

Chileans

The Chileans, sometimes known as Chilenos, are a South American people, the inhabitants of the Republic of Chile on the continent's west coast. The estimated 18 million Chileans speak the Chilean dialect of Spanish. Outside Chile there are sizable Chilean communities in Argentina, Europe, and North America. According to government studies some 70 percent of the Chilean population identifies as Roman Catholic. Most other world religions are also represented, particularly in the large urban areas.

The territory was settled by migrating peoples some 10,000 years ago. They settled in the coastal plains and the fertile valleys west of the high Andes Mountains. The Incas sought to extend their empire into the region in the 15th century CE but were stopped by the fierce resistance of the native Mapuche people. The first Europeans to see the land were members of Ferdinand Magellan's expedition in 1520. He discovered the southern passage between the Atlantic and the Pacific at the bottom of the South America continent. Entering the Pacific Ocean through the passage that now bears his name, Magellan and his expedition sailed north along the west coast. In 1535 a Spanish expedition moved south from Spanish Peru looking for gold or other treasures. The conquest of Chile began in 1540 under Pedro de Valdivia, who founded Santiago in 1541. Although the gold and silver they sought were not found, the Spanish recognized the agricultural potential of Chile's huge central valley. Settlement was gradual as the indigenous peoples resisted Spanish advances. A massive attack by the Mapuches in 1553 resulted in Valdivia's death and the destruction of many of the colonial settlements. War with the Mapuches again flared in 1598 and 1655. In 1683 the enslavement of Mapuches was abolished as it failed to cow them into submission. Isolated from the north by the Atacama Desert, from the south by the hostile Mapuches, from the west by the Pacific, and from the east by the Andes Mountains, the Chilean colony became one of the most centralized and homogeneous colonies in the Spanish Empire. The colonists not only had to mount a constant defense against the Mapuches but also guard against attacks by Spain's European enemies. The population remained largely of European descent, although it included people of mixed race, Native Americans, and black slaves.

Chilean culture is a Latin American culture based on the early Spanish traditions brought to the region, with later influences from the indigenous population and the English, French, and especially German immigrants who settled in Chile in the 19th century. German influence remains strong in southern Chile with German-style architecture and a regional cuisine that combines German recipes with local produce. Music and dance are important cultural elements and range from folkloric to popular to classical. The national dance is the *cueca*. Traditional Chilean musical forms include the *tonada*, which developed from the music imported by the Spanish colonists. A revival of Chilean culture and folklore between 1950 and 1970 saw a rebirth of folk music that remains very popular to

the present. Chileans like to refer to their country as the country of poets due to the large number of writers and poets that their culture has produced. The cuisine also reflects the various cultural influences, with contributions from the early Spanish culinary traditions and later influences from European and North American cuisines. Sports are also very important with association football being the most popular sport. Chileans have also triumphed in international sports such as tennis and polo. The modern Chilean culture increasingly manifests influences of popular American culture.

The conquest of Spain by the French during the Napoleonic Wars in 1808 began a movement in Chile for separation from the Spanish Empire. A local junta proclaimed Chile an autonomous republic under a future restored Spanish monarchy, but the autonomy movement soon gave way to a popular uprising for full independence from Spain. Patriot leaders rallied the population as Spanish attempts to re-impose colonial rule led to heavy fighting. Intermittent warfare continued in Chile until 1817 when an army from newly liberated Argentina crossed the Andes to defeat the royalists. Chile was proclaimed an independent republic in 1818. Independence did little to change Chilean society, which retained a colonial social structure dominated by family politics and the Roman Catholic Church. Between 1861 and 1883, the Chilean military fought against Mapuche resistance to occupy the southern Mapuche homeland known as Araucania. The Mapuches had resisted conquest for over 300 years before their final defeat in the 1880s. The newly conquered lands were opened to settlement, bringing new immigrants pouring into the country from various European countries and the Middle East. Basques from Spain and France were particularly drawn to the region. In 1848 heavy German immigration began, particularly to the southern regions of the country. Sponsored by the Chilean government, tens of thousands of German-speaking immigrants came to Chile from Germany, Switzerland, Alsace, and Austria. The German colonists greatly influenced the ethnic composition and the culture of Chile's southern provinces. Relations between Chile and the neighboring Spanish-speaking republics were often tense. Between 1879 and 1883 Chile fought the War of the Pacific. Taking territory from defeated Peru and Bolivia, the Chileans eliminated Bolivia's access to the sea by annexing the coastal region of the country and took control of large nitrate deposits from Peru and Bolivia that led to an era of prosperity in the late 1800s. The Chilean economy remained under the control of a system of powerful families, but in the 1920s, the emergence of a strong middle class and the organization of workers destabilized the country. A military coup overthrew the civilian government in 1924. Constitutional government was restored in 1932 under a government supported by the growing middle class. A growing leftist movement in the 1960s resulted in the election of a government of socialists, communists, and other dissidents under President Salvador Allende. An economic depression began in 1972 further destabilizing the country. Nationalization of many industries further divided Chilean society. By early 1973 inflation was out of control and unrest was widespread. Finally a military coup overthrew Allende in September 1963, reportedly with aid from the United States' CIA. A military government led by Gen. Augusto Pinochet took control and began a systematic elimination of known leftists and other opponents of the coup. The first years of military rule were marked by massive human rights violations. Pinochet became president of the country in 1980, but was denied a second term as president in a referendum held in 1988. A transitional government took control in 1990 and Chile adopted a democratic system. In January 2010, Chile was struck by a massive earthquake, one of the largest ever recorded. As many as 500 people died, with thousands injured and many more homeless. The Chileans are slowly recovering and a strong economy has allowed for rebuilding and recovery much more quickly than anticipated.

Further Reading

Collier, Simon and William F. Sater. *A History of Chile, 1808–2002*. Cambridge: Cambridge University Press, 2004.

Constable, Pamela. *A Nation of Enemies: Chile under Pinochet*. New York: W. W. Norton & Company, 1993.

Rector, John L. *The History of Chile*. Basingstoke, England: Palgrave Macmillan, 2005.

Chinantecs

Chinantecs, sometimes known as Chinantlas, Chinantecas or Tsa Jujmi, are a Mexican ethnic group living primarily in the southeastern Mexican state of Oaxaca and adjacent areas of Veracruz state. Outside the region there are sizable Chinantec communities in Mexico City, in other parts of Mexico, and in the United States. The estimated 150,000 Chinantecs speak at least 14 distinct dialects of the Chinantec language, which is the Chinantecan branch of the Oto-Manguean language family. The majority of the Chinantecs are Roman Catholics, often blending earlier pre-Christian rituals and ceremonies with their Christian belief system.

The origin of the Chinantec people is unknown. Some scholars believe that they migrated from the west near the Tehuacán Valley to their present homeland as recently as 1000 CE. Historically the Chinantec homeland lay in northern Oaxaca in the basin of the Papaloapan River. By the early 15th century the Chinantecs were expanding through the well-watered and fertile lowland valleys. The Chinantec culture was adapted to the lowland and riverine areas of settled agriculture and a stratified society. Their name derives from the Nahuatl word *chinamitl*, meaning "enclosed space" or "near the canes." The Chinantecs traditionally lived in autonomous communities although they were aware of their cultural and linguistic affinities to the other related groups. The Chinantec homeland was invaded by the Nahuatl-speaking Aztecs in 1454–1455. The Aztecs maintained the Chinantec hierarchy but took many prisoners annually—as slaves and for human sacrifices—part of the Aztec religious beliefs. In the early 16th century the Aztec Empire was conquered by the invading Spanish and their indigenous allies. After establishing firm control of the former Aztec heartland, the Spanish moved south into the Chinantec region in 1520–1521. Three epidemics of European-introduced diseases such as smallpox and measles, in rapid succession, decimated the Chinantec population. An estimated 80 percent of the preconquest population perished. By the 1570s many Chinantec survivors were living in dispersed villages, often in the higher elevations, to escape the epidemics and the Spanish slave hunters. To facilitate their political control and the religious conversion to Roman Catholicism, the colonial authorities forcibly congregated the Chinantecs in concentrated towns in the highlands. In the process, the Chinantecs were ordered to destroy all physical vestiges of their former villages, effectively eradicating all structural reminders of their history. A major result of the Spanish conquest was a simplification in the social structure. The former elite comprising chiefs and priests mostly disappeared. Although the Spanish hunted for gold and other treasures in the region they found little of immediate value. By the mid-17th century the Spanish had begun to value the Chinantec region for its production of cotton and cochineal.

The Chinantec culture is subdivided by dialect, culture, and habitat into four or possibly five major groups. Subsistence farming is the major occupation, subsidized in the lowlands by the cultivation of cash crops of coffee and tobacco. Most contemporary Chinantec communities administer communal lands in addition to the small holdings of subsistence farmers. Some of the highland communities also control extensive communal forests. Substantial tracts are worked in some communities as *ejidos* or common lands. Although there is considerable variation among the Chinantec communities, the core social organization is the nuclear family with an extended family through the Roman Catholic tradition of *compardrazgo*, godparenting, which forms an important social structure in each community. Until the 1950s, the barrio was an important center of social organization, but since that time the dispersal of the Chinantecs into the lowlands and into other areas of Oaxaca has resulted in other forms of organization. The political organization of Chinantec life is based on a civil-religious hierarchy. Many younger Chinantecs now reject the traditional authorities and are attracted to greater income-earning opportunities outside the traditional rural communities. The obligation to use Spanish in administration and education has placed great importance on bilingualism, education, and literacy. Recognition of the value of experience has replaced the historic respect for elders and shamans. The power that accrues to individuals sending regular remittances in support of family and community enterprises has led to the creation of semiofficial advisory groups of Chinantec men living in other parts of Mexico or in the United States. The growth of these groups underlines the shift in power from older men respected for their links to Chinantec traditions to men who are more sophisticated and more effective in dealing with the outside world. The Chinantec language remains the language spoken among the Chinantecs themselves, with younger people also speaking fluent Spanish. The Roman Catholicism originally introduced by the Spanish conquerors remains an important part of the culture and religious holidays form an important part of each yearly cycle. Many pre-Christian rituals have become part of the Catholic ceremonies, particularly in the more remote highlands.

By the early 19th century the best and most fertile lands had been taken by foreign companies, displacing many lowland Chinantecs. The companies, mostly large agricultural concerns overseeing coffee and tobacco plantations, brought many workers into the region from outside the Chinantec region. Friction between the imported workers and the indigenous people continued for several decades, often leading to violence. Even after the Mexican Revolution in 1910 the coffee, banana, and tobacco plantations remained under foreign control. The Chinantecs and other workers on the plantations often worked in deplorable conditions for very low wages. Subsistence farming continued as the major economic activity for the majority. The Mexican government expropriated many of the banana plantations in the first decades of the 20th century. Much of the expropriated lands were given back to the Chinantecs as communal lands. Development programs, beginning in 1947, by the Papaloapan River Commission, including dams, power plants, and other installations, displaced even more of the Chinantecs living in the lowlands. Since the 1960s, many Chinantec municipalities have formed alliances to protect their respective communal lands and forests from foreign exploitation. They have also hired young Chinantec lawyers to challenge government policies regarding the displacing of populations for construction of the large Cerro de Oro dam. Significant numbers of Chinantecs who reside in Mexico City or in the United States have organized and collaborated with other indigenous groups in efforts to protect the civil and political rights of their home communities. Remittances from many of the Chinantecs living away from their homeland form an important economic resource in the Chinantec communities. Education, particularly secondary education, has been extended to even the most remote communities. Many Chinantecs view education as a means to learn how to deal with the outside world and how to protect themselves and their communities from the abuses they suffered in the past.

Further Reading

Bartolome Barabas, Alicia and Miguel Bartolome Barabas. *Hydraulic Development and Ethnocide: The Mazatec and Chinantec People of Oaxaca, Mexico.* Copenhagen: IWGIA, 1973.

Caplan, Karen. *Indigenous Citizens: Local Liberalism in early National Oaxaca and Yucatan.* Palo Alto, CA: Stanford University Press, 2009.

Yannakakis, Yanna. *The Art of Being In-Between: Native Intermediaries, Indian Identity, and Local Rule in Colonial Oaxaca.* Durham, NC: Duke University Press, 2008.

Chipewyans

The Chipewyans, also known as Dené-soliné, are a North American ethnic group mostly living in the Arctic regions around Hudson Bay in northern Canada, including communities in Manitoba, the Northwest Territories, northern Alberta, and northern Saskatchewan. The estimated 15,000 Chipewyans speak Standard English with many still using their own language, which is a Northern Athapaskan language of the larger Athapaskan language family.

Historically the Chipewyan territory extended west from Hudson Bay along the Seal River to Lake Athabasca, and north to above the Arctic Circle around Coronation Gulf. The indigenous peoples living near the Chipewyans included the Crees to the south, the Inuits to the north, and the Dogrib, Beaver, and Slavey tribes to the west. The Chipewyan bands living in the northwest were usually identified as Yellowknife. Historically the Chipewyans considered the Inuits and the Crees as enemies. Wars were often fought over hunting grounds, women, or resources. The seasonal migrations centered on the movement of the caribou herds. The first direct contact that the Europeans had with the Chipewyans was with Chipewyan women and children who had been taken captive by the Crees. French and English traders, using information from the captives, began to move into Chipewyan territory in the late 17th century. Direct trade between the Chipewyans and the English was established in 1715, and in 1717 the English traders established a post, known as Prince of Wales Fort, at modern Churchill on Hudson Bay. Diseases brought to the region by the Europeans decimated the indigenous peoples, particularly the smallpox epidemic that spread through the Chipewyan communities in 1781–1782.

The Chipewyans are a sub-Arctic people whose name is derived from a Cree word meaning "pointed skins," which refers to the cut of the caribou-skin hunting shirts traditionally worn by Chipewyan men. The Chipewyans refer to themselves as *Dene*, meaning simply "humans" or "the people." Many of the Chipewyans now live in towns and villages that are also home to other regional peoples. Even today, in communities with Chipewyan and Cree residents, the ancient enmity continues and ethnic relations are often strained. The modern Chipewyans include two cultural and regional groups. The Boreal Forest Chipewyans live in the south below the tree line where spruce forests provided hunting and furs. The Chipewyans who continue to occupy the forest edge and the more barren territory farther north are known as the Caribou Easter Chipewyans. The Chipewyan language, known as the Dene Suline language, belongs to the Athabaskan linguistic family. Their name for themselves, Dene, meaning "the people," or Denésoliné, meaning "the people of the barrens," is the preferred name. Many consider the name Chipewyan, which is derived from the Plains Crees, to have derogatory undertones. The majority of the Chipewyans are Christians, mostly Roman Catholic, with many of their pre-Christian rituals being incorporated into their modern belief system.

A second serious smallpox epidemic swept through the Chipewyan territory in 1819, affecting even communities that had been spared by the earlier epidemics. In response to the pressures of European traders for furs and the Chipewyan desires for European trade goods, during the late 18th and early 19th centuries some groups moved south to permanently settle into the boreal forest zone, where fur-bearing animals were more plentiful. These groups became the Boreal Forest Chipewyans, and those that continued to live at the forest edge and the barren, wind-swept lands to the north where they continued their traditional pursuit of the caribou herds became known as the Caribou Eater Chipewyans. Early missionaries brought the Christian religion to the region but gained few converts until a Roman Catholic mission was established at Lake Isle à la Cross. The missionaries introduced modern education and often brought modern medicines to the tribes. In 1912 an Anglican mission was established at Churchill. Treaties between the Chipewyans and the Dominion of Canada in 1899 and 1907 ended Chipewyan land titles, which were exchanged for annual payments and other goods and considerations. Many of the historical cultural ways of the Chipewyans disappeared among the southern communities but persisted among the Caribou Easter Chipewyans well into the 20th century. European diseases continued to take a toll, particularly the influenza outbreaks in the 1920s and a severe measles epidemic in 1948. During the 1950s and 1960s, well-meaning but ill-conceived government efforts to relocate, settle, and assimilate the traditional Chipewyan communities resulted in many rapid and disruptive cultural changes. Life in the new towns and villages often resulted in social problems such as family dysfunction, alcoholism, and poor educational standards. Tuberculosis has been a major health problem in all the Chipewyan regions. In the late 20th century many Chipewyans mobilized to protect their threatened culture and language. Younger Chipewyans now often speak the language as a matter of pride.

Further Reading

Savishinsky, Joel S. *The Trail of the Hare: Environment and Stress in a Sub-Arctic Community.* London: Routledge, 1994.

Volo, James M. *Family Life in Native America.* Westport, CT: Greenwood, 2007.

Younkin, Paula. *Indians of the Arctic and Subarctic.* New York: Facts on File, 1991.

Chippewas

See Ojibwe

Chiquitanos

The Chiquitanos, sometimes known as Chikitos, Churapas, Cikitanos, Manasis, Paicas, Tamacocis, Tarapecosis, or Zúbacas, are a South American ethnic group, the largest indigenous group in the lowlands of eastern Bolivia and a small adjacent area of Brazil. The estimated 200,000 Chiquitanos speak Spanish with a minority continuing to use their own language, which is considered a language isolate. The majority of the Chiquitanos are Roman Catholics, often blending Catholic rituals with their pre-Christian shamanism and reverence for spirits.

The early Chiquitanos were largely dependent on foraging in the fertile plains and rain forests. Hunting for meat animals was an important part of the culture, with the spirits of the animals being thanked for their contribution to the well-being of the bands. Contact with the more advanced civilizations of the Andean highlands led to some trade contacts but the Chiquitano bands remained seminomadic autonomous bands. The Chiquitanos were first contacted by a Spanish expedition led by Domingo Martínez de Irala, but relations quickly soured and the Spanish were forced to leave the region. In 1560 a second Spanish expedition with a larger number of armed men under Ñuflo de Chávez defeated the Chiquitano warriors. The Spanish attempted to force the bands to live in villages by the newly established Roman Catholic missions, but by the end of the 1500s many Chiquitanos had fled the mission villages and some bands turned to raiding Spanish settlements. In 1692, when the first Jesuit mission was founded in Chiquitano territory, their society underwent radical social and economic changes. Their common conversion to Catholicism and their confinement to the mission towns under the authority of the Jesuits greatly influenced their culture and way of life. In the years following the founding of the first mission, the Jesuits founded another nine missions in Chiquitano territory. Different tribes were represented at the missions, but because the Chiquitanos were in the majority, the Jesuits used the Chiquitano language as the language of Christian conversion. It became the lingua franca in which the Jesuit missionaries preached and translated the bible and other religious texts. The Jesuits imposed a strict regime of work and prayer, while protecting their charges from slavers crossing the border from Portuguese Brazil. Trained and armed by the Jesuits, the Chiquitanos were able to resist many of these raids. In 1767, a religious dispute in Spain led to the expulsion of all Jesuits from the Spanish colonies. At that time there were over 37,000 Chiquitanos and others at the mission stations, with nearly 25,000 baptized as Christians. After the Jesuits were forced to leave, the missions became towns controlled by the growing mestizo population who exploited the Chiquitanos' disciplined work habits and economic dependency learned from the Jesuits. The mestizos controlled the land, establishing farms and cattle ranches where the Chiquitanos worked and lived. Some Chiquitanos abandoned the mission towns to found independent villages where many of them remain to the present.

The Chiquitano culture is based on the agriculture that accounts for the way of life for most Chiquitanos. Once mostly dependent on foraging and hunting, the Chiquitanos are now farmers, horticulturists, domestic servants, or wage laborers. Those living in the traditional villages sell ocelot skins, chickens, rice, eggs, pigs, and woven goods such as hammocks; they are often better off materially than those Chiquitanos who work as rubber tappers or as farm or ranch laborers. The Chiquitanos still gather fruits and honey, but hunting is no longer an important part of their lives as most of the land is fenced for ranches and farms and the game has largely disappeared. The Chiquitanos live in stucco houses often roofed with palm fronds or thatch. Traditionally they lived in beehive-shaped huts that had very low doorways to restrict the entrance of mosquitoes. Because of these small doors the early Spanish called them Chiquitos, meaning "little ones." Most present-day Chiquitano villages are, to a great extent, self-governing communities. Each one has a chief and a council that is elected by the villagers. Those elected to the councils are often younger men selected for their ability to speak Spanish and to deal with outsiders. The councils have little authority in village affairs. Chiquitano society is divided into *sibs*, each with a separate family name. Each *sib* is headed by its oldest member, but his authority is limited to the *sib*. When

a couple marries, it is traditional for the husband to move into his wife's household and relations with the wife's family usually remain close. In essence, this political and social organization is based on that which prevailed under the Jesuits, with the local civil authorities taking the place of the missionaries. Labor exchange is an important part of community life. Work parties cooperate in building houses, harvesting, and clearing fields. The Roman Catholicism of the Chiquitanos is basically the religion they were taught by the Jesuits over two centuries ago. The Chiquitanos memorized the religious texts that the Jesuit missionaries translated into their language and have transmitted them orally from generation to generation. Shamans are respected and powerful and exercise a great deal of social control in Chiquitano culture. Shamans derive their authority by contact with spirits representing the forces of nature, which demonstrates the continued reverence for the ancient pre-Christian beliefs. Despite their long experience of close contact with the mestizo Bolivians, they have resisted assimilation and preserved a strong ethnic identity into the 21st century.

The mestizos often used debts to control Chiquitano laborers and to tie them to farms and ranches with little hope of paying off the debt or of escape to the free Chiquitano villages in the less accessible regions. Beginning in the 1880s, Bolivian and Brazilian rubber trappers recruited thousands of Chiquitanos to accompany them north to tap rubber in the tropical forests. The rubber workers lived under conditions of forced labor. Many generations, trapped into debt peonage on farms, ranches, or rubber camps, often died of beriberi, malaria, abuses, and overwork before they could escape. Between 1945 and 1955 many Chiquitanos were hired to help build the railroad line from Santa Cruz, the largest city in lowland Bolivia, to Corumbá in Brazil. Many still work on the railway, with the families living in the region served by the rail lines being the most assimilated into modern Bolivian society. During the 1970s, political activism began to gain popularity across South America. Several Chiquitano leaders formed activist groups to protest the exploitation of their people, including denouncing the traditional debt system that forced many Chiquitanos into near slavery for life. In the 1990s, a new organization became a grassroots political movement with representatives in most towns and cities in the region. The Chiquitano Indigenous Organization (Organizacíon Indigena Chiquitana) is the most important group representing the interests of the Chiquitano people. In recent years indigenous peoples from the Andean highlands of Bolivia have settled in the region, offering competition for jobs and political power. The promises of the Bolivian government under Evo Morales, an indigenous politician from the highlands, to promote the interests of Bolivia's indigenous peoples has not resonated in the Chiquitano region. Despite their position as the most numerous of the indigenous peoples of the lowland eastern Bolivia, they have not benefited greatly from new government policies that favor the indigenous peoples of the Altiplano, the Andean highlands.

Further Reading

Mitchell, Juri. *Chiquitano.* Little Rock, AR: Baptist Trumpet Press, 1984.

Postero, Nancy. *Now We are Citizens: Indigenous Politics in Postmulticultural Bolivia.* Palo Alto, CA: Stanford University Press, 2006.

Riester, Jürgen. *Indians of Eastern Bolivia: Aspects of Their Present Situation.* Copenhagen: IWGIA, 1972.

Choctaws

The Choctaws, sometimes known as Chacktaws, Chaquitas, Chat-Kas, Tchatakes, or Tchiactas, are a North American ethnic group, one of the so-called Five Civilized Tribes that also includes the Creeks, Chickasaws, Cherokees, and Seminoles. The estimated 165,000 Choctaws speak Standard English with many, often the elderly, speaking the Choctaw language, one of the languages of the Muskogean language family. The majority of the Choctaws are Christians, with both Protestant and Roman Catholic churches represented, along with a minority that continues to adhere to traditional beliefs or to mix those beliefs with Christian rituals.

The Choctaws are believed to have originated west of the Mississippi River. They later moved with the related Chickasaws to the eastern shore to settle in the valley of the Mississippi and its tributaries. The ancestors of the Choctaws are often linked to the advanced Mississippian culture in the lower Mississippi River valley. The early settlers built large mounds that held temple complexes and other sacred buildings, usually with a sizable town built around the huge mounds. The greatest of the mounds, Nanih Yaiya in present-day Mississippi, built before 300 CE, is still considered sacred by the Choctaws and

Chickasaws. The two groups, once considered one people, split into two distinct tribes. The Choctaws coalesced as a separate people in the 17th century. They developed three distinct geographic and political divisions corresponding to the east, west, and south. The Choctaw towns, often with many temple-topped mounds, covered a wide territory and were divided into numerous autonomous chiefdoms. The first encounter with Europeans took place in the fall of 1540. A Spanish expedition led by Hernan De Soto entered Choctaw territory from the Florida Peninsula. The looting of temples and abuse of Choctaw women ended in an armed conflict but the Choctaw's arrows and bows did little against the Spanish armor and their guns. The rampaging Spanish killed an estimated 1,500 Choctaws before withdrawing. This conflict was the last contact with Europeans for over 150 years. The French began to enter the region in 1692 and established good relations with the area's tribes. French aid against the British slave traders raiding in the region resulted in an alliance against the British and their allies in the colonial wars for control of North America in the early 18th century. Shifting alliances between the three geographic Choctaw bands and the Europeans in each area resulted in a civil war among the Choctaws in 1748. One of the bands favored the British and the related Chickasaws. The French aided the Choctaws to defeat the British and their Choctaw and Chickasaw allies, but a new treaty stipulated that the Choctaws must never again ally themselves with the British. Following the French defeat and British supremacy in the region in 1763, the Choctaws began trading relations that lasted until 1781, but rejected all attempts at an alliance. The Choctaws adhered to this during the Revolutionary War in 1775–1783, when many fought with the American colonists against the British. Relations with the newly independent United States continued on good terms. The Choctaws ceded lands to the new government in exchange for paying off Choctaw debts or lavishing gifts to chiefs. The first American president, George Washington, believed that the Native American people should be assimilated. He formulated a policy for civilizing the tribes and assumed that once the Native Americans adopted the practice of private property, built homes, educated their children, and embraced Christianity they would win acceptance from Americans of European descent. In 1786 the Choctaws signed the Treaty of Hopewell, which recognized them as a nation. The Choctaws remained friendly and resisted alliances offered against the United States.

The Choctaw culture is a modern blend of their traditional culture and European-American influences. The Choctaws are known for their rapid incorporation of modernity. They developed a written language, left their traditional practices to embrace yeoman farming, and accepted European-Americans and African-Americans into their culture. Within Choctaw culture there are two distinct groups, the *Imoklashas* and the *Inhulalatas*. The first comprises the elders, respected for their wisdom and experience, and the second is made up of the Choctaw youth. Traditionally the society was matrilineal, with inheritance and status through the female line. Children belonged to the mother's clan with the most important male influences being her brothers and other male relatives. Sport is an important cultural element. Choctaw stickball, the oldest field sport in North America, is still played and is sometimes referred to as the "little brother of war" because of the roughness of play. When disputes arose between different Choctaw communities, stickball often offered a civil way to settle outstanding issues. The Choctaw language is very closely related to Chickasaw, with speakers able to understand each other. The language belongs to the Muskogean language family, which includes several of the indigenous languages spoken in the southeastern United States. Many Choctaw adults learn to speak the language before they learn English, the language of formal education. While the early Choctaws did not believe in any higher being, they did believe that all things had a soul and that spirits were everywhere. Most Choctaws are practicing Christians but many also respect and participate in traditional rituals and ceremonies. The most remarkable characteristic of the traditional religion is the seeking of complete peace and harmony between all peoples. Every summer since 1949, the Choctaws have hosted the Mississippi Choctaw Indian Fair in Pearl River, Mississippi. Thousands of people attend every year, including Choctaws and other Native Americans and many others who come for the cultural events and other attractions. The fair promotes tourism but also helps the Choctaws to maintain their heritage and customs. Another fair is held yearly at Tuska Homma, Oklahoma, which draws over 100,000 visitors each year.

In 1811, Tecumseh, a Shawnee chief, in an attempt to recover land from the growing number of American and European settlers, rallied many tribes, but a joint Choctaw-Chickasaw council rejected his overtures and warned that they would fight any group that fought the United States. When war broke out between the British and the Americans in 1812, the Choctaws honored their alliance. During the 1820s the Choctaws signed several treaties ceding more territory to the United States. Younger leaders, educated in European-American schools, led a cultural adaptation that greatly changed Choctaw society. Many of the chiefs and other traditional nobles acquired plantations worked by African slaves, while most others adapted to wooden homes, new farming methods, and education. Unrelenting pressure by settlers convinced many Choctaw leaders that the removal of their nations was inevitable. In 1830 the U.S. Congress passed the Indian Removal Bill. The Treaty of Dancing Rabbit Creek represented one of the largest transfers of land by an indigenous group to the United States without warfare. The Choctaws agreed to accept new lands in Indian Territory although the treaty allowed a small number to remain in Mississippi. The Choctaws emigrated west in what became known as the Trail of Tears. Between 1831 and 1833 over 15,000 Choctaws moved west, with about 2,500 dying along the trail. Between 4,000 and 6,000 remained in Mississippi, where they suffered legal conflicts, racism, intimidation, and harassment. Removals of the Mississippi Choctaws continued, with some 1,000 sent to Indian Territory in 1846, and several hundred more in 1903. By 1930, only

1,665 Choctaws remained in Mississippi. The Choctaws formed an alliance with the Confederacy in 1861, although not all Choctaws agreed to fight the United States. The defeat of the Confederacy in the American Civil War led to reprisals against the Choctaws. The black slaves held by Choctaw owners were freed, and became members of the tribe in 1885. In 1894, the Dawes Commission was established to register Native American families in Indian Territory, and it allotted lands to each family. The U.S. government then proposed to end the tribal governments of the Five Civilized Tribes and to combine Indian and Oklahoma territories in a new state.

In 1905 a convention of the Five Civilized Tribes met to draft a constitution for an autonomous state to be known as the State of Sequoyah. The proposal was ignored or rejected and Oklahoma was admitted to the Union in 1907. The Mississippi Choctaws reorganized as a federally recognized tribe in 1945; they still faced discrimination and segregation as nonwhites in an officially segregated Southern state. In 1959, the Choctaw Termination Act was passed by Congress, effectively ending Choctaw status as a sovereign nation. Many Choctaws mobilized during the Civil Rights Movement to demand greater rights as American citizens. New legislation in the 1970s

Choctaw family at Savanna, Indian Territory (later Oklahoma), ca. 1900. (USGS)

provided for greater self-determination. In the 1980s federally recognized tribes, including the Mississippi Choctaws, were granted the right to develop casinos. The Mississippi Band of Choctaw Indians has one of the largest casino resorts in the country, located at Philadelphia, Mississippi. Other casino operations were created by the Oklahoma Choctaws. After nearly two centuries, the Choctaws regained control of the ancient site of Nanih Waiya in 2006.

Further Reading

Haag, Marcia and Henry Willis. *Choctaw Language and Culture: Chahta Anupa.* Norman, OK: University of Oklahoma Press, 2007.

Kidwell, Clara Sue. *The Choctaws of Oklahoma: From Tribe to Nation, 1855–1970.* Norman, OK: University of Oklahoma Press, 2008.

Tingle, Tim. *Walking the Choctaw Road: Stories from Red People Memory.* El Paso, TX: Cinco Puntos Press, 2005.

Colombians

The Colombians are a South American people, the multiethnic inhabitants of the nation of Colombia in northwestern South America. Most of the estimated 49 million Colombians speak Spanish, the official language of the country, with smaller groups speaking Native American languages. Outside Colombia there are large Colombian communities in the United States, Venezuela, Spain, Canada, Italy, Argentina, and the United Kingdom. The Colombians are predominately Roman Catholic, with Protestant and other religious minorities, and with a small group of people of Middle Eastern origin who are Muslims or Druze.

The territory of present-day Colombia, a geographic location that served as a corridor between the ancient regions of Mesoamerica, the Andes Mountains, the Amazonian lowlands, and the Caribbean, was settled by ancient peoples moving south from North America. The oldest indications of settlement date to around 20,000 BCE. A number of indigenous groups developed in the region with early hunter-gatherer societies gradually evolving a sophisticated political and social structure. Advanced farming methods allowed for a large settled population. Skilled in textile weaving and as goldsmiths, they developed trading relations with neighboring nations. Contact with Europeans began on the Caribbean coast as early as 1499, but the first permanent Spanish settlement was not established until 1525. Moving into the highlands, the Spanish founded Bogota in 1549. European diseases, abuses, and slavery decimated the indigenous peoples. To repopulate the region colonization directly from Spain was begun and African slaves were imported to work in the large plantations and mines. Many Basques and Jewish refugees from the Inquisition were drawn to the protection of the less accessible highland valleys. Most of the indigenous population was gradually absorbed into the growing mestizo population. The Viceroyalty of New Granada was established in 1717 with Bogota as its capital. Until 1740 the government was subordinate to the Viceroyalty of Peru. Bogota became, along with Lima and Mexico City, one of the major centers of colonial administration and colonization. The government at Bogota administered territories in present-day Colombia, Venezuela, Ecuador, and Panama. The colonists from Spain, including Basques and other Spanish minorities, mostly settled in the highlands as free farmers. Large families quickly expanded the population, which spread throughout the fertile valleys of the highlands and into the Caribbean lowlands. The relative isolation of the various settler groups resulted in the creation of a number of regional cultural groups, including the *paisas* of the Antioquia region in the highlands, the *costeños* of the Caribbean coast, the *llaneros* of the eastern plains, the people of the Pacific coast, and the groups living in the vast Amazon region in the southeast.

Much of modern Colombian culture can be traced back to the early Spanish settlers, although Colombia's position as a geographic crossroads has brought many other influences. The long conflict between conservatives and liberals, often leading to civil wars, resulted in the isolation of many regions until the 19th century. Regional cultures remain an important part of the Colombian culture with marked differences in speech and lifestyle from region to region. After World War II, a sizable immigration of new settlers from Europe and the Middle East brought new influences that were adapted to the Colombian culture. Most Colombians continue to live in the Andean highlands high above sea level with climates ranging from temperate to cool. The treacherousness of the geography and the sheer variety of climates that made communication and travel very difficult fostered an intense regionalism that remains to the present. French influence during the 19th century and North

American cultural influences starting in the 20th century have greatly shaped modern Colombian society. The country has a diverse population that reflects its unique history and the many peoples that have settled in the region from ancient times to the present. The Colombians now include the mestizos—of mixed European and Native American heritage—who form an estimated 58 percent of the population, the descendants of European immigrants, Native American peoples, descendants of slaves brought from Africa and mulattos of mixed ethnic background, people of Asian and Middle Eastern descent, and other recent immigrants from Europe and other parts of the world. The overwhelming majority of Colombians speak the Colombian dialect of Spanish, which includes influences from indigenous languages and in recent decades, many borrowings from English. An estimated 95 percent of the Colombians are Christians, mostly Roman Catholic but with an increasing number adopting Protestantism, mostly evangelical sects. Small groups of Jews, Muslims, Hindus, and Buddhists are also present.

Since the early 17th century various groups have attempted to throw off Spanish rule; the last of the groups seeking outright independence formed around 1810. War in Europe weakened the Spanish hold on the region with various regions being liberated from Spanish rule. The formation of two rival governments led to a period of civil unrest known as La Patria Boba. In 1811 the United Provinces of New Granada was created but despite the success of the anti-Spanish rebellion two distinct ideologies emerged with conservatives favoring a highly centralized state and liberals supporting a loose federal system giving the historically distinct regions more local power. The conflict between the two allowed the Spanish to reconquer the region and reestablish the viceroyalty. Reprisals against those who supported the rebellion stoked renewed unrest and uprisings. A successful rebellion led by Venezuelan-born Simón Bolivar resulted in independence being proclaimed in 1819. The new state, known as Gran Colombia, included present-day Colombia, Ecuador, Venezuela, and Panama, which formed part of Colombia. The new republic was very unstable and Venezuela seceded in 1829, followed by Ecuador in 1830. Colombia, known as New Granada, created the first constitutional government in South America although the founding of the Liberal political party in 1849 and the Conservative party a year later undermined stability. After a two-year civil war ending in 1863, the United States of Colombia was created as a federal state. Federalism lasted until 1886, when a unified Republic of Colombia was formed. Internal divisions between Liberals and Conservatives occasionally erupted in bloody civil wars, the most significant being the Thousand Days' War in 1899–1902. Influence from the United States, involved in the construction of the Panama Canal, led to the secession of Panama in 1903. In the 1930s a relative degree of stability and economic prosperity rapidly modernized the society. The period of stability was interrupted by the mounting tensions between the two leading political parties that finally led to widespread violence. The period, known as *La Violencia*, spread throughout the country and claimed the lives of over 180,000 Colombians. After the war, military governments ruled until the Liberals and Conservatives agreed to a formula to jointly govern the country. Despite the attempts at cooperation many social and political problems persisted, and guerrilla groups were organized to fight the government political apparatus. In the 1970s, powerful and violent drug cartels formed in several regions. The cartels became so powerful in the 1980s and 1990s that they exerted political, economic, and social influence on the society as a whole. A new constitution, ratified in 1991, included human, political, gender, and human rights. Despite the advances since the new constitution and the reforms that were adopted, the Colombians remain under threat due to guerrilla insurgencies, paramilitary groups, the powerful drug cartels, and smaller factions that continue to engage in armed conflicts. Many Colombians, despairing of the continued instability and insecurity in their homeland, have opted to leave the country to settle in the United States and elsewhere.

Further Reading

Bouvier, Virginia M. *Colombia: Building Peace in a Time of War.* Washington: United States Institute of Peace Press, 2009.

Bushnell, David. *The Making of Modern Colombia: A Nation in Spite of Itself.* Berkley: University of California Press, 1993.

Safford, Frank and Marco Palacios. *Colombia: Fragmented Land, Divided Society.* New York: Oxford University Press, 2001.

Comanches

The Comanches are a North American ethnic group living mostly in the states of Oklahoma and Texas. The Comanches call themselves Numinu or Numunuh, which means "The People." The estimated 14,000 to 30,000 Comanches speak Standard English with a minority still able to speak the Comanche language, a northern or Numic language of the Uto-Aztecan language group.

The Shoshone people were primarily hunter-gatherers up to the late 1600s. The Comanches emerged as a distinct people in the late 17th century when they separated from the Shoshone people living in the area of the upper Platte River in present-day Wyoming. This separation coincided with their acquisition of horses, which allowed them to hunt better and have greater mobility. Around 1680 the Comanches acquired horses from the Pueblo people to the south after the Pueblo Revolt against Spanish rule. Other Comanche bands acquired horses from the Utes, who brought them to Spanish traders. The Ute name for the migrants was transformed by the Spanish into "Comanche." The original Comanche migration was to the southern Great Plains. Their population increased dramatically due to the abundance of buffalo, an influx of related Shoshone migrants, and the adoption of significant numbers of captives taken from other tribal groups. The Comanches never formed a single tribal unit but lived in nearly a dozen autonomous bands. These bands shared a common culture and religion and rarely fought each other. Horses were a key part of the emergence of a distinctive Comanche culture. They may have been the first of the Plains peoples to incorporate the horse into their culture. They introduced horses to many of the other peoples of the Great Plains. As the Comanches moved south they displaced other Plains peoples, particularly the Apaches, who were driven from the southern plains. Once established as the "Lords of the Southern Plains" the Comanches split into five major groups or bands. The Comanche population at the end of the 18th century may have been as high as 45,000. Although the five bands were independent they often came together to fight a common enemy, particularly the Apaches, or to take land, horses, and captives from other peoples, including the Spanish. The Spanish sought to convert the Comanche to Roman Catholicism and wanted Comanche land for its gold and other precious items. European diseases, particularly smallpox, decimated many of the Comanche bands; French traders, unlike the Spanish, had no religious or social intent, were interested in the furs trapped in the northern parts of the Comanche territory, and maintained good relations with the various bands. The French traded guns and ammunition, and forged metal goods such as pots and knives. Following the French defeat by the British in the French and Indian War of 1763, most of the French traders left the continent, and the Comanche bands lost valuable trading partners. A serious smallpox epidemic swept the region in 1780–1781 and so weakened the Comanches that they could no longer fight the Spanish. Some of the bands made peace with the Spanish, while others, not part of the negotiations, continued to raid Spanish settlements.

Comanche culture is a modern culture based on their traditional culture and many borrowings from the American society that surrounds them. In recent decades many younger Comanches have, like the rest of

American society, urbanized; they often live in urban and suburban areas of the Southwest. Only about half of them live in the region of their old homeland in Oklahoma and Texas. Traditional Comanche culture looked upon children as a precious gift. Children are rarely punished although sometimes an older sister or other relative will be called upon to discipline a child. Because of their former nomadic lifestyle, the Comanche did not use breakable pottery but relied on the buffalo for most of their needs. They made nearly 200 distinct articles from the hides, bones, horns, and bones of the buffalo. The Comanches speak standard American English, the language of education and administration, with a small minority still able to speak their own Comanche language. The language belongs to the Uto-Aztecan language family. Many older Comanches learned the language, but during the 1920s education was in the hands of the Bureau of Indian Affairs (BIA) schools that suppressed traditional languages. Today a new program is teaching pre-school children the Comanche language as part of an immersion program to ensure the survival of the language. A Comanche Language Preservation Committee also works to preserve the language and culture. In comparison to other Plains peoples, the Comanches had few ceremonies. The Comanche war dance, held the night before the warriors were to go into battle, was the most important of the religious ceremonies. Most Comanches are Christians but many continue to revere their pre-Christian religious beliefs. After being forced to settle on reservations, many Comanches began practicing the ritual use of peyote learned from neighboring peoples.

The Comanches expanded throughout the southern plains, displacing other peoples to control a vast area called by the

Quanah Parker

Quanah Parker is one of the most famous of the Comanche chiefs. He was a war leader during the Indian Wars, and later the leader of the reservation and the Native American Church. He was born between 1845 and 1852, the son of Comanche chief Peta Nocona and Cynthia Ann Parker, a young European-American girl who had been captured at the age of nine and assimilated into the Comanche tribe. As a young warrior Parker formed his own band, which became the largest of the Comanche bands. In the 1960s he led his warriors against the American cavalry, but gradually lost ground and finally surrendered in 1875. Parker helped to settle the Comanches on a new reservation in southwestern Indian Territory. Parker was named chief of all the Comanches on the reservation and proved a resourceful and able leader. Through wise investments he became one of the wealthiest Native Americans of his time in the United States. He became a friend of President Theodore Roosevelt, who often visited him. Even though he embraced much of American culture, he rejected traditional Christianity in favor of the Native American Church, of which he was a founder.

Spanish and later the Mexican authorities as the "Comancheria." The Comanches often supplied horses to other tribes and to settlers. They even supplied horses to the American settlers heading to California during the Gold Rush of 1849. The Comanches often maintained contradictory relationships with the European settlers and later the American settlers attempting to colonize their homeland. They were valued as trading partners, especially for their herds of horses, but were feared for their raids on settlements throughout the frontier. The Comanches managed to maintain their independence and carried on wars with nearly all the neighboring peoples, including the Spanish, the Mexicans, and the Americans, but in the mid-19th century they faced near annihilation because of a new wave of epidemics to which they had no immunity. Outbreaks of smallpox in 1817 and 1848 and a severe cholera epidemic in 1849 took a serious toll on the Comanches, whose population dropped from an estimated 20,000 to just a few thousand survivors in the 1870s. The American government began efforts years after the American Civil War to force the Comanches into reservations. The Treaty of Medicine Lodge, signed in 1867, provided for churches, schools, and monetary payments in return for ceding a vast tract of Comanche land totaling over 60,000 square miles (160,000 sq. km.). The government promised to stop the indiscriminate slaughter by hunters who were decimating the great buffalo herds, but the killing of buffalo continued. Some Comanches retaliated by leaving the reservation and attacking American settlements. The U.S. Cavalry drove the remaining Comanche groups onto reservations. Within just a few years, the buffalo were on the verge of extinction, which effectively ended the Comanches' traditional way of life. In 1875, the last band of free Comanches surrendered and was moved to a reservation in Oklahoma. A new agreement, signed in 1892, further reduced the area of the Comanche reservation. Allotments were given out to each family with the surplus lands opened to white settlement. This agreement brought the end of the Comanche reservation system. Entering the modern American economy presented many challenges to the former nomads. Many were defrauded of whatever remained of their lands and possessions. Elected chief of the entire Comanche people, Quanah Parker, in the early decades of the 20th century, campaigned for better deals for his people and for the right to practice the peyote ritual of the Native American Church. During World War II, many Comanches left the tribal lands in search of jobs and financial opportunities in the cities of California and the Southwest. To the Comanches, survival meant adapting to the prevailing American society. Education, particularly higher education, became a way to advance since the 1960s and 1970s. Today Comanches live in many parts of the country, with diverse occupations and professions, but most retain important ties to their culture and their history as the Lords of the Southern Plains.

Further Reading

Fehrenbach, T. R. *Comanches: The History of a People.* New York: Anchor, 2003.

Hamalainen, Pekka. *The Comanche Empire.* New Haven, CT: Yale University Press, 2009.

Wallace, Ernest and E. Adamson Hoebel. *The Comanches: Lords of the South Plains.* Norman, OK: University of Oklahoma Press, 1987.

Costa Ricans

The Costa Ricans, sometimes known as Costaricans or Ticos, are a Central American people, the inhabitants of the Central American Republic of Costa Rica. The estimated 4.3 million Costa Ricans speak a dialect of Spanish known as Costa Rican Spanish. Around 10 percent of the population, mostly descendants of Jamaican black immigrants, speaks an English patois along the Caribbean coast. The majority of the Costa Ricans are Roman Catholics, the official religion of the country. The Mormons and evangelical Protestant sects have gained many followers in recent decades. The Costa Ricans also include over 40,000 Buddhists and smaller numbers of Hindus, Jews, Baha'is, and Muslims.

The region of Central America was a historically important meeting ground for cultural influences from the Mesoamerican civilization that controlled territory south to the Nicoya Peninsula area and the Chibcha cultures that dominated northwestern South America. Christopher Columbus on his fourth and last expedition to the Americas sighted the coast in 1502. The Spanish named the region Costa Rica or the "rich coast," probably due to the heavy gold ornaments worn by the indigenous population. The gold was the product of trade and the disappointed Spanish never found gold or other treasure in the region. The first permanent Spanish settlement, Villa Bruselas, was established in 1524, but the lack of gold or silver, the distance from the seats of Spanish power, and a legal prohibition on trade with settlements in neighboring Panama, which formed part of a separate Spanish province, made the region a poor, isolated, and sparsely populated outpost of the Spanish Empire. Costa Rica was described by a local administrator as the poorest and most miserable of the Spanish possessions in America. Another significant factor in Costa Rica's poverty was the lack of a large indigenous population available for slavery or forced labor. The settlers had to work their own lands, preventing the establishment of large haciendas as in other colonies. The Costa Ricans evolved into an autonomous and individualistic society that gradually absorbed the small indigenous population. Costa Rican society became a "rural democracy" with no downtrodden mestizo or indigenous underclass. The European settlers soon migrated into the hills, where they found a milder climate and fertile volcanic soil. With relatively few new immigrants during the 1700s, the population expanded due to large families and readily available food crops.

Costa Rican culture is based on the Spanish culture brought to the region by settlers in the 16th and 17th centuries. The cornerstones of Spanish culture, the Spanish language and the Roman Catholic religion, are strong elements of the Costa Rican culture. Costa Ricans are the most prosperous and stable society in Central America. One of the popular phrases of the Costa Rican Spanish dialect is *Pura Vida*, meaning pure life or good life. It is often used as a salutation meaning "hello" or as a response to questions such as "how are you?" Costa Ricans abolished their army in 1949, and since that time they have concentrated on improving the lives of their people. The literacy rate is one of the highest in Latin America because, as they like to say, the "army was replaced by an army of teachers." Costa Rica is the only Latin American country included in the list of the world's oldest democracies. The country is consistently among the top Latin American countries in the Human Development Index, where it ranked 69th in the world in 2011. Costa Rica has been cited by United Nations agencies as having attained much higher human development than other countries having the same income levels. Environmental concerns have become part of the culture with popular support for the preservation and study of the country's rain forests. The Spanish dialect spoken in the region includes some archaic Spanish forms and influences from Spanish language television from Mexico. Some 50,000 blacks, the descendants of laborers brought to the region from Jamaica, speak an English patois as their first language. There are also small indigenous groups speaking their own languages along with Spanish. Although more than 90 percent of the Costa Ricans are baptized Catholics, only about half actively practice the religion. Roman Catholicism is the official national religion but freedom of religion is guaranteed.

Costa Rica, along with the other provinces in Central America, never fought for independence from Spain. In September 1821, after the decisive Spanish defeat in the Mexican War of Independence, the authorities in Guatemala declared the independence of Central America. Costa Rica became a province of the new Federal Republic of Central America in 1823. The government of the federation exercised only loose authority over the remote and poor province of Costa Rica. While civil wars raged in other parts of the federation, Costa Rica remained largely peaceful and isolated. In 1838, after the federation had ceased to function, the Costa Ricans proclaimed the sovereignty of their own republic. Coffee, first planted in the early 19th century, began to be shipped in commercial quantities in 1843. Coffee quickly became the most important crop but transportation to the ports on the east coast was hazardous and slow. The Costa Rican government contracted with a U.S. businessman, Minor C. Keith, to build a railway from the highland centers of population and coffee production to the Caribbean port of Limón. The Americans imported laborers and their families from Jamaica to work on the railway, and many of these laborers settled along the coast. Despite many difficulties with construction, financing, and disease, the railroad connection was completed in 1890. Keith also began banana production on the tracts of land along the railway. As a result bananas became an important export crop to the United States and foreign-owned companies, including the United Fruit Company, began to play major roles in the Costa Rican economy. Throughout their history the Costa Ricans have generally enjoyed greater peace and more political stability than their Latin American neighbors. Since the late 19th century Costa Rica has experienced two significant upheavals. During 1917–1919, a military dictator ruled until he was overthrown and forced into exile. The unpopularity of the dictatorial regime resulted in a marked decline in the size, political influence, and wealth of the Costa Rican military forces. In 1948, an armed uprising in the wake of a disputed presidential election led to a 44-day civil war that left several thousand dead, the bloodiest event in Costa Rican history. The victorious rebels abolished the military completely, and oversaw the drafting of a new democratic constitution in 1949. Since then, Costa Rica has held 14 presidential elections, all of them widely regarded as peaceful, fair, and transparent. Costa Rica's traditions of democratic government and the absence of class or racial tensions has allowed the country to become one of the most peaceful in the world and one of the most prosperous in the Americas.

Further Reading

Biesanz, Mavis Hiltunen, Richard Biesanz, and Karen Zubris Biezanz. *The Ticos: Culture and Social Change in Costa Rica.* Boulder, CO: Lynne Rienner Publishers, 1998.

Helmuth, Charlene. *Culture and Customs of Costa Rica.* Westport, CT: Greenwood, 2008.

Palmer, Steven and Iván Molina, eds. *The Costa Rican Reader: History, Culture, Politics.* Durham, NC: Duke University Press, 2004.

Creeks

The Creeks, sometimes known as the Muscogees, Muskogees, or Mvskokes, are a North American ethnic group, one of the historic Five Civilized Tribes. The estimated 75,000 Creeks live primarily in Oklahoma, Alabama, Georgia, and Florida.

The Creek language, known as Mvskoke, is a language of the Muscogean language family. The majority of the Creeks belong to Protestant sects, and some adhere to the traditional Four Mothers Society or the Native American Church.

The early hunter-gatherer groups in the Southeast probably settled the region at least 12,000 years ago. New technologies, such as pottery and small-scale horticulture, spread across the region. The population growth made possible by the cultivation of corn, beans, and squash led to the rise of urban centers and great mounds constructed to hold temples and other sacred buildings. Stratified indigenous societies developed regional hierarchies of chiefs and priests that flourished in what is now the Midwest, East, and South of the United States between 800 and 1500 C.E. The early Creeks were probably descendants of the collapsed Mississippian culture first noted along the Tennessee River in present-day Tennessee, Georgia, and Alabama. The first Europeans, a Spanish expedition led by Hernan De Soto, rampaged through the mostly Creek territories between 1540 and 1543. Brutal excesses, looting of temples, taking captives for slaves, and the rape of kidnapped Creek women forced the Creeks to defend themselves. After several indecisive battles against the better-armed Europeans, the Creeks faced the Europeans at the Battle of Mabila, after which the Europeans turned the town of Mabila and killed most of its inhabitants. However, the battle cost the Europeans the lives of 22 men and 45 horses, a crippling blow to their morale. The De Soto expedition continued but his failure to find gold or silver or to found a colony were considered failures. De Soto died in 1542 and the survivors of the expedition made their way to the coast and eventually to Spanish Mexico. De Soto's expedition, particularly the infectious European diseases it introduced, caused a high rate of fatalities among the indigenous peoples. Historians believe that the epidemics that swept through the region contributed to the final depopulation and collapse of the Mississippian culture. Some of the survivors and descendants regrouped in the Muscogee or Creek Confederacy, a loose alliance of Muskogean-speaking groups. The social unit of the confederacy was the town. Abihka, Coosa, Cusseta, and Coweta were the four "mother towns" that are still revered by the Four Mothers Society. Spain, France, and England all established colonies in present-day southeastern United States. The Spanish established missions for the control and conversion of the indigenous peoples. The French and British were more interested in trade. The Creeks quickly acquired horses and guns, giving them greater mobility and defense. The Europeans often engaged in taking captives for sale as slaves, which further decimated many bands. In the early 1700s the Creeks joined an alliance of tribes to wage war against the newcomers. In 1718, Creek leader Brim invited representatives of the three colonial powers to his town. There he declared a policy of Creek neutrality in the ongoing colonial wars. At the end of the French and Indian War in 1763, the French were forced to give up most of their colonial claims. The British became the colonial power, founding towns and trading posts across the South. British-American settlers began to move inland in search of

free land. During the American Revolution (1776–1783) the Creeks were divided, some joining the Americans while others remained loyal to their British allies. At the end of the war, the Creeks were dismayed to learn that the British had ceded their ancestral lands to the new United States. In 1786, some of the Creeks mobilized to attack settlers in Georgia. President George Washington invited Creek leaders to New York, the American capital, for negotiations. The Treaty of New York resulted in the cession of a large portion of their lands to the federal government and a promise to return fugitive African slaves in exchange for federal recognition of Creek sovereignty and promises to evict American and European settlers. With the invention of the cotton gin, planters in the coastal regions and on the frontier clamored for more cotton lands in the indigenous territories.

Modern Creek culture is the product of a long evolution over centuries, combining the traditional culture with the later European-American traditions and customs. The Creeks, known for the rapid incorporation of technology and modernity, developed a written language, accepted strangers into their society, and made a rapid transition to yeoman farming, earning them a place among the so-called Five Civilized Tribes. Today young Creeks, preferring to call themselves by the name Muscogee, continue to preserve and share their vibrant culture through annual events, language classes, and gatherings. The Green Corn Ceremony is an annual ritual that remains an important cultural event. The traditional clan system, made up of extended families, continues as the basis of society. Traditionally the Creeks were matrilineal, with inheritance from the mother's family. The Creek language is an important member of the Muskogean language family and was well known among early frontiersmen. The Creeks were mostly converted to Protestant sects by missionaries who arrived in their homeland in the early 1800s. The religious beliefs of the Creeks include many pre-Christian rituals and reverence for the Four Mothers Society, a religious and political grouping.

In the early 19th century the Creeks signed a number of treaties ceding lands to the states or the federal government. A number of Creek chiefs acquired cotton plantations and slaves for labor. The New Madrid earthquake in 1812 convinced many Creeks that it was a sign that they should join many other tribes to follow Tecumseh, a Shawnee chief. In 1813 a civil war broke out between Creek factions, but American forces became involved after attacking a Creek party. The war continued until the defeat of the Creeks in 1814. The peace included the cession of over 20 million acres of fertile land in Georgia and Alabama, lands belonging to both the combatant Creeks and other bands not involved in the war. In the late 1810s and the early 1820s, the Creeks established written laws and formed the National Creek Council. The Council, following the cession of more land in Georgia by some Creeks, decreed the death penalty for tribesmen who surrendered additional lands. In 1825, some Creek chiefs signed an agreement ceding more land to Georgia, with funds allotted for the removal of all Creeks west of the Arkansas River. By the terms of the new treaties the Creeks were confined to a small strip of land in east central Alabama.

Andrew Jackson was elected president of the United States in 1829 and government policies toward indigenous groups became harsher. Jackson actively pursued the removal of all indigenous tribes to the west of the Mississippi in lands set aside as Indian Territory. Under pressure from both the federal and state government, particularly in Georgia, the Creeks finally signed away their last remaining lands and accepted relocation. Many refused but rampaging mobs moved through the Creek lands, taking over plantations, looting, and forcing many Creeks out of their homes. Crowded into unsanitary camps many Creeks died before they were forced west onto the Trail of Tears in 1834. Thousands died on the trail before the survivors arrived in Indian Territory. Anger and resentment against the American authorities led many to support the South in the American Civil War in the 1860s. At the end of the war they were often punished. Thousands of black slaves were freed and in the 1880s were enrolled as members of the Creek tribe. In 1907, the U.S. government forced the Creeks to give up their common lands and to accept single family allotments. The surplus lands were confiscated and opened to white settlement. Today the Creeks are among the most advanced of the indigenous peoples of North America. The largest population continues to live in Oklahoma, with smaller groups in Louisiana and Alabama.

Further Reading

Debo, Angie. *The Road to Disappearance: A History of the Creek Indians.* Norman, OK: University of Oklahoma Press, 1979.

Ethridge, Robbie. *Creek Country: The Creek Indians and Their World.* Chapel Hill, NC: University of North Carolina Press, 2003.

Littlefield, Daniel F. Jr. and James W. Parins, eds. *Encyclopedia of American Indian Removal.* Westport, CT: Greenwood, 2011.

Crees

The Crees, sometimes known as Nēhilaws, are a North American ethnic group concentrated in Canada in the provinces of Ontario, Manitoba, Saskatchewan, Alberta, and the North West Territories. Outside their traditional homeland there are sizable Cree communities in eastern Quebec and in the United States, where they share a reservation with the Ojibwe people in Montana. The estimated 190,000 Crees mostly speak English as their first language, or French in Quebec, and many speak the Cree language, which is closely related to the other Algonquian languages spoken in northern and eastern Quebec, Labrador, and the Maritime Provinces of Canada. The majority of the Crees are Roman Catholic, with a sizable Protestant minority. Many continue to practice traditional religious customs.

The earliest Crees are believed to have inhabited the subarctic region south of Hudson Bay since the glaciers receded some 5,000 years ago. The Crees spread to the south, some turning east to settle in present-day Quebec and the Maritimes, others turning west to settle in the Great Plains north and west of Lake Superior. The western migrants adapted to the plains culture and traded for horses with the tribes further to the south. The horses allowed greater mobility and easier hunting. The Crees became skilled horsemen and lived by hunting the bison that roamed the plains in enormous herds. The Plains Crees often allied with the Assiniboine and the Saulteaux peoples for defense and war. The Plains Crees became known as a warlike people while those farther east, the Woodland Crees, remained mostly settled farmers. The name "Cree" is derived from an Ojibwe word used for the people living around Hudson Bay. French Jesuits first encountered the Cree bands around 1650, east of James Bay. The Crees generally maintained friendly relations with both the French and the British. Fur traders and trappers, attracted to the potential wealth of the fur-bearing animals in the Cree homeland, began to expand their operations into the territory. Obtaining firearms from Europeans in the 1670s, the Crees continued to migrate westward, reaching the Mackenzie River and the Rocky Mountains. A smallpox epidemic greatly reduced their population in 1781. Wars with the Blackfoot and the Sioux and another severe smallpox epidemic decimated the scattered Cree bands in 1784. The Plains Crees, raiding and warring with other plains peoples, developed a warrior society. Divided into 12 autonomous bands, each with its own chief, the Plains Crees evolved an integrated military society that united the 12 bands. Eventually the Crees became geographically and regionally divided into the James Bay Crees, living in the site of the Grand Council of the Crees, in the James Bay region of northern Quebec; Moose Crees, living near the mouth of the Moose River at the southern end of James Bay; the Swampy Crees, occupying the lands along Hudson Bay and inland in northern Manitoba, Saskatchewan, and Ontario; the Woods or Woodland Crees, living in northern Alberta and Saskatchewan; and the Plains Crees, in Manitoba, Saskatchewan, Alberta, and Montana. The French were expelled from North America in 1763, ending a long relationship of trading and religious conversions.

The Crees are one of the largest Native American ethnic groups in North America and form the largest of the First Nations in Canada. The Crees are traditionally divided into two broad groups, those of the eastern woodlands culture and the Crees of the Great Plains. Both groups are further subdivided by bands that are differentiated by slight differences in dialect and cultural traditions. Social organization is traditionally based on the bands or clans of related families. The old belief system, hunting customs, and kinship traditions persisted throughout the Cree homeland during the fur-trading years but began to fade as the Crees modernized and urbanized in the second half of the 20th century. The Cree language belongs to the Algonquian language group that is spoken in large parts of eastern and central Canada and the United States. The language is spoken in a number of distinct dialects that over time have borrowed many words and influences from neighboring peoples—French, or English. In October 2001, a two-volume Cree dictionary was published in an effort to standardize the language. French Jesuits converted many of the Cree bands to Roman Catholicism in the 17th and 18th centuries. A minority were converted to Protestant sects by missions established in the Cree regions in the

1820s. Traditionally the Crees believed in a supernatural hero known as Wisukatcak. Conjuration and witchcraft were important elements of their religious beliefs, as was the important and powerful priestly order. Their greatest religious ceremony was the annual Sun Dance ceremony, which is still celebrated today.

The scourges of European diseases, war, and abuse by the growing number of settlers colonizing their traditional lands further reduced the Cree population in the first years of the 19th century. The first permanent religious mission was established at St. Boniface, opposite modern Winnipeg, in 1818. The missionaries translated religious tracts into the Cree language and produced a Cree grammar and a Cree-French dictionary. A Protestant missionary, Reverend James Evan, invented a Cree syllabary that allowed the Crees to read and write in their own language. The Cree lands were mostly included in the vast territorial claims of the Hudson Bay Company. The Company's territorial claims were purchased by the Canadian government in 1870. The Canadian government's presence in the Cree lands was slow to be felt but as conflict grew and grievances went unanswered Cree resentment also grew. The Plains Crees, led by Chief Poundmaker, joined the mixed race Métis in the Riel Rebellion in 1885. Provincial governments began to intervene in the Cree regions in the 1920s, particularly to defuse a crisis brought on due to overtrapping by non-Cree trappers. Canadian government policies aimed at the assimilation of Native Canadians led to the separation of thousands of Cree children from their parents and the creation of many boarding schools where the Cree language and culture

Chasin Thompson,12, of the Cree nation, wears traditional clothing during an event by Manito Abhee celebrating National Aboriginal Day in Winnipeg, Manitoba, June 21, 2011. More than 1 million Canadians are of Aboriginal origin, and the nation has more than 600 recognized First Nations governments. (AP Photo/Kevin Frayer)

was suppressed. Schooling away from the Cree reserves created a sense of dislocation and opened a serious division between traditional parents and acculturated children. In 1975 the Crees signed the James Bay and Northern Quebec agreement, the first modern treaty signed with an indigenous people in Canada. The agreement provided for construction of water systems and sanitary facilities but they were never provided. Only after Cree representatives presented their case to the United Nations in 1981 did the Canadian government begin to provide clean and reliable water supplies. Representatives of the Grand Council of the Cree presented their case for territorial and resource rights to the Commission on Human Rights in Geneva in 1985. Their traditional way of life—hunting, trapping, and fishing—was greatly disrupted by modern constructions such as dams and hydroelectric plants. Questions of land rights and legal jurisdictions have come up among many of the Cree bands in Canada in the 1990s and 2000s. The Crees claim that Canada, with its well-respected democratic traditions, does not protect indigenous rights or recognize formal territorial settlements negotiated in the 1970s and 1980s. The Crees, to the present, have never relinquished their long-standing claims to jurisdiction over their historic homeland and its far-flung territories.

Further Reading

Stout, Mary. *Cree*. Milwaukee, WI: Gareth Stevens, 2003.

Riehecky, Janet. *The Cree Tribe*. Mankato, MN: Capstone Press, 2002.

Robinson, Deborah B. *The Cree of North America*. Minneapolis, MN: Lerner Publishing, 2002.

Crows

The Crows, sometimes known as Absarokas, Apsalookas, or Apsáalooke, are a North American ethnic group living primarily in southern Montana but with communities in many large cities in the western states. The estimated 16,000 Crows speak English and many of them also speak the Crow language, which belongs to the Siouan language family. The majority of the Crows are Christians, the largest denominations being the Catholics, the Pentecostals, and the Baptists.

The Crows are thought to have originated near the headwaters of the Mississippi River in present-day Minnesota or Wisconsin. Some scholars believe they originated farther north in Manitoba. The tribe migrated south to the Devil Lake region of present-day North Dakota. Cultural anthropologists believe the tribe split into two parts between 1400 and 1500, but according to linguistic anthropologists the split was much earlier, between 900 CE and 1000 CE. The Crows split from the Hidatsa people, who remained farmers and gatherers, to move out into the northern plains where the buffalo provided most of their needs. The Crows were driven farther west by the migration of the powerful Sioux people in the 18th century. The Sioux moved west as settlers from the east invaded their territory seeking open farm land. In 1743 the Crows encountered French traders from Canada. The name of the tribe was translated into French as *gens du corbeaux* or "people of the crows." The name Apsáalooke means "children of the large-beaked bird," a name given to them by the related Hidatsa people. The French began to refer to them as Crows and the name is still in use. The Crows adopted the horse around 1740 and moved west across the plains in search of game, bison, and more horses. The Crows settled in the Valley of the Yellowstone River and its tributaries on the northern plains in present-day Wyoming and Montana. There they eventually divided into three groups, the Mountain Crows, the River Crows, and the Kicked in the Bellies. The nomadic lifestyle of the plains was adopted. They became hunters and gatherers using dog or horse travois for carrying goods. The huge herds of buffalo, also known as bison, became the source of food, clothing, shelter, and nearly 200 implements made of bone and other buffalo products. Known as horse breeders and dealers, the Crows often suffered raids by tribes seeking to steal horses rather than to acquire them through trade. The Crows developed a strong warrior tradition in defense of their herds of horses. To control the large territory they claimed they warred against the Shoshone bands as allies of the local Kiowas. The Kiowas later migrated south, leaving the Crows as the dominant tribe in the region through the 18th century.

Crow culture changed greatly when their ancestors gave up the village life of their Hidatsa kinsmen. They stopped farming, only growing the crops of the sacred tobacco. They exchanged earth lodges for buffalo-hide tipis and ceased making pottery. On the Great Plains they lived a nomadic life following the buffalo herds and other game. The horse revolutionized Crow methods of hunting and warfare, allowing bands to travel faster and farther over long distances. Like many of the plains peoples, the Crows participated in the Sun Dance and believed in visions. They had special societies, particularly the Crow Tobacco Society, with rituals based on their one crop. Historically the Crows had a matrilineal system, with young couples living with the wife's parents. Women were respected and played a significant role in tribal life. The modern Crows in Montana are mostly farmers or ranchers or work in the coal mines on tribal territory. The Little Bighorn Battlefield National Monument is situated on traditional Crow territory adjoining the Crow Reservation. The Crows hold reenactments of the battle, which they call the Battle of the Greasy Grass; it is one of the most famous battles of the Indian Wars of the 19th century. The annual Crow Fair, held in August, recreates the historic Sun Dance along with a rodeo, dances, and parades. Many Crow families still use the traditional tipis, especially when traveling, so the annual Crow Fair is often described as the largest gathering of tipis in the world. Many younger Crows now live in larger urban areas in the western states where educational and professional opportunities are available. Modern Crow culture is part of the culture of the American West with ranches, rodeos, and cowboys, but it also includes entertainment, television, and other technologies of modern

American life. The relentless movement of Americans of European descent to the west brought a gradual end to the bison herds and threatened the way of life of the Crow people. By the early 1800s many bands of Lakota Sioux and Cheyennes had migrated west, and by the mid-1800s they were established just to the south and east of Crow territory in Montana. These tribes, the traditional enemies of the Crows, wanted the fine hunting grounds and during a series of wars took control of the Crows' eastern hunting territory, pushing the less numerous Crows to the west and northwest along the Yellowstone River. Around 1860 the Lakota Sioux claimed all of the traditional Crow lands lying east of the Big Horn Mountains and whites coming into the region were required to deal with them and not the Crows. The Sioux went to war against the American cavalry on the Bozeman Trail between 1866 and 1868. The victorious Sioux, in the Treaty of Fort Laramie, were confirmed in their control over all the northern plains from the Big Horn Mountains east to the Black Hills, most of which was ancestral Crow territory. Bands of Sioux and Cheyennes hunted and raided across Crow territory. War again broke out between the Sioux and their Cheyenne allies and the American military. The Crows often served as guides for the cavalry units in the region. In June 1876, the Sioux and the Cheyenne defeated and massacred an army force under Gen. George Armstrong Custer at the Battle of the Little Big Horn. Custer sent his Crow scouts to the rear of the column so they survived while Custer and his 70 soldiers were massacred. The victory gave way to defeat and the Sioux and Cheyenne abandoned eastern Montana and Wyoming, either to migrate to Canada or by forced removal to distant reserved lands. Increasing numbers of miners and settlers moved into Crow territory, building forts and railroads, and depleting the buffalo herds. The nomadic life of the Crows ended with the near extinction of the bison. The Crows, although they had remained friendly with the U.S. government, were treated no differently than those tribes that had resisted and warred against the American onslaught. After a series of treaties up to 1888, they were forced to cede most of their lands and to settle on a small reservation. The Crows, as breeders and traders of horses, had more horses than any other plains tribe. In 1914, the Crow horse herds numbered between 30,000 and 40,000. By 1921, the number of horses had dwindled to just a few thousand. In the 1950s, the Crow Reservation in south-central Montana was further reduced so that the Yellowtail Dam could be in the Crows' Bighorn Canyon. Although the remaining reservation lands were rich in natural resources, including farm and grazing land and coal reserves, many individual Crows had a difficult time earning an adequate living because of earlier unjust leasing deals or a lack of tribal funds to develop mines. Many left the reservation to seek work and education in the large cities of the region. Most of the Crows living in urban areas are not enrolled as members of the tribe but maintain contact with their culture and heritage. Nowadays, one coal mine provides royalties and employment for many tribal members. In 2001 the Crow Tribe, with some 12,000 enrolled members, adopted a new constitution that established guidelines for elections and a tribal legislature.

The seat of government and the capital of the reservation is Crow Agency, Montana. President Barack Obama visited the Crow Nation during the presidential campaign in 2008, the first presidential candidate to visit the Crow people.

Further Reading

Ditchfield, Christin. *The Crow.* New York: Children's Press, 2006.

Lowie, Robert H. *The Crow Indians.* Lincoln, NE: University of Nebraska Press/Bison Books, 2004.

Medicine Crow, Joseph. *From the Heart of Crow Country: The Crow Indians' Own Stories.* Lincoln, NE: University of Nebraska Press/Bison Books, 2000.

Cubans

The Cubans are a Caribbean people, the inhabitants of the large island of Cuba just south of the Florida Peninsula in the Caribbean Sea. Outside Cuba there are sizable Cuban communities in the United States, Spain, Italy, Mexico, Venezuela, and Canada. The estimated 12.5 million Cubans speak Cuban Spanish, a Caribbean dialect that incorporates borrowings from other languages. The majority of the Cubans are Roman Catholic, with smaller Jewish, Protestant, and Santeria minorities.

The first known inhabitants of the island of Cuba were the Ciboney, a Native American people. Later the island was settled by the Taíno people, who formed the main population of Cuba and the other islands of the region when Christopher Columbus sighted the large island which became known as Cuba in 1492. Columbus claimed the island for Spain and soon Spanish settlements were founded. The indigenous peoples quickly disappeared, decimated by European diseases, European abuses and brutality, and slavery. The Taíno staged their last significant uprising against Spanish rule in the mid-1500s. The Taíno population, estimated to number some 350,000 at the end of the 15th century, had dwindled to just a few thousand by 1600. Waves of Canary Islanders, Catalans, Galicians, and Asturians emigrated from Spain to Cuba. Other immigrants included the English, the Scots, the Russians, the Portuguese, the Poles, the Italians, the Germans, the Greeks, the French, and the Irish. Spanish Jews often migrated to the island to escape the Spanish Inquisition. In the 1700s the need for labor on the Spanish plantations was met by importing large numbers of slaves from Africa. Most of the Africans came from the Congo region of Central Africa, but a significant number also came from the Yoruba and other peoples of West Africa. The fusion of the Spanish culture with other European cultures began the evolution of the Cuban people. The Taíno mostly disappeared by the mid-7th century but some of their traditions and foods became part of the Cuban culture. The colonial economy of the island was based on plantation agriculture, coffee production, and mining and the export of coffee, sugar, and tobacco to Europe. In the 18th century slaves, sugar, coffee, and tobacco were exported to the nearby mainland American territories. A small land-owning aristocracy of Spanish settlers controlled the social and economic life of the island, supported by a growing population of Spaniards, known as Creoles (Criollos), born on the island, and other Europeans, supported by a growing population of mixed race and numerous black slaves.

The Cuban culture reflects the influences of the various cultures that were brought to the island, but it remains primarily a mixture of European—mostly Spanish—and African cultures. Prior to the Cuban Revolution in 1959 Cuban culture was heavily influenced by the United States. American influence on Cuban music, sports, architecture, and finances were evident and many Cubans viewed Cuban culture as more closely related to American culture than to the other cultures of Latin America. During the period of the revolution, when Cuba was abruptly and surprisingly declared a communist republic, the Cubans became isolated. The Russian presence was felt in the structuring of the Stalinist-like Cuban regime but it had very little impact on the Cuban culture. The large number of Cubans who fled the island in the early 1960s took their culture with them. Areas with large Cuban populations, such as Miami, have contributed to the maintenance of the vibrant prerevolutionary Cuban culture. Music and dance are very important parts of the culture and are well known outside the country. Internationally known forms of music such as salsa, mambo, rumba, cha cha, bolero, and son mostly originated in Cuba. Cuban music mixes the original Spanish and West African musical forms with American musical instruments such as the trombone and the clarinet. Other elements of Cuban culture include the famous Cuban cigars, most of which are exported as they are too costly for the majority of Cubans.

The Spanish language spoken by Cubans is known as Cuban Spanish. The dialect is characterized by the reduction of a number of consonants, a feature first brought to the island by immigrants from the Canary Islands. Many of the Cuban-Americans, while fluent in Spanish, increasingly use American English as one of their daily languages. Most Cubans are Roman Catholic. The Catholic religion is often practiced in tandem with Santeria, a mixture of Catholicism and African, and mostly Yoruba traditions, brought to the island by African slaves. A form of the Yoruba language known as Lucumi is the liturgical language for practitioners of Santeria. A growing number of Cubans have converted to Protestant sects, particularly the Pentecostal sect, which has grown rapidly in recent years.

The island census of 1817 showed a total population of 630,980, of which 291,021 were listed as European or of European descent, 115,691 as free blacks, and 224,268 as black slaves. Many of those listed as free blacks formed part of the growing mixed population of people having European fathers and slave mothers. In the 1810s and 1820s, when most of the other American colonies of Spain rebelled and formed independent states, the Cubans remained loyal. Although there was some agitation for independence, the Cubans depended on Spain for trade, protection from pirate attacks, and the military presence that prevented slave uprisings. They also feared the rising power of their neighbor to the north, the United States. Unrest, particularly among the influential plantation elite, resulted in a serious rebellion known as the Ten Years' War from 1868 to 1878. The war ended with greater autonomy for the Cubans but not independence. The abolition of slavery, maintained in Cuba after the Spanish officially outlawed the practice, was not completed until the 1880s. Discontent among the ruined planter class added to the discontent that spread at the end of the 19th century. An exiled dissident, José Martí, founded the Cuban Revolutionary Party in New York in 1892. In early 1895 Martí traveled to Cuba to join a growing uprising. Fighting against the Spanish army, Martí was killed in the Battle of Dos Rios in May 1895. His death immortalized his place as Cuba's national

Fidel Castro

Fidel Castro holds the record for the longest period in office of any ruler in the Americas. The leader of the Cuban Revolution in 1959, he served as prime minister from 1959 to 1976, and then as president from 1976 to 2008. His brother Raul took over the reins of government on Fidel's retirement. Fidel Castro also held the position of First Secretary of the Communist Party of Cuba from the time of the declaration of a communist state in 1961 until 2011. Tight censorship, harsh treatment of dissidents, and the flight of many of the Cubans opposed to communist rule kept challenges to his leadership to a minimum during the decades of his rule.

hero. The Spanish troops greatly outnumbered the rebels as fighting spread. A campaign of intimidation and suppression was begun, targeting the civilian population. Concentrations camps eventually held hundreds of thousands of Cubans in deplorable conditions. Estimates of the number of people who died from starvation and disease range from 200,000 to 400,000. American and European protests against the Spanish conduct were politely ignored. The U.S. battleship *Maine* sailed into the Havana harbor to protect the 8,000 American residents in Cuba, but the Spanish saw the *Maine* as intimidation and provocation. On the evening of February 15, 1989, the *Maine* blew up, killing over 250 crew members. Although the facts of the destruction of the *Maine* are still disputed, war was soon declared between the United States and Spain. Defeated Spain ceded Puerto Rico, the Philippines, and Guam to the United States and relinquished all claims to Cuba. Cuba gained nominal independence from the United States in 1902. The United States leased the Guantánamo Bay naval base in the east of the island. Following a disputed presidential election in 1906, violence broke out. The United States occupied the island for two years until a new president was elected in 1908. Instability and American intervention in the politics and finances of the island continued until the 1930s when a long series of military coups, weak presidents, and corruption sent the first large wave of Cuban migrants to the United States and Europe. Fulogencio Batista, democratically elected in 1940, later attempted to return to the presidency but with little chance

of winning he staged a coup in 1952. An attempted army coup against Batista's dictatorship in 1956 ended with hundreds of officers being imprisoned. In 1958, Cuba was a relatively prosperous country by Latin American standards. A large and growing middle class enjoyed the modern fixtures of American culture, telephones, radios, and automobiles. But Cuba was affected by the most extensive labor privileges in Latin America, obtained largely at the expense of the unemployed and the peasants, which led to wide disparities. A small rebel group led by Fidel Castro established an armed resistance in the mountains east of Havana. Batista's dictatorship, crippled by an American arms embargo, was unable to stem the tide of revolution. Breaking out of the mountains, the rebels launched a popular insurrection supported by most of the middle class and the peasants. The trade unions remained loyal to the dictatorship until the end. Batista fled from Havana on January 1, 1959, leaving Cuba to the revolutionaries. Widespread support for the revolution quickly waned as private properties were expropriated without compensation, public services were nationalized, tight controls stifled the private sector, and the mafia-controlled gambling industry was closed down. By the end of 1960 a steady flow of refugees left the island for the United States and Europe. The sudden declaration of a communist state and a close alliance with the Soviet block countries convinced most of the professionals and the middle class to flee the island. A one-party state with Fidel Castro as the ultimate leader executed tens of thousands of people and imprisoned anyone opposing the revolution. The construction of sites for Soviet nuclear missiles resulted in one of the most serious crises of the Cold War and nearly brought on a nuclear holocaust. The Soviet missiles were finally removed but the Cuban regime remained firmly in the communist bloc. A United States trade embargo was put in place and restrictions on travel and other exchanges were adopted. In the 21st century some 1.2 million people of Cuban background live in the United States, about a tenth of the total Cuban population. The Cuban population of the island is now among the poorest in Latin America, dissidents are still imprisoned, private enterprise is mostly suppressed, and those who are able continue to leave the island.

Further Reading

Barrett, Pam, ed. *Cuba.* Singapore: APA Publications, 2008.

Chomsky, Aviva. *The Cuba Reader: History, Culture, Politics.* Durham, NC: Duke University Press, 2004.

O'Reilly Herrera, Andrea, ed. *Cuba: Idea of a Nation Displaced.* Albany, NY: State University of New York Press, 2007.

Curaçaoans

The Curaçaoans are a Caribbean people of mixed background, the inhabitants of the Dutch island of Curaçao in the southern Caribbean. Outside the island there are sizable Curaçaoan communities in the Netherlands, the United States, and Canada. The estimated 160,000 Curaçaoans speak Papiamentu, the national language, with many also being able to speak Dutch, the other official language of the island. Many also speak English or Spanish. About 85 percent of the Curaçaoans are Roman Catholics, with a large Protestant minority. Some Curaçaoans practice *Montamentu*, a religion based on African religious beliefs, and there are small but influential Jewish, Muslim, and Hindu minorities.

Arawak people from the nearby mainland of South America settled the island possibly as early as 200 BCE. The Arawaks were mostly farmers and fishermen, living in small peaceful villages. A Spanish expedition, led by Alonso de Ojeda, visited the island in 1499. The Spanish took most of the Arawaks as slaves and forcibly relocated the remainder of the population to other Spanish colonies where workers were needed. Spanish interest in the island quickly waned as no gold or other treasure was found and agriculture was difficult due to a lack of fresh water. The Dutch occupied the island in 1634 and the Dutch West India Company founded the settlement of Willemstad. The natural harbor of Willemstad proved ideal for trade with commerce, shipping, and piracy quickly becoming the island's most important economic activities. The salt ponds that prevented irrigation for agriculture proved to be an asset as salt became an important commodity. Plantation agriculture was begun and African slaves were imported as laborers. Curaçao became a center of the African slave trade in 1662. The slave trade and plantation agriculture made the island rich. Impressive buildings and plantation mansions blending Dutch and Spanish colonial styles were built in Willemstad and across the island. A major slave revolt broke out in 1795 with some 4,000 slaves joining the uprising before it was crushed a month later. Tula, one of the leaders of the revolt, is considered a national hero.

The Curaçaoan culture reflects the island's polyglot society. The Papiamentu name for the island is Kursow, which indicates a strong cultural identity. The island's ties to the Netherlands remain strong but it has evolved a more Caribbean culture, a blend of Dutch, Spanish, African, and North American influences. The culture retains its historic ties to its African roots through the Curaçaoan language, music, and dance. One of the strongest demonstrations of the island's African slave past is *tambu*, an ancient form of dance and music. Slaves brought the rhythmic structure of *tambu* from West Africa and passed it down from generation to generation. African-style drums are the basis of *tambu*, which is usually accompanied by a form of dance known as *baila ban* or "the dance of the drum." The Curaçaoans have also adapted the European music and dances of the colonials to the syncretic beat of Africa. The French quadrille, waltzes, and polkas are often performed to a Caribbean rhythm. The Curaçaoans' first language is Papiamentu, a creole language based on Portuguese, Spanish, Dutch, and several dialects brought from Africa. Most islanders also speak Dutch, the language of administration, and Spanish and English are widely spoken. Most Curaçaoans are Roman Catholics, with smaller numbers of Seventh-day Adventists and Methodists. Some of the islanders practice *monamentu*, a blend of Christian teachings and African rituals.

Curaçao's proximity to the coast of South America meant that many Curaçaoans were involved in the independence wars against the Spanish in the early 19th century. During the Napoleonic Wars the island changed hands several times before being returned to Dutch rule in 1815. The island, along with Bonaire and Aruba, was governed from Dutch Suriname from 1828 to 1845 when the three were combined to form a single political unit ruled from Willemstad. The Dutch abolished slavery in their colonies in 1863, bringing financial hardship to many. Many of the island's inhabitants left for other islands or returned to Europe. Most of the former slaves remained as workers on the plantations in the *paga tera* system, a form of sharecropping. This system lasted until the beginning of the 20th century. When oil was discovered in Venezuela, oil refining on the island quickly reversed the economic decline. Curaçao was an ideal site for refining as it was away from the endemic civil and social unrest of the South American mainland. In 1954 Curaçao became part of the Netherlands Antilles, which represented all the Dutch Caribbean territories in an autonomous federation as part of the Kingdom of the Netherlands. A tourist boom in the 1960s brought much needed jobs and modest prosperity. Cruise ships began to call regularly at Willemstad. A serious labor dispute in 1969 escalated into rioting and widespread protests. The unrest fuelled a social movement that allowed the Afro-Curaçaoans to attain more influence over the political process in the island. The decolonization of the British islands of the Caribbean raised the question of independence for Curaçao but in 1993, the islanders voted against following Aruba in separating from the Netherlands Antilles. In 2005 the Curaçaoans voted to become a separate autonomous state, known locally as Pais Kòrsou, within the Kingdom of the Netherlands. The new status was approved by a slim majority in 2009. Due to an economic downturn in recent years, emigration to the Netherlands has been growing.

Further Reading

Icon Group International. *Curaçao: Webster's Timeline History, 1634–2007.* San Diego: Icon Group International, 2009.

Rupert, Linda M. *Creolization and Contraband: Curaçao in the Early Modern Atlantic World.* Athens, GA: University of Georgia Press, 2011.

Wolfert, Sinaya R. *Curaçao: Religions, Rituals and Traditions.* Amsterdam: KIT Publishers, 2010.

D

Dominicans

The Dominicans, sometimes known as Dominicanos, are a Caribbean people, the inhabitants of the Dominican Republic on the eastern side of the large island of Hispaniola. The estimated 11.4 million Dominicans speak standard Spanish along with a Caribbean patois that blends Spanish with Native American, African, and French influences. The Dominicans are predominately Roman Catholic although in recent years Protestant evangelical sects have gained popularity.

The early inhabitants of Hispaniola, the Taíno, settled the island around 600 CE. The island's population, divided into five chiefdoms, lived mostly by farming, hunting, and fishing. Christopher Columbus landed on the island during his first voyage to the New World in 1492. His name for the island, La Española, gradually became Hispaniola. In 1496 Bartholomeo Columbus, his brother, founded the settlement of Nueva Isabella, later called Santo Domingo, the first European settlement in the New World. The Taíno chiefs valiantly resisted the Spanish conquest of their homeland. They led their warriors in fighting the Spanish, but infectious diseases to which they had no immunity, combined with slavery, abuses, starvation, and violence decimated the island population. The Spanish established a plantation economy that required numerous laborers. The surviving Taíno proved unfit for forced labor so African slaves were imported. Hispaniola became the center of the Spanish colonization in the Caribbean and the later settlement of the American mainland. The conquest of advanced empires in Mexico and Peru became the focus of Spanish attention. Santo Domingo was neglected and rapidly declined. French buccaneers defied the Spanish claim to the island and settled in the western half. The Spanish government ceded the western half of the island to Spain in 1697. The French took control of the Spanish half during the French Revolution and its aftermath. The Spanish ceded their claims to France, but rebellious slaves in the French half captured Santo Domingo and took control of the entire island.

The Dominican culture is a Caribbean culture that blends the influences of European colonists, African slaves, and the original Taíno population. Like the other Caribbean cultures, the Dominicans have developed distinctive music and dance forms. The most famous of the Dominican musical styles is merengue, a lively and fast-paced rhythm that accompanies the dance, a unique creation of the Dominican culture. Another type of music, known as bachata, that originated in the rural districts and poor neighborhoods of the large cities has become very popular in recent years. American influence is especially evident in sports. Baseball is the most popular sport and many players have been integrated into the major league teams of the American mainland. American influence is also evident in entertainment, music, films, and television. The Spanish language spoken by the Dominicans, known as Castellano or Castilian, is the official language of the country although other European languages, particularly English, are widely spoken. The Spanish influence is predominant in religion with the majority of the Dominicans belonging to the Roman Catholic Church. Protestant groups, often from the American mainland, are gaining followers, particularly the evangelical groups.

The capture of the colony by rebellious slaves from the French half of the island in 1801 sent many colonists fleeing to Cuba and other Spanish possessions. An army dispatched from Europe by Napoleon captured the slave leaders, but a yellow fever epidemic and a renewed slave uprising ended in a French defeat. The French half of the island was declared an independent state (as the Republic of Haiti), while the French recovered the Spanish half of the island. In 1808, following Napoleon's invasion of Spain, the people of Santo Domingo rose against the French, and with British and Haitian aid the eastern half of the island was returned to Spanish rule. The independence movements in the Spanish colonies resulted in several years of turbulence before Santo Domingo was declared independent, but Haitians invaded and ended the movement. The Haitian occupiers declared the end of slavery on the island in 1821. In 1838 Dominican patriots defeated the Haitians and declared the independence of the eastern half of the island. The first constitution of the republic was approved in 1844, and was modeled on that of the United States. The next decades were times of great instability, tyranny, factionalism, economic problems, and renewed Haitian invasions in 1844, 1845–1849, 1849–1855, and 1855–1856. Pedro Santana, a wealthy rancher and a hero in the fight against the Haitians, signed a pact in 1861 that returned Santo Domingo to colonial status, the only Latin American country to do so. His actions were ostensibly to protect against Haitian invasions, but opponents launched the War of the Restoration in 1863. Spain finally abandoned the island in 1865. Political strife and economic upheavals continued for many years while the country amassed huge foreign debts, mostly with European nations. American troops occupied the country in 1916 resulting in widespread resistance. Despite Dominican opposition, the occupation largely pacified the country, reduced the massive public debt, revived the economy, and built a network of roads that at last connected all parts of the country. Following the American withdrawal the political, social, and economic life of the island again reverted to chaos. In 1930 a military coup placed Gen. Leonidas Trujillo at the head of a dictatorial government. Although Trujillo inaugurated a pension plan, negotiated a definitive border with Haiti in 1935, and made the country debt-free, his rule was accompanied by repression and violence. Trujillo was finally assassinated in 1961, and American marines were landed to restore order. The marines stayed long enough to oversee the elections, which were won by Joaquín Balaguer, whose rule was a period of renewed repression. Several decades of relative freedom and respect for human rights ended when Balaguer returned to office by means of fraudulent elections in 1986. He was reelected in 1990 and 1994. Balaguer finally stepped down in 2000, leaving the Dominicans among the poorest of the peoples of the Caribbean. Although peaceful elections and economic expansion are gaining ground, many Dominicans continue to leave the island for better lives in Puerto Rico, the U.S. mainland, or Spain.

Further Reading

Candelario, Ginetta E. B. *Black behind the Ears: Dominican Racial Identity from Museums to Beauty Shops.* Durham, NC: Duke University Press, 2007.

Gregory, Steven. *The Devil behind the Mirror: Globalization and Politics in the Dominican Republic.* Berkeley, CA: University of California Press, 2006.

Wucker, Michele. *Why the Cocks Fight: Dominicans, Haitians, and the Struggle for Hispaniola.* New York: Hill & Wang, 2000.

Dominicas

The Dominicas, sometimes known as Dominicans, are a Caribbean people of the island nation of Dominica in the Lesser Antilles region of the Caribbean Sea. The es-timated 95,000 Dominicas speak English, the official language of the island, along with a French creole language known as Dominican Creole French. Outside Dominica there are sizable Dominica communities in the United States and the United Kingdom. About 80 percent of the Dominicas are Roman Catholics, though in recent decades a number of Protestant churches have been established in the country.

The early inhabitants of the island, probably related to the Arawak peoples, had disappeared or had been absorbed by later Carib settlers from South America. In 1660, the French and the English agreed that the islands of St. Vincent and Dominica should not be colonized, but instead left for the Caribs as neutral territory. Dominica was officially neutral for the next century, but the attraction of its natural resources led to exploitation. Rival expeditions of English and French foresters were harvesting timber by the beginning of the 1700s. In 1715 the French established the first permanent settlement in Dominica with groups of "poor European" smallholders from Martinique. The island became a French colony in 1727. The French imported African slaves to work the plantations that were established. As part of the terms of the 1763 Treaty of Paris that ended the Seven Years' War, Dominica became a British possession. A legislative assembly was created, representing only those of European descent. In 1778, during the American Revolution, the French, with the active participation of many of the islanders, mounted a successful invasion. The island was again returned to British rule in 1783. French invasion attempts in 1795 and 1805 ended in failure.

The culture of Dominica reflects the fact that the island is home to a wide range of people. The culture is a unique mixture of British, French, African, and Carib traditions. The remaining Caribs now occupy a small territory on the east coast of the island under the authority of an elected chief. Music and dance are important elements of the culture. The annual independence day celebrations showcase the local music and dance forms. Local music styles include creole music, jing ping, and cadence. The official language of Dominica is English, which is spoken throughout the island and is the language of education and administration. A patois handed down from the early French-speaking African slaves, part of a group of languages known as Antillean Creole, is spoken mostly by older people although efforts are underway to preserve the use of the Dominica Creole French language. In recent decades it has gone from being seen as a sign of lower status, banned in school playgrounds, to a mark of pride. Most Dominicas are Roman Catholic, the result of early French missionary settlements, with smaller congregations belonging to a number of Protestant churches.

The British continued to import slaves, but by the early 1800s most were brought to Dominica from other islands. In 1831 a change in official British racial policies, summarized in the Brown Privilege Bill, granted political and social rights to free nonwhites. Three free men of African descent were elected to the island legislature the following year. The abolition of slavery in 1834 resulted in the power to vote by the former slaves. Dominica became the first British Caribbean colony to have a legislature controlled by people of African descent in 1838. The planters of European descent, reacting to a perceived threat, lobbied for a return of direct British rule. In 1865, after much tension and agitation, the British colonial authorities replaced the elective assembly with one that had one half of its members elected and the other half appointed. Dominica became part of the Leeward Islands Federation in 1871 and the power of the African-descent majority progressively eroded. Government as a British Crown Colony was reestablished in 1896. All political rights for the majority of the population were effectively curtailed. The African-Dominicas began to mobilize after World War I, winning a growing number of seats in the island assembly in 1924 and 1936. The island became part of the West Indies Federation in 1958 but after the larger members opted for separvate independence Dominica became an associated state of the United Kingdom in 1967. The Commonwealth of Dominica became an independent state on November 3, 1978. Many of the islanders of European descent returned to the United Kingdom but a small number remained. Eighty-six percent of the population of the new state comprised people descended from African slaves; 9 percent was made up of people of mixed background; Caribs made up about 3 percent; and people of European descent made up about 0.8 percent. In recent years banana exports have fuelled a modest economic upturn. Democratic multiparty elections and peaceful changes of government have given the Dominicas an unusual level of stability in the Caribbean.

Further Reading

Atwood, Thomas and J. Johnson. *The History of the Island of Dominica.* Charleston, SC: BiblioLife, 2010.

Baker, Patrick L. *Centering the Periphery: Chaos, Order, and the Ethnohistory of Dominica.* Montreal: McGill-Queen's University Press, 1994.

Honychurch, Lennox. *The Dominica Story: A History of the Island.* London: Macmillan, 1995.

E

Ecuadorians

The Ecuadorians are a South American people, the inhabitants of the Republic of Ecuador on the west coast of the continent. Outside Ecuador there are sizable Ecuadorian populations in the United States, Spain, the United Kingdom, Italy, Australia, and other South American countries. The estimated 17 million Ecuadorians speak a version of South American Spanish and often speak one of the two widely spoken Native American languages, Quechua and Aymara. Some 95 percent of the Ecuadorians are nominally Roman Catholic with small groups of Protestants, Jews, Orthodox Christians, Muslims, Buddhists, and Baha'is.

Several advanced civilizations emerged in the region of present-day Ecuador beginning in 3500 BCE. After years of resistance by the peoples of the region they were finally defeated by the invading Incas in 1453 CE. The final battle, known as the Battle of Yahuarcocha or Blood Lake, ended with the slaughter of thousands of warriors whose bodies were thrown into the lake. The conquered region was made part of the Inca Empire in 1463 and was loosely controlled from the Inca heartland in Peru. The Inca Empire was ruled by Huayna Capac, who had two sons, Atahualpa and Huáscar. Upon Huayna Capac's death in 1525, the empire was divided into two parts. Atahualpa ruled the north from his capital at Quito while Huáscar ruled his half from Cuzco. Atahualpa defeated his brother in 1530 and gained control of the entire Inca Empire but his victory was short-lived. He was captured by Spanish invaders and was later executed. European diseases devastated the indigenous peoples in the first decades of Spanish rule. The survivors were forced into the *encomienda*, a system of forced labor in mines and haciendas. Quito became the seat of an administrative district of the Viceroyalty of Peru, but most of Ecuador remained poor and neglected as the Spanish concentrated on the territories that yielded gold or other treasure.

Ecuadorian culture is defined by its mestizo majority; like the mestizos' mixed ancestry, the culture is a blend of Spanish heritage, influences from the Native American peoples, and some elements of African culture on the coast. A later immigration of people from a number of European countries, North America, and Asia has also added cultural elements. Ecuador's indigenous peoples are integrated into the national culture to varying degrees. Particularly the cultures of the indigenous peoples of the remote Amazon basin. European influences in art, music, dance, and especially sports remain strong to the present. The most popular sport is association football with intense rivalries among the regional teams. Education is often limited, especially in rural areas, so oral traditions among the mestizo and indigenous groups are important cultural displays. Spanish is spoken as a first language by about 90 percent of the population, with many more speaking it as a second language. Some 2 percent of the Ecuadorians speak only a Native American language. The Ecuadorians are overwhelmingly Roman Catholic, with small numbers practicing other religions. Evangelical Protestant groups have gained popularity in recent decades.

Inspired by war in Europe and the ideals of the American Revolution, the population of the coastal regions rebelled in 1809, but despite many sacrifices Ecuador did not achieve independence until 1822 as part of Simón Bolivar's Republic of Gran Colombia. In 1830 the Ecuadorians withdrew from the state that also included Colombia and Venezuela to become a separate republic. Rivalries between the coastal peoples and those of the Andean highlands, economic instability, and a succession of poor rulers greatly impeded progress. The country was not completely unified until the 1860s. The Roman Catholic Church and wealthy landowners controlled the country until a liberal revolution reduced their power in 1895. The liberals ruled the country until a military takeover in 1925. Instability and the emergence of populist politicians continued in the 1930s and 1940s. Following a brief war with neighboring Peru in 1941, repression and unrest resulted in the return of populist politics that promised much but delivered little

in the way of good government. Military interventions in areas of unrest began in the 1960s, while foreign oil companies developed petroleum resources in Ecuador's Amazon basin region. An oil pipeline was finished in 1972, quickly making Ecuador South America's second largest oil producer. Military governments took power during the 1970s, often undermining the Ecuadorians' basic rights. The Ecuadorians welcomed a return to democracy in 1979 although populist politics quickly dominated. Tensions with Peru continued over claims to the oil-rich Amazonia region, again leading to war in 1995. In 2006 another populist, Rafael Correa, gained the presidency. Instability led to a police revolt in 2010 and continuing unrest in various parts of the country. Correa's closeness to the communist Cuba and populist Venezuela are matters of concern for many Ecuadorians. The ongoing economic and political instability in Ecuador has convinced many Ecuadorians to leave the country to live in the United States or Spain.

Further Reading

De la Torre, Carlos and Steve Shriffler. *The Ecuador Reader: History, Culture, Politics.* Durham, NC: Duke University Press, 2009.

Franklin, Albert B. *Ecuador: Portrait of a People.* Franklin, PA: Franklin Press, 2007.

Roos, Wilma and Omer Van Renterghem. *Ecuador in Focus: A Guide to the People, Politics, and Culture.* London: Latin American Bureau, 2000.

F

Falkland Islanders

The Falkland Islanders, sometimes known as Kelpers, are an Atlantic people, the inhabitants of the Falkland Islands, an archipelago in the South Atlantic lying 290 miles (460 km.) east of the southern tip of South America. The estimated 5,000 Falkland Islanders speak English, the official language of the islands, with many also speaking Spanish or other languages. The majority of the Falkland Islanders are Protestants, mostly Anglican, United Free Church, or Lutheran with a sizable Roman Catholic minority.

In 1592 the English ship *Desire* under Capt. John Davis visited the remote islands. This visit is believed to have been the first visit by Europeans to the uninhabited islands. Captain John Strong of the English ship *Welfare* was driven off course and reached the islands in 1690. He named the channel between the two largest islands "Falkland Channel" in honor of Anthony Cary, Viscount of Falkland, who was the Commissioner of the Admiralty that had financed the expedition. The island group later took its English name from this body of water. A French settlement was founded on East Falkland in 1764. A British expedition explored the islands and created a settlement in 1766. Unaware of the French presence in the islands, the islands were claimed as English territory. The Spanish acquired the French colony in 1767, placing the islands under the administration at Buenos Aires on the South American mainland. Spanish ships attacked the British settlement and expelled its inhabitants in 1770, bringing the two nations close to war. A peace treaty allowed the British to return to their settlement. Under economic pressure leading up to the American Revolutionary War, the British withdrew the settlers in 1774, leaving behind a plaque asserting the continuing British claim.

The culture of the Falkland Islanders is based on the British culture brought with the settlers from the British Isles. The culture has been influenced by the Spanish-speaking cultures of the South American mainland but remains mostly British in language, religion, and outlook. Some 61 percent of the islanders claim Falkland Islander nationality; 29 percent are British; 2.5 percent are Spanish-speaking people, mostly Chileans; and there are smaller groups of Japanese, Gibraltarians, Scandinavians, and others. Recent immigration from the United Kingdom, Saint Helena, and Chile has reversed a former gradual decline in the island population. The major language is standard British English, the language of education, administration, and entertainment. Television and radio are mostly in English, often with programs from the United Kingdom. The major economic activities include fishing, tourism with some 30,000 tourists visiting the islands each year, and sheep farming that produces high-quality wool. The possibility of large oil deposits in the islands' territorial waters has added to the conflict between the United Kingdom and Argentina over the sovereignty of the islands. The Falkland Islanders became British citizens in 1983.

The Spanish government maintained a governor in the islands until 1806. On his departure he also left behind a plaque asserting Spain's claims to the islands. Storm damage forced the privateer *Heroina* to stop in the uninhabited islands in 1820. The captain of the *Heroina* raised the flag of the United Provinces of the River Plate and read a proclamation claiming the islands. The proclamation became known in Buenos Aires a year later. After several failures a settlement was established by a European merchant of Huguenot descent, Luis Vernet, with the authorization of both the British and Argentine governments. Vernet was proclaimed governor of the islands by the Argentine authorities in 1829 although he made a pact with the British at the same time. The Argentines attempted to create a penal colony in 1832 but were expelled by British forces. Vernet's settlement continued until 1833 when British authority was firmly established. A permanent British colony was established in 1840. A new harbor was constructed at Stanlay, the capital, and the islands became a strategic stop on the navigation route around Cape Horn from Europe to the west coast of the Americas, particularly during the California Gold Rush in the late 1840s. The issue of sovereignty over the islands was raised by the Argentines after World War II. Talks between the British and the Argentines in the 1960s failed to reach an accord. The major sticking point in all the negotiations was the fact that the Falkland Islanders were adamant that they preferred to remain a British territory. The military dictatorship of Argentina, partly to redirect growing public unrest, sent an invasion fleet in April 1982. The United Nations called on the Argentines to withdraw the occupation forces and for both parties to seek a diplomatic solution. An Argentine refusal resulted in the dispatch of a British expeditionary force to retake the islands leading to the Falklands War. After rapid but fierce naval and air battles, the British landed on the islands. The Argentine forces surrendered in June 1982. The war brought an end to the Argentine military government and diplomatic relations were reestablished with the United Kingdom in 1990, but no new negotiations were undertaken. The possibility of large petroleum deposits in the sea around the islands reopened the sovereignty controversy in recent years. The British base their claim on the continuous administration of the islands since 1833 and the islanders' right to remain British if they so wish. The Argentines based their claim to the islands—which they call the Malvinas—on the inheritance of the earlier Spanish claim when they achieved independence in 1816. The Falkland Islanders reject the Argentine claim on the grounds that the early Spanish claim stemmed from the notorious Treaty of Tordesillas that, in 1494, divided the entire Western Hemisphere between Spain and Portugal.

Further Reading

Cawkell, M. B. R., D. H. Maling, and E. M. Cawkell. *The Falkland Islands.* New York: St. Martin's Press, 1960.

Gustafson, Lowell S. *The Sovereignty Dispute over the Falkland (Malvinas) Islands.* New York: Oxford University Press, 1988.

Hastings, Max and Simon Jenkins. *The Battle of the Falklands.* New York: W. W. Norton & Company, 1984.

G

Garifunas

The Garifunas, sometimes known as Garinagu, Garifunes, Karaphunas, Black Caribs, or Black Karibs, are a Central American ethnic group living mostly on the west coast of Central America in Honduras, Belize, Guatemala, and Nicaragua. Outside the region there are sizable Garifuna communities in the United States, the United Kingdom, and the island state of St. Vincent in the eastern Caribbean. The estimated 600,000 Garifunas normally speak the languages of the countries they inhabit, including English and Kriol (Belizean Creole) in Belize and parts of Nicaragua, English in St. Vincent, and Spanish in the other countries. Among themselves the Garifunas usually speak the Garifuna language, a blend of the Native American Arawak and Carib languages with English, French, and Spanish borrowings. Most of the Garifunas are officially Roman Catholic, with small groups of Protestants and other religions.

The Garifunas trace their history to the Kalinagus or Kalifunas, an Arawak agricultural people originally found in the northern parts of South America. Around 1000 CE, some of the Kalinagus migrated up the Orinoco River to the Caribbean coast eventually spreading north through the chain of islands in the Caribbean Sea. Later the more warlike Caribs also migrated north from South America to overrun the islands. The Arawaks living in the islands were mostly displaced or absorbed by the newcomers. In the mid-1600s Spanish slave ships were wrecked in the islands. The Caribs helped to save many of the Africans, who gradually adopted the Carib-Arawak culture and language. The mixture of the Caribs and the Africans, known as Black Caribs, grew in number and began to compete with the Caribs for land and resources. They eventually drove the Caribs into a small zone in the eastern part of the island, where they remain to the present. Both the English and the French claimed the island of St. Vincent in the late 17th century. The governor of French Martinique sent a force to occupy the island in 1719 but the Caribs prevented the force from landing. A British attempt to settle in 1723 was also repelled. The Europeans agreed in 1748 to put aside their territorial claims and St. Vincent, along with Dominica, was declared a neutral island. Throughout this period unofficial French settlements were established. The 1763 Treaty of Paris awarded St. Vincent to the British. A series of conflicts, known as the Carib Wars, finally ended with the surrender of the Black Caribs in 1796. The British considered the Black Caribs as dangerous and deported them to Roatán, a British-held island off the coast of Honduras.

The Garifuna culture is a unique blend of African, Carib, Arawak, Caribbean, British, French, and Spanish influences.

Formerly known as Black Caribs, the Garifunas call themselves Garinagu, a corruption of the name of the early Arawak Kalinagu people. The descendants of African slaves, indigenous Arawaks and Caribs, and Europeans, the Garifunas have a range of physical appearances although most of them closely resemble their African ancestors in skin color and features. Culturally the Garifunas have evolved a unique language that—along with their music and dance—was declared one of the Masterpieces of the Oral and Intangible Heritage of Humanity by UNESCO in 2001. Garifuna music is quite distinct from other music forms in Central America. The most famous style is known as *punta*, which later evolved into a more modernized form known as *punta rock*. The Garifuna language is considered an Arawakan language as it is primarily derived from Arawak and Carib. Almost all Garifunas are bilingual or multilingual, usually speaking Garifuna and one or two of the other regional languages. Most of the Garifunas are officially Roman Catholic although their rituals and traditions combine many pre-Christian customs. Rastafarians and a small Muslim minority are also found in the region.

Only about half the Black Caribs originally forced to leave St. Vincent survived the deportation. The survivors, dumped on Roatán, were left without adequate water or food. The Garifuna leaders petitioned the Spanish authorities on the mainland for permission to settle. They found employment as laborers and settled the coast in small villages. Disgusted with the corrupt and inefficient Spanish authorities in Honduras, many Garifunas left the area

in 1807. They gradually spread north and south along the Caribbean coast of Central America. Slavery was abolished in Central America in 1824 and many freed slaves joined the Garifuna communities. Continued instability resulted in a new migration of Garifunas seeking to settle in British territory in 1832. The British territory, known as British Honduras, became a crown colony in 1862. The beginning of the commercial fruit industry in Central America provided employment and new Garifuna communities grew up in the areas of banana and fruit production in the Spanish-speaking countries. In the 1930s the British authorities in British Honduras set up reserves in the Garifuna areas to protect subsistence farmers and fishermen. The neighboring Honduran government, fearing the Garifuna ties to the British, attempted to suppress the culture in Honduran territory in the 1920s and 1930s. In 1937 the Hondurans carried out a massacre of most Garifuna leaders in the region. Emigration from Central America to the United States and the United Kingdom began in the 1950s. Garifuna communities in these countries led a revival of the Garifuna culture by publishing in the Garifuna language, including a Garifuna dictionary, a working orthography, and an increasing literature. Beginning in the 1990s activists have worked for the unity and ethnic consciousness of all the Garifuna communities in Central America, the Caribbean, North America, and Europe. Annual events such as the Settlement Day festival in Belize have become informal gatherings of Garifuna from far-flung diaspora and a reaffirmation of the Garifunas' unique culture.

Further Reading

Anderson, Mark. *Black and Indigenous: Garifuna Activism and Consumer Culture in Honduras.* Minneapolis, MN: University of Minnesota Press, 2009.

Ávila, Tomás Alberto. *Black Caribs.* Providence, RI: Milenio Publishing, 2008.

Palacio, Joseph O. *The Garifuna: A Nation across Borders.* Belize City, Belize: Cubola, 2005.

Gitxsans

The Gitxsans, sometimes known as Gikisans, Gitksans, Gityskyans, or Interior Tsimchians, are a North American ethnic group living in the historic Skeena Country in western Canada's British Columbia province. Outside their traditional territory there are Gitxsan communities in Vancouver and other regional cities. The estimated 15,000 Gitxsans speak the English language along with their own language known as Gitxsanimaax. Most of the Gitxsans are Christians, including both Protestants and Roman Catholics.

The early Gitxsan society was based on matrilineal forms with inheritance through the mother's line. Traditionally they were divided into four clans, the Frog, the Eagle, the Wolf, and the Fireweed, each with a high chief and traditional territories and fishing grounds. Marriage between the clans was important to the maintenance of the culture and the unity of the culture. Marriage within a clan was forbidden. The historic homeland of the Gitxsans is around the headwaters of the Skeena River. Their name means "People of the River Mist" and archaeological evidence supports the Gitxsan claim that they have inhabited the region continuously for at least 10,000 years. The traditional Gitxsan society was based on the trading of salmon, other natural resources, and the products from these resources. The Gitxsan and the coastal peoples along the so-called grease trails traded salmon from the Skeena River for *oolichan*, a grease extracted from candlefish. The society revolved around the *huwilp* or house groups as the clans were known. During the 1770s, smallpox brought by European visitors to the coast swept through the region killing an estimated 30 percent of the Gitxsan people. The epidemic was only the first of several that followed.

Gitxsan culture is considered part of the civilization that evolved on the Pacific Northwest coast even though the Gitxsan homeland lies in the interior rather than on the coast. Trade and cultural exchanges with the Tsimshian people of the coast led many early chroniclers to call the Gitxsans the Interior Tsimshian, due to the similarities in art, music, and dance. The neighbors to the east, the Wet'suwet'en, an Athapaskan people, also influenced the culture through centuries of close relations and a shared political and cultural community to the present. A museum known as 'Ksan is located on the Gitanmaax reservation near Hazelton, British Columbia. The museum displays traditional and modern Gitxsan art and history. The Gitxsan language is a Tsimshianic language closely related to the neighboring Nisga'a language. The two groups are politically separate and prefer to separate the two languages as distinct, although there are only slight dialectical and vocabulary differences. Gitxsanimaax is considered an endangered language even though over 1,500 people are able to speak it.

Fur traders entered the region in the early 1800s. The traders charted the maze of rivers and mountain ranges between the Canadian Prairies and the Pacific. The Europeans were primarily interested in extending the fur trade rather than political considerations. The establishment of trading posts by the North West Company and the Hudson's Bay Company brought the region under effective British control in the mid-1800s. A second serious smallpox epidemic further decimated the Gitxsans in 1862. Tensions and violence accompanied the settlement of people of European descent in the region. The seeds of hatred and distrust began as a dispute between neighboring villages. In the winter of 1887–1888 a measles epidemic swept through the population. Over 200 children are reported to have died of the disease, with some families wiped out entirely. The inhabitants of one Gitxsan village blamed the epidemic on a shaman of the neighboring village. Violence broke out between the villagers and soon led to the involvement of other Canadians; Canadian constables were dispatched to arrest the culprits. The Gitxsans resisted and the provincial government mobilized a military unit; a warship was sent to the mouth of the Skeena River in 1888. But in the meantime the villagers had made peace and the event was archived as the Skeena Uprising of 1888. Loggers and trappers continued to settle in the region raising the question of sovereignty over the historic Gitxsan region. The provincial government claimed jurisdiction but Gixtsan leaders disputed the claim. The Canadian government's land claims process proved extremely slow and cumbersome and the British Columbia provincial government would not participate. In 1984 legal proceedings were begun by the Gitxsan and Wet'suwet'en peoples. They claimed ownership and legal jurisdiction over some 133 hereditary territories totaling 53,000 square kilometers (over 20,000 sq. mi.) in the Skeena watershed region. The aboriginal rights of the two neighboring peoples were affirmed by the Supreme Court of Canada in 1997. In recent years many younger Gitxsans have left the rural communities to seek work and opportunities in Vancouver or other nearby cities, but they often return for tribal events and are among the most active members of the Gitxsan society.

Further Reading

Adams, John W. *The Gitksan Potlatch: Population Flux, Resource Ownership and Reciprocity.* Toronto: Holt, Reinhart and Winston, 1973.

Muckle, James. *The First Nations of British Columbia: An Anthropological Survey.* Vancouver: University of British Columbia Press, 2006.

Penikett, Tony. *Reconciliation: First Nations Treaty Making in British Columbia.* Vancouver: Douglas & McIntyre, 2006.

Grenadians

The Grenadians are a Caribbean people, the inhabitants of the island of Grenada and six other small islands at the southern end of the Grenadines in the southeastern Caribbean Sea. There are Grenadian communities in the United States and the United Kingdom. The estimated 115,000

Grenadians speak English, the language of government and education, but the daily language is Grenadian Creole with a smaller number speaking a French patois. The majority of the Grenadians are Roman Catholic, with smaller congregations of Anglicans and other Protestant sects. There are small Rastafarian, Hindu, Muslim, Buddhist, and Baha'i groups as well.

Peaceful Arawak people from the South American mainland may have settled the islands as early as 1000 CE. They lived in small villages and sustained their people by farming, fishing, and hunting. Between 1300 and 1400 the warlike Caribs, also from the South American mainland, took control of the islands. Christopher Columbus sighted Grenada in 1498. Columbus named the island Concepcíon. He later changed the name to Granada, after the city in southern Spain. The Spanish attempted to colonize the island in 1609 but were repulsed by Carib warriors. The Spanish decided to concentrate on other islands, opening the way for a failed English attempt to settle. In 1650 the French landed a large military force that defeated the Caribs. Calling the island La Grenade, the French established sugar plantations and began to import African slaves as labor. Grenada's natural harbor became an important stop on the slave routes between Africa and the Caribbean. European diseases decimated the remaining Carib population. In 1763 the French were forced to cede the island to the British. The population of the island, largely of African descent, retained the French patois and other French influences on the food and dress of the islanders.

Grenadian culture is a Caribbean culture of blended African, British, and Carib influences. The French influence from early French colonization is much less visible than it is on some of the neighboring islands. French words lace the local patois and French influence is still found in the spicy food and styles of cooking that are similar to those found in New Orleans.

Big Drum

The idyllic island of Carriacou, a dependency of Grenada, is known for a unique style of Afro-Caribbean music known as Big Drum. The style dates back to at least the late 18th century when the island was under French influence. Each of the African-descended groups on Carriacou is known as a nation and Big Drum glorifies the ancestors of these nations. The nations include Manding, Temne, Chamba, Moko, Igbo, Arada, Banda, Kongo, and Cromanti. As the largest of the nations, the Cromanti always begins the Big Drum ceremony with the song "Cromanti Cudjo" or Beg Pardon. This is followed by a song by each of the other nations, with choruses, and accompanied by two boula drums and a single high-toned cut. Both types of drums are made from old rum barrels. Big Drum is often performed to honor the dead, and music played at funerals is a major part of the island's folk music.

The island culture is heavily based on the African roots of the majority, but the influences of the Caribs and the later immigrants from India are evident in the cuisine with cassava from the Caribs and *rotis*, *dhal puri*, and curries from the Indian immigrants. An important aspect of Grenadian culture is folk tales passed from generation to generation often featuring characters from both African and French folklore. As in most Caribbean cultures, music, dance, and festivals are very important. The British influence is especially evident in sports with cricket being the national and most popular sport. Religion is an important part of the culture with religious festivals now considered national festivals.

The plantation system and European and European-descended plantation owners dominated the island in the early 19th century. In 1833 Grenada became part of the British Windward Islands. Slavery was abolished in the British Empire in 1834 leading to the disintegration of the plantation system. Many of the ruined planters and their families left the island. The freed slaves were on their own and were dependent on a few local industries and their own small holdings. Nutmeg was first introduced from a ship sailing between the East Indies and the United Kingdom in 1843 and quickly became a major agricultural produce and cash crop. The first immigrants from India arrived in 1858 as indentured workers. The first secondary school was constructed in 1872. In 1877 Grenada became a British crown colony. A large wooden jetty was built to accommodate large ocean-going ships in 1882. Local leaders founded the Representative Government Association (RGA) in 1917 to agitate for a greater say in the affairs of the island for the Grenadians. A modified crown colony government with limited local representation was created in 1921. Electricity was installed in the island capital, St. George's, in 1928, beginning the modernization of island life. An airport was opened in 1943 allowing for faster and easier access to the island. In 1951 workers on the island called a general strike to demand better working conditions. The labor movement, led by Eric Gairy, became the most popular political organization and led Grenada to full independence in 1974. Gairy won the first general election in 1976 but the opposition refused to accept the outcome. The New Jewel Movement launched an armed revolution that overthrew the government and installed a dictatorship with close ties to Cuba and Nicaragua. A military coup in 1983 ended the one-party state but as violence and instability spread a joint U.S.-Caribbean military force landed to restore order and constitutional government. Between 2000 and 2002 a truth and reconciliation commission heard testimony about the abuses, violence, and violation of rights during the 1970s and early 1980s. Hurricane Ivan hit Grenada directly on September 7, 2004, destroying about 85 percent of all structures on the island. A second serious hurricane, called Emily, again ravaged the northern part of the island in June 2005. The Grenadians celebrated 35 years of independence in 2009 but the celebrations were muted due to the worldwide economic slump and the aftereffects of the two hurricanes.

Further Reading

Heine, Jorge. *A Revolution Aborted: The Lessons of Grenada.* Pittsburgh: University of Pittsburgh Press, 1991.

O'Shaughnessy, Hugh. *Grenada: An Eyewitness Account of the U.S. Invasion and the Caribbean History that Provoked It.* New York: Dodd Mead, 1985.

Steele, Beverly A. *Grenada: A History of Its People.* London: Macmillan, 2003.

Guadeloupeans

The Guadeloupeans are a Caribbean people, the inhabitants of the French island of Guadeloupe in the Lesser Antilles in the Caribbean Sea. The estimated 435,000 Guadeloupeans speak standard French, the language of education and government, but the language of daily life is Antillean Creole French. Over 91 percent of the Guadeloupeans are nominally Roman Catholic and about 5 percent belong to various Protestant sects.

As happened in the other Caribbean islands, the early inhabitants of Guadeloupe were the peaceful Arawaks, who were later displaced or absorbed by the more aggressive Caribs; the Caribs then gave their name to the surrounding sea. The second expedition led by Christopher Columbus visited the islands in 1493. He named the large island after the image of the Virgin Mary in the monastery of Villuercas, in Guadelupe, a town in the Extremadura region of southern Spain. Columbus is credited with the discovery of pineapple on the island. He called the large fruit *piña de indias*, meaning "pine of the Indians" or "pine cone of the Indians." Not finding gold, the Spanish mostly ignored the islands. Attempts to establish a settlement failed in 1604 and again in 1626. A French expedition was sent to take control of Guadeloupe, which they did by nearly wiping out the Carib population. Guadeloupe and the nearby smaller islands were annexed to the French kingdom. Colonization began in 1674 based on plantation agriculture. The need for labor was met by importing numerous African slaves. The smaller islands were settled in the 18th century by colonists from Brittany and Normandy. During the chaos that followed the outbreak of the French Revolution in 1789, the planter aristocracy of Guadeloupe attempted to retain control but a slave rebellion and the guillotine mostly eliminated the upper class Europeans in the colony.

The culture of the Guadeloupeans is a Caribbean mixture of African and French influences blended with other traditions adopted from the early Native Americans, the later Indian immigrants, and the influence of American popular culture. Music and dance are very important and demonstrate a unique interaction of African, French, and Indian traditions that has given birth to new forms specific to Guadeloupe. Local dance styles such as *zouk*, *zouk-love*, and *kompa* as well as international dances remain popular. Music has also evolved in Guadeloupe with the mixture of the island's various cultures. One of the best-known facets of Guadeloupe's culture is the island literature. Many notable writers have come from the islands, including Saint-John Perse, who won the Noble Prize for Literature in 1960. The French language is the official language although some 99 percent of the Guadeloupeans use Antillean Creole French, a patois mixing African, French, English, and Indian words and forms in a simplified language first developed by the African slaves who were taught rudimentary French by their owners. Most Guadeloupeans are nominally Roman Catholic, 86 percent in official surveys, with smaller Protestant, Hindu, and other denominations. Many Guadeloupeans blend their Christian religion with traditions and beliefs brought to the island from Africa by their ancestors.

The island's remaining population of freed slaves, a small number of mixed race, and some poor Europeans attempted to repulse the return of French rule. Napoleon Bonaparte restored slavery but a group of mulattos and freed slaves led by Louis Delgrès attempted to fight the return of French rule. He and some 300 followers killed themselves rather than submit. The French expedition took control of the island, killing some 10,000 Guadeloupeans in the process. During the Napoleonic Wars the island changed hands several times before being returned to France in 1815. Slavery was not abolished until 1848. To replace the slave labor indentured laborers were imported from India. A worldwide glut of sugar brought poverty to many Guadeloupeans dependent on the industry in 1870. New products such as bananas, which began to be exported in 1923, helped to stabilize the economy, but subsidized budgets paid for by the French government became a tradition as the islanders, mostly poor descendants of African slaves, were unable to generate enough revenue to support themselves. Guadeloupe became a department of the French Republic in 1946, bringing more French social programs to the island. In the 1950s and 1960s many activists supported independence for Guadeloupe but the generous French subsidies convinced many Guadeloupeans that remaining part of France made better financial sense. In the 2000s the growing disparity between the European administrators—whose inflated salaries allow the ostentatious consumption of imported luxury goods—and the poor Guadeloupeans continues to fuel unrest. Strikes and demonstrations demanding economic reforms have become part of island life.

Further Reading

Berrian, Brenda F. *Awakening Spaces: French Caribbean Popular Songs, Music, and Culture.* Chicago: University of Chicago, 2000.

Goslinga, Marian. *Guadeloupe.* Santa Barbara, CA: ABC-Clio, 1999.

Icon Group International. *Guadeloupe: Webster's Timeline History, 1503–2007.* San Diego: Icon Group International, 2010.

Guahibos

The Guahibos, sometimes known as Guaicas, Goahibas, Goahivas, Guaiguas, Guajibos, Sicuanis, or Sikuanis, are a South American ethnic group inhabiting the *llanos* or plains in eastern Colombia and southwestern Venezuela. The estimated 37,000 Guahibos include the Chiricoas, who speak a closely related Guahiboan language but are culturally indistinguishable from the Guahibos. Many of the Guahibos have converted to Christianity, mostly Roman Catholicism, but a significant part of the population continues to adhere to their traditional belief system.

The Guahibos, during their long history, have been hunter-gatherers in the region of the vast flatlands known in Spanish as the *llanos*. They had fairly extensive trade links with the settled farming peoples to the south. At one time the nomadic peoples supplied the sedentary tribes with slaves taken in warfare from other tribes. As nomads they developed a complex culture, making painted ceramic pottery, woven hammocks, and many kinds of baskets. The nomads had a close relationship with the rivers of the basin, using them as a source of food as well as for communication and transportation. Conflict with other tribal peoples was nearly constant, often undertaken for resources, women, captives, or to protect their territory.

Guahibo culture is a Native American culture based on the environment and traditions of their homeland. Modern Guahibos, when they visit towns, wear European-style clothing, but in their own villages most continue to wear traditional loincloths which are either made of cloth or a vegetable bark known as *marima*. Traditional clothing includes body ornamentation, such as necklaces of glass beads or shamanistic amulets for ceremonial use, usually made of animal teeth, beaks, or hooves. Textile weaving is an important part of their material culture. Using handmade looms, they weave high-quality hammocks using plant fibers. Historically basket weaving was a male occupation but of late women have begun making baskets for commercial sale. The decline in pottery making caused by the introduction of aluminum pots and plastic containers is a loss to the culture. Music and dance are important and popular. Wind and percussion instruments for festivals and ceremonies, such as three-hole flutes made from deer bones, are still made by hand. Pan flutes, made from cane tubes, are often played with another instrument made from the skull and antlers of deer. The Guahibo language is a Guahiboan language related to a number of other languages spoken in the region. Spanish is also spoken as a second language by many of the bands. Roman Catholicism, introduced by Spanish-speaking missionaries, is the primary religion. It is often blended with their pre-Christian beliefs. Catholicism has had a profound influence on their art, with most artwork now having a religious theme.

In the 1800s widely scattered ranches known as *hatos* were established in the ancestral lands of the Guahibos. A few villages and mission stations along the lower courses of the region's rivers also brought increasing contact with outsiders. The discovery of oil and gas in the plains initiated industrial and urban development in a region that had been sparsely populated for centuries. An expansion of intensive agriculture began to spread across the region in the 1950s. This pattern of settlement quickly impacted the Guahibos' nomadic lifestyle. Government programs promoted the settlement of the nomads in small villages where education and other services could be provided. Population increase and settlements quickly overwhelmed most of the Guahibos living in Venezuela but in the west, in Colombia, many continue to live as nomads as population increase has been modest in most areas. The activities of the insurgent group known as FARC in Colombia have further disrupted the Guahibo culture.

Further Reading

Garcia, Andres Hurtado. *Unseen Colombia.* Bogota, Colombia: Villegas Editores, 2004.

Olson, James S. *The Indians of Central and South America: An Ethnohistorical Dictionary.* Westport, CT: Greenwood, 1991.

Sosa, Marcelino. *The Value of the Person in the Guahibo Culture.* Dallas: SIL International, 2000.

Guajajaras

The Guajajaras are a South American ethnic group living in the northeastern Brazilian state of Maranhão. The estimated population of 23,000 makes the Guajajaras the most numerous surviving indigenous people in Brazil. The Guajajaras speak their own language, which belongs to the Tupi-Guarani language family, and many now also speak Portuguese. Missionary activity in the region is recent, so the Guajajaras mostly adhere to their traditional tribal religion.

The Guajajaras have inhabited the Amazonian lowlands in the region of the Pindaré and Zutiua rivers. The region consists of high Amazonian forests and lower less-tropical forests that form a transitional region between the Amazonian forests and the savannah regions. The Guajajaras never occupied the savannahs, the homeland of the Jê people. Some migrated from the Pindaré region to escape Portuguese slave-hunting expeditions. The slavers left the territory with the establishment of Jesuit missions across the region between 1653 and 1755. The missions offered some protection from slavers, but gave rise to a system of dependency and serfdom with the Guajajaras tied to the mission lands. In the late 18th century the Guajajaras began to expand their territory to the Grajaú and Mearim rivers where they settled shortly before the arrival of the first European and Brazilian explorers in the region. The expulsion of the Jesuits from Brazil in 1755 allowed the Guajajaras to return to their former independence by carefully avoiding contacts with outsiders.

Guajajara culture is an indigenous culture that has evolved through centuries of living with nature in the untouched wilderness. Today the principal activity is agriculture and in the dry season they often work on clearing brush and trees. Some villages have common planting lands usually set aside for the cultivation of commercial crops such as fruit. Fishing is important in the villages along the rivers. The Guajajara used to fish some 36 different species but the construction of dams has greatly reduced the varieties available. Hunting is a traditional occupation but is less productive as competition with other hunters and limitations on their territory have reduced the number of animals. Collecting and gathering are still important, particularly of forest honey.

In the early 19th century the Guajajaras continued to migrate and to dispute the hunting and fishing grounds with the various Timbira tribes. About 1850, a part of the Guajajaras migrated to the north and formed a group that was later called Tembé by the regional population. The Tembé and the Guajajaras are together known as the Tenetehara people. The Guajajaras were gradually integrated into regional systems of patronage that often included abuses and near-slavery. The indigenous peoples of the 19th century were not protected from such excesses. The Guajajaras sometimes reacted violently, but for the most part they remained obedient. The greatest Guajajara uprising was provoked by a Capuchin missionary colony started in 1897. The abuse of Guajajaras by the missionaries provoked a violent reaction. In 1901, Chief Cauiré Imana was able to unite a great number of villagers to destroy the mission and to expel all of the outsiders from the region. Some months later a military expedition moved into their territory. Skirmishes and attacks took a heavy toll on the Guajajara population. The revolt represents one of the most important incidents in Guajajara history and is regarded as the last Brazilian "war against the Indians." In the 1960s and 1970s the uncontrolled expansion of huge rural properties in the center of Maranhão pushed many peasants off small holdings without clear land titles into the Guajajara lands. The illegal settlers established a town, São Pedro dos Cacetes, which existed from 1952 until it was finally dismantled and dispersed by Brazilian federal authorities in 1995. The Guajajaras resisted the settlement for over four decades with only sporadic help from the Federal Government. Beginning in the 1980s new threats arose with the construction of dams and the overrunning of much of the territory by avid regional logging companies.

Further Reading

Bendor-Samual, David Harold. *Hierarchical Structures in Guajajára.* London: University of London Press, 1966.

Gomes, Mércio Pereira. *The Ethnic Survival of the Tenetehara Indians of Maranahão, Brazil.* Gainesville, FL: University of Florida Press, 1977.

Gross, Daniel R., ed. *Peoples and Cultures of Native South America.* New York: The American Museum of Natural History Press, 1973.

Guaranis

The Guaranis are a South American ethnic group traditionally inhabiting a large territory in Paraguay, northern Argentina, southern Brazil, and parts of Uruguay and Bolivia. The estimated 320,000 Guaranis speak the Guarani language, which belongs to the Guarani branch of the Tupi-Guarani language family. Although many Guaranis are monolingual, the second language spoken by about half the population is Spanish or Portuguese. An estimated 5 million people speak Guarani as their first or second language as Guarani is an official language in Paraguay and is spoken by virtually the entire population of the country. Most Guaranis are nominally Christian, with a Roman Catholic majority and a growing Protestant minority. Some, particularly in rural areas, continue to adhere to their pre-Christian belief system.

Early Guarani villages most often consisted of large communal houses, each meant for 10 to 15 families. Larger tribal groups were usually a grouping of many bands speaking the same dialect. The estimated Guarani population of around 400,000 consisted mostly of sedentary agriculturalists when they first encountered the Europeans. In 1537, Gonzalo de Mendoza led an expedition through present-day Paraguay to the present Brazilian border. On his return he established relations with the Guaranis and founded the settlement of Asunción, later the capital city of Paraguay. The first Spanish government of the territory known as Guayrá initiated the enslavement of the Guarani people and the intermarriage of European men and Guarani women. The descendants of these marriages characterize the nation of Paraguay today. The first Jesuits entered Guarani territory in 1585. Others soon followed and a Jesuit college was created in Asunción. In 1608, in response to a Jesuit protest against the enslavement of the Guaranis, King Philip III of Spain granted them authority to convert and colonize the indigenous tribes. The first Jesuit mission was established in 1610. The mission provided the only real protection against the Portuguese slave hunters, and the Guarani flocked there in such numbers that 12 more missions were established in rapid succession, ultimately sheltering some 40,000 Guaranis. In 1629, an army of slave hunters and pirates from São Paulo attacked one of the missions and carried off thousands into slavery. Within two years all but two of the missions were destroyed and over 60,000 Christian converts were marched off for sale in São Paulo and Rio de Janeiro. In the 1630s and 1640s the missionaries gained permission to arm the Christian Guaranis. When the next slaver attack neared they were met by guns and a determined Guarani militia. By 1732, at the time of their greatest prosperity and extent, the 30 Guarani missions were guarded by an army of over 7000 well-armed and well-drilled Guarani warriors. Two years later, in 1734, a smallpox epidemic killed over 30,000 people. A second epidemic killed another 12,000

in 1765. In 1750, a treaty between Spain and Portugal transferred the territory of the seven missions on the Uruguay River to Portuguese control. The Portuguese closed the missions and ordered the Guaranis to leave. They refused and initiated seven years of guerrilla warfare known as the Guarani War. Thousands died before the Jesuits secured a royal decree returning the territory to Spanish control. The Jesuits were expelled from the Spanish colonies by royal edict in 1767. The missions were turned over to priests of other orders, but under a new set of regulations drawn up by the Spanish viceroy.

Guarani culture comprises a number of linguistically and culturally related groups often called by local names. The culture is a blend of their traditional culture and the European cultures brought to the region from Spain and Brazil. Most of the modern Guaranis are farmers, although hunting and fishing also remain important. The Guaranis are integrated into the surrounding society, particularly in Paraguay where most of the population has at least some Guarani ancestry and nearly all of the population is bilingual, speaking both Spanish and Guarani. The Guarani language was once dismissed as a peasant language but in recent decades it has become a matter of pride and of national distinction. The Guarani language is spoken in all parts of the region and has official status in Paraguay, in Argentina in the Corrientes province, and as a regional language in Brazil. Guarani is the only indigenous language in the Americas that is spoken by a large population of nonindigenous people. The mostly Roman Catholic Guaranis have begun to convert to Protestant evangelical sects in recent years.

Guarani boy smokes a traditional pipe. (AP Photo/Douglas Engle)

exiles returned to their forests and plains. The Guarani language, which had been the official language of the missions under the Jesuits, retained vigor to become an official language of Paraguay. In the early and middle 20th century Paraguay's dictators sought isolation and for a time closed the country's borders, thereby protecting the local Guarani culture and language. The missions were declared part of the patrimony of humanity by UNESCO in 1993. In 2006 over 1500 leaders of the Guarani peoples of Uruguay, Brazil, Argentina, and Paraguay met at the site of the ruins of Mission São Gabriel to celebrate the memory of the Guarani peoples of the missions and their resistance against slavers, outlaws, hostile tribes, and unsympathetic governments. The meeting was celebrated as the first Guarani summit meeting where decisions were taken to strengthen their bonds and their united will in respecting their historic rights, including recognition of their claims to traditional Guarani lands by the various national governments.

Further Reading

Abou, Sélim. *The Jesuit "Republic" of the Guaranis, 1609–1768*. New York: Crossroad, 1997.

Garson, Barbara. *The Guarani under Spanish Rule in the Rio de la Plata*. Palo Alto, CA: Stanford University Press, 2005.

Icon Group International. *Guarani: Webster's Timeline History, 1523–2007*. San Diego: Icon Group International, 2010.

The missions rapidly declined under a chaotic political system that rescinded most of their former prerogatives. The official census of 1801 showed that fewer than 45,000 Guaranis remained in the region of the missions. The former herds of cattle, sheep, and horses had disappeared. The fields and orchards were quickly overgrown or cut down and the churches and mission buildings were in ruins. The long wars for independence completed the destruction of the missions. By 1814 fewer than 8000 Guaranis still clung to the limited protection of the old missions. In 1848 the few who remained were declared citizens. The descendants of the mission

Guatemalans

The Guatemalans are a Central American people, the inhabitants of the Republic of

Guatemala. Outside Guatemala there are over a million Guatemalans in the United States, and a sizable group in Canada, Mexico, Venezuela, Europe, Australia, and the Middle East. The estimated 15 million Guatemalans speak Spanish, the official language of the country, although it is often spoken as a second language by the large indigenous population. The majority of the Guatemalans are Roman Catholics, with smaller numbers of Protestants and many indigenous people who continue to practice the ancient Maya religion.

More than 1000 years before the European presence in the Americas, the Mayas established a number of autonomous city-states in the territory of present-day Guatemala. The city-states were centers of an advanced culture that perfected the arts and sciences, but they often warred amongst themselves. By 1000 CE -the Mayan civilization had collapsed, the cities had been abandoned, and most of the population had migrated to the highlands. Soon after conquering Mexico in 1521, the Spanish moved south to conquer the Maya peoples. Spanish contact with the Mayas resulted in epidemics of European diseases that devastated the indigenous populations. Guatemala became the center of government for most of Central America for the next three centuries. The surviving Mayas were often taken as slaves to work in mines and on Spanish plantations. The capital of the region was moved several times due to Maya uprisings or earthquakes. Guatemala City was founded as the new capital in 1776.

The Guatemalan culture reflects the traditions of the two largest population groups, the indigenous Maya groups and the ladinos (people of mixed Spanish and indigenous background or Mayas who have adopted the Spanish language, the national culture, and the dress and lifestyle of the large mestizo population). Only about one percent of the Guatemalans are of unmixed European descent. Descendants of African slaves and Garifunas, often English speaking, live along the Caribbean coast. As the traditional center of power in Central America, Guatemala has a long history of art, literature, and music. Guatemalan music comprises a number of different styles and forms. One popular and unique music form is *nueva canción*, which blends together popular issues, histories, political values, and the struggles of Guatemala's common people. The Spanish language is the official language of the country but it is not universally spoken, even as a second language. There are 21 Mayan languages still in use that are recognized as national languages. Since 1996 some official documents are permitted in other languages and there is a provision for interpreters in legal cases for non-Spanish speakers. The 1996 accord also permitted bilingual education. Some 50–60 percent of the Guatemalans are Roman Catholics, and an estimated 40 percent are Protestants, mostly Evangelicals and Pentecostals. Mayan rituals are often incorporated into the modern Christian traditions. Smaller religious groups include the Eastern Orthodox group, Jews, Muslims, Buddhists, and others.

Wars in Europe and a loosening of Spanish authority resulted in independence movements throughout the Spanish Empire in the Americas. In 1821, the authorities in Guatemala City declared the independence of Central America, including Chiapas, Guatemala, El Salvador,

Nicaragua, Costa Rica, and Honduras. Central America joined the new Mexican state, which was dissolved two years later. All but the Chiapas soon seceded from Mexico to form a Central American federation. The federation dissolved in civil war between 1838 and 1840. Guatemala became a separate republic dominated by the Roman Catholic Church, large landowners, and the conservative descendants of the early European settlers. A "liberal revolution" began in 1871 with the modernization of the country, improved trade, and the introduction of new commercial crops and limited manufacturing. During the late 19th century coffee became an important export. From 1898 to 1920, Guatemala was under the dictatorial rule of Manuel Estrada Cabrera, supported by the United Fruit Company, which quickly became a major force in the country. A series of weak governments and dictators finally ended with a military coup in 1944 followed by the country's first free election. The United States, engaged in the so-called Cold War with the communist states from the 1950s to the 1990s, directly supported Guatemala's army with money, training, and weapons as a bulwark against communism in Central America. In the 1970s indigenous rights groups agitated for better treatment and small guerrilla groups led attacks against the army. The Guatemalan military initiated a widespread reign of terror. The United States, in 1979, ended all aid to the Guatemalan military due to widespread and systematic abuses. Massacres of Maya civilians, particularly in the rural highlands, continued unabated. A bloody campaign of disappearances, torture, and a "scorched earth" policy made Guatemala a pariah state internationally. Tens of thousands of refugees, displaced or forced from their homes, fled across the border into Mexico. Many students, activists, professionals, and opposition leaders also fled the country. Rigoberta Menchú, a native Maya activist, received the Nobel Peace Prize in 1992 for her efforts to focus attention on the government-sponsored genocide perpetrated on the indigenous population. The Guatemala Civil War ended in 1996 with a peace accord that finally recognized the basic human rights of the Maya and other indigenous groups. In the 1990s a Truth Commission worked to review the police and military archives as many families searched for the remains of the disappeared or the victims of the massacres. Since the peace accord of 1996, the Guatemalans have witnessed successive democratic elections, most recently in 2011.

Further Reading

Grandin, Greg, Deborah T. Levenson and Elizabeth Oglesby, eds. *The Guatemala Reader: History, Culture, Politics.* Durham, NC: Duke University Press, 2011.

Sanford, Victoria. *Buried Secrets: Truth and Human Rights in Guatemala.* Basingstoke, England: Palgrave Macmillan, 2004.

Wilkinson, Daniel. *Silence on the Mountain: Stories of Terror, Betrayal, and Forgetting in Guatemala.* Durham, NC: Duke University Press, 2004.

Guaymis

The Guaymis, sometimes known as Ngabes, Ngawbes, Ngäberes, Ngäbere-Buglé, or Ngobe-Bugle, are a Central American ethnic group living in the western provinces of Panama, with a small community in neighboring Costa Rica. The estimated 280,000 Guaymis speak the Guaymi language, a language belonging to the Chibchan language family. Most Guaymis adhere to their traditional belief system with small Roman Catholic and Protestant Evangelical minorities.

The original settlers of the rainforests of southern South America were influenced by the more advanced civilizations in the highlands of South America and central Mexico. The Spanish explorers encountered three distinct Guaymi tribes in the early 16th century. Each of the tribes was led by a chief and each spoke a distinct language. Those following Chief Urraca in the Veraguas region became famous for defeating the Spanish several times, finally forcing the Spanish to sign a peace treaty recognizing the tribe's sovereignty and territory in 1521. Urraca was betrayed and sent to the Atlantic coast in chains. He later escaped, returned to the mountains, and became so feared that the Spanish left his tribe in peace until his death in 1531. The Guaymis united in the face of Spanish aggression but remained divided between the lowlanders along the Atlantic coast and those living in the tropical forests in the highlands of Veraguas and Chiriqui. The Guaymis never surrendered to the Spanish, who feared entering Guaymi territory.

Guaymi culture is a traditional culture only slightly influenced by the Spanish-based culture of most of Central America. The modern Guaymis are mostly subsistence farmers or agricultural laborers on large farms. The majority is considered as living in poverty but they continue to live much like their ancestors. Because of the rugged terrain, efforts to build roads and bring new infrastructure to the Guaymi lands have been limited. Many Guaymis must enter the cash economy in order to survive. Working on large farms or ranches, harvesting bananas, or picking coffee are the main sources of money. In recent years some Guaymis have moved north into Costa Rica to work on the coffee plantations. Guaymi women are artisans and have continued with their many traditional crafts, both for their own use and to sell commercially. The Guaymi language remains the first language for the majority although many younger Guaymis now also speak Spanish. The language has a long oral tradition and recently a writing system was devised. The majority of the Guaymis continue to follow their traditional religious beliefs, which include the belief in spirits and witchcraft. Smaller numbers have converted to Roman Catholicism and recently some have embraced the Baha'i religion.

The Guaymis continued to live in small jungle villages and to identify with their communities rather than with their ethnic or linguistic group. The independence of the Spanish colonies ended Spanish attempts to encroach on their lands but as part of newly-independent Colombia's territory they faced renewed pressure. In the mid-1800s many of the Guaymis moved deeper into the jungled hills to escape abuses or forced labor. In 1903 Panama separated from Colombia and the Guaymis were faced with yet another new government and its policies. In 1972 a new Panamanian constitution required the government to establish reserves for the indigenous peoples. The Guaymi reserve, created in 1997, finally gave the tribesmen some relief from loggers, well-meaning missionaries, ill-advised government policies, and other abuses. The loss of many of their traditional lands caused some Guaymis to leave their homeland to join Panama's migrant workforce. These workers are often given the lowest paid and most dangerous jobs. In the late 20th century development projects such as the Cerro Colorado mining project and hydroelectric dams forced many Guaymis to unite to fight the threats to their traditional homeland.

Further Reading

Gjording, Chris N. *The Cerro Colorado Copper Project and the Guaymi Indians of Panama.* Cambridge, MA: Cultural Survival, 1981.

Gjording, Chris N. *Conditions Not of Their Choosing: The Guaymi Indians and Mining Multinationals in Panama.* Washington, D.C.: Smithsonian Institution Press, 1991.

Young, Philip D. *Ngawbe: Tradition and Change among the Western Guaymi of Panama.* Champaign, IL: University of Illinois Press, 1971.

Guianans

The Guianans, sometimes known as Guyanans, Guyanais, Guyanes, or French Guyanese, are a South American people, the inhabitants of Guyane, French Guiana in English, an overseas region of the French Republic. Outside French Guiana there are Guianan communities in France, Martinique, Guadeloupe, and the other French islands of the Caribbean. The estimated 235,000 Guianans speak French, the official language and the language of government and education. A French patois known as French Guiana Creole is widely used, plus six indigenous languages, four Maroon dialects, and Hmong Njua are spoken as regional languages.

The region was inhabited by a number of distinct indigenous groups before 1450 CE. The tribes mostly lived by hunting, fishing, gathering, and subsistence farming. Often warring among themselves, the tribes never unified. On his third voyage to the New World, Christopher Columbus sighted the coast in 1498. The Spanish claimed the region but the resistance of the native peoples and the lack of gold or other treasure persuaded the Spanish to ignore the region for richer takings in other parts of the Americas. The French attempted to establish a settlement but left when threatened by the Portuguese. In 1608 the Grand Duke of Tuscany organized an expedition to create an Italian colony but the scheme ended with his sudden death. A French expedition returned in 1630 and in 1643 managed to establish a settlement at Cayenne as a center of a number of plantations. The colony was abandoned following a series of attacks by hostile tribes. The French returned in 1664 to reestablish the settlement at Cayenne. The colony changed hands several times during the European colonial wars. After 1763 when the French lost all their American colonies except Guiana and a few Caribbean islands, the French government sent thousands of settlers to

Guiana with stories of plentiful gold and easy fortunes. Instead of gold the settlers found a territory of tropical diseases and hostile native tribes. Within a year and a half only a few hundred remained alive. The French survivors fled to three small islands just off shore, calling them the Iles de Salut or the Islands of Salvation. The three islands, known as Royal Island, St. Joseph, and Devil's Island, allowed the French settlers to survive long enough to take the ship back to France. The terrible stories they told left a lasting impression on the French public. During the French Revolution many opponents of the revolutionaries were sent to the region as prisoners. Gradually plantations were established and African slaves imported as labor. Exports of sugar, hardwood, and Cayenne pepper, along with other spices, brought a limited prosperity to the colony for the first time.

The Guianan culture reflects the mixed population of those living along the coastal regions of the territory. Most of the population is of mixed African and European descent, known as mulattos or creoles, with a large immigrant population from Haiti that is closely related both culturally and linguistically. Together these two groups make up 60–70 percent of the Guianan population. Some 15 percent of the population is of European ancestry, mainly French, although there are also people of Dutch, Portuguese, Spanish, and British ancestry. The Asian population includes the Chinese, who make up about 3.5 percent of the Guianans, and the Hmong from Laos, who make up some 1.5 percent. Other smaller groups are from the Caribbean islands, mainly St. Lucia and Dominica, and there are small numbers of Hindus and Muslims from India, Lebanese people, and Vietnamese people. In the interior there are the Maroons, formerly called "Bush Negroes," who are racially African, the descendants of escaped slaves, and the Native American groups that make up 3–4 percent of the population. The many cultural influences have been absorbed into a unique culture that shows its French roots along with all the

---

Devil's Island

Devil's Island, known in French as île du Diable, is one of the three Salut Islands some 7 miles (11 km.) off the coast of French Guiana. The island was first used as a penal colony by the government of Emperor Napoleon III in 1852. Prisoners sent to the island ranged from political prisoners to the most hardened thieves and murders. Most of the 80,000 prisoners sent to Devil's Island were never seen again. The horrors of the penal colony on Devil's Island became notorious following the publicity surrounding the plight of French army captain Alfred Dreyfuss, who had been unjustly convicted of treason and sent to the island in 1895. In 1938 the French government stopped sending prisoners to the island, and in 1952 the infamous penal colony was finally closed.

other traditions and the modern American and European influences from television, films, and music. The dominant religion of the Guianans is Roman Catholicism with smaller groups of Protestants and other religions. The Maroons and some of the indigenous groups maintain their traditional religions. Most of the Chinese are Buddhists or Taoists but the Hmongs are mainly Christian owing to the influence of the Christian missions that helped them to reach French Guiana.

During the Napoleonic Wars an Anglo-Portuguese naval group took control of the

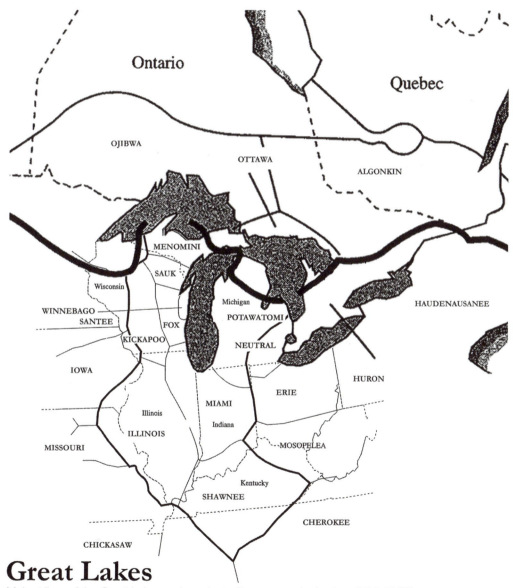

Great Lakes

Major tribes of the Great Lakes region prior to European colonization. (ABC-CLIO)

colony, which was added to Portuguese Brazil. The colony returned to French control in 1817. The French abolished slavery in their empire in 1848 and many of the freed slaves fled into the rainforest to join earlier escaped slaves in communities similar to those they had known in Africa. Called Maroons, they formed a buffer between the Europeans and the Creoles on the coast and the often hostile tribes of the interior. Without slaves many of the plantations were soon overgrown and the planters ruined. In 1850 several ships landed groups of Indians, Malays, and Chinese to work the plantations, but instead the newcomers set up shops in Cayenne and other settlements. The struggling colony became the site of a failed French experiment with its large criminal population. In 1852 the first groups of chained convicts arrived in the colony from France. In 1885, to rid France of habitual criminals and to increase the number of settlers in French Guiana, a new law was passed for the deportation of criminals to the colony where they were to be imprisoned for six months and then released to become colonists. The experiment was a dismal failure as the released convicts were unable to live off the land and were forced back into crime or died of disease, exposure, or starvation. The convict system led to the creation of prisons and camps throughout the territory. French Guiana became an overseas department of France in 1946, giving most of the population French citizenship. In 1964 Kourou was chosen as the launch site for the rockets of the French space program. Kourou later became the center of the European Space Agency. In the 1970s some groups formed to support demands for greater autonomy or even independence. Widespread violence accompanied pro-autonomy demonstrations in 1996–1997 and 2000. While many Guianans support calls for greater autonomy from France, support for full independence has waned as people fear a future without the generous French subsidies that give the Guianans one of the highest incomes in South America.

Further Reading

Kline, Michael. *Issues in the French-Speaking World.* Westport, CT: Greenwood, 2004.

Redfield, Peter. *Space in the Tropics: From Convicts to Rockets in French Guiana.* Berkeley, CA: University of California Press, 2000.

Spieler, Miranda Frances. *Empire and Underworld: Captivity in French Guiana.* New Haven, CT: Yale University Press, 2012.

Guyanese

The Guyanese, sometimes known as Guyanans, are a South American people, the inhabitants of the Co-operative Republic of Guyana on South America's northern coast. The estimated 775,000 Guyanese speak English, the official language of the country, with many also speaking the national language, known as Guyanese Creole. About 52 percent of the Guyanese are Christians, mostly Roman Catholic and Anglican, some 35 percent are Hindus, and about 10 percent are Muslims.

The early inhabitants of the area were Arawak, Carib, and possibly Warao peoples who survived by farming, fishing, and hunting. Christopher Columbus sighted the coast on his third voyage to the New World in 1498, but although the Spanish claimed the region settlement was difficult so the region was mostly ignored. The region between the Orinoco and Amazon deltas became known as the Wild Coast. During the 16th and 17th centuries, the European colonial powers fought to control the territory for the establishment of the important sugar industry. The territory changed hands frequently, mostly as a result of wars between the French and the English. The Dutch were the first Europeans to establish colonies, Essequibo in 1616, Berbice in 1627, and Demerara in 1752. Unrest among the slave population finally erupted in a widespread slave rebellion led by a slave named Cuffy in 1763. Many slaves escaped into the interior to live much as their ancestors had in Africa. Upheavals in Europe resulted in the capture of the Dutch colonies by the British in the late 18th century. The sugar plantations taken by the British required a constant supply of laborers so African slaves continued to be imported to the region as they had been under Dutch rule.

The Guyanese culture is one of the four non-Hispanic cultures of South America. The culture is similar to those of the English-speaking Caribbean states and Guyana has historically been tied to that part of the British Empire. The culture is a unique blend of Indo-Guyanese and Afro-Guyanese traditions and customs, and is similar to the culture of Trinidad. Cultural traits that Guyana shares with the Anglophone Caribbean are similar foods, festivals, music, and sports. The British heritage is evident in the language, politics, and

sports, with cricket considered the national sport. Guyana's population originally came from many parts of the British Empire, although a small population of indigenous peoples still lead seminomadic lives in the inland forests. The Afro-Guyanese are the descendants of African slaves and form about a third of the population. The Indo-Guyanese, who came as indentured laborers when African slavery was abolished, make up about half the Guyanese population. Smaller groups of Portuguese, Chinese, and others make up the rest of the population. The religious beliefs of the Guyanese also reflect their backgrounds with most of the Afro-Guyanese and some of the Indo-Guyanese belonging to Christian sects and the majority of the Indo-Guyanese following the Hindu or Muslim religions. Some African religious beliefs and rituals are also practiced.

The British outlawed the importation of new slaves to the colonies in 1804 but chattel slavery continued. The Dutch government formally ceded the three colonies to the British in 1814. The three distinct colonies were united into a single colony known as British Guiana in 1831. The abolition of slavery in the British Empire in 1834 caused a severe shortage of laborers, which was met by importing indentured Indians from the British territories in India. The Indian population grew to eventually become the largest segment of the colonial population. The neighboring country of Venezuela, since its independence in 1824, laid claim to part of British Guiana. In 1899 the overlapping territorial claims were submitted to an international tribune that ruled against Venezuela and affirmed

Britain's legal control of the disputed districts. The practice of importing laborers was officially ended in 1917. Over the next decades, many of the Afro-Guyanese urbanized while the large Indo-Guyanese populations remained in the rural areas. Two political blocks emerged in the 1950s representing the two largest segments of the Guyanese population. Local British officials, in an effort to divert the drive to full independence, incited violence between the two groups. Serious riots resulted in the destruction of a large part of the capital, Georgetown. Strikes, instability, and interference by Venezuela and other foreign governments marked the period known in Guyana as "the Disturbances." Guyana became independent in 1966 under a socialist government. The period of state socialism, press censorship, and tight one-party rule finally came to an end in 1985. Governments dominated by the Afro-Guyanese finally gave way to a government led by an elected Indo-Guyanese administration in 1999. Venezuela renewed its old territorial claims to three-quarters of Guyana's national territory when it was found to be potentially oil-rich. Neighboring Suriname also claims parts of Guyana. In 2006 the first nonviolent elections were held in more than 20 years. Close cultural and linguistic ties are maintained with the Anglophone countries of the Caribbean, but in 2008 the Guyanese signed a new treaty bringing the country into closer contact with the other nations of the South American continent.

Further Reading

Bisnauth, Dale. *Settlement of Indians in Guyana: 1890–1930.* Leeds, England: Peepal Tree Press, 2001.

Senauth, Frank. *The Making of Guyana: From a Wilderness to a Nation.* Bloomington, IN: AuthorHouse, 2009.

Williams, Brackette F. *Stains on My Name, War in My Veins: Guyana and the Politics of Cultural Struggle.* Durham, NC: Duke University Press, 1991.

Gwich'ins

The Gwich'ins, sometimes known as Kutchins or Gwitchins, are a North American ethnic group living mostly above the Arctic Circle in the Northwest Territories and the Yukon Territory in northwestern Canada and in adjacent parts of the American state of Alaska. The estimated 10,000 Gwich'ins speak English, often also speaking their own language belonging to the Athabaskan language family. Most Gwich'ins are Christians, primarily Anglican or Roman Catholic, with many blending their traditional beliefs with modern Christian rituals.

The history of the Gwich'in people is mostly unknown due to the lack of a written language. An extensive oral history is mostly myths and parables. Historically the Gwich'ins controlled a very large territory south of the lands of the Inuit peoples. The northernmost of the Athabaskan peoples, the Gwich'in traditionally occupied a vast expanse of land covering portions of present-day northern Canada and Alaska. Most of their historic homeland lies above the Arctic Circle just to the northern tree line. The forests offered a wide range of resources and the caribou herds afforded sustenance, tools, and shelter. The semi-nomadic way of life divided the Gwich'ins into several distinct bands, each associated with the territory around a major river. In 1789, the Gwich'in territory was explored by Alexander MacKenzie, who gave his name to one of the major rivers in Gwich'in territory during an unsuccessful expedition in search of an overland route to the Pacific.

Gwich'in culture reflects the influences of Inuit and modern Canadian and Alaskan culture on their traditional society. The harsh winter climate resulted in innovations such as snowshoes and birch bark canoes well adapted to their homeland. They maintained a seminomadic lifestyle using sleds, rather than the more common Subarctic toboggans, for transportation. The caribou herds provided much of their daily needs as they lived in dwellings covered in caribou hides, wore clothing made from caribou skins, and the bones were used for needles and other tools. The Gwich'ins lived in a number of bands or tribes united by language, culture, and a clan system that extended across the Gwich'in territory. Modern Gwich'ins usually divided the year into hunting, fishing, and seasonal wage employment. The Gwich'in language is spoken in two major dialects that roughly correspond to the Canada-Alaska border. The language, according to UNESCO, is severely endangered with less than 400 speakers. Most Gwich'ins are Christians, although they retain their traditional relationship with the natural world, especially the caribou.

The Gwich'ins had for centuries been the intermediaries in trade between the Inuit peoples on their northern borders and the tribes to the south. European traders began to take over the trade and the Gwich'ins traveled to trading posts outside their territory to trade for goods they needed. In 1840 Fort McPherson was established as a trading post on the Peel River in Gwich'in territory. The Hudson's Bay Company established Fort Yukon in 1847. Even though the Gwich'ins resented the European trading posts in their territory they soon became accustomed to goods and resources available only at the posts. In the 1850s smallpox and other diseases further reduced the Gwich'in population. The estimated population of 5000 in 1800 had declined to just 1300 by 1900. Roman Catholic and Anglican missions were established in the 1860s with many Gwich'ins converting to Christianity. Over 1000 Gwich'ins died of an influenza epidemic in 1865. A severe scarlet fever epidemic again devastated the territory in 1897. A year later the Klondike gold rush began with thousands of outsiders moving into Gwich'in territory. Conflicts with the miners led to abuses, land grabs, and violence. The miners brought new diseases to which the Gwich'ins had no immunity including two serious influenza epidemics in 1921 and 1928. Treaties with the Canadian government in 1921 defined Gwich'in territory and such rights as hunting and fishing. Treaty Indians, as defined by the Canadian government, were granted Canadian citizenship in 1960. Alaska recognized territorial claims by indigenous peoples in 1972. In the 1990s the Gwich'ins, along with other related peoples, began negotiations with the provincial and Canadian governments to obtain their own self-governing territory.

Further Reading

Bass, Rick. *Caribou Raising: Defending the Porcupine Herd, Gwich'in Culture, and the Arctic National Wildlife Refuge.* San Francisco: Sierra Club Books, 2004.

Heine, Michael. *That River, It's Like a Highway for Us: The MacKenzie River through Gwichya Gwich'in History and Culture.* Yellowknife, N.T., Canada: Gwich'in Social and Cultural Institute, 1977.

Nelson, Richard K. *Hunters of the Northern Forest: Design for Survival among the Alaska Kutchin.* Chicago: University of Chicago Press, 1973.

Gypsies

See Romanis

H

Haidas, Tlingits, and Tsimshians

The Haidas, Tlingits, and Tsimshians are closely related North American ethnic groups that inhabit the mainland and the islands of southern Alaska and northern British Columbia. The estimated 32,000 tribal members, including some 17,000 Tlingits, 10,000 Tsimshians, and 5,000 Haidas and Kaigani Haidas (Alaskan Haidas), speak the closely related Tlingit and Tsimshian languages, which belong to the Na-Dene language group, and Haida, which is considered an isolated language. Most also speak English, the language of government and education. The Haidas, Tlingits, and Tsimshians are mostly Christian, with many, especially in Alaska, being members of the Russian Orthodox Church.

The islands and the mainland of northwestern North America were the center of a sophisticated culture with a dense population. The forests provided cedar for dwellings and carvings and the abundant salmon was the staple food. Living in a resource-rich region, the Haidas and Tlingits had time to develop elaborate rituals and ceremonies and to craft ritual and daily objects such as masks, totem poles, and cedar-plank canoes. The cultures evolved into highly stratified societies of chiefs, nobles, commoners, and slaves. Warfare between different bands or tribes often included the taking of captives for slaves.

Large ocean-going canoes allowed the warriors to raid distant peoples taking slaves and other resources as far as Mexico. In the early 17th century a group of Haidas drove the Tlingits away to settle the southern half of present-day Prince of Wales Island. The colonists called themselves Kaigani, but unlike the other Haidas to the south they found the streams in their new territory too small for salmon spawning, so they took to the sea like the Tlingits in search of salmon, halibut, and cod. A Russian expedition explored part of the northern coast in 1741, followed by a Spanish expedition in 1755. Over the next decades other Europeans visited the region, marveling at the sophisticated cultures. George Vancouver, an Englishman, surveyed and mapped the coast in detail between 1792 and 1794. Russian trappers and traders established settlements in the northern islands and in 1799 they established a fortified post in Tlingit territory but were driven out by a series of attacks.

The culture of the Haidas, Tlingits, and Tsimshians is closely related though the Haidas, due to the isolation of their home islands, have been able to preserve more of their traditional culture, including customs and ceremonies that have disappeared from the mainland cultures. The ancient tradition known as *potlatch*, a public dispensation of personal wealth characterized by the giving of gifts, brought great community respect for the giver. Both cultures are divided into two major clans, or moieties, which are assigned at birth and are based on maternal lineage. Totem poles, formerly used to mark important events in family or clan histories, are still an important cultural expression. English is now the major language with only a small number speaking the Haida and Tlingit languages and over 2000 still able to speak Tsimshian. Younger people have taken a new interest in recent decades and in 1991 language courses in the indigenous languages were begun in area schools. The majority of the population is Christian, with many retaining the Orthodox religion brought to the region by Russian colonists. Pre-Christian beliefs are often blended with modern Christian rituals.

The Russians, despite continued resistance by the Tlingits, extended their control south to Haida and Tsimshian territories in 1802. In 1821 the Russians claimed all territory south to the 51st parallel. A compromise in 1824 between the British and Russian governments established the border at 54 40' north latitude, the present international boundary between Alaska and British Columbia. The compromise effectively partitioned the homelands of the three closely related peoples. European diseases and especially brutal colonial methods in the Russian territories decimated the population, which dropped from an estimated 30,000 in 1750 to some 8,000 in 1850. Christian missionaries established missions and schools between the 1850s and the 1870s, winning many converts and aiding the cultural survival of the two small peoples. A long decline in population and traditions began to reverse after World War II. Work in the factories established for canning and processing the region's rich fish harvests helped to stabilize the local economy. In the 1950s the Haidas, Tlingits, and Tsimshians began to press tribal land claims in both Canada and Alaska. Salmon fishing, considered part of their cultural heritage, became a question of agreements and negotiations between the tribes and the governments of Canada and the United States in the 1980s. Tribal claims to sovereignty include the management and control of the natural resources in the region, including the salmon population. The Central Council of the Tlingit and Haida, headquartered in Juneau, Alaska, has become a champion for the rights of the two peoples both in U.S. territory and in Canada. A recent campaign to revert to the indigenous names of islands, territories, and other landmarks has united

Haida Eagle dance. (AP Photo/M. Spencer Green)

activists representing the three peoples, who argue that two centuries of colonialism is embodied in the foreign names.

Further Reading

Johnson, Michael and Jane Burkinshaw. *Native Tribes of the North and Northwest Coast.* Milwaukee, WI: Gareth Stevens, 2004.

Kosh, A. M. *Alaskan Native Cultures: Tlingit, Haida, Tsimshian.* Santa Barbara, CA: Albion Publishing, 1994.

Worl, Rosita. *Celebration: Tlingit, Haida, Tsimshian Dancing on the Land.* Juneau, AK: Sealaska Heritage Institute, 2008.

Haitians

The Haitians, sometimes known as Haytians or Ayitians, are a Caribbean people, the inhabitants of the Republic of Haiti on the western third of the island of Hispaniola. Outside Haiti there are millions of Haitians living in other countries, including large communities in the Dominican Republic, the United States, Canada, France, the Bahamas, Cuba, the French Antilles islands, Jamaica, Puerto Rico, Trinidad and Tobago, Venezuela, and French Guiana. The estimated 13 million Haitians speak two official languages, standard French, the language of administration and education, and Haitian Creole, a French-based patois closely related to Louisiana French. Some 80 percent of Haitians are Roman Catholics, with an estimated 16 percent belonging to various Protestant churches. Many Haitians combine Christian beliefs with elements of voodoo. Besides the large Christian population there are important minorities of Baha'is and Muslims.

The island of Hispaniola, inhabited by the Arawakan-speaking Tainos, was politically divided into five chiefdoms, each ruled by a *cacique.* The island, called Ayiti or Kiskeya by the Taino peoples, was visited by Christopher Columbus on his first voyage to the New World in 1492. Columbus claimed the island for Spain and Spanish settlements were established over the next few decades. The colonists exploited the island for its gold deposits, worked chiefly by local Tainos. Those Tainos who refused to work in the mines were killed or sold into slavery. European diseases brought to the island by the colonists devastated the indigenous peoples, already weakened by ill treatment, malnutrition, and a rapid drop in their birthrate due to the disruption of their society. As the Taino population dwindled, the Spanish began to import slaves from Africa. As the gateway to the Caribbean region, Hispaniola became a center for pirates. French pirates settled the western part of the island in the 1600s. Some of the pirates settled and began to grow tobacco. French colonial families from Martinique and Guadeloupe settled in the region and established sugar plantations. France and Spain settled the ownership of the disputed island in the Treaty of Ryswick in 1697. France received the western third, which was named Saint-Domingue. More French colonists arrived due to the high potential for profit from agriculture. Sugar, coffee, and indigo plantations required the importation of thousands of African slaves. By 1790, the French colony had greatly overshadowed the Spanish colony of Santo Domingo. Some 40,000 French immigrants were greatly outnumbered by the slave population, which was nearly ten times more numerous. A population of mixed race, often freed by their owners, became the free people of color, forming a class of artisans, shopkeepers, and tradesmen. Inspired by the ideals of the French Revolution, the free people of color and many slaves pressed for greater civil rights and freedom. A slave revolt broke out in the north in 1791, sending many French planters and their families to the relative safety of Port-au-Prince. The French revolutionary government abolished slavery. Toussaint Louverture, a former slave, achieved peace in the territory in 1794 after years of war against both invaders and internal dissension. Napoleon's rise to power in France brought pressure, mostly by the island's French planters, to rethink the stand on slavery. Louverture created a separatist constitution that prompted Napoleon to send an expedition of 20,000 soldiers to retake the island and reestablish slavery. The French, at first victorious, began to succumb to yellow fever, which eventually killed most of the 50,000 soldiers, including 18 generals. Toussaint Louverture was invited to negotiate but was kidnapped by the French and sent to France, where he died in prison. In Haiti the local population of people of color and slaves continued to fight against the return of French rule.

Haitian culture is mostly derived from France, with elements from Africa, and influences from the original Taino population and the colonial Spanish. The customs and traditions are a blend of cultural beliefs that are derived from the various ethnic groups that inhabited the island. Cultural elements such as music, dance, and cuisine are derived from the French and African influences but have borrowed many forms from the neighboring Spanish-speaking peoples. Much of the Haitians' music is blended with music derived from voodoo ceremonial traditions, particularly the Haitian music known as rara, a parading music, troubadour ballads, and the extremely popular compas, called konpa in the Creole language. Haitian art is known for its color and symbolism and is often divided into regional "schools" representing various parts of the country. Haitian cuisine, although sharing many elements with other Caribbean cuisines, is unique in the region with its mixed French, African, Taino, and Spanish influences. Sports are an important part of Haitian culture with association football (soccer) being the most popular sport. Many small soccer clubs throughout the country compete at the local level. Most Haitians speak both French, the language of administration, education, and the upper classes, and the patois known as Haitian Creole, which was recently standardized. Both languages are official languages of the country. About 85 percent of the Haitians are Christians, mostly Roman Catholic. Many Haitians mix their Christian rituals with the traditions of voodoo, which is derived from the beliefs brought to the island by the African slaves. Voodoo is more widespread in the rural areas; it is estimated that around half of all Haitians continue to practice voodoo rituals and ceremonies. The Baha'i faith was brought to the island in the 1920s and 1930s and the first assembly was organized in 1942. The small Muslim population is mostly descended from Muslim slaves brought from Africa.

The freed slaves, mostly led by free people of color, largely mulattos, fought for their independence against the Europeans. Jean-Jacques Dessalines led the Haitians to victory over the French at the Battle of Vertières. The Haitians declared the independence of Saint-Domingue on January 1, 1804. They called their new country Ayiti, meaning home or homeland in the Taino Arawak language and also the language of many of the slaves, the Fon language from West Africa. The slave revolt and the subsequent wars are believed to have cost the lives of over 100,000 rebels and some 24,000 of the 40,000 French colonists. In 1809 nearly 10,000 refugees, mostly the French and free people of color, along with many slaves, arrived in New Orleans where they doubled the city's population and helped to maintain its French heritage for several generations. Voodoo, brought with the slaves from Hispaniola, became part of the slave culture of Louisiana. In Haiti Dessalines was proclaimed emperor but was killed by rivals. The country split into two countries that were finally reunited in 1821. The Haitians took control of the neighboring Spanish colony of Santo Domingo after it declared its independence from Spain, and Haitians ruled the entire island of Hispaniola until 1844. The French government sent a large fleet to reconquer the island in 1825 but a compromise led to French recognition of Haitian independence in exchange for a large monetary payment for the loss of plantations and slaves by the French government and colonists. Instability and poverty led to incursions by American and European troops several times before the United States sent an occupation force in 1915. The U.S. Marines remained in the country until 1934. The American government paid off Haiti's huge debts while the American military forces maintained the peace and put down several small rebellions. The American occupation transformed the Haitian militia into a modern police force, public health care was inaugurated, education was supported, and ports and roads were built. The Americans supervised the operation of the client Haitian government and emphasized American-style modernization and universal education. Many of the conservative Haitian elite resisted the reforms and the growing upper classes, mostly of mixed background, wanted more control. The end of the American occupation brought new disputes with the neighboring Dominican Republic, with the large Haitian population in that country targeted for discrimination and persecution. Flawed elections and military interventions led to the election of Dr. François Duvalier in 1957. From then until 1986 the country was ruled as a hereditary dictatorship that maintained control by terrorizing the population. The overthrow of Duvalier's son, known as Baby Doc, in 1986 was followed by a new round of coups and unfair elections. In 2004 a revolt forced the government to flee with the United Nations sending peacekeepers to maintain order. New elections resulted in more stability but a severe earthquake in 2010 killed nearly 316,000 Haitians and left 1.6 million homeless. Earthquake relief has been slow and often inept with most of the earthquake damage still evident and the homeless still living in tents two years after the event.

Further Reading

Dubois, Laurent. *Haiti: The Aftershocks of History.* New York: Metropolitan Books, 2012.

Girard, Philippe. *Haiti: The Tumultuous History – From Pearl of the Caribbean to Broken Nation.* Basingstoke, UK: Palgrave Macmillan, 2010.

Heinl, Robert Debs and Nancy Gordon Heinl. *Written in Blood: The Story of the Haitian People 1492–1995.* Lanham, MD: University Press of America, 2005.

Hawaiians

The Hawaiians, sometimes known as Native Hawaiians or Maoli, are the indigenous Polynesian people of the Hawaiian Islands and their descendants. About a third of the Hawaiians live outside their islands, mostly in California, Nevada, Oregon, and Washington. The estimated 530,000 Hawaiians are American citizens usually speaking English as their first language but often using the Hawaiian language or a patois known as Pidgin English. Many of the people who identify themselves as Hawaiian are of mixed ancestry but are at least part-Hawaiian. Most Hawaiians are Christians, with Protestant churches being the most popular; there is also a sizable Roman Catholic minority.

The original settlement of the islands is not completely understood with archaeological evidence of settlement, probably by Marquesans, no later than 800 CE. Some scholars believe that a second wave of settlement came between the 1100s and 1300s from Tahiti, with the newcomers conquering the islands. Others maintain that a single, extended period of settlement brought settlers from several areas of the Polynesian islands of the South Pacific. Contacts with Tahitians and other Polynesian peoples resulted in a number of influences on the Hawaiian language, oral traditions, and lifestyles. Long distance journeys by outrigger canoe are believed to have been less frequent from about 1200 CE; they were little more than legends and oral memories by the time the first Europeans visited Hawaii. The chiefdoms expanded to encompass whole islands of the archipelago. War among the various island kingdoms was frequent, often involving taking captives for slaves or human sacrifices. The early Hawaiians adopted a caste system with each person born into a specific social class. The chiefs controlled all the land in a system that has many parallels with the feudal system of medieval Europe. A strict religious system, known as the *kapu*, held the society together, making traditions, lifestyles, work methods, laws, and social policy part of the religious system. In 1778, British explorer Capt. James Cook landed on Kaua'I, and then sailed to the south to explore the other islands of the archipelago. Captain Cook was later killed in a confrontation between the Europeans and the Hawaiians. The Hawaiian population, variously estimated to number between 200,000 and 1 million, declined rapidly due to European diseases, particularly smallpox.

The Hawaiian culture is a Polynesian culture that has been strongly influenced by modern American culture. Traditional Hawaiian philosophy does not consider the spiritual and physical aspects of the world to be separate, which offended the early Christian missionaries. Hawaiian culture was discouraged and sometimes banned completely by Calvinist missionaries active in the islands beginning in 1819. During the reign of King David Kalakaua I, between 1875 and 1887, a movement was encouraged that saved the culture, particularly such elements as the *hula* that had so offended the early missionaries. A second resurgence of the culture, known as the Second Hawaiian Renaissance, occurred between the 1960s and the 1980s, with a renewed sense of national pride among the Hawaiians. The Hawaiian language is a Polynesian language of the Marquesic language family. Nearly submerged by English in the early decades of the 20th century, the language is now taught in some schools and is one of the two official languages of the state of Hawaii. The majority of the Hawaiians are Christians, and they include both Protestants and Roman Catholics. In recent decades a resurgence of interest in the ancient religious beliefs of the islands, particularly *ho'oponopono*, a practice of reconciliation and forgiveness, often combined with prayer, have been blended into the Christian rituals.

After Cook's expedition and the publication of accounts of his voyage, the islands were visited by many other explorers and traders and eventually whalers, who found the islands to be a convenient and safe harbor and source of needed supplies. These visitors introduced diseases to the once-isolated Hawaiians. The population declined rapidly because the indigenous populations had no resistance to smallpox, influenza, measles, and other imported diseases. Using European weapons the islands were subjugated under a single ruler, King Kamehameha the Great, who established a dynasty that ruled until 1872. American missionaries converted many Hawaiians to Christianity in the 1820s and 1830s. Their influence ended many ancient cultural practices, including the *hula* and other cultural expressions found offensive by the Calvinists. Many of the missionaries stayed in the islands and became active in commercial and political affairs. Political unrest and succession conflicts led to the landing of American and British troops, who supported the House of Kalakaua. In 1887, King Kalakaua was forced to sign a constitution, which stripped the monarchy of much of its authority. The constitution included a property qualification for voting, which excluded most Hawaiians and the growing number of immigrant laborers and favored the wealthier Americans and Europeans. In 1893, the Euro-American commercial elite mobilized to overthrow the Hawaiian monarchy. The U.S. government, responding to a request by the group, sent a company of armed marines. The last monarch, Queen Lili'uokalani, was overthrown and replaced by a provisional government composed of businessmen and former missionaries. A Republic of Hawaii was proclaimed in 1894 over the protests of the Hawaiian population of the islands. Immigrants from Japan, Puerto Rico, the Philippines, Portugal, Korea, and other areas soon outnumbered the Hawaiians, who became the poorest segment of the population. American members of the republican government signed an annexation agreement with the U.S. government, and Hawaii became a U.S. territory despite the opposition of the Hawaiians. In the 1950s the power of the plantation owners and businessmen was finally broken by the descendants of the immigrant laborers who formed the largest part of the island population. Hawaii became a state of the United States in 1959 and quickly modernized as the rapidly growing tourist industry became the leading part of the economy. In the 1960s and 1970s, the Hawaiians, as the poorest and least advantaged of the state's population, began to mobilize. New programs promoted Hawaiian culture. In recent decades some of the benefits of federal assistance available to Native American peoples were extended to the Hawaiians. In 1993, U.S. president Bill Clinton signed the Apology Resolution, which apologized to the indigenous Hawaiians on behalf of the people of the United States for the illegal overthrow of the Kingdom of Hawaii. In the early 2000s, a bill that would have permitted the Hawaiians to form a government entity to negotiate with state and federal government agencies was obstructed and failed to pass. Some Hawaiians have become activists in a number of organizations seeking full independence or the legal restoration of the Hawaiian kingdom.

Further Reading

Kauanui, J. Khaulani. *Hawaiian Blood: Colonialism and the Politics of Sovereignty and Indigeneity.* Durham, NC: Duke University Press, 2008.

Silva, Noenoe K. *Aloha Betrayed: Native Hawaiian Resistance to American Colonialism.* NC: Duke University Press, 2004.

Young, Kanalu G. Terry. *Rethinking the Native American Past.* London: Routledge, 1998.

Hispanic Americans

The Hispanic Americans are Americans whose origins are in the Hispanic countries of Latin America and Spain; in general, they include all persons in the United States who self-identify as Latino or Hispanic. The estimated 55 million Hispanic Americans speak Spanish with the majority also speaking standard American English. Hispanic Americans encompass a very racially and culturally diverse group composed of dozens of subgroups reflecting their national origins. The majority of the Hispanic Americans are Roman Catholic, with a large and growing minority of Protestants, particularly the evangelical sects.

The first Spanish settlers in the territory of the present mainland United States came to St. Augustine, Florida, in 1565. Spanish settlers also founded settlements in New Mexico in 1598. Spanish settlements in New Mexico, Arizona, and California were founded from the late 17th century through the 18th century. In 1540 Hernando de Soto undertook an extensive expedition through the present southeast United States. In the same year, Francisco Vásquez de Coronado led an expedition of 2,000 Spaniards and Mexican Indians north as far as central Kansas. From 1528 to 1536, Álvar Núñez Cabeza de Vaca and three companions journeyed all the way from where they were shipwrecked in present-day Florida to the Gulf of California, 267 years before the legendary expedition of Lewis and Clark. The Spanish settlements remained small and often isolated from the larger Spanish populations of central Mexico and other colonies to the south.

Hispanic American culture is a mixture of the 28 sub-groups considered part of the Hispanic American population. The largest groups are of the Mexican-Americans, the Puerto Ricans, Cuban-Americans, Salvadorean-Americans, Dominican-Americans, Guatemalan-Americans, Colombian-Americans, Spanish-Americans, Honduran-Americans, Ecuadorian-Americans, Peruvian-Americans, and smaller numbers with roots in Nicaragua, Argentina, Venezuela, Panama, Chile, Costa Rica, Bolivia, Uruguay, Paraguay, and other parts of Latin America. Each of the sub-groups has a distinct culture mixing the Spanish elements with local indigenous cultures that have flourished in all parts of Latin America. Texas and California account for over half the total population of Hispanic Americans in the Unites States. Racially, 53 percent of the Hispanic Americans self-identify as being of European descent; 42 percent of them self-identify as being of mixed background, with smaller numbers of Hispanic Blacks, Hispanic Native Americans, and Hispanic Asians. The Spanish language is the main unifier, as it is spoken by most Hispanic Americans though younger generations usually grow up speaking English. The Roman Catholic religion, another heritage of Spanish colonialism, is an integral part of most Hispanic cultures though in recent decades evangelical Protestant groups have gained many converts.

In 1809 the first revolt against Spanish rule in the Americas quickly spread to all the Spanish colonies, which became independent nations with the exception of Cuba and Puerto Rico. From 1810 to 1848 the present-day Southwest formed part of the territory claimed by independent Mexico. The region developed very slowly largely because of the distance between the settlements and the capital at Mexico City. During the Mexican War, the United States gained the Southwest. In the Treaty of Guadalupe-Hidalgo the U.S. government promised to protect the rights of the Hispanic population in the newly won territories. The huge region was largely assimilated into the Anglo-American culture between 1849 and 1910. Huge tracts of land were taken from the Hispanic population by dubious legal means. Small Hispanic settlements grew quickly into American towns and cities. Around 1910 massive emigration from Mexico began, both legal and illegal, that continues to the present. Immigrants also began to arrive from other Latin American nations and from Spain. From 1910 to 1939 the Hispanics remained largely rural, unassimilated, poor, and Spanish-speaking. Partly due to the civil rights movement in the 1960s, Hispanic groups began to assert their distinct cultures and to demand rights as citizens of the United States. Many Hispanics immigrated to the United States seeking economic opportunities or to escape persecution and oppression in their homelands. Since 1940 the Hispanic population has shifted from a mostly rural to a mostly urban environment. Conflicts such as the Cuban Revolution, dictatorships in most Latin American countries, ongoing wars, a lack of economic advancement or educational opportunities, and abject poverty added to the growing number of immigrants between the 1960s and 1980s. Since the 1980s Hispanic Americans have prospered, often joining the large middle class, gaining higher education, and becoming notable members of the armed forces, the professions, sports, politics, and the entertainment industry.

Further Reading

Garcia, Jorge J. E. *Forging People: Race, Ethnicity, and Nationality in Hispanic American and Latino/a Thought.* Notre Dame, IN: University Press of Notre Dame, 2011.

Kanellos, Nicolas. *Chronology of Hispanic-American History: From Pre-Columbian Times to the Present.* Farmington Hills, MI: Gale Research, 1995.

Ollhoff, Jim. *Identity and Civil Rights.* Edina, MN: Abdo Publishing, 2011.

Ho-Chunks

The Ho-Chunks, sometimes known as Winnebagos, Hocaks, Hochungras, Hotcangaras, or Oochangras, are a North American ethnic group living in the states of Iowa, Nebraska, and Wisconsin. The estimated 12,000 Ho-Chunks speak English, with a small minority that is able to speak their traditional language, Hoc k. The majority of the Ho-Chunks are nominally Christian with a sizable minority that adheres to the Native American Church, also known as the Peyote Religion.

The oral history of the Ho-Chunks tells of their origins at the Red Banks on Green Bay in present-day Wisconsin. The Ho-Chunks' name for themselves, Ho-chungra, means "people of the parent speech," or "people of the big voice." The name Winnebago comes from a Fox name, "Ouinipegouek," meaning "people of the dirty or stinking water," referring to the algae-rich waters of the Fox River and Lake Winnebago. A French expedition led by Jean Nicolet entered Ho-Chunk territory in 1634. At that time the Ho-Chunks occupied lands in present-day Wisconsin, Iowa, South Dakota, Nebraska, and Illinois and had a population between 8,000 and 20,000. The French adopted the Fox name for the Ho-Chunks, which they translated as "stinking people," and shortened the name to Puants. In English their name became Stinkard or Stinky. In the 1640s the Beaver Wars, a conflict between the Iroquois tribes and the Algonquian peoples for control of the fur trade with the Europeans, sent a wave of Algonquian refugees into Ho-Chunk territory. The refugees from the Beaver Wars, one of the bloodiest conflicts in North American history, pushed several Ho-Chunk groups westward to become separate tribes. The resulting wars and the epidemics that accompanied the wars brought the Ho-Chunks to the point of extinction. In the process of rebuilding their society after 1670, many Ho-Chunks intermarried with their Algonquian neighbors, reinforcing the already strong Algonquian influences on their culture. When peace was finally reestablished in 1701, many of the Algonquian peoples returned to their homelands, relieving pressure on the Ho-Chunks. From a population of perhaps only 500 survivors, the tribal population gradually increased. By 1736 they had increased to some 700 and had regained much of their traditional territory in present-day Wisconsin. The Ho-Chunks fought against the British in the French and Indian Wars that ended in 1763 and later sided with the British against the American revolutionaries in 1775–1783.

The name given to the Ho-Chunks by the neighboring Algonquian-speaking peoples does not have the negative overtones of the later French and English translations of "stinky people." Traditional Ho-Chunk

Ho-Chunk (Winnebago) in a dance contest at Wisconsin Dells, WI, in 1956. (AP/Wide World Photos)

culture revolved around hunting, farming, and gathering. The sweat lodge, a purification ceremony, formed an important part of the early culture. Modern Ho-Chunk culture is a blend of traditional customs and American popular culture. Due to the forced relocations of the 19th century the Ho-Chunks are now divided into two geographic groups, the Ho-Chunks in Wisconsin and the Winnebagos in Nebraska. The two groups consider themselves one tribe culturally though the two tribes are politically independent. The language of the Ho-Chunks is English though some, mostly elders, also speak their traditional language. Most Ho-Chunks are nominally Christian with many adhering to the Native American Church.

In 1805, the Ho-Chunks joined the Shawnee Prophet, Tenskwatawa, and his brother, Tecumseh, in a widespread uprising against American settlement of their lands. This anti-American sentiment persisted and Ho-Chunk warriors fought alongside the British in the War of 1812. Forced to cede lands to the United States, many Ho-Chunks moved north of the Wisconsin River in the 1830s. A dubious treaty, signed in 1837, ceded all lands in Wisconsin and gave the Ho-Chunks just eight months to leave their ancestral homeland. Many refused and stayed in Wisconsin, others were forced to leave, first to Minnesota, then South Dakota, and finally to a government reservation in Nebraska in 1865. During 1873–1875 the state and federal authorities again attempted to force the Wisconsin Ho-Chunks to leave. Some 900 were rounded up and shipped to Nebraska, but within a year most had returned to Wisconsin. By the 1880s, the government decided to allow the Ho-Chunks to take up 40-acre farms and to remain in Wisconsin. Christian missionaries helped to build the first Ho-Chunk school in 1875 that was later expanded into a boarding school. In the late 1800s and early 1900s, the tribal members generally worked as migrant agricultural workers in the summers and hunted and trapped in the winters. Gatherings of Ho-Chunks from both Wisconsin and Nebraska for dances, ceremonies, and lacrosse games reinforced the shared culture of the two groups. The Peyote Religion, now called the Native American Church, first appeared in Nebraska and in 1908 was carried to the Ho-Chunks of Wisconsin. In the years that followed, many Ho-Chunks adopted the rituals. Religious differences created problems between the different Ho-Chunk groups for many years. New economic activities, including crafts and performances for the growing number of tourists in the region, greatly changed tribal life. Many Ho-Chunks settled at Wisconsin Dells and developed cultural performances and craft sales. In 1934, the reorganization of the Indian affairs by the federal government allowed the Wisconsin Ho-Chunks to gain recognition as a tribe. A territorial claims committee was formed in 1949 to press for claims to traditional territories. In 1994, the Ho-Chunks of Wisconsin officially changed their name from Winnebago to the traditional name, Ho-Chunk, or People of the Big Voice.

Further Reading

Hunter, Sally M. *Four Seasons of Corn: A Winnebago Tradition.* Minneapolis, MN: Lerner, 1996.

Loew, Patty. *Indian Nations of Wisconsin: Histories of Endurance and Renewal.* Madison, WI: Wisconsin Historical Society Press, 2001.

Radin, Paul. *The Winnebago Tribe.* Lincoln, NE: University of Nebraska Press, 1970.

Hondurans

The Hondurans, called Hondureños in Spanish and sometimes known as Catrachos, are a Central American people, the inhabitants of the nation of Honduras on the Caribbean coast south of the Yucatan Peninsula. The estimated 10 million Hondurans speak Spanish, with many Hondurans living in the United States and other countries speaking English or other languages. Most Hondurans are Roman Catholics with a small but growing number of Protestants.

The early inhabitants of the region formed part of the Maya civilization, particularly in the west where advanced city-states flourished for hundreds of years. In the early ninth century CE the lowland Maya culture collapsed, leaving scattered tribes living as farmers, hunters, and gatherers. Christopher Columbus, on his fourth and final voyage, visited the Honduran coast in 1502. A Spanish expedition moving south from Mexico began the conquest of the region in 1524. Most of the region came under Spanish rule and was added to the government established at Guatemala City. Silver was the reason for the conquest and settlement of Honduras. The mines, originally worked by the indigenous peoples and later by imported slaves, proved to be less productive than anticipated and the region was mostly ignored. The poor leadership of the colony provoked rebellions by the colonists and rebellions against the colonists by the abused and exploited indigenous peoples. Honduras was placed under the authority of the Spanish colonial government at Guatemala City, creating resentment among the colonists of the region. Mining declined rapidly after the first decades leading to a lessening of the importance of Honduras. On the east coast the Miskitos and some other indigenous peoples remained outside Spanish authority. The English from Jamaica formed close ties to the Miskitos, whose territory was declared a British protectorate in 1740. Attempts to assert Spanish control of the east coast led to several conflicts. An Anglo-Spanish agreement, signed in 1786, acknowledged Spanish control of the Caribbean coast though the Miskitos continued to maintain their independence of Spanish rule.

The Hondurans are often referred to as Catrachos and Catrachas, terms coined by the Nicaraguans in the mid-19th century. The word derives from the Honduran general Florencio Xatruch, who led the armed forces against an attempted invasion by American adventurer William Walker in 1857. The culture of the Hondurans is similar to the other Hispanic cultures of Central America, a complicated mixture of Spanish colonial and indigenous cultures with later influences including American and European popular cultures. The Honduran population is about 70 percent Mestizo (mixed background); 6–7 percent of the population is of Native American descent, about 2 percent is descended from African slaves, and about 1 percent is Caucasian, mostly of Spanish descent. Popular celebrations, referred to as *punta*, are events that draw large crowds. The celebrations include traditional dances and music that is particularly Honduran. Roman Catholic holidays are important to the culture, particularly the celebrations of Holy Week and Christmas. Most Hondurans are nominally Roman Catholic though the membership in the Church is declining as converts to Protestantism, particularly evangelical sects, are increasing rapidly. Many Hondurans attend Protestant services, particularly the Honduran diaspora in the United States, but retain their ties to the Catholic Church. The Spanish language, the official language of Honduras, is spoken by the majority of the Hondurans along with some indigenous languages and English in the Bay Islands off the northern coast.

Honduras gained independence from Spain in 1821 as part of Mexico. Separate independence was achieved in 1838. In the 1840s and 1850s, the Hondurans often supported attempts to restore the unity of Central America. The Hondurans eventually adopted a republican government but the idea of a Central American union continued and Hondurans were among the most ardent supporters of regional government. Most Hondurans remained poor, undereducated, and neglected with modernization taking place only among the small urbanized elite. International trade and investment, particularly in tropical fruits, brought modest prosperity in the 1870s. American fruit-growing companies developed the neglected northern coast in the late 19th century with banana plantations, railroads, and port installations. The prospect of steady employment brought many Hondurans to the north to work in the fruit economy. Political crises in the 1940s resulted in a gradual reform of labor laws, including the right to organize and join unions. The boom in the fruit industry drew in tens of thousands of immigrant Salvadoreans, which raised tensions in the 1960s. Following a three-round football elimination match as a preliminary to the Football World Cup in 1969, relations between the two countries rapidly deteriorated. The Salvadorean military invaded Honduran territory in what would become known as the Football War. A negotiated ceasefire ended hostilities after a week of fighting. In the wake of the Football War, some 130,000 Salvadoreans were expelled from Honduras. Hurricanes have periodically caused severe damage to the country's infrastructure adding to the reasons for the country being the poorest in Central America. Many Hondurans leave every year, mostly for the United States, seeking greater opportunities and a better life away from Honduras' chronic instability and poverty. In 2009 a new constitutional crisis led to a virtual coup d'etat, which was condemned by countries throughout the world. A general election eventually ended the crisis but the political and economic instability remain as major impediments to greater prosperity and opportunities for the Honduran people.

Further Reading

Leonard, Thomas M. *The History of Honduras.* Westport, CT: Greenwood, 2011.

Pine, Adrienne. *Working Hard, Drinking Hard: On Violence and Survival in Honduras.* Berkeley, CA: University of California Press, 2008.

Shields, Charles J. *Honduras.* Philadelphia, PA: Mason Crest Publishers, 2007.

Hopis

The Hopis are a North American ethnic group living mostly in the southwestern United States. The Hopi reservation is located in northeastern Arizona. Encompassing more than 1.5 million acres, it is made up of 12 historic villages on three flat mountains or mesas. The region, known as Hopituskwa, is mostly an arid table land but supports dry farming and herding. The estimated 14,000 Hopis are mostly bilingual, speaking English and their own language of the Uto-Aztecan language group. The majority of the Hopis believe themselves to be the caretakers of the earth. They perform traditional rituals and follow a set of religious laws in order to keep the world in balance. These laws and rituals are called the "Hopi Way."

The Hopis are believed to be descendants of the ancient Puebloan cultures of the region. The Puebloan peoples constructed large apartment house complexes in northeastern Arizona and northwestern New Mexico, especially from the 1100s to around 1400 CE. For reasons not fully understood by modern scholars, the Puebloan peoples abandoned their towns around the turn of the 16th century, probably due to the drying up of water sources. The Puebloans dispersed, becoming the Hopi and Zuni peoples. The Hopi town of Oraibi is one of the four original Hopi settlements, and one of the oldest continuously inhabited places within the United States. In the 1540s Oraibi was a sizable town of between 1500 and 3000 inhabitants. The first recorded contact with Europeans occurred in 1540 when a Spanish expedition explored the Hopi and Zuni territories. The Hopis welcomed the visitors and gave them information and directions for their journey. The early Spanish settlements in the region were well away from Hopi territory and visits by Spaniards were not frequent. The Spanish colonies were founded near the Rio Grande so Spanish troops were not garrisoned in Hopi territory, which did not have rivers that gave access to the Rio Grande region. Between 1519 and 1650 many previously flourishing Hopi pueblos were wiped out by European diseases or violence by the Spanish looking for treasure. In 1629, a group of 30 Spanish friars arrived in the Hopituskwa. A mission station and church were built but most Hopis resisted conversion to Roman Catholicism.

Thirteen-year-old American Indian Smiling Sun has his hair braided by Hopi tribeswomen before the hair-cutting ceremony as he enters manhood, March 9, 1955. (F. Roy Kemp/BIPs/Getty Images)

The Spanish persecuted the Hopis for their refusal to accept Christianity. Forced labor and confiscation of Hopi goods and products harmed formerly cordial relations. In 1680 the Pueblo people of the Rio Grande region rebelled against Spanish rule and most Hopis joined the rebellion in the first recorded alliance of indigenous peoples in the region. The Hopis attacked the Spanish and destroyed the Catholic Church and mission in their homeland. The rebellion destroyed Spanish control of the territory but by 1700 Spanish friars had begun to rebuild their church and mission. The Hopis moved their villages to the top of the impregnable mesas where the Spanish were unable to penetrate. Throughout the 18th century the Hopis remained in their high village strongholds nearly untouched by the world below.

The Hopi culture is based on the agricultural cycle, an important part of their society. They have always viewed their ancient territory as sacred land. The name Hopi is an abbreviated form of their name for themselves, Hopituh Shi-nu-mu, meaning "the peaceful people." The name Hopi now is considered to apply to anyone who adheres to the Hopi Way, a concept deeply rooted in the culture with its religious aspects, spirituality, and the Hopi view of morality and ethics. To be Hopi is to strive toward a state of total reverence and respect for all things, to be at peace with all things, and to live in accordance with the teachings of Maasaw, the creator or caretaker of the earth. Traditionally the Hopis are organized into important clans that are based on matrilineal inheritance. These important clans extend across the Hopi villages and are a key cultural element. Many Hopis continue to live in their traditional stone pueblos at the tops of the mesas though others now prefer the modern communities at the mesas' bases. The Hopi culture is very adaptable, allowing the Hopis to maintain their traditional ways while adopting elements of modern American culture. Traditional healing arts are used in conjunction with modern medicine. The Hopi language, a Uto-Aztecan language, is not related to any of the other Pueblo languages. Each of the three mesas of the Hopi homeland has its own dialect. Protected by their mesas in a relatively inaccessible region, the culture and language remain integral parts of modern Hopi society.

The Hopis often traded corn and other produce for meat and hides with the neighboring Navajos. Despite the trade links, the Navajos continued to expand their range seeking grazing lands for their herds of sheep. Conflicts between the two peoples often ended in violence. The advance of the Americans into the region following the Mexican-American War in 1846–1848 brought the Hopis under the Bureau of Indian Affairs, which established a presence at Santa Fe, New Mexico. In 1850 four Hopi leaders traveled to Santa Fe seeking protection against the marauding Navajos. The American authorities established Fort Defiance in Arizona in 1851 to deal with Navajo threats to the Hopi farmers. Mormons, having created a Mormon colony to the north in 1847, sent missionaries to the region in 1858. The early Mormons were on good terms with the Hopis. In 1875 the first Latter-day Saints Church was built in Hopi territory. Modernization, including the first schools, gradually came to the Hopis in the last decades of the 19th century. A Hopi reservation was established in 1882, a territory surrounded by the Navajo reserved lands. During the 1880s, the U.S. government divided up the Native American peoples between religious groups. The Hopis were assigned to the Mennonites and the Baptists. A Mennonite minister, Rev. H. R. Voth, arrived in 1893. He immediately attempted to destroy the Hopi Way and to replace it with Mennonite Christianity. The Hopis despised the minister, who was eventually removed, and still recount with horror about both Voth and what he attempted to do. The Native American peoples were declared American citizens in 1924, giving them greater rights and privileges. From the 1940s to the 1970s, the neighboring Navajos continued to move their villages closer and closer to Hopi lands. The Hopis raised the land issue with the state and federal authorities but attempts to set up joint-use areas or to delimit the boundaries of the two reservations failed. The land and water disputes continue to the present. The Hopis now earn most of their income from natural resources, tourism, and farming. Many younger Hopis leave the area to attend colleges and universities but often return to add their new knowledge to the good of the Hopi people.

Further Reading

Clemmer, Richard O. *Roads in the Sky: The Hopi Indians in a Century of Change.* Boulder, CO: Westview Press, 1995.

Koyiyumptewa, Stewart B. *The Hopi People.* Mt. Pleasant, SC: Arcadia Publishing, 2009.

Page, Jake and Susanne Page. *Hopi.* Tucson, AZ: Rio Nuevo Publishing, 2007.

Huastecs

The Huastecs, sometimes known as Téeneks, Huaxtecs, Wasteks, Wastekos, or Huastecos, are a North American ethnic group concentrated along the Pánuco River and the coastal regions on the Gulf of Mexico in the historic region of La Huasteca, now forming parts of the Mexican states of San Luis Potosí, Veracruz, Tamaulipas, and Hidalgo. The estimated 180,000 Huastecs speak Spanish and their own language, known as Téenek or Wastek, a language belonging to the Mayan language family. Most of the Huastecs are nominally Roman Catholic, with many blending pre-Christian traditions and customs with their Catholic rituals.

The Huastecs are thought to have migrated north from the Mayan heartland in Guatemala around 2200 BCE. The other Mayan peoples later retreated south and east as other peoples expanded their territories, leaving the Huastecs as the most northerly of the Mayan-related peoples. The early Huastecs created an advanced civilization based on agriculture and fishing. Between 750 CE and 800 CE the Huastecs became the dominant people in the region, expanding their authority west to the Sierra Madre Oriental and along the coast. The Huastecs built small cities and ceremonial centers, but they never reached the size or complexity of others in ancient Mexico. The armies of the Aztec empire began to take Huastec territories in the south and west, and in 1458 the Aztecs took control of an important territory known as Chicoaque or Tzicoac. The first Huastec contact with Europeans was in 1518, when Spanish ships explored the Gulf of Mexico coast and entered the Pánuco River. The Spanish, taking advantage of the war between the Huastecs and the Aztecs, quickly took control of much of the region they called La Huasteca. Reportedly the conquerors burned alive some 460 Huastec nobles and chiefs while hunting treasure in the region. Over 20,000 Huastecs were captured and sold as slaves in the Antilles. European diseases and war decimated the Huastec population. Many fled south from Tamaulipas to the less accessible areas of Veracruz and San Luis Potosí. The introduction of cattle ranching forced many Huastecs from their traditional farmlands. Other indigenous peoples were imported to work the large ranches and by the late 18th century a large mestizo population occupied much of the former Huastec lands along the gulf coast. Spanish abuses, including high taxes, debt serfdom, and land confiscations, resulted in serious Huastec uprisings in 1750 and 1784.

Huastec culture has remained distinct due to the difficult communications with the outside world. Despite over 4,000 years of separation, the Huastecs have maintained their Mayan cultural beliefs and patterns. The Huastecs refer to themselves as Teenek, meaning "the laughing people." The name Huastec or Wastek derives from the Nahuatl name given to them by the Aztec invaders. The Huastec homeland now forms only a part of their traditional homeland, which is currently populated by a number of distinct ethnic groups. Many of the Huastecs continue as farmers or ranchers and are known as rancheros. Since 1970, the Huastec population has nearly doubled though the number of people reported as monolingual has remained the same. At present an estimated 10 percent of the Huastecs are unable to speak Spanish fluently. The Huastec language remains the primary language of the society with most also speaking Spanish as a second language. The language forms the fifth largest Mayan language in Mexico, but is the most linguistically isolated. Huastec culture values stories and storytellers and there are many well-known storytellers throughout the region. Almost all Huastecs are nominally Roman Catholic, though some are quite anticlerical while others are devout. Pre-Christian ceremonies and celebrations remain an important part of the distinctive Huastec culture.

Large cattle ranches dominated the region in the early 1800s. Coffee was introduced to the inland mountainous regions giving the Huastec highlanders a new commercial agricultural product. Land and agrarian conflicts continued throughout the 19th century, with local elections often based on land use issues. The discovery of oil in the northern districts of Veracruz resulted in serious environmental damage that made subsistence farming impossible in some areas. In the early 20th century the development of roads and railroads began to connect the Huastecs to the rest of the world. The roads allowed for seasonal or permanent emigration of younger Huastecs looking for work. Schools were established in the larger towns and villages, raising literacy rates and spreading the Spanish language to the isolated Huastec communities. Despite the name of the large region known as La Huasteca, in the early 21st century the Huastecs only occupy a fraction of their former homeland. Most Huastecs live on a wide strip of land stretching from northwest Querétaro east into northern Veracruz on the Gulf of Mexico. The largest Huastec communities are located in the highland areas of Veracruz and San Luis Potosí.

Further Reading

Coe, Michael D. *Mexico: From the Olmecs to the Aztecs.* London: Thames & Hudson, 1994.

De Vidas, Anath Ariel. *Thunder Doesn't Live Here Anymore: The Culture of Marginality among the Teeneks of Tanoyuca.* Boulder, CO: University Press of Colorado, 2004.

Leon-Portilla, Miguel. *The Broken Spears: The Aztec Account of the Conquest of Mexico.* Boston, MA: Beacon Press, 2006.

Huaves

The Huaves, sometimes known as Huavis, Huabis, Guabis, Wabis, Wabes, Ikoots, Kunajts, or Mareños, are a North American ethnic group inhabiting the Pacific coast of the Isthmus of Tehuantepec in the southern Mexican state of Oaxaca. The estimated 17,000 Huaves speak their own language, also known as Huave, which is considered a language unrelated to any other regional language. Spanish is often spoken as a second language. The Huaves are nominally

Roman Catholic, but most do not practice their doctrinal beliefs as more emphasis is given to worshiping their ancestors, often as altars in Huave homes.

The Huaves are thought to have settled their present homeland some 3000 years ago, possibly having originated farther south in Central America. The region, made up of inland thorn forests teeming with wildlife, savanna lands used for pasture and farming, and mangrove swamps along the coast that supplied fish allowed the Huaves to prosper with a surplus of products for trade with other indigenous peoples. Around 1000 BCE Zapotec peoples began migrating into the region from the north. While they never displaced the Huaves completely they took much of the best farm lands and became the predominant ethnic group in the region. They built important cities and ceremonial centers often using forced labor from the subject peoples. The Spanish entered the region in the 16th century and quickly conquered the Zapotecs and other indigenous peoples. The Huaves joined the Zapotec and Spanish trading system in the 17th century, trading their fish, produce, and animal products for iron tools and other goods. Roman Catholic missionaries came to the Huave villages in the mid-17th century but the Huave converts continued to revere the spirits of their ancestors, often at altars hidden in their homes. Even under Spanish rule the Huaves continued to lose large portions of their traditional lands to the more numerous Zapotecs and the large Mestizo population of mixed Spanish and Zapotec ancestry.

The Huave culture is a mostly peasant culture based on five important villages and dozens of hamlets in southern Oaxaca. Ancient trade patterns continue with the Huaves trading marine products, fish, agricultural produce, and textiles with their inland neighbors. The Huave culture is a patrilineal society with inheritance through the father's family. The extended family is an important part of the culture with kinship an important part of every village. The Huave language is not related to the neighboring languages and is spoken in five main dialects, each associated with one of the five major villages. The language has been significantly altered with borrowings from Spanish. Religious activity is often considered a household matter. Many rituals are conducted directly by the head of the household at the home altar. There are also Roman Catholic chapels and periodic visits by missionaries and priests.

In the early 19th century the Huaves had been forced to relinquish most of their ancestral lands and to settle in five large villages and a number of smaller settlements. They continued to live by hunting, grazing their herds on communal pastures, and farming. Land encroachments by large landowners, neighboring Zapotec and Mestizo communities, and large companies continued into the early 20th century. The land losses were legalized following the Mexican Revolution. Occupying a small strip of territory just east of the city of Tehuantepec, the Huaves were introduced to a modern market economy on which they based their production of commercial wares and services. Tourism began in the region in the 1960s bringing needed income and employment. The Huaves, in the 21st century, continue to live much as their ancestors did with the traditional occupations of hunting, fishing, and farming occupying most of their population. Seasonal work on nearby farms or in the tourist industry also helps to sustain the local economy.

Further Reading

Blanton, Richard, Gary M. Feinman, Stephen A. Kowalewski, and Linda M. Nicholas. *Ancient Oaxaca.* Cambridge: Cambridge University Press, 1999.

Campbell, Howard. *Mexican Memoir: A Personal Account of Anthropology and Social Politics in Oaxaca.* Westport, CT: Praeger, 2001.

Yannakakis, Yanna. *The Art of Being In-between: Native Intermediaries, Indian Identity, and Local Rule in Colonial Oaxaca.* Durham, NC: Duke University Press, 2008.

Huichols

The Huichols, sometimes known as Wixáritaris, are a North American ethnic group living in the highlands of the Sierra Madre Occidental Mountains in the Mexican states of Nayarit, Jalisco, Zacatecas, and Durango. The estimated 30,000 Huichols speak their own language, which belongs to the Uto-Aztecan language family, with many also speaking Spanish as a second language. Though the Huichols are nominally Roman Catholic, the majority continue to revere their pre-Christian deities and the shamans who interpret the signs of nature and attend to most Huichol medical needs.

Historically the Huichols are believed to have been divided into four or five tribal groups, each with distinct regional traditions. Little is known about the origins of the Huichols and several theories have been proposed. Some scholars believe they migrated to the rugged highlands to escape incursions by the Aztecs of central Mexico. Because of the rugged terrain and the physical resistance of the Huichol warriors, they held out against direct Spanish subjugation until the 1720s. By the time they came under direct Spanish rule the Huichols had lost much of their territory and population due to the wars and European diseases. Franciscan missionaries set up centers in the region that became outposts of Spanish authority. The Huichols were allowed to retain their own tribal government and were exempt from paying tribute.

The Huichol culture retains many of the traditions and customs of the precolonial era while absorbing much of the modern Mexican culture. Peyote is an important part of many religious rituals and forms a part of the traditional culture. Many Huichols spend significant parts of their lives working in the region's tobacco fields, which has been disastrous for the health of the tribesmen. Owners of the large tobacco plantations are no longer allowed to use pesticides too toxic for use in countries where they are manufactured. Living in the mountains around the coastal resorts on the Pacific coast has given the Huichols a market for their arts and crafts. Many Huichols work in the tourist towns during the season but when the rains come they return to their farms known as ranchos. Extended families usually live together in rancho settlements. Each settlement has a communal kitchen and a family shrine, which is dedicated to the ancestors of the rancho. Most of the Huichols retain their traditional belief system that honors the spirits of all living things and holds their departed ancestors in great reverence.

Intensive Roman Catholic missionary influence declined in the Sierra Madre region after Mexican independence in 1821. By 1860 virtually all priests and missionaries had left the Huichol region because of increasing tensions over land rights. Mexican independence also annulled the Spanish-chartered indigenous communities in the mountains, which were consequently opened to Mestizo colonists and ranchers. The Huichols, joined by the neighboring Coras, rebelled in a 10-year conflict under the leadership of Lozada. The rebels attempted to protect their ancestral lands from further encroachments by outsiders. Until the arrival of anthropological expeditions at the end of the 19th century little was known about the Huichols or their culture. The Mexican Revolution began in the early 20th century and by 1913 violence had spilled into the Huichol region. The large Mestizo population that had been attempting to take Huichol lands mostly sided with Pancho Villa. So the Huichols supported their chief, General Mesquite, who allied to the rival group. Mezquite and his Huichol warriors were successful in driving the Mestizos from their territory but their victory was short-lived. The Mestizos later returned to take lands for farming and herding. In the 1950s the Catholic Church began to make inroads among the Huichols and in the 1960s government schemes began to integrate the Huichols into the modern Mexican culture. Airstrips and roads connected the isolated Huichol communities to the outside world. In the 21st century projects have focused on improving cattle and livestock in the Huichol communities. Medical clinics and schools have been built, often run by bilingual Huichol doctors and teachers.

Further Reading

Furst, Peter T. *Rock Crystals & Peyote Dreams: Explorations in the Huichol Universe.* Salt Lake City, UT: University of Utah Press, 2006.

Liffman, Paul M. *Huichol Territory and the Mexican Nation: Indigenous Ritual, Land Conflict, and Sovereignty Claims.* Tucson, AZ: University of Arizona Press, 2011.

Schaefer, Stacy B. and Peter T. Furst, eds. *People of the Peyote: Huichol Indian History, Religion, and Survival.* Albuquerque, NM: University of New Mexico Press, 1997.

I

Ingas

The Ingas, sometimes known as Highland Ingas, are a South American ethnic group living in the Putumayo region of southwestern Colombia. Outside their homeland there is a small Inga community in Bogota, the Colombian capital. The estimated 26,000 Ingas speak a Quechua language known as Inga Kichwa, being part of the large population speaking Quechua languages in the northern Andean region of South America. The majority of the Ingas are Roman Catholics with small numbers of Protestant evangelicals; about a third of the population adheres to their traditional belief system.

The early Ingas inhabited a larger territory than the one being inhabited by the present-day Ingas, a homeland that encompassed the territories around the Putumayo and Japurá rivers. In the 14th century their territory was invaded by the Incas coming north from Peru. Forcibly incorporated into the Incas' vast empire, the Ingas were made to give annual tribute, often consisting of slaves or treasure. In the early 16th century Spanish explorers came into contact with the Ingas. The overthrow of the Incas freed the Ingas but Spanish authority was soon established. European diseases, slavers, and abuses decimated the population. The Quechua language spoken in Peru and other territories to the south was apparently introduced to the Ingas by the Spanish and their Quechua allies. The language gradually replaced the earlier Inga dialect. Roman Catholic missionaries and priests came to the Inga territory in the early 18th century. Many Ingas accepted the new religion but quietly retained their former belief system as well.

Despite their distance from the Quechua heartland to the south, the Ingas have numerous cultural characteristics brought to the region by early Quechua travelers. Traditionally Inga identity is local and often linked with the local economic system, farming in the lower altitudes and pastoral farming in the highlands. Many Inga communities extend over several altitude ranges and include a variety of agricultural products and livestock. The land is usually owned by the local community and is either worked jointly or redistributed annually. The Inga language, known as Inga Kichwa, is one of the Quechua languages and is spoken in two distinct dialects—Highland Inga and Jungle Inga. Most of the Ingas are nominally Roman Catholic, but usually blend their rituals and traditions with their pre-Christian rituals.

The struggle for land rights continued to mark Inga society in the 19th century. Encroachments by large landowners and foreign agricultural firms forced many Ingas off their traditional lands. In the mid-20th century the Ingas began to mobilize. Led by activists the Ingas sent petitions, marched in demonstrations, and sometimes occupied their former lands. Some of the lowland Inga territory was taken for government petroleum extraction in the last decades of the century. The spread of the Spanish language began with the construction of schools in the region. By the early 21st century the majority of the Ingas were bilingual and many younger Ingas spoke only Spanish. The predominance of the Spanish language has alarmed many Ingas who fear the extinction of their own Kichwa language.

Further Reading

Rappaport, Joanne. *Intercultural Utopias: Public Intellectuals, Cultural Experimentation, and Ethnic Pluralism in Colombia.* Durham, NC: Duke University Press, 2005.

Reichel-Dolmatoff, Gerardo. *Indians of Colombia: Experience and Cognition.* Bogota, Colombia: Villegas Editores, 1991.

Ulloa, Astrid. *The Ecological Native.* London: Routledge, 2010.

Innus

The Innus, sometimes known as Naskapis or Montagnais-Naskapis, are a North American ethnic group inhabiting parts of the Labrador Peninsula of Newfoundland and eastern Quebec in eastern Canada. The Innu homeland, partitioned by colonial borders, is known as Nitassinan. The estimated 30,000 Innus include the three closely related tribes known as the Montagnais, the Naskapi, and the East Main Crees. The Innus usually speak French or English with many, particularly the elders, also speaking the Innu-aimun language, which forms part of the Cree-Montagnais-Naskapi dialect continuum.

According to Innu oral history, the three peoples formed a powerful federation that controlled a vast territory further to the south. Often at war with the Iroquois, the Innu peoples were forced to flee north about 2,000 years ago. They gradually adapted themselves to the woodlands and the harsh climate of their new homeland. The Innus had little tribal organization beyond semi-nomadic bands made up of extended families. The Innus learned to use every resource, including the products of their large herds of caribou. European expeditions visited the coast in the late 15th century, with English, Spanish, and French explorers mapping the coastal regions. Henry Hudson and his English expedition sailed into the huge bay that now bears his name in 1610–1611. His expedition proved to be the first contact with Europeans for the Innus. Samuel Champlain met a group of Innus at the mouth of the Saguenay River, far to the southeast. The French explorers called the Innu bands the Montagnais, meaning "mountaineers." The French fur trade brought many Innus to settle near the St. Lawrence River in the early 17th century. Roman Catholic missionaries entered Innu territory as early as 1615, bringing Christianity and European contacts with the southern bands. The French and the British established huge territorial claims and entered into treaty relations with the various Innu bands as rivalry for the North American territories grew. Smallpox, brought by the Europeans, decimated the Innu bands in the 18th century. Frequent conflicts between the French and the British finally ended with the French defeat in the French and Indian War in 1763, bringing all the Innus under nominal British rule.

INDIAN CESSION OF LANDS IN THE UNITED STATES

Indian Cessions
By 1784
By 1810
By 1835
By 1868
By 1890

ATLANTIC OCEAN

PACIFIC OCEAN

Gulf of Mexico

Caribbean Sea

Native American territories ceded to or incorporated into the United States in the 18th and 19th centuries. (ABC-CLIO)

The Innu culture is a composite culture encompassing the three divisions, the Montagnais, the Naskapis, and the East Main Crees, also known as Atikemeks. The three groups, speaking related dialects of the same language, share a common culture. Geographic divisions and their respective adaptations to different environments determine their affiliations. Poor soil and a short growing season gave the Innus a traditional culture of hunters and gatherers. The history of colonial interference in their lives severely demoralized the Innus, who now have the world's highest suicide rate and very high levels of drug abuse and alcoholism. The Innus speak dialects of an Algonquin language with three major dialects that correspond to the three tribal divisions. French and English are used by different bands depending on their geographic location. In the late 20th century an Innu dictionary was published, along with other works on the grammar and structure of the language. The majority of the Innus are Roman Catholics, but historically there is no clear separation between Innu spirituality and tribal society. Even today tribal elders are generally respected, both as the civic leaders and the spiritual leaders of the Innu communities.

The booming fur trade occupied the Innus during the early 19th century. Beaver hats gave way to silk during the 1830s, finally ending the traditional fur trade that had sustained the Innus for two centuries. Lumber companies moved into Innu territories in the latter half of the 19th century, bringing many non-Innu settlers. The newcomers took much of the more fertile land while exposing the Innus to constant epidemics against which they had no immunity. By the late 19th century the Innus had declined to just 2,000 people. Colonial borders left the Innus divided between the English-speaking Labrador and the French-speaking Quebec. The Innus refused to recognize the partition of their homeland but colonial governments simply took possession of their tribal lands and parceled them out to mining and forestry companies. After World War II, the Canadian government forced the seminomadic Innus to settle in permanent communities. In the 1980s, activists began to work for cultural and linguistic rights and to press for the resolution of long-standing land claims. In the late 20th century and the early 21st century, the Innus have put forward demands for more self-government, control over the natural resources in their territory, and the right to restrict environmentally damaging construction projects.

Further Reading

Cohn, Ronald and Jesse Russell. *Innu People.* Paris: VSD Publications, 2012.

Samson, Colin. *A Way of Life that Does Not Exist: Canada and the Extinguishment of the Innu.* New York: Verso Books, 2003.

Wadden, Marie. *Nitassinan: The Innu Struggle to Reclaim Their Homeland.* Vancouver, BC: Douglas & McIntyre, 1991.

Inuits

The Inuits are an Arctic ethnic group inhabiting the Arctic regions of Canada, Alaska, and northern Greenland. Other small Inuit communities are found in northern Siberia in Russia. The estimated 100,000 Inuits speak languages belonging to the Eskimo-Aleut language family. The majority of the Inuits are nominally Christian, primarily Anglican or Roman Catholic, though traditional beliefs are still revered.

Nunavut

The territory of Nunavut is the self-governing Inuit homeland in northern Canada. The territory, with a population of about 32,000, encompasses most of the Canadian Arctic region, a vast expanse nearly four times larger than France. Activists first put forward a plan for an autonomous Inuit homeland in Canada in the 1970s. The inhabitants of Canada's Northwest Territories voted in 1982 to divide the region to accommodate a new Inuit homeland. Negotiations often stalled over the desire of other Inuit groups in northern Labrador and Quebec for inclusion, but in 1989 the Nunavut settlement was finally adopted. The agreement gave the Inuits considerable control over mineral development and set aside special tracts for traditional activities such as hunting and trapping. In 1999, Nunavut officially became an autonomous Inuit state within Canada.

The ancient ancestors of the Inuit peoples are believed to have crossed into the North American continent from Asia some 4,000 years ago. The migrants used the now-disappeared land bridge across the Bering Strait between Alaska and Siberia. The Inuits and the Aleuts separated around 2000 BCE when the Aleuts moved to the south while the Inuits spread across a vast territory above the Arctic Circle. The migrants adjusted to the frozen lands north of the tree line in an adaptation unequaled by any other northern ethnic group. The ancestor group, known as the Thule Inuits, migrated across the Arctic lands of North America between 1000 CE and 1400 CE, with groups leaving the main migration to settle in present-day Alaska, northern Canada, the Canadian Arctic islands, and Greenland. The Inuit descent from this one migration gives the modern Inuits a surprising uniformity of language and culture. The Inuits, unaware that other peoples existed except for some sub-Arctic peoples with whom they carried on a lively trade, were astounded when Europeans first began exploring their homeland in the 16th century. Most of the Inuit bands encountered Europeans for the first time only in the 1770s, when British, Russian, and Spanish expeditions explored the Arctic regions. The arrival of Christian missionaries in the late 18th century began a gradual conversion to various Christian sects.

The Inuit culture is based on their traditional occupations, hunting and fishing. They were formerly known as Eskimos, a name derived from the Algonquin language and adopted by the early European explorers to denote any of the Arctic peoples. The name Eskimo is now considered derogatory and all bands now call themselves Inuit, simply meaning "the people." Traditional Inuit culture was completely adapted to the harsh climate with fish and sea mammals as the major food sources. Modern Inuit culture has again adapted to adopt a wider range of foods, including vegetables that were formerly unknown, while snowmobiles have replaced dog sleds and rifles have replaced harpoons for hunting. Modern houses have replaced the traditional igloos and imported tools are now used instead of items made of animal hides, driftwood, or bone. Most Inuits now speak English in Canada and the United States, Danish in Greenland, and Russian in Siberia, though a sizable minority continues to use their traditional Inuit dialects. The Inuit dialects are closely related but are not always mutually comprehensible, though they form a language continuum from coastal Siberia to northern Greenland. The Inuits are largely Christian, the result of early missionary activity in the Arctic region, but since the 1970s and 1980s there has been a revival of traditional customs and rituals that form part of the Inuit cultural revival. In Greenland the Inuits are mostly found in the northern districts while the Greenlanders, though related to the Inuits, are of mostly mixed ancestry and consider themselves a separate ethnic group.

The Inuit communities were known to missionaries and explorers but were mostly ignored by the governments that controlled their home territories. Many Inuits remained isolated from modern culture until after World War I. The decline of traditions such as infanticide and blood feuds resulted in a steady population increase in the 1920s and 1930s. The Inuit lifestyle changed very little until the

1950s, when paternalistic government agencies began to move the Inuits into planned housing projects with schools and health facilities. Though the change from a nomadic or seminomadic way of life was accepted many of the ills of modern society accompanied the change. Alcohol abuse, the breakup of traditional family units, and poverty became serious social problems. Activists demanding redress of old abuses began to mobilize the Inuits in the 1960s and 1970s. In Canada the Inuits won a long battle to gain control of their ancient homeland when the new territory of Nunavut was officially recognized in 1999. Inuits from around the Arctic Circle now gather for annual conferences to discuss common problems and share experiences and solutions.

Further Reading

Burgan, Michael. *Inuit.* Milwaukee, WN: Gareth Stevens, 2004.

Fleischner, Jennifer. *The Inuit: People of the Arctic.* Minneapolis, MN: Millbrook Press, 1995.

Lassieur, Allison. *The Inuit.* Mankato, MN: Bridgestone Books, 2000.

Iroquois

The Iroquois, sometimes known as Haudenosaunee or Hodinoshones, are a North American ethnic group comprising six sovereign nations—Mohawks, Oneidas, Cayugas, Onondagas, Senecas, and Tuscaroras. The estimated 170,000 Iroquois inhabit parts of their historic homeland in upstate New York, with smaller groups in Wisconsin, Oklahoma, and North Carolina in the United States, and southern Quebec and southern Ontario in Canada. The total population, including people of Iroquois descent and people of mixed ancestry who identify with Iroquois culture, may be as high as 500,000. The Iroquois generally speak English or French along with their own six languages. The majority of the Iroquois adhere to their own Longhouse religion, a Quaker-influenced belief system that spread through the region in the 19th century. Smaller numbers belong to Protestant and Roman Catholic churches.

The Iroquois bands are thought to have originated in the central part of present-day New York state. They created a settled culture in the region some 1,000 years ago. Agriculture allowed a culture to adopt a new form of society, with a stratified caste system, sophisticated artisans, a powerful military, and large, fortified towns. The various tribes, often warring among themselves, began to unite sometime between 1350 CE and 1600 CE. Some scholars believe that unification was achieved over a thousand years earlier, though the general consensus places the formation of the confederacy around 1570. The confederacy became the most sophisticated and powerful entity north of central Mexico. The united Iroquois extended their political power over a huge area stretching from eastern Canada south to the Carolinas. The first contacts with Europeans occurred in the region of the Great Lakes when French expeditions entered the region. The French supported the fur trade and became the allies of the Iroquois' enemies, the Hurons. The arrival of the Dutch in 1610 provided the Iroquois a rival source of firearms with which to counter the French threat.

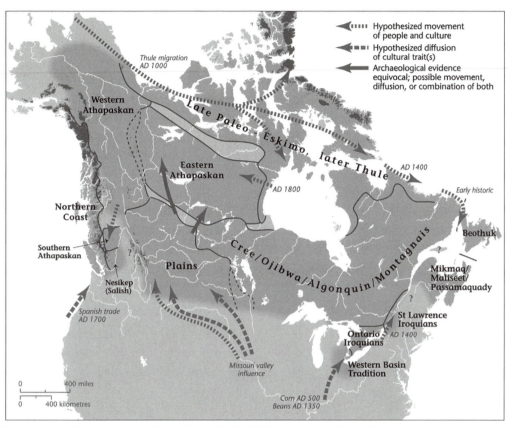

Movements of peoples and cultures in pre-Colonial Canada according to theories put forward by historians and anthropologists. (Eric Leinberger)

The Iroquois destroyed the Huron confederacy in 1648–1650, and then began a decade of raids on French settlements in New France. The Iroquois' inland location protected them from the first epidemics of European diseases but by the mid-17th century diseases and war had greatly depleted the Iroquois population. The depletion of the local beaver population resulted in the so-called Beaver Wars that lasted some 70 years as the Iroquois waged war against ever more distant tribes to procure the furs they traded to the Dutch and English for iron goods and guns. The confederacy, strengthened by the addition of the Tuscaroras in 1772, played a vital role in the British victory in the French and Indian War in 1763. The outbreak of the American Revolution nearly destroyed the historic confederacy. Four of the tribes eventually supported their traditional British allies while the Oneidas and Tuscaroras mostly aided the Americans. Oneida chief Shenendoah (Oskanondonha) brought 3,000 bushels of white corn to Valley Forge and even provided an instructor to show the starving American troops how to prepare it. Following the end of the war in 1781, many Iroquois joined the Loyalists moving north into British Canada.

The Great Peacemaker

The Iroquois Confederacy was formed through the efforts of Dekanawida or Dega-nawida, known as the Great Peacemaker, and Hiawatha, a leader of the Onondagas or Mohawks. Dekanawida was a prophet who counseled peace among the warring tribes, particularly the closely related tribes that now form Haudenosaunee or the People of the Longhouse. With Hiawatha, his first convert, Dekanawida gathered together leaders of the five tribes that shared a common culture and closely related languages to bring peace to the region. He planted a white pine, the Tree of Peace, under which the tribal leaders buried their weapons of war. The Tuscarora joined the confederacy later to become the sixth Iroquois tribe. The Great Peacemaker's original instructions formed the basis of an oral constitution, the Great Law of Peace, which is still honored by the Iroquois. Benjamin Franklin is believed to have modeled parts of the new American constitution on the Iroquois' Great Law of Peace.

The Iroquois culture is a mixture of traditions and customs contributed by each of the six member tribes. Calling themselves Haudenosaunee, the "People of the Longhouse," the Iroquois have blended and adopted cultural patterns common to all the Iroquoian peoples and the modern Iroquois are united by historical, clan, and family ties that cut across the tribal divisions. Each of the six tribes traditionally occupied a distinct geographical and political position within the confederacy. The Mohawks (Kahniankehaka) are known as the "keepers of the eastern door," because their territory occupied the eastern part of the confederacy. The Cayugas (Gweugwe-hono) are called the "keepers of the Great Pipe," the symbol of peace. The Oneidas (Onayotekaono) are known as the "stone people." The Onondagas (Onundagaono) are called the "keepers of the fire." The Senecas (Nundawaono) are the "keepers of the western door." The Tuscaroras (Akotaskororen) joined the confederacy as a nonvoting member in 1722. The Iroquois

were historically a matrilineal society, with women owning all property and inheritance through the female line. The modern Iroquois have mostly adopted modern culture with most living and working in large cities or in communities near the reservations. Most of the Iroquois are bilingual, speaking English or French along with their own languages that form part of the Hokan-Siouan language group.

The confederacy effectively disintegrated around 1800. The tribes, in spite of numerous treaties insuring their traditional lands, gradually lost territory and were forced into ever-dwindling reservations in the United States and Canada. The Iroquois, desiring peace with their white neighbors, adopted a pacific religion known as the Longhouse religion or creed in the early 19th century. Begun by a Seneca prophet and believed to have roots in Quaker ideals of pacificism, the new religion quickly spread through the scattered remnants of the confederacy. The Iroquois gradually adapted to North American

Iroquois in traditional dress in Quebec, 1940. (AP/Wide World Photos)

culture and many pursued education as a way for their people to survive. The sizable urban populations in New York City, Buffalo, and Montreal began to form in 1896 when Iroquois workers showed no fear of heights and rapidly became involved in the construction of major bridges and skyscrapers. Increased education renewed an appreciation for their unique history and culture. By the 1960s militants, mostly led by young Iroquois lawyers, put forward land claims and demands for sovereignty. Taking the position that the confederacy predated the United States and Canada the Iroquois filed numerous court cases in an attempt to force the governments to honor the treaties made between sovereign political entities. Iroquois representatives presented a petition to the United Nations in 1977 seeking official recognition of Iroquois sovereignty. Passports issued by the government of Haudenosaunee have been honored by dozens of countries. The confederacy, though physically dispersed, still holds a special place as a concept in Iroquois culture. It has been responsible for the Iroquois being able to retain much of their traditional culture in spite of modernization and acculturation.

Further Reading

Engler, Mary. *The Iroquois: The Six Nations Confederacy*. Mankato, MN: Capstone Press, 2006.

Graymont, Barbara. *The Iroquois*. New York: Chelsea House, 2005.

Snow, Dean. *The Iroquois*. Hoboken, NJ: Wiley-Blackwell, 1996.

J

Jamaicans

The Jamaicans are a Caribbean ethnic group living in the island nation of Jamaica in the Greater Antilles. There are also sizable Jamaican communities in the United Kingdom, the United States, Canada, Cuba, and Belize. The estimated 4.5 million Jamaicans speak English, the official language of the country, but in daily life they speak a language of mixed English and African origins known as Jamaican Patois. Most of the Jamaicans are Christian, divided into a number of different sects. Smaller groups adhere to the Rastafarian movement or to other non-Christian religions.

The island was home to indigenous Tainos who migrated to the island from South America between 4000 BCE and 1000 BCE. The island was split between some 200 small chiefdoms when Christopher Columbus visited in 1494. Columbus claimed the island for Spain and Spanish settlers began to colonize in the early 1500s. The Tainos were decimated by European diseases and the forced labor imposed by the Spanish, though a few Tainos survived when the English took control. The European wars were often mirrored in the Caribbean. In the mid-17th century the English evicted the Spanish authorities and took control of Jamaica in 1655. The Spanish colonists fled the island leaving their freed slaves behind. Many of the slaves escaped to the mountains to join an already sizable group of escaped slaves living with the Tainos. The runaway slaves, known as Maroons, resisted colonial authorities to maintain free communities in the mountains. British Jamaica became one of the world's leading sugar producers, which required large numbers of imported African slaves. By the late 1700s the slave population of the island far outnumbered the European planters and colonists.

The Jamaican culture is an Afro-Caribbean culture influenced by British and later popular American culture. The island's musical styles including reggae, ska, mento, dub, and others have made Jamaican music known throughout the world. Other important aspects of Jamaican culture are sports, particularly cricket and track and field sports, and the island's distinctive cuisine, which is characterized by Jamaican jerk spice. Since independence in the 1960s Jamaica has experienced a very high rate of criminal activity, including one of the highest rates of murder in the world, and an ongoing wave of hate crimes against people of non-African descent, particularly whites and Orientals, and mob attacks on gay people, prompting human rights groups to call the island the "most homophobic place on earth." In spite of the high crime rate most Jamaicans are nominally Christian, with many sects represented on the island, including a number of indigenous churches. Like the Afro-Caribbean churches, Jamaica's most widely used language is a blend of English and African influences that became known through the global popularity of Jamaican reggae music.

The sugar industry continued to dominate the colony in the 19th century. The abolition of slavery, beginning in 1807, was offset by the importation of Chinese and Indian indentured laborers and their families. In the early 1800s Jamaica's heavy reliance on African slaves resulted in a population of some 20 blacks to each white on the island. Measures to improve the lives of the slaves were resisted by the plantation owners until the slave trade was completely outlawed in 1833–1834. The freed slaves mostly settled as subsistence farmers while many of the plantation families left the island. Poverty and a lack of development kept most of the island's Afro-Caribbean majority tied to the land until the mid-20th century. British development schemes aided the spread of education and greater opportunities but poverty forced many Jamaicans to leave for the United Kingdom, the United States, and Canada beginning in the 1950s. The island slowly gained self-government and achieved full independence in 1962. The first years of independence were marked by rapid economic growth but by 1970 the Jamaicans were again mired in poverty. Criminal gangs proliferated and Jamaica became one of the least secure countries in the world. Economic deterioration continued into the 21st century prompting new generations of Jamaican immigrants to leave the island, including many of the best educated.

Further Reading

Hope, Donna P. *Inna de Dancehall: Popular Culture and Politics of Identity in Jamaica.* Mona, Jamaica: University of the West Indies Press, 2012.

Mason, Peter. *Jamaica: A Guide to the People, Politics, and Culture.* London: Latin America Bureau Books, 2000.

Sheehan, Sean and Angela Black. *Jamaica.* Salt Lake City, UT: Benchmark Books, 2005.

Jewish Americans

Jewish Americans, also known as American Jews, Jewish North Americans, or Jewish Canadians, are Americans and Canadians of Jewish faith or ancestry. The estimated 7 million Jewish Americans are found primarily in the large metropolitan areas of the northeastern states, the West Coast, South Florida, the upper Midwest, and in the major metropolitan areas of Canada. Jewish Americans mostly speak North American English with minorities that speak Hebrew, Yiddish, or Russian. Jewish Americans are considered an ethnoreligious group, as being a Jew is considered an ethnic identity as well as a religious one.

Jewish emigrants from Europe arrived in North America as early as the 17th century. Their numbers were small and they were almost exclusively Sephardic immigrants of Spanish and Portuguese ancestry. The French colony of New France had no official Jewish population because only Roman Catholics were permitted to enter the French territories. The early Sephardic communities in the Dutch colonies were later joined by other Sephardic Jews eager to leave Europe, even the tolerant Netherlands. Most of the early Sephardic Jewish immigrants had settled first in the Netherlands following their expulsion from Spain and Portugal. The Sephardic Jews prospered as merchants and artisans in the Dutch colony of New Amsterdam, which later became the British colony of New York. In the 1700s, the Jews from England and other British colonies began to settle in the British colonies on the east coast of North America. At the end of the French and Indian War in 1763 a number of Jews settled in the former French territories. By the end of the 18th century the larger towns in the British colonies usually had a small and thriving Jewish community. Many of the Jews supported the American cause during the Revolutionary War that led to American independence. Though denied the right to vote or hold public office, the Jews became active in community affairs in several American states in the 1790s, after they were granted political equality in the five states with the largest Jewish populations.

Jewish American culture is integrated in almost every way with the broader North American culture. Many aspects of traditional Jewish culture have become part of the popular culture of North America. The early Sephardic communities that once dominated Jewish life in North America have long since been eclipsed by the number of Ashkenazi Jews who settled in North America in the late 19th century and early 20th century. The modern Jewish population of North America is now overwhelmingly of Ashkenazi descent, from northern Europe and Russia. Other communities include the Sephardic Jews from Turkey,

Morocco, and Algeria, and the Misrahi Jews from the Middle East, North Africa, Central Asia, India, and the Caucasus. The Jewish Americans manifest a wide range of cultural traditions, apart from encompassing the full range of Jewish religious observances. The language of the Ashkenazis, Yiddish, was formerly widely spoken by the large immigrant community but most now speak English though the more orthodox sects, such as the Hadisic Jews, continue to speak the language. The Yiddish language is a High German dialect that developed as a fusion of German dialects with Hebrew and Slavic languages. The language is still spoken in Jewish communities throughout the world though assimilation usually includes the adoption of the language of the majority population. Other languages still in use as first or second languages include Ladino, the language of the Sephardic Jews, and Farsi, spoken by the numerous Persian Jews concentrated in the Los Angeles and New York metropolitan areas. Many from the most recent wave of Jewish immigrants to North America come from the countries of the former Soviet Union and often speak Russian at home though younger people quickly adapt to English.

Jewish immigration continued mostly from the British Isles in the early years of the 19th century. Until about 1830, the city of Charleston, South Carolina, had the largest Jewish population in North America. Large scale Jewish immigration began with Jews fleeing restrictive laws and violence in Germany. Most of the immigrants were secular Ashkenazi Jews who settled as merchants and shopkeepers. By the 1880s, the Jewish population of North

America had reached nearly 300,000, most concentrated in the cities of New York, Boston, Philadelphia, and Montreal. The majority of the Jewish population comprised educated and largely secular Ashkenazi Jews, although a minority of the older Sephardic Jewish families remained influential. Jewish immigration increased dramatically in the last decades of the 19th century as a result of increased persecution in parts of Eastern Europe and Russia. North America and its culture became an easy escape into the "melting pot" that created a commonality of culture and political values. This open culture allowed the Jewish immigrants to flourish in predominately Christian North America. Between 1880 and the beginning of World War I in 1914, over 2 million Jews migrated from Eastern Europe. The vast numbers of Jewish immigrants eventually resulted in restrictions and quota systems that greatly reduced the number of new immigrants. Despite the worsening conditions for European Jews that culminated in the Holocaust, these quotas remained in place with only minor alterations until 1965. Jewish leaders urged assimilation and integration into the wider North American culture and Jews quickly became part of American and Canadian life. During World War II over 500,000 enlisted and served in the armed forces. After the war, as the Jews became more prosperous, they joined the new suburbanization of the older urban areas. The Jewish communities expanded to other major urban areas such as Los Angeles, Miami, San Francisco, Toronto, and Vancouver. Intermarriage with non-Jews accelerated a trend that had begun in the 19th century. During the 20th century the Jews mostly joined the middle class, with many becoming wealthy as bankers and manufacturers. Jews were prominent in the civil rights movements of the 1960s and often supported liberal political ideals. By the 1980s, Jewish family incomes were the highest of any ethnic group in North America. The latest wave of immigration began as a trickle in the late 1960s and became a massive movement following the disintegration of the Soviet Union in the early 1990s. Jewish Americans continue to prosper in the 21st century and are widely represented in business, academia, and politics. Many of the richest families of North America are of Jewish origin and Jewish philanthropists are known for their generous support for cultural activities and the arts. Demographically, the Jewish population of North America is not increasing. Assimilated into North American culture and with high rates of intermarriage the actual number of Americans and Canadians who self-identify as Jews is decreasing and the Jewish population will probably experience an actual decline in the decades ahead.

Further Reading

Goren, Arthur A. *The Politics and Public Culture of American Jews.* Bloomington, IN: Indiana University Press, 1999.

Heinze, Andrew R. *Jews and the American Soul: Human Nature in the Twentieth Century.* Princeton, NJ: Princeton University Press, 2006.

Swierenga, Robert P. *The Forerunners: Dutch Jewry in the North American Diaspora.* Detroit, MI: Wayne State University Press, 1994.

Jivaros

The Jivaros, sometimes known as Shuars, Híbaros, Gívaros, Mainus, Jívaras, or Chívaris, are a South American ethnic group inhabiting the tropical forests of the eastern slopes of the Andes in Ecuador, southwestern Colombia, and northern Peru. The estimated 15,000 to 50,000 Jivaros speak a variety of related languages of the Jivaroan group of languages, which some scholars believe is a single language with several dialects. Most of the Jivaros retain their traditional belief system that revolves around a great many deities or gods. A minority of the Jivaros have adopted the Roman Catholic religion.

The Jivaros lived a seminomadic life in separate households in the rain forest with each band or extended family identifying themselves by the local names for "people" or by the names of their local rivers. The bands were linked by very loose kin or political ties. Traditionally the men hunted, made war, and wove cloth while the women gardened or gathered food in the forest. War between the many autonomous bands was endemic, with headhunting a traditional part of the ritual of warfare. The Jivaros' history as violent warriors goes back to the time of the expansion of the Inca Empire when the Jivaros fought to remain free of Inca authority. When the Jivaro peoples were contacted by the early Spanish explorers in the 16th century they entered into peaceful trade relations. Spanish attempts to collect taxes or to take slaves resulted in a violent confrontation that drove the Spanish from the region in 1599. The Spanish later alleged that the Jivaros massacred nearly 50,000 Spanish colonists in the conflict. In the 17th and 18th centuries the Jivaros continued to resist successive waves of missionaries. A few adopted the new Christian faith but the majority withdrew to their inaccessible villages. The fame of the savagery of the Jivaro warriors persuaded the Spanish to mostly leave them to their traditional way of life. The name Jivaro entered the Spanish language as "jibaro," meaning "savage," or in more modern usage "rustic" or "uncivilized."

The Jivaros live in the rain forests on the eastern slopes of the Andes, where the mountains meet the headwaters of the Amazon River. The Jivaro region is characterized by frequent and heavy rains and dense tropical vegetation. The Jivaros developed a rain forest type of farming that allows them to grow different crops such as maize, cassava, manioc, and sweet potatoes. Fishing, hunting, and gathering fruits and other forest products are also important cultural pursuits. The Jivaros are known for their rich mythology with a variety of myths passed orally from generation to generation to explain the origins of the Jivaro peoples. The modern stories are a blend of their historic myths and the stories brought to the region by missionaries. The myths are part of the traditional belief system that reveres the spiritual forces all around, spirits that are responsible for real-world occurrences. Spiritual significance is seen in all animals, plants, and objects. Missionary activity in the 19th century converted some Jivaros to Christianity, mostly Roman Catholicism, but later missionaries introduced the various Protestant sects. The Jivaros' language is considered by some as a language family while other scholars believe it is a single language with a number of distinct dialects.

In the early 1800s representatives of the newly independent nations of Ecuador, Peru, and Colombia attempted to bring the Jivaros under government control. The Jivaros, as wary of outsiders as they are of nearby tribal peoples, resisted government controls or moved to even less accessible areas. The Jivaros became famous for their elaborate process of shrinking the heads of slain opponents. In the late 19th and early 20th centuries outsiders began trading manufactured goods, including guns, for shrunken heads. The heads were sold as souvenirs in the Americas and Europe. The trade, particularly the introduction of guns, increased local warfare, including the traditional head-hunting that contributed to the notoriety of the Jivaros as a violent and savage people. Prior to the increase in mission influence in the 1940s and 1950s, Jivaro culture functioned as an organized warrior society. Roman Catholic missionaries promoted Jivaro settlements known as *centros* that facilitated conversions to Christianity and became a means of defending Jivaro land claims against non-Jivaro settlers. In the 1960s representatives of the *centros* formed several political organizations to represent their interests to

Jivaros dressed in their Sunday best on a jungle trail in Sucua, Ecuador. The Jivaros are the headhunters who kill with poisoned blowgun darts (curare) and then shrink the victim's head to the size of an orange. (USGS)

the national governments. The Jivaros' reputation as warriors prompted the military, particularly in Ecuador, to form elite military units made up of Jivaro soldiers. These units distinguished themselves in the 1995 war between Ecuador and Peru known as the Cenepa War. In recent decades the Jivaros have largely settled in peaceful communities and are no longer completely isolated from modern culture.

Further Reading

Down, Frank and Marie Down. *Mission to the Headhunters: Life among the Head-Shrinking Jivaro Indians of Ecuador.* Grand Rapids, MI: Zondervan, 1974.

Harner, Michael J. *The Jivaro: People of the Sacred Waterfalls.* Berkeley, CA: University of California Press, 1984.

Stirling, M. W. *Historical and Ethnographical Material on the Jivaro Indians.* New York: Library Reprints, 2007.

K

Kaingangs

The Kaingangs, sometimes known as Caingangs, Caingangues, Guayanás, Botocudos, or Aweikomas, are a South American ethnic group living in the southern Brazilian states of São Paulo, Paraná, Santa Catarina, and Rio Grande do Sul. There is a small community of some 2,000 Kaingangs in the areas adjacent to the Misiones province of Argentina. The estimated 36,000 Kaingangs are largely bilingual, speaking both their Kaingang language—which belongs to the Gê or Jê language family—and Portuguese and Spanish. About 60 percent of the Kaingangs are Christian, mostly Roman Catholic but with a growing number belonging to evangelical Protestant sects.

The Kaingangs believe that their origins began with two founding brothers, Kamé and Kairu. Following a huge flood, the two brothers climbed out of the top of the Crinjijimbés Mountain to create a new world. They named the plants and animals and brought order to the world. Scholars believe that the ancestors of the Kaingangs first settled in the Amazon rainforest, but some 2,900 years ago they started to spread to the south and gradually occupied the jungled highlands of the Atlantic coast. The Kaingangs were mostly hunters, fishermen, and farmers raising cassava, corn, sweet potatoes, beans, tobacco, peanuts, cotton, and squash. The early Kaingangs were not unified despite the fact that they belonged to a single ethnic group with a distinct culture and language. Like the other cultures living in the forests along the Atlantic Ocean, the Kaingangs were first contacted by Europeans in the early 16th century. The bands living in territories coveted by the Europeans were usually enslaved or simply exterminated by the colonists and the Bandeirantes, the Portuguese colonial scouts. As the Portuguese rarely brought their families to the New World, many took indigenous women. By the end of the 18th century there was a large population of mixed background while the tribal groups were forced into smaller and smaller territories.

Kaingang culture varies from band to band with each displaying influences borrowed from neighboring peoples, and increasingly, from popular Brazilian and Argentine culture. Historically the Kaingangs experienced frequent warring among the different bands; so weapons such as bows, arrows, spears, and clubs were highly evolved. Modern Kaingangs no longer make war but produce decorated weapons to sell as souvenirs. Kaingang pottery is also highly prized although the art of ceramic making is declining rapidly. The legend of the origins of the Kaingangs continues to direct modern Kaingang society. The division between Kamé and Kairu is a cultural concept that is applied to the people, the structure of Kaingang society, and their surrounding environment. A natural phenomenon such as the sun is Kamé, while the moon is Kairu; pinewood is Kamé and cedar is Kairu; lizards are Kamé, while monkeys are Kairu. In Kaingang society Kamé represents perfection, achievement, and permanence, and Kairu signifies imperfection, a lack of achievement, and impulsivity. Individual Kaingangs belong to one of the two groups with strict traditions. A Kamé man must marry a Kairu woman and vice versa. Kaingang culture is matrilocal, but patrilineal in inheritance. The Kaingang language remains the language of daily life with most also speaking Portuguese or Spanish. In some areas, particularly in São Paulo state, the Kaingangs speak only Portuguese. Most of the Kaingangs are Christians, primarily Roman Catholic although in recent decades evangelical Christian groups have gained followers.

Most of the Kaingangs moved deeper into the forests to escape slavers and abuses by colonists. In the early 19th century contacts with non-Kaingangs increased as the colonists moved inland from the coastal settlements. In the 1840s several local chiefs signed a treaty with the Portuguese authorities. Despite the treaties the expropriation of Kaingang lands continued; intergroup conflicts, exacerbated by the colonial authorities, grew to serious proportions. By the 1930s the Kaingangs had been forced to give up their seminomadic existence and to settle on reservations that represented a small part of their traditional lands. Divided by the boundaries of four states and an international border, the conditions of the Kaingang reservations varied greatly. At the end of the 20th century the Kaingangs lived in 30 reservations that were insufficient to maintain their population. Many younger Kaingangs left the reservations to seek work in São Paulo, Porto Alegre, and other large regional cities. Kaingang activists, educated in Portuguese, lead modern Kaingang organizations that demand restitution of stolen lands and more control over their territories. In 2006, Brazil's state-owned power company agreed to compensate the Kaingangs with a payment of $6.5 million for the operation of a small power plant on one of the reservations. Activists had threatened to destroy the plant unless they were compensated for its construction on reserved lands.

Further Reading

Elmo, Timoteus. *Kaingang People.* Saarbrücken, Germany: Loc Publishing, 2012.

Gomes, Mercio Pereira. *The Indians and Brazil.* Gainesville, FL: University of Florida Press, 2000.

Henry, Jules. *Jungle People: A Kaingang Tribe of the Highlands of Brazil.* New York: Vintage Books, 1964.

Kalaallits

The Kalaallits, sometimes known as Greenlanders or Grønlanders, are a North American ethnic group, the inhabitants of the autonomous country of Greenland, known as Kalaallit Nunaat, the "Land of the Kalaallit." Though physically part of North America, Greenland has been politically and culturally associated with Europe for more than a millennium. The estimated 62,000 Kalaallits constitute a majority of Greenland's population, which also includes sizable European—mostly Danes—and Inuit populations. Outside their island homeland there is a sizable Kalaallit population in Denmark. The Kalaallit language is classed as an East Inuit dialect of the Inuit-Aleut language family that mixes Inuit and Scandinavian words and forms. The majority of the Kalaallits are Protestants, mostly Evangelical Lutherans.

Known in Europe from about 3000 BCE, the island was called Thule or Ultima Thule—the "farthest land"—by the Romans. Stories about the island, often fanciful, became part of Europe's folklore before the island gradually faded into myth and legend. Norse explorers, led by Eric the Red, rediscovered the island in 982 CE. To make the island more attractive to colonists, Eric called the frozen land "Greenland." The Vikings established a number of settlements in the narrow plains of the south, where agriculture was possible. The number of Norse settlers grew to some 10,000 by the 12th century. In the 13th century the Norse colonists reported the first contacts with the Inuits, part of the great Inuit migration across the polar lands to northern Greenland. The island was ruled by Norway until it came under the rule of the Danish king in 1380. Sometime in the 14th century the island's weather grew colder, with a rapid decline in agriculture and livestock breeding. Plagues brought from Europe decimated the settlements. The Black Death is estimated to have killed at least half the colonists. Inuits moving south attacked the colonies in the mid-14th century. The last official report of the colonists arrived in Europe in 1410; afterward there was only silence. The colonists disappeared without a trace, either dying out as agriculture collapsed, decimated by plagues or Inuit attacks, or

perhaps joining the Inuits in order to survive. In 1721, the Norwegians, then ruled by the Danes, began to resettle Greenland but the European influence remained isolated in the far south.

The majority of the Kalaallits are of mixed Inuit and European background, though in the northern districts there is a sizable population of seminomadic Inuits. The designation of the Greenlander or Inuit is based on culture; the settled population, mostly of mixed ancestry, is known as Kalaallits or Greenlanders, while those who retain their traditional culture in the north are known as Inuits, part of the wider transpolar Inuit culture. Politically all the inhabitants of the island are known as Kalaallits. Over centuries the Inuits of the southern districts mixed with the Norwegian and Danish settlers from Europe, with the result being that the modern Kalaallits have a variety of features, from Inuit to European. The Kalaallit culture incorporates both European and Inuit traditions and customs. Important elements of the local culture are based on the traditional pursuits of whaling and fishing. Some 90 percent of the island's population inhabits the ice-free coastal regions in the southern districts. The large Danish population is concentrated in the island capital and the other important towns in the south. The language of the Kalaallits, known as Kalaallisut, has been the official language of the territory since 2009. The language, only partially intelligible to speakers of Inuit, is a unique mixture of influences, with various words for different conditions of snow, ice, weather, and other natural phenomena. Danish is also widely spoken and is taught in the island's schools. Though the majority of the Kalaallits are Protestants, many traditions and beliefs, particularly those connected with hunting, fishing, and whaling, are often mixed with their Christian rituals.

In 1815 the Danish kingdom lost Norway to Sweden, though it retained the island known as Greenland through an oversight at the Congress of Vienna. Economically unimportant and sparsely populated, Greenland remained a forgotten outpost mostly ignored by the Danish government. Matthew Perry, the American naval officer who would become famous for opening Japan to foreign trade in 1853–1854, explored the northern coast of the huge island in the early 19th century. American claims to northern Greenland were not relinquished until 1917, when the United States purchased the Danish Virgin Islands. During World War II the Americans returned to establish military bases following the occupation of Denmark by German forces. At the end of the war the United States offered to buy the island. The Danish government refused but allowed the maintenance of the military bases as part of a mutual defense agreement. In the 1950s the benefits of the Danish welfare system were extended to the Kalaallit population. Immigration from Denmark increased with extensive intermarriage and ethnic mixing. The generous welfare system created a culture of dependence by the 1960s. Kalaallit activists mobilized to oppose the system that was decimating their culture and later extended their opposition to foreign investments and the development of the Arctic oil deposits found on the island. Opposition to Danish rule that was seen by many as the death of their own indigenous Kalaallit culture resulted in demands for autonomy and greater control of their island's natural resources. Modern cultural problems such as urban living, high rates of alcoholism, and the spread of venereal diseases became part of the Kalaallit campaign to protect their culture. The politics of the Kalaallit population reflects their situation as an autonomous country within the Danish kingdom. Some groups support greater self-government, others support full independence, while a minority wants to retain the island's historic ties to Denmark and the generous government subsidies that make life on the island comparable to the lifestyle of European Denmark.

Further Reading

Hibbert, Alex. *Kalaalit-Nunaat: Land of the People.* Portsmouth, UK: Tricorn Books, 2012.

Jensen, Ole G. *The Culture of Greenland in Glimpses.* Copenhagen, Denmark: Milik Publishing, 2007.

Loukacheva, Natalia. *Arctic Promise: Legal and Political Autonomy of Greenland and Nunavut.* Toronto, Canada: University of Toronto Press, 2007.

Kiowas

The Kiowas, sometimes known as Kauigus, are a North American ethnic group mostly living in the U.S. state of Oklahoma. Outside the region there are Kiowas living in Texas and in a number of large cities in the lower Midwest. The estimated 15,000 Kiowas generally speak English with a minority that can still speak the Kiowa language, a language of the Tanoan language family. Kiowans are divided into a number of Christian sects with some adhering to the Native American Church.

The Kiowas originated in the Columbia River basin in the Kootenay region of present-day British Columbia. Around the time the first European traders and explorers entered the area, they migrated south to the Upper Yellowstone region of western Montana. Shortly after their arrival in the Yellowstone area a dispute between two prominent chiefs resulted in the division of the tribe with one group moving to the northwest while the main body of the Kiowas migrated to the southeast. Accompanied by the Plains Apaches, also known as Kiowa Apaches, they reached the Black Hills by 1775. Moving out onto the Great Plains, the Kiowas came into contact with the Crows in 1790. An alliance with the Crows allowed the Kiowas to acquire two things that were to become indispensable to their future, the horse and the sacred Sun Dance. The Sun Dance became the center of Kiowa religious beliefs and an important symbol of Kiowa unity. The tribe, made up of small autonomous bands, gathered together once a year to celebrate the Sun Dance and to reaffirm their culture and tribal unity. The annual Kiowa gathering would be accompanied by many weddings, tribal councils, and reunions of extended Kiowa families. The Sun Dance was always preceded by a great tribal buffalo hunt.

Kiowa culture is a Native American culture that blends traditional culture with the customs and language of modern American society. Historically Kiowa artists have maintained a unique record of their culture. Originally painting hides, the artists became known for their ledger art, graphic depictions of Kiowa life and important events in Kiowa history. The "Kiowa Five" were among the earliest Native Americans to receive international recognition in the 1920s and 1930s. Traditional cultural skills are also showcased by bead artists who continue the historic art of beadwork. Kiowa music was noted for its hymns that were traditionally accompanied by a flute, which is the basis of modern Kiowa music. Historically the Kiowas occupied a large

The Kiowa Five

Kiowa prisoners held at Fort Marion in Florida from 1875 to 1878, at the conclusion of the Red River War, continued a tradition of hide painting but substituted the lined pages of record-keeping books for the unavailable natural materials. Known as the ledger artists, they kept the tradition going after their release and return to Oklahoma. The ledger artists fostered an artistic tradition that was followed by the artists known as the Kiowa Five, who later became the Kiowa Six. The artists, Spencer Asah, James Auchiah, Jack Hokeah, Stephen Mopope, Lois Bougetah Smoky, and Monroe Tsatoke, all studied at the University of Oklahoma. Lois Smoky left the group in 1927 when her place was taken by James Auchiah. The Kiowa artists gained international fame following exhibitions of their works at the 1928 International Art Congress in Czechoslovakia and were invited to participate in the Venice Biennale in 1932.

territory in western Oklahoma, the Texas panhandle, and northeastern New Mexico. The Kiowa bands were seminomadic, moving seasonally to follow the buffalo herds. The modern Kiowa reservation is located in Oklahoma where some 12,000 Kiowas are enrolled members. Others who identify with Kiowa culture but live away from the reservation or have less than the quarter Kiowa descent necessary for tribal membership also consider themselves as Kiowas. The Kiowa language is a member of the Kiowa-Tanoan language group. The Sun Dance, which is still the highlight of annual Kiowa gatherings, was the center of traditional Kiowa religious beliefs. The modern Christian beliefs are often blended with traditional rituals in the Kiowa belief system.

The Kiowa reliance on the bison herds required a vast territory and a seminomadic lifestyle. They never wantonly killed the buffalo but took only what they needed. They were disgusted by the wholesale slaughter of buffalo by American and European sportsmen beginning in the early 19th century. Moving south with the herds the Kiowas came into contact with the powerful Comanches. A tribal alliance made the Kiowas, the Plains Apaches, and their Comanche allies the dominant inhabitants of the southern Plains. By 1840 the Kiowas had forged alliances with the Lakotas, the Cheyennes, the Arapahos, and the Osages. In 1870 a new technique for tanning buffalo hides became available commercially. In response, American and European hunters systematically eliminated the huge herds. Originally numbering in the tens of millions, by 1878 the buffalo was nearly extinct. Facing a crisis as the buffalo disappeared and white settlements continued to expand, the Plains peoples fought against the hunters, the settlers, and the American cavalry. The U.S. Army launched a campaign against the Plains peoples in 1874 in an effort to remove the tribes from the southern plains and to relocate them to reservations in Indian Territory. The Kiowas and other Plains tribes, unable to sustain the fight against the modern military might of the United States, surrendered band by band in 1874–1875. At first held in captivity in Florida, the Kiowas were later resettled in Oklahoma on reserved lands. A new agreement, signed in 1892, reduced their holdings to individual plots and allowed the surplus to be opened to white settlement. The Kiowas adapted to American society, learned the English language, and attempted to live in peace. In the 20th century activists led the fight for self-determination. In 1968 the Kiowa Tribal Council became the governing body of the Kiowa Tribe of Oklahoma. In the early 21st century only a minority of the Kiowas continues to live on reservation lands; most of them live in urban and suburban areas across the country.

Further Reading

Lookingbill, Brad D. and Philip Earenfight. *A Kiowa's Odyssey: A Sketchbook from Fort Marion.* Seattle, WA: University of Washington Press, 2003.

Mayhall, Midlred P. *The Kiowas.* Norman, OK: University of Oklahoma Press, 1984.

Meadows, William C. *Kiowa Military Societies: Ethnohistory and Ritual.* Norman, OK: University of Oklahoma Press, 2010.

Kitteans

The Kitteans, sometimes known as Kittitians, are the people of the Caribbean island of Saint Kitts, part of the island country made up of the two islands Saint Kitts and Nevis. Outside their home island there are Kittean communities in the United Kingdom, the United States, and Canada. The estimated 45,000 Kitteans speak English along with a dialect that mixes English, West African, and French elements—known as Saint Kitts Creole. Most Kitteans are Christians, with an Anglican majority and smaller numbers belonging to other Protestant churches and the Roman Catholic Church.

Around 800 CE the indigenous people of the island were replaced by the Igneri people, a part of the Arawak peoples who migrated north through the islands from their original homeland along the Orinoco River in present-day Venezuela. Around 1300 war-like Caribs, also from the South American mainland, invaded the island. They quickly killed or dispersed the earlier inhabitants. Christopher Columbus sighted the island in 1493, claiming it for the growing Spanish Empire. The Spanish ignored the island in favor of richer prizes, so in 1538 the French established a short-lived colony but were soon driven out by the Caribs. The first English colony was founded in 1623, followed by a second French settlement in 1625. The English and the French briefly united to massacre the local population, and then partitioned the island between the two colonial authorities. A Spanish expedition drove the English and French settlers from the island in 1629, but a year later the English

settlement was rebuilt following peace between England and Spain. The French also returned to claim the island. Saint Kitts became the principal base for the English and French colonization of other Caribbean islands. Sugarcane cultivation began in 1640 resulting in the large-scale importation of slaves from West Africa. Sugar production was the island's only important export with the island mostly divided into numerous sugar plantations. By the end of the 18th century the slaves on the island far outnumbered the Europeans. Control of the island alternated between English and French authority until it became permanently British in 1783.

The Kittean culture is an Afro-Caribbean culture incorporating influences from the former colonial cultures of Britain and France along with traditions and rituals brought to the island by their ancestors from West Africa. The culture is known for its music and dancing and for the number of annual musical festivals and celebrations. These celebrations usually feature parades, street dances, and island musical forms such as salsa, soca, jazz, calypso, and steelpan. The Kittean cuisine is another important cultural element, featuring a blend of European and African cooking techniques along with the island's abundant seafood. Cricket is the national sport and is played throughout Saint Kitts. Though English is the official language and is spoken throughout Saint Kitts, a local dialect known as Saint Kitts Creole is the language of daily life. The dialect blends English, French, and words and structures brought from West Africa. The Anglican faith brought to the island by the English is still the largest of the denominations in Saint

Kitts. Other groups, particularly evangelical Protestants, have gained followings in recent decades. The Roman Catholic minority comprises mostly the descendants of slaves held on French plantations in the 17th and 18th centuries.

Sugar cultivation continued as the only important economic activity in the early 19th century. In 1807 the British government outlawed the importation of new slaves from Africa but slaves from other islands were still imported. After 1834, when slavery was finally abolished, the sugar industry quickly declined in spite of the importation of indentured laborers from India and elsewhere. In 1882 the islands of Saint Kitts, Nevis, and Anguilla were joined in a federation of British Caribbean islands over the protests of the Kittean leaders. By the early 20th century the Kittean economy was floundering and discontentment with British rule was spreading. After World War II several attempts at forming a federation in the Caribbean failed, and in 1967 Saint Kitts, Nevis, and Anguilla were joined in a self-governing federation. Anguilla withdrew and the federation of Saint Kitts and Nevis gained full independence in 1983. Even though the sugar industry had been the historic mainstay of the island economy, the last of the industry was closed down in 2005. Most of the Kitteans live as subsistence farmers, though a growing number are employed in the tourist industry that is now the largest employer in Saint Kitts.

Further Reading

Cameron, Sarah and Ben Box, eds. *Caribbean Islands Handbook*. Chicago, IL: Passport Books, 1995.

Dyde, Brian. *Out of the Crowded Vagueness: A History of the Islands of St. Kitts, Nevis and Anguilla*. Oxford, UK: Macmillan Caribbean, 2005.

Dyde, Brian. *St. Kitts: Cradle of the Caribbean*. Oxford, UK: Macmillan Caribbean, 2009.

Kollas

The Kollas, sometimes known as Collas or Qullas, are a South American ethnic group inhabiting the *yungas* or high altitude forests at the edge of the Amazon rainforest in western Bolivia, northern Chile, and northern Argentina. The estimated 125,000 Kollas speak a dialect of Southern Quechua known as Northwest Jujuy Quechua, which is related to the numerous Quechua dialects spoken from southern Colombia to northern Argentina. Most Kollas continue to adhere to their traditional religious beliefs though there is a sizable Roman Catholic minority and a growing number belonging to evangelical Protestant groups.

The Kollas inhabited the region of the highlands east of the Andes Mountains for centuries. Divided into several distinct groups they were united by language and culture. The majority lived in villages or small towns as farmers, herders, or hunters. The flourishing Kolla culture was influenced by the sophisticated Inca Empire to the north. Stone sculptures, cloth weaving, and advanced farming techniques were practiced. In the 15th century the Inca armies moved south to incorporate the Kolla territories into the expanding empire. Inca rule lasted the arrival of the Spanish in the region in 1540. The Kollas resisted Spanish invasions for 110 years but ultimately lost their territory, known as the Santiago Estate, to the Spanish. Various leaders led Kolla rebellions against harsh Spanish laws and forced labor. One particularly famous rebel leader named Ñusta Huillac fought the Spanish in northern Chile in 1780. She was nicknamed *La Tirana* or The Tyrant because of her abuse of Spanish prisoners. She reportedly fell in love with Vasco de Almeida, one of the Spanish prisoners, and pleaded with her people to spare his life. After her father's death she led a group of Kollas brought to Huantajaya in Chile to mine silver. Many Kollas were killed in the mass genocide of indigenous peoples that continued into the 19th century.

Kolla culture retains much of its traditions and beliefs though modern South American customs have been widely adopted. Isolated in the rural areas the Kollas are some of the poorest people of the region. Their primary employment is agricultural or seasonal labor. Because the Kollas traditionally held their lands in common, they do not have titles of ownership to their ancestral lands, and this has resulted in many Kollas being displaced. In recent decades many Kollas have abandoned their traditional lands in the *yungas* to seek employment and a better life in the large cities of Argentina and Chile. In the cities they are often engaged in cleaning or behind-the-scenes kitchen work. The Kolla language is a Quechua dialect known as Northwest Jujuy Quechua or simply as Kolla. The language is only partially intelligible to the speakers of Quechua in other parts of western South America. Many Kollas continue to practice their ancestral

religion, which includes shamans and belief in spirits. Missionaries converted some of the Kollas to Roman Catholicism in the 18th and 19th centuries though in recent decades evangelical Protestant sects have become popular.

The independence of Argentina, Chile, and Bolivia in the early 19th century did not improve the situation of the Kollas. Most continued to work as seasonal laborers or on farms and ranches for minimal wages. Many Kollas worked as forced labor on the so-called Santiago Estate, the last of the Kolla lands to fall to the Spanish conquerors. The majority of the Kollas continued to live in *ayllus* or separate Kolla communities and mostly rejected contacts with the outside world. The governments of the countries with Kolla populations mostly ignored and neglected the indigenous populations. In the decades just before World War II Kolla activists began to mobilize the population. In 1945, representatives of the Kolla communities in northwestern Argentina demanded the restitution of their traditional lands in compliance with previous laws. Several Kolla organizations were formed in the 1950s and 1960s to work for the return of their stolen lands and to protect their culture and language. In 1985 the Argentine government officially recognized the indigenous peoples but for the Kollas there was little change. In 1996 Kolla activists occupied parts of their ancestral lands, blocked roads and highways, and fought with the local police. The Santiago Estate was finally returned to Kolla control in 1997. Unrecognized land claims, widespread poverty, and abuses by local governments and large agricultural and forestry companies continue to threaten the future of the Kollas in the 21st century.

Further Reading

Archibald, Priscilla. *Imagining Modernity in the Andes.* Lewisburg, PA: Bucknell University Press, 2011.

Coronado, Jorge. *The Andes Imagined: Indigenismo, Society, and Modernity.* Pittsburgh, PA: University of Pittsburgh Press, 2009.

Rodriguez-Piñero, Luis. *Indigenous Peoples, Postcolonialism, and International Law.* New York: Oxford University Press, 2006.

Kunas

The Kunas, sometimes known as Cunas, Dules, or Tules, are an indigenous people of Panama. The estimated 65,000 Kunas live in three politically autonomous *comarcas* or reservations in Panama, with a few small villages in Colombia. There are communities of Kunas living in Panama City, Colón, and other Panamanian cities. The Kuna language, called Dulegaya, meaning "people speak" or "people mouth," is still widely spoken with Spanish often spoken as a second language. The majority of the Kunas are Christian, with both Protestant and Roman Catholic churches represented; most Kunas maintain their traditional beliefs alongside the Christian ceremonies.

The largest Kuna populations occupied the territory around the Gulf of Urabá in present-day Colombia with others farther north in Panama. The Kunas were an important group living in federated clan villages. The Kuna clans often engaged in warfare among themselves and with the neighboring Catio tribe. The Kunas were mostly farmers but also conducted an extensive maritime trade, mainly by canoe, along the coast. The Kunas had a well-developed and stratified class system. Important chiefs were carried by their retainers in elaborate hammocks. The Kuna artisans produced fine ceramics, ornaments of shell and bone, and woven cloth. Europeans visited the region in 1510. The Kunas at first welcomed the strangers, but as the Spanish took many for slaves and engaged in mistreatment of the Kunas, many moved to less accessible regions or migrated north to escape the Spanish and their enemies—the Catios. In their new homeland, called Kuna Yala or "Kuna Land," they settled in the Darién region of what is now Panama. Contacts with Europeans were mostly with pirates on the coast or with traders from the European settlements around the Isthmus of Panama. In 1787 the Kuna leaders signed a treaty with the Spanish that began a century of profitable trade. The Kunas began to specialize in farming coconut, which is still their most important cash crop.

The culture of the Kunas is a traditional culture with some influences from modern Central American society. Descent among the Kunas is reckoned bilaterally, with individuals tracing their ancestry through both the male and female lines. Marriage is matrilocal with extended families of several generations living together. Traditionally there are two cultural subgroups, the Mountain Kunas and the San Blas Kunas; there had been little contact between the two until the 1960s. The Kunas are famous for their brightly colored *molas*, a Kuna textile art form made using the techniques

Kunas in Panama, 1996. (AP Photo/Scott Dalton)

of appliqué and reverse appliqué. Mola textiles are also made into clothing, particularly the blouses of Kuna women. Music—particularly chants—usually accompanies Kuna ceremonies and festivals. The chants are of three types—historical, religious, and political. Kuna healers also use chants and herbs to treat their patients. Beginning in the 1970s modern health clinics were established in the Kuna region. The Kuna language is the primary language though many also speak Spanish, Panama's official language. Officially many of the Kunas are Christians, including both Roman Catholics and Protestants, though their Christian beliefs are often blended with pre-Christian rituals and traditions.

Pressure from the growing population pushed many Kunas off the most fertile lands in the early 1800s. To escape the growing conflicts over land and the disease-bearing insects on the mainland, as early as the mid-1800s whole villages migrated to the sandy San Blas Islands off the northern coast. Settling on the islands gave the Kunas easier access to trading vessels on the coastal routes and greater protection against the abuses of the rapidly increasing Latino population of mixed indigenous and European ancestry. Mistreatment by government officials resulted in a widespread Kuna revolt in the late 19th century. The revolt, centered on the San Blas Islands and the rugged San Blas Range on the mainland, continued for several decades. In 1903, under pressure from the United States, the Colombian government recognized the secession and independence of Panama. The new Panamanian government attempted to forcefully impose a "national culture" on the Kunas. In 1925 the

Kunas again rebelled and, with the backing of the Americans, were able to negotiate a semiautonomous status for their homeland. The region was officially recognized as a Kuna reserve in 1938. A Kuna constitution was adopted in 1945. Tensions increased resulting in a Kuna uprising in 1962, which was quickly put down. Claims to mainland territories became more important as the Kuna population grew by some 60 percent between 1950 and 1980. In 1972 the boundaries of Kuna Yala were expanded to include part of the mainland territories. The growing number of illegal Latino squatters on Kuna lands led to conflicts and protests in the 1990s and the early 2000s.

Further Reading

Howe, James. *A People Who Would Not Kneel: Panama, the United States, and the San Blas Kunas.* Washington, DC: Smithsonian, 1998.

Howe, James. *Chiefs, Scribes, and Ethnographers: Kuna Culture from Inside and Out.* Austin, TX: University of Texas Press, 2009.

Salvador, Mari Lyn. *The Art of Being Kuna.* Seattle, WA: University of Washington Press, 1997.

L

Latino Americans

See Hispanic Americans.

Lencas

The Lencas are a Central American ethnic group living on the Pacific Coast of Honduras and the adjoining areas of El Salvador east of the Lempa River. Outside their homeland there are Lenca communities in the large cities of Honduras and El Salvador. The estimated 145,000 Lencas speak Spanish as their own language, formerly spoken across the region, is now considered extinct. Most of the Lencas are Roman Catholic, though some Lenca communities still retain and practice their pre-Christian rituals.

The Lencas are thought to have migrated north from present-day Colombia to settle the forested highlands in the 11th century CE. The center of Lenca settlement was the Comayagua Valley, a highland basin in southwestern Honduras. Historically the Lencas located their settlements along major rivers. Large constructions were normally military fortifications while most buildings were constructed of adobe rather than stone. Contacts with the Mayan cities to the north greatly influenced Lenca arts, sciences, and religious beliefs. With a population of between 500,000 and 600,000, the Lenca empire consisted of four distinct regions: Potón in present-day El Salvador,

Care, Cerquin, and Lenca in Honduras. By the time the Spanish entered the region, in 1537, the Lenca culture showed many cultural features shared with other cultures of Mesoamerica. Lempira, a Lenca chief, led a decade-long war of resistance to Spanish rule. Lured from his hilltop stronghold with promises of negotiations, Lempira was ambushed and killed. He is considered a national hero in Honduras and the Honduran currency is called the lempira. In the first years following the Spanish conquest, European diseases and forced labor greatly reduced the Lenca population. By 1550 only about 25,000 Lencas survived, mostly in highland villages. In contrast to other indigenous peoples the Lencas were able to retain some of their communal lands and continued their agricultural way of life. Lenca agriculture was based on corn and beans with communal labor and shares in the harvest. The Lencas mostly shunned contacts with outsiders well into the 18th century.

Lenca culture is an indigenous culture heavily influenced by the Hispanic culture of Central America. The Lencas maintain a number of ceremonies and rituals taken from both Roman Catholic and traditional practices. The most sacred day of the year in any Lenca community is when the statue of the patron saint is carried through the streets on the saint's day. The day is normally celebrated with a great festival and various annual rituals. The culture remains a mainly rural culture with the Lencas being among the poorest and least educated peoples of Central America. There are few doctors or other medical personnel in Lenca areas as they are mistrusted, and most people prefer to remain under the care of traditional healers. Death rituals are particularly important. When a person dies, the community holds a feast featuring large amounts of *chichi*, a fermented maize drink, and the mourning often goes on for nine days. The Lencas' language mostly disappeared as Spanish was adopted by the early 19th century. Some elders remember a few words but the language is officially listed as extinct. Like the language, the Lencas also lost most of their religious beliefs and are now largely Roman Catholic. Many Lencas continue to revere "the old religion," parts of which are often blended with Catholic ceremonies and rituals.

The postconquest population of some 25,000 remained stable for most of the colonial period. Isolation, little medical care, and high rates of infant mortality and diseases limited the Lenca population until the mid-19th century. Spanish authority, weakened by long wars in Europe, was finally overthrown in Central America in 1821. Instability and civil wars continued to impact the Lencas, who were often forced to leave their highlands in search of seasonal agricultural labor or other low-paying work. The new republics of Honduras and El Salvador were ruled by European-descended elites along with a large population of mixed European and indigenous ancestry. The native peoples, including the Lencas, remained marginalized and mostly ignored. In the 1920s, greater contact with surrounding peoples and the local and national governments accelerated the acculturation of the Lencas. Having lost their language, the Lencas also lost many of their ancient traditions and customs as they adopted the wider Central American culture. The Lencas were caught in the middle when El Salvador and Honduras fought a brief war in 1969. Thousands were displaced, particularly Lencas born in El Salvador who were expelled along with the other Salvadorians living in Honduras. The Cold War period brought renewed violence to the region as local wars repeatedly intruded into Lenca districts. Peace in the 1990s allowed the Lencas to advance economically. Education became more available and younger, educated Lencas began to take over the leadership of their people. Despite the advances the Lencas remain among the poorest and least educated of the indigenous peoples of the Americas.

Further Reading

Adams, Richard E. W. *The Cambridge History of the Native American Peoples of the Americas.* Cambridge, UK: Cambridge University Press, 2000.

Forte, Maximilian C. *Indigenous Cosmopolitans.* Bern, Switzerland: Peter Lang Publishing, 2010.

Witschey, Walter R. T. and Clifford T. Brown. *Historical Dictionary of Mesoamerica.* New York: Scarecrow Press, 2011.

Lumbees

The Lumbees, sometimes known as Croatans or Croatoans, are a North American ethnic group concentrated in Robeson

County and adjacent counties on the southern border of the U.S. state of North Carolina. Outside the region there are Lumbee communities in South Carolina and in the cities of Greensboro, Baltimore, Philadelphia, and Detroit, although the Lumbee migrants do return to their traditional homeland. The estimated 55,000 Lumbees are native English speakers, speaking both Standard English and the unique dialect known as Lumbee English.

Lumbee legends connect the modern Lumbees with the lost colony on Roanoke Island whose colonists mysteriously disappeared in the late 16th century, but these legends are refuted by many Lumbees and most historians. The oral tradition identifies the Lumbees with Croatan people whose name was found carved on a tree, the only clue to the disappearance of the European colonists. The Lumbees claim descent from the Cheraw people who originally lived around the area of Danville in present-day Virginia. The loss of traditional lands and conflicts with the growing European population resulted in the migration of the Cheraws south to the region of the Pee Dee River in South Carolina in 1703. Wars with the Tuscaroras and participation in the Yamassee War decimated the Cheraws and several other indigenous peoples. In 1737 the Cheraws sold their lands in South Carolina to the European colonists and mostly settled along Drowning Creek, now known as the Lumber River, in southern North Carolina prior to 1750. The area, dominated by swamps and other marginal lands, was of little interest to white settlers. The survivors of a number of tribes joined the settlers while intermarriage with Europeans and free blacks was frequent. The

settlers also took in many runaway slaves who became part of the community. The remnants of the several tribes adopted English as a lingua franca while their own languages fell into disuse and mostly disappeared. Between 1775 and 1783 many Lumbees joined the American forces in the Revolutionary War. In 1790, the U.S. Census listed the people of the settlements as free, giving them a status equal to that of their white neighbors.

The people known as the Lumbees are mostly of mixed white and black ancestry with some Native American mixture. The unknown and complex lineage has made the issue of identity of prime concern. The Lumbees have been known by a number of names during their long history in North Carolina. They are the largest and best known of the so-called American isolates made up of mostly rural peoples of mixed racial background. Lumbee culture is a mixture of traditions such as agricultural life, family, hunting and gathering, and their religion that have been blended with modern American culture. Arts and crafts have been handed down from generation to generation so that items such as Lumbee patchwork quilts, rugs, and clothing often contain the same designs used over a century ago. A desire for education has traditionally been of prime concern, particularly following a state law in 1885 that recognized the Lumbees as the Croatan Tribe and allowed the Lumbees separate schools and the right to select their own teachers. A teacher training school was established in 1887. The many languages spoken by the ancestors of the Lumbees resulted in the adoption of English as a common language. The unique dialect known as Lumbee English contains many words, phrases, and structures that have disappeared in modern standard American English. Religion is an important part of the culture and has historically played a primary role in the evolution of the Lumbees. The majority belongs to the Baptist or Methodist churches with smaller numbers that attend other Protestant churches or are Roman Catholic.

The Lumbees shared a common culture and lifestyle with their white neighbors that included the English language, land ownership, agriculture, and religious affiliations. Because they lived and worshiped like their white neighbors, the Lumbees were mostly accepted and were exempted from laws that governed the rights of African Americans or indigenous peoples. In 1835 the laws were changed, stripping the Lumbees of most of those rights and beginning decades of discrimination and impoverishment that persisted until well after the Civil War. Officially the state of North Carolina listed them as "free people of color" in state censuses

Lumbees in North Carolina, ca. 1936. (USGS)

and other documents. The Lumbees lived in their isolated settlements in relative obscurity for much of the 19th century. During the Civil War the Lumbees endured many privations and injustices,

Henry Berry Lowrie

Following a complex series of accusations during the Civil War, the Home Guard shot Henry Berry Lowrie's father and brother while he watched from hiding. Leading a mixed-race band of supporters, Lowrie began an eight-year war to avenge his family and the other injustices suffered by the Lumbees. The group, known as the Lowrie Band, fought skirmishes with Home Guard units from 1865, and in 1868 they were officially outlawed and were pursued by local, state, and federal agents and bounty hunters. To the Lumbees he is a hero; he is seen as a Robin Hood–type who distributed stolen goods to starving Lumbee settlements across the region. During the years from 1865 to 1872, Lowrie and his gang killed 18 men associated with the Home Guard or the suffering of the Lumbees. He disappeared mysteriously in 1872, and his followers were mostly captured or killed.

including forced labor on coastal fortifications and harsh treatment by the local militia, the Home Guard. Their treatment resulted in the rise of the most famous of Lumbee heroes, Henry Berry Lowrie. In 1885 the state of North Carolina recognized the Lumbees as an indigenous tribe called the Croatans, referring to the belief that they were descended from the lost colonists of Roanoke Island. Citizenship rights were returned to the Lumbees in 1888, following years of privations and injustices. The name of the tribe was officially changed from "Croatan" to "Indians of Robeson County" in 1911. Several scholars studied the people between 1914 and 1933 concluding that they were descended from the Siouan speaking Cheraws and other related peoples. Embracing their identity as indigenous peoples rather than as mixed race, the Lumbee leaders joined the National Congress of American Indians in 1934. The members voted to adopt the name Lumbee in 1952, taking the name from the Lumber River that runs through their traditional territory. The Lumbees were recognized as an indigenous tribe by the Federal Government in 1956. The Lumbees received national attention in 1958 when over 500 armed Lumbees routed a group of Ku Klux Klan members. The event, remembered as the "Battle of Hayes Pond," ended Klan intimidation of the Lumbees. In 1987 the Lumbees petitioned the U.S. Department of the Interior for federal recognition. A new tribal government was organized and sworn in 2001. New legislation, proposed in 2009, would extend federal recognition for the tribe, but the official recognition is still pending due to controversy over their mixed racial ancestry.

Further Reading

Blu, Karen I. *The Lumbee Problem: The Making of an American Indian People.* Lincoln: University of Nebraska Press, 2001.

Dial, Adolph L. and David K. Eliades. *The Only Land I Know.* Syracuse, NY: Syracuse University Press, 1995.

Lowery, Malinda Maynor. *Lumbee Indians in the Jim Crow South: Race, Identity, and the Making of a Nation.* Chapel Hill: University of North Carolina, 2010.

M

Machiguengas

The Machiguengas, sometimes known as Matsigenkas, Machigengas, or Matsiguenkas, are a South American ethnic group inhabiting the Amazon region of southeastern Peru, with smaller numbers in adjacent areas of Brazil and Bolivia. The estimated 15,000 Machiguengas speak a language of the Campa group of Arawakan languages. Most Machiguengas retain their traditional religious beliefs with a minority of them being Christians, mostly Roman Catholics.

The Machiguengas evolved as a traditionally nomadic people, migrating through the Amazon rain forest on a seasonal basis. Once they exhausted the resources of an area, they would move on in search of new resources. Though their society was based on a hunter-gatherer culture augmented by the cultivation of cassava and other crops, the Machiguengas also developed attributes usually exhibited only by advanced societies, such as weaving textiles, cultivating numerous food and fiber crops, and making fine ceramics. The Machiguengas had no central authority but lived in small extended family groups led by a "headman." Though the Machiguengas inhabited the jungled eastern foothills of the Andes Mountains along the Rio Urubamba and its tributaries just east of Machu Picchu, they were never conquered by the Incas; instead, they established trade relations providing the highland Incas with

cacao, bird feathers, cotton, herbal medicines, tropical fruits, and palm wood. In exchange they received stone and metal tools and silver for use in jewelry. The Machiguengas maintained their self-imposed isolation when the Spanish took control of the Inca Empire in the early 16th century. Spanish military columns and Catholic missionaries soon learned to avoid the region, which held little interest for the colonial authorities.

The culture of the Machiguengas is an Amazonian culture based on their hunter-gatherer way of life. Shifting agriculture is also important with cassava as the main crop. Traditionally Machiguenga society is often polygamous, with a man often having several wives. Some anthropologists believe that the culture is matriarchal with women dominating family life. The Machiguengas are only now in the process of allowing contact with the outside world, so few scholars have studied the culture. Traditionally the Machiguengas believe in the sacredness of the nature around them, ascribing spirits to all living things. They believe the Amazon forest is there to nurture them, its herbs, plants, animals, and fish, along with the earth itself, all working in harmony to sustain everything in the world. Belief in evil spirits helps to explain accidents and natural phenomena. The Machiguenga language is spoken with only slight variations by a number of small related groups united by culture, language, and history. The language is spoken in two main dialects and differs greatly from the languages of other neighboring indigenous peoples.

The Machiguengas remained isolated from modern society until the 1960s when American missionaries were flown into the region in small planes. However, due to the inaccessible locations of some Machiguenga groups they have survived and continue to live in voluntary isolation to the present. Scholars have also begun to study their traditional herbal lore, which may hold new cures and medicines unknown to the outside world. The missionaries moved into outposts in the jungle near the Machiguenga villages but the new Christian religion, with its new value system, and imported diseases have disrupted the culture. Critics claim that the indigenous Amazonian peoples are not allowed to feel proud of their history, culture, or ancestry but other anthropologists point out that indigenous societies are adaptable and capable of resisting the modern world provided that the core cultural values and their native language are maintained. Though the Machiguengas live in an area that is easily accessible from the Machu Picchu ruins, few organized tours involve a visit to the region and fewer visitors come to the isolated Machiguenga villages. The Machiguengas are renowned for being nonviolent and for their warm reception of visitors.

Further Reading

Davis, Patricia M. *Reading for Knowing: Literacy Acquisition, Retention, and Usage among the Machiguenga.* Dallas, TX: SIL International, 2004.

Johnson, Allen. *Families of the Forest: The Matsigenka Indians of the Peruvian Amazon.* Berkeley, CA: University of California Press, 2003.

Miller, Frederic P., Agnes F. Vendome, and John McBrewster, eds. *Machiguenga People.* Saarbrücken, Germany: Alphascript Publishing, 2011.

Macushis

The Macushis, sometimes known as Macuxis, Makuxis, Makushis, Makusis, Macusis, Macussis, Teweyas, Pemons, or Teueias, are a South American ethnic group living in southern Guyana and northern Brazil. There is also a small community in the adjacent area of Venezuela. The estimated 40,000 Macushis speak a language belonging to the North Amazonian branch of the Cariban language family. The Macushis are now mostly Christian though they continue to adhere to their traditional religious beliefs, including shamanism.

The early Macushis were a people of the savannas that now lie in the northern part of the Brazilian state of Roraima and in southern Guyana. The region was inhabited by a number of distinct tribal groups living in the neighboring Kanuku Mountains, in the tropical forests, and along the major rivers. Villages were usually populated with between 100 and 600 people, the number that could be sustained by the territory controlled by the village for farming, hunting, and fishing. Trade between the tribes was mostly in foods from regions outside the savannas and for wood and metals. The Macushis harvested many products from the savannas and forests, including foods, medicines, and fibers. Contact with European explorers was probably sometime in the 17th century, though accounts of the Macushis are mostly from expeditions exploring the interior from Brazil and the Caribbean coastal region in the early- to mid-18th century. European diseases brought to the region by the explorers decimated the indigenous peoples who had no natural immunity. By the end of the 18th century the Macushi population is thought to have declined to half the number living in the region prior to the Spanish conquest.

The Macushis view themselves as descendants of the sun's children, the ancestors who created the fire needed for life as well as diseases. They credit the sun's children with the discovery of *washacá*, the tree of life. The Macushis live according to the life principle, the *stkaton*, which was a gift of the sun. The modern Macushis live in villages with houses built around a central square. The culture is patrilineal, with inheritance through the male line, but is also matrilocal so that when married, a Macushi couple lives with the wife's extended family. The father-in-law is of great importance in Macushi society. Despite having contact with outsiders for over two centuries, the Macushis have maintained their language and culture while adopting parts of the modern South American cultures. Hunting and fishing are the most important occupations for both men and women and provide the major sources in the diet. Women are also occupied with weaving, making pottery, and crafting jewelry. Women also care for the farms and do most of the food-preserving and cooking. Though nominally Christian, mostly Roman Catholic, the Macushis also revere the *piaiman* or shamans, whose powers are believed to cause or remove diseases;

it is also believed that spirits speak through these "medicine men." The Macushis now teach their children their traditional language, a member of the Carib language related to the languages once spoken throughout the Caribbean area.

The Macushis mostly shunned contacts with outsiders during the 19th century. Memories of epidemics, slavers, and abuses resulted in their villages being built in inaccessible regions. They traded with neighboring tribes but contacts with representatives of the governments that claimed their homeland were minimal. In 1909 a Jesuit missionary, Cuthbert Cary-Elwes, studied the Macushis of southern British Guiana while living with the tribe for 23 years. He later returned to the United Kingdom, and through lectures, he made the Macushis better known and respected. In the 1960s miners, loggers, and others began to move into Macushi territory, often resulting in conflicts and abuses. Aided by the Roman Catholic missionaries the Macushis organized to protect their lands from encroachments. Since the 1980s over 20 Macushis have been killed and hundreds injured in attacks by people hired by mining and agribusiness companies. In 2005 the Macushi region known as Raposa-Serra do Sol was set aside as a tribal reserve. Many Macushi children now attend government schools and health clinics established in the last decade.

Further Reading

Balkaran, Lal. *The Rupununi Savannas of Guyana: A Visual Journey.* Bloomington, IN: AuthorHouse, 2005.

Plotkin, Mark J. *Tales of a Shaman's Apprentice: An Ethnobotanist Searches for New*

Medicines in the Amazon Rain Forest. London: Penguin Books, 1994.

Saizano, Francisco M. *Lost Paradises and the Ethics of Research and Publication.* New York: Oxford University Press, 2003.

Mapuches

The Mapuches, sometimes known as Maputongos, Arucanians, Arucanos, or Mapuchs, are a South American ethnic group inhabiting both sides of the Andes Mountains in southern Chile and western Argentina. The estimated 1.8 million Mapuches speak a number of related dialects collectively known as Mapudungun, with most speaking Spanish as their second language. The Mapuches are nominally Roman Catholic, usually blending Christian rituals with traditional beliefs and customs.

The origin of the Mapuches is not well known and is disputed by scholars studying the language and culture. The Mapuches controlled a large territory in southwestern South America perhaps for thousands of years. They mostly lived in distinct regional groups, each with its own dialect and cultural traditions. From the 12th century CE the Mapuches came under constant pressure from the expanding Inca Empire to the north. The various Mapuche groups united to face the invading Inca warriors and over time they evolved a strong warrior tradition. They halted the southern expansion of the Incas, defeating invasions led by Tupai Yupanqui between 1448 and 1482. The Inca troops, unable to defeat the fierce Mapuche resistance, finally withdrew leaving the Mapuches as the most powerful nation in the southern part of the continent prior to the arrival of the Europeans. Mapuche territory stretched from the Pacific Ocean to the Atlantic, a vast area traversed by the high Andes Mountains. Though they controlled a huge territory, the Mapuches did not recognize any central political or cultural authority above the village level. Spanish military forces under Pedro de Valdivia moved south from present-day Peru in 1540. The Spanish founded Santiago in 1541 and eventually crossed the Bío-Bío River that was the northern boundary of Mapuche territory. Meeting only minimal resistance the Spanish continued south in the Mapuche heartland in 1552. Having established a number of permanent settlements, the Spanish considered the conquest of Chile complete and the people they called the Arucanos completely pacified. Led by their warrior chief Lautaro, the Mapuches launched a massive attack on the Spanish settlements in 1553, beginning a long series of conflicts known as the Arucanian Wars. The victorious Mapuches surged north intent on driving the Spanish back to Peru, but the death of Lautaro and a severe smallpox epidemic—a disease brought to the area by the Europeans—saved the colony. The Mapuches withdrew to the south of the Bío-Bío and continued to repulse Spanish incursions. The Mapuches had defeated the world's most powerful state, the Spanish Empire of the 16th century. Unable to overcome Mapuche resistance, the Spanish, a century after the first invasion of Mapuche territory, negotiated a treaty that guaranteed Mapuche independence and prohibited further Spanish settlements south of the Bío-Bío River. In spite of the Spanish treaty, the Mapuches were forced to unite to defeat renewed Spanish invasions in 1725, 1740, and 1766, as well as numerous raids by Spanish slavers.

The Mapuches comprise 14 distinct castes or clans, each with its own dialect and cultural traditions. The following are the most important of the clans: the Mapuches, the "people of the land," who are mostly farmers; the Moluches, the "people of O," who are traditionally warriors; the Pipuche, the "people of the pines," who are traditionally mountain dwellers; the Huilliche, the "people of the south"; the Pehuenche, the "people of the north"; and the Liquenche, the "people of the coast." Despite advances in recent decades discrimination continues to affect the Mapuches, with an estimated third of the total population now living in urban areas where alcohol, illiteracy, disease, and poverty continue to be major problems. The Mapuche language, Mapudungun, meaning "language of the land," is a group of closely related dialects that make up a separate language family of disputed origins. Until recently the language was an oral tradition; Spanish was used as the literary language. A number of scholars and organizations are working toward the creation of a Mapuche alphabet in order to standardize the dialects and to sustain and preserve the oral tradition. The Mapuches were mostly converted to Roman Catholicism in the 19th century but have also retained their traditional beliefs, including the belief in spirits and the reliance on the shaman or *machi*, who is the spiritual leader of each village.

Mapuche woman weaving a blanket, 1998. (AP Photo/Santiago Llanquin)

Chile and Argentina gained independence from Spain in 1810, though the Mapuches retained their independence in their traditional homeland. The new national governments revived the struggle to conquer the Mapuches, whose territory they claimed and divided by the new national boundaries. In Argentina, the so-called Campaign of the Desert devastated and nearly exterminated the Mapuche population east of the Andes. In Chile the Mapuches repeatedly defeated Chilean military incursions but having decided to colonize the region the Chilean government began selling land grants to European immigrants in Mapuche land. In the 1850s the Mapuches retaliated by raiding the settlements established in their territory by German immigrants. In 1866 the Chilean government passed a law declaring Mapuche lands as "public land" to be sold to the growing number of immigrants arriving from Europe. The Chileans sent a large military force south in 1873, determined to take control of the entire Mapuche region of Arucania. Once again defeated, the Chileans withdrew but returned in 1880 with the entire national army. Finally defeated in 1881, the Mapuches were forced to surrender, ending over three centuries of successful resistance. The Mapuches were the last indigenous nation in South America to fall to the conquerors. Most of Chile's Mapuches were forced to settle on small reservations in 1884. Over the next decades they lost nearly all their lands to the colonizers while the reservations set up in Chile and Argentina were unable to adequately support the surviving Mapuches. The continuing loss of the productive lands and a tripling of the Mapuche population

between 1927 and 1961 caused severe poverty, disease, and hunger forcing many to leave their homes to migrate to the cities in search of work. During the 1970s the Mapuches gave their support to the leftist Salvador Allende, who was elected president of Chile in 1970. His procommunist ideals appealed to the Mapuches with their ancient communal traditions. The Allende government passed new laws allowing the Mapuches to recover lost lands. Allende's overthrow and the establishment of a right-wing dictatorship under Augusto Pinochet ended concessions to the Mapuches, whose leaders and many followers were murdered and their bodies thrown into mass graves. Most of the lands recovered during the Allende years were again taken away. Mapuche life under the dictatorship was harsh and poverty was widespread. Younger activists began to mobilize the population in the 1980s following the abolition of the reservations, the prohibition of their religious practices, the ban on using their language in public, and punishments for educating their children about their language and culture. The Mapuche clans, formerly autonomous and traditionally disunited, had become a viable tribal group by the early 1990s. Demands for greater autonomy and for the unification of the Mapuches' traditional territory in Chile and Argentina have won widespread support among the growing Mapuche population. Activists continue to demand that the Spanish, Chilean, and Argentine governments honor the many treaties that recognized Mapuche sovereignty over territories south of the Bío-Bío River in Chile and the Colorado River in Argentina.

Further Reading

Bacigalupo, Ana Mariella. *Shamans of the Foye Tree: Gender, Power, and Healing among Chilean Mapuche.* Austin, TX: University of Austin Press, 2007.

Course, Magnus. *Becoming Mapuche: Person and Ritual in Indigenous Chile.* Champaign, IL: University of Illinois Press, 2011.

Ray, Leslie. *Language of the Land: The Mapuche in Argentina and Chile.* Copenhagen, Denmark: IGWIA, 2008.

Martinicans

The Martinicans, sometimes known as Martiniquans, Martiniquais, Madianans, Martinecos, or Martinique Creoles, are a Caribbean ethnic group whose homeland is Martinique, an island in the Lesser Antilles in the Caribbean Sea. Outside their home island there are Martinican communities in France and the other French Caribbean islands. The estimated 600,000 Martinicans speak French, the language of education and administration, but the language of daily life is an Antillean Creole dialect. An estimated 95 percent of the Martinicans are nominally Roman Catholic although the Catholic traditions are generously blended with customs and rituals that originated in Africa.

Migrants from the South American mainland, known as Arawaks, are believed to have settled the island around 130 CE. They called the island Madiana, the "island of flowers." An eruption of Mount Pelée decimated the island population in the year 295. Around 400 CE, Arawaks from other Caribbean islands repopulated Madiana and established a flourishing society based on farming and fishing. Around 600 CE another ethnic group moving north from the South American mainland, the warlike Caribs, invaded the island. They exterminated or absorbed the Arawaks and took over the farms, fisheries, and other Arawak enterprises. The island was charted by Christopher Columbus in 1493 although the first contact was made during a later voyage in 1502. The expedition

Aimé Césaire

Postwar Martinican politics was greatly influenced by Aimé Césaire, a Martinican writer and one of the founding members of the black Martinican emancipation group known as the Negritude movement. Césaire was elected mayor of Fort-de-France, the island's capital, and deputy to the French National Assembly for Martinique in 1945. He resigned in 1956 and later founded a new Martinican political party, the Progressive Party of Martinique. The party's pro-independence platform gathered widespread support and in 1957 the party won island elections by a wide margin. Aimé Césaire is considered the father of the Martinican equality movement. Césaire died in Fort-de-France in 2008. He was honored with a state funeral attended by French president Nicolas Sarkozy.

left several pigs and goats on the island, a population that expanded rapidly. A group of between 80 and 100 French colonists arrived in 1635. Their guns quickly overcame Carib resistance to the landing. The colony grew rapidly and settlers arrived from other Caribbean islands and also directly from France. European diseases, slavery, and violence decimated the Carib population with the survivors fleeing to the least accessible parts of the island. The establishment of sugar plantations in the late 1600s resulted in a great demand for labor. With few surviving Caribs to enslave, the French began importing slaves from Africa. In 1674 the island became a dominion of the French crown. Slavery and slave revolts became major influences on the politics and economy of Martinique. By 1750 the slave population of the island numbered over 60,000 out of a population of about 75,000. Many of the slaves were of mixed European and African background, often freed by their European fathers to form a free population of artisans and laborers. The French planter aristocracy dominated island society; it's most famous representative, Josephine Rose Tascher de La Pagerie, gained fame as Napoleon's wife, the empress of France. The outbreak of the French Revolution in 1789 prompted a small, unsuccessful slave revolt but the threat remained. The island's leaders voluntarily placed the island under British authority until the French monarchy could be reestablished. The revolutionary government in Paris officially abolished slavery in 1794, but the implementation was forestalled by the British occupation. The planters regained control of their plantations and their slaves. The island changed hands several times during the Napoleonic Wars before returning to permanent French rule in 1814. Slavery was finally abolished in 1848 with over 48,000 slaves suddenly having the status of free men. The former slaves mostly settled on small plots as subsistence farmers or fishermen. The island's capital, Saint-Pierre, became the center of French culture in the Caribbean. A sophisticated city nicknamed the "Paris of the West Indies," Saint-Pierre was destroyed by the eruption of Mount Pelée in 1902. Over 40,000 people in the city and its surroundings perished as ash covered the region. The colony, dominated by Békés, the descendants of the colonists, and the Metros, French officials and business people from continental France, flourished prior to World War II on the trade in sugar and tropical fruit. The European elite mostly ignored the majority Creoles, who were relegated to the most menial occupations. In the late 1940s the island's status was changed to that of an overseas department, giving the Martinicans the same rights as the inhabitants of the departments of continental France. Emigration to France became the only outlet for the many Martinicans seeking jobs or greater opportunities. A local writer, Aimé Césaire, greatly influenced Martinican politics in the postwar era. Support for independence was balanced by the material prosperity allowed by generous French welfare state benefits. In the 21st century the Martinique Creole population, with a birthrate twice that of continental France, suffers endemic unemployment and few economic opportunities with many younger Martinicans leaving the island each year. The island's Békés, the white minority, control a majority of the island's economy.

Further Reading

Burton, Richard D.E., and Fred Reno, eds. *French and West Indian: Martinique, Guadeloupe, and French Guiana Today.* Charlottesville, VA: University of Virginia Press, 1995.

Icon Group International. *Martinique: Webster's Timeline History, 1615–2007.* San Diego, CA: Icon Group International, 2010.

Schloss, Rebecca Harthopf. *Sweet Liberty: The Final Days of Slavery in Martinique.* Philadelphia, PA: University of Pennsylvania Press, 2009.

Martinois

The Martinois, sometimes known as Saint Martins or Saint Martiners, are a Caribbean people, the inhabitants of the northern half of the island of Saint Martin in the northeastern Caribbean. There are Saint Martin communities in France, other Caribbean islands, and the United States. The estimated 40,000 Martinois speak French, the language of education and administration, and many also speak English, which is widely spoken across the island. Minorities also speak Spanish, mostly among the growing number of immigrants to the territory. The largest religion is Roman Catholicism, which was introduced by the early French colonists, with smaller numbers of Jehovah's Witnesses, people belonging to several Protestant groups, and Hindus.

Originally settled by Arawak migrants from the South American mainland between 800 CE and 1000 CE, the island was known as Sualouiga, the land of salt, for its abundant saltpans. Around 1,300 warlike Caribs, also from South America, took control of the island, absorbing or killing the Arawak population. Christopher Columbus sighted the island in 1493 on his second voyage to the New World. Claimed by the Spanish, the island remained mostly uninhabited due to the epidemics of European diseases. The Spanish ignored the island in favor of richer pickings in Mexico and Peru. Some French settlers from Saint Kitts moved to the island and began to cultivate tobacco between 1620 and 1624. A small Dutch settlement was founded on the southern half of the island in 1631. The Spanish, not wanting to lose territory to either France or the Netherlands, sent an expedition to take control of Saint Martin in 1633. Losing interest in the unprofitable island, the Spanish abandoned it in 1648. Both the French and the Dutch reestablished their settlements and territorial claims. To avoid a conflict over Saint Martin, the two colonial powers agreed in 1648 to divide the island with the French in control of the north and the Dutch in the south. In the later 17th and 18th centuries, the island changed hands several times, including periods of French, Dutch, or English control of the entire island. French planters established cotton, tobacco, and sugar plantations and began importing slave laborers from Africa for the grueling manual labor.

The culture of Saint Martin is a Caribbean blend of French culture and traditions and customs brought to the island by the African slaves. Following the abolition of slavery many of the Europeans left the island so the majority, of African or mixed ancestry, evolved a culture that retained the French language and culture mixed with the traditions of the Afro-Caribbean population. French influence remains strong and the island is known for nude beaches, French fashion, extensive shopping facilities, and a rich island cuisine. Though the language of the territory is officially French, which is spoken by most of the population, the language of daily life is a French Caribbean patois that blends French with the structures, expressions, and vocabularies of several West African languages. French influence is also felt in religion with the Roman Catholic Church being the most important of the numerous religions represented in Saint Martin.

During the Napoleonic Wars in Europe the conflict was extended to the Caribbean territories. From 1795 to 1801 the French took control of the entire island. The British occupied Saint Martin in 1801–1802 and again from 1810 to 1816. On the Dutch side English was adopted by many of the inhabitants, but in French Saint Martin the inhabitants clung to their French language and heritage. French Saint Martin was returned to French rule in 1816 following Napoleon's final defeat and the end of the European wars. In 1848 the French government outlawed slavery in all its colonial possessions, bringing an economic decline to Saint Martin's plantation economy. The former slaves mostly settled on small plots of land as subsistence farmers or fishermen. Some became laborers in the island's saltpans. The Martinois often resented rule from Guadeloupe, a larger French Caribbean island that is the center of government and administration for several of the French islands. In 1939 the island of Saint Martin was declared a duty-free port, which stimulated the local economy and brought work for many of the Martinois. Guadeloupe and its dependencies, including French Saint Martin, became an overseas department of France in 1946. The new status gave the Martinois the rights to health care, welfare, and educational subsidies, the same as residents of departments in continental France. The Martinois became citizens of France and in 1957 became citizens of the European Economic Community. In 2002, as part of the French Republic, the Martinois began to use the Euro as their local currency. Dissatisfaction with the administration of the island resulted in a Martinois vote in a referendum on separation from Guadeloupe in order to form a separate country within the French Republic. In 2007 Saint Martins became an overseas collectivity with greater powers of local government.

Further Reading

Burton, Richard D.E. and Fred Reno, eds. *French and West Indian: Martinique, Guadeloupe, and French Guinea Today.* Charlottesville, VA: University Press of Virginia, 1995.

Greey, Madeleine. *Saint Martin/Sint Maarten: Portrait of an Island.* Oxford, UK: Macmillan Caribbean, 2005.

Russell, Jesse and Ronald Cohn. *Saint Martin.* Paris: VSD, 2012.

Mayans

The Mayans, sometimes known as Mayas, Quiches, Tzeltals, or Tsotzils, are a Native American ethnic group living in southern Mexico and northern Central America. Outside this region there are sizable Mayan communities in other parts of Mexico and in the United States, particularly in California. The name Mayan or Maya is a collective name for the peoples of the region who share cultural and linguistic ties but have their own particular traditions, historical identities, and cultures. The estimated 7–10 million Mayans mostly speak Spanish though some traditional groups often speak one of the Mayan languages as their primary language. Most Mayans are nominally Christian, with a Roman Catholic majority and a growing Protestant minority, though Christian beliefs are often blended with the earlier Mayan belief system.

The origins and early history of the Mayan peoples is not well known, though scholars agree on the existence of three major epochs in the Mayans' long history—the Pre-Classical Era from about 1500 BCE to 300 CE, the Classical Era from around 300 CE to 900 CE, and the Post-Classical Era from 900 CE to 1697 CE. The Pre-Classical Mayan civilization developed in the highlands of present-day Guatemala and El Salvador as a sedentary agricultural society. Its sophisticated arts and sciences included advanced agricultural methods, inventions such as an extremely accurate calendar and a hieroglyphic writing system, and major art forms. In the early Classical period Mayan culture spread over a much larger territory. Large cities were dominated by great stone temples, pyramids, and large central markets. During the Post-Classical Era the centers of Mayan civilization shifted north to the city-states of the Yucatan Peninsula. The Mayan culture, considered the most advanced culture of pre-Columbian America, reached its apex between 600 CE and 900 CE. Discoveries in astronomy and

mathematics were comparable to similar achievements in ancient Egypt and Mesopotamia. Mayan developments in ceramics, sculpture, painting, and weaving were often more advanced than those of their European contemporaries. In spite of their brilliant advances, the Mayans never developed machines such as the wheel, which was used for children's toys but was never adapted to any practical application. All labor was done by human manual laborers, overseen and directed by a religious and military elite. Mayan civilization began to decay in the ninth century due to unknown causes. Scientists estimate the Mayan population at that time to have been around 14 million, living mostly south of the Yucatan Peninsula. Two large migrations moved north to settle the Yucatan Peninsula and the highlands of Chiapas. New city-states arose in the region, which enjoyed a long period of stability and prosperity. That stability crumbled around 1440 when a civil war erupted. Whole populations fled, abandoning fields, towns, and cities. When the Spanish began to visit the coast the Mayan civilization was thoroughly in decline, yet they managed to resist subjugation longer than either the Aztecs of central Mexico or the Incas of Peru. The Spanish launched a military expedition against the Mayans during 1531–1535. The last Mayan strongholds fell to the Spanish invaders in 1546 except for the Itzá, the last free Mayan nation, whose people were driven from their capital at Tayasal in 1697, bringing an end to the last important Mayan state. The Spanish authorities and priests systematically destroyed the Mayan culture and religion. Zealous Roman Catholic missionaries gathered and burned all Mayan

MAYA CIVILIZATION, 200 BCE – 800 CE

0		200 km
0	100 miles	

N

Dominant Maya city of the Postclassic period

Komchen • Dzibilchaltún •
Izamal •
Acaneh •
Chichén Itzá ■
Oxkintok • Cobá •
Loltun •
Uxmal • Chacchob Yaxuná
Jaina • Kabah ◻
Xcalumkin Sayil • Labná
Xcocha Keuic Xcichmook
Xtampak • Yucatán
Dzibilnocac •
Edzná • Huntichmul
Hochob • **NORTHERN AREA**

Gulf of Mexico

Pechal ◦

Becan Xpuhil
Bellote Hormiguero ◦ Pasión del Cristo
Comalcalco Jonuta *Dominant Maya city of the Preclassic period* Cohunlich Cetros
Oxpemul ◦ Rio Bec Nohmul
Calakmul ★ El Palmar Cuello
Naachtún ◦ Colhá
CENTRAL Ucal ◦ Balakbal Lamanai
AREA Balancán Morales El Mirador ◦ Rio Azul Altun Ha
Tortuguero ★ La Honradez
Palenque ★ Pomoná *The largest Classic* Xullún San José
Chinikha *Maya city* Uaxactún ◻
El Porvenir **Petén** El Péru Tikal ★ Nakum Baking Pot
La Mar ◦ Piedras Negras Xunantunich
Toniná ◦ Motul de Yakhá Naranjo Pomona
San Yaxchilán ◦ San José Caracol Mountain
Augustin Lacanhá • Bonampak Cow
Chiapa de Itzán Sacul Nimli
Corzo Agua Escondida Seibal Ixtutz Punit
Santa Elena Altar de Sacrificios Lubaantún
Santa Cruz Poco Uinic Aguateca Pusilha
Chinkultic Machaquilá
Quen Santo Cancuén
Lagartero Salinas de los
Chamá Nueve Cerros Lago de Izabal
Nebaj •
Guatemalan Highlands Quiriguá Santa
SOUTHERN La Lagunita Los Higos Rica
AREA San Agustin
Izapa Acasaguastián El Paraíso
El Jobo • Takalik Motagua Copán
Salinac Kaminaljuyú
la Bianca Chucumuk Amatitlán Yarumela
El Baul Pantaleón
Tiquisate Monti Obero Asunción
Alto Chalchuapa Mita
Finca Tazumal
Arizona Lake Ilopango

PACIFIC OCEAN

Usulután

Classic Maya

★ Pre-eminent regional centres

• Major Classic city-states

◦ Other Classic sites

■ Late Preclassic sites with monumental sculpture, 300 BC–AD 300

◻ Other late Preclassic sites, 300 BC–AD 300

◻ Classic Period AD 300–800

— Conjectural borders of Maya city-states c. AD 790

Tikal Cities whose dynastic histories have been deciphered

The Mayan homeland in the Yucatan and Central America during the rise and fall of the region's most advanced civilization. (ABC-CLIO)

books and archives; only a few scattered examples survived the disaster. The inventors of advanced mathematics, arts, astronomy, and sciences were relegated to the status of a subject people, many of them enslaved or forced to work on Spanish plantations. European diseases, abuses, and the social disruption of the Spanish conquest wiped out a large portion of the Mayan population during the 16th century. By 1700 the population of millions had declined to fewer than 250,000.

The Mayan culture encompasses a wide area populated by a number of culturally and linguistically related peoples, all descendants of the great Mayan empire. The Mayans of the Yucatan Peninsula were the first to call themselves and their language "Mayan," which was eventually applied to the related peoples of southern Mexico and Central America. The chief division in Mayan culture is between the inhabitants of the highlands and the lowland groups. Land is the key element in modern Mayan culture, particularly among the 80 percent that still lives in rural areas. Many Mayans have assimilated into the Hispanic culture, often speaking Spanish as a first or second language and participating in their shared Catholic faith. The indigenous Mayan populations in Mexico, Guatemala, El Salvador, Honduras, and Belize are the poorest of a generally relatively poor regional population. Socially the indigenous peoples are considered inferior to those of European or mixed ancestry, and discrimination is rife. Their Roman Catholic faith is often seen as a refuge by some but as part of the problem by others. Elements of their pre-Christian religion remain as important parts of the culture, particularly the ceremonies and rituals that are often mixed with Christian traditions. Belief in the powers of shams or curers and both good and evil spirits is also widespread.

The overthrow of Spanish rule in Mexico and Central America did little to better the lives of the Mayan population though slavery was gradually abolished. Newly independent Mexico claimed most of Central America in 1821, one of the wealthiest regions of Spanish America dominated by plantations worked by Mayan debt slaves following the abolition of slavery. By 1839 the Central American states had broken away from Mexico, including the Yucatan. Mexican troops ended the Yucatan secession in 1843 but failed to recover the other Central American regions. The Yucatan secession roused the downtrodden Mayans against the cruel European and Mestizo (mixed race) landlords. A new rebellion broke out in 1847 and quickly escalated to civil war. Called the War of the Castes, it pitted the poorly armed Mayans against the oppressive landlords and their Mestizo supporters. The war ended in a Mayan defeat in 1848 though part of the Yucatan Peninsula remained under Mayan rule until 1902. Another Mayan revolt broke out in 1910 but after initial successes the rebels fled to the less accessible parts of the region. Revolution and civil war left Mexico without a central government from 1914 to 1919. A separatist revolt again swept through the Yucatan region with widespread Mayan support. A socialist republic was declared in 1916, the first socialist state in the world a year before Lenin proclaimed a socialist state in Russia. The secessionist state was defeated but a renewed Mayan revolt began in 1923. A new Yucatan government

Mayans greet the north during the celebration of the Mayan New Year. (AP Photo/Carlos Lopez)

declared the Mayan language an official language for the first time since the Spanish conquest. The return of centralized Mexican rule ended the experiment in equality and socialism. The legacy of large estates, both in Mexico and in Central America, effectively excluded most Mayans from participation in the local economies. This remained a well-established mechanism for dominance and subordination well into the 1960s. From the late 1960s military governments, particularly in Guatemala and El Salvador, targeted the Mayan population leaving tens of thousands dead and many more displaced. In the 1990s democracy was restored in Guatemala and El Salvador but violence against the Mayans continued.

The Mayans began to cast aside their legendary patience in the early 1990s. Activists led groups demanding the return of stolen lands and cultural rights. The Mayans of the Chiapas region of Mexico were the last to mobilize against centuries of depravation and abuse. In the 2000s Mayans were leading protests and publishing demands for equality and redress of past outrages.

Further Reading

Ellington, Kristine. *Tales from the Yucatan Jungle: Life in a Mayan Village.* Foster, VA: Sun Topaz, 2012.

Guzaro, Tomás and Terri Jacob McComb. *Escaping the Fire: How an Ixil Mayan Pastor led his People out of a Holocaust during the Guatemalan Civil War.* Austin, TX: University of Texas Press, 2010.

Sharer, Robert and Loa Traxier. *The Ancient Maya.* Palo Alto, CA: Stanford University Press, 2005.

Mayos

The Mayos, sometimes known as Yoremes, are a Mexican ethnic group living in the northwestern Mexican states of Sonora and Sinaloa. Outside their homeland there are Mayo communities in other parts of Mexico, particularly the large urban areas, and in the United States. The estimated 70,000 Mayos speak a language of the Piman branch of the Uto-Aztecan language group. The majority of the Mayos are nominally Roman Catholic, blending Christian rituals with pre-Christian customs and traditions.

The Mayos are believed to have migrated north from central Mexico, possibly to escape the wars and the expansion of the Aztec empire. They settled in the valleys of the Mayo and Fuerte rivers near the coast of the Pacific Ocean. They lived as farmers and fishermen occupying villages that were autonomous and ruled by local chiefs. The Mayos normally united to face a common enemy but never united to form a structured tribal group. Contact with Europeans began in 1532 when a Spanish expedition led by Diego Hertado de Mendoza landed at the mouth of the Fuerte River. Their arrival frightened the Mayo villagers, so when the Spanish sailed upriver they watched and waited. When the Spanish made camp and settled down to sleep the Mayos attacked and killed the invaders. A second Spanish expedition traversed

the Mayo territory in 1533 but Spanish aid against their Yaqui enemies resulted in an informal alliance. In 1609–1610 they aided the Spanish against the Yaquis. The Spanish victory brought peace to the region as part of the peace agreement stipulated that the warlike Yaquis should live at peace with the Mayos. The first Roman Catholic mission was founded in Mayo territory in 1613 with over 3,000 Mayos baptized within the first few weeks. Within a short time seven mission stations were established in the Mayo towns, beginning a long history of regular mission work in the region. The discovery of precious metals led to the exploitation of the Mayos and their lands. In 1740 the Mayos joined the Yaquis in a widespread revolt, apparently with the aid of Spanish officials jealous of missionary influence. The rebels burned the churches and drove the priests and settlers from their historic lands. The revolt was put down following hard fighting but the missions never regained their former influence and were mostly abandoned following the expulsion of the Jesuits in 1767. After the departure of the missionaries the Mayos were left without priests or religious teachers and many lapsed back into their traditional religious beliefs.

The culture of the Mayos is a Native American culture that has been greatly influenced by the Hispanic culture of northern Mexico. Most of the Mayos live in 15 regional towns and numerous villages. The major occupations are farming and fishing, though some villages are devoted to traditional pottery or weaving. Many Mayos work on large agribusiness farms that have irrigated lands and use modern agricultural techniques although in the villages agriculture is more traditional. The major annual celebrations are based on the Roman Catholic calendar. The largest religious festival is during Easter week, when the Mayos traditionally recreate the passion of Christ. Their traditional dances, particularly the deer dance and the Pascola dance, are well known. The Mayos continue to use their own language with many speaking Spanish as a first or second language. Their language is classified as a Nahua-Cuitlateco language of the Uto-Aztecan language group. They speak a dialect of the Cáhita branch, which also includes the neighboring Yaqui language. Their religious beliefs are primarily Roman Catholic with some belief systems from their pre-Christian religion still in use.

The independence of Mexico in 1821 did little to change the Mayo way of life. Many Mayos labored on the large ranches and farms established in the region. Discrimination and debt slavery were widespread as were abuses by local Mestizo (mixed race) populations. During 1825–1827 the Mayos again joined the Yaquis in a revolt against discrimination and mistreatment. Led by the war chief Juzucanea, known as Bandera in Spanish, the rebels initially routed the local garrisons and drove many landlords and townspeople from the region but the arrival of troops from Mexico City ended the rebellion. Though the Mayos joined the Yaquis in several subsequent uprisings, by 1900 most had settled as sedentary farmers, fishermen, mine workers, and artisans. The farmers cultivated corn, beans, squash, tobacco, cotton, and manguey, the main ingredient in tequila and mescal liquors. The *ejido* or communal land system was established as part of the Mexican Revolution

during 1914–1919, but it was not until the 1920s and 1930s that the Mayos were able to consolidate the *ejido* lands and revive their traditional culture in relative peace. The traditional self-government system of the Mayos, based on the village community with a headman and tribal chiefs, is now breaking down as many younger Mayos leave the villages to seek jobs and greater opportunities in the nearby cities or as far away as Mexico City, Guadalajara, and the southwestern states of the United States. The Mayo language is one of 62 indigenous languages designated by the Mexican government as having the same validity in their territory as Spanish. Education is bilingual in local schools, and a Mayo university is located in the town of Mochicahui.

Further Reading

Crumrine, Ross. *The Mayo Indians of Sonora: A People Who Refuse to Die.* Tucson, AZ: University of Arizona Press, 1977.

Yetman, David. *Scattered Around Stones: A Mayo Village in Sonora, Mexico.* Tucson, AZ: University of Arizona Press, 1998.

Yetman, David and Devender Thomas Van. *Mayo Ethnobotany: Land, History, and Traditional Knowledge in Northwest Mexico.* Berkeley, CA: University of California Press, 2002.

Mazahuas

The Mazahuas, sometimes known as Hñathos, are a Mexican ethnic group inhabiting the northwestern districts of the state of Mexico and northeastern Michoacán. In recent decades many of them have migrated to the Federal District and the suburbs of Mexico City. The estimated 350,000 Mazahuas speak a language of the Oto-Manguean language family with most also speaking Spanish as their first or second language.

The history of the Mazahuas is an oral record, so much of their early history has been lost. They are thought to descend from the large Otomí tribe of central Mexico, having migrated to their present homeland during the 13th century CE, part of the great migration of the five tribes that made up the Chichimec migrations to the Valley of Mexico. The Mazahuas came under the rule of the Aztec empire in the 15th century. The Aztecs demanded annual tributes, including goods and captives for human sacrifice. Mazahua cities were garrisoned by Aztec warriors to ensure loyalty to the empire. In 1521 Hernán Cortés, having conquered the Mexica or Aztec empire, consolidated Spanish power in central Mexico by sending troops to subdue the neighboring peoples including the Mazahuas. Domination by the Spanish included the instruction by Franciscan missionaries to convert the Mazahuas to Roman Catholicism. The large Mazahua population declined rapidly due to epidemics of European diseases to which they had no immunities, forced labor and slavery, and the disruption to their society caused by the Spanish. By the mid-1700s most of the Mazahuas lived in villages near large Spanish haciendas where they worked as ranch hands, farmers, or house workers, or worked their own small plots as subsistence farmers. The subjugation of the Mazahuas by the Spanish was even more onerous than their subjugation under Aztec rule. The system of tribute and slavery continued with Spanish institutions that insured the colonists access to forced indigenous labor. The concentration of extensive lands in vast Spanish haciendas, the development of mines, and the establishment of workshops were Spanish colonial ways of subjugating the Mazahuas and other peoples.

The name Mazahua, meaning "deer people," was given them by the neighboring peoples. In their own language they call themselves "Teetho ñaatho jñaatho," meaning "real people." Mazahua culture has been greatly influenced by the larger Hispanic culture that surrounds them and the Roman Catholic religion they adopted shortly after the Spanish conquest. The Catholic year dictates much of Mazahua life with each village or town holding its major yearly festival on the day of its patron saint. Though nominally Catholic, the Mazahuas continue to rely on traditional specialists for their medical needs, among them midwives, sorcerers, and bonesetters. To the Mazahuas the supernatural world is the source of many illnesses and of death. Another tradition that remains a strong cultural element is the custom of holding land in common, the *ejido*. Municipal and *ejido* authorities are officially responsible for conflicts and for solving problems. Traditionally the Mazahuas married within their local group, often their cousins, but with the growing number of Mazahuas living away from their homeland marriage to outsiders has become more common, particularly in the large urban areas. About half the Mazahuas still use their own language as their first language. Closely related to Otomí, the neighboring language group, its use in daily life is widespread. Many

Mazahuas speak Spanish but not all are fluent in the language.

The independence of Mexico from Spain in 1810 did not improve the lives of the Mazahuas. The consolidation of the large haciendas left many Mazahuas working on them as peons. Later Mexican governments expropriated the remaining *ejido* lands forcing the Mazahuas to abandon the communal property system that had given them some protection since colonial times into the hands of the large land owners. It was only after the Mexican Revolution of 1910 that some of the *ejido* lands were returned to the Mazahuas. A small plot of land was apportioned to each Mazahua family as part of the agrarian reforms of the 1930s. These reforms ushered in a mixed economy in which the Mazahuas produced basic subsistence foodstuff, bought industrially produced goods, and remained a pool of low-paid seasonal workers in the cities, farms, and cattle ranches. The modern Mazahuas are mostly employed in agriculture, growing maize, squash, beans, and maguey. The Mazahuas are one of the largest of the Native American ethnic groups in Mexico and their language is one of the most widely spoken. In 2000 they represented the sixth largest ethnic group in Mexico. The patience of the Mazahuas in the face of continued discrimination and abuses five centuries after the conquest began to give way in the early 21st century. In 2006 a group of about 300 Mazahuas briefly took over a water treatment plant in Mexico City's western suburbs, cutting off one of the main sources of water to the capital and its surrounding cities. The protesters demanded more government development aid and water plants to provide the

Mazahua villages and towns with potable water.

Further Reading

De Haan, Mariette. *Learning as Cultural Practice: How Children Learn in a Mexican Mazahua Community.* West Lafayette, IN: Purdue University Press, 2000.

Hidalgo, Margarita. *Mexican Indigenous Languages at the Dawn of the Twenty-First Century.* Berlin, Germany: Mouton de Gruyter, 2006.

Iwanska, Alicja. *Purgatory and Utopia: A Mazahua Indian Village in Mexico.* Piscataway, NJ: Transaction Publishers, 2006.

Métis

The Métis, sometimes known as Metis, Métiss, Metiffs, Mistchiffs, or Michifs, are a North American ethnic group who trace their ancestry to mixed Native American and European heritage. The estimated 450,000 Métis are concentrated in the prairie provinces of Canada with smaller communities in Ontario, Quebec, and other provinces and in the northern United States. The Métis usually speak standard French and English but also retain their own dialect known as Michif (Mitchif) or French Cree. The majority of the Métis are staunch Roman Catholics though evangelical Protestant groups have gained converts in recent decades.

The indigenous peoples of North America, now known as First Nations in Canada, were divided into a large number of tribal groups that maintained a trading network that reached from the eastern coast to the vast prairies in the west. French trappers and traders began exploring the territories west of the French colony of New France in the early 16th century. The first records of mixed-race children are found as early as 1600 on Canada's eastern coastal regions. The Frenchmen moving into the fur-rich regions between the Great Lakes and Hudson Bay began to marry women from the Cree, Ojibwe, Algonquin, Saulteaux, Menominee, Maliseet, or Micmac (Mi'kmaq) peoples in the mid-1600s. The majority of the early trappers and traders were French or Scottish and Catholic, so their offspring were raised as Roman Catholics. Later the English, the Scandinavians, the Irish, and other Europeans added their mixed-race offspring to the emerging Métis population. During the height of the North American fur trade, in the 18th century, indigenous wives formed a link between the Europeans and the First Nations, acting as interpreters, guides, and companions. The largest of the fur companies, the Hudson's Bay Company, attempted to discourage unions between its fur traders and indigenous women while its rival, the North West Company, supported the mixed marriages. The Métis were valuable employees of both companies due to their skills as trappers, buffalo hunters, and interpreters and due to their knowledge of the lands and peoples of the region. As the number of mixed-race offspring, called Métis in the French dialect of the trappers, expanded they began to develop their own unique culture, a mixture of the customs and traditions of the indigenous peoples, the French trappers, and the later English, Irish, and other Europeans who joined the Métis communities. As the buffalo herds dwindled, the Métis expanded, settling a vast area of the upper Great Plains.

The Métis culture is a blend of indigenous and European influences. At times rejected by both the indigenous peoples and the Europeans, the Métis, whose name comes from the Latin *miscere*, meaning "to mix," evolved a strong sense of separate identity on the vast North American plains. The dispute over the origins of the Métis is often heated. The Métis consider themselves a distinct indigenous people who developed on the Great Plains in the 18th and 19th centuries. In Canada the Métis demand the same rights and privileges accorded to the First Nations. The majority of the Métis once spoke, and many still speak, a dialect that mixes archaic French, English syntax, and borrowings from several indigenous languages. Most Métis now speak standard French, with English also spoken in many Métis communities. The use of the Métis dialect is growing due to the efforts of the provincial Métis councils. Most Métis, particularly the French-speaking majority, are Roman Catholic, often tempering their Christian traditions with customs and beliefs acquired during the evolution of the Métis culture. In recent decades Protestant denominations, particularly the evangelicals, have had some success among the scattered Métis communities but the majority remains devoutly Roman Catholic.

The Hudson's Bay Company obtained a grant of land in the Great Plains in 1811. The new colony, known as the Red River Settlement, encompassed much of present-day southern Manitoba, a region where the majority of the population consisted of Métis employed by the rival North West

Company. European settlers, mostly the Scots and the Irish, were recruited to settle the region. Seen as a threat, the Métis attacked the new settlements in 1816, forcing most of the colonists to abandon the region. A number of violent incidents finally led to a truce between the rival fur companies and a merger of the two in 1821. The territories of the fur companies were transferred to the British government, but the many European settlers and the large Métis population were forgotten in the transfer. A Métis leader, Louis Riel, educated in Montreal, organized resistance to the land transfer in the Red River region without the consent of the peoples living in the Northwest Territories. Riel led a large group of Métis to take control of the Red River colony and forced the Canadian and British governments to postpone the territorial transfer. The rebellion, known as the Red River Rebellion of 1869, ended with the entry of Manitoba into the Canadian Confederation and the exile of Louis Riel to the United States. In 1885, when news reached the area that a large force of North-West Mounted Police was heading west the Métis formed a separate government supported by several of the First Nations. This resulted in a series of incidents and conflicts known collectively as the North West Rebellion. Riel was later hanged for his part in the uprising and became the Métis' first national hero. In the 1930s activists mobilized the Métis of Alberta and Saskatchewan over land rights. The Alberta government passed the Métis Betterment Act in 1938, providing for funds and land for the Métis communities. The militancy of the 1960s and 1970s saw the emergence of Métis political organizations. A national organization, the Métis National Council, was formed in 1983, following official recognition of the Métis as an aboriginal people in Canada. A new political organization, the Métis Nation of Canada, was organized in 2009 to protect and preserve the unique Métis culture, to promote communications and understanding between the Métis and the general public, to facilitate communications between the various Métis communities, to initiate and affirm land claims, and to establish mobility rights for the Métis of Canada and the United States. The Métis now include both the larger French-descended communities and the later Anglo-Métis, more commonly known as Countryborn, the descendants of 19th century Scots, English, and Irish trappers and traders and indigenous women. The Métis flag, representing all Métis communities, is one of the oldest patriotic flags in Canada, though there are actually two flags with both having the centered infinity symbol but on different backgrounds, red or blue. Red was the color of the Hudson's Bay Company while blue was the color of the North West Company.

Further Reading

Brown, Jennifer S. Hl, Jacqueline Peterson, Robert K. Thomas, and Marcel Giraud. *New Peoples: Being and Becoming Métis in North America.* St. Paul, MN: Minnesota Historical Society Press, 2001.

Gordon, Irene Ternier. *A People on the Move.* Victoria, British Columbia: Heritage House Publishing, 2009.

Jackson, John C. *Children of the Fur Trade: Forgotten Métis of the Pacific Northwest.* Corvallis, OR: Oregon State University Press, 2007.

Mi'kmaqs

The Mi'kmaqs, sometimes known as Inus, Micmacs, Miigmaqs, Mi'gmaqs, Migmaqs, are a North American ethnic group living in Canada's Atlantic provinces, the Gaspé Peninsula of Quebec, and the northern part of Maine in the United States. Outside their traditional homeland there are Mi'kmaqs communities in Montreal, Boston, and New York. The estimated 42,000 Mi'kmaqs speak English with a French-speaking minority in Quebec. Many also speak their own language, which is an Eastern Algonquian dialect of the Algonquian language family.

Little is known of the early history of the Mi'kmaqs prior to the arrival of the Europeans in North America. Because their Algonquian language differs greatly from that of the neighboring Algonquian peoples, many scholars believe they were latecomers to the region in prehistoric times. According to Mi'kmaq traditions they occupied their present homeland for a considerable period prior to 1500 CE. Traditionally they were led by a *saqamaw* or chief, who served for life. The succession of the chiefs was through the male line and was restricted to a few families. Though geographically scattered the Mi'kmaqs were united in a confederacy based on clans or bands. The seminomadic Mi'kmaqs ranged over the present-day Maritime Provinces and the Gaspé Peninsula and later spread to Newfoundland and New England. European ships began to regularly visit their shores in the early 16th century. The first indigenous peoples of the region to come into contact with the Europeans, the Mi'kmaqs welcomed the visitors. Sebastian Cabot probably visited the coastal region in 1497, followed shortly by a French expedition. Jacques Cartier recorded Mi'kmaqs in the St. Lawrence Gulf region in 1534. The French negotiated an alliance with the Mi'kmaqs, whose hostility toward the English delayed the settlement of Nova Scotia and New Brunswick. Samuel de Champlain established the first European settlement in Mi'kmaq territory in 1604. French missionaries introduced the Roman Catholic religion, quickly gaining many converts. In 1633 several Mi'kmaq chiefs and their families visited Rome and were received by the Pope. The Mi'kmaq population, estimated at between 20,000 and 30,000 at the time of European contact, had been reduced to less than 4,000 by 1620. European diseases swept through the clans decimating whole villages. By 1760 their numbers had fallen to around 3,000. Though greatly reduced in numbers, the Mi'kmaqs proved to be valuable allies in the French and British wars of the 18th century. Hostility toward the British was widespread when France ceded the Maritimes to British rule in 1713. The defeat of their French allies at Quebec in the French and Indian War ended French rule in the region. In 1761 the Mi'kmaq leaders formally submitted to the British conquerors. In 1778 the rebel American colonies attempted to incite the Mi'kmaqs against the British, but they remained carefully neutral in the conflict that eventually divided their historic homeland between British Canadian and American territories.

Mi'kmaq culture is a Native American culture that has absorbed many of the traditions and norms of modern North

American society. Traditionally the culture was an open democratic society where the people collectively made the decisions. Honor was the basis of all relationships and events and looking after the welfare of the entire community was the most important requirement of all tribal members. The easternmost of the Algonquian peoples, the Mi'kmaqs have a long history of interaction with European culture. Only a minority live on the officially designated reservations and increasingly younger Mi'kmaqs are moving to the larger urban areas for work or greater opportunities. Even the urbanized minority maintains close ties to its culture and the tribe. Because of the traditionally close relations with the French-speaking population of eastern Canada, Mi'kmaq culture has absorbed many French influences. The offspring of mixed marriages usually identify with the Mi'kmaq culture though many are not registered as tribal members. Though the Mi'kmaqs speak the English or French languages, in recent decades they have devised programs to revive and extend the use of their own Algonquian language. Traditionally written in a hieroglyphic script it now utilizes the standard Latin alphabet. The Mi'kmaqs are staunchly Roman Catholic, the result of early French missionary activity. Some Protestant sects have won converts, but the majority steadfastly retains its Catholic heritage.

During the 19th century the Mi'kmaqs slowly recovered from the devastation of the European colonization and the diseases that devastated their nation. Usually ignored by provincial and federal governments, most Mi'kmaqs settled as farmers or fishermen. In the late 19th century the Canadian government established a number of reservations, mostly in New Brunswick and Nova Scotia, but the large number of Mi'kmaqs living in other areas were not obliged to move into them. Many Mi'kmaqs became involved in the illegal transfer of liquor from Canada to the prohibition-era United States in the 1920s and 1930s. Access to liquor worsened a problem with alcoholism that had persisted since colonial times. In the 1980s, the ideal of "Red Power" began to spread among the formerly acquiescent Mi'kmaqs. Demands were voiced for the right to fish, hunt, and gather on traditional Mi'kmaq lands as recognized in treaties with the British in 1760 and 1761. In the 1990s activists led a concerted campaign to win territorial rights for the Mi'kmaqs. In 1997, the Canadian Supreme Court ruled that indigenous nations continued to exercise aboriginal title to their traditional territory. The Mi'kmaqs rushed to take advantage of their rights to fish, hunt, and gather, often meeting resentment from other Canadian fishermen. Conflicts extended to many areas along the coast. Leaders on both sides brought the conflict under control in the early 2000s and pressed for negotiations that the Mi'kmaqs hope will validate their rights to the land and resources that were historically theirs.

Further Reading

Davis, Stephen A. *Mi'kmaq: People of the Maritimes.* Rockport, ME: Down East Books, 1997.

Leavitt, Robert. *Mi'kmaq of the East Coast.* Markham, Ontario: Fitzhenry and Whiteside, 2000.

Poliandri, Simone. *First Nations, Identity, and Reserve Life: The Mi'kmaq of Nova Scotia.*

Lincoln, NE: University of Nebraska Press, 2011.

Miskitos

The Miskitos, sometimes known as Moskitos, Miskitus, Mostiques, or Marquitos, are a Central American ethnic group occupying the Mosquito Coast region on the Caribbean coasts of Nicaragua and Honduras. The estimated 325,000 Miskitos include the smaller closely related Sumo and Rama peoples. The Miskito language belongs to the Misumalpan language group, which is part of the Macro-Chibchan language family. The majority of the Miskitos are Protestants, mostly Moravian but with a sizable Baptist minority and a smaller Roman Catholic group.

The ancestors of the Miskitos are believed to have migrated north from present-day Colombia to settle the Caribbean lowlands. They developed a society based on fishing and agriculture living in a number of autonomous groups. Christopher Columbus sighted the coastal region on his fourth voyage to the New World in 1502. Fierce Miskito resistance to Spanish incursions precluded the colonization of the Caribbean coastal areas. Some 500,000 people, members of tribal groups west of the mountains in Nicaragua and Honduras suffered massive epidemics of European diseases, enslavement, and abuses and effectively disappeared as distinct peoples. Only the Miskitos and the related groups successfully prevented the Spanish conquest of their homeland. In the early 17th century Dutch pirates established bases in the region, preying on Spanish shipping from their settlement at Bleuwvelt, later called Bluefields. English Puritans established a colony on Providence Island in 1630, beginning Miskito contacts with the English. The Spanish destroyed Providence Island in 1641 but many English traders and pirates remained in the region. A slave ship floundered on the coast in the mid-17th century. The Miskitos rescued and adopted the surviving slaves—the origin of the tribe's characteristic Afro–Native American appearance. The Miskitos' status as an ally of the English was institutionalized in 1687 with the foundation of the Miskito kingdom and the crowning of the first Miskito monarch. The British formally claimed the Mosquito Coast, the Miskito kingdom, as a protectorate in 1740. Conflicts with the Spanish continued through the 18th century. The Miskitos often raided Spanish settlements for loot and slaves to sell to the English.

The Miskitos are a Native American culture influenced by the admixtures of African and European strains. There are five subgroups among the Miskitos not including the smaller Sumo and Rama tribes, who are closely related but are not considered part of the Miskito culture. Miskito culture has always been egalitarian, with status based on kinship, age, and parenthood. Each Miskito village is politically autonomous, tied by relatively weak links through the village headman to the Nicaraguan or Honduran states. In contemporary Central America a clear ethnic hierarchy assigns the Miskitos and other indigenous peoples to the lowest rank of society. They remain the least educated and impoverished in the relatively poor countries of the region. An estimated unemployment rate of 80 percent has perpetuated poverty and the underdevelopment of the Caribbean coast region. The Miskito language is still widely spoken though most Miskitos speak Spanish, the language of education and administration, along with a mixed dialect known as Miskito Creole English. The religious beliefs of the Miskitos are primarily the mission instruction they received from Protestant missionaries in the 19th century. Moravian ministers remain important figures in Miskito society.

The independence of the Central American countries from Spanish rule in the early 19th century did little to improve relations between the Miskitos and the Spanish-speaking mostly Mestizo population on the other side of the mountains. In 1844 the British sent a representative to the Miskito kingdom, formalizing its status as a British protectorate. The governments of Nicaragua and Honduras, supported by the United States, formally claimed the region as part of their national territories. German Moravian missionaries arrived in the area in 1849, soon followed by Baptists and other denominations. The Miskitos' conversion to Protestant sects and the introduction of education in the English language solidified the region's separate culture and character. Under U.S. pressure, the British ceded the northern district to Honduras in 1859

A Miskito family in Waspan, Nicaragua, 2005. (AP Photo/Esteban Felix)

and the larger, southern districts to Nicaragua in 1860. The two governments promised not to impose the Spanish language, to respect the religious and political autonomy of the Miskitos and the smaller groups, and not to interfere in their internal affairs. Abrogating the agreement, Nicaraguan troops occupied the region in 1894 ending Miskito autonomy in Nicaragua. American interest in a possible canal route dictated support for the Nicaraguan government. American troops landed on the Mosquito Coast in 1910, provoking widespread Miskito resistance. With the aid of a rebel peasant army led by Augusto Cesar Sandino, the Americans were finally expelled between 1928 and 1930. The Miskitos were later defeated by troops sent by dictator Anastasio Somoza, installed as president of Nicaragua by the Americans in 1934. Generally ignored, the region remained isolated and largely English-speaking. The Nicaraguans, known as "the Spanish" by the Miskitos, garrisoned only the major towns. The Miskitos continued to live their traditional way of life. They took little part in the revolution that overthrew the Somoza regime in 1979. The rebels, known as Sandinistas after the former peasant leader of the 1920s and 1930s, implemented a plan to integrate the Miskito homeland and its rich natural resources into the new Sandinista state. The Miskitos, Sumos, and Ramas joined together to resist the Sandinistas. Heavy fighting swept the region in the 1980s until a negotiated truce led to limited Miskito autonomy. Conflicts and violent incidents continued into the 2000s, particularly following the Sandinista electoral victory in 2006.

Further Reading

Conzemius, Eduard. *Ethnological Survey of the Miskito and Sumu Indians of Honduras and Nicaragua.* Rockville, MD: Wildside Press, 2010.

Garcia, Claudia. *The Making of the Miskitu People of Nicaragua: The Social Construction of Ethnic Identity.* Uppsala, Sweden: Uppsala Universitet, 1996.

Stonich, Susan C. *Endangered Peoples of Latin America: Struggles to Survive and Thrive.* Westport, CT: Greenwood, 2001.

Mixes

The Mixes, sometimes known as Mijes or Ayuuk, are a Mexican ethnic group concentrated in the state of Oaxaca. Known as the "people of the mountains," the Mixe inhabit the Sierra Mixe highlands but also the midlands and tropical lowlands. The estimated 190,000 Mixes speak a language of the Mixe-Zoque language family spoken around the Isthmus of Tehuantepec. Mixe religious beliefs are largely a syncretic blend of Roman Catholicism and the earlier traditions of their pre-Christian belief system. In recent years evangelical Protestant missionaries have gained followers in the region.

The Mixes are believed to be descendants of the Olmecs, the first advanced civilization of Mesoamerica. However, Mixe traditions claim that their ancestors originated in the Andes Mountains of South America and arrived in Mexico by boat. The migrants then settled around the holy mountain of Cempoaltepetl, where the legendary king Condoy built an advanced kingdom. Little is known of the history of the Mixes as few archeological sites remain and written sources were mostly destroyed by the Spanish in the 16th century. Scholars agree that the Mixes were such an organized and strong society that neither the Zapotecs nor the Aztec empire were able to fully conquer the region. The Mixes were latecomers to the region, having arrived in several waves of migrants between 1300 and 1533. The newcomers quickly came into conflict with the established states of the Mixtecs and the Zapotecs. By 1522, the Mixes had become tributary to the Zapotec ruler of Tehuantepec. The Spanish, believing tales of gold in the region, pushed south from the newly conquered central Mexico. Most of the indigenous peoples chose not to fight the invaders but negotiated to keep their chiefly hierarchies with ultimate authority given to the Spanish. The Mixes were the most powerful of the peoples who resisted Spanish incursions. They continued to fight the Spanish through the 16th century. The last major Mixe war was in 1570, when they burned and looted Zapotec communities and threatened Spanish control of the lowlands. The Spanish, aided by other indigenous warriors, finally defeated the Mixes, who retreated into the mountains where many are still living. In 1555 Dominican missionaries managed the first peaceful contact with the Mixes. The Dominicans built churches and missions that were maintained even during times of Mixe-Spanish conflict. Cruelty, slavery, and other abuses resulted in Mixe uprisings against the Spanish in 1660–1661. European diseases such as typhoid, smallpox, and influenza decimated the Mixe population. Even though slavery and forced labor were discontinued, tribute in goods continued to impoverish the Mixes as late as 1789. The Dominicans were withdrawn in 1780, to be replaced by secular priests.

The Mixe culture is a blend of their traditional culture, Spanish colonial influences, and modern Hispanic society. Spanish influences are most evident in religion, construction, and village layout. Traditional cultural elements such as music, dance, and art forms are unique to the Sierra Mixe region and reflect the preconquest Mixe culture. Since the 1960s the construction of roads leading into the region has facilitated the introduction of new foods, modern industrial goods, and the replacement of traditional thatched roofs with corrugated metal. Most Mixes are subsistence farmers although some communities engage in textile weaving, ceramics, or basketwork. Great attention is given to their music, dance, and dress, which are exhibited primarily during community and religious fiestas. While the Roman Catholic faith dictates the yearly cycle of saint's days and feasts, Mixe religious beliefs encompass elements of the Spanish Catholic teachings blended with the belief in spirits, demonic beings, and supernatural serpents that are often held responsible for diseases or other calamities. The Mixe language is a language of the Mixean branch of the Mixe-Zoque languages that is spoken in several regional dialects that reflect the geographic diversity of the Mixes grouped into highland, midland, and lowland communities.

The Mixes generally supported the War of Independence against the Spanish that culminated in Mexican independence in 1810. The new Mexican authorities in Oaxaca expelled the Spanish priests. For many years the Mixes were served by just one Mexican priest, who visited the villages only for the annual religious festival on the day of the village's patron saint. The Mixes remained isolated in their highland communities but as the population expanded many left to settle in the lower valleys and later moved into the tropical lowlands of the Isthmus of Tehuantepec. In the 20th century Mixe migrants seeking work or greater opportunities moved to the large urban centers, especially Mexico City. In the 1960s the construction of roads, the intervention of development agencies, and renewed Roman Catholic missionary activity began a marked economic, political, and religious change in the Mixe homeland. Since the 1980s tourism to the lowlands of Oaxaca has increased dramatically, giving the lowland Mixes new sources of income. Tourists began to visit the Sierra Mixe highlands in smaller numbers but goods such as woven cloth, ceramics, and other souvenirs became important to the Mixe economy. In 2006 many Mixes joined the popular revolt against the state government led by the Popular Assembly of the Peoples of Oaxaca (APPO). The conflict continues, though the reduction in tourists that occurred in the early stages of the protests in 2006 returned to record levels by 2011, with ever greater numbers of Mixes gaining a living in the thriving tourist trade.

Further Reading

Lipp, Frank J. *The Mixe of Oaxaca: Religion, Ritual, and Healing.* Austin, TX: University of Texas Press, 1991.

Schmieder, Oskar. *The Settlements of the Tzapotee and Mije Indians: State of Oaxaca, Mexico.* Berkeley, CA: University of California Press, 1968.

Yannakakis, Yanna. *The Art of Being In-Between: Native Intermediaries, Indian Identity, and Local Rule in Colonial Oaxaca.* Durham, NC: Duke University Press, 2008.

Mixtecs

The Mixtecs, sometimes known as Mixtecas, are a Mexican ethnic group mostly living in the Mexican states of Oaxaca, Guerrero, and Puebla, a region known as La Mixteca. Outside the region there are sizable Mixtec communities in other parts of Mexico and in the United States. The estimated 520,000 Mixtecs speak dialects of the Mixtec language, the largest of the Mixtecan language branch of the Oto-Manguean language family.

The Mixtecs are the descendants of the early Otomanguean peoples who settled the region in prehistoric times, possibly as early as 4400 BCE. By about 1500 BCE the Otomangueans had divided into at least nine distinct cultural and linguistic groups. By 500 BCE, the central valleys of Oaxaca were mostly inhabited by the related Zapotecs, with the Mixtecs concentrated in the western valleys and the foothills. The two groups were often in conflict over territory, slaves, and treasure. Archaeological evidence indicates that between 750 CE and 1521 CE, there may have been a population of some 2.5 million Zapotecs and Mixtecs in Oaxaca's central valleys. The Zapotecs were the first to gain control of central Oaxaca, flourishing from 500 BCE until 750 CE. The Mixtecs, known as the "cloud people," expanded in the

14th century to take control of many Zapotec cities, including the capital at Monte Albán. Though divided into a number of autonomous states, the Mixtecs evolved one of the major civilizations of Mesoamerica. At the height of their civilization the Mixtec artisans produced fine stone, wood, and metal artworks and tools that were well regarded throughout ancient Mesoamerica. The Mixtec conquest of the Zapotec region was never completed as the Aztecs of central Mexico began to mount military invasions of the region in the 14th and 15th centuries. The Mixtecs and Zapotecs formed a military alliance to face the powerful intruders and to maintain their territories and the valuable trade routes between central Mexico and Central America. The Spanish conquest of the Aztec empire ended the Aztec invasions but the Spanish soon became a new threat. Hearing that the region was rich in gold, the Spanish turned their attention south. The Zapotecs, hearing of the conquest of the Aztecs, sent an offer for an alliance. Spanish expeditions explored the region in 1521, looking for gold and trade routes to link the Pacific with the Atlantic. The Mixtecs mostly chose not to fight the powerful newcomers, instead negotiating a peace that allowed the Mixtec hierarchy to maintain its position with ultimate authority held by the Spanish. Diseases, abuses, slavery, and the loss of much of the most fertile land decimated the Mixtecs. Owing to the severe population decline due to the plagues, as well as the region's lack of gold or other treasure, relatively few Spanish colonists settled in the area. Pressure to assimilate into the new Hispanic culture, though substantial, was not as great as in other parts of conquered Mexico.

Mixtec culture is mostly a peasant culture mixing the traditional indigenous culture with later borrowings from the Spanish and modern Mexican influences. The basic level of social unity in modern Mixtec villages is the household. Households are linked through a historic tradition of reciprocal exchanges of goods and labor, marriage and kinship ties, and economic interests. Intervillage conflicts are widespread and often violent, even among Mixtec communities. The conflicts, mostly over land boundaries, have continued for hundreds of years. Traditionally Mixtec parents selected their offspring's mates, with marriages often taking place before the couple was sexually mature. Mixtec society is patrilineal, though custom dictates that all sons inherit equally. Even today *compadrazgo*, or ritual kinship, remains an important relationship in all Mixtec areas. There are several kinds of *compadrazgo* although those resulting from baptisms and marriages are considered the most significant. In recent decades the need to leave their homeland to find work or opportunities has resulted in large Mixtec communities in Mexico City, Tiajuana, and a number of large American cities. The Mixtec migrants are known for maintaining strong familial and cultural ties to their homeland. Most Mixtecs speak their own language, the most widely spoken of the Mixtecan languages, along with Spanish which is the language of education and administration. A growing number of Mixtec migrants in the United States are also using English.

The Mexican uprising against Spanish rule divided Oaxaca into warring groups by 1810. The large towns, particularly the capital city of Oaxaca, remained strongholds of the growing Mestizo population and were mostly loyal to the Spanish cause. The Mixtecs usually joined the rebels, who promised equality and greater economic opportunities. Most of the state eventually fell to the rebel forces, but the capital remained in royalist hands until the end of the independence war. During most of the 19th century the state of Oaxaca was split between two opposing factions, the liberals and the conservatives. The Mixtecs and the other indigenous peoples mostly avoided politics but were often the victims of outrages by armed groups from both sides. In the early 20th century modernization with new agricultural techniques and commercial enterprises mostly benefited the national and international companies while the Mixtec and other workers worked long hours for very little salary. Many Mixtecs joined the Mexican Revolution that eventually resulted in a new government but the gains of the revolution were mostly lost during two major earthquakes in 1928 and 1931, and then during the Great Depression that prompted large scale immigration of poor Mixtecs to Mexico City and other urban areas. In the 1940s and 1950s new roads were built that allowed the Mixtecs to sell commercial crops such as coffee and tobacco. In the 1980s tourism became a major factor in the local economy. In 2006 many Mixtecs joined a protest movement against the heavy marginalization of the indigenous peoples of Oaxaca. A new state government, elected in 2010, promised to integrate the needs of the indigenous peoples into the new political structure.

Further Reading

Flannery, Kent V. *The Cloud People: Divergent Evolution of the Zapotec and Mixtec Civilizations.* Clinton Corners, NY: Percheron Press, 2003.

Joyce, Arthur A. *Mixtecs, Zapotecs, and Chatinos: Ancient Peoples of Southern Mexico.* Hoboken, NJ: Wiley-Blackwell, 2009.

Spores, Ronald. *The Mixtecs in Ancient and Colonial Times.* Norman, OK: University of Oklahoma Press, 1985.

Montserratians

The Montserratians are a Caribbean people, the inhabitants of the island of Montserrat in the Lesser Antilles islands in the West Indies. There is a larger number of Montserratians living in the United Kingdom than on the island. The estimated 17,000 Montserratians speak English, the official language of Montserrat, with many also using an island creole dialect known as Montserratian English. The majority of the Montserratians are Christians, mostly Anglican, Roman Catholic, or belonging to other Protestant denominations.

Arawak migrants from the South American mainland settled the island. In the eighth century CE warlike Caribs, also moving north from South America, overran the island and killed or absorbed the Arawaks. Christopher Columbus sighted the island in 1493, claiming it for the Spanish crown. He named the island Santa María de Montserrat, after the Monastery of Montserrat in Catalonia. The Spanish mostly ignored the island once they found it had no gold or other treasure. In 1632 a group of Irish Catholics, fleeing anti-Catholic violence in the island of Nevis, settled on Montserrat. The island became a haven for Irish Catholics escaping religious persecution on other Caribbean islands and in Virginia. By 1648 there were over a thousand Irish families in Montserrat. Most of the Irish had been forcibly transported from Ireland as slaves or indentured servants. English control of the island was acknowledged by the other colonial powers and plantations were soon producing sugar, rum, arrowroot, and Sea Island cotton for export. The labor demands of plantation agriculture resulted in the importation of African slaves. By the late 1700s there were many plantations worked by African and Irish slaves, many political prisoners taken to the West Indies after a failed Irish rebellion. A planter elite, based on slave labor and sugar production, controlled the island. Slave uprisings occurred several times, most notably the Saint Patrick's Day rebellion of March 17, 1768. The uprising is now celebrated as a public holiday on the island.

Montserratian culture is a unique blend of Anglo-Irish and Afro-Caribbean influences. Although the majority of the Montserratians are of African or mixed African-European background, Montserrat is often referred to as "the emerald isle of the West Indies" because the Irish figured so prominently in its early history. The island's cuisine, music, dance, and art forms all reflect the mixture of cultures, particularly the Irish and African heritage of the Montserratians. Following the devastation of Hurricane Hugo and the eruption of the Soufriere Hills Volcano in the 1990s, an estimated two-thirds of the Montserratians were evacuated to the United Kingdom. Very few of the refugees have returned to the island but the overseas communities maintain close ties to the culture and their island homeland. The Montserratians normally use Standard English but among themselves they speak a Caribbean patois known as Montserratian English that incorporates archaic English, Irish Gaelic, and African words and expressions. The religious beliefs of the Montserratians are an important part of the culture, often mixing rituals and traditions that developed on the island with the Christian belief system.

The plantation economy of Montserrat, based almost exclusively on sugar production, allowed the planters and their families to live in mansions and to send their children to England for education. However, the majority of the population consisted of black slaves, the descendants of the early African slaves, or people of mixed race. Unrest erupted several times in the early 1800s. When slavery was abolished in 1834 most of the former slaves settled on small plots as subsistence farmers and fishermen. Many of the plantation families left the island as the sugar economy ended. British rule insured a democratic government and minimal health care and education in the late 19th and early 20th centuries. Most of the island was owned by the descendants of former slaves in small holdings that supported a growing population, which reached 13,000 in 1989. Tourism became the major industry. Two events devastated the island, ending the prosperity and well-being the Montserratians had enjoyed. Hurricane Hugo struck the island in 1989, damaging over 90 percent of the structures on Montserrat. Within a few years the island recovered, only to be struck by a second disaster. Montserrat's Soufriere Hills Volcano, dormant for centuries, erupted in 1995. Lava and ash covered the southern two-thirds of the island, including the island's capital and airport. Over 8,000 Montserratians were evacuated to the United Kingdom while the rest remained in the northern part of the island. The volcano has been relatively quiet since 2010 and a new capital and airport have been constructed, but limited land and opportunities has restricted the number of Montserratians the island is able to sustain.

Further Reading

Akenson, Donald Harman. *If the Irish Ran the World: Montserrat 1630–1730.* Montreal, Canada: McGill-Queens University Press, 1997.

Greenaway, Sharmen. *Montserrat in England: Dynamics of Culture.* Bloomington, IN: iUniverse, 2011.

Prospere, Dr. Irene S. *Memories of Montserrat.* Bloomington, IN: Trafford Publishing, 2009.

Mormons

The Mormons, also known as Latter-day Saints, are a North American religious and cultural group concentrated in the U.S. state of Utah. Outside the Mormon heartland there are large Mormon populations in Mexico, Brazil, the Philippines, Chile, Peru, Argentina, parts of Europe, and Oceania. The estimated 6 million Mormons in the United States speak Standard English and form part of the greater American culture. The Mormon Church is an American religious denomination centered on the Mormon complex in Salt Lake City, Utah.

The origin of the Mormons began with the establishment of a small church by Joseph Smith in Seneca County, New York, in 1830. According to Mormon teachings, Joseph Smith was 14 when he was visited by celestial beings in human form who told him to prepare himself for important tasks. About 30 years later, in 1827, the beings appeared again and directed Smith to a nearby hill where golden plates had been buried 14 centuries earlier by Moroni, identified as the son of Mormon, their compiler and a member of an ancient civilization. The engraved plates, which later came to be known as the *Book of Mormon*, contain a history of the American Indians as the direct descendants of ancient Hebrews who sailed to the Western Hemisphere to live in the Americas from 600 BCE to 421 CE. According to Mormon beliefs, Smith translated the plates from "reformed Egyptian" with the aid of special translator stones. First published in 1830, the translations were offered by Smith as scientific evidence of his special divine calling. Many scholars, to the present, consider the book a collection of local legends of indigenous origins, fragments of Smith's autobiography, and contemporary religious and political controversies, particularly the anti-Masonic movement of the early 19th century. Although skeptical, many scholars admit that the contents were transformed with great ingenuity into a religious tract. Religious leaders at the time of the organization of Smith's church, in 1830, rejected his claim that his church restored the ancient, primitive Christian faith. The practice of polygamy and Smith's "revelation" on polygamy, revealed in 1852, proved to be one of the most controversial aspects of the new Mormon teachings. Smith governed the growing Mormon community by announcing periodic revelations on widely divergent matters. Smith combined direct communication with God and Jewish and Christian mysticism with the goal of perpetual prosperity and sought to establish the Mormon beliefs as a complete way of life.

The Mormons are considered to be the only indigenous American cultural group other than the Native Americans. They developed as a distinct religious-cultural group through the suffering and persecutions of their early adherents. The story of the Mormon trek out of the territory of the United States has for them the same influence as the story of the Exodus on the Jews. Mormons self-identify as a Christian people, though many of their beliefs differ considerably from mainstream Christian traditions. The Mormon culture evolved during the 19th-century migration and later in the isolation of their new homeland on the Great Salt Lake. The majority of Mormons are of Caucasian descent, with minorities of Native Americans, Pacific Islanders, Hispanics, and blacks. Until 1978 black Mormons were excluded from church office. The Mormons retain their clannish traditions and continue to adhere to a strict social order. The Mormon tradition of isolation and self-sufficiency remains to the present. Very few Mormons receive public assistance, as the self-help tradition remains a strong cultural element. The Mormon way of life is distinguished by religious activism, order and respect for authority, strong group conformity, and vigorous proselytizing and worldwide missionary activity. A continuing stream of immigrant converts from all over the world is being rapidly assimilated into Mormon society. Mormon traditions such as large families are still respected; the Mormons have the highest birthrate in the United States, twice the national average. Like their non-Mormon neighbors, known as gentiles, the Mormons speak the western American dialect of English, written in the Latin alphabet. A phonetic alphabet for the writing of English was promulgated by the Church of Jesus Christ of Latter-day Saints in the 19th century, but it never came into common use. The Mormon script consists of 38 letters, with upper- and lower-case pairs that differ only in size, not in shape. A Mormon is a member of any of the several denominations and sects that trace their origins to the religion founded by Joseph Smith in the 1830s. The largest is the Church of Jesus Christ of Latter-day Saints, with around 11 million members, just over half living in the United States. The next largest Mormon church is headquartered in Missouri, with a membership exceeding 200,000. The Mormon Temple in the center of Salt Lake City, built between 1853 and 1893, is the focus of Mormon religious beliefs and culture. All Mormon males over the age of 12 are required to join the priesthood.

Converts to Joseph Smith's new religion soon experienced persecution. Smith, his brother Hyrum, and their followers left New York and moved west to Ohio, but wherever they settled they were persecuted and mistreated for their beliefs. From Ohio they migrated to several areas of Missouri, where their clannishness, polygamy, and openly antislavery stance led to violence in 1833. On October 27, 1838, the governor of the state of Missouri proclaimed that the Mormons "must be exterminated or driven from the state if necessary to the public peace." Three days later the local Missouri militia killed 17 Mormon men and boys. Despite the persecution, the Mormons continued to make converts, and their numbers continued to increase. The Mormons again migrated, many to Nauvoo, Illinois. At Nauvoo the Mormons constructed a new city, which soon had a population of over 20,000—the largest city in Illinois and among the most organized and modern in 19th-century America. Tensions and violence between the Mormons and their neighbors continued in Illinois. Their commercial successes and their growing political power provoked renewed hostility from the gentiles. Joseph Smith and his brother were killed by a mob during anti-Mormon rioting in Carthage, Illinois, in 1844. At Nauvoo the Mormon leadership, as a protective measure, formed a defensive unit known as the Nauvoo Legion. Following Smith's death and amid growing anti-Mormon hysteria, the majority of the Mormons abandoned Nauvoo and determined to leave the territory of the United States. They undertook a mass migration some 1,100 miles (1,800 km) into the wilderness. Led by Brigham Young, long wagon trains moved westward into the mostly uninhabited lands west of the Rocky Mountains in territory claimed by Mexico. They planned to establish a sovereign commonwealth where they could live and worship without persecution. The first Mormon wagon trains, after a long and dangerous journey, arrived in the valley of the Great Salt Lake in 1847. The new Mormon homeland, called Deseret, came under American government authority through the Treaty of Hidalgo, which ceded large tracts of land from Mexico to the United States in 1848. The Mormon Deseret initially claimed most of the present-day southwest of the United States and parts of northern Mexico. The territorial claims were rejected by the U.S. authorities so a reduced territory of Utah was organized. Congress and the American administration refused to consider statehood for Utah until the church ended its economic policies and discontinued the practice of polygamy. The Mormon migrations became part of the lore and culture of the developing Mormon society. In 1852, the majority of the Mormons left behind in Ohio and Missouri also moved west to the new Mormon homeland. Beginning in the 1850s, a stream of Europeans converted by Mormon missionaries began to arrive in the Atlantic ports and to continue directly to the Great Salt Lake valley. In 1857 the U.S. authorities attempted to stamp out the Mormon practice of polygamy, an integral part of Mormon culture. Tensions also increased over Mormon territorial claims to Nevada. Tensions increased until the government dispatched troops against the Mormons. The brief war, known as the Winter War or the Mormon Rebellion of 1857, ended with more territorial concessions that left even more Mormon communities outside the Utah heartland. Those living outside Utah came to be known as Deseret Mormons. Over the next decades the U.S. government passed increasingly severe anti-Mormon legislature. Many Mormon men were imprisoned for refusing to renounce their extra wives. Mormon families were known for the number of children, the largest recorded being 65. The Mormon leadership finally banned the practice of polygamy in 1890, and six years later Utah was admitted to the Union. The Mormon Church has officially been neutral in Utah's state politics since the early 1900s. Large families and continued immigration of Mormon converts added to the rapidly increasing population in Utah. Modern Mormon doctrines are no longer controversial and Mormons live in peace with the large "gentile" population of Utah, but Mormon wealth and political influence continues to be felt. The Mormon Church continues to exert a profound influence on many facets of daily life and on the Utah economy. The separation of church and state is not clearly defined in Utah, where Mormon devotion to their religion and culture supersedes all other loyalties.

Further Reading

Abanes, Richard. *One Nation under Gods: A History of the Mormon Church.* New York: Basic Books, 2003.

Bowman, Matthew. *The Mormon People: The Making of an American Faith.* New York: 2012.

Linn, William Alexander. *The Story of the Mormons from the Date of their Origin to the Year 1901.* Whitefish, MT: Kessinger Publishing, 2010.

Mapuche woman weaving a blanket (1998). (AP Photo/Santiago Llanquin)

N

Nahuas

The Nahuas, sometimes known as Nahuat-lacas, Aztecs, or Aztecas, are a Mexican ethnic group inhabiting an extensive area in central Mexico. Outside the region there are Nahua communities in many other parts of Mexico and in the United States, primarily in California and New York, and Canada. The estimated 2.6 million Nahuas speak a number of dialects and variants of the Nahuan or Aztecan branch of the Uto-Aztecan language family. The Nahuas are overwhelmingly Christian, mostly Roman Catholic, though their traditional religious rituals and ceremonies are still practiced.

The Nahuas are believed to have originated in the desert areas of northern Mexico and adjacent areas of the United States. They probably migrated south into central Mexico in several waves. Around 400 CE the first groups began to split from the Nahuas to settle on the Pacific Coast and other parts of central and southern Mexico. From around 600 CE the Nahuas quickly overcame the resistance of the earlier inhabitants and rose to power in central Mexico. Between 800 and 1000 the Nahuas, known as Toltecs, established their rule over much of Central America. During this period the Nahua people were the dominant group in the great Valley of Mexico and in territories far beyond the heartland, augmented by continuing migrations of Nahuas from the north. After the fall of the Toltecs a period of instability and movements scattered the Nahuas as far south as present-day Nicaragua. In central Mexico different Nahua groups formed powerful city-states that fought for political dominance. One of the last of the Nahua migrations to arrive in the Valley of Mexico, probably in the 13th century, settled on an island in Lake Texcoco, from which they proceeded to subjugate the surrounding cities and tribes. This group, known as the Mexica, was the dominant Nahua group for the next three centuries. In 1519 a Spanish expedition from Cuba arrived on the Mexican gulf coast. Moving inland in search of treasure the Spanish were opposed by the Tlax-caltecs, a Nahua people that had avoided subjugation by the Mexica Aztec empire. Defeated by the Spanish, the Tlaxcaltecs entered into an alliance—with the Spanish leader Hernán Cortés—that proved invaluable in the struggle against the Aztecs. The Spanish and their allies "liberated" a number of Nahua cities before arriving in the Valley of Mexico. At the Aztec capital of Tenochititlan they were welcomed by Montezuma II, but once in the city they took the Aztec emperor prisoner. Led by the Aztec nobility the Mexica warriors drove the Spanish from the city. Over the next year the Spanish and their Tlax-caltec allies besieged Tenochititlan, which finally fell to the invaders. After the fall of the Aztec capital alliances with Nahua leaders aided the Spanish subjugation of the extensive Aztec empire, renamed New Spain. The Nahuas of New Spain were recognized as allies of the Spanish rulers and were granted privileges and a degree of independence not granted to other indigenous peoples of the region. From 1519 to around 1550 the Spanish conquerors emphasized conversion to Roman Catholicism and the organization of an indigenous tributary system. During this period contact between the Spanish and the indigenous peoples was limited, except for women taken as wives or concubines. As the Spanish extended their political domination to the farthest territories of Mesoamerica, the Nahuas accompanied them as foot soldiers. Nahua warriors formed the bulk of the military expeditions that conquered other Mesoamerican states, such as the Mayans, Zapotecs, and Mixtecs. Mass baptisms were performed and the Nahuas were given Spanish names. Those that clung to their pre-Christian religion were severely punished or even executed. The Nahua converts often incorporated pre-Christian practices and beliefs into their Christian rituals without the Spanish authorities noticing it. Smallpox and other European diseases swept through the Nahua population leaving millions dead. The deaths caused by the smallpox epidemics of the 1520s are believed to have begun the rapid growth of Christianity in Mexico. Believing that the epidemic proved the superiority of the Christian god, they mostly accepted their fate as subjugated people and ceased their resistance to Spanish rule. During the 16th century, some 240,000 Spaniards immigrated to New Spain to be joined by an estimated 450,000 in the 17th century. Unlike the English-speaking colonists to the north, the majority of the Spaniards were single men who married or lived with indigenous women. As a result a vast number of *mestizo* or mixed-race people became the largest part of the population. During the colonial period much of the identity, traditions, arts, and architecture of Mexico evolved from a fusion of the indigenous traditions and the Spanish-European culture. The Nahuas usually spoke their own language along with Spanish but they gradually adopted the lifestyle and culture of the numerically predominant *mestizo* population.

The Mexican government does not categorize the country's citizens by ethnicity, but rather by language. Information about the Nahuas usually deals only with the estimated 1.5 million Nahuatl speakers though the actual numbers of Nahuas may be twice that figure. The largest concentrations of Nahuas are in the Mexican states of Veracruz, Puebla, Hidalgo, San Luis Potisí, and Guerrero with significant populations in México state, Morelos, and the Federal District around Mexico City, Tlaxcala, Oaxaca, Michoacán, and Durango. The Nahua culture is a regional mixture of their indigenous preconquest traditions and the later Spanish culture that was imposed during the colonial era. The Nahuatl language is still spoken in many areas though the various dialects, often heavily influenced by Spanish, are not all mutually intelligible. A new language law, adopted in 2003, recognized Nahuatl and other indigenous languages as national languages in the areas where they are spoken, with the same status as Spanish within their region. The introduction of the Latin alphabet by the Spanish resulted in a written language that has a history stretching back to within 20 years of the initial Spanish conquest. Modern activists continue to advocate the use of the language as the first language in the Nahua areas. Forcibly converted to Roman Catholicism in the early years of Spanish rule, the majority of the Nahuas are now nominally Roman Catholic though evangelical Protestant groups have gained converts in recent decades. Pre-Christian rituals and ceremonies, thinly disguised as Christian traditions, continue as part of the Nahua belief system.

In the early years of the 19th century, as wars swept across Europe, the Mexican leaders led the fight for Mexican independence from Spain. In 1810 Mexico was declared independent but the life of the poor, marginalized Nahuas remained the same. Most worked as seasonal workers, menials, or subsistence farmers with little interest in the politics that occupied the Spanish-speaking elite. The first decades of independence were marked by economic instability, which impacted the Nahua communities. In 1857 Mexico was established as a secular state, bringing many Nahuas to support the opposition in the conflict known as the Reform War in 1858. The war ended in 1861 with the victory of the liberals led by Native American president Benito Juaréz. In the 1860s the country was occupied by France with many Nahuas joining the resistance forces. Over the next decades, under Porfirio Díaz, Mexico was characterized by remarkable economic advances, investments in the arts and sciences, and modernization, but for the Nahuas it was a period of economic inequality and political repression. The Mexican Revolution, beginning in 1910, ended the Díaz regime but initiated a widespread civil war. A new constitution, adopted in 1917, included many of the social and economic demands of the rebels, including equality for the Nahuas and other indigenous peoples. Despite modest gains, the Nahuas remain largely marginalized and among the poorest of Mexico's citizens. Each year many young Nahuas are forced to leave their home districts to seek work and opportunities in the large urban areas or even in the United States and Canada. Successive Mexican governments have promised redress and equality but little has changed for most Nahuas despite the modernization and economic advances of the 20th and early 21st centuries. The greatness of the Nahuas and the Aztec empire that once dominated central Mexico are now only seen in museums or in the collective memory of the Nahua people.

Further Reading

Osowski, Edward W. *Indigenous Miracles: Nahua Authority in Colonial Mexico.* Tucson, AZ: University of Arizona Press, 2010.

Schroeder, Susan. *The Conquest All Over Again: Nahuas and Zapotecs Thinking, Writing, and Painting Spanish Colonialism.* Eastbourne, UK: 2011.

Smith, Michael E. *The Aztecs.* Hoboken, NJ: Wiley-Blackwell, 2012.

Navajos

The Navajos, sometimes known as Dine, Dineh, Diné, or Navahos, are a North American ethnic group concentrated in the southwestern American states of Arizona and New Mexico with smaller communities in

Utah and Colorado. The estimated 305,000 Navajos speak the Navajo language, which belongs to the Southern Athabaskan language group of the Athabaskan languages. The majority of the Navajos are Christians belonging to a number of denominations, with some 20,000 belonging to the Native American Church.

Early Athabaskan nomads, moving south from their original homeland in western Canada, settled the high plateau region of the American southwest around 1000 CE. The nomads gradually split into several distinct bands, the most important ones becoming the Navajos and the Apaches. The Navajos settled near the Pueblo peoples, from whom they adopted agriculture, weaving, sand painting, and some religious beliefs. By 1500 the Navajos had evolved a distinct culture that blended their original Athabaskan heritage with the indigenous traditions of their new homeland in the southwest. The Navajos, probably numbering no more than 9,000 in the early 16th century, controlled a vast territory and received tribute from many non-Navajo peoples. The Spanish, searching for the legendary cities of gold, reached the Navajo territory in 1539. Unable to fully subdue the fierce Navajo warriors the Spanish generally left them to their traditional way of life. The Christian missions established across the region had a greater impact on the Navajos than did the Spanish administration. The missions brought with them European farming methods and domesticated animals, including horses and sheep. Sheep, till then unknown to the Navajos, profoundly changed their way of living. They adopted a seminomadic tradition based on large herds of sheep. By the early 1600s the Navajos of the Colorado Plateau had achieved a relatively organized and settled way of life. Toward the end of the 17th century, Spanish settlers and Pueblo peoples attempted to establish communities in territory traditionally claimed by the Navajos. The Navajos developed a strategy of spreading into and then preying on the newly settled communities to acquire food, sheep, horses, and cattle. The movement of Navajo bands westward into and around the lands of the Hopis seriously threatened the precarious economic situation of that tribe.

The name Navajo comes from the Spanish usage, Apaches de Navajó, which is derived from a name given to the Navajos by the Tewa peoples meaning "fields adjoining a ravine." The Navajos call themselves Diné, which simply means "the people."

Early photo of Navajos in New Mexico. (USGS)

Divided into some 60 clans, the Navajos are traditionally a matriarchal people, with inheritance through the female line. Marriage within a clan used to be considered incestuous, though modern Navajo culture has adopted the marriage traditions of American culture. The most numerous of the Native American peoples of the United States, the Navajos call their homeland Diné Bikeyah or Dinetah, a territory larger than many American states. The Navajo Reservation, known as the Navajo Nation, is home to about half the total Navajo population as the generally arid land will not provide a livelihood for everyone. Many Navajos live outside the reservation, mostly in other parts of Arizona and New Mexico but increasingly in the large urban areas of the southwestern states. Sheep remain an important part of the Navajo culture, although tourism is now the largest industry. Modern problems such as alcoholism, a chronic problem, and a high suicide rate continue to impact Navajo society. The Navajo language belongs to the Navajo-Apache branch of the Athabaskan languages that are more widely spoken in northwestern Canada and Alaska. The language has been tenaciously preserved and most Navajos speak it as their first or second language along with English. The majority of the Navajos belong to various Christian denominations with a minority adhering to the Native American Church, which combines Christian and traditional beliefs, including the use of hallucinogen peyote.

The Navajos remained under nominal Spanish rule and then under Mexican authority until the territories in the southwest were ceded to the United States by Mexico in 1848. The traditional Navajo resistance to outside authority quickly led to clashes and conflicts with the new American authorities. The clashes escalated into a widespread war that continued until 1864 when the Navajo territory was invaded by the U.S. cavalry led by Kit Carson. The invaders destroyed everything in their path, including the vast Navajo sheep herds. Captured Navajo families, numbering over 8,500, were forced to march under guard to Fort Sumner, in New Mexico, a harrowing journey of over 350 miles. Those who survived the hardships of the "Long Walk" were then imprisoned in a squalid camp for four years. The survivors were finally allowed to return to their homeland in 1868. The destruction of their homeland and the years of horrible captivity left a legacy of bitterness and distrust that is still evident today. A formal treaty signed in 1868 recognized the Navajo nation in exchange for the cession of vast tracts of land. The Navajos retained a reservation of some 3.5 million acres. The terms of the treaty were quickly broken, beginning a century of humiliation, degradation, and neglect. Diseases, crop failures, and attacks by neighboring tribes further decimated the tribe. Finally provided with sheep and cattle, the Navajos began to recover and gained a modest prosperity. In 1884 the reservation boundaries were extended to accommodate their growing herds. During the late 19th century the Navajo population doubled. Since the lands of the reservation were generally poor for farming, few attempts were made by outsiders to encroach on Navajo land. In 1921 the Indian Agency began to give out leases to oil and power companies on reservation lands without consulting the Navajos. The leases, though contravening the existing reservation laws, began the development of the enormous natural resources on the reservation lands but the Navajos received nothing. The Navajo tribal government, organized in 1923, lobbied for greater say over their land and lives. Granted U.S. citizenship in 1924, few of the poor and uneducated Navajos were able to exercise their citizenship rights. In the early 1930s Navajo leaders began a concerted effort to end their long isolation. Between 1935 and 1940 a Navajo alphabet, devised for the Navajo language, allowed the spoken language to become a literary language and greatly aided the spread of education across the Navajo territory in the 1940s and 1950s. Despite continuing poverty, the birthrate grew spectacularly. By the early 1960s the Navajos numbered some 85,000 and in 1980 their numbers had climbed to over 150,000. The increasing population severely strained the limited resources of the reservation, forcing many Navajos to seek work outside their homeland. Activists in the 1960s and 1970s introduced Navajo history and language to reservation schools and founded the first community college run by a Native American people. Granted self-government in 1972, the Navajos, for the first time in over a century, were free of outside political control. In the late 20th century, on the basis of the reservation's natural resources, the Navajos are one of the world's wealthiest nations, but the wealth is only on paper. The reality of Navajo life is mostly poverty, unemployment, and neglect as it has been since their homeland became part of the United States in the mid-19th century.

Further Reading

Bruchac, Joseph. *Navajo Long Walk: Tragic Story of a Proud Peoples' Force March from Their Homeland.* Washington, D.C.: National Geographic Books, 2002.

Iverson, Peter. *Diné: A History of the Navajos.* Albuquerque, NW: University of New Mexico Press, 2002.

Sundberg, Lawrence D. *Dinétah: An Early History of the Navajo People.* Santa Fe, NM: Sunstone Press, 1995.

Ndyukas

The Ndyukas, sometimes known as Djukas, Njukas, Alukus, Aukans, or Okanisis, are a Maroon ethnic group inhabiting the interior districts of Suriname, French Guiana, and Guyana in South America. Outside their homeland there is a Ndyuka community in the Netherlands. The estimated 52,000 Ndyukas speak the Ndyuka language, an English-based creole language, with many also speaking English, Dutch, or French. The Ndyukas are nominally Christian, with a growing number adhering to evangelical Protestant denominations.

Dutch and English plantations producing coffee, cocoa, sugarcane, and cotton were established in the early 17th century in the fertile Guyana plains of northeastern South America. The planters relied heavily on slaves imported from West Africa to cultivate the plantation crops along the region's rivers. Treatment of the African slaves was notoriously bad, particularly on several of the larger plantations. Many of the Africans escaped the plantations by fleeing into the rain forests just beyond the cultivated areas. With the help of the indigenous tribes in the area the slaves established small settlements on the inland rivers, particularly along the Tapanahony River. The resourceful escaped slaves not only survived, but thrived and established their own unique culture and language. Known collectively in English as Maroons, in Dutch they were called *Bosnegers*, meaning "forest negroes," and in French *Nèg'Maroons*, the Africans established several independent tribes in the inaccessible interiors of British, Dutch, and French colonies. Taught by the indigenous inhabitants of the rain forests, the Africans, many from similar forested regions in West Africa, quickly adapted to life as independent tribes. One of the groups of Maroons took the name Ndyuka as the name of their new tribe. The Maroons often raided the plantations in order to help other Africans to escape and to acquire women, food, and weapons. The Ndyuka attackers often killed the European planter families and several unsuccessful campaigns were launched against the Maroons. The Dutch authorities of Dutch Guiana, unable to subdue the Ndyukas, finally signed a peace treaty with the Maroon tribe on October 10, 1760, that recognized them as a distinct tribal group and guaranteed their territorial autonomy.

The Ndyuka culture is based on the cultures of the escaped slaves originally brought from West Africa. Later English, Dutch, French, and indigenous influences were adopted or adapted to the basically African society. Modern Ndyuka culture has incorporated much from the modern cultures of the region particularly due to the increasing numbers of Ndyukas leaving their ancestral villages to move to the coast, especially in large urban areas such as Paramaribo, Suriname's capital. The Ndyukas are often subdivided into two regional and cultural groups, the *opu*, who live in the upstream regions, and the *bilo*, the inhabitants of the downstream areas of the Tapanahony and Marowinjne rivers in Suriname. About 35,000 Ndyukas live in interior Suriname, around 10,000 in French Guiana, and smaller communities in Guyana and the Netherlands. The Ndyuka language is based on an archaic English vocabulary, with strong African influences in the sounds and grammar. During 1908–1910 a distinct script of 56 letters was devised by Afáka Atumisi. The script, known as the Afaka Syllabary, is the only known script in use that was designed specifically for a creole dialect of English. The Ndyukas' Christian beliefs, acquired during the period of slavery and later from European and American missionaries, is often blended with African traditions and rituals handed down from generation to generation.

In the early 19th century the British and French authorities also signed treaties and agreements with the Ndyukas granting sovereign status and trade rights. Slavery was abolished in British Guiana in 1834 and in French Guiana in 1848, but in Dutch Guiana slavery remained legal until 1863. The Dutch slaves were not fully freed until 1873, after a mandatory 10-year transition period during which they were required to remain as laborers on the plantations for minimal pay. Escaped slaves continued to join the Ndyuka communities during this period giving the Dutch colony the largest number of Ndyuka settlements of the

NATIVE AMERICAN NATIONS PRIOR TO COLONIZATION

Major tribes of the Americas prior to European colonization. (Robert Cronan/Lucidity Information Design)

three European colonies. When the plantation slaves of Dutch Guiana were finally freed, they largely abandoned the hated plantations to settle in Paramaribo. Still heavily dependent on manual labor, the Dutch authorities imported contract laborers from the Dutch East Indies and India, and later from China and the Middle East. The Ndyukas mostly avoided contact with the coastal population well into the 20th century. Christian missionaries introduced some aspects of modern culture and education. As the two largest ethnic groups in the colony—the Hindustanis and the Creoles of African or mixed African and European background—competed for power in the colony the Creoles sought to establish ties with the Maroon peoples of the interior to increase the influence of the African-descended population. In 1975, Dutch Guiana was granted independence as the Republic of Suriname. The majority of the Dutch population returned to the Netherlands, along with many other Surinamese who feared for the future in the ethnically divided state. In 1980 a military coup overthrew the democratic government and declared a socialist republic. Increasing conflicts between the military government and the Ndyukas erupted into a full-scale guerrilla war in 1986. The Surinamese army rampaged through the Ndyuka region demolishing villages and destroying roads, water pipelines, power lines, public buildings, schools, health clinics, and many Ndyuka businesses. The most intensive fighting, between 1986 and 1989, was mostly over control of eastern Suriname and the trade in cocaine with the Ndyuka homeland as the theatre of war. In 1992 a peace agreement was signed,

allowing many Ndyukas to return to their homeland. A democratic government aided the recovery of the Ndyuka region and in 1998 established the Central Suriname Nature Reserve to protect the unspoiled rain forest that is home to the Ndyuka people. The reserve became a UN World Heritage Site in 2000. In 2009 violent conflicts and rioting broke out between the Ndyukas and illegal Brazilian gold diggers invading their territory.

Further Reading

Kambel, Ellen-Rose. *The Rights of Indigenous Peoples and Maroons in Suriname.* Copenhagen, Denmark: IWGIA, 1999.

Price, Richard. *The Guiana Maroons: A Historical and Bibliographical Introduction.* Baltimore, MD: Johns Hopkins University Press, 1976.

Van Velzen, H. U. E. Thoden and Ineke van Wetering. *In the Shadow of the Oracle: Religion as Politics in a Suriname Maroon Society.* Long Grove, IL: Waveland Press, 2004.

Nevisians

The Nevisians, sometimes known as Nevis Islanders, are a Caribbean people whose home island, Nevis, forms part of the Federation of Saint Kitts and Nevis. The estimated 30,000 Nevisians are divided between the island of Nevis, with a population of some 12,000, and sizable Nevisian populations living on other Caribbean islands and in the United Kingdom, the United States, and Canada. English is the official language of Nevis though most Nevisians use a local creole language known as Nevisian English in daily life.

Nevis was originally settled by peaceful Arawak peoples migrating north from the South American mainland over 2,000 years ago. The Arawaks had been killed or driven from the island by the later migration of the warlike Caribs, also from South America, when the island was first sighted by Christopher Columbus in 1493. Columbus named the sparsely populated island Nuestra Señora de las Nieves, Our Lady of the Snows, probably for the white clouds that usually cover Nevis Peak. The Native American population of the island probably perished from diseases introduced by the Europeans. Though claimed by Spain, the Spanish had little interest in agriculture so the island, with no gold or other riches to attract the Spanish, remained uninhabited for over a century. The English established their first Caribbean colony on nearby Saint Kitts in 1623, with settlers crossing from Saint Kitts to colonize Nevis in 1628. The Spanish name of the island, Nieves, was retained as "Nevis" as the early settlers believed that Nevis Peak resembled Ben Nevis Mountain in Scotland. The settlers established plantations for the production of sugar and began importing African slaves for the intensive manual labor. In the 18th century, Nevis became a famous resort for the plantation aristocracy of the British Caribbean islands. The opulent way of life of the European planter society earned Nevis the reputation and name of "Queen of the Caribbees." The growing population of slaves from Africa or of African descent formed the largest part of the island population in the early 1700s. Pierre Le Moyne d'Iberville, the founder of the French colony of Louisiana, led a French force of soldiers and French pirates in an invasion of Nevis in 1706. Faced with the notorious French pirates most of the English militia fled. Some of the planters burned their plantations rather than let the French pillage them. Others fled to other islands or hid in the mountains. It was the African slaves who held the French force at bay by taking up arms to defend their families. The French offered the pirates the right to capture as many slaves as they could take to be resold in the slave markets of Martinique. During the fighting, 3,400 slaves were captured and shipped off to Martinique, but about 1,000 slaves, poorly armed and untrained, held the French troops off until help arrived 18 days after the invasion. Of the Nevisian slaves carried off by the invaders, six were later sent to Louisiana, the first persons of African descent to arrive in the colony. The invasion decimated the island's lucrative sugar industry. During the hard times that followed many absentee planters allowed their slave families to farm small plots of land to stave off starvation. Between 1776 and 1783, during the American Revolutionary War, food supplies for the plantation slaves failed to arrive in Nevis, causing 300–400 of them to die of starvation.

The Nevisian culture is an Afro-Caribbean culture with many British influences and traditions. The later arrival of East Indians added another layer to the island culture, particularly in terms of cuisine and the arts. The majority of the Nevisians are the descendants of black slaves though there is a considerable European admixture. The Nevisian culture also includes small East Indian and white Nevisian communities.

The high level of emigration offsets the natural population increase and enables Nevis to maintain a fairly stable population. The Nevisian populations in the United Kingdom and elsewhere maintain close family and political ties to the island. Remittances from Nevisian emigrants form an important source of the island's income. Nevisian versions of Caribbean music and dance forms are important parts of any celebration on the island, particularly the Emancipation Day celebrations during the Nevis Culturama held each August and the Christmas Sports, a festival of music and theatre held around Christmas. A series of earthquakes severely damaged most of the colonial-era stone buildings in the 18th century. When they were rebuilt a particularly Nevisian architecture was developed with a wooden upper floor over a stone ground floor; the new architectural style proved to be much more earthquake resistant than the earlier style. The Nevisians speak Standard English along with the creole dialect known as Nevisian English, a mixture of archaic English with African words and structure. Most Nevisians belong to Protestant denominations such as the Anglican or Methodist denominations, with smaller groups of Moravians, Roman Catholics, and converts to evangelical sects active in Nevis since the 1960s. Religion is an important part of the island culture.

The sugar industry never fully recovered from the French invasion, leaving many of the island's slaves in control of small plots of land as subsistence farmers. Slavery was officially abolished in the British Empire in 1834, and some 8,815 slaves were officially freed, although they were forced to work out a four-year apprenticeship on their home plantations. The Nevisian planters were given monetary compensation for the loss of their slaves while the slaves themselves received nothing for their two centuries of labor. Because of the early distribution of plots and the departure from the island of many planter families when sugar cultivation became unprofitable, a relatively large part of the Nevisian black population already owned or controlled farm land at emancipation. Others settled as subsistence farmers on crown land. This early development of landowning farmers and entrepreneurs created a distinct culture with a stronger middle class than in other Caribbean islands. Nevis was united with Saint Kitts and Anguilla in 1882, over the protest of the Nevisian leaders. The three islands became an associated British state with full autonomy in 1967, though the people of the island of Anguilla supported secession from the federation in 1971. Nevis and Saint Kitts, separated only by a narrow strait, became an independent nation in 1893. Nevisians, seeing themselves as a culture distinct from that of nearby Saint Kitts, pressed for greater self-government and control of their own economy and culture. In 1998, the Nevisian activists organized a referendum on separation that failed to gain the two-thirds of the votes necessary. Many Nevisians are content with the autonomy accorded their island in the federation but others see the island as a separate nation and continue to work for the legal separation of Nevis from the federation. Many Nevisians see a structural imbalance with greater shares of the revenue from tourism and exports and developmental funds going to Saint Kitts.

Further Reading

Gordon, Joyce. *Nevis: Queen of the Caribees.* Basingstoke, England: Macmillan Caribbean, 2005. Hubbard, Vincent K. *Swords, Ships and Sugar: A History of Nevis to 1900.* Corvallis, OR: Premier Editions International, 1996.

Olwig, Karen Fog. *Global Culture, Island Identity: Continuity and Change in the Afro-Caribbean Community of Nevis.* London: Routledge, 1996.

Nicaraguans

The Nicaraguans, sometimes known as Nicas, Nicoyas, or Pinoleros, are the inhabitants of the Central American nation of Nicaragua. Outside Nicaragua there are sizable Nicaraguan communities in neighboring Costa Rica and in the United States. The estimated 7.5 million Nicaraguans mostly speak the Central American dialect of Spanish though minorities speak several indigenous languages and English or English Creole.

The early inhabitants of Nicaragua were influenced by both of the great indigenous civilizations of the Americas, the Mesoamerican civilization to the north and the Andean civilization to the south. By the end of the 15th century CE, western Nicaragua was inhabited by several indigenous groups related culturally and linguistically to the Azteca and the Mayans. The inhabitants were primarily farmers living in villages and towns, organized into small, often-warring kingdoms. East of the mountains, on the Caribbean coast, other groups—mostly belonging to the Chibchan linguistic and cultural tradition—lived as fishermen, hunters, and gatherers. These people traded with the indigenous peoples of the Caribbean, which was reflected in their culture and way of life. Christopher Columbus and his ships were the first Europeans to sight the present Caribbean coast of Nicaragua. Mostly ignoring the Caribbean area, Spanish expeditions explored the area west of the mountains, gathering gold in the fertile valleys and often taking indigenous women from their villages. Despite active resistance they soon controlled the larger western districts from the Pacific Ocean to the mountains. The estimated population of some one million declined rapidly in the region due to the spread of smallpox and measles, to which they had no immunity. The Spanish colonizers, leaving families behind in Spain, often took indigenous women as wives, beginning the large population of mixed race that forms the majority of the present population of western Nicaragua. Included in the Captaincy General of Guatemala, the southern part of New Spain, the area of western Nicaragua was divided into a number of large land holdings worked by indigenous people enslaved by the Spaniards. English loggers and fishing communities were established on the Caribbean coast where the indigenous peoples had mostly escaped the horrors of the Spanish conquest.

Nicaraguan culture is a Central American culture with strong folklore elements in the traditional music and dance. The mixture of the indigenous and European traditions is evident in all facets of the culture, which is similar to other cultures of Latin America. The racial background of the multiethnic Nicaraguans is approximately 69 percent mestizo, 17 percent European descent, 5 percent Native American, and 9 percent black, mostly descendants of early Jamaican settlements on the Caribbean coast. Nicaraguan literature has gained international fame with famous writers known throughout the Spanish-speaking world. The distinctive histories and cultures of the western half of the country, dominated by the large mestizo population, and the eastern Caribbean region where indigenous cultures are still evident along with the English language and influences from Jamaica and other parts of the Caribbean make up the two major influences in the country's culture. The influences brought to Nicaragua by the large population living in the United States have become part of modern Nicaraguan culture, particularly American musical forms, food, and the Nicaraguans' national sport, baseball. Nicaraguan Spanish, one of the Central American dialects of Spanish, has many indigenous influences with words and syntax adopted from indigenous languages now being used in everyday speech. Religion is an important element in the Nicaraguan culture and is confirmed in the country's constitution. Nicaragua has no official religion though the majority of the Nicaraguans identify themselves as Roman Catholics. The number of practicing Roman Catholics has been declining, while membership in evangelical Protestant churches and the Mormon denomination have been growing rapidly since the 1990s. The Roman Catholic year—particularly the patron saints of each city, town, and village—dictates the celebrations and fiestas held on an annual basis.

Unrest and resistance to continued rule by Spain began a series of conflicts that culminated in independence as part of the first Mexican empire in 1821. The overthrow of the Mexican monarchy in 1823 resulted in the secession of Central America and the formation of the United Provinces of Central America, later called the Federal Republic of Central America. Tensions and conflicts between the member states ended the federation with Nicaragua becoming an independent republic in 1838. Rivalries between regional power centers degenerated into civil war, particularly violent and destructive in the 1840s and 1850s. Invited by one of the factions, an American adventurer named William Walker set himself up as the new president of the republic. The neighboring Central American republics united to drive Walker out of Nicaragua in 1857. The British, having claimed the eastern part of the country as a protectorate since 1655, transferred the region to Nicaragua in 1860. The region, known as the Mosquito Coast, remained self-governing until 1894 when President José Santos Zelaya negotiated the annexation of the region and it's largely indigenous population to Nicaragua. A sizable number of Europeans, particularly Germans, Italians, Spanish, French, and Belgians, arrived in the 19th century to establish plantations, open banks or hotels, and establish newspapers. Throughout the 19th century the United States, along with several European countries, considered a scheme to build a canal across Nicaragua to link the Atlantic and the Pacific oceans. A bill was put before the U.S. Congress in 1899 but failed to pass; construction of the Panama Canal was begun as an alternative. In 1909 the

United States began providing aid to opponents of President Zelaya due to differences over the proposed Nicaraguan canal, the country's destabilizing influences in Central America, and Zelaya's attempts to regulate foreign control of Nicaragua's natural resources. Following the mass execution of 500 revolutionaries, including two Americans, the United States intervened leading to Zelaya's resignation. Another rebellion erupted in 1912 and the government requested American aid in protecting American citizens and others in the republic. The U.S. Marines occupied the country from 1912 to 1933 except for some nine months in 1925. From 1927 to 1933, Augusto César Sandino led a large guerilla force against the corrupt Nicaraguan government and subsequently against the U.S. Marines. When the Marines withdrew in 1933 they left behind an American-trained military force and put pro-American Anastasio Somoza García in charge of the government. Despite a peace agreement Somoza distrusted the rebel leader Sandino. In 1934 Somoza invited Sandino to a meeting where Sandino was assassinated. Hundreds of Sandino followers were also rounded up and executed. The Somoza dictatorship lasted from 1936, when democracy was dissolved, until 1979. In 1961 anti-Somoza groups formed the Sandinista National Liberation Front (FSLN), named in honor of Augusto César Sandino. A devastating earthquake destroyed much of Managua, the republic's capital. The Somoza regime's alleged mishandling of relief aid, the ongoing corruption, and the government's refusal to rebuild Managua resulted in thousands of disaffected Nicaraguans joining the antigovernment Sandinistas. The Sandinistas, supported by a majority of the Nicaraguans and aided by several Latin American governments, finally took power in 1979. Fearing Soviet influence in the leftist Sandinista government of Nicaragua, the United States began financing, arming, and training the anti-Sandinista rebels known as the Contras. The civil war eventually drew in other Central American countries as violence spilled over the Nicaraguan borders. Both sides were accused of dealing in drugs to finance the conflict and of brutality to noncombatant villages, massacres, and other abuses of human rights. Tens of thousands of refugees fled the brutal conflict. In the 1990s elections were held that ended the Sandinista government and ushered in a more moderate government but with the economy in ruins and the country politically divided instability drove thousands of Nicaraguans to migrate to other Central American countries or the United States. After several weak governments, the Sandinistas won the 2006 elections and were reelected in 2011. The populist politics of the Sandinistas, while popular with the country's majority of poor peasants, continues to drive many educated professionals and business people to abandon Nicaragua.

Further Reading

Hagene, Turid. *Negotiating Love in Post-Revolutionary Nicaragua*. Bern, Switzerland: Peter Lang, 2008.

Walker, Thomas W. *Nicaragua: Living in the Shadow of the Eagle*. Boulder, CO: Westview Press, 2011.

White, Steven F. *Culture and Customs of Nicaragua*. Westport, CT: Greenwood, 2008.

Odawas

The Odawas, sometimes known as Odaawaas, Ottawas, or Anishinabes, are a North American ethnic group concentrated in the U.S. states of Oklahoma and Michigan and the Canadian province of Ontario. The estimated 20,000 Odawas speak English, with about half the Odawa population still able to speak their tribal language. The majority of the Odawas are Christians, including both Protestants and Roman Catholics, with a minority adhering to the Native American Church.

Odawa history tells of an early migration from the present Atlantic coast to a new homeland on the Great Lakes, where the migrants divided into three separate tribes or bands, the Odawas, the Ojibwes, and the Potawatomis. Tribal scholars believe the three tribes formed the Council of the Three Fires around 796 CE. The three tribes continued to use the collective term Anishnaabeg to refer to the three closely related peoples. In this council, the Ojibwes were addressed as the "older brother," the Odawas as the "middle brother," and the Potawatomis as the "younger brother." The French made contact with the Odawas and the other tribes in 1615, with French trading posts and Roman Catholic missions established over the next decades. In the 1640s the Iroquois, armed by the Dutch and the English, sought to expand their territory and to monopolize the lucrative fur trade between the Europeans and the tribes of the Great Lakes region. The Iroquois warriors drove the Odawas from their home territory on sacred Manitoulin Island in Lake Huron by 1650, killing many of the survivors of the diseases introduced by the Europeans. Following a peace treaty with the Iroquois, the Odawas recovered and prospered from the fur trade, mostly trading with the French colonists. The Odawas were widely known as traders; their towns on the Great Lakes water routes and their negotiating skills enabled them to become the middlemen in intertribal and French commerce. From about 1615 to 1763 the Odawas were one of the most important tribal groups in North America. During the French and British wars for control of northeastern North America the Odawas fought on the side of the French. The defeat of the French in 1763 allowed British military occupation of the Great Lakes region. Odawa chief Pontiac led a widespread uprising against the British that came to be known as Pontiac's Rebellion; it united a number of tribes against British authority. The rebellion ended in 1766 when Pontiac finally made peace with the British authorities. A decade later the Odawas fought the American rebels as British allies. In the 1790s, the Odawas again fought the U.S. military in a series of battles and campaigns known as the Northwest Indian War.

The Odawa culture is a Native American culture that blends traditional society with the customs and language of modern American and Canadian cultures. Traditionally the Odawas were seminomadic, traveling from Michigan's Upper Peninsula and the other areas on the Great Lakes to present-day southern Michigan where the climate was more hospitable during the winter months. In the spring, the Odawas returned to their homelands to collect maple syrup, fish, and plant the spring and summer crops. After the European settlement of the region the Odawas' southern lands were colonized by farmers and the Odawas ceased their annual migrations. In their homelands around the lakes the Odawas erected permanent housing, schools, churches, and administrative buildings. Most of the modern Odawas are farmers or run small businesses. Only about 15,000 of the Odawas are registered as tribal members while an estimated 5,000, mostly urbanized, are not registered. The Odawas maintain many traditions such as storytelling, artwork, traditional music and dance, and a folklore of herbal medicine. Modern Odawa artisans are known for traditional arts such as beadwork and basketry. The Odawa language is considered a dialect of the Ojibwe language, possibly the dialect that has undergone the most change. To maintain their language as English increases and fluent speakers decline, the Odawas have begun second language learning in the area's primary and secondary schools. The Odawas are mostly Christians, with many Roman Catholics, a legacy of their long alliance with the French.

In 1807 the Odawas and their allied tribes ceded 7 million acres of southeastern Michigan to the new U.S. government. The Odawas were given an annuity of $800 for 10 years and a reservation in Ohio on the Maumee River. The Odawas again honored their alliance with the British during the War of 1812, which ended with a total defeat of the Odawas. Treaties signed with the American government over the next decades pushed the Odawas into ever smaller reserved lands. Many moved north to British territory in Canada. Following the passage of the Indian Removal Act in 1830, pressure grew to force the removal of the tribes still living east of the Mississippi. Some Odawa bands ceded their lands and agreed to move to Kansas or Indian Territory. Treaties signed by the remaining Odawas in Michigan in 1836 and 1855 allowed massive fraud that eliminated their tribal status and declared the Odawas legally dead. The result of the two treaties has been almost 150 years of legal battles. In 1905 the Michigan Odawas successfully sued the United States for redress for fraud and treaty violations, but the Indian Reorganization Act of 1934 prohibited the Michigan Odawas from reorganizing as a tribe. Only two small bands regained federal recognition but it took them until 1980 to do so. The Odawas in Kansas mostly moved to Indian Territory in the 1860s where they purchased lands that were mostly lost in 1891 under the terms of the Dawes Act. A lawsuit to recover the value of the lands was finally settled in 1965. The various bands of the Odawas, often living on reserved lands with their Ojibwe or Potawatomi cousins, have maintained contact as members of the same ancient tribe and continue to maintain their culture and language even though they are increasingly urbanizing and younger tribal members often leave in search of work or greater opportunities.

Further Reading

Bellfy, Phil. *Three Fires Unity: The Anishnaabeg of the Lake Huron Borderlands.* Lincoln, NE: University of Nebraska Press, 2011.

Blackbird, Andrew J. *History of the Ottawa and Chippewa Indians of Michigan.* Charleston, SC: Nabu Press, 2010.

Cleland, Charles E. *Rites of Conquest: The History and Culture of Michigan's Native Americans.* Ann Arbor, MI: University of Michigan Press, 1992.

Ojibwes

The Ojibwes, sometimes known as Ojibwas, Ojibways, Chippewas, Chippeways, Asinhinabes, or Asinhinaabes, are a North American ethnic group, one of the largest Native American groups north of Mexico. The estimated 225,000 Ojibwes live in scattered bands from Michigan west to Montana in the United States and from western Quebec to eastern British Columbia in Canada. There are sizable urban Ojibwe populations in Minneapolis, Duluth, and Green Bay in the United States and in Owen Sound, Fort Frances, and Sault Ste. Marie in Ontario. Many Ojibwe also live in smaller towns across the region. The Ojibwe usually speak English, or sometimes French, with a large number that is fluent in their own language, Anishinaabemowin or Ojibwemowin. The Ojibwes are nominally Christian, belonging to both Protestant and Roman Catholic denominations, though they often combine Christian beliefs and traditions with their earlier pre-Christian rituals.

The Ojibwe, part of the Anishinaabe, migrated west from the Atlantic coast with many Ojibwe sites continually inhabited since the Middle Woodland period, from about 200 BCE. In the area of the Great Lakes the migrants split into three closely related tribal groups, the Ojibwes, the Odawas, and the Potawatomis. The three groups united in the Council of the Three Fires, thought to have been sealed by leaders of the three groups in 746 CE. Each year the three tribes gathered for an annual celebration of the Great Medicine Society, a secret organization open to both men and women. In the early 1600s French explorers visited Ojibwe territory and trade in furs and French manufactured goods assured peaceful relations. At the end of the 17th century the Ojibwes had settled in a region adjacent to northern Lake Huron and eastern Lake Superior. In a series of migrations and conquests, they expanded to the west and north. They drove the Sioux from present-day Michigan, Wisconsin, and Minnesota and by the mid-1700s the Ojibwes had settled in the Mil Lacs region of present-day Minnesota. The Ojibwe population was estimated at between 25,000 and 30,000 in the 1770s. The Ojibwes mostly settled in villages and lived by hunting, fishing, and gathering, particularly the cereal later known as wild rice. Small bands, beginning at the end of the 18th century, moved out onto the northern plains where they adopted many traditions and traits from the plains tribes, including the buffalo hunting economy. The Ojibwes were not prominent in the wars between the French and the British or in other events in colonial history because of their remoteness from the frontier during the colonial wars.

The Ojibwes, popularly called Chippewas in the United States and Ojibwas in Canada, often call themselves Anishinabe or Anishinaabes, meaning "true people" or "original men." The related Odawas and Potawatomis also call themselves Anishinabe as the three tribes are closely related in culture and language. Within the Ojibwes there is a division between the eastern Woodlands Ojibwes and the Plains Ojibwes with distinct cultural traditions and dialects, but all maintain their ties to the Ojibwe nation. The Woodlands Ojibwes maintain the classic Ojibwe culture, which has been immortalized in the 1855 epic poem by Henry Wadsworth Longfellow, "The Song of Hiawatha." The stories related in the poem are nearly all Ojibwe even though the name Hiawatha is probably of Iroquois derivation. Ojibwe traditions include the complex kinship system that includes not only the immediate family but also the extended family. The system reflects the Ojibwe's philosophy of the interconnectedness and balance among all living things and generations, both past and future. The Ojibwe language is a Central Algonkian language that is shared with the related Odawas and Potawatomis. Due to the territorial dispersal and the relatively large Ojibwe population there are some regional dialectical differences. English is replacing the language in many areas, particularly among the Ojibwes who have urbanized since the 1950s. Historically the Ojibwes have a unique system of picture writing that is used in the scrolls and other archives connected with the Midewiwin society, the "Medicine Society." The Ojibwe religious beliefs often combine Christian rituals with their pre-Christian customs and traditions. Many converted to Christianity in the 19th and 20th centuries though some never gave up their traditional beliefs.

British influence in the Ojibwe lands, including trading posts in Wisconsin and Minnesota that continued to operate until 1815, worried the new U.S. government. A military expedition in 1805–1806 led by Lieutenant Zebulon Pike attempted to undermine British influence and to end the Ojibwe-Sioux wars but with little success. Like many tribes the Ojibwes generally favored the British due to fears that the U.S. government would take their lands for settlement. White settlers moving west in the early 1800s threatened Ojibwe lands and resources. Several treaties were negotiated with the United States that ceded traditional territories in Michigan, Wisconsin, and Minnesota in return for monetary payments and parts of their land set aside as reserved lands or reservations. In 1862, some Ojibwes joined the Sioux in fighting the encroaching American settlers, but others, including the Ojibwes in the Mil Lacs region, remained carefully neutral and often protected their white neighbors. For this they were classified as "nonremovable" and when other bands were forced to leave their historic homelands, they remained. Unable to support themselves

Ojibwe (Chippewa) Centennial Pageant, 1949. (AP/Wide World Photos)

on the small reservations, many Ojibwes found work as lumberjacks or miners. In 1887 the Dawes Act was passed, breaking up the reservations into individual plots with the surplus lands confiscated and sold to white farmers or lumber companies. Unaware of the value of their lands, many Ojibwes sold their plots to lumber companies or were tricked into selling. On some reservations, over 90 percent of the land passed into white ownership. By 1930 over half the Ojibwes lived off the reservation lands and many were living in abject poverty. Alcohol abuse became a serious problem, as did petty crime. Because of their relative isolation, the Ojibwes escaped the great epidemics that decimated the tribes to the east in the early colonial period, but they later suffered great losses from the diseases brought west by the

white settlers. By 1910 their numbers had fallen to some 30,000 in the United States and 20,000 in Canada. The 1930 census showed a further drop, with just 21,500 Ojibwes in the United States. Well into the 20th century the Ojibwes were forbidden from practicing their traditional religion, teaching their language to their children, or having any control over their own lives. The 19th-century treaties reserved the right of Ojibwes to hunt and fish on the ceded lands. Many were arrested or detained while hunting or fishing off the reservation lands in Wisconsin and Minnesota until a landmark court case in the federal district court of Chicago affirmed their right to hunt and fish on their traditional lands in 1983. Land claims and court cases in both the United States and Canada in the 1980s and 1990s mostly

Hanging Cloud

Hanging Cloud was an Ojibwe woman who was accepted as a warrior among her people. Her Ojibwe name, Aashawigiizhigokwe, meaning "Goes across the Sky Woman," is registered by the Wisconsin Historical Society as the only Ojibwe woman to ever become a full warrior or *ogichidaakwe* in the known history of the Ojibwe. She was the daughter of a chief of an Ojibwe band living near Lake Superior. Shortly after her father's death in 1855, her village was attacked by her uncle and his clan. She defended her people and killed her cousin during the fighting. In 1857 she married Edward Dingley and later had a son. She later worked as a housekeeper for a local lumber baron. When she died in 1919 she was buried with all the ceremony and rites reserved for the tribe's full warriors.

confirmed government policies in the United States and Canada that they had no legal right to lands stolen during the colonial period. The opening of casinos in the United States, illegal in the surrounding territories but allowed on the sovereign territory of the reservations, proved to be an economic boon to the Ojibwes, creating jobs, opportunities, and hope. In the early 21st century the scattered Ojibwe bands have begun to organize into larger units that allow them to use their numbers and their votes for the betterment of the Ojibwe tribe. Some bands are still seeking redress for the loss or theft of hunting and fishing grounds stemming from the unequal 19th-century treaties. The traditional Council of the Three Fires of the Ojibwes, Odawas, and Potawatomis has been renewed and revitalized as the Nation of the Three Tribes.

Further Reading

Greene, Jacqueline Dembar. *The Chippewa*. New York: Franklin Watts, 1993.

Lucas, Eileen. *The Ojibwas: People of the Northern Forests*. Brookfield, CT: Millbrook Press, 1994.

Peacock, Thomas and Marlene Wisuri. *Ojibwe Waasa Inaabidaa: We Look in All Directions*. Saint Paul, MN: Minnesota Historical Society Press, 2009.

Otomis

The Otomis, sometimes known as Otomís, Otomies, or Hña-hñu, are a Mexican ethnic group inhabiting the central plateau region of Mexico. The Otomis are concentrated in the Mexican states of Hidalgo, Mexico, Querétaro, Puebla, Veracruz, Guanajuato, Tlaxcala, and Michoacán. There are sizable Otomi communities in Mexico City and other large urban areas and in the United States. The estimated 320,000 Otomis speak at least four closely related languages, all of which are known as Otomi. A sizable number of Otomis no longer speak their ancestral language but continue to self-identify as Otomis.

The Otomis are predominately Roman Catholic, often mixing Christian ceremonies and rituals with customs and traditions from their pre-Christian belief system.

The Otomis inhabited the valleys of Toluca, Tula, and Mexico where they lived as sedentary farmers or they lived in market towns and cities. The advanced Otomi civilization spread through the region but lived in peace with the Olmecs and the other peoples of central Mexico. Around 800 CE Nahuas from the deserts to the north began to infiltrate the Otomi state. Waves of Nahuas gradually pushed the Otomis into the highlands as they took control of the valleys. The first Nahuas were the Toltecs who established themselves in the region by force, founding a new capital city at Tula. The Otomis became subjects of the Toltec empire. In the 12th century a nomadic Nahua people known as the Chichimecas invaded the central valleys and destroyed Tula around 1200. After the fall of Tula, the Otomis settled in the Toluca valley and in 1220 they moved east to found the city-state of Xaltocan to the north of the Valley of Mexico. In 1395 their territory was overrun by another Nahua, the Tepanecs. Fleeing the Nahua invasions, many Otomis migrated northeast and east to settle in the semidesert highlands. Another Nahua group, known as the Aztecs, conquered much of central Mexico, making the Otomis pay tribute as subject people. The Aztecs did not interfere much with the local Otomi authorities in the Valley of Mezquital because it was largely a desert and unproductive, and therefore of little interest to the Aztec empire. In the early 16th century the Spanish invaded the region, moving inland from where their ships had landed in Veracruz. The Otomi of the Mezquital formed an alliance with the Spanish in the hope of freeing themselves from Aztec rule. European diseases decimated the Otomi communities in the valleys but those living in the more inaccessible mountains mostly escaped the epidemics. During the later 16th century and in the 17th century the Otomis played an intermediary role between the Spanish authorities and the nomadic tribes to the north, thus avoiding serious conflicts with the conquerors. At the beginning of the 1700s silver mining in the Otomi territory drew in a number of colonists, who fought a war against the nomadic Chichimecas, a war that ended with their extermination. The Otomis were conscripted to work in the mines, with many fleeing into the more arid regions to escape the Spanish soldiers.

The Otomi culture is divided into two main groups: the Highland Otomis, living mostly to the north of the Valley of Mexico, and a smaller group known as the Sierra Otomis, who live in the mountains of eastern Hidalgo and in adjoining parts of the states of Puebla and Veracruz. Although divided into two main divisions and a number of regional groups, the culture of the Otomis is fairly uniform. Social organization is based on family relationships and the network of mutual help that forms part of the *compadrazgo* system. Religious festivals, which are annual celebrations based on the Roman Catholic calendar, create cohesion and social identity. Many migrants return to their home communities at fiesta time and participate in cultural events and family reunions. The immediate family is the most important kin group, but extended families are also important. The Otomi language is an Oto-Manguean language, one of the largest spoken indigenous languages in Mexico. The language is spoken in many different dialects, not all of which are mutually intelligible. Some older Otomis are monolingual but the majority also speaks Spanish. Increasingly Spanish is the first language for the growing number of Otomis living in the large urban areas. The majority of the Otomis are Roman Catholic, though their world is filled with many invisible spirits, both good and bad, that can affect every aspect of daily life. Failure to perform their Christian religious duties is believed to make the saints and the dead angry, bringing misfortune and hardships. Folk medicine is an important part of the culture and the most widely used means of dealing with illness or death.

By 1800 most of the Otomis were forced to serve the Spanish under the *encomienda*, the labor-tribute system. But the Otomis benefited from the fact that their lands were not rich and did not attract a large number of European immigrants. A low population density allowed the Otomis to retain extensive landholdings. Many Otomis joined the uprising against Spanish rule in 1808 but Mexican independence two years later did little to alleviate the hardships of their daily lives. Large Spanish estates were divided into small plots that became the property of the Mexicans of European descent, the *criollos*, and the mestizos, but the majority of the Otomis remained as poor laborers. As a result of the agrarian reform carried out in the 1930s, the Otomis were given lands of very poor quality and low productivity, in the form of *ejidos*, lands held and worked in common. Beginning in 1975, the semiarid lands north of the Valley of Mexico began to be developed, with new drainage and sewage waters diverted from the Mexico City urban area. By the late 1970s the Otomis had dramatically increased their crops of maize, squash, and maguey from their newly irrigated lands. In the higher elevations, populated by the Sierra Otomis, the people are primarily subsistence farmers or they herd goats or cattle. Traditional crafts such as pottery, weaving, and furniture-making have gained favor with collectors and tourists in the 21st century, giving the Otomis additional income. Market towns in the region now display a range of Otomi arts and crafts. Historically the Otomis, with their poor semidesert lands or mountain plots, were among the poorest of the peoples of central Mexico but in recent decades they have enjoyed a modest prosperity.

Further Reading

Carrasco, David, ed. *The Oxford Encyclopedia of Mesoamerican Cultures: The Civilizations of Mexico and Central America.* New York: Oxford University Press, 2001.

Galinier, Jacques. *The World Below: Body and Cosmos in Otomi Indian Ritual.* Boulder, CO: University Press of Colorado, 2004.

Granberg, Wilbur J. *People of the Maguey: The Otomi Indians of Mexico.* Westport, CT: Praeger, 1970.

P

Pacific Islander Americans

The Pacific Islander Americans, sometimes known as Pacific Islands Americans, Pacific people, Oceanian Americans, or South Pacific people, are Americans whose ancestry is connected with the many island cultures of Oceania. The estimated 358,000 Pacific Islander Americans include a number of subgroups, including Polynesian Americans, Samoan Americans, Tongan Americans, and Micronesian Americans. The Pacific Islands Americans usually speak English as their first language while many also speak the indigenous languages of their island ethnic group.

The history of the Pacific Islands is as vast and varied as the islands themselves. Originally settled by waves of migrants sailing large double-hulled canoes from the Asian mainland from 3000 BCE to 1000 BCE, the settlers of the many islands were divided among three large island groups, Micronesia, Melanesia, and Polynesia. While similar cultures and languages prevailed in each of the three regions, each island often constituted a distinct cultural and linguistic ethnic group. The Micronesian cultures include the islands of Kiribati, Nauru, the Marianas (Guam and the Northern Mariana Islands), the Marshall Islands, Palau, and the Micronesian federation. Melanesia comprises the large island of New Guinea, the Bismarck and Louisiade islands, the Admiralty group, Bougainville, the Solomon Islands, New Caledonia and the Loyalty Islands, Vanuatu, Fiji, and Norfolk Island. The largest of the three cultural regions is Polynesia, which includes the Maoris of New Zealand, the Samoan Islands, the Cook Islands, French Polynesia, Niue, Tokelau, Tuvalu, Tonga, Wallis and Futuna, and Pitcairn Island. Altogether there are approximately 25,000 islands, atolls, and islets in Oceania. Life in the Pacific Islands changed dramatically in the early 17th century when European explorers and traders first encountered the islands. By the end of the 18th century the majority of the islands had been claimed and controlled by European colonial powers. Christian missionaries followed the colonizers, gaining many converts among the islanders in the late 1700s.

The Pacific Islander Americans represent a large group of distinct island cultures blended with modern American culture. Traditions and customs originally brought from their island homes have been adapted or modified by contact with popular American culture and the mixture of cultures that make up the overall American society. The blending of Pacific Island culture and modern popular culture has resulted in many distinct art forms, musical blends, and dialectical innovations. Music and dance, important elements in the island cultures, have been adapted to include a wide variety of skilled musicians, dancers, and athletes who have entered and enhanced mainstream American culture. The shared experience of immigrants to Hawaii and the American mainland has resulted in many cultural borrowings and the construction of lasting community relationships that include the Pacific Islander Americans as a distinct part of American society. The largest Pacific Islander American communities are in Hawaii, Alaska, and the states of the American West Coast, particularly in California and Utah. The overall Pacific Islander population in the United States numbers over 1.3 million, which also includes Pacific Island groups such as the Hawaiians, the Chamorros, and the Samoans of American Samoa who are the American citizens of American territories in the Pacific and are therefore not included as part of the immigrant community known as Pacific Islander Americans. Since Pacific Islanders had no written languages, music was a means of expression and remains an important cultural manifestation. The Christian religion that plays an important role in Pacific Islander American communities also includes music in the form of hymn singing and church choirs. The rapid assimilation of the Pacific Islanders into American society included the adoption of English as part of their new mixed culture. Though English is often the language used in the home, many Pacific Islander Americans retain and use their traditional languages. The majority of the island migrants are Christians, often belonging to the Mormon faith or Roman Catholicism, with a growing number embracing evangelical Protestant sects or other religions,

including the ancient religions of their island ancestors.

In the 1800s the various European colonial powers divided the islands of the vast Pacific among themselves with little thought of the welfare or wishes of the islanders themselves. Small numbers of Europeans settled in the islands as administrators or Christian missionaries, who often engaged in trade or other lucrative businesses. By the end of the 19th century most of the islands were administered as colonies of the United Kingdom, France, Spain, Germany, and the Netherlands. According to immigration records and family histories, the first Pacific Islander, from Tonga, came to the United States as the companion of a Mormon missionary in 1924. The first families began to settle in Utah and California in the 1950s. The first immigrants included the Tongans in Utah, three Fijians who entered the United States in 1953, and then three more Fijians plus three people from French Polynesia in 1954. Waves of Pacific Islander immigrants arrived in Hawaii and the U.S. mainland in the late 1950s and 1960s. By the 1970s several thousand Pacific Islanders had settled in the United States, often choosing to live close to others from the same island or island group to form communities in many cities and towns in Hawaii and the western United States. The Mormon Church, through active missionary activity in the vast region, received a steady stream of immigrants wishing to settle in the Mormon heartland in Utah. Other islanders chose large urban areas such as Honolulu, San Diego, Los Angeles, Long Beach, San Francisco, Sacramento, Portland, and Seattle before moving east to northern Texas during the 1970s and 1980s, particularly the Dallas–Fort Worth urban area. Language proved to be the first barrier for the Pacific Islander immigrants. A limited knowledge of English resulted in problems when the islanders sought housing, employment, legal representation, and health care. Though the Pacific Islander Americans faced serious challenges to assimilation, their traditional cultural concept of community proved a valuable support for new arrivals. Cultural events, such as the Pacific Island Festival, a weekend cultural event held annually in California since 1990, enabled the Pacific Island Americans to meet other immigrants and to maintain their cultural ties to their homelands. For centuries the Pacific Islanders regarded obesity as a sign of wealth and nobility, but excess weight has led to diabetes, hypertension, and other health problems. The need for and benefits of higher education were not fully understood by the immigrant communities until the 1990s when programs were instituted to aid students to attend universities, provide tutors, and make financial aid more widely available. Though the Pacific Islander Americans have assimilated they retain much of their traditional cultures, which are closely interwoven with their religions and religious services. The integration into a technological society proved difficult for many immigrants whose traditional values were often at odds with the American idea of success. No longer living as part of an extended family, the Pacific Island Americans had to learn to prosper as individuals instead of working for the good of the group. American military service is often the route to immigration for Pacific

Islanders, who later bring their families to the United States. In the early 21st century a number of cultural and help groups are active among each of the many distinct Pacific Islander American communities. Radio and television programming helps to keep them informed about events in areas where they live while specifically Pacific Islander programs address everyday problems and provide news of their Pacific homelands.

Further Reading

Hune, Shirley and Gail M. Nomura, eds. *Asian/ Pacific Islander American Women: A Historical Anthology.* New York: New York University Press, 2003.

Russell, Jesse and Ronald Cohn. *Pacific Islander American.* Seattle, WA: VSD, 2012.

Spickard, Paul R. *Pacific Islander Americans: An Annotated Bibliography in the Social Sciences.* Provo, UT: Brigham Young University Press, 1995.

Paez

The Paez, sometimes known as Páez, Páes, Paes, Nasas, or Nasa Yume, are a South American ethnic group living in the southeastern highlands of Colombia. The estimated 124,000 Paez speak the Paez language, which is a language isolate with up to 40,000 monolinguals, though Spanish is increasingly spoken as a second language. The majority of the Paez continue to adhere to their traditional religious beliefs but there is a growing number of converts to Roman Catholicism.

The early inhabitants of the Tierradentro region of the Andes Mountains, the Paez traditionally lived in a series of chiefdoms often warring amongst themselves or against the other ethnic groups of the region. The Spanish, moving inland from their bases on the coast, invaded the region in 1537. The estimated Paez population of some 10,000 was halved through war and imported European diseases by 1600. The Spanish forced the Paez into centralized villages where they could be more easily controlled and exploited as a source of labor and tribute. Paez resistance to Spanish rule resulted in bloody battles that mostly ended in Paez defeats. Some Paez migrated to the less accessible western slopes of the cordillera, where they established new villages outside Spanish control. The rugged mountains protected the Paez from destruction by the Spanish or assimilation into the general population under Spanish control. In the early 1700s Paez chiefs validated their political authority over their peoples and the territories under their authority through the creation of *resguardo* or reservations with titles granted by the Spanish authorities. Jesuit missionaries established themselves in the Paez territory but failed to win many converts.

Paez culture is an indigenous culture that has adapted by adopting traits and customs from the Hispanic culture that dominates Colombia. Traditionally the nuclear family is the core of Paez culture. The father has nearly absolute authority in a Paez family, and a family often has more than three children. The Paez are a reserved people who prize formality and respect. Small children are allowed much freedom but from the age of six or seven they are expected to behave more obediently and

quietly. Marriage customs blend both Paez and Spanish traditions. A prospective bride is chosen; then the boy's parents and godparents, his *compadres*, visit the girl's family to arrange the marriage. If accepted the boy and his family take the girl into their home for a year of trial marriage, after which if both parties agree they are usually married in the Catholic Church. Because of the cold climate of their Andean homeland, the Paez mostly live in brick and cement homes. Paez women raise and shear varieties of sheep for wool, which they clean, spin, dye, and knit cloths and blankets with. Most Paez are now nominally Roman Catholic with each Paez community celebrating a number of Catholic saints' days, including that of the patron saint of each community. Belief in spirits and in the traditional healing of shamans, many of who are now confirmed Roman Catholic priests, remains an important part of their mixed religious beliefs. The Paez language is thought to be related to other indigenous languages that mostly died out during the 20th century, leaving the Paez language as an isolated dialect.

During the early years of the 19th century the communal Paez holdings of the *resguardo* were challenged by nonindigenous landowners, by gatherers of quinine bark, and later by the ravages of wars. Colombian independence in 1819 began a long series of conflicts over new legislation that sought to privatize land ownership in place of the Spanish *resguardo* system. In the early 1900s, Roman Catholic Lazarist missionaries constructed missions in the Paez region. Learning the Paez language and traditional customs they converted many to the Catholic religion. The Paez evolved a syncretic form of Catholicism that absorbed much of their pre-Christian religious beliefs. The Paez lived in poor farming communities and survived with only the basic necessities but they resisted the division of their communal lands. At the turn of the 20th century many Paez joined a political movement led by share-cropper Manual Quintín Lame, who led a movement to reclaim lost tribal lands and to free the Paez sharecroppers from paying rent on the plots they tilled. Non-Paez sharecroppers evicted from their lands by large landowners in neighboring regions began to settle in the Tierradentro in the 1930s, triggering a strong reaction among the land-poor Paez. During the 1950s, Colombia's civil war swept the region with many Paez casualties. Some Paez communities were forced to disperse in order to survive. In the 1970s and 1980s a system of unpaved roads was constructed to link the various Paez villages and towns. Around 1970 the Paez adopted a pacifist philosophy toward Colombia's long-running armed conflicts. In the early 21st century they have some 7,000 men and women who stand guard in their territory armed only with ceremonial three-foot batons. These guardians persuade combatants of both sides to leave their lands.

Further Reading

Larson, Brooke. *Trials of Nation Building: Liberalism, Race, and Ethnicity in the Andes, 1810–1910.* Cambridge: Cambridge University Press, 2004.

Pittier, Henry. *Ethnographic and Linguistic Notes on the Paez Indians of Tierra Adentro, Cauca, Colombia.* Whitefish, MT: Kessinger Publishing, 2009.

Rappaport, Joanne. *The Politics of Memory: Native Historical Interpretation in the Colombian Andes.* Durham, NC: Duke University Press, 1998.

Panamanians

The Panamanians are a Central American people and are the inhabitants of the Republic of Panama, the most southerly of the Central American states. The largest Panamanian community outside the country is in the United States. The estimated 3.6 million Panamanians mostly speak Spanish, though there are communities that speak English or one of several indigenous languages. Roman Catholicism is the religion of about 85 percent of the Panamanians with sizable evangelical Protestant groups and smaller numbers of Baha'is, Jews, Muslims, Hindus, Buddhists, and Rastafarians.

The regions that form part of present-day Panama were once the home of Chibchan, Chocoan, and Cueva peoples. The largest of the groups, the Cueva, were widely dispersed so that population estimates for the whole region in precolonial times ranges from about 200,000 to over 2 million. Rodrigo de Bastidas, sailing westward from present-day Venezuela in 1501 in search of gold, is considered the first European to explore the region of the Isthmus of Panama. A year later, Christopher Columbus explored the isthmus and established a short-lived Spanish settlement at Darien. Vasco Núñez de Balboa led an expedition across the isthmus from the Atlantic to the Pacific in 1513, demonstrating that the isthmus was a connection between the two great oceans. Panama quickly became a trade center and crossroads of Spain's empire in the Americas. Gold, silver, and other looted treasures were brought by ship from western South America, hauled across the isthmus to the Atlantic, and then loaded aboard ships bound for Spain. The route became known as the Camino Real, the Royal Road, as all treasure theoretically belonged to the Spanish king. From the beginning the narrowness of the isthmus inspired the idea of a canal but the Spanish, jealous of their domination of the Pacific trade routes, were reluctant to build one. The Cueva people resisted Spanish domination and were massacred. The other indigenous peoples suffered epidemics of European diseases, forced labor, and the kidnap of indigenous women. From the beginning of colonization, Panamanian identity was based on the geographic position of the isthmus and the Panamanian economy fluctuated with the geopolitical importance of the isthmus as a center of Spanish trade in the Americas. The route across the isthmus was often vulnerable to attacks by Dutch and English pirates or by cimarrons, escaped African and indigenous slaves who lived in hidden communities along the trade route. In 1717, the viceroyalty of New Granada was created with Bogota as its administrative center. In 1739 the authority of New Granada was extended to Panama. The remoteness of Bogota proved a great obstacle as the authority of New Granada was weak prompting local initiatives of self-government by the Panamanians. The uneasy relationship between Panama and Bogota persisted until the early 20th century. By the mid-1700s the largest segment of the population was mestizo, of mixed Spanish and indigenous or African descent. The centuries of prosperity due to the colonial transshipment and trade in the isthmus and the pivotal role played by the Panamanians at the height of Spanish power in the Americas helped to define a distinctive sense of a regional and national identity well before most of the other Spanish colonial territories.

The culture of the Panamanians is a Central American Hispanic culture that blends Spanish traditions with local customs and influences from the Caribbean, North America, and Europe. The Panamanians, both rural and urban, share certain cultural values. One is *personalismo*, a system of interpersonal trust and individual honor. The most valued unit is the extended family and a tradition of self-help within the family. Another cultural tradition emphasizes *machismo*, the belief in the male dominance of the culture and the image of men as strong and daring. Women are expected to obey and be gentle, forgiving, and dedicated to their homes and families. The majority of the Panamanians, about 70 percent, are mestizos of mixed ancestry, followed by blacks, mostly of West Indian ancestry; about 14 percent of the Panamanians are white, mostly of European ancestry (10%), and indigenous peoples make up about 6 percent. The Panamanians are mostly concentrated in the urban areas of the Panama City-Colón metropolitan corridor. The Spanish language is spoken by 93 percent of the Panamanians with many speaking both English and Spanish, one of the indigenous languages, or languages spoken by the immigrant populations, such as French, Arabic, or one of several Chinese dialects. The majority of them are Roman Catholic, following the religion of the historic Spanish Empire, with an estimated 85 percent of the Panamanians identifying themselves with the Catholic Church. Evangelical Protestant groups and Mormons have won many converts in recent decades as the number of Roman Catholics has fallen.

The Spanish were forced to abandon Bogota as the independence of New Granada in 1819 moved the viceroyalty to Panama City, and they ruled there for two years. The Spanish control of the isthmus area ended in 1821 with the Colombian occupation of the region. The California Gold Rush in the 1840s renewed interest in travel between the Atlantic and the Pacific. In 1845, the United States financed the first transcontinental railroad that crossed Panama; in the meanwhile France, the United Kingdom, and the United States studied the possibility of a canal to join the two oceans by way of the Isthmus of Panama or farther north in Nicaragua. The French began to dig a canal across the isthmus in 1879, but after 20 years of struggle with diseases, the jungle, financial problems, political uncertainty, and the sheer enormity of the project, they were finally forced to abandon it. Between 16,000 and 22,000 workers, many imported from Caribbean territories, had died in the effort. In the early 1900s civil war erupted in Colombia. The war, known as the War of a Thousand Days, threatened American interests in Central America. In 1902, the United States intervened in the war and forced the combatants to sign a truce. When the Colombian senate rejected the truce, the U.S. administration began to support the Panamanian independence movement. In 1903, supported by the United States, Panama was declared independent of Colombia. A treaty between the new Panamanian government and the U.S. government granted rights to a zone roughly 10 miles wide and 50 miles long for the construction of a canal. American engineers and tens of thousands of workers completed the Panama Canal in 1914. The presence of the canal changed the lives of the Panamanians. A people that had previously survived as subsistence farmers now mostly gained their incomes from the canal. The canal quickly became one of the wonders of the world and radically changed world trade routes. Income from the canal sustained a modest prosperity for the Panamanians though immigration to the United States allowed many to seek work or more opportunities than were available in Panama. The United States administered the canal and the Canal Zone, including a sizable Panamanian population. During the 1950s, the Panamanian military began to challenge the traditional political class in the country. In the early 1960s a sustained pressure began for the renegotiation of the Panama Canal treaty. A military coup overthrew the civilian government of Panama in 1968, beginning a long period of instability. In 1977 the treaties governing the Panama Canal were changed to make way for joint Panamanian and American administration of the Canal Zone with a stipulation for the canal and the Canal Zone to be turned over to Panamanian control in 1999. In 1988 Panama's military ruler, General Manuel Antonio Noriega, was accused of trafficking in drugs. The U.S. administration invoked emergency powers and froze all Panamanian government assets in all U.S. banks and institutions. In 1989, the Panamanians overwhelmingly voted for the anti-Noriega candidates. The Noriega regime overturned the election and embarked on a new round of repression. In the United States, President George H. W. Bush decided to use force, declaring that a military operation was necessary to safeguard Americans in Panama, defend democracy and human rights, combat drug trafficking, and secure the safety and functions of the canal as required by the 1977 treaties. Operation Just Cause was launched with urban warfare in Panama City leaving between 400 and 4,000 civilians dead and 20,000 displaced by bombardments. The large Panamanian urban population, many living below the poverty level, was greatly affected by the invasion. A new democratic government launched social welfare programs aimed at improving the lives of the Panamanians. The Canal Zone came under complete Panamanian administration as agreed in 1999. Democratic government and economic incentives revived the postinvasion Panamanian economy. The Panamanians are now among the most prosperous in Central America with an economy that is one of the fastest growing in the world.

Further Reading

McCullough, David. *The Path between the Seas: The Creation of the Panama Canal, 1870.* New York: Simon & Schuster, 1978.

McDaniel, Felix. *Revolution: The Panamanian Quest for Independence and National Sovereignty.* Bloomington, IN: AuthorHouse, 2008.

Seales Soley, La Verne M. *Culture and Customs of Panama.* Westport, CT: Greenwood, 2008.

Paraguayans

The Paraguayans, sometimes known as Paraguayos, are a South American ethnic group, the inhabitants of the Republic of Paraguay, a landlocked country in the southern part of the continent. Outside Paraguay there are sizable Paraguayan communities in neighboring Argentina and Brazil and an estimated 15,000 concentrated in the New York City area of the United States. The estimated 7 million Paraguayans speak Spanish and Guarani, both of which are official languages. About 90 percent of the Paraguayans are Roman Catholic, with a growing number of evangelical Christians, and smaller numbers of mainstream Protestants, Jews, Mormons, Muslims, and Baha'is.

The largest group of indigenous origins, the Guaranis, lived in the region as horticulturists organized in chiefdoms based on an extensive network of kinship. Though the Guaranis traced descent through the male line, they had settlement patterns reflecting matrilineal descent. Alliances were often formalized through the exchange of women between the chiefdoms. In 1537 a Spanish expedition entered Guarani territory to establish the fort of Nuestra Señora de la Asunción. As few women accompanied the Spanish colonists to the New World an alliance between the Spanish and the Guarani chiefs in the region included the exchange of women for Spanish arms and other goods. The Paraguayans traditionally trace their origins to the children of the unions of the Spanish colonists and the Guarani women. Distant from the centers of colonial administration and lacking the gold or silver of other regions, the Paraguay colony remained isolated and impoverished. Colonial politics was often tumultuous, with intense rivalries between the large Spanish landowners and their economic rivals, the Jesuit missions established to convert the Guaranis to Christianity. Both utilized Guarani labor either as paid workers or as slaves. Left to defend themselves, the inhabitants of the region raised citizen militias to face the threat of hostile indigenous tribes, Brazilian slave raiders, and Portuguese attempts to annex parts of the colony. Until the late 1700s the impoverished Paraguayans used bartering as the normal means of exchange and the local economy was largely based on subsistence farming. The Jesuit missions in the eastern part of Paraguay flourished until the Jesuits were expelled from Spanish America in 1767.

The Paraguayan culture is a South American Hispanic culture heavily influenced by the indigenous Guarani culture. Approximately 95 percent of the Paraguayans are of mestizo ancestry, mostly of mixed Spanish and Guarani background. The population also includes a number of small indigenous groups, some 15,000 Mennonites, and about 8,000 Japanese with smaller numbers of Korean, Chinese, and Brazilian immigrants and their offspring. The most powerful cultural symbols are the Guarani language and the imagery derived from Paraguay's national history, particularly the wars. Guarani cultural influence and the Guarani language are powerful markers of Paraguayan national identity that unite Paraguayans of disparate social classes and political affiliations. The national territory and sovereignty and the many sacrifices the Paraguayans made

historically to defend that territory and the culture figure prominently in the national identification and tradition. The modern culture has adopted many elements of popular American culture while retaining its essence from the extensive intermarriage between the early Spanish colonists and Guarani women, a cultural fusion with two bases: one European, the other Southern Guarani. The Spanish language is the language of administration though more than 80 percent of Paraguayans speak both Guarani and Spanish. Jopara, a mixture of Spanish and Guarani, is also widely spoken. Paraguayan arts, music, and dance reflect the cultural fusion that symbolizes the country. Poverty remains a national problem with 30–50 percent of the Paraguayans living in poverty. In some rural areas over 40 percent of the people lack the means to cover basic necessities.

Unrest and resentment of Spanish authority resulted in the overthrow of the local Spanish administration in 1811. Attempts by the Argentines to incorporate Paraguay into their newly independent republic were repulsed but threats by the neighboring countries remained. A dictatorship was established under Jose Gaspar Rodriguez de Francia, who ruled from 1814 to 1840. Very little outside influence or contacts allowed the creation of a utopian society based on Rosseau's *Social Contract*. Francia's nephew was declared dictator in 1840. He quickly modernized the country and opened the economy to foreign commerce. The expansionist policies resulted in the Paraguayan War, also known as the War of the Triple Alliance, in 1864. The Paraguayans fought against the combined forces of Brazil, Argentina, and Uruguay in one of the bloodiest wars in South American history. Defeated in 1870, the prewar population of between 450,000 and 900,000 had dwindled to only 220,000, of which only 28,000 were adult males. The Paraguayans also suffered extensive territorial losses to Brazil and Argentina. An attempt to gain control of the fertile Gran Chaco region led to war with Bolivia in the 1930s. Political and economic instability continued to keep the majority of the Paraguayans living in near abject poverty. Between 1904 and 1954 the country had 31 presidents, most of who were removed from office by force. A new dictatorship under Alfredo Stroessner was established that ruled Paraguay from 1954 to 1989. Stroessner oversaw an era of economic expansion, but brutalized segments of the Paraguayan population. Torture and the killing of political opponents were routine, forcing many Paraguayans to leave the country, often to the United States. Following Stroessner's overthrow in 1989 his political party continued to dominate the country's politics until 2008. A former Catholic bishop, Fernando Lugo, in a historic vote defeated the conservative candidate, ending 61 years of conservative rule. In recent years the Paraguayans have experienced a modest prosperity as the government's efforts to reduce corruption, extend the prosperity of the capital region to the rest of the country, and promote economic equality have begun to change the lives of many Paraguayans.

Further Reading

Leuchars, Christopher. *To the Bitter End: Paraguay and the War of the Triple Alliance.* Westport, CT: Praeger, 2002.

O'Shaughnessy, Hugh. *The Priest of Paraguay: Fernando Lugo and the Making of a Nation.* London: Zed Books, 2009.

Thompson, George. *The War in Paraguay: With a Historical Sketch of the Country and Its People and Notes upon the Military Engineering of the War.* Whitefish, MT: Kessinger Publishing, 2010.

Peruvians

The Peruvians, sometimes known as Peruanos, are a South American people, the inhabitants of the Republic of Peru on the continent's west coast. The estimated 31 million Peruvians speak Spanish, the official language of Peru, along with several indigenous languages that are official languages where they predominate. The majority of the Peruvians are Roman Catholic, with a growing number belonging to the Mormon Church and smaller numbers of other Protestant denominations, Baha'is, and Muslims.

Evidence of human habitation in the region is dated at approximately 9000 BCE. The oldest known advanced society, the Norte Chico civilization, flourished in the coastal regions from about 3000 BCE to 1800 BCE. Other civilizations rose and fell in the region until the 15th century CE when the Incas emerged as a powerful state. Within the span of a century, the Incas expanded to form the largest empire in the pre-Columbian Americas. The Inca society was based on agriculture, using advanced techniques of irrigation and terracing. A vast network of roads connected all parts of the growing empire, including advanced engineering techniques, bridges, and tunnels. In 1525, the Inca

Huayna Capac died in an epidemic that may have been smallpox or measles, European diseases introduced by the Spanish to which the indigenous populations had no immunity. Because Huayna Capac had failed to designate a successor, two of his sons became co-rulers for a time, but tensions soon led to civil war that lasted for a number of years, severely weakening the empire just as the Spanish began to penetrate the empire. In 1532, Francisco Pizarro, at the head of an expedition looking for plunder and territory landed on the Peruvian coast. Aware of the civil war, Pizarro was able to use the chaos to gain control of the empire. For a number of years several leaders battled the Spanish invaders until their last leader was executed in 1572. The Spanish ruled Peru as a viceroyalty for nearly 300 years after the conquest, often treating it as a huge reserve of gold and silver to be plundered to fill the crown's coffers. The Spanish felt that as a superior culture their culture and particularly their religion must be adopted by the conquered peoples. An influx of Spaniards seeking to gain from the riches of the Peruvian region resulted in a stratified society. The European-born Spanish were at the top, the Peruvian-born Spanish or Creoles were next, and the urban working class, African slaves, and the indigenous peoples were at the bottom. Lima, the capital of the viceroyalty, became one of the most important centers of Spanish authority in the Americas. Practices such as debt peonage, where indigenous peoples were trapped in an unending cycle of indebtedness were widespread. In 1780 a descendant of the last Inca, known as Tupac Amaru, led a widespread rebellion against Spanish corruption and abuses that failed to reestablish indigenous independence.

Peruvian culture is a South American Hispanic culture that blends Spanish traditions and customs with elements of the pre-Columbian indigenous cultures. Peruvians maintain a strong sense of national identity that is supported by cultural elements such as their Spanish language, Roman Catholic religion, distinctive foods, and their art forms, including music and dance. Until the 1960s when roads and railways began to unite the country, various regional cultures existed. A massive internal migration to the urban areas resulted in the homogenization of the Peruvian culture. As the culture is rooted in indigenous and Spanish traditions these two influences remain the major parts of the culture though later influences from various Asian, African, and European cultures added new elements. Peruvian artistic traditions date back to the elaborate textiles, pottery, jewelry, and sculptures of the Inca and pre-Inca civilizations. During the colonial period most art focused on religious subjects, a tradition that remains to the present. Peruvian literature, music, dance, and cuisine all display the fusion of the Spanish and indigenous traditions. Peruvian culture is most firmly represented among the elite of European descent and the large mestizo communities. The indigenous peoples, blacks, and Asians tend to adapt Peruvian culture to their own traditions. The indigenous peoples, after five centuries of discrimination and genocidal practices, are still portrayed as backward and inferior and fit only for manual labor. Spanish and Quechua, the language of the Incas, are the two most widely spoken languages with Spanish dominating in the urban areas. The Peruvian constitution recognizes the Roman Catholic Church's role as "an important element in the historical, cultural, and moral development of the nation." Catholic clergy and laypersons are paid state salaries in addition to the stipends paid them by the Church. An agreement signed with the Vatican in 1980 grants the Church special status in Peru, giving it preferential treatment in education, tax benefits, immigration of religious workers, and in other areas. Though Peru claims to respect religious freedom, laws mandate that all schools, both public and private, include Roman Catholic religious education as part of the curriculum. Despite its overarching influence in Peru, in recent decades many Peruvians have abandoned the Church in favor of Mormonism or other denominations.

In the early 1800s, while most of the Spanish colonies in the Americas were swept by wars of independence, Peru remained a royalist stronghold. While the elite of Lima hesitated and remained loyal to Spain, Peruvian independence was achieved by the occupation of the territory by the forces of José de San Martin and Simón Bolivar. Peru was declared independent in 1821, though the royalist forces were not finally defeated until 1824. The early years of the republic were marked by the return to Spain of many of the educated elite and endemic struggles for power among military leaders and various political factions. Peruvian national identity was forged during the 1840s and 1860s as projects such as a Latin American confederation floundered and a political union with Bolivia was quickly abandoned. In the 1870s, following a period of stability,

political infighting increased once again. Tensions with neighboring republics led to war with Chile during 1879–1883, resulting in the loss of the southern provinces of Arica and Tarapacá. The humiliating defeat led many Peruvians to call for improvement in the lives of the indigenous Peruvians so that they may contribute more fully to society. In the late 19th and early 20th centuries efforts were made to modernize the economy and society. Immigrants from Asia began to settle in the country, adding a new element to the culture. During the hardships of the Great Depression popular political movements embraced radical ideals borrowed from Marxist ideology or Italian fascism. A military government ruled the country from 1968 to 1975 with many innovations, including the breaking up of the large holdings of the landed aristocracy and the distribution of the land to cooperatives and individual families. Political and economic instability continued to send a steady stream of emigrants to the United States and other countries. Economic problems were compounded by the social disruption of leftist terrorist groups and the excesses of the Peruvian military in the 1980s and 1990s. The Sendero Luminoso, the Shining Path, utilized assassinations and the violent intimidation of the rural peasants to control larger districts of the interior. In less than 20 years an estimated 30,000 Peruvians were killed. Another group, the Tupac Amarú, carried out equally violent attacks in Peru's large urban areas. Under the presidency of Alberto Fujimori, elected in 1990, Peru began to recover, but accusations of corruption, authoritarianism, and human rights violations forced his resignation in 2000. Since the end of the Fujimori era, the Peruvian government has attempted to fight corruption while sustaining economic growth. Even though the country has recovered from the violence and instability of the last decades of the 20th century many Peruvians "vote with their feet" and leave the country, primarily for the United States, which counts a Peruvian community of immigrants and their offspring of up to 1 million.

Further Reading

Ferreira, Cesar and Eduardo Dargent-Chamot. *Culture and Customs of Peru.* Westport, CT: Greenwood, 2002.

Polla, Mario. *Peru: An Ancient Andean Civilization.* Vercelli, Italy: White Star Publishers, 2010.

Starn, Orin, Ivan Degregori, and Robin Kirk. *The Peru Reader: History, Culture, Politics.* Durham, NC: Duke University Press, 2005.

Piaroas

The Piaroas, sometimes known as De'aruas, Wothuhas, Guaguas, Kuakuas, Quaquas, Adoles, Atures, or Wo'tihehs, are a South American ethnic group concentrated in the rain forests of Venezuela and Colombia in the upper Orinoco River region. The estimated 20,000 Piaroas, including the closely related Wirõs, speak dialects of the Piaroa language, which belongs to the Saliban language family. The Piaroas are mostly Christian, around 80 percent of them, though their Christian customs are blended with their earlier pre-Christian rituals and ceremonies.

The Piaroas settled in the rain forests of the upper Orinoco River region in prehistoric times. They were considered as among the most peaceful of societies by their neighboring tribes. The Piaroas often avoided contact with outsiders. The Europeans settled the coast around the mouth of the Orinoco in the early 16th century. European expeditions sailed up the Orinoco in the 1530s, claiming the vast territory for Spain, but the rain forests and their peoples remained hidden from the colonizers. Though unknown to the Spanish colonizers along the coast, the small tribes of the rain forests were not immune to the European diseases introduced to the continent by the Spanish settlers. Smallpox and measles swept from tribe to tribe, often decimating whole bands. In the mid-18th century the Spanish pushed inland along the Orinoco River. Though they never encountered the Piaroas, the neighboring Makiritares organized resistance against the European invaders in 1775 and 1776.

Piaroa culture is an Amazonian culture well adapted to life in the rain forests. The mode of transportation is a canoe known as a *bongo* that is used to navigate the tributaries of the Orinoco. The Piaroas are considered one of the most peaceful societies in the world. Seeing competition as an evil and always stressing cooperation, the Piaroas are both strongly egalitarian and very supportive of individuals. Piaroa culture is strongly antiauthoritarian and is opposed to the hoarding of resources. Murder as a concept is both unknown and nonexistent. Though the local chiefs are traditionally male, domination by the males of the tribe is not part of the culture. The basis of their peaceful society lies in their religious beliefs. They believe that the ancient gods were greedy, violent, and arrogant. The village shamans control that violence by chanting and blowing words into a mixture of water and honey, which the people of the villages consume the next morning ensuring their safety for another day. Traditionally the Piaroas mummified their dead and kept the mummies and their belongings in caves, but as most Piaroas are now Christians, underground burial has mostly ended this practice. Sickness and death are considered punishments for disobeying the values of Piaroa society. The Piaroas consider tarantulas and other large jungle spiders as food delicacies, a practice the missionaries have tried and failed to curtail.

The end of the Spanish control of South America in the early 19th century did little to change the lives of the Piaroas, whose territory was first explored by a Venezuelan expedition in 1897. The demarcation of the international border between Venezuela and Colombia divided the Piaroa territory leaving a small community on the western bank of the Orinoco in Colombian territory. In the 1950s Roman Catholic missionaries established small missions in the Piaroa territory. Teaching a peaceful version of the Catholic religion they won the first Piaroa converts in the 1950s. Later Protestant missionaries entered the area, leading to much confusion among the Piaroas. By the mid-1960s an estimated 80 percent of the Piaroas were considered at least nominally Christian though traditional beliefs, shamanism, and cultural patterns changed very little. In the 1990s some Piaroas settled in the towns that have grown up along the river. Their traditional crafts, religious beliefs, and customs are gradually disappearing as their culture is influenced by the modern Hispanic culture of Venezuela and Colombia. In 2011 Piaroa leaders expressed their frustration with the Venezuelan government following repeated requests for the demarcation of their lands as reserved lands as oil prospectors and other outsiders invade their territory.

Further Reading

Gordon, Nick. *Tarantulas, Marmosets and Other Stories: An Amazon Diary.* London: John Blake Publishing, 1997.

Guss, David M. *To Weave and Sing: Art, Symbol, and Narrative in the South American Rainforest.* Berkeley, CA: University of California Press, 1990.

Kaplan, Joanna Overing. *The Piaroa: People of the Orinoco Basin.* Oxford, UK: Clarendon Press, 1975.

Pierrois

The Pierrois, sometimes known as Saint Pierreans or Pierrotins, are a North American people, the inhabitants of the small French islands of Saint Pierre and Miquelon just off the coast of Newfoundland in southeastern Canada. The estimated 8,000 Pierrois include some 5,800 living in the islands with the remainder living in mainland France or Canada. The language of the Pierrois is French, the official language of the islands, though English is also widely spoken. The majority, estimated at 98 percent, are Roman Catholics, with small Protestant and other religious groups.

The islands were known to the Mi'kmaq people living along the coast of present-day Newfoundland and were accessible by canoe. Though they used the islands to hunt and fish the Mi'kmaq did not establish permanent settlements. Later, beginning in the 15th century, Basque and Breton fishermen began to utilize the islands as bases for fishing in the Grand Banks. In 1520, a Portuguese expedition sighted the islands and officially noted their location. Saint Pierre and Miquelon were claimed for France by Jacques Cartier in 1536. The population of the islands grew slowly. Only four permanent settlers were counted in 1670 and just 22 in 1691. By the early 1700s the few settlers had left the islands for the colony of New France on the mainland, leaving the islands once again uninhabited. France ceded the islands to the English in 1713, at the end of one of Europe's many wars. In 1763, following defeat in the Seven Years' War, France ceded all its North American territories, retaining only Saint Pierre and Miquelon, as well as fishing rights on the coasts of Newfoundland. As the last French territory in North America, the islands witnessed a significant rise in importance and population in the 18th century. French support for the rebellious American colonies led to a British occupation and the deportation of all the French colonists in the islands in 1778. During the French Revolutionary Wars, in the late 1700s, the British again landed and expelled all the French population and promoted the settlement of British colonists. French troops sacked the British settlement in 1796 but under the terms of the Treaty of Amiens, the islands were returned to French rule though they were again occupied by British forces when hostilities recommenced later the same year.

The Pierrois culture is a French culture combining the culture brought to the islands from metropolitan France with traditions and customs borrowed from the mainland culture of Canada, particularly the French culture of Quebec. National resources are limited to fish and deep water ports but new industries are being promoted, including tourism, fish farming, crab fishing, and some forms of agriculture. Many of the traditional elements of the Pierrois culture evolved from the Basques, Bretons, and Normans who settled the islands in the 19th century. The influence of these three cultures is evident in many of the traditions and customs of the islands and their traditional flags form part of the unofficial flag of Saint Pierre and Miquelon. Centuries of cod fishing remains a strong influence and the local cuisine, based on French food, relies heavily on fresh or salted cod. Fish and seafood chowders are very popular. *Tiaude*, a highly seasoned stew of cod fish, vegetables, and other local ingredients is considered the islands' most typical dish. Sports play an important part in the culture, particularly ice hockey and association football. The language of the Pierrois is French, spoken in an island version that is closer to metropolitan French than it is to the Acadian or Québécois French spoken in Canada. Roman Catholicism remains the religion of the majority of the islanders though in recent years Protestant sects have won some converts.

Finally returned to France by the victorious British in 1814, government-sponsored colonization brought an influx of Basques, Bretons, and Normans from the French regions on the Atlantic. Only in the 1850s did increased fishing bring a modest prosperity to the small colony. During World War I the young men of the colony were conscripted leaving the fishing industry without its most productive workers. Already crippled by the decline of the fisheries, the adoption of steam trawlers in the 1920s and 1930s also contributed to the reduction of employment. Smuggling, always an important economic activity, became especially prominent following the prohibition of alcohol in the United States in the 1920s. The end of prohibition in 1933 ended a decade of prosperity and began a severe economic depression. During World War II the islands were ruled by the Fascist Vichy government following the fall of France to the invading Germans in 1941. A military expedition of Free French forces took control of Saint Pierre and Miquelon on Christmas Day 1941. The islanders quickly voted to support the takeover as most young Pierrois were fighting with the Free French forces. After the war attempts were made to diversify the economy as fishing declined. In 1958 the French government gave the Pierrois the options of being fully integrated with France, becoming a self-governing state of the French Community, or preserving their status as a French territory. The islanders voted to retain their territorial status with increased measures of self-government. The two islands became an overseas collectivity in 2003 with a special autonomous statute. In the 21st century the Pierrois enjoy all the benefits of French citizenship and are represented in the National Assembly in Paris.

Further Reading

Cohn, Ronald and Jesse Russell. *Saint Pierre and Miquelon.* Paris: VSD, 2012.

Rannie, William F. *Saint Pierre and Miquelon.* Beamsville, Ontario: Rannie Publications, 1977.

USA International Business Publications. *Saint Pierre and Miquelon: Country Study Guide.* Washington, DC: International Business Publications, 2000.

Pipils

The Pipils, sometimes known as Pipiles, Nawats, Nahuats, or Southern Nahuans, are a Central American ethnic group concentrated in western El Salvador and adjacent parts of Honduras. The estimated 220,000 Pipils mostly speak Spanish with only a few elders still able to speak the Pipil language. The majority of the Pipils are Roman Catholics, with a growing number converting to Mormonism or evangelical Protestant sects.

During the waves of Nahua migrations from the arid northern parts of present-day Mexico that eventually settled most of central Mexico, some migrant groups continued further south into Central America. The Pipils, a subgroup of the Nahua peoples, are believed to have settled in western El Salvador as early as 3000 BCE. Another group of Nahua migrants arrived in the 10th century CE. Known as the Izalco Pipils, they occupied the lands west of the Lempa River. At first they lived in settled autonomous communities, but by the 11th century the Pipils had united in a flourishing civilization in the region they called Cuscatlán, the "Land of the Jewel." The Pipils developed vast irrigated agricultural lands and supported a large urban population living in towns and cities. Known as fierce warriors, the Pipils staunchly defended Cuscatlán and their culture. The Pipil civilization, though it retained the

Nahua culture and language, was influenced by the advanced Mayan civilization in the region. The religious cults of the early Pipils more closely resembled those that developed among the related Aztecs of central Mexico, though human sacrifice was abandoned early in Pipil history. Spanish conquistadors began venturing south from Mexico, then known as the colony of New Spain, in the early 16th century. After subduing the Mayan city-states, the Spanish moved west to the lower Atlantic region of the Pipils, then under the authority of the powerful city-state of Cuscatlán. Accompanied by thousands of Mayan allies, the Spanish invaded the region in 1524. Though the Pipil warriors were defeated in two major battles by superior Spanish weapons, the invaders were unable to overcome the resistance of the surviving Pipil warriors who retreated into the mountains. A sustained guerrilla war forced the Spanish to retreat but renewed invasions in 1525 and 1528 finally overcame the remaining Pipil resistance. The defeated Pipils were no longer referred to as Pipils but simply as *indios* or Indians. The name Pipil has remained associated, in local Salvadorean history, with the preconquest indigenous culture but not the *indios* of the country. Many of the Mayans of Central America were able to live in relative isolation through much of the colonial period, but for the Pipils the terrain of El Salvador offered little protection. As a result, the Pipils were assimilated into the colonial economy. Realizing that the region they called El Salvador (the savior) had little in terms of gold or silver, the Spanish set about developing the land. The European confiscation of the land that sustained the Pipils, combined with European diseases that swept the region, resulted in the rapid decline of the Pipils.

The Pipil culture had a strong influence on modern Salvadorean culture, as a large portion of the country's population is descended from the Pipils or other indigenous peoples. Pipil culture has a rich heritage of folk beliefs and customs that evolved in the villages, fields, forests, and mountains of the Pipil homeland. The introduction of cash crops such as coffee required large landholdings that further displaced the Pipils. This has left a legacy of the landed and the landless and an economy in which Pipil laborers can be hired and fired without consideration of working conditions or a livable salary. The Pipil language, usually known as Nawat, was spoken by only some 20 speakers in the 1980s. Language programs and a new interest among younger people raised the number to 200 in the 1990s and up to some 3,000 speakers in 2010. The revival of the language has given the Pipils hope that their language and culture can be pulled back from the brink of extinction. The renewed interest in the culture has aided the preservation of traditional beliefs and cultural practices and brought about a greater openness among Pipil communities to perform their music, dances, and ceremonies in public and to wear traditional clothing, once prohibited by the Salvadorean government.

The system of *repartimiento* allowed Spanish landowners nearly unlimited power over the Pipil populations on their lands. The colony's isolation, the ease of paying corrupt royal officials, and the prevailing disregard among the landed elite for the plight of the Pipils and other indigenous peoples prevented any substantial improvement in the Pipil living conditions well into the 20th century. Cash crops such as cacao and indigo were replaced by coffee in the early 20th century. Pipil workers usually lived on the coffee plantations, held in debt bondage or other forms of forced labor. The Napoleonic Wars in Europe weakened the Spanish hold on the Americas resulting in the independence of El Salvador in 1821. Like the Spanish authorities, the Salvadoreans emphasized a one-crop economy geared for export rather than for subsistence. The boom or bust cycles of coffee mostly impacted the poor, landless indigenous workers, who could be fired easily whenever the landowners wished to do so. Most of El Salvador's land was controlled by an oligarchy known as the "Fourteen Families." The unstable social order often led to violence. The country became known for repeated rebellions, each one followed by massive and bloody retaliation against the landless poor. In 1833 an indigenous leader, Anastasio Aquino, led an unsuccessful peasant revolt. Successive governments, dominated by the landed oligarchy, either ignored the Pipils or allowed massive abuses and mistreatment. The government abolished titles to all indigenous communal lands in 1881, leaving most Pipils as landless peasants and manual laborers. In 1912, the National Guard was created as a rural police force to maintain strict control of the Salvadorean peasants and the indigenous peoples. A military coup in 1931 installed a new government that brutally suppressed growing rural resistance. An uprising of peasants, including many Pipils, was put down in 1932 and then the army rampaged through the indigenous villages targeting those who wore traditional dress or spoke indigenous languages. An estimated 30,000 to 35,000 people were killed, including thousands of Pipils, often with whole villages wiped out. The government then eliminated all references to indigenous people, claiming that they had disappeared through assimilation. Over the next decades the Salvadorean military dominated politics just as the small land-owning elite dominated the economy while the Pipils and the other indigenous peoples and the landless peasants lived in abject poverty as agricultural workers. In the 1960s opposition to the centuries of oppression resulted in the formation of dissident organizations working to better the lives of the poor. As the opposition to the government grew stronger, so did the official government repression. Death squads assassinated opposition leaders and other "subversives" including most of the Pipil leadership. Instability and leftist ideals began to undermine the military and the landed elite's hold on the country in the late 1970s, finally leading to a bloody civil war from 1980 to 1992. Guerrilla groups, including Pipils, fought against the Salvadorean military that was trained and equipped by the United States. An estimated 75,000 people died in the conflict, most of them civilians or victims of government death squads. The Pipils began to recover as younger leaders and activists demanded redress for past crimes against their people. In the post–civil war era the Pipils experienced a resurgence of Pipil identity. New interest, particularly among young Pipils, in the language and culture marked an end to the humiliation and shame they had been taught to feel for their traditions and history. Language classes raised the numbers of people able to speak Pipil, saving the language from total extinction. Renewed interest in the preservation of traditional beliefs and cultural manifestations spread across the Pipil areas of western El Salvador. In Honduras, where a small Pipil population had nearly lost its culture and language through assimilation, new ties to the larger Pipil centers in El Salvador have aided the reculturation of the Honduran Pipils.

Further Reading

Fowler, William R. *The Cultural Evolution of Ancient Nahua Civilizations: The Pipil-Nicarao of Central America.* Norman, OK: Oklahoma University Press, 1989.

Tilley, Virginia O. *Seeing Indians: A Study of Race, Nation, and Power in El Salvador.* Albuquerque, NM: University of New Mexico, 2005.

White, Christopher M. *The History of El Salvador.* Westport, CT: Greenwood, 2008.

Potawatomis

The Potawatomis, sometimes known as Neshnabés, Potewatmis, Pottawatomies, or Pottawatomis, are a North American ethnic group living in scattered bands in Michigan, Wisconsin, Kansas, and Oklahoma in the United States and Ontario in Canada. The estimated 33,000 Potawatomis usually speak English as their first language as their traditional language, belonging to the Ojibwe-Potawatomi branch of the Algonquian languages, is nearly extinct. Most Potawatomis are Christians, with the largest denominations being the Roman Catholics and the Methodists.

According to Potawatomi traditions, some 500 years ago they, along with the related Ojibwes and Odawas, lived as one people near the mouth of the St. Lawrence River. Around 1660 they migrated westward, guided by visions, until they reached the Straits of Mackinac, the channel that connects Lake Huron with Lake Michigan. The tribe split into three divisions. The Potawatomis moved south to settle in the region between Lake Michigan and Lake Huron. The Odawas settled north of Lake Huron, and the Ojibwes settled along the eastern shore of Lake Superior. The three tribes maintained close linguistic and cultural ties in a historic alliance known as the Council of Three Fires. The French were the first Europeans to explore the region, making contact with the Potawatomis in southwestern Michigan. In the mid-17th century the Beaver Wars disrupted the entire Great Lakes region. Armed by the English and Dutch, the Iroquois sought to extend their control of the lucrative fur trade. The Potawatomis fled Iroquois attacks to settle in the area around present-day Green Bay, Wisconsin. In the mid-1700s the Potawatomis, as allies of the French, fought the British in the French and Indian wars. In 1769, they formed an alliance of several tribes to defeat the Illinois tribe that blocked expansion to the west. During the American Revolution, the Potawatomis fought as British allies against the American rebels. The Potawatomis then fought in a series of unsuccessful wars to stop the American settlers from overrunning their lands. The first of the conflicts, known as Little Turtle's War of 1790–1794, began a long period of conflicts between the Potawatomis and the new United States.

Potawatomis at Rush Lake Mission near Watervliet, Michigan, in 1906. (T. R. Hamilton/Buyenlarge/ Getty Images)

The traditional culture of the Potawatomis stressed generosity, honesty, endurance, strength of character, and wisdom through religious traditions, and by example within the tribe. The modern culture still stresses these traditional values while living within the larger modern American culture. The traditions that formed during the time of seminomadic wanderings were heavily influenced by the natural terrain of their forest homelands. In the 20th century the culture was transformed through contact with non–Native Americans. By the 1940s, only the elderly were bilingual as education in English replaced the traditional language. The rate of acculturation varied from band to band but all Potawatomis now live in a culture that blends their traditions with the modern popular culture of North America. Potawatomi culture is currently experiencing a renaissance as tribal members and non-natives are studying traditional botany, crafts, myths, and religious beliefs. Many Potawatomis are concerned about the degradation of the environment by industry and mismanagement. Traditional occupations such as wild rice harvesting, fishing, and maple syrup collection have all suffered from pollution, housing construction, boat traffic, and the incursion of alien species. The Potawatomi language, a Central Algonquian language, is now spoken by fewer than 1,300 mostly elderly people. In recent years an effort has been made to revitalize and extend the usage of the language. Because of early French missionary influence the largest denomination among the Potawatomis is Roman Catholicism. In the 19th century Protestant missionaries, mostly Methodists, gained followers among the Potawatomi bands.

The Potawatomis formed an important part of Tecumseh's confederacy of tribes that waged war against the new United States from 1811 and later as a British ally in the War of 1812. The conflict continued as the Peoria War, fought mostly in Illinois Territory, then encompassing parts of Minnesota, Michigan, Wisconsin, and Illinois. In August 1812, a large tribal force, mostly Potawatomis, attacked a group of American soldiers and civilians at Fort Dearborn, on the site of present-day Chicago. A Potawatomi chief, Mucktypoke, opposed the attack and later saved some of the civilian captives. In the 1820s a series of treaties with the United States created reservations covering small parts of traditional Potawatomi land. In exchange the Potawatomis ceded most of their lands in Wisconsin and Michigan. The reservations were reduced as land-hungry settlers moved west into the region. The Treaty of Chicago, signed in 1833, led to forcible removal of the Potawatomis to areas west of the Mississippi River. The forced removal, known as the Potawatomi Trail of Death, was a harrowing journey on foot for hundreds of miles. Exhaustion, hunger, and typhoid killed many of the children and elderly before they finally arrived in areas set aside in the west. Many Potawatomis found ways to remain, particularly those in Michigan, while others fled to Odawa settlements or crossed into Canada to avoid removal. Most Potawatomis lived in poverty on small plots of land. Younger people often left the limited opportunities of the reservations for the large urban areas, where a sizable urban Potawatomi

population now resides. Since the end of World War II the spread of education and ethnic activism have allowed a revitalization of the culture and language. Though many still live in poor areas, the majority have achieved a modest prosperity through sound business investments, including gambling casinos on reservation lands. With more tribal funds efforts are being put into reviving the language, traditional arts, and crafts.

Further Reading

Clifton, James A. *The Prairie People: Continuity and Change in Potawatomi Indian Culture, 1665–1965.* Iowa City, IA: University of Iowa Press, 1998.

Edmunds, R. David. *The Potawatomis: Keepers of the Fire.* Norman, OK: University of Oklahoma Press, 1987.

Gibson, Karen Bush. *The Potawatomi.* Mankato, MN: Bridgestone Books, 2002.

Potiguáras

The Potiguáras, sometimes known as Potyguaras, Pitiguaras, Potivaras, Potiguars, Cannibals, or Cannibaliers, are a South American ethnic group concentrated in the Brazilian state of Paraíba. The estimated 15,000 Potiguáras speak Brazilian Portuguese as their first language. There are no known speakers of their traditional language, a member of the Tupi-Guarani language family. The majority of the Potiguáras are Roman Catholic, but Baptist and other Protestant denominations have gained followers in recent decades.

The Potiguáras, possibly numbering more than 90,000 people, inhabited the coastal regions of present-day Brazil north of the Goiana River. Known as fierce warriors, they controlled the fishing ground and the inland area along the region's rivers for hundreds of years. The Portuguese began to encroach on Potiguára territory in the mid-1500s when settlers from Pernambuco founded Filipéia de Nossa das Nieves, later renamed João Pessoa, at the mouth of the Paraíba do Norte River in Potiguára territory. Finding the region perfect for the production of the lucrative sugarcane, other Europeans, particularly the French and the Dutch, contested Portuguese control of the Paraíba region. The Potiguáras fought the Portuguese invaders and allied themselves with the French in the late 16th century. When the French left the region they became Dutch allies in hopes of expelling the Portuguese invaders. Between 1603 and 1654, supplied with arms by the Dutch, the Potiguáras fought a long and devastating war with the Portuguese. European diseases and the violent confrontations decimated the Potiguára population. Jesuit missionaries entered the territory in the late 16th century winning many converts among the Potiguáras. By the middle of the 17th century the Potiguáras had given up their fight and formed an alliance with the Portuguese against other Europeans and indigenous tribes. As a reward for their allies, the Portuguese granted the surviving Potiguáras substantial land grants. In the 1700s the Potiguáras began to assimilate into the growing mestizo population and Portuguese colonial culture. They adopted the Portuguese language, the Roman Catholic faith, and the colonial cash economy.

Traditional Potiguára culture was an egalitarian society that gave women substantial decision-making powers within their communities. The imposition of the colonial culture required male domination as traditional social structures and family roles were changed. The modern Potiguára culture is a part of the mestizo Brazilian culture that combines European and indigenous influences with customs brought to the region by African slaves. Though acculturated into the regional society the Potiguáras remain aware of their indigenous heritage and maintain many customs and traditions. The Potiguára language is now considered extinct as the Portuguese replaced it during the colonial era. The Potiguáras mostly live in villages scattered along the coast of the state of Paraíba, especially around Traição Bay. The Roman Catholic faith, adopted as part of the colonial culture, remained the largest denomination among the Potiguáras until the 1960s when evangelical Protestant groups began to win converts. The Christian ceremonies are often blended with pre-Christian rituals and the belief in the local shamans and curers remains strong among the Potiguáras.

In 1808, the Portuguese royal family and the majority of the Portuguese nobility, fleeing the French invasion of Portugal, established themselves in Rio de Janeiro; when the king returned to Europe in 1821 the Portuguese colonists refused to return to colonial status. Brazil became independent in 1822, but fighting in the northeast spilled into Potiguára territory before the last Portuguese soldiers surrendered in 1824. Mostly ignored as part of the majority peasant population for most of the 19th century, the Potiguáras mostly lived as subsistence farmers and fishermen. In the 20th century new laws were passed that treated the indigenous peoples of Brazil in a patronizing, often corrupt fashion. Official programs handed out food and medicine instead of encouraging traditional occupations. Modern problems such as alcoholism, family violence, and later drugs, invaded the territory of the Potiguáras. For decades they were legally considered wards of the state, unable to make decisions for themselves. A new Brazilian constitution, adopted in 1988, did away with that tutelage, guaranteed indigenous rights, and required demarcation of all indigenous territories. Few of the provisions of the new laws have been implemented. Of the traditional Potiguára territory of 57,600 hectares, just 21,600 hectares were demarcated, leaving 36,000 hectares in a legal limbo. In 1996, a further 7,300 hectares were demarcated as land traditionally occupied by the Potiguáras. Since that time nothing more has been done while a large refinery and its sugarcane plantations have been established in the disputed territory bringing the Potiguáras into conflict with the refinery company. The Potiguáras traveled to the Brazilian capital, Brasilia, to plead their case and to ask for protection following attacks by refinery employees and threats by the management. The problem continues to overshadow Potiguára life in the early 21st century as government responses remain extremely slow or nonexistent. Demands for the demarcation of all their traditional territory are voiced annually but with little reaction from public officials.

Further Reading

French, Jan Hoffman. *Legalizing Identities: Becoming Black or Indian in Brazil's Northeast*. Chapel Hill, NC: University of North Carolina Press, 2009.

Jones, Shirley, ed. *Simply Living: The Spirit of the Indigenous People*. Novato, CA: New World Library, 1999.

Rogers, Thomas D. *The Deepest Wounds: A Labor and Environmental History of Sugar in Northeast Brazil*. Chapel Hill, NC: University of North Carolina Press, 2010.

Puerto Ricans

The Puerto Ricans, sometimes known as Puertoricans, Puertorriqueños, or simply Ricans, are the people or descendants of the inhabitants of the Caribbean island of Puerto Rico. Located in the northeastern Caribbean Sea, Puerto Rico comprises an archipelago that includes the island of Puerto Rico and a number of smaller islands. The estimated 8.8 million Puerto Ricans include an estimated 3.7 million living in Puerto Rico and a larger diaspora, numbering over 5 million, living in the continental United States. Puerto Ricans are U.S. citizens and the majority of them are bilingual, speaking both Spanish and English, though there are a number of Puerto Ricans who speak only Spanish. The Puerto Ricans are predominately Roman Catholic with a sizable and growing Protestant minority.

Puerto Rico is believed to have been settled as early as 2000 BCE though there is little in the way of archeological or written history. The Igneris, a tribe from the Orinoco River in northern South America, settled the islands between 120 CE and 400 CE. The Igneris and the earlier inhabitants, known as Arcaicos or Archaics, may have shared the islands between the 4th and 10th centuries. Sometime between the 7th and 11th centuries the Taino culture developed, becoming the dominant culture by approximately 1000 CE. When Christopher Columbus arrived in 1493, there were an estimated 30,000–60,000 Tainos. The first Spanish settlement was established in 1508, beginning the colonization of the island. The Tainos were taken as slaves, massacred, or decimated by European diseases. By 1520 the Tainos' presence had nearly vanished from the islands. Columbus named the largest island in the group after Saint John the Baptist, San Juan Bautista, though later settlers and traders referred to the island as Puerto Rico, with the name San Juan used for its largest settlement. The elimination of the Tainos required a new source of labor so African slaves were imported. Puerto Rico became an important colony, a strategic Spanish stronghold, and a key port for the region known as the Spanish Main. During the 17th and 18th centuries Spanish attention shifted to the treasures of the conquered civilizations of the mainland regions. Puerto Rico declined and was left virtually unexplored, undeveloped, and except for the port towns, largely unsettled until the 19th century.

Puerto Rican culture is a unique Caribbean culture that blends Spanish European influences with African and Taino customs and traditions and more recent influences from modern North American culture. About 75 percent of Puerto Ricans are of European ancestry, 13 percent are of African or Afro-Caribbean ancestry, and the remainder are of mixed race, Asian, or of other backgrounds. Some 99 percent of the Puerto Ricans consider themselves Hispanic or Latino. The Spanish cultural heritage includes the Spanish language, the Roman Catholic religion, and the majority of the cultural values and traditions. Music is a key element in the culture and much of Puerto Rican culture centers on the influence of music. Like Puerto Rico itself, Puerto Rican music evolved by mixing the music of other countries with local and traditional rhythms. Early Puerto Rican music showed strong Spanish and African traditions, but

Marcos Xiorro

Marcos Xiorro was a bozal, a slave recently brought to Puerto Rico from Africa. He was purchased by the owner of a sugar plantation near San Juan. In 1821, believing a story that slavery had been abolished in the Spanish possessions, the slaves on the sugar plantations waited impatiently for freedom. When they learned that slavery was not to be abolished, Marcos Xiorro planned and organized a rebellion against the slaveholders and the colonial government of Puerto Rico. Betrayed by a slave loyal for his freedom and 500 pesos, Xiorro's uprising was suppressed and its leaders captured. Marcos Xiorro was quickly executed, but he gained legendary status among the slave population and later entered Puerto Rican folklore as a hero fighting for freedom. Slavery in Puerto Rico was not abolished until 1873.

modern island music displays the cultural movements across the Caribbean and North America. Though the cultural mixture of Spanish and Afro-Caribbean is shared with other Caribbean and Latin American cultures, Puerto Rican culture has absorbed educational, political, and economic systems imported from mainland North America. Puerto Rican identity remains strong; they rarely refer to themselves as Americans though they are legally American citizens. The Puerto Ricans' attachment to their island homeland has endured despite large-scale emigration to the mainland since 1917, the year they were granted American citizenship. The Spanish language, spoken in Puerto Rico in a Caribbean dialect, remains the primary language with English spoken mostly as a second language. The teaching of English in the islands' primary and secondary public schools has been a subject of heated debate in Puerto Rico. Many view English as an encroachment upon Puerto Rican cultural autonomy. Like the Spanish language, the Roman Catholic religion remains an important part of the culture even though increasingly Puerto Ricans are abandoning Catholicism for evangelical Protestant sects, Mormonism, or other imported religions.

In the early 1800s as Napoleon's forces overran Spain, independence movements quickly developed in Spain's American colonies. In 1809, in an effort to secure the loyalty of the Puerto Ricans, the Spanish government recognized the colony as an overseas province with representation in the recently convened Spanish parliament. The parliamentary and constitutional reforms that granted Puerto Rico greater rights were in force from 1810 to 1814 and

again from 1820 to 1823, but were twice reversed when the Spanish monarchy was restored and Puerto Rico reverted to the status of a colony. The growing number of African slaves led to several minor slave revolts; however, the revolt organized by Marcos Xiorro in 1821 was the most terrifying for the Spanish colonists. The Puerto Rican independence movement of the early 1800s was suppressed and its members imprisoned or exiled. The loss of most of the colonies in the Americas resulted in increased immigration to Puerto Rico from Spain and trade reforms that favored the island's European population and economy. The Spanish culture of the island was reaffirmed by the large numbers of European immigrants who continued to migrate to the colony throughout the 19th century. A royal decree of 1815 allowed non-Spanish Europeans to settle in the colony with free land offered as an incentive. Hundreds of Roman Catholic European families immigrated to Puerto Rico, including Corsican, French, German, Irish, Italian, and Scots people. In the 1860s the United States offered to purchase Puerto Rico and Cuba from Spain but the offer of 160 million dollars was rejected. An independence uprising in 1868 was subdued but the exiled leaders in the United States formed the Puerto Rican Revolutionary Committee. The Committee supported another independence uprising in 1897, when the Puerto Rican flag was used for the first time. The Spanish government granted autonomy in 1898 and granted overseas province status. In July 1898, during the Spanish-American War, Puerto Rico was invaded by American troops and was later ceded to the United States, along with the

Philippines and Guam. In 1900 new laws granted the Puerto Ricans a certain amount of self-government and a popularly elected House of Representatives. American judicial and monetary systems were introduced. Later the laws were amended to allow greater autonomy and in 1917 Puerto Ricans became U.S. citizens. Natural disasters, including a major earthquake, several hurricanes, a tsunami, and the effects of the Great Depression impoverished Puerto Rico in the first decades of the 20th century. Many Puerto Ricans left the islands for the American mainland seeking work, greater opportunities, and specialized education. After World War II, the U.S. government granted the Puerto Ricans the right to elect their own governor; however, other laws made it illegal to display the Puerto Rican flag, to sing a patriotic song, or to promote the independence of Puerto Rico. Puerto Rican nationalists attempted to assassinate President Harry S. Truman in 1950, emphasizing the extent of feeling among the Puerto Ricans. A new constitution was approved in 1952 making Puerto Rico a freely associated autonomous state—the Commonwealth of Puerto Rico—with its own government, flag, and identity. Rapid industrialization beginning in the 1950s transformed the state and along with tourism gave the Puerto Ricans the highest standard of living in the Caribbean. Since the 1950s the Puerto Ricans have voted several times on the status of their homeland. Consistently the Puerto Ricans voted for continued autonomy as a freely associated state or statehood while a small minority supported full independence. Continued emigration from the island, mostly to the American mainland, resulted in large Puerto Rican populations in the urban areas of the Northeast, the southern states, and the upper Midwest. The number of Puerto Ricans living in mainland United States now outnumbers the total population of Puerto Rico.

Further Reading

Ayala, Cesar J. and Rafael Bernabe. *Puerto Rico in the American Century: A History since 1898.* Chapel Hill, NC: University of North Carolina Press, 2009.

Mihelich, T.J. *Puerto Rico: Land of Lost Dreams.* Bloomington, IN: iUniverse, 2010.

Monge, Jose Trias. *Puerto Rico: The Trials of the Oldest Colony in the World.* New Haven, CT: Yale University Press, 1999.

Purépechas

The Purépechas, sometimes known as Purhepechas, P'urhépechas, P'orhépechas, Tarascans, Tarascos, or Porhés, are a Mexican ethnic group centered in the northwestern parts of the Mexican state of Michoacán. There are also sizable Purépecha communities in Guadalajara, Mexico City, Tiajuana, and the United States. The estimated 200,000 Purépechas speak a language isolate that is unrelated to the other languages of Mesoamerica. Most Purépechas also speak Spanish, the language of administration and education. The majority of the Purépechas are Roman Catholic, with smaller groups of Protestants, particularly evangelicals, and a minority that adheres to their traditional belief system.

The Purépechas, who speak a language that may be distantly related to Quechua, may have migrated north from the Andes

Mountains in South America. Purépecha traditions claim that they traveled by boat on the Pacific Ocean before settling in their current territory. Their homeland, the earlier Purépecha or Tarascan empire, occupied most of the present-day state of Michoacán and some of the lower valleys of neighboring Guanajuato and Jalisco. By 1324 CE the empire had become the dominant force in western Mexico. The empire, with its capital at Tzintzuntzan, was known for the knowledge of metalworking and feather mosaics made of hummingbird feathers that were highly regarded throughout central Mexico. Because of their metal weapons the Purépechas were never conquered by the Aztecs (the Mexica people) and also fought off incursions by the fierce Chichimecas from the north. The Aztecs invaded the empire several times, including a fierce war in 1479. The Aztecs called the Purépechas the Michoacanos, meaning "masters of fish," a reference to the large Lake Pátzcuaro and its abundant fish species. Though enemies, the Purépechas and the Aztecs carried on a lively trade in food, slaves, copper arms, and feather capes. European diseases, brought to the region by travelers, decimated the Purépechas before any Spanish entered their empire. After word came of the conquest of the rival Aztec empire, the Purépecha ruler, Tangaxuan II, formed an alliance with the Spanish in 1525. The Spanish, instead of acting as allies, entered the territory as conquerors, taking captives for slaves, plundering temples, and kidnapping women. Purépecha legend tells of a bloody war against the Spanish led by a 16- or 17-year-old Purépecha princess, Erendira. Using the horses stolen from the invaders, the Purépechas learned to ride into battle. In 1529–1530, a Spanish force of some 500 European soldiers and 10,000 indigenous allies invaded the empire, plundering the cities and capturing and executing Tangaxuan II. In 1533 the Spanish managed to establish a lasting colonial order, ending the Purépecha empire that had flourished for hundreds of years. Spanish missionaries established missions that gave Purépechas some protection from the excesses of Spanish colonial rule. The missionaries directed the tearing down of Purépecha temples and platforms to use the building materials in the construction of churches and monasteries leaving few archeological remains. Through the missions the Purépechas adopted the Catholic religion and the Spanish language. The Purépecha language, adapted to the Latin alphabet, became a literary language in the early colonial period. From about 1700 the status of the Purépechas changed and their language was banned as the colonial government pursued a policy of *castellanización*, with the Purépechas actively encouraged to abandon their language in favor of Spanish. The city of Tzintuntzan, with a population of over 40,000 when the Spanish arrived, dwindled to a small village. The "Place of Hummingbirds" was mostly deserted, with even the hummingbirds gone, hunted to extinction for their iridescent feathers. The Spanish called the Purépechas by the name Tarascos, derived from a Purépecha word meaning "relative" or "brother-in-law," a term used by the Purépechas to mock the Spanish who regularly raped Purépecha women. By the mid-17th century the Purépecha population had declined by half. In 1776 the territory of the former Purépecha empire was divided into the provinces of Michoacán and Colima. The economy of the region was concentrated in the hands of the ruling elite, those born in Spain, who held vast lands, haciendas, and mines. The Purépechas were exploited for their labor, and slavery was common. Education was restricted to the elite and their descendants, and was controlled by the Roman Catholic Church. At the end of the 18th century, Enlightenment ideas from Europe began to infiltrate the educated classes. Some of the more restrictive laws concerning indigenous peoples were amended or abandoned but the Purépechas continued to live in poverty as farmers, fishermen, and day laborers.

The Purépecha culture is a highland culture centered on Lake Pátzcuaro, including the highland forests to the west of the lake, a region known as the Sierra Purépecha, and the valley of the Río Duero to the north. Called Tarascos or Tarascans by the Spanish, the name was used for hundreds of years but in recent decades younger Purépechas have rejected the name as colonial; all but the older generations now use the name Purépecha. During the early colonial period the Purépechas were congregated in towns organized along religious-communal lines. Crafts such as basket weaving, metal working, and ceramics were established in different towns so that today each Purépecha town has its own special arts and crafts. The Purépechas have retained their language, as well as cultural elements such as their cuisine, arts, and crafts though they have adopted the basic Spanish peasant culture with regard to religion, economy, and traditions. Despite the importance of the precolonial

Purépecha empire, historical knowledge of the Purépecha situation during the Mexican colonial period is amazingly limited. Only at the end of the 19th century did a systematic study of Purépecha ethnohistory and linguistics begin. Relatively isolated in the highlands until the second half of the 20th century, the Purépechas retained a self-sufficiency and a unique aesthetic sense drawn from both their historical roots and the later colonial culture. Traditional songs, known as Pirekuas or Pirecuas, are the songs of daily life and are sung at every type of regional festival or ceremony. The songs play an important role in keeping the Purépechas together as a culture.

The Europeans and the Criollos, the offspring of Europeans born in Mexico, were inspired by the American and French revolutions to take up arms when Spain was invaded by the French during the Napoleonic Wars in Europe. The fighting often targeted the Purépechas as both sides sought to dominate the indigenous populations during the long war of independence. At the end of the war Mexico was recognized as an independent country in 1821. The state of Michoacán was formed as part of the new nation in 1824. During most of the 19th century the struggle between centralists and federalists dominated Mexican politics with the Purépechas mostly left to their subsistence farming, fishing, and hunting. In the 1860s, the French intervention in Mexico resulted in the capture of Michoacán in 1863. The Purépecha resistance to the French, in alliance with the educated elite of the state, was particularly strong. French punitive acts, such as the burning of the city of Zitácuaro, drove many Purépechas to seek shelter in the higher elevations. The Mexican Revolution swept through the region in 1911, with fighting between the various factions again targeting Purépecha communities suspected of supporting an opposing faction. In 1918, the state adopted a new constitution that gave limited recognition to the indigenous population. The Purépechas again took up arms during the Cistero War in the 1920s, a rebellion against the Mexican government's anticlerical stance and the persecution of the Roman Catholic Church. The war, which affected agricultural production and distribution, raged from 1926 to 1929, though the Purépechas only began to recover from the devastation and hunger in the early 1930s. Roads, electricity, and the spread of education ended the isolation of the Purépechas from the 1960s onward. Today the Purépechas look back on their history with pride, and a new appreciation of the culture and language has helped to revitalize the cultural traditions and the Purépecha society. Most Purépechas continue to live in the cool, rainy highlands though many young Purépechas go to the United States as migratory workers or to other parts of Mexico. They bring back new ideas that have become part of the local culture, which has modernized rapidly though a movement has gained widespread support in the appreciation of their ancient culture and language.

Further Reading

Boyer, Christopher. *Becoming Campesinos: Politics, Identity, and Agrarian Struggle in Postrevolutionary Michoacan, 1920–1935.* Palo Alto, CA: Stanford University Press, 2003.

Pollard, Helen Peristein. *Tariacuri's Legacy: The Prehispanic Tarascan State.* Norman, OK: University of Oklahoma Press, 1993.

Warren, J. Benedict. *The Conquest of Michoacan: The Spanish Domination of the Tarascan Kingdom in Western Mexico, 1521–1530.* Norman, OK: University of Oklahoma Press, 1985.

Québécois

The Québécois, sometimes known as French Canadians, are a North American ethnic group, the inhabitants of the province of Québec in eastern Canada. The estimated 6.1 million Québécois speak French as their first language with many also speaking English, the language of the province's largest minorities. In total, about 98 percent of the population of Québec is able to speak French as a first or second language. The majority of the Québécois are Roman Catholic, with small Protestant and other religious minorities.

Algonquian, Iroquois, and Inuit peoples inhabited the region when the first Europeans reached North America. In the 16th century Basque fishermen and whalers traded European goods for furs with the coastal tribes. In 1534, Jacques Cartier planted a cross in the Gaspé Peninsula and claimed the land in the name of King Francis I of France. Initial French colonization attempts failed though French fishing fleets continued to sail to the Atlantic coast and into the St. Lawrence River, making alliances with the indigenous peoples. Lured by the lucrative fur trade, the French government decided to secure and expand its influence in North America. Samuel de Champlain explored the coast and the St. Lawrence River in 1603. He returned in 1608 with an expedition that founded a settlement on the upper

St. Lawrence, later known as Québec City. The new colony forged trading ties, and later military ties, with the Algonquian and Huron peoples who traded furs for French goods such as metal objects, guns, alcohol, and clothing. The royal government of the colony of New France was created in 1663. By 1700 over 12,500 French colonists, mostly farmers and fishermen, had settled in the fertile southern districts and along the coast. In the early 18th century the colony grew rapidly with continuing European settlement and immigration sponsored by the French government. French and British rivalry in Europe and North America resulted in a series of wars that culminated in the French defeat on the Plains of Abraham outside Québec City's walls in 1759. The colony of New France, with its 70,000 French citizens, was ceded to the British empire under the terms of the 1763 Treaty of Paris. After a failed attempt to assimilate the Québécois into an English-speaking colony, and with rebellion spreading in the 13 British colonies further south, the Parliament passed the Québec Act of 1774, which divided British Canada into French-speaking Lower Canada or Québec and English-speaking Upper Canada. The new laws guaranteed the Québécois their lands and cultural, linguistic, and religious rights. The Québécois culture and legal system were thereafter protected under British colonial law. The arrival of 10,000

Loyalists, the pro-British refugees from the new United States, in Québec in 1784 altered the French domination of the province and augmented unrest and conflicts between the French and English speakers.

The Québécois, the descendants of the early French colonists of Québec, are a modern French-speaking North American culture. The Québécois culture, a New World French culture, is a unique blend of traditional French culture and modern North American influences. The fundamental values of the culture emphasize equality between men and women, primacy of the French language, and separation of church and state. Music has always played an important role in Québécois society. The modern cosmopolitan culture of Québec continues the tradition with all types of music, from folk music to hip-hop. Québec government departments promote film and television in the French language. Like the other arts, Québécois literature draws on the history and traditions of Québec to maintain a strong literary tradition. Other cultural elements, such as Cirque de Soleil, are among the most visible internationally. Like their arts, the gastronomy of the Québécois is a unique North American cuisine that evolved through the influences of the early colonists from France and the later Canadian experience of the people of Québec. Until the 1960s the Québécois had one of the highest birthrates in the industrialized countries, but since then it has declined to the levels of the neighboring English-speaking Canadians. The low Québécois birthrate is offset by a constant stream of immigrants moving into the province. The culture and laws of the province set it apart from other North American regions. The Québécois retain much of their colonial culture of the 18th century, with a modern evolution into a French-speaking, advanced industrial society with a modern culture and a high standard of living. Many Québécois have embraced nationalism, the demand for an independent Québec, as a means to survive in a predominately English-speaking continent.

In the early years of the 1800s dissatisfaction with the unilateral control of the British governors spread throughout the Québécois population. In 1837, led by Louis Papineau, the leader of the French Canadian Reform Party, the Québécois rebelled and attempted to create an independent republic to be known as Laurentia, after the Laurentian Mountains in the province. Defeated in 1838 the rebels, known as Patriotes, were dispersed though unrest remained. French-speaking Lower Canada was dissolved in 1840 to become part of a united province known as East Canada, which also included English-speaking Ontario. In 1867, Québec was again constituted as a separate province, which joined with three English-speaking provinces to form the new Canadian confederation. The Québécois, mostly poor, rural, and staunchly Roman Catholic, looked to Québec City as the bastion of their culture and language. The province's largest city, Montreal, became one of North America's great immigration melting pots; French, Italian, English, Portuguese, Irish, Jewish, and Eastern European immigrants crowded into the city. English gradually replaced French as the language of business and society in the city. The

Québécois, responding to threats to their culture and language, began to organize in militant groups to press for political and linguistic autonomy. Political unrest resulted in two short-lived rebellions in 1870 and 1884. As discontent with domination by the English-speaking Canadians surged in the 1890s the Québécois pressed for increased provincial powers. A massive urbanization of the Québécois population between 1901 and 1921 reinforced the language and culture, particularly the influence of the conservative Catholic hierarchy. The severe economic hardships of the Great Depression in the 1930s were particularly felt in Québec, where families having a dozen children were common. The influence of the Church extended to all aspects of Québécois society; books from France were censored, and Québécois women were denied the vote until 1940. The only careers open to women in the province were motherhood or the convent, until the Quiet Revolution of the 1960s when church power declined as education and greater opportunities began to spread. Traditions were put aside to the extent of allowing women to enter the workforce. The culture liberalized as urbanization accelerated and a burgeoning Québécois middle class entered business and the professions. The Québécois finally attained a standard of living equal to that of the English-speaking North Americans. The Quiet Revolution transformed Québec from an underdeveloped backwater—Catholic, agrarian, and very conservative—into an advanced, French-speaking industrial society. Beginning in 1963, a paramilitary group known as the Front de liberation du Québec (FLQ)

launched a decades-long struggle for an independent Québec, utilizing propaganda and terrorism that included bombings, robberies, and attacks. The targets of the FLQ were most often English-speaking institutions. The murder of Pierre Laporte, a provincial minister, in 1970 marked the end of the FLQ as membership rapidly declined along with public support. Though the Québécois rejected political violence, support for secession from Canada remained strong. The Canadian government made French the second official language across the federation and a renovated constitution spelled out in detail the quality of French and English in Canada. In 1974 French became the sole official language of Québec, sparking violent opposition by English speakers and immigrant groups that supported bilingualism. An openly nationalist political party, the Parti Québécois, won provincial elections in 1976 vowing to hold a referendum on Québécois independence. A French-only language law, adopted in Québec in 1978, drove out much of the province's powerful English-speaking business community, raising fears that independence would aggravate the province's economic problems. A 1980 referendum failed 58.2 percent to 41.8 percent, but the nationalists continued to work for separation from Canada. Between 1976 and 1996 an estimated 400,000 people, mostly English-speaking, left Québec. A second referendum, held in 1995, resulted in a larger "yes" vote but the anti-secession voters still rejected independence if only by a small margin, 50.56 percent against and 49.44 percent in favor. In the 1990s the independence fervor waned as the Québécois shared the

North American way of life in a stable, advanced, and liberal Canada. High technology revitalized the economy of Montreal, one of the world's most important French-speaking cities. Concessions to Québécois sensibilities and the economic downturn in the 21st century dampened enthusiasm for secession from Canada. The Québec Liberal Party, considered moderate yet promoting Québécois culture, won provincial elections in 2003 and again in 2007. The pro-independence Parti Québécois now forms part of the opposition though it promises to hold another referendum on independence should it return to government.

Further Reading

Grescoe, Taras. *Sacre Blues: An Unsentimental Journey through Quebec.* Toronto, Canada: Macfarlane Walter & Ross, 2001.

Lacoursiere, Jacques. *A People's History of Quebec.* Montreal, Canada: Baraka Books, 2009.

Moogk, Peter N. *La Nouvelle France: The Making of French Canada—A Cultural History.* East Lansing, MI: Michigan State University Press, 2000.

Quechuas

The Quechuas, sometimes known as Quichuas or Kichwas, are a South American ethnic group living in the Andean regions of Peru, Bolivia, Ecuador, Argentina, and Chile. The estimated 14 million Quechuas speak various dialects of the Quechua language with the majority speaking Spanish as a second language. Most Quechuas are Roman Catholics, often mixing the Christian rituals and ceremonies with the pre-Christian Andean customs.

The foothills of the Andes Mountains are believed to have been settled at least 21,000 years ago. Historical records are fragmentary but suggest that settled agriculture was developed around 3000 BCE and the smelting of metals, especially copper, began some 1,500 years later. By 600 BCE, the first great Andean empire had developed among the neighboring Aymaras in the high plateau region later known as the Altiplano. The empire, called Tiahuanacan, was centered on Lake Titicaca and included urban centers and enclaves in different zones from the eastern valleys of the Andes to the Pacific Coast. The Aymara empire collapsed suddenly around 1200 CE to be succeeded by several smaller states, but by the 15th century the Aymaras had been brought under the rule of the Incas of the Quechuas. After the collapse of Tiahuanacan, a small state emerged in the Cuzco Basin ruled by a god-king known as the Sapan Inca. As the Aymara empire weakened, the Quechuas of Cuzco began to expand by absorbing neighboring peoples around 1100 CE. The Quechua economy was based on intensive terracing of mountain slopes and a highly engineered irrigation system. The civilization of the Cuzco Quechuas developed large urban centers, an extensive road system, and subject states, all overseen by a well-organized and efficient administration. Expanding from the empire's capital at Cuzco the Incas, taking their name from that of their ruler, ruled the largest and most advanced state in the Americas before the arrival of the Europeans. The Inca empire expanded to the highlands to the south to incorporate the Aymaras and other indigenous peoples, to become an empire of many distinct nations. At its height in the 15th century the Inca empire, known as Tawantinsuyu, extended from northern Ecuador into central Chile and from the Andes Mountains to the coastal lowlands. The empire's population in 1500 is estimated at between 9 million and 16 million inhabitants. The empire was remarkable, as it was created without the benefit of either the wheel or a formal system of writing. Instead of a written script, the Incas used a highly accurate *khipu* (knot-tying) system for record keeping and communications. The achievements of the Quechua Incas were even more remarkable considering the brevity of the period during which the empire was built and the region's formidable geographic obstacles. Inca society was very organized with the Sapan Inca and his wife, traditionally his sister, at society's peak, followed by the high priest and the military commander and then the four *apus*, the rulers of the four quarters of the empire. In 1470, several Aymara states rebelled against Inca rule. The rebels were defeated and to pacify the region Quechua colonies were planted in traditionally Aymara territory, especially in the southern valleys and the Aymara valleys east of the Andes. The present Quechua population of Bolivia comprises the descendants of the early Inca colonies. A Spanish expedition led by Francisco Pizarro, sailing south along the Pacific Coast from Panama, sought to confirm the legendary existence of a land of gold. They first encountered the people

of the Inca empire in 1526. Finding a wealthy empire with the prospects of great treasure, Pizarro returned to Spain to seek royal approval for the conquest of the Inca empire. Appointed the governor of all potential conquered lands in Peru, or New Castile as the Spanish called the region, Pizarro returned with a military expedition. Armored soldiers and horses gave Pizarro great technological superiority over the Inca forces. Smallpox, spreading south on the efficient Inca road system, decimated the population, killing 60–94 percent of the total population. The Inca empire, weakened by civil war and epidemics, fell to the Spanish following the capture and execution of the Inca ruler, Atahualpa. Resistance continued for many years until the last Inca stronghold fell to the invaders in 1572. After the conquest of the empire many aspects of Quechua culture were systematically destroyed, including their sophisticated farming systems. The Spanish colonial administration, often arbitrary and brutal, forced one member of each Quechua family to work in the gold and silver mines. When the miner died, usually within a year or two, the family was required to send a replacement. The Quechua language and culture were banned from politics and education. Smallpox was only the first of the epidemics; typhus swept the population in 1546, influenza and smallpox in 1558, smallpox again in 1589, diphtheria in 1614, and measles in 1618. According to Spanish archives, the Quechua population declined by 75 percent between 1561 and 1796, mostly due to the epidemics but also because of the disruption of their ordered society and the brutality of the conquerors. The rapid loss of population further disrupted the social and economic systems. In some districts two-thirds of the surviving Quechuas were conscripted for forced labor. Another estimate, archived in 1800, counted the Quechua population at just 10 percent of their preconquest population.

Quechua culture encompasses a number of related cultures among the large Quechua population of western South America. Despite their diversity and distinctive dialects the various Quechua groups have numerous cultural characteristics in common. Traditionally Quechuas see themselves as people of a certain town or region and an overall Quechua identity began to be developed only in the latter half of the 20th century. Quechua culture is believed to have developed at least a thousand years before the rise of the Inca empire in the early 15th century. Quechua culture is based on the efficient and sustainable use of limited resources and is centered upon community and *ayni* or mutual assistance. The social system is based on reciprocity; helping a neighbor to be helped in return. Even marriages are often subject to community approval. Farming is an integral part of Quechua society, from the harvesting of food crops to raising alpacas and llamas. The Quechuas pioneered advanced farming techniques to adapt to the demands of the varied Andean terrain, a combination of high plains, steep mountain slopes, and warm valleys. Traditional handicrafts are an important aspect of Quechua material culture. The disintegration of traditional society—regional through mining activities and the accompanying social structures—and the steady migration to the large cities have resulted in acculturation into Hispanic mestizo society and often led to the loss of both ethnic identity and the Quechua language. The Quechua language, belonging to the Andean branch of the Andean-Equatorial language family, is spoken in some 46 dialects, many not mutually intelligible. A standardized dialect, based on Southern Quechua, now forms part of the educational system in many Quechua communities. Quechua and Aymara are now official languages in Bolivia and Quechua is an official language in Peru. Officially the majority of the Quechuas are Roman Catholics, with 95 percent identifying the faith as their principal belief system. In recent years Protestant sects, particularly Evangelical Methodists, have gained converts. The pre-Christian beliefs are often combined with the Christian rituals in a unique blend that bridges the two distinct traditions.

Spanish rule created a highly stratified colonial society in which whites and mestizos controlled the "inferior" Quechua population. The harsh treatment was often justified as a means of tying the indigenous population to the plantations, mines, and haciendas of the ruling elite. The independence of the Spanish colonies in the early 19th century transferred power into the hands of the Creole descendants of the European colonizers and the larger mixed or mestizo population, with no changes made to the system of peonage that controlled Quechua lives. In the late 19th century various Quechua movements were organized in an attempt to redress over four centuries of abuse and discrimination. Between 1879 and 1965 there were 32 peasant revolts and movements, denying the traditional view that the Quechuas passively accepted serfdom. Few of the uprisings seriously threatened the hold of the white minority on the region, but they testified to the burgeoning feelings of frustration, alienation, and anger built up over centuries. Demands for redress of the most flagrant abuses resulted in the establishment of the official Indian Community in Peru in 1920. Quechua communities that could prove that they held colonial title to lands were permitted to put forward claims, a long and arduous bureaucratic process. Up to the present the Quechuas continue to be victimized by political conflicts and persecution. In the Peruvian civil war of the 1980s, fought between government forces and the Sendero Luminoso rebels, some three quarters of the 70,000 killed in the conflict were ethnic Quechuas, whereas the soldiers and rebels were without exception either white or mestizo. In the late 1990s a forced sterilization policy was begun under Peru's President Alberto Fujimori that almost exclusively affected indigenous women, a total exceeding 200,000. Although Quechua was made an official language in Peru in 1969, when two newly elected members of parliament chose to swear their oath of office in Quechua in 2006 they were rejected. Access to the courts and regional societies required the learning of Spanish. Between 1950 and 1975, the number of monolingual Quechuas dropped by nearly 40 percent and though education was predicated on the "Hispanization" of the Quechua populations the majority have retained a strong positive orientation toward their ethnic roots. A well-educated minority formed the nucleus of a Quechua intelligentsia in the 1970s and 1980s, when a renewed interest in their traditional culture and their unique history fostered a strong cultural movement and reinforced demands for lands stolen during the colonial period. Support for cultural rights and an end to the discrimination that rules their lives has spread throughout the Quechua communities in all South American countries. They reject the Spanish version that the conquistadors conquered a continent of primitive peoples in South America, instead claiming that the conquistadors plundered the territories of a highly advanced civilization symbolized by the remarkable Incas and their empire.

Further Reading

Cleary, Edward L. and Timothy J. Steigenga, eds. *Resurgent Voices in Latin America: Indigenous Peoples, Political Mobilization, and Religious Change.* Piscataway, NJ: Rutgers University Press, 2004.

Krogel, Alison. *Food, Power, and Resistance in the Andes: Exploring Quechua Verbal and Visual Narratives.* Lanham, MD: Lexington Books, 2010.

Osborne, Harold. *Indians of the Andes: Aymaras and Quechuas.* London: Routledge, 2004.

R

Romanis

The Romanis, sometimes known as Gypsies, Romanys, Romanies, Romas, or Roms, are related to the Romani people of Europe. The estimated 3 million or more Romanis in the Americas speak various languages of the Romani-Domari branch of the Indo-European languages. The Romanis are primarily Christian, mostly Roman Catholic or Orthodox but with a growing number adhering to Protestant sects. With regard to religion the Romanis have historically adapted to local traditions, so the Romani populations in the Western Hemisphere display a wide variety of religious beliefs.

Romani legends place their original homeland in the present province of Sindh in southwestern Pakistan. Nomadic groups are thought to have migrated westward between 500 BCE and 600 BCE, though the main migrants moved into present-day Iran in the first millennium CE. Many believe the migrations began with refugees fleeing the Muslim conquest of the Sindh region in 711–712 CE. During their time in Iran the migrants split into three groups—the Gitanos, the Kalderash, and the Manush—the forefathers of the modern Romani tribes. Some Romani nomads later migrated into Egypt and North Africa. By 835, Romani nomad groups were reported in parts of the Byzantine empire. In the 10th century, Rom nomads turned north into Russian territory. The nomadic groups moved into Eastern Europe in the 14th century and first appeared in Western Europe in the 15th century. In the late 15th century, some Romanis crossed the English Channel to reach the British Isles. Many of the former nomads settled as sedentary farmers and tradesmen, but others, moving into regions where the attitudes of the local government were less tolerant, were hounded from place to place. Smithing and metalworking evolved as the primary occupations, valuable skills to offer settled populations. The name Gypsy, still commonly used to refer to the Romanis, began with the name "Egyptian" arising from the mistaken belief that the Romanis originated in the mythical land of Little Egypt—although some Romanis in fact entered southern Europe from North Africa, having previously passed through Egypt. The name Gypsy was eventually applied to all the distinct Romani groups in Europe. By the mid-15th century hostility toward the Romani peoples was widespread, and anti-Gypsy laws affected most of Europe's Romani population. Their eastern origins gave rise to many misconceptions and myths associated with the Romanis. Romani women were famed as fortune-tellers and were consulted by many of the same people who supported persecutions and discrimination. By the 16th century the Romanis, in most parts of Europe, had been reduced to persecuted minorities or despised outcasts. In many regions local laws allowed the enslavement of Romanis while in other areas they were tied to large landholdings as serfs or forced laborers. In England, under the reign of Henry VIII, the Egyptians Act of 1530 banned Romanis from entering the kingdom and required those already there to leave within 16 days. The hidden nature of the Romani communities allowed most to escape deportation. A new law offered Romanis in England and Wales the possibility of citizenship, if they voluntarily assimilated into the local populations. Regarded with suspicion and fear probably because of their dark complexion and foreign appearance, they were often deported to other parts of Europe. Christopher Columbus brought several Romanis to the New World, most forcibly transported. In 1603 the first Romanis were transported to the Americas from Britain. In Portugal the persecution of *Ciganos* also resulted in forced transportation to the Brazilian colonies. Many Romanis voluntarily or forcibly migrated to the Spanish and French colonies in the New World in the 17th and 18th centuries. The Romanis adapted to the new territories in the Americas though the prejudices, discrimination, and misconceptions of Europe were also transported to the New World.

The Romani culture is considered the traditional culture of the original Romani nomads of the Middle Ages in Europe. Historically the Romanis preferred to remain anonymous and unrecognized, except to each other. The Romanis were in the Americas with the very earliest settlers and have retained their culture and traditions for a millennium. The Romanis,

or Gypsies as they are still often called by non-Romanis, have their historic origins in the Indian subcontinent and are often characterized as having dark complexions and black hair, but a thousand years of co-existence in Europe has resulted in a variety of subcultures and physical appearances with all shades of skin and hair. Many Romanis do not send their children to school, or send them only for a few years, for fear that their offspring will lose their culture. There are four primary Romani "tribes," the Kalderash, the Machavaya, the Lovaris, and the Churaris. Subgroups include the Romanichals, the Gitanoes or Calé, the Sinti, the Rudaris, the Manush, the Boyash, the Ungaritzas, the Luris, the Bashaldé, the Romungros, and the Xoraxais. Each of the groups and subgroups represent a distinct cultural tradition and often speak dialects that are not mutually intelligible. In the Americas most Romanis speak En-glish, Spanish, Portuguese, or French along with their traditional dialects. The Romanis refer to all outsiders as Gadjo, meaning "a person who is not part of the Romani culture." The term is also used to refer to ethnic Romanis who have assimilated and no longer participate in the distinct Romanic culture. The cultural elements that are shared by most Romani groups are the distinctive music, dance, and various art forms. Like the linguistic influences religion is also an aspect of local Romani cultural heritage. While often preserving aspects of their older belief systems and forms of worship, the majority of the Romanis in the Americas adopted the Christian religions that predominated in the majority of the countries and territories of North and South America. Romani populations in North America are mostly Roman Catholic or Protestant with smaller groups of Orthodox denomination or Muslims. In the Spanish-speaking countries the majority are Roman Catholic though evangelical Protestant groups such as the Pentecostals have gained followers.

Romani immigration to the Americas accelerated in the early 19th century as wars swept Europe. Forced assimilation in many parts of Europe drove some extended families to immigrate as did the ongoing persecution and discrimination that followed them everywhere. The abolition of Romani slavery in parts of Europe, particularly in Romania, in the 1840s and 1850s increased the number of immigrants seeking a new life in the Americas. In the late 19th century Romani immigration was forbidden on a racial basis. Argentina banned all Romani immigration in 1880 and in 1885 the United States outlawed the legal entry of Romanis into the country. In Europe the persecution of the Romanis reached its peak during World War II. The Romani Holocaust, the *Porajmos*, was the genocide perpetuated by the Nazis and their allies in Croatia, Romania, and Hungary. Because of the inaccuracy of prewar census figures the actual number of Romani victims is estimated at between 220,000 and 500,000. Many survivors, determined to leave Europe, immigrated to the United States, Canada, and Latin America during the late 1940s and 1950s. Discrimination and violence continue to haunt the estimated 12 million Romanis in Europe, prompting many to leave for the Americas each year.

Many younger Romanis no longer accept the huge misunderstanding that has haunted their people for hundreds of years. These activists are adopting new survival tactics that include a more open attitude to outsiders and a desire to see themselves and their families accurately portrayed in the world around them.

Further Reading

Belton, Brian A. *Questioning Gypsy Identity: Ethnic Narratives in Britain and America.* Lanham, MD: Altamira Press, 2005.

Brown, Irving. *Gypsy Fires in America: A Narrative of Life among the Romanies of the U.S.A. and Canada.* Whitefish, MT: Kessinger Publishing, 2007.

Sutherland, Anne. *Gypsies: The Hidden Americans.* Long Grove, IL: Waveland Press, 1986.

S

Saint Lucians

The Saint Lucians, sometimes known as Lucians, are a Caribbean people, the inhabitants of the island of Saint Lucia in the eastern Caribbean Sea. There are sizable Saint Lucian communities in the United Kingdom, the United States, France, and other Caribbean islands. The estimated 200,000 Saint Lucians are mostly of Afro-Caribbean background, with smaller numbers of mixed ancestry, East Indian background, European ancestry, and others. The majority of the Saint Lucians speak English, the language of education and government, but most are bilingual, also speaking Kwéyo 'l, a creole dialect that blends French and African influences. Most Saint Lucians are Roman Catholic, though in recent years Protestant sects have gained converts in the country.

The Arawaks, moving north from the South American mainland, probably settled the island between 200 CE and 400 CE. The more aggressive Caribs replaced the Arawaks sometime between 800 and 1000 and had developed a complex society by the time the first Europeans, led by Christopher Columbus, landed on the island in either 1492 or 1502. The Spanish, the Dutch, the English, and the French all attempted to establish trading posts on Saint Lucia in the 17th century but were unable to overcome the opposition of the fierce Carib warriors. The French claimed the island in 1635 but it was the English who started the first European settlement in 1639, which was destroyed by the Caribs. A French settlement was founded in 1643 that lasted some years. In 1664, the English laid claim to the island and sent an expedition of 1,000 men but after two years only 89 survived, with most having succumbed to disease. European diseases also decimated the Carib population. The French returned and resumed control of the island in 1666. The island changed hands between the French and the English a number of times though the settlements remained and the island was considered a French colony well into the 18th century. The French again colonized the island in 1763 and introduced the sugar industry two years later. The early colonists were mostly indentured European servants under elite wealthy merchants or nobles. The sugarcane plantations' requirement of labor resulted in the importation of African slaves. Soon the African population of the island greatly outnumbered the Europeans. Wars between the French and the British often involved the island, which changed administrations several times though it remained mostly French in language and culture. News of the French Revolution prompted many of the slaves to leave the plantations to begin working small plots for themselves in 1790–1791. A guillotine was erected in Castries that was used to execute the island's plantation aristocrats and administrators. The new French government abolished slavery in 1794. Shortly thereafter the British invaded the island in response to pleas by the embattled plantation families. The British restored slavery and supported the plantation economy. The capital city was burned in 1796 as part of a battle between the British troops and an opposing force of slaves and French republicans.

The culture of Saint Lucia is a modern blend of Afro-Caribbean, French, and British traditions. The culture evolved from the intermingling of the many different groups that participated in the island's long history. Each group brought different beliefs and traditions, all of which are reflected in the modern island culture. The Saint Lucians are mostly Afro-Caribbeans though they identify as Saint Lucians, even those living or born away from the island. The cultural elements such as the cuisine, music, dance, and art forms all reflect the mingling of the island's peoples. East Indians who came as indentured laborers following the abolition of slavery added their culinary and musical traditions to Saint Lucian culture. The British contributed their language, educational system, and political and legal structures. French influences are more evident in the arts, the music, the dance, and the creole patois known as Kwéyo 'l. The patois, spoken throughout the island, combines early French with words, expressions, and structures brought from Africa. Most Saint Lucians speak both English and Kwéyo 'l, also known as Patwa, though younger Saint Lucians living outside the island often speak only English. The African traditions brought to the island by the early slaves survived the repressions of the slave period and later servitude to become the strongest element in the Saint Lucian culture. Reflecting the early French colonial control, the majority of the Saint Lucians are Roman Catholic, though Protestant sects, particularly the evangelical groups, have gained converts. Every village and many rural settlements have a Catholic church, now served by Saint Lucian rather than French priests.

The British finally took control of Saint Lucia in 1803 and acquired the island permanently in 1814. The slave trade was abolished in 1808 though slavery continued until the abolition in 1834. Most of the former slaves settled on subsistence plots though others fished or worked as laborers. Sugarcane production continued though it was modified by the *meytage* system, a plan for sharecropping devised to induce the former slaves to continue working the land. Many of the European plantation families left the island. Indentured laborers, mostly East Indians, were brought to the island in the 1850s by the British administration. Considered part of the British Windward Islands, Saint Lucia continued to maintain its French-influenced culture and patois while adapting to British forms of administration and education. The use of English increased rapidly in the 19th century but in parallel with their French-African dialect that remained the language of daily life. The culture of the island evolved through the adaptation of the traditions brought to the island by slaves, mostly from West Africa, to the colonial French and British customs. As part of the British Windward Islands the Saint Lucians continued under British administration but retained the unique French-influenced culture and dialect and the

Roman Catholic faith. Later in the 1800s, the island became a major shipping center for coal. Dependence on sugar production waned in the 20th century, leaving bananas as the major export crop. Increasing self-government was introduced giving the large Afro-Caribbean population a say in the administration of their homeland. As an associated state of the United Kingdom from 1967 to 1979, the island had full responsibility for internal self-government. Full independence was achieved in 1979 though the Saint Lucians continue as an active member of the Commonwealth of Nations. In 1994 Saint Lucia suffered great damage from Tropical Storm Debbie, which destroyed over two-thirds of the banana crop. In the 21st century bananas, tourism, and offshore banking are the mainstays of the Saint Lucian economy. Thousands left the island to seek work, opportunities, or higher education, mostly settling in the United Kingdom, the United States, other parts of Europe, and other Caribbean islands.

Further Reading

Balletto, Barbara Lawrence and Debbie Gaiger, eds. *Saint Lucia.* Guilford, CT: Globe Pequot Press, 1999.

Joseph, Tennyson S.D. *Decolonization in St. Lucia: Politics and Global Neoliberalism, 1945–2010.* Jackson, MS: University Press of Mississippi, 2011.

Palmer, Jenny and Derek Walcott. *Saint Lucia: Portrait of an Island.* Oxford, UK: Macmillan Caribbean, 2008.

Saint Maartens

The Saint Maartens, sometimes known as Sint Maartens, Maarteans, or Saint Martiners, are a Caribbean people, the inhabitants of the Dutch half of the island of Saint Martin in the northeastern Caribbean. There are sizable Saint Maartens communities in the Netherlands, Suriname, and the United States. The estimated 50,000 Saint Maartens usually speak Dutch and most are bilingual, also speaking English. Both are official languages of the autonomous state of Saint Maartens. The majority of the Saint Maartens are Christians, mostly Protestant, with Roman Catholic, Mormon, and Jewish minorities.

Sighted by Christopher Columbus in 1493, the island was named Isla de San Martin, as it was first sighted on Saint Martin's Day. Though claimed by the Spanish, the island was ignored and never colonized. The Dutch established a settlement in 1631 with French and English settlements soon following. The Spanish, as part of the Eighty Years' War with the Dutch, invaded the island and captured the Dutch settlement in 1633. At the end of the war the Spanish, finding that the island was not profitable, abandoned Saint Martin in 1648. With the island again available for colonization both the Dutch and French reestablished their settlements. Preferring to avoid a conflict, the two colonial powers agreed to divide the island. The treaty, known as the Treaty of Concordia, was signed in 1648 while a French fleet waited off shore to insure that the French received more than just half the territory. According to local legend, in order to decide on the division of the island, the two sides agreed to hold a contest. A Frenchman drank wine while a Dutchman drank *jenever* (Dutch Gin) until both were barely able to stand. Then they embarked from Oysterpond on the eastern shore to follow the coasts until they met on the western edge of the island, which would then be used to draw a dividing line through Saint Martin to Oysterpond. The Dutchman met a woman and stopped to sleep off the effects of the gin, so the Frenchman was able to cover more distance, but he apparently cheated by cutting through the northeastern part of the island, so the French ended up with more land. In spite of the treaty and protestations of good will, relations between the two sides of Saint Martin were not always cordial. Conflicts between the two populations resulted in changes being made to the dividing line 16 times. Although the Spanish had imported slaves to the island, the Dutch established plantations of cotton, tobacco, and sugar, requiring many laborers. The salt pans that supported a lively trade in salt also required many workers. African slaves were imported and the African population quickly outnumbered that of the Europeans. Often subjected to cruel treatment, the slaves staged several rebellions.

The culture of Saint Martin is a blend of Afro-Caribbean, Dutch, British, and French influences. During the colonial era, British settlers and several periods of British rule left the English language as the most widely spoken language and infused the local culture with a strong British tradition. The Saint Maartens can trace their ancestry to African slaves, Dutch plantation families and government administrators, and British settlers and soldiers. Immigration from many parts of the world during the latter half of the 20th century has added many new influences, foods, and musical styles to the island culture. Music and dance, important elements of the local culture, have absorbed traditions from other Caribbean islands so that calypso, merengue, zouk, soca, and reggae are all part of Saint Martin's musical heritage, along with old Dutch folk tunes and modern English and American music. The country's anthem, called "O Sweet Saint-Martin's Land," is a bi-national anthem used by both the Dutch and French halves of the island. French influence on the island cuisine has been incorporated into Saint Martin culture, which is known for excellent food. Sports are also important, particularly sailing. An annual yacht race known as Sint Maarten Heineken Regatta is held annually with participants from all around the world. Though both Dutch and English are the official languages, the language of daily life is a Saint Martin variety of Caribbean English, a patois blending African and English with some Dutch and French borrowings. Dutch and British religious traditions are maintained with the majority of the Saint Maartens belonging to the Methodist Church or other Protestant denominations. There are smaller Roman Catholic, Jewish, and Mormon groups and religious freedom is guaranteed.

Saint Martin changed hands several times during the wars known as the Napoleonic Wars in Europe. Finally returned to Dutch rule in 1816, the island's salt pans and agricultural exports sustained a prosperous white elite that controlled a vast slave population. From 1828 to 1845 Saint Martin, along with the other Dutch Caribbean possessions, was governed from Dutch Suriname on the South American mainland. In 1845 the Dutch Caribbean islands were formed into a separate colony known as the Netherlands Antilles. In 1848, the French abolished slavery on their half of the island forcing the Dutch to end the trade on their half of the island though slavery officially continued until 1863. The emancipation of the slaves was a severe blow to the local economy, which did not completely recover until the early 20th century. Saint Martin and the other northern Dutch islands, with less population and industry, lived mostly on subsistence farming. In the 1930s the Dutch government began to develop Saint Martin to forestall radical political movements or claims by other colonial powers. After World War II the Netherlands Antilles became a self-governing part of the Dutch kingdom. Tourism began in the 1950s and Saint Martin became an important stop for cruise ships. The differing cultures and languages of the member states of the Netherlands Antilles resulted in tensions from the 1970s between the island governments. In 1986 Aruba seceded from the Antilles federation. The domination of the federation by Curaçao was also resented in Saint Martin though the islanders voted to retain the federation during the 1990s. Saint Martin and the other member islands were largely autonomous, particularly in cultural matters. Despite reassurances and offers of increased autonomy within the Netherlands Antilles, the Saint Maartens voted in 2000 to separate from the federation. The dissolution of the federation resulted in the formation of the autonomous country of Saint Martin in 2010. The island country remains a self-governing part of the Dutch kingdom, which supports the island economy with generous welfare and economic subsidies.

Further Reading

Greey, Madeleine. *Saint Martin/Sint Maarten: Portrait of an Island.* Oxford, UK: Macmillan Caribbean, 2005.

Hillebrink, Steven. *The Right to Self-Determination and Post-Colonial Governance: The Case of the Netherlands Antilles and Aruba.* The Hague, Netherlands: T.M.C. Asser, 2008.

Russell, Jesse and Ronald Cohn. *Saint Martin.* Paris: VSD, 2012.

Salvadorans

The Salvadorans, sometimes known as Salvadoreans, Guanacos, or Salvadoreños, are a Central American people, the inhabitants of the Republic of El Salvador on the region's Pacific coast. People of Salvadoran heritage are often referred to as Cuscatlecos or Cuscatlecas. Outside their homeland there are sizable Salvadoran communities in the United States, Canada, Mexico, Guatemala, Costa Rica, Australia, Sweden, and Spain. The estimated 8.5 million Salvadorans speak Spanish with many also speaking English, especially among the 2 million living in other countries. The Salvadorans are mostly Christian, with just over half belonging to the Roman Catholic Church and about 28 percent being Protestants.

The territory that is now El Salvador was inhabited by various indigenous peoples, including the Mayan Chortis in the north, the Pipils in the western and central regions, and the Lenca, who settled the eastern territories. In the 15th century the Pipil empire of Cuscatlán became the dominant power with a wide-ranging trading network in woven fabrics and agricultural produce, particularly cacao. The Pipil cultivation of cacao involved a vast and sophisticated irrigation system and was especially lucrative. Trade in cacao reached as far north as central Mexico. In 1524 Spanish conquistadores moved south into Central America fresh from their conquest of central Mexico and the Mayan territories. Accompanied by thousands of Mayan allies, the Spanish forces using superior weapons massacred the Pipil warriors in two major battles. The surviving Pipils retreated to the mountains where they continued to resist the Spanish invaders. Two subsequent Spanish expeditions were sent to achieve the complete defeat of Cuscatlán in 1525–1526. Resistance continued as the Pipils and Lencas joined forces to again drive out the invaders from the region. For 10 years the resistance prevented the Spanish from building a permanent settlement until the Lencas and Pipils were finally overcome in 1537. The Spanish called the newly conquered region "Provincia de Nuesta Señor Jesus Cristo, El Salvador del Mundo," later shortened to El Salvador. The province formed part of the Spanish government of Guatemala as an administrative division of New Spain. The Spanish replaced the indigenous communal tradition with a system of private property. The *encomienda* system obliged the conquered peoples to work in Spanish mines and on plantations in order to pay a large annual tax. The colonial society was highly stratified with the *Peninsulares*, Spaniards born in Spain, at the top, followed by the *criollos*, Europeans born in the Americas, and then the rapidly increasing population of *mestizos* of mixed European and indigenous ancestry, who had some rights but could not own private property. The indigenous peoples, the former rulers of the territory, were relegated to the bottom of society where they were exploited and mistreated.

The Salvadoran culture is dominated by the Mestizos, who form the largest segment of the society. The culture displays many influences from both the pre-Columbian cultures and the later European Spanish traditions. The practice of Spanish men coming to the New World in search of treasure instead of as settlers resulted in a large number of marriages between the Spanish colonists and indigenous women. Traditionally the Roman Catholic Church plays an important part in Salvadoran culture. Early cultural expressions were most often based on religious themes. Painting, ceramics, and textiles that show the traditions of both the indigenous peoples and the later European groups remain the principal artistic mediums. Like the arts, Salvadoran cuisine is also a blend of influences. The most common dish is *pupusa*, hand-made corn or rice tortillas stuffed with cheese, refried beans, eggs, or meats, which reflects the indigenous food heritage. The large number of Salvadorans living in the United States and Canada and the growth of tourism in recent years have added North American elements to the culture, including shopping malls, fine restaurants, and elegant shopping districts. The Spanish language, the language of education and government, is spoken in a specifically Salvadoran dialect known as Caliche, the language of daily life. The Spanish heritage is evident in religion, with most Salvadorans belonging to Christian churches, particularly the Roman Catholic Church. The Protestant groups, especially the Mormons and Pentecostals, are growing rapidly, influenced by the Salvadoran community in North America.

In the early 19th century dissatisfaction with Spanish rule, particularly the domination of the region by European-born Spaniards, spread among the locally born Europeans and the large Mestizo population. War in Europe and other factors motivated the colony's elite to attempt to gain independence from distant Spain. The 1811 Independence Movement, supported by much of the Salvadoran population, failed. The leaders of the insurrection were arrested but another uprising was launched in 1814, though it was again suppressed. As unrest spread across Central America, the Spanish authorities finally capitulated and signed the *Acta de Independencia*, which released the Central American territories of Guatemala, El Salvador, Honduras, Nicaragua, Costa Rica, and Chiapas from Spanish rule in 1821. The Central American states joined newly independent Mexico in 1822, but soon broke away though Chiapas remained part of Mexico. The territories formed the Federal Republic of Central America, which was dissolved in 1841 and the Central American territories became separate republics. In the mid-19th century the economy was dominated by the growing of coffee, with the country suffering or prospering as the price of coffee fluctuated. The enormous profits from coffee served as an impetus for the concentration of fertile land in the hands of an oligarchy of just a few wealthy families while the majority of the population lived in poverty. The government of El Salvador, drawn from the oligarchy families, saw its primary responsibility as the support of the coffee industry. The last communal lands of the indigenous peoples were confiscated for further coffee production, and antivagrancy laws were adopted to ensure that the now landless *campesinos* and other rural indigenous or mestizo workers provided sufficient labor for the coffee plantations. In 1912, the government created a military force, the National Guard, to protect the coffee industry and to enforce the harsh labor laws. In the early 20th century political instability and conflicts with the neighboring Central American republics retarded progress and reinforced the rule of the oligarchy. A military coup overthrew the government in 1931, with the rebels later endorsed by the U.S. government that insisted on new presidential elections. Instability continued to haunt the Salvadorans with labor problems, strikes, leftist resistance groups, and economic downturns during the next three decades. During this period the social activists and revolutionary leader Farabundo Martí founded the Communist Party of Central America, which supported a guerilla revolt among the country's indigenous farmers. The government responded with the mass killing of over 30,000 people in 1932, an event that became known as *La Matanza*, The Slaughter. The communist-led rebellion, triggered by collapsing coffee prices, enjoyed initial success but was soon drowned by the bloodbath. Martí was arrested and was later shot after a perfunctory hearing. The high density of population in El Salvador contributed to ongoing tensions with neighboring Honduras and Guatemala as land-poor Salvadorans migrated to the less densely populated regions of adjacent states to establish themselves as squatters on vacant or underused lands. In 1960 two new political parties were established that continue to the present, one representing the growing urban middle class and the other dominated by the Salvadoran military. The two parties dominated Salvadoran politics, particularly following the 1969 Football War with neighboring Honduras. The conflict began with a football match that was won by El Salvador, adding to the already tense situation in the region. Fighting erupted on the border and before the short war could be stopped, over 130,000 Salvadorans were forcibly expelled or fled the anger of the Hondurans. Another military coup installed a revolutionary government in 1979 that quickly nationalized many private companies and took over much privately owned land. Unrest and violence spread as the poor took to the streets to demand the right to unionize labor, agrarian reform, better wages for their labor, primary health care, and basic freedoms such as education and the freedom of expression. Revolutionary groups, often under leftist leaders, organized students, workers, and the indigenous population. The United States supported the forces opposed to the leftist groups and began to arm the anticommunist government troops. The Salvadoran Civil War repeatedly swept across the country from 1980 to 1992. Thousands of Salvadorans fled north to the United States, Canada, and Mexico or across the borders into the neighboring republics. By the early 1990s, between 500,000 and one million Salvadorans, mostly refugees, were in the United States, where their status was disputed and regulations and laws made their status in the country uncertain. In 1992 peace agreements ended the fighting though most Salvadorans did not return to their country. Economic reforms since the early 1990s quickly improved social conditions for the poor and landless majority. Political insecurity and economic problems continue to send a steady stream of Salvadorans to other countries in the early 21st century.

Further Reading

Shields, Charles J. *El Salvador.* Bromall, PA: Mason Crest, 2007.

White, Christopher M. *The History of El Salvador.* Westport, CT: Greenwood, 2008.

Wood, Elisabeth Jean. *Insurgent Collective Action and Civil War in El Salvador.* Cambridge, UK: Cambridge University Press, 2003.

Saramaccas

The Saramaccas, sometimes known as Saramakas, Saamákas, or Saramaccans, are a South American ethnic group living in the interior regions of Suriname and French Guiana. The estimated 60,000 Saramaccas speak the Saramaccan language with a minority also speaking English, French, Dutch, or Portuguese. The traditional Saramacca religion is still practiced by about 80 percent of the population with Christian minorities including Roman Catholics, Moravians, and Evangelical Protestants.

The ancestors of the Saramaccas were African slaves captured and sold into slavery in the 17th and early 18th centuries.

Brought by ship from West Africa they were sold in slave markets to European owners of sugar, timber, sugarcane, and coffee plantations in the Dutch colonies in northeastern South America. Treatment of the slaves was notoriously bad, and many slaves escaped from the plantations and moved into the dense rain forest. Aided by the indigenous peoples, the slaves settled in villages in the upper reaches of the Suriname River and its tributaries. Individuals, small groups, and sometimes large numbers during the frequent slave rebellions escaped the harsh life of slavery on the plantations. For nearly a century they fought the Dutch forces sent to recapture them, a war of independence that was finally won in 1762, when they signed a treaty with the Dutch colonial government and were recognized as free people. Their liberty came a full century before the general emancipation of the African slaves in Suriname. In their rain forest home the escaped slaves, from many tribes and regions of West Africa, evolved a common culture and a distinct language that combined the Portuguese of many of the slave masters on the Suriname plantations with borrowings from Dutch and English and the vocabulary and structures of their African languages. The Saramaccas survived by the exploitation of the rain forest environment, with shifting agriculture, hunting, and fishing.

The Saramaccas are a Maroon people, often called Bush Negros in Suriname, though the name "Maroon" derives from the Spanish word *cimarrón*, which refers to an animal that was once domesticated but that has reverted to a wild state. The word was used from the early 1500s throughout the Americas to designate slaves who successfully escaped from their masters. Saramacca culture is strong and egalitarian, with kinship ordering the social organization. Extended families often occupy an entire village. Elders are accorded great respect and ancestors are consulted, through the help of local practitioners, on a daily basis as part of the Saramacca religious beliefs. The government-approved paramount chief is the nominal head of the tribe, assisted by local headmen and assistant headmen. The role of these officials in political and social life is dominated by various clans, based on a tradition of spiritual consultations that is quickly eroding as modern culture reaches even the most remote Saramacca villages. Saramacca men devote a large part of their time to earning wages in the coastal regions of Suriname and French Guiana in order to provide the manufactured goods considered essential to live in their remote villages, such as guns and powder, tools, iron pots, cloth, hammocks, soap, kerosene, and rum. Since the 1960s such imports as outboard motors, transistor radios, and tape recorders have become part of the local culture. The Saramacca belief system is prevalent in all aspects of daily life. Decisions such as where to plant a garden, build a house, or undertake a trip are made in consultation with the local village deities, the revered ancestors, forest spirits, and the snake gods. Gods and spirits, a constant presence in daily life, are also honored through frequent prayers, libations, special feasts, and music and dance. The Saramacca language is a mixed language that has evolved from the slavery experience blended with the many African languages spoken by the escaped slaves. About 50 percent of the lexicon derives from the various West and Central African languages, perhaps 20 percent from English, the language of the original European settlers in the region, another 20 percent from Portuguese, the language of many of the slave masters on the Suriname plantations, and the remaining 10 percent from Dutch and the indigenous languages of the rain forest peoples.

The Saramaccas lived in isolation, recreating as much as they could of the life remembered from their African homelands in the Suriname rain forest. Slavery in Suriname was officially abolished in 1863, though most slaves in the colony were not released until 10 years later. Many of the freed slaves moved into the interior to join the Maroon tribes. Like the other Maroon groups, the Saramaccas remained apart from the colonial government until the mid-20th century when the pace of outside contacts increased. A huge hydroelectric project constructed in their territory displaced thousands of Saramaccas in the 1960s. New villages were constructed for those forced from their traditional villages and they were rehoused in areas along the lower Suriname River. In 1980, a military coup overthrew the Suriname government and a socialist republic was declared. Several antigovernment activists escaped into the rain forest where they sheltered with the Maroon population. In 1986 government soldiers searching for rebel leaders attacked a Saramacca village at Moiwana leading to the massacre of 35 inhabitants, mostly women and children. Thousands of Saramaccas and other Maroons fled across the border into French Guiana. By mid-1989 over 3,000 Saramaccas were living in refugee camps in neighboring parts of French Guiana. The war between the Maroon peoples and government forces brought great hardships and devastation to the Saramaccas. The war ended in the mid-1990s but the needs of the Saramaccas were mostly ignored while the government granted large timber and mining concessions to foreign companies in traditional Saramacca territory without consulting the Saramacca authorities. An invasion of Brazilian gold miners further disrupted traditional Saramacca villages. In the 1990s the Association of Saramacca Authorities initiated a complaint before the Inter-American Commission on Human Rights in an effort to protect their land rights. In 2007 the Inter-American Court ruled in favor of the Saramaccas. The landmark decision established a precedent for all Maroon and indigenous groups in the Americas. The Saramaccas secured the collective rights to the lands on which their ancestors had settled since the early 18th century, including the right to decide on the exploitation of the region's natural resources. They were also granted compensation by the government for damages caused by previous logging grants given to Chinese companies in their territory. In another major victory, in 2005 the Inter-American Court ordered the Suriname government to pay $3 million in compensation to the 130 survivors of the Moiwana massacre.

Further Reading

Bilby, Kenneth. *True-Born Maroons.* Gainesville, FL: University Press of Florida, 2008.

Price, Richard. *First-Time: The Historical Vision of an African American People.* Chicago, IL: University of Chicago Press, 2002.

Price, Richard. *Rainforest Warriors: Human Rights on Trial.* Philadelphia, PA: University of Pennsylvania Press, 2010.

Seminoles

The Seminoles are a North American ethnic group concentrated in two regions of the United States, primarily in the states of Oklahoma and Florida. The estimated 22,000 Seminoles speak English as their first language with many also retaining their ancestral language. The majority of the Seminoles are Christians, largely Protestant but with a sizable Roman Catholic minority. Some Seminoles continue to practice the ceremonies, feasting, and religious observations associated with their pre-Christian *Posketv*, known in English as the Green Corn Ceremony.

The original inhabitants settled in the region as early as 12,000 years ago, living as hunter-gatherer bands until the woodland period of their history, from 1000 BCE to 1000 CE, an epoch that saw the development of pottery and small-scale horticulture. The cultivation of stable food crops such as beans, squash, and corn allowed for a larger population and the rise of urban centers and regional chiefdoms. The Mississippian culture, based on a stratified society with hereditary religious and political elites, flourished in the southeastern, eastern, and midwestern regions of the present-day United States from about 800 CE to 1500 CE. The early Muscogee peoples are believed to have descended from the advanced Mississippian society along the Tennessee River in present-day Tennessee, Georgia, and Alabama. The Spanish expeditions that explored parts of the southeast in the mid-1500s introduced European diseases that caused many fatalities and a sharp decline in the population leading to the collapse of the Mississippian culture. As the survivors and their descendants reorganized they formed the Muscogee or Creek Confederacy, a loose alliance of Muscogee-speaking bands. The confederacy consisted of two geographic areas populated by the Upper Creeks in the north and the Lower Creeks in the south. The bands traded with the English, French, and Spanish colonies established along the coast. British influence among the Lower Creeks resulted in French instigation of the Upper Creeks to raid their kin in the south. In 1718 the Creeks informed the European colonial powers of their neutrality in the ongoing wars between the Europeans but encroachments and conflicts continued. The Seminoles emerged as a separate tribal unit in the mid-18th century from among refugees of a number of southeastern tribes fleeing the violence into the less accessible regions of Florida. Elements from the Lower Creeks became the dominant group among the newly formed bands. The Spanish rulers of Florida, uninterested in the interior of the peninsula, mostly left the indigenous peoples in peace though contagious diseases continued to take a toll. In 1763 the English took control of Florida, and when the Spanish left for Cuba they took most of the coastal peoples with them as slaves. Returned to Spanish rule in 1783, new groups moved into the region from the new United States and expanded into their southeastern homelands. Escaped slaves from European and American plantations joined the bands in Florida.

Seminole areas were often raided by U.S. troops in pursuit of runaway slaves from the southern states.

Seminole culture is divided into two geographically distinct regions, with the larger number of Seminoles living in the state of Oklahoma and smaller numbers, divided into the Seminoles and the Miccosukees, in Florida. Though distinct politically the various bands share the historic Seminole culture. Local customs and adaptations have changed the cultures of the two regions but the historic culture has been retained by all Seminoles. Traditional Seminole culture evolved from a blending of a number of distinct cultures brought to Florida from refugees and migrants in the 18th and early 19th centuries. The culture is divided into eight traditional clans that remain an important part of Seminole society. Historically Seminole men were hunters and fishermen while women tended farms, took care of children, and prepared meals. Both men and women take part in storytelling, a way of passing on the rich oral history. Artwork, music, and traditional medicine are also shared by both genders. Although historically only men could be chiefs, modern Seminole culture allows women to participate in tribal governments. Basketry, adopted as an art form over 60 years ago, utilizes the sweet grass that grows wild in Florida. Christianity plays an important role in the culture with both Protestant and Roman Catholic faiths represented. The Green Corn Ceremony, still celebrated annually, is a pre-Christian tradition that included purification rites and transition-to-manhood ceremonies. Tribal disputes were also addressed during this time. The first language of most

Seminoles is now English with many also able to speak one or both of the traditional languages used by the Seminoles, Muscogee (Creek) and Mikasuki.

The expanding settlements of the United States increasingly encroached on indigenous lands in the early 19th century. A steady migration south into Spanish Florida continued to add to the indigenous population. Conflicts and skirmishes between the Creeks and the Americans led to the Creek War in 1813–1814, sending a new wave of refugees south into Florida. Attacks from Florida on settlements in Georgia resulted in a military campaign led by Gen. Andrew Jackson in 1817–1818. The invasion, known as the First Seminole War, ended with the U.S. forces in effective control of East Florida. A treaty, signed in 1819, ceded the Spanish colony of Florida to the United States in 1821. As American settlement increased in Florida pressure grew to remove the indigenous peoples from the most fertile lands coveted by the Americans moving into the region. In 1832, a few Seminole chiefs signed a treaty agreeing to leave Florida voluntarily for new lands west of the Mississippi River. The Seminoles who opposed the move prepared for war. A U.S. military expedition moved into the region to enforce the treaty in 1835, setting off the Second Seminole War. Led by Osceola, the vastly outnumbered Seminoles and the allied Black Seminoles, the descendants of escaped slaves, faced a modern force of army and militia. Employing guerrilla tactics with devastating effect on the American soldiers, the Seminoles continued to fight for two years. In 1837, Osceola, under a flag of truce, agreed to attend negotiations with the U.S. authorities. He and his chiefs were arrested and he died in jail less than a year later. His body was buried without the head, which was preserved as a prize of war. Other Seminole and Black Seminole leaders continued the resistance against the army. After a decade of conflict the war finally ended in 1842. Many captured Seminoles were exiled to Creek lands west of the Mississippi, others escaped south into the Everglades. In the end the government, economically drained by the long conflict, gave up trying to subjugate the surviving 500 Seminoles in Florida. As a result of the war, about 3,800 Seminoles and Black Seminoles were forcibly removed from their historic lands and sent west on the "Trail of Tears" to Indian Territory, the present state of Oklahoma. The Seminoles settled in the arid region but retained their tribal structure and culture. During the American Civil War, the Seminoles of Oklahoma were divided with some supporting the Union while others allied with the Confederacy. After the war, the U.S. government negotiated only with the loyal Seminoles, requiring them to make a new peace treaty, to emancipate their black slaves, and to extend tribal membership to the freed slaves who chose to remain in Seminole territory. Pushed into the less desirable territory as their best lands were confiscated or stolen, the Seminoles in Florida rebelled, setting off the Third Seminole War of 1855–1856. At the end of the conflict, probably fewer than 200 Seminoles remained alive in Florida, mostly in the inaccessible areas of the Everglades. After the conflict ended, the Seminoles in Florida divided into two groups: those who preferred the traditional way of life and those willing to adapt to the reservations. Those who adapted were recognized as the Seminole Tribe of Florida, while those who retained their traditional way organized themselves as the Miccosukee Tribe. The Seminoles in Florida began to move into federally designated reservation lands set aside in 1891 though many distrusted the U.S. government and feared forced removal to Oklahoma. In the 1940s, some Seminoles began to move to the reservation lands, mostly newly converted Christians. In 1957 the Seminole Tribe of Florida established formal ties with the U.S. government and set up its headquarters in Hollywood, Florida. In 1962 the Miccosukees also signed an agreement that confirmed their sovereignty over tribal lands and agreed to compensation for lost or stolen territory. In the late 20th century the Seminoles in Florida have prospered from the lucrative casinos, resorts, golf clubs, and museum attractions established on reservation lands. In 2006, they purchased the worldwide Hard Rock Café chain of restaurants and resorts. In Florida the Seminoles include two bands known as Freedmen or Black Seminoles, partly descended from escaped or freed slaves. The acculturation of the Seminoles to modern American culture has evolved a blending of the traditional and the modern that allows the Seminoles to retain their unique culture while participating fully in modern life.

Further Reading

Missall, John and Mary Lou Missall. *The Seminole Wars: America's Longest Indian*

Conflict. Gainesville, FL: University Press of Florida, 2004.

Yacowitz, Caryn. *Seminole Indians.* Mankato, MN: Heinemann Raintree, 2003.

Wesiman, Brent R. *Unconquered People: Florida's Seminole and Miccosukee Indians.* Gainesville, FL: University Press of Florida, 1999.

Shipibo-Conibos

The Shipibo-Conibos, sometimes known as Shipibo-Konibos, are a South American ethnic group living along the Ucayali River and its tributaries in the Amazon region of eastern Peru and adjacent areas of Brazil. Formerly two separate peoples, the Shipibos and the Conibos combined through intermarriage and communal rituals over several centuries. The estimated 32,000 Shipibo-Conibos speak a Panoan language, which is an official language in Peru. Many also speak Spanish, particularly the younger people. The majority of the Shipibo-Conibos adhere to their traditional belief system with a minority having converted to Christianity since the mid-19th century.

Anthropological and archaeological evidence suggests that the Shipibo-Conibos or their ancestors have inhabited the rain forests along the Ucayali River for over 1,000 years. Some elements of their material culture indicate historic contact with the advanced Inca civilization of the highlands to the west. Traditionally Shipibo-Conibo communities were linked by kinship ties and marriage. Conflicts and raids on neighboring peoples for women and slaves were common. In the 17th century Spanish Franciscan missionaries entered their territory. During this time some were converted to Roman Catholicism and many more were resettled in missionary-controlled villages. After a number of attacks on the missions the Franciscans withdrew from the area until the mid-18th century, but once again a Shipibo-Conibo uprising resulted in the destruction of a mission station.

Shipibo-Conibo culture is traditionally based on an egalitarian society, with the male heads belonging to the largest families and having the most wives exercising the greatest authority. In the 20th century the Peruvian government imposed a political structure but the elected positions carry little authority. Many of those holding office are the younger Shipibo-Conibos who speak Spanish, and this has begun to undermine the status and traditional influence of the tribal elders. The Shipibo-Conibo word for "people" is *jonibo*, and their social world is divided between themselves (*noa jonibo* [we people]) and all outsiders (*nahua jonibo* [less than people]). Though many are now Christian, their traditional beliefs are still practiced, particularly *ayahuasca* or shamanism. Traditional shamanistic chants and songs have inspired the artistic forms and decorative designs found in Shipibo-Conibo clothing, tools, pottery, and textiles. Acculturation into the largely mestizo culture and the Spanish language is more advanced among the urbanized Shipibo-Conibos living around the city of Pucallpa, the largest urban center in the region. Farther from the urbanized areas the traditional culture remains predominant. The Shipibo-Conibo language belongs to the Pano-Tacanan language family and is spo-ken in four regional dialects.

Roman Catholic missionaries were able to establish a permanent base in the region in the early 19th century though many bands did not see a white person until the early 20th century. With their strategic location on the important Ucayali River, the Shipibo-Conibos had contact with Spanish gold hunters, miners, and explorers and therefore access to guns. In the early 19th century they used the guns to raid other indigenous groups, which spread unrest and chaos throughout the region. In the 1840s, Franciscan missionaries settled several Shipibo-Conibo families at a small settlement near the Ucayali River. The settlement, isolated by the Amazonian rain forest and the Andes mountain range, remained a center of contact between the Shipibo-Conibos and the outside world until it was finally connected with the rest of Peru by a highway through the mountains in 1945. The highway allowed colonists to begin settling the region, with the Shipibo-Conibos soon forming only a small minority of the population. In the later 20th century outside influences such as logging, oil prospecting, drug trafficking, conservationists, and Protestant and Roman Catholic missionaries have threatened the Shipibo-Conibos and their way of life. Global warming is also becoming a major threat, as fruit trees have mostly died off because of the severe cycles of drought and floods.

Further Reading

Bergman, Ronald. *Amazon Economics: The Simplicity of Shipibo Indian Wealth.* Syracuse, NY: Dellplain, 1980.

Eakin, Lucille and Erwin Lauriault. *People of the Ucayali: The Shipibo and Conibo of Peru.* Dallas, TX: SIL International, 1986.

Farabee, William Curtis. *Indian Tribes of Eastern Peru.* Charleston, SC: Nabu Press, 2010.

Sioux

The Sioux, sometimes known as Lakotas, Dakotas, Dahoctahs, or Nakotas, are a North American ethnic group concentrated in the U.S. states of South Dakota, North Dakota, Minnesota, Nebraska, and Montana and the Canadian provinces of Manitoba, Saskatchewan, and Alberta. The estimated 215,000 Sioux use English as their first language, though around 40,000 speak the Sioux language, a language of the Siouan language family. Most of the Sioux are Christian, often mixing traditional beliefs with their Christian rites, with some adhering to the Native American Church.

The origins of the Sioux are not known, with several theories tracing their origins to the Black Hills region of South Dakota, an area that is still considered sacred to the Sioux. Other theories claim they migrated to the Black Hills from the woodlands of present-day Minnesota. Historically the Great Sioux Nation comprised seven member tribes known as the Seven Council Fires. Each year the Mdewakanton, Wahpeton, Wahpekute, Sisseton, Yankton, Yanktonai, and the Teton or Lakota would gather for a great summer council to renew kinships, decide on tribal matters, and participate in the Sun Dance. The seven members would select four leaders from among the tribal chiefs to lead the united tribes for the next year. The ceremonies and sharing of the great councils reaffirmed tribal ties and their common culture and language. French Jesuit missionaries first encountered the people they called the Sioux near the Great Lakes in the early 17th century. The Sioux tribes, mostly living in small agricultural villages, ranged over a large territory, including a northern group living in the valleys of the Missouri River and its tributaries and a southern group occupying the upper Mississippi Valley. In the late 17th century many of the Sioux bands migrated southwest into present South Dakota to escape hostile neighboring tribes, particularly the Ojibwes who were equipped with French firearms. The horse, first introduced to the Great Plains by early Spanish explorers, first appeared in the northern Great Plains at the beginning of the 18th century. The horse revolutionized the lives of the tribes as horse culture spread throughout the region. By the mid-18th century most of the Sioux had abandoned agriculture and moved from the woodlands into the flat northern plains, where they evolved a nomadic culture based on horses and the hunting of buffalo. The Sioux peoples, in the late 1700s, dominated a vast area of the Great Plains, with their spiritual center in South Dakota's Black Hills, which they settled around 1775.

The Sioux culture shares many traits and customs with other indigenous cultures of the Great Plains of North America while retaining many historical elements unique to Sioux society. The blending of the traditional culture with modern American culture has allowed the Sioux to function within the wider American society while retaining their own traditions and customs.

Sioux Indian "Chief Wild Horse" and family on the Pine Ridge Reservation, Shannon County, South Dakota, 1909. (USGS)

Skilled artisans, the Sioux have worked to retain their skills in beadwork, quilt making, carving, drum making, pipe making, and leatherwork. These are the crafts and skills that have been handed down from generation to generation. Many of these inherited arts are displayed each year, usually during the summer season, at annual fairs or powwows that reaffirm the cultural and kinship ties of the Sioux and give visitors a chance to learn more about the traditional culture. The basic unit of the Sioux culture is the *tiyospaye*, a group of related families that form an extended clan or family. The *tiyospaye* evolved during the time of the great buffalo hunts and worked as a highly mobile unit capable of daily movement if necessary. Acculturation, assimilation, and intermarriage with non-Sioux have diluted traditional family and community relationships, particularly among the growing number of urban Sioux. The more rural or isolated communities are usually the most culturally traditional. Most of the Sioux are Christians, both Roman Catholic and Protestant, though many continue to practice the Sun Dance, also known as the Offering Lodge ceremony. It is one of seven sacred ceremonies and is the most well known among the general population though attendance by tourists is not encouraged. Many of the rites and traditions of the historic Sioux religion are still practiced with many non-Sioux adopting parts of the religion as part of a new-age spiritual movement. Until the American Indians Religious Freedom Act of 1978, the practice of Indian religions was a crime in the United States. The Sioux language was once more widely spoken until groups of speakers developed distinct tribal cultures

and are now not considered as Sioux. The language is divided into three broad dialect groups: Eastern Dakota, also called Santee-Sisseton or Dakhóta, Western Dakota, also called Yankton-Yanktonai or Dakhóta, and Lakota, also known as Lakhóta, Teton, or Teto Sioux. The term Dakota has been used by scholars and government agencies to refer to all Sioux groups so that names such as Teton Dakota, Santee Dakota, or Ogalala Dakota are often used by non-Sioux.

By 1800 the Sioux tribes dominated a vast region of mountains, prairies, and river valleys embracing most of present-day South Dakota, and parts of North Dakota, Minnesota, Montana, Wyoming, Nebraska, Iowa, and Wisconsin in the United States and the southern plains of Manitoba, Saskatchewan, and Alberta in western Canada. Much of the region was included in the huge territory purchased by the U.S. government from France in 1803, the Louisiana Purchase. American explorers and officials found that the Sioux did not recognize the sale of their territory, leading to many confrontations and misunderstandings. The American authorities signed treaties with the Sioux in 1815, 1825, and 1851, but each time the terms of the treaties were ignored by the Americans and encroachments on Sioux lands continued. In the 1840s and 1850s a steady flow of wagon trains and parties of men passed through Sioux territory on their way to the California gold fields. They brought with them diseases such as measles and smallpox that swept through the Sioux population, which declined by an estimated one-half. The 1851 First Treaty of Laramie recognized the Sioux territory, a huge tract of territory in the unknown West, and formalized the Sioux status as an independent political community or sovereign nation. Conflicts, violence, mistrust, and the steady advance of the American frontier pushed the Sioux peoples westward. The wanton destruction of the buffalo herds on which the Sioux depended for most of their food and material culture finally provoked violence in 1856. Most of the Sioux attempted to remain at peace, roaming the plains in winter and returning to the sacred Black Hills each spring to conduct tribal business and religious ceremonies and to summer in the cooler highlands. Continued violence between the Sioux and the ever increasing number of miners, settlers, and buffalo hunters encroaching on their lands finally erupted in open warfare in 1862. Sioux warriors attacked the farms and settlements of the colonists, killing over 800 settlers and soldiers in Minnesota. Reprisals included attacks on Sioux camps and the mass trial of 303 Santee Sioux, all sentenced to be hanged. President Abraham Lincoln commuted the death sentence of 284 of the warriors, many of whom later died in jail. The execution of 38 Sioux warriors by hanging in December 1862 was the largest mass execution in U.S. history. Many Sioux fled across the border into Canada to escape attacks that did not discriminate between those who had participated in the revolt and those who remained carefully neutral or even aided beleaguered white settlers. Farther west a second conflict, known as Red Cloud's War or the Bozeman War, erupted in Wyoming and Montana territories in 1866–1869 following encroachments on Sioux territory by the U.S. military and land-hungry settlers. The war ended with the Treaty of Fort Laramie that allowed the Sioux to retain

control of much of their western lands. In the Second Treaty of Fort Laramie, signed in 1868, the U.S. government guaranteed Sioux possession of a large territory west of the Missouri River. Despite treaties, agreements, and promises settlers continued to pour into Sioux lands, including the sacred Black Hills, where gold was discovered. Gold hunters poured into the region, digging into the sacred lands of the Black Hills and often attacking Sioux camps that stood in their way. The conflicts merged into a wider war known as the Great Sioux War of 1876–1877. The war, also known as the Black Hills War, comprised a series of battles between the Lakota Sioux and allied tribes against the U.S. military. Among the famous battles the most well known was the Battle of the Little Bighorn. According to the legend of Colonel Custer and command there were no survivors of the battle, yet some 1,500 Sioux and their allies survived. Soon after the battle the hard-pressed Sioux surrendered, but in direct violation of the 1868 treaty they were expelled from their sacred Black Hills and driven west into the arid Badlands to small reservations. Poverty, neglect, alcoholism, and the disruption of family life took a heavy toll on the reservations. The Ghost Dance religion, which spread through the tribes in the late 1800s, preached the coming of a savior, a return to their traditional way of life, and a grand reunion with the dead. The Sioux, after suffering harsh privations while confined to the reservations, embraced the new religion as their only hope. The U.S. authorities, believing that the ceremonies of the new religion were disrupting the uneasy peace, ordered the arrest of the leaders. The famous Chief Sitting Bull was killed in 1890 while being taken into custody. A band of starving Sioux warriors and their families fled the reservations to take refuge in the Badlands. They were captured in December 1890 at Wounded Knee. A scuffle broke out and an army officer was wounded. Without warning the soldiers opened fire and within minutes nearly 200 men, women, and children had been shot and killed. The massacre at Wounded Knee is considered the last major conflict of the Sioux Wars. With no alternative, the Sioux settled on the reservations, with no rights and often under the authority of corrupt or dishonest officials. At first attempts were made to acculturate the Sioux, including taking children from their families and sending them to far-away schools for Indians run along military lines. Then, in the mid-20th century, attempts were made to legislate them out of existence through an official policy of "termination" of indigenous nations. Only in recent decades have there been attempts on the part of the American authorities to redress past injustices. During the 1960s, the period of the civil rights movements, some concessions were made to recognize and respect the remaining vestiges of Sioux sovereignty. Activists mobilized young Sioux to demand their rights as American citizens and to petition the government to honor at least some of the many treaties signed with the Sioux. Militants of the American Indian Movement (AIM) took over the town of Wounded Knee in 1973 to bring attention to their demands. They held the town for 71 days while various enforcement agencies, such as the FBI, laid siege. Two of the activists were killed by gunfire during the standoff. Legislation passed in 1978–1979

finally allowed indigenous peoples to practice their traditional religions. Many younger Sioux left the reservations for urban centers in search of jobs or simply to leave behind the dismal life of the reservations. In recent years the uncontrolled exploitation of reservation lands by loggers, miners, and others contracted by the U.S. government has left the lands heavily polluted; four decades of uranium mining in the Black Hills left the area's rivers poisoned. Radioactive sands from the tailings have scattered across the reservation lands, and the Sioux are suffering devastating health defects. Government funds set aside to compensate the Sioux for the loss of the sacred Black Hills, some $100 million in 1980, has grown with interest to over $700 million in 2010. The Sioux refuse to accept the money, claiming that to do so would be selling their heritage. Many local and federal officials consider the Sioux attitude as foolish pride, but Sioux leaders reply that pride is all they have left.

Further Reading

Gagnon, Gregory O. *Culture and Customs of the Sioux Indians.* Westport, CT: Greenwood, 2011.

Gibbon, Guy. *The Sioux: The Dakota and Lakota Nations.* Hoboken, NJ: Wiley-Blackwell, 2002.

Ostler, Jeffrey. *The Lakotas and the Black Hills: The Struggle for Sacred Ground.* London: Penguin Books, 2011.

Surinamese

The Surinamese are a South American people, the inhabitants or descendants of the many people who settled the Republic of Suriname in northern South America. The estimated 1 million Surinamese include some 350,000 living in the Netherlands and sizable communities in the United States, Curaçao, Brazil, and Trinidad and Tobago. Most of the Surinamese speak Dutch, the official language of the country, along with Sranan Tongo, a creole language understood by about 90 percent of the population, and Sarnami Hindustani, Javanese, Maroon languages, or Amerindian dialects. The largest segment of the population is Christian, including both Roman Catholics and Protestants, with sizable Hindu and Muslim minorities.

The indigenous peoples of the region, known as Amerindians, are believed to have inhabited the area as early as 3000 BCE. The coastal regions and rain forests were home to many distinct indigenous cultures. The first Europeans to sight the coast were the Dutch, who called the region the "Wild Coast." The first attempt to settle was by the English in 1630 and it was a financial failure. A later English expedition from Barbados founded a small colony in 1650. By 1663 some 1,000 Europeans, including Brazilian Jews drawn to the region by religious tolerance, oversaw a fort and plantations worked by indigenous peoples and some 3,000 African slaves. In 1667 the settlement was invaded by a Dutch expedition that renamed the settlement Fort Zeelandia. A later treaty confirmed Dutch control of Suriname and the cession of the Dutch colony of New Amsterdam (New York) to English control. The indigenous peoples fled into the interior to escape the European slavers so captives from Africa were imported as slave labor. By the early 1700s some 200 plantations worked by 13,000 African slaves produced sugar, cotton, coffee, and cocoa for the markets of the Netherlands. Treatment of the slaves was notoriously bad, and slaves escaped into the rain forests from the beginning. The escaped slaves, known as Maroons, formed tribes and often raided plantations to acquire needed goods and to liberate slave women. In the 1760s, a century before the abolition of slavery in the Dutch colonies, the colonial authorities signed treaties with the Maroon tribes recognizing them as free peoples of the interior districts of the colony. The colony prospered though the colonial settlements were mostly limited to the fertile coastal plains. War in Europe also involved the colonies. In 1799 the British occupied Suriname following the French invasion of the Netherlands.

The culture of Suriname is diverse, including influences from the Dutch and English, traditions brought to the region by the African slaves, and later traditions from the East Asians who settled in the colony in the 19th and 20th century. The Surinamese population includes people of European, African, East Indian, Chinese, Indonesian, Amerindian, and Maroon ancestry as well as smaller groups of Caribbean peoples. The cultural contributions of each group have been blended into the country's unique culture. The center of Surinamese culture is Paramaribo, the Surinamese capital and the country's only large city. Surinamese music, such as *kaseko*, is a fusion of many styles adopted from the folklore of Europe, Africa, and the Americas. Another important musical style is known as Indo-Surinamese, a mixture of local rhythms and the folk music that arrived with immigrants from East Asia. Sports are an important part of the culture, with association football being the most popular sport. The unique Surinamese cuisine is also a blend of dishes, incorporating influences from Indian, Creole, Javanese, Chinese, Dutch, Jewish, Portuguese, and Amerindian traditions. Like the other cultural elements, the religions of the Surinamese are diverse; the population comprises about 48 percent Christians, 27 percent Hindus, 20 percent Muslims, 5 percent people of indigenous religions, and smaller groups of Jews and others. Dutch is the official language of the country and the language of education, business, the media, and government, with some 60 percent of Surinamese speaking it as their first language and most of the rest speaking it as a second language. Sranan Tongo, a creole language, originally spoken by the Creoles, the descendants of African slaves, is the most widely used language in daily life and is spoken by most of the Surinamese population. Surinamese Hindi, also known as Sarmani, is the third most important language.

The British occupation of the colony continued until the end of the Napoleonic Wars in Europe. The return of the Dutch colonial administration in 1816 was welcomed by most of the region's inhabitants though the British abolition of slavery during their administration meant that the large African population resisted a return to servitude under the Dutch. The continued importation of slaves from Africa resulted in the Africans forming the largest segment of the colony's population in the early 1800s. The Dutch government

finally abolished slavery in 1863 though the slaves were not officially released until 10 years later. To compensate for the loss of slave labor, many indentured workers and their families were brought to Dutch Guiana from the Dutch East Indies, particularly the island of Java, and the European colonies in India. Many Chinese also settled in the colony, mostly as merchants or laborers. The exploitation of the colony's natural resources, particularly the rubber, gold, and bauxite, were undertaken in the 1930s and 1940s. To protect the bauxite production, from which aluminum is made, the United States occupied Dutch Guiana in 1941 in agreement with the exiled Dutch government. In 1945, at the end of World War II, the Americans withdrew and the Dutch resumed their control over the protests of a growing anticolonial movement. The Surinamese were granted self-government in 1954 and in 1975 the country became an independent nation, though ties to the Netherlands were maintained. Many of the Dutch, Javanese, and East Indian groups left the colony for the Netherlands. A military coup in 1980 sent another large number of Surinamese to Europe. The military government's dictatorial rule also affected the interior, where an insurgency among the Maroons resulted in a long and bloody conflict and the flight of many Maroons to neighboring French Guiana or the Netherlands. In the 1990s the war with the Maroons ended as democratic government was finally restored though most of the Surinamese living in the Netherlands remained in Europe. In the late 1990s relations between the governments of Suriname and the Netherlands again deteriorated and the important Dutch development funds were withheld. Economic growth slowed in the early 21st century with a new wave of immigrants leaving Suriname to join the large Surinamese community in the Netherlands.

Further Reading

Beatty, Noelle Blackmer. *Suriname.* New York: Chelsea House, 1997.

Clancy, Tomas. *Republic of Suriname.* Seattle, WA: CreateSpace, 2012.

Williams, Colleen Madonna Flood. *Suriname.* Philadelphia, PA: Mason Crest, 2007.

T

Tarahumaras

The Tarahumaras, sometimes known as Rarámuris or Tarahuamaras, are a North American ethnic group concentrated in the Mexican state of Chihuahua. The estimated 60,000 to 75,000 Tarahumaras speak their own language, a Uto-Aztecan language that remains the first language with Spanish often spoken as a second language. The majority of the Tarahumaras practice their traditional animist religion often mixed with Roman Catholic rites and customs.

According to Tarahumara oral history they originated farther to the east, but through several migrations settled most of the territory of the present Mexican state of Chihuahua. They mostly lived by hunting, gathering, and some agriculture. In the 15th century Aztec invaders were repulsed and the Tarahumaras were never drawn into the extensive Aztec empire. Spanish explorers entered their homeland in the late 16th century, often seeking legendary treasures or precious metals. By the beginning of the 17th century Spanish mines had been established in Tarahumara territory and Spanish slavers raided Tarahumara villages to get workers for the mines. A Jesuit mission was founded in the southern part of Tarahumara territory but uprisings by the Tarahumaras and other indigenous peoples in 1616–1618 ended missionary activity for over a decade. The founding of the settlement of Parral at the site of a large silver strike in 1629 brought an influx of Spanish people to the region. Non-Christian indigenous peoples were rounded up for slave labor and many of their women were taken by the colonists. European diseases decimated the Tarahumara people as epidemics swept the region. Slavery, rape, and other abuses also took a heavy toll on the population. In 1648 the Tarahumaras declared war on the Spanish, destroying settlements and the mission at San Francisco de Borja. The war split the Tarahumara people with those attached to the Spanish missions opposing the conflict and the non-Christian majority retreating into the high sierras and canyons. The mission Tarahumaras gradually assimilated into the growing mestizo population and lost their cultural identity. The Jesuits returned to Tarahumara territory in the 1670s and baptized thousands of new converts, but these converts retained their Tarahumara culture and identity. Continued Spanish abuses resulted in a second Tarahumara uprising during 1696–1698 leading to the military defeat of the rebels and harsh reprisals against the entire ethnic group. In 1767 the Jesuits were expelled from New Spain and the missions were turned over to other orders, but most of the missions ceased to function and were finally abandoned.

Tarahumara culture is a vibrant indigenous culture that has absorbed some Spanish and Mexican traditions but retains much of its pre-Columbian influences. The Tarahumaras are a private people who still live in the canyons that gave them refuge from the Spanish soldiers and slavers in the early 17th century. They mostly live in small adobe or wooden houses though some still inhabit caves or homes hidden under rocky outcroppings. They tend to live simple uncomplicated lives undisturbed by modern technologies. The traditional economy is based on barter and paper money is not often used. The Tarahumaras regard work as necessary for survival but believe that it lacks intrinsic moral value of its own. Tarahumara religious beliefs combine Roman Catholic and traditional beliefs, particularly during the largest of their religious celebrations, Semana Santa (Easter Week) and Fiesta Guadalupana in December. Most religious ceremonies and other types of celebration, such as harvests, are interwoven with *tesgüino*, an alcoholic beverage made of corn and grasses that is only good for a couple of days after it is brewed. Though the majority of the Tarahumaras have converted to Roman Catholicism, there are some who have refused baptism and even those who adopt Christianity have introduced their own traditional concepts into their religious practices. The Tarahumara language is spoken in five regional dialects that demonstrate the rugged terrain that makes up their homeland. The language is used in primary schools and in local administration and business transactions.

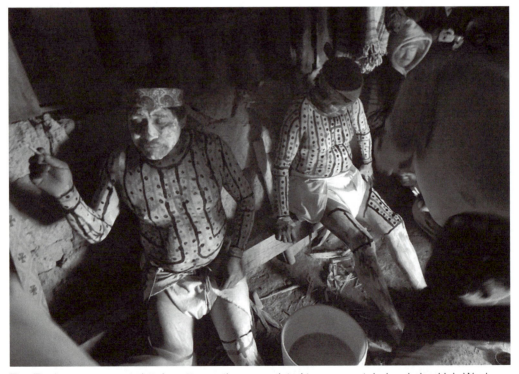

Two Tarahumara men smoke cigarettes as they are painted to represent Judas during Holy Week celebrations in the Tarahumara village of Norogachi, Mexico, March 22, 2008. (AP Photo/ Gregory Bull)

Those Who Run Fast

The Tarahumaras are renowned as runners of extraordinary endurance, a tradition that grew out of a transportation network of narrow footpaths through their home canyons. With widely dispersed settlements, the Tarahumaras developed a tradition of long distance running of up to 200 miles (320 km) in just two days for communications between settlements and transportation as well as for hunting. Their name for themselves, Rarámuri, is thought to mean "foot runner" or "those who run fast." Tarahumaras entered in international competitions have been known to irritate champion marathoners by beating them while wearing huarache sandals made of old tire treads and stopping now and then for a smoke.

Following the expulsion of the Jesuits and the closure of many of the mines in the early 19th century the Tarahumaras in their inaccessible canyons and mountains were mostly ignored and contact with outsiders was minimized. Following Mexican independence in 1821, the new government encouraged settlement of the large but sparsely populated area of Chihuahua. As a result, more Mexicans settled in Tarahumara territory, often driving the Tarahumaras further into the less desirable mountain lands. This pattern of retreating as settlers encroached on their lands functioned as their means of handling contact with nonindigenous peoples and it continued well into the 20th century. Deprived of their productive lands, the Tarahumaras kept herds of sheep, goats, and cattle to produce the manure used to fertilize the shallow soils as well as for food. The construction of the Chihuahua Pacific Railway, which was completed in 1961, brought tourists and commerce to the Tarahumara region, particularly the spectacularly beautiful Copper Canyon. Though the railroad and new roads opened up the Tarahumara territory in the 1960s and 1970s, travel through the Sierra Tarahuma mostly remained the same as it was centuries before. The inroads of modernization brought new products and advances but in the early 21st century the proud Tarahumaras, having repulsed Aztecs, Spaniards, and other conquerors, are now having to struggle to protect their homeland from being taken by the Mexican army, drug lords, or large commercial enterprises that want to exploit the region's natural resources.

Further Reading

Fontana, Bernard L. *Tarahumara: Where Night is the Day of the Moon.* Tucson, AZ: University of Arizona Press, 1997.

McDougall, Christopher. *Born to Run.* New York: Vintage, 2009.

Raat, W. Dirk. *Mexico's Sierra Tarahumara: A Photohistory of the People of the Edge.* Norman, OK: University of Oklahoma Press, 1996.

Ticunas

The Ticunas, sometimes known as Juanas, Magütas, Tucunas, Tukunas, or Tecunas, are a South American ethnic group living in the Amazon basin region that straddles the boundaries of Brazil, Colombia, and Peru. The estimated 30,000 to 56,000 Ticunas speak their own language, which is considered a language isolate not related to the languages of surrounding peoples. The majority of the Ticunas are Roman Catholic, often blending the religious ceremonies with their pre-Christian traditions.

According to the Ticuna creation myth, their ancestors originated in the Eware ravine, situated near the present border between Brazil and Colombia. Traditionally the Ticunas occupied the lowlands and tributaries on the right bank of the Amazon River while the left bank was the homeland of their enemies, the Omaguas. The arrival of the Europeans in the region in the early 17th century brought great suffering, European diseases, and conflicts between Portuguese and Spanish soldiers and missionaries. The Omaguas were decimated and other peoples also lost populations that allowed the Ticunas to expand their territory as others retreated. One of the first indigenous peoples of the Amazon to come into contact with the Europeans, the Ticunas also lost many people to the diseases the Europeans introduced though they suffered fewer deaths because of their tradition of taking refuge along the upper courses of the rivers and streams. Rivalry between the Spanish and the Portuguese for control of the region often involved the indigenous peoples and the missions founded by both Spanish and Portuguese missionaries. Portugal gained control of the majority of the region and built a fort at Tabatinga on the Amazon to control river traffic and the surrounding indigenous peoples in the 18th century. As the other indigenous groups of the region declined the Ticunas moved into the sparsely inhabited districts, often following the construction of Portuguese or Spanish missions.

Ticuna culture is one of the largest indigenous cultures to survive in the Amazon basin of South America. Formerly, the Ticunas lived in communal houses with large extended families. Each of the communal houses was built in the area known as *terra firma*, the dry land above the Amazon flood line. Later the oval-shaped communal houses were replaced by rectangular houses with no walls and thatched roofs that remain the most popular type of dwelling to the present. The change from communal living to one-family houses substantially transformed the Ticuna way of life. Ticuna culture is organized in clans and moieties (groups of clans) that oversee daily life, though the traditions are weakening as Ticunas are introduced to Western traditions. Historically marriage was only between different moieties; the preferred form of marriage involved the maternal uncle of the mother's moiety marrying his niece. Modern Ticunas mostly marry within the same generation, and often marry their cousins, which is considered incestuous by the Catholic priests. Even with over four centuries of contact with outsiders the Ticunas have managed to preserve their personal identity through the continued use of their own language, their traditional religious practices, and their cultural art forms. The Ticuna language is an isolated language unrelated to any other known language. Through centuries of contact with Roman Catholic missionaries the majority of the Ticunas are now officially Roman Catholic, though they continue to mix pre-Christian rituals with their Christian ceremonies and festivals.

Mostly ignored by the national governments during the first half of the 19th century, the Ticunas continued to live their traditional way of life. During the final decades of the century, the Amazonia region became the scene for an intense period of exploitation of the region's native rubber. The rush for "white gold" as the rubber was called quickly intruded into the Ticuna lands. Rubber trappers and wealthy families from coastal Brazil laid claim to the Ticuna territories. The Ticunas were forced to obey and to work as the government backed the newcomers and ignored Ticuna pleas and protests. The rubber bosses forced the Ticunas to abandon their traditional communal houses to disperse the population along the rivers and creeks where rubber extraction was possible. Italian Capuchin friars arrived in the region in 1910 and often attempted to aid the Ticunas against the all-powerful rubber bosses. A war between Colombia and Peru erupted in 1932, forcing most Ticunas to migrate from the left to the right bank of the Amazon. The near absolute rule of the rubber bosses was, in theory, overseen by government agencies set up to protect the indigenous peoples from 1917 onward, but it was only in 1942 that a federal agency was set up in the region.

In the 1960s the Amazonia frontier region was gradually transformed into a region of national security by the Brazilian military, whose presence undermined the absolute power the rubber bosses maintained over the Ticuna population. American Baptist missionaries arrived in the 1960s and 1970s, often buying land where the Ticunas could live and be educated under missionary control. Seeing their control diminishing, the rubber bosses supported the ideas of José Francisco da Cruz, who preached a messianic creed that reflected traditional Ticuna beliefs. His religious movement quickly became the largest in the region. Leadership of the movement often included the former rubber bosses, who were able to reestablish their old forms of authority. In the 1980s, activists demanded demarcation of their lands and education in the Ticuna language in Brazil. Education in Ticuna was available in Peru from the 1960s. In 1993 Ticuna ownership of a large part of their homeland was approved by the Brazilian government. In the 21st century serious conflicts over land have often ended in violence and bloodshed. Internally the Ticunas are also divided between Roman Catholic and evangelical groups, and between traditionalists and those who see assimilation as the way of the future.

Further Reading

Balée, William L. *Footprints of the Forest.* New York: Columbia University Press, 1999.

Davis, Wade. *One River: Explorations and Discoveries in the Amazon Rain Forest.* New York: Simon & Schuster, 1997.

Nimuendajú, Curt. *The Tukuna.* Berkeley, CA: University of California Press, 1952.

Tlapanecs

The Tlapanecs, sometimes known as Tlappanecs, Me'Phaas or Yopis, are a North American ethnic group concentrated in the Mexican state of Guerrero. Outside their homeland in Guerrero there are Tlapanec communities in Mexico City, Morelos, and the United States. The estimated 100,000 Tlapanecs speak a language of the Oto-Manghue language family, of which it forms a separate branch. Most Tlapanecs are Roman Catholic, with a growing number of Protestants, mostly evangelicals, though most Christian ceremonies are often mixed with their traditional beliefs.

Most historians believe that the Tlapanecs settled in the Guerrero area before the rise of the great civilizations of the central valley of Mexico. They settled in two geographic areas, the Costa Chica and La Montaña regions. Geographically divided they formed two bands, the northern band with its capital at Tlapa, and the southern people centered on Yopitzingo, also known as Yopes. They controlled a large territory in the eastern part of the present-day state of Guerrero. The people of Tlapa, known as Tlapanecs, began to extend their rule to the north while the southerners, the Yopes, took control of territory to the south. The expansion of the Mexicas of the Aztec empire began a long series of incursions and wars in the 15th century. In 1486 the Aztecs finally captured Tlapa and the Tlapanecs became a tributary people. In the south the Yopes repulsed Aztec attacks and were never conquered. They continued to represent the biggest problem on the southern borders of the Aztec empire until the invasion of the Spanish conquistadors. The Spanish reached Tlapanec territory in 1521 and quickly brought the region under their rule. Taking advantage of the system put in place by the Aztecs the Spanish set up the *encomienda*, a system of tribute and debt slavery. The Yopes in the south rebelled against Spanish authority in 1531 but the Spanish reprisals resulted in the almost complete annihilation of the southern group, with only a few escaping into the mountains. Franciscan missionaries entered the region but with little success. Later Augustinian missionaries established a mission and convent at Chilapa in 1534, transforming the town into a center of missionary activity. The Augustinians introduced the cultivation of cotton and indigo and promoted the weaving of textiles into shawls or *rebozos*. European diseases devastated the population, with many of the survivors rounded up as slave labor. Spanish colonists and the Roman Catholic missions took much of the most fertile lands while making the Tlapanecs a class of landless laborers. Pushed into the least desirable of their former lands, the Tlapanecs rebelled in 1716 but were defeated and punished with even more confiscations and displacements. By the end of the 18th century the Tlapanec population had declined, most of their lands were gone, and the people lived in poverty under the authority of Spanish landowners.

The Tlapanec culture is an indigenous culture that had borrowed influences and traditions from the surrounding mestizo society in southwestern Mexico. The majority are subsistence farmers cultivating maize, beans, and chili peppers. Meat is usually only eaten during fiestas. Cash crops include bananas, coffee, and sugarcane. The Tlapanec men do most of the agricultural, carpentry, and construction work while the women produce most of the cotton and wool cloth. Traditional handicrafts, such as fans, hats, saddles, and *petates* (straw mats), are now mostly produced for sale. The Tlapanecs enjoy a reputation as day workers and often work in the fields of their mestizo neighbors. Others have left the region for Mexico City or even the United States in search of work and opportunities. The primary cultural unit is the family, which is patriarchal with inheritance from father to son. The traditional council of chiefs is the highest level of Tlapanec government but the council is unable to do much without the permission of the Mexican government or the Roman Catholic authorities in Guerrero. The religious beliefs of the Tlapanecs blend the Christian rituals learned from missionaries with their pre-Christian ceremonies and customs including the belief in witchcraft, spirits, and sacred places throughout their lands. The Tlapanec language is a tonal language that forms a separate branch of the Oto-Mangue languages spoken throughout central Mexico. The geographical separation of the Tlapanec communities has resulted in the use of four regional dialects that are usually mutually intelligible. In recent decades the language has been introduced into local education and is the language of a radio station broadcasting from their ancient capital now known as Tlapa de Comonfort in Guerrero.

In the early 1800s the Tlapanecs supported the growing independence war against the hated Spanish. Many hoped that the end of Spanish rule would mean the recovery of their stolen lands. Following the independence of Mexico in 1821 they continued to suffer abuses and discrimination at the hands of local authorities and landowners. Several local rebellions culminated in a widespread rebellion in 1842–1843. The revolt was so serious that the Mexican government signed a peace treaty, the Agreement of Chilpancingo, with representatives of the Tlapanecs, but later one of the leaders was shot and the Mexican soldiers invaded the region forcing some 25 towns to surrender. In October 1844 some 4,000 Tlapanecs besieged the town of Chipala demanding redress of their land claims and an end to the abuses and persecution. The murder of the besiegers' leader soon dispersed the warriors but the problems persisted. They again rebelled in 1849 under the leadership of Domingo Santiago. Once again punished and dispersed they again rebelled in 1887 to again meet defeat. In 1910 they enthusiastically joined the Mexican Revolution, sure that they would finally regain control of their ancestral lands. At the end of the revolution, during which many Tlapanecs died, the abusive agrarian system remained in place and the promises of the revolution were quickly forgotten. During the 20th century the Tlapanecs suffered extreme poverty, neglect, discrimination, and constant violations of their human rights by the local and military authorities. In 1994 activists joined the Independent Organization of Mixtec and Tlapanec Peoples, out of which the Indigenous Me'Phaa Peoples Organization was formed in 2002. Since its foundation leaders of the group have been threatened and harassed for denouncing human rights abuses and the diversion of public resources by local and military authorities. Physical and verbal attacks escalated to violence in 2007 and over the next years a number of activists were murdered. The plight of the Tlapanecs remains a threat to their unique culture and the survival of their people.

Further Reading

Austin, Alfredo Lopez. *Mexico's Indigenous Past*. Norman, OK: University of Oklahoma Press, 2005.

Guardino, Peter. *Peasants, Politics, and the Formation of Mexico's National State: Guerrero, 1800–1857*. Palo Alto, CA: Stanford University Press, 2002.

Valdez, Norberto. *Ethnicity, Class, and the Indigenous Struggle for Land in Guerrero, Mexico*. London: Routledge, 1998.

Tobas

The Tobas, sometimes known as Guaycurues, Guaycuru, L'añagashiks, Ntocoits, Frentones, Qomis, or Qom-Liks, are a South American ethnic group concentrated in the Chaco region that extends from Argentina into Bolivia and Paraguay. The majority of the Tobas live in the Argentine provinces of Chaco, Formosa, and Santa Fe. Outside their homeland there are Toba communities in the region's large urban centers, particularly the large Argentine cities of Rosario, Santa Fe, and Buenos Aires. The estimated 50,000–60,000 Tobas speak a language of the Guaicuruan language group.

The Tobas were originally hunter-gatherers in the forests that formerly covered the Chaco region. The region was also inhabited by other related peoples and there was a history of conflicts among the bands over hunting lands, water, and resources. The arrival of the Spanish in the latter part of the 16th century quickly changed the structure of the region as European diseases ravaged the population and slavers raided villages for workers on Spanish haciendas and in mines in the Andes to the west. The peoples of the region formed alliances for the purpose of attacking Spanish settlements. The Spanish, initially uninterested in the forests and semitropical swamps of the Chaco, required over 300 years to conquer and colonize the region. Horses captured from the Spanish revolutionized warfare in the region and made it difficult for the Spanish to defeat them. Horses became a prized possession, both for use and for trade. The Spanish tried to consolidate control of roads rather than to dominate the territory. In the 18th century settlements were founded at the edges of the territory—particularly important at Tucumán, Asunción, and Corrientes—but there was no actual occupation of the Chaco until much later. The Jesuits, until their expulsion in 1767, founded several mission stations as part of a program to contain and civilize the Chaco peoples but Christianity was mostly rejected as a Spanish religion.

The Toba culture is an indigenous culture that survived centuries of contact with the European colonial society. Originally hunters and gatherers, the modern Tobas are mostly farmers, with farming often combined with hunting and gathering, rural manual labor, or work at jobs in the provincial bureaucracies. The Tobas living in urban areas most often live in slums or shanty towns and sell handicrafts, work as day laborers, or occasionally as building porters. Traditional handicrafts such as baskets, leather objects, bags, and pottery are now produced for sale in tourist areas and in the cities. Traditionally Toba men hunted, fished, warred, and built dwellings while the women gathered wild fruit, carried firewood, prepared food, and took care of the children along with producing baskets and pottery. The basic unit of the culture is the extended family, which usually formed the nucleus of local bands. Groups of bands made up the Toba tribe whose structure remains to the present. Since the middle of the 20th century new forms of land tenure and the reorganization of social relations has resulted in a process of breaking down extended families into nuclear family units. Most Toba land remains communal though there are individual plots and many Tobas now living away from their original communities. Education in the region tends to teach Western socialization and the culture of the white and mestizo populations with only a few centers of intercultural and bilingual education in the initial phases of development. It is very difficult for modern Tobas to reconcile the values and norms of their culture with those taught to the children in the region's schools. The Catholic religion, originally brought to the region by missionaries, is the primary religion though the belief system incorporates both Christian and traditional influences and rituals. The Toba language remains a vital part of the culture though exposure to Spanish in schools and among the communities living outside the Chaco has allowed Spanish to make inroads and caused the decline of the use of Toba outside the home.

Toba women carry wood for cooking. (AP Photo/Jorge Saenz)

Throughout most of the 19th century the Toba territory in the Chaco remained under their traditional chiefs with Spanish rule recognized only in the surrounding settlements and farming communities. Beginning in 1870 the Argentine military sent expeditions to try to bring the Chaco territory under the control of the national government. The Argentine military was resisted and fighting spread through the region. Tobas and their allies used guerrilla tactics to harass the Argentine columns. In 1884, General Victorica led an expedition into the region that finally defeated the Tobas. Soon settlers, cattle ranches, and lumber mills were founded in Toba territory. The mills and ranches hired the Tobas as temporary wage earners and began a tradition of seasonal migrations. The cities of Formosa and Resistencia were founded and became centers for the colonization of the Chaco. Cotton became the largest cash crop with most of the work performed by Toba workers. Beginning in the latter part of the 19th century Toba women were incorporated into the rural manual work force. Attempts to force the Tobas and the other indigenous groups to work in settlements and to leave their seminomadic lives resulted in serious confrontations with the authorities and the police in 1924. The Chaco War between Paraguay and Bolivia in 1933 modified the geopolitical map of the region with many Tobas displaced. The friction between the Toba workers and the large land and mill owners continued and confrontations again erupted in 1947. Anglican and Roman Catholic missions that were established in the early 20th century often supported indigenous demands. Laws by provincial legislatures in Argentina in the 1980s established the legal right of indigenous peoples to claim lands they had occupied historically, but this process of legal recognition has never been satisfactorily implemented. In the 21st century the Tobas face many problems in preserving their collective identity. New leaders, indigenous churches, interethnic marriages, and the continuing migration to the cities have strained the traditional culture and forced the Tobas to adapt or be lost.

Further Reading

Kersten, Rafael. *Indian Tribes of the Argentine and Bolivian Chaco: Ethnological Studies.* New York: AMS Press, 1976.

Mendoza, Marcela. *Band Mobility and Leadership among the Western Toba Hunter-Gatherers of Gran Chaco in Argentina.* Lewiston, NY: Edwin Mellen Press, 2002.

Metraux, Alfred. *Myths of the Toba and Pilaga Indians of the Gran Chaco.* Whitefish, MT: Kessinger Publishing, 2008.

Tohono O'odhams

The Tohono O'odhams, sometimes known as Papagos, Sand Papagos, Lower Pimas, or Odham, are a North American ethnic group concentrated in the Sonoran Desert near the Gulf of California in southwest Arizona in the United States and northwest Sonora state in Mexico. Outside their homeland there are sizable communities in Phoenix, Tucson, and Los Angeles. The estimated 27,000 Tohono O'odhams speak a Piman language of the Uto-Aztecan language family. The majority of the Tohono O'odhams are Christian, including both Roman Catholics and Protestants, with many still practicing elements of their pre-Christian religious beliefs.

The Tohono O'odhams originally inhabited a vast region in the U.S. Southwest, extending south into Mexico, north into present-day central Arizona, west to the Gulf of California, and east to the San Pedro River. For thousands of years the Tohono O'odhams lived a seminomadic life moving seasonally, spending the summers in "field villages" and the winters in "well villages." The Tohono O'odhams practice a unique form of irrigated agriculture growing mostly tepary beans, squash, melons, and sugarcane. The neighboring Pima peoples called them *Ba:bawiko'a*, meaning "eating tepary beans." Spanish expeditions moving north from Mexico first crossed their territory around 1550. The Spanish, hearing the Pima name for the Tohono O'odhams began to call them the Spanish version of the name, Papagos, and their territory became known as Papagueria. Though the Tohono O'odhams had less contact with the Europeans than some of the neighboring peoples they were gradually brought under Spanish control around 1700. The first Spanish mission was established in 1687, introducing Christianity, metal tools, and new crops such as wheat and fruit along with livestock. The Tohono O'odhams fought with the Spanish against their old enemies, the Apaches and the Yavapais. Throughout the 18th century the few Spanish settlements in the region were isolated and distant from the European colonies. Two major Tohono O'odham rebellions, in the 1660s and the 1750s, rivaled in scale the Pueblo Rebellion. Between 1783 and 1979 the Tohono O'odhams, under the supervision of Franciscan priests, constructed the famous Mission San Xavier del Bac in Tohono O'odham territory.

The Tohono O'odham culture is a Native American culture that today mixes traditional customs and ways with modern American culture. The Tohono O'odhams were considered scientists of their environment, using meteorological principles for planting, harvesting, and ceremonial cycles. They developed complex water storage and irrigation systems. They learned to make the best of the harsh environment of their homeland, migrating seasonally from their villages in the valleys, where they spent winters, to the cooler mountain villages for the summers. The Tohono O'odhams share linguistic and cultural roots with the related Akimel O'odhams (People of the River), also known as Pimas, whose lands are just to the north. The two peoples shared a common ancestry though historically they became two peoples. Tohono O'odham music and dance is muted in comparison to that of other Native American peoples and they have no grand ceremonies. Dancing consists of skipping and shuffling on bare feet that raises a cloud of dust believed to assist in the formation of rain clouds. Despite hundred of years under the domination of foreign administrations, the Tohono O'odhams have retained much of their traditional culture into the 21st century, though in recent decades the culture has been eroded by the surrounding environment of American mass culture. An estimated half of the Tohono O'odhams are still able to speak their traditional language though English is now the primary language. Many also speak Spanish, the language spoken by their kin living south of the international border. Little is known of the traditional religious beliefs prior to the 19th century when a remarkable religious synthesis swept the Piman peoples. The religious movement, influenced by Christianity, featured a murdered man-god and public ceremonies mirrored the Easter celebrations of Christian tribes.

The Tohono O'odhams supported the Mexican war for independence in the early 18th century but were disappointed when independence, finally achieved in 1821, failed to redress the discrimination and loss of territory they had suffered under Spanish rule. Instability and corruption marked the Mexican administration of the huge territory. Tensions between the growing number of American settlers moving into the Southwest and the Mexican authorities led to war between the United States and Mexico in the 1840s. The Treaty of Guadalupe-Hidalgo ended the war with Mexico ceding most of the present-day Southwest to the United States. The northern parts of the Tohono O'odham territory became U.S. territory while the largest districts remained under Mexican rule. An American offer to buy the territory lying along its new southern border resulted in the Gadsden Purchase in 1854. The new international boundary divided the Tohono O'odham territory in half though the Tohono O'odhams moved back and forth across the new border without hindrance. In 1882 the Gila Bend reservation was set aside for part of the Tohono O'odhams and the main reservation was created in 1917. Under American rule traditional culture was suppressed. Indian boarding schools, U.S. Indian policy, and the important cotton industry collaborated in the effort to assimilate the Tohono O'odhams into mainstream American culture. The Tohono O'odhams remained under the absolute control of the American authorities until a tribal authority was finally allowed in 1970. Since the 1960s, obesity and its offshoot, type 2 diabetes, have become commonplace among the Tohono O'odhams with half to three-quarters of them being diagnosed with the disease. To fight the obesity and its effects many Tohono O'odhams have turned to traditional foods that have been proven to regulate blood sugar and to reduce obesity. Obesity isn't the only threat to the Tohono O'odhams. The language and culture is in danger as younger Tohono O'odhams leave for urban areas and more opportunities. A cultural revitalization in the early 21st century, financed by resorts and casinos run by the Tohono O'odhams, is taking hold as a new appreciation for their traditional ways is championed by younger tribal activists.

Further Reading

Erickson, Winston P. *Sharing the Desert: The Tohono O'odham in History*. Tucson, AZ: University of Arizona Press, 2003.

Fontana, Bernard L. *Of Earth and Little Rain: The Papago Indians*. Tucson, AZ: University of Arizona Press, 1989.

McIntyre, Allan J. *The Tohono O'odham and Pimeria Alta*. Mount Pleasant, SC: Arcadia Publishing, 2008.

Trinidadians and Tobagonians

The Trinidadians and Tobagonians, sometimes known as Trinidadians and Tabagonians, are the inhabitants of the southern Caribbean islands of Trinidad and Tobago that make up the two-island nation of the same name. Outside the islands there are sizable Trinidadian and Tobagonian communities in the United Kingdom, Canada, the United States, and other Caribbean nations. The estimated 1.4 million Trinidadians and Tobagonians speak English, the official language of the country, along with local languages known as Trinidadian Creole and Tobagonian Creole. The Trinidadians and Tobagonians adhere to a number of religions, including Christianity (66%), Hinduism (26%), and Islam (6.5%), and a number of smaller sects.

The two islands were originally settled by indigenous peoples moving north from South America as early as 7,000 years ago. The island people, representing both Arawaks and Caribs, were divided into several tribal groups. Christopher Columbus, on his third voyage, sighted three peaks of an island, which he named "Trinidad" for the Holy Trinity. The expedition also sighted Tobago, which was also claimed for Spain. Intermittent contact with Europeans in the early 16th century probably reduced the island populations by half as European diseases, to which they had no immunity, ravaged the tribal peoples. The first Spanish settlement was founded in Trinidad in 1592. Neighboring Tobago was first colonized by the English in 1616 but the fierce Caribs drove them from the island. In 1632 the Dutch attempted to settle Tobago, but gave up the colony due to attacks by the indigenous tribes. From 1654 to 1693 Tobago was officially a colony of the Duchy of Courland, in what is now northern Lithuania. Throughout the 17th and 18th centuries the islands changed hands several times between the English,

the French, the Spanish, and the Dutch. By the early 1700s the indigenous peoples had mostly disappeared, killed, sold into slavery, or absorbed into the growing population of slaves brought from Africa to work the European plantations. Wars in Europe, particularly between the English and the French, included battles and territorial changes in the Caribbean as well. The English attempted to settle Tobago in 1721 but the French captured the island, which was ceded to the British in 1763, only to return to French rule in 1768. British authority over Tobago was finally established permanently in 1797. The Spanish colony of Trinidad remained an insignificant and sparsely populated outpost. In the later 18th century, during a period of alliance between the French and the Spanish, the Spanish government encouraged Roman Catholic settlers, particularly from the French islands where the Haitian Revolution, various slave uprisings, and the depredations of the French Revolution sent many French planters and their slaves to Spanish Trinidad. By 1797, the population of Trinidad had risen to nearly 18,000, including 10,000 slaves and just over 1,000 surviving Native Americans. The first sugar mill was constructed in 1787, and 10 years later the number of mills had risen to 130 to accommodate the output of the many plantations worked by slave labor.

The culture of the Trinidadians and Tobagonians is a Caribbean culture that blends the traditions and customs brought to the islands by the many ethnic groups that now make up the population. Trinidad's population is about 43 percent Afro-Trinidadian, 40 percent Indo-Trinidadian,

14 percent of mixed ancestry, 1 percent of European descent, 1 percent Chinese-Trinidadian, and 1 percent Syrian-Lebanese and Native American. The Tobagonians are primarily Afro-Caribbean, known as Afro-Tobagonians. The island culture, based on the colonial British culture, values the Euro-American ideals of religiously sanctioned marriages and monogamy but the reality is a more casual attitude to kinship and marriage. The influences of the many cultures that made up the Trinidadian culture are evident in the food, music, dance, and island art forms. Trinidad is credited as the birthplace of calypso music and the steelpan, the only acoustic musical instrument invented in the 20th century. Formal education is highly valued as a means of preparing the young for a better and more prosperous future. The complex race and social strata inherited from the British still permeate the culture, often pitting those of African descent against the Trinidadians of East Indian ancestry. Religions play an important part in the culture though it is generally accepted that all are different routes to a shared divinity rather than incompatible and rigid systems of belief. The English language, also inherited from the British colonialists, is the first language of most of the population and is an important cultural icon, allowing peoples of many different backgrounds to share the same language and cultural values.

The slave trade in the Caribbean was abolished in 1807, prohibiting the importation of more slaves from Africa but emancipation was not initiated until 1834, following a planned period of "apprenticeship." The Trinidadian population in 1810 included 20,000 former slaves, 3,200 Europeans, 16,300 mixed race people, and only 750 Native Americans. To ensure a continued supply of abundant, exploitable workers for plantation agriculture, the British began to import indentured laborers and their families from the British colonies in India in the 1840s. When the system of indentured labor was finally ended in 1917, just under 144,000 Hindus and Muslims, jointly called East Indians, had been brought to the colony. The emancipation of the slaves led to the collapse of the sugar industry in Tobago, resulting in the flight of most of the small European population. The former slaves remained on the island, surviving mostly as subsistence farmers. Trinidad and the smaller island of Tobago were joined administratively in 1889. Commercial amounts of oil were discovered and oil production began in Trinidad in 1902. The first refinery was constructed in 1911. Labor protests in Trinidad and strikes and riots on both islands in 1937 led to a grant of universal suffrage in 1945. In the years after World War II, as decolonization reached the Caribbean, the Tobagonians began to agitate for separation from Trinidad, a move opposed by the Trinidadians and the British authorities. Economic problems and a lack of opportunities prompted many islanders to immigrate to the United Kingdom in the 1950s and early 1960s. In 1962 Trinidad and Tobago were granted independence, though in the same month the British parliament passed a new immigration law restricting immigration from the newly independent Caribbean states. Migrants continued to leave the islands, mostly to the large cities of the United States and Canada. Petroleum production fueled a modest prosperity in Trinidad but tourism quickly became the major industry in the 1970s and 1980s, particularly for Tobago. The end of petroleum production, predicted for 2018, has prompted government efforts to diversify the economies of the two islands that are overly dependent on oil and tourism, two industries that continue to give the islands cycles of prosperity and downturn. Remittances from Trinidadians and Tobagonians living overseas are one of the mainstays of the country's modern economy.

Further Reading

Hernandez, Romel. *Trinidad and Tobago.* Philadelphia, PA: Mason Crest, 2009.

Stuempfle, Stephen. *The Steelband Movement: The Forging of a National Art in Trinidad and Tobago.* Philadelphia, PA: University of Pennsylvania Press, 1996.

Williams, Dr. Eric. *History of the People of Trinidad and Tobago.* New York: A & B Publishers Group, 1993.

Triques

The Triques, sometimes known as Triquis, are a North American ethnic group concentrated in the Mexican state of Oaxaca. Outside their homeland there are sizable Trique communities in several large Mexican cities, in the San Quintin valley of Baja California, and in the United States. The estimated 30,000 Triques speak a Mixtecan language of the Oto-Manguean language family along with Spanish, the language of education and government. Most Triques are Roman Catholic, though a growing number are converting to evangelical Protestant sects.

The Triques settled in the mountainous region now in the southwestern part of the Mexican state of Oaxaca. They adapted to the high elevations that are often smothered in low-lying cumulus clouds that envelope entire towns. Their mountainous homeland was surrounded by the lands of the related Mixtec peoples, who developed one of the major civilizations of pre-Columbian Mexico. During the mid-15th century the Aztecs expanded south to conquer the Mixtecs and the Triques. The Aztecs built a fort in Trique lands to better control the newly conquered territories. In the later 15th century a war between the Mixtec kings of Achiutla and Tuxtepec also involved the Triques, who fought with the Achiutla Mixtecs until the intervention of the Aztecs brought the war to a close. The Trique warriors, experienced and well-armed, resisted the Spanish conquest of the region in an alliance with the neighboring Mixtecs in the 1520s. The last rebellion, in 1570, ended with the Triques moving into the higher altitudes to escape Spanish domination. Trique communities in the mountains did not suffer the drastic changes suffered by the lowland peoples brought under Spanish rule. The Spanish took the best valley lands and the fertile lowlands along the region's rivers, but did not bother with the less productive mountains, allowing the Triques to maintain their descent groups and to hold on to many of their cultural values. The Triques formed a cultural island within a wider Mixtec region, occupying the high, cold, and misty mountains that were of no interest to the conquerors. The Triques maintained their tradition of communal lands controlled by clans. In the 18th century the Triques established a thriving trade with the growing Mestizo towns and cities in the lower territories, trading their agricultural produce for manufactured goods, tools, and other items they were unable to produce themselves.

The Trique culture is an indigenous culture based on peasant farming and a tradition of isolation in their highland communities. While coffee is the preferred crop in the surrounding lowlands, the Triques cultivate maize, chilies, beans, and squashes. The agriculture of their region is restricted by the unevenness of the terrain and the scarcity of water for irrigation. Since the mid-20th century the Triques have turned traditional crafts into products for sale to collectors and tourists. They produce women's dresses known as *huipiles*, baskets, and handbags called *morrales*. Their homeland, an enclave of the Mixteca Alta and Mixteca Baja regions, varies in elevation between 4,500 feet and 10,000 feet. Like other peoples of southern Mexico, many Trique men leave their families to seek work in Oaxaca City, Mexico City, and in recent decades in the United States. One of the most enduring elements of Trique culture is the custom of female dowries. During the precolonial and colonial eras, this was a common practice. The Trique custom is for a prospective bridegroom to offer the bride's family money, food, or animals in exchange for the bride's hand. Generally the prospective bride and bridegroom already know each other and there is no wedding without the consent of both parties. The tradition of patrilineal clans continues as the different families hold lands within the clan territories. The Trique language is still the first language of most Triques, with most also speaking Spanish and increasingly some English, a product of the increasing numbers spending time in the United States. Traditionally the Triques were converted to Roman Catholicism by missionaries in the 18th century but the majority continues to blend the Christian rituals with their traditional beliefs, including an important annual ceremony honoring the God of Lightning on April 25. The ceremony is held in the House of Lightning, a series of mountain caves. Like their religious practices, the Triques also blend forms and vocabulary from Spanish with their ancient Mixtecan language though in recent decades younger Triques speak standard Spanish in public and their own language amongst themselves.

The Triques, in their cold and misty highlands, remained isolated from the mainly mestizo lowlands and cities except for Roman Catholic priests who visited many villages to celebrate the mass on Sundays. The lower elevations of their territory proved appropriate for the cultivation of coffee beginning in the early 20th century. The commercial production of coffee offered many Trique men the opportunity to work in areas closer to their families though others began to venture farther afield in search of work. The first migrants went to Oaxaca City and other urban areas in the state but the number of workers available made finding employment very difficult. Soon Trique men were seasonally migrating north to Mexico City, Guadalajara, and other large Mexican cities where work was available. In the 1950s and 1960s they migrated to the United States to work during the agricultural harvests. After some years of seasonal migrations, many Triques moved their families from their traditional homeland to settle in urban slums in Mexico or to take up permanent residence in the United States. The Trique customs were adapted to their new surroundings but the tradition of dowries continued. Denounced by some American organizations as a form of slavery or prostitution, the tradition came under intense scrutiny. In 2009, a Trique man was arrested in California after he paid a dowry of $16,000 and food products to his bride's family. The Triques who remain in their homeland receive an average daily salary of less than $5, making their homeland the poorest region in Oaxaca. The migrants, particularly those in the United States, send remittances back to Oaxaca, and this has become one of the major sources of income for the Trique people.

Further Reading

Chomsky, Noam. *New World of Indigenous Resistance.* San Francisco, CA: City Lights Publishers, 2010.

Cohen, Jeffrey H. *Cooperation and Community: Economy and Society in Oaxaca.* Austin, TX: University of Texas Press, 2000.

Yannakakis, Yanna. *The Art of Being In-Between: Native Intermediaries, Indian Identity, and Local Rule in Colonial Oaxaca.* Durham, NC: Duke University Press, 2008.

Turks and Caicos Islanders

The Turks and Caicos Islanders, sometimes known as Belongers or Turcaicians, are a Caribbean people, the inhabitants of the Turks and Caicos Islands in the northern Caribbean Sea. The estimated 70,000 Turks and Caicos Islanders include about 45,000 living in the British-dependent state of Turks and Caicos, and most of the rest living in the neighboring Bahamas or in Florida in the United States. English is the official language of the islands and is spoken by all the islanders, though a local language known as Turks and Caicos Islands Creole is the language of daily life. The majority of the Turks and Caicos Islanders are Protestant, though religious beliefs and traditions brought to the islands by their African ancestors continue to hold the loyalty of many of the islanders.

The islands were populated by Arawak peoples migrating north from the South American mainland thousands of years ago. According to local traditions, either Christopher Columbus or Ponce de Leon was the first European to see the islands. One of Columbus's ships, the *Pinta*, is believed to have been lost in the islands in 1500. Formally claimed by the Spanish in 1512, the islands were visited by European ships but no settlements were attempted. The indigenous population, ravaged by abuses, slavery, and European diseases, disappeared by the mid-1500s. The first Europeans to live in the islands were pirates, who used the islands as bases for attacking Spanish ships. The first permanent settlers were a group of English colonists from Bermuda, who came to the islands for the extensive salt deposits. The Bermudans fought off attacks by pirates, invaders from the Bahamas, and invasions by the Spanish and French but managed to maintain their freedom until a French attack overwhelmed them in 1764. The Bermudans were rounded up and shipped to the French colony of Haiti. The British later gained control of the island, and during the American Revolution, British loyalists settled the islands and established cotton plantations. The planters imported African slaves, who quickly outnumbered the Europeans in the islands.

The culture of the Turks and Caicos Islanders, or Belongers as they call themselves, is an Afro-Caribbean culture similar to that of the neighboring Bahamas. The majority of the islanders are descendants of the early African slaves brought to the islands to work the plantations. Following the abolition of slavery they settled on small plots and developed a distinctive island culture that reflects their nearness to the Bahamas but with many local traditions and customs. Historically a poor peasant people, tourist and annual subsidies from the British government have raised the islands' standard of living to one of the most prosperous in the Caribbean. A lack of land in the eight small islands results in many people leaving the islands to seek work or opportunities in the Bahamas or the United States. The Turks and Caicos Islanders speak English, the language of government and education, but for daily life they use a local dialect known as Turks and Caicos Islander Creole, which is similar to Bahamas Creole. Religion is a major part of the island culture with participation in church services, events, and ceremonies usually involving most of the island population. The major denominations are Baptist, Methodist, and Anglican, though the Christian rituals are often mixed with beliefs and customs brought to the islands by their African ancestors.

The Caicos Islands were administered by the colonial government of the Bahamas from 1799, while the Turks Islands were annexed to Bermuda in 1804. The island plantations prospered on the cotton trade until the abolition of slavery in 1834. Most of the plantation families left the islands, abandoning their former slaves as they went. The freed slaves divided up the plantation lands into small plots which they farmed while others fished or worked in salt production. Salt remained the major export well into the 20th century. The two island groups were united to form a local government under the governor of Jamaica in 1848. Ships sailing between the United Kingdom and Jamaica made stops at the islands' ports, which were more convenient than those in the Bahamas. The frequent visits by ships brought work to the locals and modernization to the society. The poor and mostly neglected islands remained largely undeveloped and were severely damaged by hurricanes in 1925, 1928, and 1945. An American military base, established during World War II, became a major source of income. The collapse of the salt industry in 1964, and the closure of the U.S. Navy base in 1983, weakened the already poor economy sending many migrants to seek work in neighboring Bahamas or Florida. As almost all food and consumer goods were imported and even water was in short supply the cost of living in the islands drove many more to migrate. Offshore banking was established in the

1980s and by 1990 over 9,000 offshore businesses were registered in the islands. This development, along with the rapid growth of tourism, spurred the construction of a new airport, hotels, and public buildings. Some of the early migrants returned to the islands as work in the banking and tourist industries provided for the growing population. Despite the urging of the British government, the Turks and Caicos Islanders have rejected full independence for now, being content to remain under the financial and political security that the British government provides.

Further Reading

Boultbee, Paul G. *Turks and Caicos Islands.* Santa Barbara, CA: ABC-Clio, 1991.

Mills, Carlton. *A History of the Turks & Caicos Islands.* Oxford, UK: Macmillan Caribbean, 2009.

Smithers, Amelia. *The Turks and Caicos Islands: Lands of Discovery.* Madison, SD: Hunter Publishing, 2011.

U

Uruguayans

The Uruguayans, sometimes known as Uruguayos, are a South American people, the inhabitants of the Republic of Uruguay in southeastern South America. The estimated 3.6 million Uruguayans include sizable communities living outside the country in neighboring Argentina, Spain, the United States, and Australia. The Uruguayans speak a dialect of Spanish known as Rioplatense or Platellano. The majority of the Uruguayans are Roman Catholic, with large Protestant groups and smaller numbers of Jews, Muslims, and others.

The Charrúas, a small tribe driven south by the Guaranis, settled the region around 4,000 years ago. Uruguayans often refer to themselves as *charrúas*, particularly in the context of a competition or battle against a foreign rival. Little is known of the Charrúas except for the information from the surviving documents of the Spanish explorers. The Charrúas fiercely resisted the Spanish invaders in 1515–1516. The hostility of the indigenous peoples, combined with the absence of gold or silver, limited Spanish interest and settlement in the 16th century. The territory was claimed by both Spain and Portugal as part of their colonial empires. In 1603 the Spanish introduced cattle, which became a source of wealth for the region. The first permanent settlement was founded by the Spanish at

Soriano in 1624. To press their claim, the Portuguese founded a settlement at Colonia del Sacramento in 1669–1671. The Spanish colonization expanded as they sought to limit Portugal's colonies to neighboring Brazil. Montevideo was founded as the center of Spanish colonization in 1726. European diseases and the brutal treatment of the Charrúas decimated the indigenous population as Spanish colonization was extended across the territory.

The Uruguayan culture is a Hispanic culture that has evolved from the traditions of the many ethnic groups that settled in Uruguay. The country's multiethnic population is united by culture though the country, like the United States or Canada, is a melting pot of peoples from many backgrounds. About 88–90 percent of the population is of European descent, largely of Spanish and Italian descent, but with peoples from all parts of Europe. Many of the Europeans migrated to Uruguay during the 19th century and heavily influenced the life and culture of Montevideo and the other cities so that urban Uruguayan culture is reminiscent of southern Europe. The remainder of the Uruguayan population is made up of the descendants of the mestizos (6–8% of the total), Afro-Uruguayans, Asians (mostly of Lebanese and Syrian ancestry), and smaller numbers of Japanese people, Chinese people, and people of Native American descent. Historically the Uruguayans have identified with the figure of the Gaucho. The original Gauchos were an equestrian group, mostly of Mestizo background, similar to the American cowboys or the Ukrainian Cossacks. Cattle, horses, and other livestock introduced by the Spanish in the 16th and 17th centuries roamed freely over the grasslands of Uruguay with some of the population adopting a seminomadic lifestyle based on horses and wild cattle. The Gauchos later served in the militias during the struggle for independence from Spain and became the embodiment of the Uruguayan national character. The idealized Uruguayan Gaucho is brace, strong, loyal, proud but humble, straightforward, generous, clever, patient, free, and independent. The Uruguayans speak Spanish, the national language, using a local variety of Spanish known as Rioplatense or Platellano, sometimes known as Uruguayan Spanish, that is similar to the dialect spoken across the Rio Plate in Argentina. The majority of the Uruguayans identify themselves as Roman Catholics though regular church attendance is low. Smaller numbers belong to various Protestant groups with minorities of Jews, Muslims, and others. Uruguay is considered the most secular nation in South America.

The Napoleonic Wars in Europe loosened the Spanish hold on their American colonies in the early 19th century. In 1811 José Gervasio Artigas, who is now considered the country's national hero, launched a successful uprising against the Spanish authorities. In 1813, representatives of the Spanish colonies of the Rio Plate region convened a constituent assembly in Buenos Aires with Artigas championing a federal system and autonomy for each region, particularly the Banda Oriental as Uruguay was then known. The assembly rejected federalism and troops from Buenos Aires laid siege to Montevideo, finally taking the city in early 1815. Once the troops from Buenos Aires were withdrawn, the residents of the Banda Oriental formed the first autonomous government. In 1816, the region was invaded by Portuguese troops from Brazil. After four years of fighting, the Portuguese annexed the region as a province of Brazil. In response, a group known as the Thirty-Three Orientals declared the independence of Uruguay in 1825. The declaration triggered the 500-day war known as the Cisplatine War. In 1828 the Treaty of Montevideo, promoted by the United Kingdom, recognized Uruguay as an independent nation. The remaining Charrúas were massacred at Salsipuedes Creek in 1831 by a group led by the nephew of Uruguay's first president, Fructuoso Rivera. The Uruguayans invited the Charrúas to negotiate, then ambushed them, killing men, women, and children. Four months later a second massacre left most of the survivors dead. Four Charrúas were captured and were later sent to Paris, where they were exhibited to the public. They soon died of exposure, cold, and abuses. A monumental sculpture known as The Last Charrúas was later built in their memory in Montevideo. Political splits between Blancos (Whites) and Colorados (Reds) representing conservatives and liberals fostered political instability, war, and foreign military interventions between the 1830s and the 1850s. In the 1870s and 1880s the military became the center of political power leading to authoritarian rule but also a period of organization with an economic and social transformation into a modern state. In the latter part of the 19th century and the first decades of the 20th century, tens of thousands of immigrants came to the region, mostly from Europe, but also from Lebanon, Syria, Turkey, Armenia, and other areas. This mass immigration greatly influenced the character and culture of the country. Continued political instability in the 1930s and 1940s and a sharp drop in demand for their agricultural products in the 1950s resulted in a rapid decline in the formerly prosperous standard of living. Student militancy and labor unrest culminated in the 1970s in an urban guerrilla movement known as the Tupamaros and a severe police and military response with a suspension of civil liberties. A return to civilian government in the 1980s began a period of economic expansion and prosperity that continued until the worldwide economic downturn of the early 21st century.

Further Reading

Jermy, Leslie. *Uruguay.* New York: Benchmark Books, 2009.

Shields, Charles J. *Uruguay.* Broomall, PA: Mason Crest, 2007.

Tetley, William C. *Blanco y Colorado: Old Days among the Gauchos of Uruguay.* Charleston, SC: Nabu Press, 2010.

V

Venezuelans

The Venezuelans, sometimes known as Venezuelanos, are a South American people, the inhabitants and descendants of the peoples who settled in the Bolivarian Republic of Venezuela on the northern coast of the continent. The estimated 31 million Venezuelans include the 27.3 million living in Venezuela and sizable communities living in the United States, Spain, Italy, Portugal, Colombia, Canada, France, Panama, Germany, Mexico, the United Kingdom, Cuba, and Australia. The Venezuelans speak standard Spanish, the language of administration and education, with a growing number speaking English as their second language. Most Venezuelans, some 92 percent of the population, self-identify as Roman Catholics, though church attendance and devotion are quite low. Evangelical Protestant groups have won a large following, possibly as high as 10 percent of the Venezuelans.

The northern coastal regions of South America have been inhabited for at least 15,000 years. By the early 15th century CE there may have been as many as 500,000 to 1 million indigenous people living in the territory of present-day Venezuela. In 1499, a Spanish expedition led by Alonso de Ojeda visited the coastal areas. According to local tradition, the stilt houses built over water on Lake Maracaibo reminded the navigator Amerigo Vespucci of the city of Venice, so the region was named Veneziola, in Vespucci's Tuscan dialect meaning "little Venice." The Europeans brought with them many diseases to which the native peoples had no immunity. Even before Spanish colonization began in 1522 epidemics had greatly reduced the indigenous population. The indigenous chiefs attempted to resist the invaders but superior arms and the debilitating diseases soon ended the resistance. The settlement of Caracas, founded in 1567, became a center of colonization and a stronghold against pirate attacks and encroachments by other colonial powers. Because of a lack of gold or other treasure, the region was largely ignored as the Spanish empire concentrated on the wealthier parts of the continent. In 1717 Venezuela was placed under the Viceroyalty of New Granada, which covered most of the northern part of South America. The early settlements focused colonization on the coast, but by the mid-18th century the Spanish pushed inland along the Orinoco River. In 1775–1776 the Spanish met serious resistance from the Ye'Kuana people of the inland area. By the end of the 1700s resistance to Spanish colonial rule had spread through the colony.

The culture of the Venezuelans is a Hispanic-American culture combining traditional Spanish society with influences from the other immigrant groups in Venezuela and modern American culture. Venezuelan culture encompasses four groups: mestizos, also known as *pardos*, of mixed European and indigenous ancestry make up about 67 percent of the population; people of European descent, primarily Spanish, Italian, and Portuguese descent, make up some 21 percent of the total; Afro-Venezuelans, both of African and Afro-Caribbean ancestry, form about 10 percent; and surviving indigenous peoples, mostly in the interior rain forests, make up about 2 percent. The Venezuelan culture owes much to the Spanish colonial heritage, which is maintained by the white and mestizo populations that are concentrated in the country's cities. The black population is mostly concentrated along the Caribbean coast, where Afro-Caribbean influence is evident in the local culture. In recent decades an influx of rural migrants, both from within Venezuela and abroad, have swelled the populations of the urban areas, especially the many shanty towns known as *ranchos*. Modernization and the Americanization of Venezuelan culture have increasingly diminished the presence of rural traditions in the large cities. The blend of modernist American influences and local customs, including the remnants of colonial architecture, has evolved a unique Venezuelan style. Despite the country's vast deposits of oil and natural gas, Venezuela remains a mostly poor country due to mismanagement of resources, government instability, widespread corruption, unemployment, and a lack of professional skills. Many Venezuelans have migrated to the United States or other countries seeking better opportunities or higher education, or just to escape the violence and poverty of Venezuela's cities. Though the Venezuelans are mostly monolingual Spanish speakers, many languages are spoken in the country,

particularly English, which has become an unofficial second language. English is seen by many Venezuelans as the language of advancement, science, and upward mobility. The large immigrant population in North America has added to the spread of the English language. According to the Venezuelan government, at least 92 percent of the Venezuelans are nominally Roman Catholic, with the remainder either being nonreligious or belonging to various Protestant sects or to other religions. Many Venezuelans see themselves as Roman Catholic but in practice church attendance and participation in church activities has fallen drastically since the 1970s.

A series of unsuccessful uprisings followed the occupation of Spain by French troops during Europe's Napoleonic Wars in the early 19th century. A national hero, Francisco de Miranda, finally declared independence in 1811, beginning the Venezuelan War of Independence. Political instability and the ongoing war against the Spanish forces in the region continued until Simón Bolivar finally defeated the Spanish at the Battle of Carabobo in 1821. The newly independent Venezuela was added to Bolivar's Gran Colombia, which also included Colombia and Ecuador. Conflicts between the regions resulted in a Venezuelan uprising and separate independence in 1830. The long independence war cost Venezuela between a quarter and a third of its total population, which by 1830 had fallen to just 800,000. Following independence in 1830, most of the rest of the 19th century was characterized by political turmoil and rule by local dictators. A civil war, known as the Federal War, was fought from 1859 to 1863, and killed hundreds of thousands of people. The discovery of huge oil deposits in Lake Maracaibo during World War I soon transformed the country's economy. By 1935 Venezuela's national income was Latin America's highest, prompting an economic boom that lasted until the 1980s. The wealth of the country, mostly held by a small European-descended elite, promoted the growth of a middle class in the 1960s and 1970s. However, political instability continued as the military involved itself in national politics with long periods under military or civilian dictatorships. Thousands of Venezuelans, for both political and economic reasons, left the country to live in North America, Europe, or neighboring countries. A severe economic crisis in the 1980s and 1990s led to political upheavals that left hundreds dead in widespread rioting in 1989. Several coup attempts in the 1990s continued the turmoil, one of them led by Hugo Chávez, who was later pardoned and elected to the presidency in 1998. He then launched the "Bolivarian Revolution" that included close political ties with Cuba and other leftist governments in Latin America and such pariah states as Iran and North Korea. Chávez remains in power, having changed the constitution that would have prevented so many successive terms as president. Many of Chávez's domestic programs are aimed at maintaining the unqualified support of the poor majority of the country. Meanwhile instability, urban violence, official corruption, and high unemployment push thousands to migrate each year.

Further Reading

Corrales, Javier and Michael Penfold. *Dragon in the Tropics: Hugo Chavez and the Political Economy of Revolution in Venezuela.* Washington, DC: Brookings Institution Press, 2010.

Maslin, Jamie. *Socialist Dreams and Beauty Queens: A Couchsurfer's Memoir of Venezuela.* New York: Skyhorse Publishing, 2011.

Tarver, H. Michael and Julia C. Frederick. *The History of Venezuela.* Basingstoke, UK: Palgrave Macmillan, 2006.

Vincentians

The Vincentians, sometimes known as Saint Vincentians or Vincys, are a Caribbean people, the inhabitants of the Caribbean islands that make up the independent state of Saint Vincent and the Grenadines in the southeastern Caribbean. The estimated 135,000 Vincentians include sizable communities in the United Kingdom, the United States, and Canada. The majority of the Vincentians are Christian, largely Protestant though there are sizable Roman Catholic congregations, Seventh-day Adventists, and smaller Hindu and Muslim populations.

The island was originally settled by peaceful Arawaks moving north across the Caribbean from the South American mainland. They were later driven out or absorbed by the more warlike Caribs, also originating in South America. The European exploration of the West Indies, beginning in the late 15th century, eventually led to the colonization of many of the Caribbean islands. The Caribs of the island they called Hairouna (The Land of the Blessed) aggressively prevented European settlements in the 16th and 17th centuries. Escaped or shipwrecked African slaves, many fleeing plantation slavery in Barbados, Saint Lucia, and Grenada, fled in canoes to Saint

Vincent, where they intermarried with the Caribs and became known as Garifuna or Black Caribs. The French, in 1719, finally defeated the Caribs and took control of the island. They extended plantation agriculture to the island and imported slaves from Africa. In 1763 the island was ceded to the British, who instituted a program of colonial plantation development that was resisted by the native Caribs. A representative assembly was authorized in 1776, though membership was restricted to the small European population. Between 1783 and 1796, the Black Caribs fought British efforts to enslave them. Eventually some 5,000 Black Caribs were deported to the island of Roatán, off the coast of Central America. By the end of the 18th century the slave population of Saint Vincent and the smaller Grenadines far outnumbered the European popultion. The Carib population, decimated by European diseases and abuses, survived as a small minority.

The Vincentian culture is a Caribbean culture combining the colonial influences from the British and the French with the traditions and customs brought to the island by African slaves in the 18th and early 19th centuries. The population of the country is primarily rural with most Vincentians living in small villages of 100 to 500 people. The only urban area is that around the capital, Kingstown. Bananas and tourism are the mainstays of the island economy while most Vincentians live as subsistence farmers on small plots of land. About 66 percent of the Vincentian population is made up of people of African descent, 20 percent is of mixed ancestry, 6 percent is East Indian, 4 percent is of European ancestry, 2 percent is Carib, and 2 percent comprises others, including a growing Chinese minority. Each of the racial groups has been successfully integrated into the Vincentian culture and identity. The Afro-Caribbean influences are evident in the island music, dance, religious practices, food, and dialect. The official language is English; however, most Vincentians use a creole language locally known as "dialect," which is unintelligible to English speakers though it is based on English vocabulary. Most Vincentians are Christians, mostly Anglican or Methodist with some Roman Catholic representation; Mormon, Hindu, Muslim, and other groups are also represented in the population. Christian traditions are often blended with early African customs in a unique Caribbean belief system.

Under British rule of the islands of Saint Vincent and the Grenadines, the number of imported slaves continued to increase until the import of new slaves was prohibited in 1807. The abolition of slavery was finally legislated in 1834. Thousands of freed slaves settled as subsistence farmers and many plantation families returned to Europe. To make the shortfall in labor, indentured laborers from the British colonies in India were imported though the sugar industry was restricted by the development of the sugar beet industry in Europe. The economy of the islands remained depressed until the turn of the 20th century and the introduction of banana production. Other workers, such as Madeirans, settled in the islands as banana production spread and rapidly became the most important export. In 1877 the islands became a crown colony with wider powers of self-rule. The eruption of the volcano Soufrière in 1902 killed over 2,000 Vincentians and damaged the most productive agricultural lands. A new legislative council was created in 1925, though universal suffrage was not granted to the Afro-Caribbean majority until 1951. Attempts to join the various British Caribbean islands in a unified administration were unsuccessful, including the West Indies Federation, which collapsed when the larger islands opted for separate independence in 1962. Many Vincentians left their islands to settle in the United Kingdom or mainland North America in search of greater opportunities, beginning a long tradition of migration. The Vincentians were granted associate statehood within the British Commonwealth in 1969, giving them complete control over the internal affairs of their island state. In early 1979 Soufrière erupted again and though there were no casualties, thousands had to be evacuated and there was extensive damage to the banana plantations. Following a yes vote in a referendum in 1979, Saint Vincent and the Grenadines became the last of the Windward Islands to gain full independence. Severe hurricanes devastated the banana and coconut plantations in 1980, 1987, and 1999. In the 20th century bananas remain the most lucrative export and the island's economy remains a combination of subsistence farming and plantation agriculture that was established following the abolition of slavery in the early 19th century. Due to the heavy reliance on banana exports, the Vincentians are very dependent on the trade policies of the United States, the United Kingdom, and the European Union.

Further Reading

Bobrow, Jill and Dana Jinkins. *St. Vincent and the Grenadines: A Plural Country.* New York: W. W. Norton & Company, 1985.

Potter, Robert B. *St. Vincent and the Grenadines.* Santa Barbara, CA: ABC-Clio, 1992.

Toy, Mike. *St. Vincent and the Grenadines.* Oxford, UK: Macmillan Caribbean, 2003.

Virgin Islanders

The Virgin Islanders, sometimes known as Crucians, are a Caribbean people, the inhabitants of the United States Virgin Island and the British Virgin Islands in the Caribbean just east of Puerto Rico. The estimated 140,000 Virgin Islanders include sizable communities outside their home islands in the mainland United States, Puerto Rico, and the United Kingdom. The official language of the islands is English though Spanish and other languages are also spoken. The Virgin Islanders are mostly Christian, largely Protestant, with a large Roman Catholic minority, mostly in the U.S. Virgin Islands.

Ciboney people, moving north by canoe from the South American mainland, settled the islands between 300 BCE and 400 BCE. A later wave of migrants, the agricultural Arawaks, settled the islands between 100 CE and 200 CE. In the 14th century a new group moved north from mainland South America, the warlike Caribs, who gave their name to the warm sea that surrounded the islands they quickly overran. The Caribs were notorious as they supposedly feasted on their adversaries, spawning the English word "cannibal," derived from the name given them by the

Spanish, "Caribal." Blown off course during his second voyage to the New World, Christopher Columbus landed on Saint Croix, and then continued his exploration of the other islands of the group. The Spaniards named the major islands after saints, Santa Cruz, San Tomas, and San Juan, and counted so many cays and islets that they called the archipelago Santa Ursula and her 11,000 virgins, after the legend of Saint Ursula. The name was later shortened to Las Virgenes or The Virgins. In 1555, a Spanish force was dispatched to take control of the islands though the Spanish did not attempt to colonize the group. European diseases, conflicts with the Spanish, and the capture and export of many for slaves decimated the indigenous population. Charles V of Spain declared the indigenous peoples enemies and most of the survivors were forced to leave the islands. By 1596 the indigenous peoples had mostly disappeared. The islands became a center for piracy as the English, Dutch, French, Spanish, and Danish colonial forces jostled for domination. The Dutch established a permanent settlement on Tortola in 1648, which was captured by the English in 1672. The other major islands of Anegada and Virgin Gorda were annexed by the English in 1680. The Danes took control of the western islands in 1666 to supply the mother country with sugar, cotton, indigo, and other island products. Slaves from Africa were first imported as plantation laborers in 1673, and the English and Danish territories became important sugar producers with a prosperous planter aristocracy and thousands of African slaves. The Danes occupied St. John in

1684 and bought St. Croix from the French in 1733, the same year that a very serious slave revolt erupted on St. John. The slave revolt lasted for eight months, and many European plantation families were killed before the Danes were able to retake control of the island. In 1755, the capital of the Danish West Indies, Charlotte Amalie, was declared a free port open to all international shipping. The neutrality of the Danish islands during the Napoleonic Wars in Europe made them the center of Caribbean trade and the largest slave market in the Western Hemisphere.

The majority of the Virgin Islanders are of African or mixed African-European descent, so the culture of the islands is an Afro-Caribbean culture similar to that of the other English-speaking islands in the region. Though the islands are politically separate they maintain close cultural and family ties. The island culture is a blend of West African, European, and American influences. Some traditions were adopted from the early French, Danish, and Dutch colonial cultures and later immigrants from the U.S. mainland, the United Kingdom, and the countries of the Middle East, India, and other Caribbean cultures. The culture continues to be under a process of creolisation, the result of a continuing migration to the islands from elsewhere in the Caribbean. English is the official language in both territories; however, a local dialect known as Virgin Islands Creole is the language of daily life. Because of the growing number of immigrants from other Caribbean islands, the usage of Spanish and some French creole dialects has increased since the 1970s. The islanders are overwhelmingly Christian with the largest denominations being the Methodists, the Anglicans, the people following the Church of God, and the Roman Catholics. There are smaller Muslim and Jewish groups and some other minority religions as well.

The continuing wars in Europe resulted in a British occupation of the Danish islands in 1801 and during 1807–1815, though they were later returned to Danish rule. A series of disastrous hurricanes and the expansion of the beet sugar industry in Europe and North America significantly reduced sugarcane production and led to a serious economic decline in 1820. The production of sugar was further damaged by the abolition of slavery in the British territories in 1834 and in the Danish islands in 1848. American interest in the Danish islands began during the Civil War, but the U.S. Senate refused to approve the purchase of St. Thomas and St. John in 1870. A firm American offer to purchase the Danish West Indies came during World War I, when they were seen as strategically important to the control of the major strait through the Caribbean to the Panama Canal. The Danes, fearing the territory's seizure by the Allies or an invasion by Germans, decided to accept the offer. In 1917, the United States purchased the three Danish islands for $25 million. The British Virgin Islands were made part of the colony of the Leeward Islands in 1872, though ties with the Danish and later American islands remained stronger than ties to the other British islands in the Caribbean. In 1927 a citizenship law granted U.S. citizenship to most of the inhabitants of the U.S. Virgin Islands, and another law in 1932 extended citizenship rights to Virgin Islanders and their descendants living elsewhere in the Caribbean or on the U.S. mainland. A revised government statute provided for substantial self-government in the American territory in 1954. A new election law, adopted in 1970, provided for direct elections for the governor and other territorial officials. The British Virgin Islands were separated from the other British territories to become a separate colony in 1956 and the U.S. dollar was adopted as the British territory's official currency in 1959. The unification of the British Caribbean territories in the West Indies Federation was rejected by the citizens of the British Virgin Islands in order to retain their close cultural and economic ties to the neighboring American islands. Tourism, beginning in the 1960s, quickly became the major industry in both territories though the diversification of the local economies promoted other industries. A lack of opportunities forced many islanders to migrate each year, mostly to the United States and the United Kingdom, though in recent years many have settled in nearby Puerto Rico. In the 1990s both territories were granted greater autonomy as their per capita income became the highest in the Caribbean. A substantial middle class, unusual in the Caribbean area, has precluded widespread support for independence or any changes that might upset their prosperous lifestyle. Since the 1990s tensions have increased between the Virgin Islanders and the growing number of newcomers from other Caribbean islands. Called "Down Islanders" or Garotes, after the tropical bird that migrates annually from island to island in the Caribbean, the newcomers now represent over 30 percent of the total population of the two territories. There is also a movement among the Virgin Islanders, particularly the Afro-Caribbean majority, for a greater role in the social and economic decisions traditionally made by the minority of European descent.

Further Reading

Boyer, William. *America's Virgin Islands: A History of Human Rights and Wrongs*. Durham, NC: Carolina Academic Press, 2010.

Dookhan, Isaac. *A History of the Virgin Islands of the United States*. Mona, Jamaica: University of the West Indies Press, 1994.

O'Neal, Michael E. *Slavery, Smallholding and Tourism: Social Transformations in the British Virgin Islands*. New Orleans, LA: Quid Pro Books, 2012.

W

Waraos

The Waraos, sometimes known as Waroas, Guaraúnos, Guaraos, or Warraus, are a South American ethnic group living in the delta of the Orinoco River in Venezuela with smaller numbers in neighboring Guyana and Suriname. The estimated 24,000 Waraos speak their own language, which is considered a language isolate, unrelated to any other known language. The majority of the Waraos adhere to their traditional belief system though missionaries have converted some of them to Roman Catholicism or Protestant sects.

The indigenous peoples settled the vast delta region of islands and swamps thousands of years ago. According to Warao oral histories, their relations with the neighboring Lokonos, an Arawak-speaking tribe, were always peaceful and friendly, but relations with the Carib-speaking Cariñas (Red Faces) were often violent and the Cariñas are still feared today. Christopher Columbus explored the delta of the river the Waraos called the Wirinoko in 1498 during his third voyage to the New World. A Spanish expedition led by Diego de Ordaz sailed upstream with several ships in 1531 in search of the legendary El Dorado. The river, called Orinoco by the Spaniards, became the main entrance to the interior for explorers, missionaries, and scientists interested in the fabled El Dorado, which was believed to lie farther

upriver. The Waraos often worked for and traded with the Spanish and the Dutch in northern Brazil but maintained their independence in their inaccessible islands and swamps. Though their homeland officially formed part of the New Andalusia province of New Spain, the Waraos were one of the few indigenous peoples to remain free of Spanish control. European diseases to which they had no immunity decimated many Warao villages bringing the population down to about 8,000, a figure that remained fairly constant during the colonial period. The Waraos lived by hunting, fishing, and gathering, particularly the starch pith of the moriche palm, which is similar to the sago palm of the South Pacific region.

The Warao culture is an indigenous culture little changed from the traditional culture of the pre-Columbian period. Most of the Waraos, which means "canoe people," live in villages of extended families. Their houses and other buildings are normally built on stilts over the swamps and rivers of the Orinoco delta region. Modern Warao society is still a hunter-gatherer society though wage labor in lumbering and fishing has become one of the major sources of income. Hammocks and other handicrafts are increasingly produced for sale to collectors or to stores in tourist areas or for trade for axes, machetes, fish hooks, iron pots, and other manufactured goods, including cloth. Kin groups are based on a group of real or classified sisters, led by a principal woman, the *kanoko orotu* or "owner of the house," who enjoys special prestige. Work groups of men related to the "sisters" are important social and economic activities. Descent is bilateral and fictive kinships are frequent. Marriage is traditional within descent groups and young couples normally move into the bride's mother's house. The Warao religious beliefs include spirits in all living things that can work for good or evil. Shamanistic practices help control the bad spirits and maintain contact with the spirit world. Though Roman Catholicism, and in some areas of the western delta, evangelical Protestantism, have made inroads the majority of the Waraos continue to adhere to their traditional beliefs. All of the Waraos speak dialects of the same language, which is considered an isolated language or possibly having distant relationships with other languages in northern South America. About half the Waraos now speak Spanish, particularly those who engage in seasonal work or in the local industries.

The Waraos remained isolated, often intentionally, from the mostly mestizo population of Venezuela during the colonial period. The independence of Venezuela in the early 19th century changed little for the indigenous peoples, who were often abused, defrauded, or attacked. In the late 19th century, from the early 1880s, Brazilian and Venezuelan rubber trappers invaded the region as the Amazonian rubber boom extended into the rain forests of the Orinoco region. Many of the rubber trappers took Warao men as forced labor. The decline of the rubber industry, during 1912–1914, ended the excesses of the rubber trappers but left many Warao villages devastated and depopulated. In 1922 an agreement between the Roman Catholic Capuchin order and the Venezuelan government allowed for Spanish missionaries to enter the Warao region. The missionaries established several missions in 1925, the first organized effort to penetrate the Warao heartland in the Orinoco delta. The importation by a migratory Warao of the taro-like *ocumo* or *ure*, a cultigen suitable for growing in the swampy delta, ended Warao dependence on the palm starch as a staple food. The *ocumo* revolution allowed the Waraos to construct villages along the rivers away from the palm groves as they had traditionally been doing. It also made them available as a cheap labor pool for the newly established sawmills and palmetto factories as well as for commercial rice production. Improved diet, health care, and a decrease in infectious illnesses resulted in a rapid growth in population. However, in the late 20th and early 21st centuries, imported diseases such as tuberculosis continue to ravage many Warao villages. In the last decade there has been a mass migration of mestizo Venezuelans into the region looking for jobs in the important delta and offshore oil production. The influx threatens the Waraos and their traditional homeland especially as the Venezuelan government mostly ignores the indigenous peoples and their many problems.

Further Reading

Davis, Wade. *Light at the Edge of the World: A Journey through the Realm of Vanishing Cultures.* Vancouver, Canada: Douglas & McIntyre, 2007.

Heinen, H. Dieter. *Oko Warao: We are Canoe People.* Stuttgart, Germany: Föhrenau, 1988.

Olsen, Dale A. *Music of the Warao of Venezuela: Song People of the Rain Forest.* Gainesville, FL: University of Florida Press, 1996.

Wayuus

The Wayuus, sometimes known as Wayus, Wayúus, Wahiros, Goajiros, Guajiras, or Guajiros, are a South American ethnic group inhabiting the La Guajira Peninsula on the Caribbean coast of northern Colombia and northwestern Venezuela. The estimated 450,000 Wayuus make it one of the most numerous of the indigenous peoples of northern South America. Outside their homeland there are Wayuu communities south of the peninsula and in the Maracaibo urban area in Venezuela and in the city of Riohacha, the capital of the Guajira department of Colombia. The Wayuus speak a language belonging to the northern branch of the Arawakan language group. The religious life of the Wayuus is a mixture of Catholicism and traditional beliefs though officially the majority of them belong to the Roman Catholic Church.

The origin of the Wayuus is not known, though they are believed to have settled their present homeland thousands of years ago. The Wayuus lived in autonomous villages under a dominant male leader, the *alaüla*, considered the keeper of Wayuu traditions and the coordinator of economic life. All members of the group contributed to the payment of compensation for a misdeed by a group member, the cost of funeral rites and burial fees, and the bride-price obligations of young male members. The arrival of the Spanish in the early 16th century brought waves of epidemics of European diseases and raids by slavers and women-hunters. Though the Spanish never subjugated the Wayuus, there was a more or less permanent state of war in the region. Most of the Spanish preferred to avoid the region though Roman Catholic missionaries set up several mission stations in the late 1600s. In 1701 the Wayuu warriors attacked and destroyed a Capuchin mission in their territory. In 1718 local governor Soto de Herrera called them "barbarians, horse thieves, godless, without law or king, and only worthy of death." Continued Spanish encroachments led to serious clashes in 1727, 1741, 1757, 1761, and 1768. Of all the indigenous peoples in the northern part of the continent, the Wayuus were unique in having adopted and learned to use firearms and horses. In 1769 the Spanish captured 22 Wayuus in order to use them as forced labor for building the fortifications of the Spanish town of Cartagena. The reaction of the Wayuus of the village of El Rincón was unexpected. They burned their village, including the church and two Spaniards who took refuge in it. A Spanish force sent to quell the disturbance was killed. As news of the uprising spread, other Wayuus joined the revolt. Soon there were over 20,000 Wayuus, often armed with firearms acquired from the English and the Dutch, and sometimes even purchased from the Spanish. The rebels overran nearly all the Spanish settlements in the region, which were sacked and burned with more than 100 Spaniards killed and many others taken prisoners. Troops were sent to fight against the Wayuus but a dispute that split the warriors into two warring groups caused the rebellion to collapse, albeit not before the Wayuus had gained much additional territory.

The Wayuu culture is an indigenous culture based on their traditional seminomadic way of life. The Wayuus are divided into clans with each clan made up of several family groups, with leaders who are recognized as both the spiritual and secular heads of the clans. The Wayuu homeland, the La Guajira peninsula, is made up of a long coastline on the Caribbean, dry lands in the interior, and even mountains that rise in the center. The peninsula is divided by the international border between Colombia and Venezuela though the Wayuu cross without papers or problems. Members of the same clan may live in areas as different as the remote desert areas of the peninsula and the barrios of the region's large cities. Though the Wayuus have had contact with Spanish-speaking people for centuries, they continue to use their own language. The younger Wayuus and the increasing urban Wayuu population generally speak Spanish fluently while retaining their own language within the family or the community. Over the years the Wayuus were gradually converted to Christianity, though some beliefs and practices from their earlier belief system persist and most ceremonies and rites blend Catholic traditions with those of their pre-Christian beliefs.

The Wayuus were mostly ignored during the early part of the 19th century as Colombia and Venezuela gained their independence from Spanish rule. Trade between the Wayuus and the neighboring mestizo communities increased but government attempts to control the Wayuus failed. The process of Christianization of the Wayuus was restarted in 1887 when the Capuchin friars returned to the region for the first time since 1701. Capuchin missions introduced modern education, the Spanish languages, and Christianity. In 1905, Pope Pius X supported the creation of the Vicariate of La Guajira in an attempt to "civilize" the Wayuus. The Capuchin friars set up orphanages for Wayuu children beginning in 1903. The orphanages became centers of Spanish-speaking influence for the many Wayuu Rancherias or extended villages. The friars moved around the territory inviting the Wayuus to attend mass and to accept baptism. Wayuu children in the orphanages were educated in Spanish and traditional European customs. Conflicts between the Wayuus and the national governments of Colombia and Venezuela decreased in the 1930s. In 1942, the town of Uribia, mostly settled by Wayuus, celebrated its first Christmas and New Year as a Christian town. Many Wayuus migrated to the region's mestizo towns or even farther to the large city of Maracaibo in search of work and greater opportunities. In the early 21st century the urban Wayuus continue to live in certain neighborhoods or ghettos in the slums of the large cities while the majority of the population continues to live in villages grouped into Rancherias. The influence of the urbanized Wayuus is particularly felt in education, which is more widely available in the cities. Many young Wayuus do not stay in school beyond the primary grades. Others have just a few years of schooling as many parents feel it is more important for their offspring to learn to herd, hunt, fish, build simple shelters, and weave. In recent years paramilitary groups have invaded the Colombian part of their territory seeking plunder, land, or as the forerunners of government agencies or large companies seeking to exploit the mineral wealth of the region. Many Wayuus have been killed, and thousands displaced by the violence of the paramilitary groups. The governments of Venezuela and Colombia have both ignored the pleas of the Wayuus and of international aid agencies who have denounced the state-sanctioned violence and ethnic cleansing.

Further Reading

Russell, Jesse and Ronald Cohn. *Wayuu People.* Saarbrücken, Germany: VSD, 2012.

Villegas, Benjamin. *Wayuu: People of the Colombian Desert.* Bogota, Colombia: Villegas Editores, 1998.

Wilbert, Johannes, ed. *Encyclopedia of World Cultures: Volume VII South America.* New York: G. K. Hall & Company, 1994.

Y

Yanomamis

The Yanomamis, sometimes known as Yanomamö, Guaicas, Guajaribos, Shidishanas, Shiranas, Shoris, Waicas, Waikas, Yanoamas, Yanomamas, or Xirianas, are a South American ethnic group whose territory straddles the border between southeastern Venezuela and northwestern Brazil. The estimated 32,000 Yanomamis speak dialects of the Yanomaman languages that are not usually connected to any other language family. The majority of the Yanomamis adhere to their traditional beliefs, a form of shamanism.

The ancestors of the Yanomamis moved into the present-day Venezuelan-Brazilian border region of South America, probably in the Parmia highlands. There has been little research done on Yanomami anthropology and history though many believe they moved into the rain forests to escape attacks by the Carib-speaking peoples who occupied the upper Orinoco and its tributaries. The Yanomamis established villages of large single houses that resemble a giant circular lean-to. Traditionally families lived in quarters not separated by internal partitions. Violent conflicts with neighboring peoples gained them the name the "fierce people." They lived by foraging, hunting, and fishing. Moving seasonally they planted crops such as bananas and plantains that supplemented their diet. Many trekked for a month or more each year, living in provisional camps some distance from their village. They depended heavily on the wild resources of the rain forests. The first Europeans, probably Portuguese expeditions, entered their homeland in the 1750s, but contacts were avoided and the Yanomamis became part of the legends of the rain forests.

Yanomami culture is an indigenous culture little affected by modern Venezuelan or Brazilian culture as the Yanomamis have avoided contact with outsiders for hundreds of years. The Yanomamis continue to depend on the rain forests for their survival. They practice "slash and burn" horticulture, growing bananas, cassava, and plantains; they also gather fruit and sustain themselves by hunting and fishing. Yanomami collective villages are frequently moved to avoid overusing a particular area, a practice known as shifting cultivation. Most Yanomami families are part of extended families living within a single *shabono*, a single building built around a large common area. Rituals are very important in Yanomami culture. A good harvest is celebrated with a great feast to which nearby villages are invited. Though women are excluded from many ceremonies and rituals, they are an important part of the preparation. Traditional marriage practices include polygamy with many Yanomami men having many wives. Violence and abuse between wedded couples in Yanomami culture is very common. Each Yanomami village is an autonomous entity, free to live in peace or to make war on neighboring villages. Violence in Yanomami society is reportedly widespread and many traditions involve violence or conflict. The Yanomami language, believed to be spoken in four dialects, has many variations and local dialects that are not all mutually intelligible. The origin of the language is unknown and most scholars believe that it is an isolated language, not related to any other language of the region. Traditional religious beliefs remain the most important among the Yanomamis. Roman Catholic and evangelical Protestant missionaries have been in contact with the Yanomamis since the 1950s, but they have had very little success in winning converts.

Though the Yanomamis had occasional contact with outsiders in the 19th and early 20th centuries, it was not until the mid-1950s that anthropologists and missionaries made sustained contact. Violent conflicts with neighboring villages or tribes result in many deaths each year. In the mid-1970s, *garimpeiros*, independent gold diggers, started to enter Yanomami lands. The *garimpeiros* often settled along rivers leading to conflicts with the Yanomamis over land and resources. Abusive mining techniques led to massive pollution and environmental degradation. By the early 1990s, over 40,000 outsiders were in lands recognized by the Brazilian government as Yanomami territory. The story was repeated on a smaller scale in the Yanomami territory in Venezuela. Both governments claim they are unable to enforce laws and programs to prevent the outsiders from invading the reserved lands. The invasion of their lands has resulted in

Yanomamis in Venezuela's Amazon region in 2012. (AP Photo/Ariana Cubillos)

a spreading wave of violence against the poorly armed Yanomamis. In 1993 near Haximu, Brazil, a group of gold miners killed at least 16 Yanomamis in an incident known as the Haximu Massacre. The *garimpeiros* also introduced a variety of diseases to which the Yanomamis have no immunity. The diseases have taken a huge toll on the Yanomami villages. The Yanomami territory, at over 9.6 million hectares in Brazil and 8.2 million hectares in Venezuela, is the largest forested indigenous territory in the world.

Further Reading

Chagnon, Napoleon. *Yanomamö: The Fierce People.* New York: Holt, Rinehart & Winston, 1983.

Schwartz, David M. *Yanomami.* Boston, MA: Lothrop Publishing, 1995.

Tahan, Raya. *The Yanomami of South America.* Minneapolis, MN: Lerner Publishing, 2001.

Yaquis

The Yaquis, sometimes known as Yormes, Yoremes, or Cahitas, are a North American ethnic group concentrated in the northern part of the Mexican state of Sonora. The estimated 32,000 Yaquis include a sizable Yaqui community numbering some 6,000 living in the United States, mostly in the states of Arizona, California, and Texas. The Yaqui language, spoken by most of the modern Yaquis, is a Uto-Aztecan language. Most Yaquis also speak Spanish and most of the community in the United States also speaks some English. The Yaquis are mostly Roman Catholics, blending their Christian teachings with the older pre-Christian beliefs.

The early ancestors of the Yaquis are thought to have practiced irrigation farming for centuries, cultivating the staple crops of maize, beans, and squashes. To supplement their diet they also hunted and fished. Traditionally they lived in a long coastal valley opposite the Sea of Cortez, living mostly in small and dispersed settlements. The Yaqui territory formed part of the Chichimeca, a territory on the fringes of the advanced civilizations of central Mexico to the south. Because of their geographical isolation, the Yaquis had contact with but were never conquered by the Toltecs or the Aztecs. By the early 15th century they lived in a fixed territory with well-defined borders. A Spanish expedition led by Diego de Guzman, seeking the legendary treasure cities of the north, encountered the Yaquis in 1533. The expedition was confronted by a large number of Yaqui warriors. The Yaqui leader drew a line in the dirt and told the invaders not to cross it. He also denied the Spanish request for provisions. A battle ensued and though the Spanish claimed victory, they quickly retreated. The confrontation began over four centuries of struggle against domination by outsiders. The lack of silver or gold in their territory probably saved the Yaquis from a Spanish invasion. In 1608 the Yaquis defeated the Spanish and their Mayo allies in two battles. A peace agreement, signed in 1610, was sealed by the presentation of gifts by the Spanish. Jesuit missionaries entered the region in 1617, beginning a long relationship between the Yaquis and the Jesuits. Most of the Yaquis converted to the new religion while maintaining their pre-Christian beliefs. Jesuit control through the missions was stern but allowed the Yaquis to retain their lands and their unity. The missionaries introduced wheat and livestock, particularly cattle and horses. The Jesuit success was facilitated by the isolation of the missions as the nearest Spanish settlement was many days travel, so the Yaqui were able to avoid interaction with the Spanish and mestizo settlers, soldiers, and miners. The epidemics of European diseases that decimated many tribal groups did not seriously impact the Yaqui people. The reputation of the Yaquis as fierce warriors and the protection of the Jesuit missions shielded the Yaquis from raids by Spanish slavers. Labor was directed by the missionaries and the Yaquis achieved a modest prosperity. However, dissatisfaction with the missionary regime led to a Yaqui uprising in 1740. In 1741 a new treaty was signed that allowed them to maintain their own traditions and customs, carry out administration by themselves, and have the right to total possession of their lands and to retain their weapons; the treaty was recognized by the Spanish authorities. The expulsion of the Jesuits from the Spanish American colonies in 1767 brought an end to the long peace in the region. Franciscan priests replaced the Jesuits but never gained the confidence of the Yaquis. Franciscan influence resulted in the Yaquis losing large territories to the colonists.

The culture of the Yaquis is an indigenous culture with borrowings from the mestizo culture that dominated in most of Mexico. In the past the Yaquis survived on agriculture but modern Yaqui culture has also incorporated influences from modern North American society. Through 120 years of close relations between the Yaquis and the Jesuits, their culture is closely tied to the religious teachings and practices learned from the missionaries. Saints days and other Roman Catholic feast days are celebrated with song, music, and dancing. The best known of all the celebrations is the *maso bwikam*, the deer song that accompanies the deer dance. The dance is performed by a deer dancer known as a *pascola*, a name that is derived from the Spanish word for Easter, *Pascua*. The *pascolas* perform at religious and social functions many times during the year, but particularly during Lent and Easter. The Yaqui deer song and dance are a central part of the culture and are closely tied to their Roman Catholic rites and practices. The combination of Roman Catholic and Yaqui traditions remains strong, and many Yaquis believe that the existence of the world depends on their annual performance of the deer dance as part of the Lenten and Easter ceremonies. The Yaqui language is still spoken by many as their first language though among younger Yaquis, Spanish, or in the United States, English, is replacing Yaqui as the first language.

The dissatisfaction of the Mexican elite with Spanish rule culminated in the Mexican war of independence in the early 19th century. Considering themselves independent of Spanish rule, the Yaquis remained neutral. When Mexico became independent in 1821 the Yaquis refused to pay taxes to the new Mexican government. Mexican attempts to take control of the Yaqui territory led to a Yaqui revolt led by Juan Banderas in 1825. Allied to the neighboring tribal groups, the Yaquis drove the Mexicans from the region, but they were eventually defeated and Banderas was executed in 1833. This began a series of Yaqui uprisings as the Mexicans attempted to gain control of the Yaquis and their lands. The Yaquis supported the French occupation of Mexico during the 1860s and continued their resistance to Mexican rule under the leadership of Jose Maria Leyva, known to the Yaquis as Cajemé. The Yaquis continued to wage war against the Mexicans until 1887 when Cajemé was captured and executed. The Yaqui Wars were characterized by brutality on both sides, but featured a series of atrocities by the Mexican authorities, including the massacre of 1868 when the Mexican Army burned 150 Yaqui men, women, and children to death inside a church. The wars impoverished the Yaquis but they continued to resist as the government confiscated and distributed Yaqui lands to settlers. Thousands of Yaquis remained in mountain strongholds and carried on a guerrilla war against the Mexican authorities. In the early 1900s, after the official campaign of "extermination, military occupation, and colonization" had failed to end Yaqui resistance, the government rounded up thousands of Yaquis who were deported to the henequen plantations of the Yucatan, far to the south. Many Yaquis fled the deportations and crossed into the United States. The Yaquis were finally defeated in 1917, though some guerrilla bands continued to fight until 1927. The 10,000 surviving Yaquis were resettled on the north bank of the Yaqui River where a dam was constructed to provide irrigation for their crops. Even though they settled into peaceful communities the Yaquis maintain a degree of self-determination from Mexican rule. In the United States the Yaqui refugees settled in the urban areas around the cities of Tucson and Phoenix where they continued to

perform the Lenten and Easter ceremonies so important to their culture. In the 1960s the Yaquis of Arizona asked anthropologists for help. Congressman Morris Udall agreed to aid the Yaquis in their quest for a land of their own. The government set aside a territory southwest of Tucson, and with the help of Congressman Udall and others they received federal recognition as the Pascua Yaqui Tribe. Many of the Yaquis moved to the Phoenix area, settling in a neighborhood near Tempe named after Our Lady of Guadalupe. The town was incorporated under the name Guadalupe, Arizona, in 1979 and today around 44 percent of the town's population is Native American, mostly Yaqui.

Further Reading

Erickson, Kristin C. *Yaqui Homeland and Homeplace: The Everyday Production of Ethnic Identity.* Tucson, AZ: University of Arizona Press, 2008.

Radding, Cynthia. *Wandering Peoples: Colonialism, Ethnic Spaces, and Ecological Frontiers in Northwestern Mexico, 1700–1850.* Durham, NC: Duke University Press, 1997.

Shorter, David Delgado. *We will Dance our Truth: Yaqui History in Yoerme Performances.* Lincoln, NE: University of Nebraska Press, 2009.

Yupiks

The Yupiks, sometimes known as Yu'iks or Yuplit, are a North American ethnic group concentrated in southern and western Alaska in the United States. There is a sizable Yupik community across the Bering Strait in the Russian Far East. The estimated 25,000 Yupiks in the United States speak several dialects of the Yupik languages along with English, the language of education and government. The majority of the Yupiks are Russian Orthodox though their pre-Christian shamanism is still practiced, often in conjunction with Christian rituals and ceremonies.

The ancient peoples of eastern Siberia, the common ancestors of the Inuits, the Aleuts, and the Yupiks, are believed to have crossed the land bridge over the Bering Strait about 10,000 years ago, somewhat later than the ancestors of most of the Native American peoples. About 3,000 years ago the ancestors of the Yupiks had settled the coastal regions of western Alaska and up the coastal rivers. Around 1400 CE migrating Yupiks arrived at the upper reaches of the Yukon and Kuskokwim rivers in present-day Canada. Historically the Yupiks were seminomadic, migrating according to the season to villages and seasonal camps that followed the migrations of fish, game, and plant life. The Yupik camps and villages were made up of extended families or small groups of families. All males lived in a *qasgiq*, or men's house, that served as a community center. Boys old enough to leave their mothers joined male relatives in the *qasgiq*, where they lived, slept, and learned the things needed to be a Yupik man. Women and girls lived in an *ena*, a smaller version of a *qasgiq*, which also provided space for cooking. The lifestyle of the Yupiks was highly adapted to survival in the subarctic environment. Social behavior was geared toward survival and compatibility among the extended family-village groups. Roles and social stature were largely determined by individual skills and gender. Successful hunters, known as *nukalpiit*, usually became village leaders. Women were in charge of child rearing, food preparation, cultural ceremonies, and sewing. The coastal Yupiks carried on a lively trade with the inland Yupiks and other indigenous peoples, trading seal oil—highly valued by the interior groups—for moose and caribou meat and furs such as mink, marten, beaver, and muskrat. In the 1740s Russian ships began to explore the coastal regions but the hostility of the Yupiks prevented contact between the indigenous peoples and the Russian expeditions.

Yupik culture has much in common with the related cultures of the Inuits and Aleuts, though it developed many unique traits and practices. Though they were often lumped together with the Inuits as Eskimos, the Yupiks see themselves as a separate people with a distinct culture. Traditionally Yupik extended families spent the spring and summer at a fishing camp, then joined other groups to winter in a larger village. The modern Yupiks mostly live in villages and small towns in cement block houses with iron or ceramic roofs. Community centers now play the same role as the traditional *qasgiq*, with many ceremonies and festivals, and community singing, dancing, and storytelling. Some Yupiks continue to build traditional homes of lumber and driftwood that are partly subterranean to maintain heat in winter and coolness in summer. Unlike their relatives, the Inuits, who live in a land of barren, icy wastes, the Yupik lands are below the Arctic Circle, a region of mostly flat marshy plains crisscrossed by many waterways, which the Yupiks use in place of roads. The relatively moderate climate supports a wide variety of vegetation and a rich population of birds, mammals, and fish. The abundance of food resulted in a tradition of permanent communities as hunting and fishing continued for most of the year. The Yupiks speak five dialects of the Yupik language, which separated from the Inuit languages around 1000 CE. The number of Yupiks able to speak their traditional dialects is estimated at 75 percent, a very high number for Native American peoples. English is also widely spoken, though the Yupiks continue to use their traditional dialects for daily life. The language became a literary language in the late 19th century when Moravian missionaries translated scripture into the language. Converted to Russian Orthodox in the 18th century, the majority of the Yupiks identify themselves as Christians though traditional beliefs are still revered, particularly the roll of the shamans.

Contact between the Yupiks and the Europeans happened much later than it did with the Inuits to the north. It was not until the early 1800s that Russian explorers visited the coastal communities. This late contact was largely due to the lack of resources deemed commercially valuable by the Russians. The Yupiks continued to live their traditional way of life though epidemics of European diseases decimated some villages in the mid-19th century. Because of the absence of European contact until late in the colonial period, the 19th-century explorers, unlike their earlier counterparts who described the Inuits as savages, had a more favorable view of the Yupiks. Russian Orthodox missionaries founded mission

stations in Yupik territory in the late 1800s, beginning the conversion of the Yupiks to Christianity. The Yupiks were selective as to the parts of the Christian teachings they adopted, depending on whether or not the teachings were compatible with their traditional belief system. Because European contact has been relatively recent, the Yupiks have been able to retain much of their traditional culture and dialects. The extended family remained as the focus of Yupik society unlike the disintegration of culture that happened to other Native American peoples. In 1867, the Russians sold Alaska to the United States. American administrators, missionaries, and teachers came to the region. By the end of the 19th century the Yupiks had settled in permanent small towns with churches, schools, and community centers. In the 20th century American welfare systems created a dependency on government rather than on the traditional Yupik practice of self-sufficiency. In the 21st century area schools began to offer courses in the language and culture in response to requests by Yupik leaders who fear the loss of their culture and dialects to the pervasive attractions of modern American culture.

Further Reading

Fienup-Riordan, Ann. *Eskimo Essays: Yup'ik Lives and How We See Them.* Piscataway, NJ: Rutgers University Press, 1991.

Fienup-Riordan, Ann. *Yuungnaqpiallerput: The Way We Genuinely Live.* Oakland, CA: Oakland Museum of California Press, 2007.

Jolles, Carol Zane. *Faith, Food, and Family in a Yupik Whaling Community.* Seattle, WA: University of Washington, 2002.

Z

Zapotecs

The Zapotecs, sometimes known as Ben 'Zaa, Binii Gula'sa', Tsapotecatl, Za, or Zapatecos, are a North American ethnic group concentrated in the Mexican state of Oaxaca. Outside their homeland in Oaxaca there are Zapotec communities in the large cities of central Mexico and in California, particularly in Los Angeles and the Central Valley regions. The estimated 800,000 to1 million Zapotecs include the more than 100,000 living in the United States. The Zapotecan language group is made up of over 60 regional dialects that all belong to the Zapotecan branch of the Oto-Manguean language family.

Archaeological evidence confirms that the Zapotec civilization goes back at least 2,500 years. The highly advanced Zapotec culture had its beginnings in the central valley of Oaxaca, one of the few areas of level plains in southern Mexico. In the late sixth century BCE, three branches of the Zapotecs formed societies in the central valley. Between 700 BCE and 500 BCE something happened, as many towns were deserted and a large new city was constructed on top of a mountain in the center of the valley. The new city, Monte Albán, was constructed with elaborate public buildings, ball courts, and magnificent tombs. Finely worked gold statuary and jewelry were manufactured as well as elegant pottery, metal weapons and tools,

and finely woven cloth. Between 400 BCE and 100 BCE the Zapotec state centered on Monte Albán began to expand beyond the large central valley to encompass territories outside its traditional homeland. As the political, military, and economic power of the region, the Zapotec empire flourished from around 200 BCE to 700 CE. The Zapotecs, known as the Cloud People, conquered or colonized areas far beyond the central valley of Oaxaca, often bringing non-Zapotecs under Zapotec rule. The Zapotec culture and language was often adopted by the non-Zapotec peoples resulting in the wide variety of Zapotecan dialects spoken in southern Mexico today. The advanced civilization included irrigation agriculture, a complicated system of imperial and local governments, an accurate calendar, and a written language, known as a logosyllabic writing system. The Zapotec writing system is thought to have been the predecessor of the writing systems later developed by the Mayans, the Mixtecs, and the Aztecs. Around 900 CE the empire declined, splitting into a number of competing states. The Aztecs began to encroach on the region around 1250, but not until the 15th century did most of the Zapotec states fall to the expanding Aztec empire. The Aztecs demanded tribute and established military outposts in the region but most left the Zapotec hierarchy to rule under the scrutiny of the

Aztec rulers of central Mexico. The Aztec rule in the Zapotec territories would only last a little more than 30 years. Soon after the conquest of the Aztec empire by the invading Spanish in 1519, a Spanish expedition moved south into Oaxaca looking for gold. The Zapotecs of the central valley chose not to fight the newcomers, but negotiated to keep most of their traditional ruling elite under the authority of the Spanish. Resistance to Spanish rule in other Zapotec areas continued for several decades. In the 1520s Roman Catholic missionaries began to establish missions in the region to begin the conversion of the Zapotecs to Christianity. The conquest and subsequent colonization of the Zapotec territory had a devastating effect on the population. European diseases, the capture of women, and forced labor and slavery decimated the Zapotecs. The Zapotec population, estimated at 1.5 million in 1520 had declined to just 150,000 in 1650. The abuses, discrimination, and slavery continued throughout the colonial period. For most of the 17th and 18th centuries the province of Oaxaca was relatively isolated, with few roads or other forms of communication. Despite Spanish colonization and domination, the Zapotecs maintained much of their culture and identity, more so than the peoples in other areas of Mexico. This is partly due to the rugged geography of the regions beyond the central valley where isolated communities continued to live and worship as their ancestors had.

The modern Zapotec culture is a peasant culture of farmers practicing a mixture of subsistence and commercial agriculture with some herding and animal husbandry. The nuclear family is the basis of the society and is the basic production unit that is linked to the outside world by an elaborate, cyclical system of markets that has operated in the region for centuries. Though the majority of the Zapotec communities are dedicated to agriculture, some communities are specialized by craft or industry. In the central valley many villages specialize in pottery, wool serapes, *mutates* (grinding stones), baskets, woven belts, and other goods. The Zapotecs are renowned for their commercial activities in the region's markets. Traditionally the Zapotec kinship ties were bilateral, with descent from both the male and female line, but modern culture emphasizes the male and inheritance from father to son. One ancient tradition, known as *compadrazgo*, the system of ritual co-parenthood or godparents, is still widely used. There is considerable variation in the customs and traditions of the various Zapotec regions in southern Mexico. The Zapotec languages belong to the Oto-Manguean language family, with probably as many as nine separate, mutually unintelligible Zapotec dialects. Most Zapotecs are fluent in Spanish, the language of education and administration, though their own dialects remain the languages of daily life. Many of the Zapotecs spend time in the Zapotec communities in the United States where English is often used as the second language.

During the Mexican War of Independence, in the early years of the 19th century, many Zapotecs joined the rebels in hopes of ending the centuries of abuses and discrimination. The rebels gained some ground in parts of Oaxaca but the capital, Oaxaca City, with a mainly mestizo population, remained loyal to the Spanish until the end of the war in 1821. The new Mexican government, controlled by the small European or European-descent elite, did little to alleviate the suffering and poverty of the indigenous peoples. During the 19th century, Oaxaca, along with the rest of Mexico, was split between liberal and conservative factions. Conflicts often led to violence and attacks on Zapotec villages. The constant warfare had a negative effect on the region's economy, particularly the towns and villages with large indigenous populations. In 1847, a young lawyer, a full-blooded Zapotec named Benito Juarez became the governor of Oaxaca with the support of the liberals and most of the indigenous peoples. His success in organizing the economy and ending the most outrageous excesses against the Zapotecs and other indigenous peoples resulted in a second term as governor. He worked to remove privileges and to redistribute lands to the indigenous peoples long held by the Church and the landed gentry. In 1857 Juarez left Oaxaca to become president of the Mexican republic during a turbulent era that included the French invasion of Mexico and the opposition, often violent, of the country's most conservative factions. A rebellion that began in Oaxaca in 1872 continued as Juarez died in office. Porfirio Diaz, a former ally, led the rebellion and finally took the presidency, which he held until the Mexican Revolution in the early 20th century. The overthrow of Diaz began

a long civil war among various factions that often included depredations among the villages thought to support one faction or other. In 1920 a new state government was installed that attempted to address some of the demands and pleas of the Zapotecs and other indigenous groups. A series of major disasters worsened the condition of village life in Oaxaca beginning with a serious earthquake in 1928, an even more devastating quake in 1931, followed by the Great Depression, which prompted many Zapotecs to migrate to Mexico City or even further to work in the harvest of fruits and vegetables in the United States. The tourist industry, drawn to the ruins of the Zapotec empire cities, brought with it jobs and a market for Zapotec handicrafts. In the latter 20th century and early 21st century political instability, government corruption, and the marginalization of the poor continued to disrupt life for most Zapotecs. Many continue to migrate, most going north to the United States where work is more easily found, education is available, and the traditional abuses and marginalization they suffer in their homeland is replaced by the acceptance of a multiethnic society and the community spirit, and the Zapotec culture is kept alive in the Zapotec communities in several areas of the United States. In Mexico the Zapotecs are among the poorest and least advantaged of Mexican citizens.

Further Reading

Flannery, Kent V. and Joyce Marcus. *Zapotec Civilization: How Urban Society Evolved.* London: Thames and Hudson, 1996.

Flannery, Kent V. and Joyce Marcus. *The Cloud People: Divergent Evolution of the Zapotec and Mixtec Civilizations.* Clinton Corners, NY: Percheron Press, 2003.

Joyce, Arthur A. *Mixtecs, Zapotecs, and Chatinos: Ancient Peoples of Southern Mexico.* Hoboken, NJ: Wiley-Blackwell, 2009.

Zoques

The Zoques, sometimes known as Soques, Tsoques, Tzoques, or Zoc, are a North American ethnic group concentrated in the southeastern Mexican states of Tabasco, Oaxaca, and Chiapas. Outside their homeland there are Zoque communities in Mexico City, Veracruz, Guadalajara, and the United States. The estimated 70,000 Zoques speak a language of the Mixe-Zoquean language family that is spoken in several distinct dialects. Most Zoques are Roman Catholics but mix their Christian rituals and ceremonies with traditions from their pre-Christian religion. Seventh-day Adventists became active in the Zoque communities in the 1930s and today are the only Protestant denomination in the Zoque villages and towns.

The Zoques are believed to be the descendants of the people of the Olmec civilization who migrated south to Chiapas and Oaxaca from present-day Veracruz and Tabasco, probably between 400 BCE and 350 BCE. The migrants brought with them many of the traits and traditions of the advanced Olmec culture, founding new communities in southern Tabasco, Chiapas, and as far away as the Isthmus of Tehuantepec in Oaxaca. The Zoques were settled agriculturalists with cultivation based on maize and other crops. The towns and cities were mostly autonomous units ruled by hereditary rulers or chiefs. The lack of unity resulted in some Zoque city-states coming under the rule of neighboring peoples. Despite a long trading relationship with the expanding Aztec empire, in 1494 the Aztecs invaded and defeated the Zoques. The Aztecs set up garrisons in the region to ensure the payment of tribute to the Aztec overlords but otherwise left the Zoques to their traditional rulers and way of life. The Spanish, having defeated the Aztecs, entered Zoque territory in 1523, under the leadership of Luis Marin. The conquerors divided up the Zoque lands in large land grants worked by Zoque slaves or Zoques trying to pay the tribute demanded by the Spanish. European diseases, exploitation, rampant abuses, and the miserable working conditions under which they lived contributed to a sharp decline in the Zoque population between 1530 and 1700. Beginning in 1549, the Spanish destroyed the Zoque settlement pattern of dispersed towns and villages in order to resettle them in communities more suitable for the collection of tribute and the conversion of the heathens to Christianity. Continued mistreatment, branding, and the taking of Zoque women resulted in several uprisings, the most serious ones in 1693 and 1722. The rapid loss of the Zoque culture due to Spanish pressure to assimilate into the growing mestizo population was particularly severe in some parts of Chiapas but Zoque culture survived in the more remote areas.

The culture of the modern Zoques is based on the pre-Columbian culture that flourished from the 13th to 15th centuries, before the Aztec and Spanish conquests. The traditional culture has borrowed from Mexico's dominant mestizo culture and from modern North American culture brought back to the area by migrants returning from the United States. The settlement patterns imposed by the Spanish conquerors in the 16th century continue to the present though the mestizo population outnumbers the indigenous population in the larger towns. The major activity continues to be farming, primarily the cultivation of maize, beans, squash, cacao, bananas, tobacco, oranges, and coffee. Cattle herding is also an important economic activity though most of the herds are owned by outsiders. Textiles, a handicraft that was widespread during the colonial period, began to die out as cheaper manufactured cloth became available in the 1940s, but since the tourist boom began in the 1960s and 1970s hand-crafted textiles have again become important. Other handicrafts such as pottery making have been revitalized by the tourist industry. Traditionally Zoque babies were named after a relative from the previous generation, in a sense taking his or her place in the community, but this practice has died out since the 1870s. Other religious practices have survived to become part of the Zoques' modern Christian ceremonies. Belief in spirits and the power of shamans or witch-doctors remains widespread. The linguistic affiliation of the Zoques is still a subject of research, but recent evidence shows the existence of a Mixe-Zoque-Popoluca language family of which the Zoque languages form a separate branch. Many believe that the three languages of the group all derive from the ancient language spoken by the Olmec culture that flourished in Veracruz and is considered the forerunner of the later Mesoamerican civilizations.

Despite the breakup of their traditional communities by the Spanish, the Zoques maintained their contacts with other Zoque communities and with their Mayan neighbors to the south through commercial and ritual exchanges. Many Zoques supported the overthrow of Spanish rule in the Mexican War of Independence in the early 1800s. But Mexican independence, finally won in 1821, did little to change the abuses, mistreatment, and poverty suffered by the Zoques. The Mexican Revolution in the early 1900s brought some changes but it was only in 1922, when they were assigned *ejidos* or common lands to work, that their living conditions began to improve. Commercial crops such as tobacco, oranges, and coffee allowed many Zoque farmers to modestly prosper but widespread poverty forced many to migrate to the large urban areas in search of work or greater security. Some joined the immigrant flow to the United States to work at harvesting fruits and vegetables on a seasonal basis. The traditional pattern of Zoque life included the traditional system of civil-religious hierarchy that made all decisions and controlled daily life. In the 1930s, the establishment of local village governments removed political power from the traditional hierarchies as Zoque political systems adapted to the institutions created by the national and state governments. In the last decades the production of textiles, traditional masks, and pottery, which was practically nonexistent for most of the 20th century, has become a flourishing cottage industry, mostly for sale to tourists and to shops in Mexico's large cities. The dispersal of the Zoque population made communications between communities very difficult until the arrival of modern communications technology in the early 21st century. Most communities are now linked by web pages and other forms of direct contact, which has stimulated a renewed interest in the traditional Zoque culture and dialects.

Further Reading

Call, Wendy. *No Word of Welcome: The Mexican Village Faces the Global Economy.* Lincoln, NE: University of Nebraska Press, 2011.

Montemayor, Carlos and Donald Frischmann. *Words of the True Peoples: Anthropology of Contemporary Mexican Indigenous-Language Writers.* Austin, TX: University of Texas, 2007.

Trejo, Guillermo. *Popular Movements in Autocracies: Religion, Repression, and Indigenous Collective Action in Mexico.* Cambridge: Cambridge University Press, 2012.

Zunis

The Zunis, sometimes known as Zuñis, are a North American ethnic group that is considered one of the Pueblo peoples. Most Zunis live in the Pueblo of Zuni on the Zuni River, a tributary of the Little Colorado in western New Mexico in the southwestern United States. The estimated 15,000 Zunis include the 10,000–12,000 enrolled tribal members and the Zuni communities in Albuquerque, Santa Fe, and other regional cities and towns in New Mexico and Arizona. The Zuni language, still widely spoken, is considered a language isolate, unrelated to any other regional language. The majority of the Zunis continue to adhere to their traditional beliefs, which also integrate some aspects of Roman Catholicism.

Archaeological evidence and Zuni traditions suggest that the Zunis have been farmers in their present homeland for 3,000 to 4,000 years. Complex irrigation systems along the Zuni River have been dated to about 3,000 years ago. Later the Zunis, like the other Pueblo peoples, became the descendants of the ancestral Pueblo peoples who lived in the arid lands of present-day New Mexico, Arizona, Utah, and southern Colorado. Most of the Zuni settlements were small and dispersed until the 12th and 13th centuries when the population and the size of the settlements began to increase. By the 14th century, the Zunis inhabited over a dozen pueblos of between 180 and 1,400 rooms each. The "village of the great kiva" near the modern Zuni Pueblo was built in the 11th century. All of the pueblos were abandoned by 1400 except for Zuni, and a series of nine large new pueblos were founded. These were the "seven cities of Cibola" sought by the early Spanish explorers of the region. Rumors of great cities filled with treasure in this Kingdom of Cibola had spread through Mexico in the early 16th century, soon after the Spanish conquest of the wealthy civilizations of central Mexico. In 1539 a Spanish expedition entered Zuni territory to make the first contact between the Zunis and the Europeans. The Spanish marveled at the high buildings of the Zunis and the other peoples of the region, calling them *pueblos*, the Spanish word for towns. The

Zunis tried to expel the disruptive Spanish missionaries in 1623 but were stopped by well-armed Spanish soldiers. A mission was established at Hawikuh in 1629 and another at Halona in 1643. The Zunis lived in six large pueblos in the mid-1600s but during the great Pueblo Revolt of 1680 they abandoned their towns to take refuge in a defensive position atop a large and steep mesa, where they stayed until 1692. After the end of the revolt they returned to their present area on the Zuni River, only briefly taking refuge again during upheavals in 1703. The self-sufficient Zuni farmers were often the target of raids by nomadic Apaches, Navajos, and other indigenous peoples. European diseases, mistreatment by the Spanish, and the dispersal of the population resulted in a rapid decline in the Zuni population in the 16th and 17th centuries. The surviving Zunis, in the 18th century, settled into the Zuni Pueblo on the site of ancient Halona where they farmed and fished. Since the uprising of the Pueblo peoples in 1680 the Zunis have lived in peace.

The Zuni culture is a traditional indigenous culture incorporating ancient customs, modern traditions and adaptations, and elements of modern American and Mexican cultures. The Zunis are a peaceful, deeply traditional culture that survives by means of irrigated agriculture and the raising of livestock. The success of their agricultural economy is due to their careful management and conservation of the

Zuni reservation in New Mexico, 1940. (AP/Wide World Photos)

limited local resources and a complex system of community involvement. Many contemporary Zunis still live in the traditional pueblo structures while others have moved to single-family homes, mostly flat-roofed structures constructed from adobe and concrete blocks. The Zuni homeland remains in relative isolation but in recent decades the reluctant Zunis have welcomed respectful tourists. The growing number of visitors has revitalized ancient handicrafts such as the famous Zuni pottery, unique jewelry designs, and the kachina dolls that were traditionally made to represent a spirit being in Zuni cosmology and religious practices. The kachina cult and kachina dancers are part of the Zuni religious system as masked dancers dress as kachinas for religious ceremonies and kachina dolls are given as gifts to children. The Zunis, despite missionary pressure to adopt Christianity, continue to practice their traditional religion with its regular ceremonies and dances. The Zuni Tribal Fair and Rodeo is an annual event held in August to showcase the Zuni culture and to share their ancient traditions with the growing number of visitors to the region.

The Zunis, living in self-sufficient pueblos, were mostly unaffected by the end of Spanish rule and the independence of Mexico in 1821. Mexican officials attempted to integrate the Zunis into a system of production for trade but the Zunis mostly preferred to work their irrigated farms and to keep contacts with outsiders to a minimum. Mexican rule lasted from 1821 until 1848 when most of the present Southwest was ceded to the United States. The arid lands held little attraction for the American and European settlers moving into the new territories in the west so the Zunis continued to live an isolated and peaceful existence. The U.S. military forces, in the latter part of the 19th century, ended the raids of the nomadic Apaches and Navajos, who were confined to new reservations. The Zuni reservation was officially recognized by the U.S. government in 1877. In the early 20th century many Zunis left farming and turned to herding sheep or cattle as a means of economic development. In the late 20th century water rights became a serious issue as growing urban areas upstream appropriated available water. In 2003, the Zuni Indian Water Rights Settlement Act provided for the financial resources to acquire water rights in the basin of the Little Colorado River. Another controversy arose over the development of a coal mine near the Zuni Salt Lake, which is considered sacred to the Zunis and is under Zuni control. The mine would have required extracted water from the aquifer below the lake and would have involved construction projects on Zuni lands. Young Zuni lawyers filed several lawsuits and finally the plan was scrapped, leaving the Zuni in peace.

Further Reading

Bunzel, Ruth R. *The Zuni: Southwest American Indians.* Charleston, SC: Forgotten Books, 2008.

Tedlock, Barbara. *The Beautiful and the Dangerous: Encounters with the Zuni Indians.* Albuquerque, NM: University of New Mexico Press, 2001.

Wyaco, Virgil. *A Zuni Life: A Pueblo Indian in Two Worlds.* Albuquerque, NM: University of New Mexico Press, 1998.

Geographical Index

Index

Note: **Bold** page numbers refer to the main entries.

About the Author

James B. Minahan has written a number of reference books on international statehood and identity, including ABC-CLIO'S *Ethnic Groups of South Asia and the Pacific*, *The Former Soviet Union's Diverse Peoples*, Greenwood's *Encyclopedia of the Stateless Nations, One Europe, Many Nations*, and *Miniature Empires*.